THE SUNDAY TIMES

ILLUSTRATED HISTORY OF

TWENTIETH CENTURY

SPORT

THE SUNDAY TIMES
ILLUSTRATED HISTORY OF
TWENTIETH CENTURY
SPORT

CHRIS NAWRAT   STEVE HUTCHINGS   GREG STRUTHERS

HAMLYN

DEDICATION

Dedicated to Pierre de Coubertin, a visionary
whose dream was conceived in the nineteenth century,
blossomed in the twentieth, and enters the next a little
battered and bruised, but as the flag-bearer of all
our sporting aspirations.

Editors: Martin Corteel, Peter Arnold, Conor Kilgallon, Trevor Davies
Assistant Editor: Tarda
Art Director: Keith Martin
Design Manager: Bryan Dunn
Original design: Christopher Matthews
Additional Design: Gwyn Lewis, Paul Webb
Jacket design: Vivek Bhatia
Picture research: Jenny Faithfull, Maria Gibbs
Production: Karyn Claridge

Published by Hamlyn
an imprint of
Reed International Books Limited
Michelin House, 81 Fulham Road
London SW3 6RB
and Auckland, Melbourne, Singapore and Toronto

A catalogue record for this book is available from the British Library.

ISBN 0 600 59379 7

Typeset by Dorchester Typesetting Group Ltd

Printed and bound in Great Britain by
Butler & Tanner Ltd, Frome and London

Contents

Introduction

As the century draws to a close there will be billions of words, millions of photographs and thousands of documentaries devoted to the events of the past hundred years. In all this, sport will get a cursory mention as prime ministers are re-assessed, the origins of wars debated and revolutions debunked. This book hopes to redress the balance.

For when the serious matters of the day are addressed, sport is too easily pushed into the hinterland. And even there sport is an also-ran, never being deemed as important as other so-called peripheral pursuits such as opera, ballet, art, poetry, literature and cinema. Parnassus is definitely off limits.

Yet great sport moves people in the same way as great art; and certainly more are moved. An historian may say that Picasso was the most important painter of the twentieth century, but did Muhammad Ali have the greater influence on the entire population of the world? Possibly not: perhaps it was Pele. Sport may not win the argument, but with the year 2000 on the horizon it is firmly entrenched as the major cultural interest of modern times, whether playing, watching or reading about it. And unlike the communist regimes of Eastern Europe who failed to go the distance in the twentieth century, its grip on popular support is based on affection.

The history of sport in the past hundred years is much the same as the history of all other human activity. Unparalleled growth, awe-inspiring technological innovation and staggering achievements. The Olympic motto: "Higher, further, faster" perfectly sums up our sporting times. In this chronicle we record all these events, year by year, accompanied by contemporary and archive photographs, but like any history we had to be selective, and no doubt many readers will disagree with our choices.

In selecting the most newsworthy events we have been guided by what we believe to be the major sports that most interest the British public: football, cricket, golf, rugby union, athletics, racing, tennis, boxing, rugby league and motor racing. This list does not preclude other sports, and in fact more than 50 different sports grace these pages, but it does reflect the general policy of the sports sections of British newspapers.

Sport and newspapers have enjoyed a symbiotic relationship for over two centuries. From the earliest days of newspapers the public were avid to read about racing and pugilism. By the beginning of this century few towns of any size did not boast a football special. And as sport mushroomed, became professional and then global so did the amount of space and resources that papers devoted to it. The Sunday Times prints more than a million words a year plus all the results, tables and scoreboards in its sports section. This book draws on that expertise. As well as a year-by-year chronicle of the major occurrences, and some of the quirky happenings, there are profiles of the people that shaped our century of sport by Sunday Times contributors, statistics on who won what and when, and an essay that seeks to put each decade and its underlying trends in perspective.

That perspective, inevitably, is from the 1990s. It would have been impossible to ignore the benefit of hindsight and pretend we were writing as if we had no knowledge of the future. So, in a sense, this book is not innocent. Frequently, certain people or events are chosen because of what happens next. But this, we believe, makes the work more valid as a history.

As we sifted through the myriad events of the century the choices of what to leave out became more difficult and more painful. But then, to do justice to every sporting feat or scandal would have consumed an entire Scandinavian forest and filled the library of the British Museum. Books, like newspapers, have to be edited. What you have here is the best of the best. For obvious reasons the balance of the book is tilted towards the modern era. Each year until the start of the Second World War is covered in two pages, from 1946 to 1959 each year is covered in four pages and from 1960 each year is covered in six pages.

Readers may find some of the views expressed in these pages contentious. We make no apology for this. Sports writing is about controversy. Were the Spurs Double team better than Arsenal's? Jack Nicklaus a greater golfer than Arnold Palmer? Martina Navratilova a more significant tennis player than Rod Laver? Sobers a better all-rounder than Botham? Sugar Ray Robinson the best pound-for-pound fighter? Juan Manuel Fangio to beat Ayrton Senna? Would Red Rum have trounced Arkle? The arguments are endless, and, of course, a lively element in the passion that sport engenders. However we do apologise for any omissions or errors that have crept in. We have made every effort to be as comprehensive and authoritative as possible.

This book would not have been possible without the help and co-operation of friends and colleagues. For devotion above and beyond the call of duty we would like to thank: Peter Bryan, Rod Carr, Richard Eaton, Tom English, Clive Everton, John Karter, Harry Mullan, Bernadine Phelan, Stewart Roberts, the late Cliff Temple, David Thomas and Carolyn Wigoder; Christine Boyle and Claire Struthers, long-suffering wives who had to put up with endless late nights and interminable discussions about the copy, our editors and designers at Reed Books who had to endure our obsession on a daily basis, and sportsmen and women, past and present, who have enriched our lives and made this book possible.

■ Len Hutton	■ Muhammad Ali	■ Suzanne Lenglen
■ Jack Nicklaus	■ Pele	■ Bobby Charlton
■ Martina Navratilova	■ Juan Fangio	■ Rod Laver

1900s

Fundamental agenda for the century

"The Empire stretching round the globe has one heart, one head, one language, one policy."

British newspapers, hailing the arrival of the new century, had unbounded optimism. The Empire was at its zenith and all that was good in the world was there to be embraced, enjoyed and expanded.

Britain was confident that the sun would never set on its glorious empire. But within a year Queen Victoria, who had presided over the industrial transformation of the country in her 63-year reign, had died. And dramatic social changes, changes that would shape the world as we know it, were already under way.

The industrial, urban working class had emerged as a significant numerical body and were starting to unite as a cohesive social force. As a result, the dawn of the century also saw the founding of the Labour Party. Radical politics were hardly novel, but the organic links that the fledgling party forged with the trades unions were.

Modernity was on the march. In Paris, a 19-year-old painter from Malaga, Pablo Picasso, enjoyed rave reviews for his first international show in 1901. The motor car was quickly becoming the fashionable form of transport. Although the masses could never aspire to owning a car until the second half of the century, railway lines criss-crossed the country and were the envy of Europe. Affordable mobility opened up ordinary people's horizons, and with the introduction of Bank Holidays leisure became a factor in people's lives.

Travelling to sport, in particular football, where cheap excursions were often specially laid on, was commonplace. Watching sport was now something that was budgeted in to everyday life. Thus, working men would save throughout the year for their annual trip to the Cup final. Sport had become, as the century unfolded, a significant part of the fabric of working class culture, as both entertainment and healthy activity. So much so that in 1906 sport was included in the school curriculum. Although professional sport had existed for nearly 25 years it was, in reality, still in its infancy. As it was growing up in the first decade of the century it was still learning and innovating. And those changes were mainly for the better.

Until 1902 the penalty area in football was kidney-shaped, and golf balls were made of hard rubber. In that year the penalty area was changed to the modern size and shape, and an American dentist introduced elastic thread into golf balls, which dramatically increased the distance they flew.

At Oxford University, Bernard Bosanquet made his mark on cricket. He took a peculiar student pastime and adapted it to cricket, thereby inventing the googly. The "wrong 'un" made its debut with startling effect in a county championship match in 1900. A year later in America, Mr Gillette was unveiling the first replaceable razor. Little did he know that in 1963 his company would change the face of English cricket for ever when they sponsored the first one-day Cup competition.

Britain was not the only forward thinking country. American football cast off the last remains of its historical association with rugby when it legalised the forward pass in 1906. And three years earlier baseball had conceived the World Series. In France, the first Grand Prix was held at Le Mans in 1906, and the Tour de France was first staged in 1903.

Thanks to royal intervention (the starting point of the race was moved so that the youngest royals could watch from their nursery window at Windsor), the marathon was formalised at 26 miles 385 yards for the London Olympics of 1908. Those games marked yet another watershed — the first time that a modern Olympics had not been an organisational shambles.

The new order was beginning to take shape. Amazingly enough, it was an order that most people would recognise today. Perhaps the traditions started in the first decade of the century were planted so deep that they took root. Wales and Yorkshire were the dominant forces in rugby and cricket; and in football the comparisons with today are unbelievable.

In 1901, Tottenham, then in the Southern League, won the FA Cup. As the century would unfold they were to win it seven more times. And in the same year Liverpool won their first League title. They went on to win it 17 more times. Both are records.

Meanwhile, in 1908, another club destined to become a household name, Manchester United, won their first championship. And Celtic won the Double in 1907, the first Scottish club to achieve the feat.

Transfer fees were then, as now, a subject of much controversy. When Alf Common moved from Sunderland to Middlesbrough for £1,000 in 1905 there was a public outcry everywhere apart from Middlesbrough. He may have been expensive but Middlesbrough supporters thought he was worth every penny. Their team immediately won away from home for the first time in two years and avoided being relegated from the First Division.

Sadly, the unacceptable face of football was also in evidence. In 1902 25 people died and more than 500 were injured when a wooden stand collapsed at Ibrox during the match between Scotland and England. Seven years later at Hampden, another 100 people were injured in a riot after the Scottish Cup final replay between Celtic and Rangers. So did those 10 years set the agenda for the rest of the century? On the face of it, it would seem so. Victorian Britain gave way to a brave new world, a world of sweeping changes, both scientific and social. Those changes would release forces so powerful that they engendered further changes, changes that would so transform things that Queen Victoria could not comprehend the world in which we now live.

Obviously sport would also be caught up in this revolution. But, uniquely, much of the inheritance of the past would be so deeply embedded that if a Victorian candlestick-maker came to Wembley today for the Cup final he would, after all, recognise it as just another football match.

ATHLETICS

■ *British Olympic gold medals*
1900 *800m* Alfred Tysoe; *1500m* Charles Bennett; *3,000m steeplechase* J Rimmer
1908 *400m* Wyndham Halswelle; *10,000m* E Voight; *3,000m steeplechase* A Russell; *triple jump* Timothy Ahearne

BASEBALL

■ *World Series*
1903 Boston Red Sox
1905 New York Giants
1906 Chicago White Sox
1907 Chicago Cubs
1908 Chicago Cubs
1909 Pittsburgh Pirates

BOXING

■ *British world champions*
1903 *Light-heavyweight.* Bob Fitzsimmons
1904 *Bantamweight.* Joe Bowker
1907 *Bantamweight.* Owen Moran

CRICKET

■ *County championship*
1900 Yorkshire
1901 Yorkshire
1902 Yorkshire
1903 Middlesex
1904 Lancashire
1905 Yorkshire
1906 Kent
1907 Nottinghamshire
1908 Yorkshire
1909 Kent

CYCLING

■ *Tour de France*
1903 Maurice Garin
1904 Henri Cornet
1905 Louis Troussellier
1906 Rene Pottier
1907 Lucien Petit-Breton
1908 Lucien Petit-Breton
1909 Francois Faber

FOOTBALL

■ *Football League*
1900 Aston Villa
1901 Liverpool
1902 Sunderland
1903 Sheffield Wed
1904 Sheffield Wed
1905 Newcastle
1906 Liverpool
1907 Newcastle
1908 Manchester Utd
1909 Newcastle

■ *FA Cup*
1900 Bury 4 Southampton 0
1901 Tottenham 3 Sheffield Utd 1 (after 2-2)
1902 Sheffield Utd 2 Southampton 1 (after 1-1)
1903 Bury 6 Derby 0
1904 Manchester City 1 Bolton 0
1905 Aston Villa 2 Newcastle 0
1906 Everton 1 Newcastle 0
1907 Sheffield Wed 2 Everton 1
1908 Wolverhampton 3 Newcastle 1
1909 Manchester Utd 1 Bristol City 0

■ *Scottish League*
1900 Rangers
1901 Rangers
1902 Rangers
1903 Hibernian

1904 Third Lanark
1905 Celtic
1906 Celtic
1907 Celtic
1908 Celtic
1909 Celtic

■ *Scottish Cup*
1900 Celtic 4 Queen's Park 3
1901 Hearts 4 Celtic 3
1902 Hibernian 1 Celtic 0
1903 Rangers 2 Hearts 0 (after 1-1 and 0-0)
1904 Celtic 3 Rangers 2
1905 Third Lanark 3 Rangers 1 (after 0-0)
1906 Hearts 1 Third Lanark 0
1907 Celtic 3 Hearts 0
1908 Celtic 5 St Mirren 1
1909 Cup withheld

GOLF

■ *The Open*
1900 J H Taylor
1901 James Braid
1902 Sandy Herd
1903 Harry Vardon
1904 Jack White
1905 James Braid
1906 James Braid
1907 Arnaud Massy
1908 James Braid
1909 J H Taylor

■ *US Open*
1900 Harry Vardon
1901 Willie Anderson
1902 Laurie Auchterlonie
1903 Willie Anderson
1904 Willie Anderson
1905 Willie Anderson
1906 Alex Smith
1907 Alex Ross
1908 Fred McLeod
1909 George Sargent

RACING

■ *The Derby*
1900 Diamond Jubilee
1901 Volodyovski
1902 Ard Patrick
1903 Rock Sand
1904 St Amant
1905 Cicero
1906 Spearmint
1907 Orby
1908 Signorinetta
1909 Minoru

■ *Grand National*
1900 Ambush II
1901 Grudon
1902 Shannon Lass
1903 Drumcree
1904 Moifaa
1905 Kirkland
1906 Ascetics Star
1907 Eremon
1908 Rubio
1909 Lutteur III

ROWING

■ *Boat Race*
1900 Cambridge
1901 Oxford
1902 Cambridge
1903 Cambridge
1904 Cambridge
1905 Oxford
1906 Cambridge
1907 Cambridge
1908 Cambridge
1909 Oxford

RUGBY LEAGUE

■ *Challenge Cup*
1900 Swinton 16 Salford 8
1901 Batley 6 Warrington 0
1902 Broughton 25 Salford 0
1903 Halifax 7 Salford 0

1904 Halifax 8 Warrington 3
1905 Warrington 6 Hull KR 0
1906 Bradford 5 Salford 0
1907 Warrington 17 Oldham 3
1908 Hunslet 14 Hull 0
1909 Wakefield 17 Hull 0

RUGBY UNION

■ *Five Nations championship*
1900 Wales
1901 Scotland
1902 Wales
1903 Scotland
1904 Scotland
1905 Wales
1906 Ireland and Wales
1907 Scotland
1908 Wales
1909 Wales

SAILING

■ *America's Cup*
1901 *Columbia* (US, Charlie Barr)
1903 *Reliance* (US, Charlie Barr)

TENNIS

■ *Wimbledon*
1900 Reginald Doherty *bt* Sidney Smith; Blanche Hillyard *bt* Charlotte Cooper
1901 Arthur Gore *bt* Reginald Doherty; Charlotte Sterry *bt* Blanche Hillyard
1902 Lawrence Doherty *bt* Arthur Gore; Muriel Robb *bt* Charlotte Sterry
1903 Lawrence Doherty *bt* Frank Riseley; Dorothea Douglass *bt* E W Thomson
1904 Lawrence Doherty *bt* Frank Riseley; Dorothea Douglass *bt* Charlotte Sterry
1905 Lawrence Doherty *bt* Norman Brookes; May Sutton *bt* Dorothea Douglass
1906 Lawrence Doherty *bt* Frank Riseley; Dorothea Douglass *bt* May Sutton
1907 Norman Brookes *bt* Arthur Gore; May Sutton *bt* Dorothea Lambert Chambers
1908 Arthur Gore *bt* H Roper Barrett; Charlotte Sterry *bt* A M Morton
1909 Arthur Gore *bt* Josiah Ritchie; Dora Boothby *bt* A M Morton

■ *Australian championship*
1905 Rodney Heath
1906 Tony Wilding
1907 Horace Rice
1908 Fred Alexander
1909 Tony Wilding

■ *US championship*
1900 Malcolm Whitman; Myrtle McAteer
1901 William Larned; Elisabeth Moore
1902 William Larned; Marion Jones
1903 Lawrence Doherty; Elisabeth Moore
1904 Holcombe Ward; May Sutton
1905 Beals Wright; Elisabeth Moore
1906 William Clothier; Helen Homans
1907 William Larned; Evelyn Sears
1908 William Larned; Maud Barger-Wallach
1909 William Larned; Hazel Hotchkiss

Southern League Tottenham won the FA Cup in 1901

Vardon triumphed on both sides of the Atlantic

Start of the 100 metres at the 1906 Interim Games

JANUARY

1900

DECEMBER

De Coubertin: French farce

Relegated to a sideshow: competitors in the standing jump

French Games degenerate into farce

PIERRE DE COUBERTIN, the innovative French baron who resurrected the ancient Games of Greece in 1896, hoped his country would put the Olympics on the world stage. Instead, his dream became a French farce. The baron's plan was to combine the five-month sporting spectacle with the Universal Paris Exposition. That was when things went wrong. The organiser of the exposition, Alfred Picart, viewed sport as an absurd activity and relegated the Games to a sideshow. The result was a muddle of recognised and non-recognised events and a confused audience soon lost interest.

The facilities were primitive. The discus and hammer were held in a narrow lane flanked by two rows of trees which several competitors hit. One of the hurdles in the steeplechase was a stone wall. The swimmers struggled through swirling currents in the muddy River Seine and the rowing was described by a writer from Sport Universal as "a sport only practised by coarse fellows who,

under the name of boatmen, spread terror among the peaceful riverside inhabitants". The marathon runners sweated through the back streets of Paris and for years afterwards there were allegations of Frenchmen

> **' It's a miracle that the Olympic movement survived that celebration '**
>
> **Pierre de Coubertin**

obstructing their foreign rivals. Michel Théato, a French gardener, won in 2hr 59min 45sec, nearly 40 minutes ahead of the first foreigner, Ernest Fast of Sweden. Dick Grant, an American who finished sixth, claimed a cyclist knocked him down when he was about to overtake the winner.

A decision to have the track and field programme on a Sunday brought howls of protest from many of the Americans,

who were representing their colleges and were not allowed to compete on the Sabbath. The American athletes agreed to withdraw. But amid the chaos and controversy there emerged one of the greatest opportunists in Olympic history. Alvin Kraenzlein decided to compete, despite his earlier agreement to withdraw. He became the first man to win four Olympic titles, clinching the 110m hurdles, the 200m hurdles, the 60m and the long jump. When his fellow American Myer Prinstein, the long jump world record holder, heard about Kraenzlein's deception he is alleged to have punched him.

Britain dominated the middle-distance events, the water polo and the football, the first team event to be included in the Olympics. Britain, represented by Upton Park FC, beat France 4-0 in the football and Alfred Tysoe and Charles Bennett won the 800m and 1500m respectively. Britain finished with 17 gold medals, seven silver and 12 bronze.

De Coubertin was not in

favour of women competing and their role was restricted to tennis. Britain's Chattie Cooper was the first woman to win an Olympic title, beating Helene Prevost of France 6-1 6-4.

There were no accurate records kept and such was the confusion that some sportsmen were not even aware they had competed in the Olympics. It had taken the world 1,503 years to revive the Games and only five months to destroy the Olympic spirit.

Wales enter golden era

WALES started an 11-year domination of the home internationals with the first of their six Triple Crowns in the "Golden Era". They lost only seven matches in 11 seasons. Their great rivals of the time were Scotland, but that winter the Scots had to settle for 0-0 draws with both Ireland and England in a fortnight.

Davis Cup launched

DWIGHT FILLEY DAVIS was a student at Harvard University with a talent for tennis. But, more significantly, the left-handed son of a wealthy St Louis family was intrigued with the idea of an international team competition. So he approached the Boston silversmiths Shreeve, Crimp and Low, who produced a magnificent punchbowl with 217 troy ounces of sterling silver, trimmed with gold, valued at $700 and capable of holding 37 bottles of champagne. Davis donated the trophy to the United States Lawn Tennis Association and the most prestigious team competition in tennis was born. But the Davis Cup made an inauspicious start. Only Britain took up the initial challenge and they were without their leading pair, the brothers Laurie and Reggie Doherty, for the five-match tie at the Longwood Cricket Club in Boston on August 8-10.

It was a whitewash. The British were unable to come to terms with the long grass, the soft, egg-shaped balls and a net that sagged three inches. The Americans dropped one set in an emphatic 3-0 victory and only a thunderstorm on the third day prevented them wrapping up the reverse singles, which were cancelled. Davis, who was a member of the American team, went on to win three US doubles titles. He then became the president of the USLTA, Governor-General of the Philippines and the Director-General of the US Army Specialist Corps in the Second World War.

Reggie and Laurie Doherty

FOR THE RECORD

BOXING
■ Jim Corbett narrowly failed to regain the world heavyweight title from James Jeffries in Coney Island.

HOCKEY
■ The England women's team started a remarkable scoring spree against Wales. They had 13-0 victories in 1900 and 1901 and a 15-0 triumph in 1902. Scotland and Ireland did not escape either. Scotland were beaten 11-0 in 1903 and 7-2 in 1904, and Ireland went down 7-1 in 1903 and 7-3 in 1907.

RACING
■ The Prince of Wales won the Triple Crown and the Grand National in the same year, a feat never to be repeated by an owner. Diamond Jubilee was so bad-tempered that two jockeys refused to touch him, so he was ridden by his stable lad in all the Triple Crown races.

RUGBY UNION
■ A tablet commemorating William Webb Ellis was erected at Rugby school.
■ The first Sydney premiership match was held.

Smith learns his lines well but fails the final exam

WHEN the one great scorer comes to write about how Sidney Smith played tennis he will have only one description: he played from the baseline. Smith of Stroud, as he was called, was forced to wear an iron support because of a leg disability. To compensate for his lack of mobility he developed a powerful, flat forehand which became known as the "Smith Punch".

Smith was a colourful character who was as good a badminton player as he was a tennis player. He won the first men's singles title at the Badminton Association tournament, which was soon to be renamed the All-England championships and become the most important event in the world. And despite his weak leg he fought his way through to the men's singles challenge round at Wimbledon. But he failed to deliver the knockout blow against the defending champion Reggie Doherty, who came from behind to clinch his fourth successive crown 6-8 6-3 6-1 6-2.

Yorkshire outclass their peers

YORKSHIRE, with the seventh Lord Hawke at their helm, clinched the first of three consecutive county championship titles. They were also the first unbeaten side in a season. Their supremacy was masterminded by two great all-rounders, George Hirst and Wilfred Rhodes. Hirst made 5,323 runs in the three years and Rhodes took 685 wickets at an average of 13.21. Yorkshire won 49 matches, drew 29 and lost only twice in three summers.

Almost impossible to beat: Yorkshire under Lord Hawke

Champion jockey finally reined in

AMERICAN jockeys had fast got a name this side of the Atlantic as a disreputable bunch. English jockeys disliked their aggressive riding style, and they were often suspected of being involved in betting coups by doping horses and fixing races.

Lester Reiff, the leading jockey in 1900, won a bruising Derby on Volodyovski. But in September he was reported to the Jockey Club for stopping a horse at Manchester in a race won by his brother. The Jockey Club wasted no time in making an example of Reiff. The next month he had his licence withdrawn and was warned off Newmarket Heath, ending his career.

Riding for a fall: Lester Reiff wins a rough and tumble Derby on Volodyovski

CRICKET

Swinging Barnes mines a rich seam

ARCHIE MACLAREN was an astute captain who had taken over the England leadership from W G Grace in 1899. However, he failed to win the Ashes that year and was given little hope of success when he set off for Australia without a cluster of leading players: C B Fry, George Hirst, Stanley Jackson, K S Ranjitsinhji and Wilfred Rhodes. Faced with a dearth of talent, he had chosen a relatively unknown medium-fast bowler named Sydney Barnes, who earned his surprise selection by impressing MacLaren in the nets at Old Trafford. And the skipper raised a few more eyebrows when he gambled on his tall protégé leading the attack in the first Test in Sydney.

Barnes did not let his captain down. He wrapped the new ball in his large right hand, made a short, springy approach to the wicket and bowled England to their only victory in an 18-match spell against Australia. He took five for 65 in the first innings on his debut, inspiring England to an innings and 124-run victory. Although Australia came back to win the series 4-1 Barnes had stormed on to the Test arena. In the next 13 years he became one of the greatest bowlers in history, taking 189 wickets for

Seam supremo: Sydney Barnes bowled England to victory

3,106 runs at an average of 16.43 in 27 Tests. He was one of the first to use the seam of the ball to swerve his deliveries, a tactic regarded alongside googly bowling as the most innovative addition to the sport in the early 20th century.

FOR THE RECORD

ATHLETICS

■ Peter O'Connor, of Ireland, broke the world long jump record with a leap of 24ft 11¾in Dublin. His record stood until 1921, when Edward Gourdin, of the United States, beat it by 3in.

BADMINTON

■ The hour-glass court, which was 5ft narrower at the net than at the baselines was abolished. It was thought to have originated at an Indian army base where inward-opening barrack-room doors would, otherwise, have hit the net.

BICYCLE POLO

■ Ireland beat England 10-5 at Crystal Palace.

CRICKET

■ Nottinghamshire were dismissed for 13 by Yorkshire at Nottingham. It was their lowest total ever, and the second-lowest in all first-class cricket.

GOLF

■ Willie Anderson beat Alex Smith 85 to 86 in the first ever play-off at the US Open. They both finished on 331 after 72 holes.

■ Harold Hilton was the first player since 1887 to successfully defend the British amateur title and the last player to do so until Lawson Little in 1935.

■ The Professional Golfers' Association was founded.

Spurs come from nowhere to win Cup

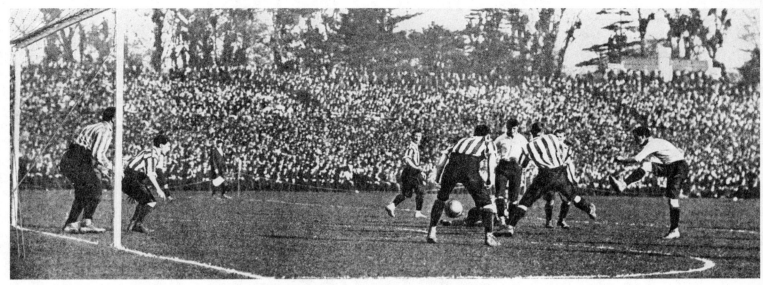

Under pressure: Tottenham attack the Sheffield United goal in the first match of the Cup final at Crystal Palace

TOTTENHAM HOTSPUR of the Southern League won the FA Cup when they defeated Sheffield United of the First Division 3-1 at Burnden Park, Bolton, in a replay. It was an amazing achievement by Spurs, who became the first non-League club to win the Cup since the formation of the Football League.

As in the semi-final and the final, it was their striker Sandy Brown who rose to the occasion. And as they did a week earlier at Crystal Palace in the first match, Spurs soon went a goal down. But three goals in the second half, the third from Brown — who had scored all four in the semi-final and both goals in the match at Crystal Palace — clinched the trophy. It was no more than Tottenham deserved. The pictures from Crystal Palace, the first match to be filmed, proved conclusively that the referee was wrong to ignore his linesman. The ball was not within a foot of the goal-line and Bennett's equaliser for Sheffield United should have been a corner, as the linesman correctly signalled. The first six-figure crowd, more than 110,000, crammed into Crystal Palace.

Unfortunately, few of the Tottenham faithful were able to make the long trek north to Burnden Park. Because of the weather and the refusal of the Lancashire and Yorkshire Rail Company to issue any cheap tickets, only 20,000 were present to see an historic replay.

Tottenham's FA Cup campaign was brilliantly masterminded by their player-manager John Cameron. It was hailed as a breakthrough against northern domination, even though the team was a collection of one Irishman, two Welshman, five Scots and three Englishmen, none of whom was born within 100 miles of White Hart Lane. Tottenham's success gave the game fresh impetus in London. Spurs had to beat four powerful First Division sides: Preston, Bury (the Cup holders), West Bromwich, and, finally, the mighty Sheffield United, who had been champions and runners-up in the previous four seasons and who had nine full internationals in their team.

At the celebratory dinner jubilant Tottenham officials tied their colours, dark blue and white, to the handles of the Cup, a tradition that has persisted.

Bloomer a popular shooting star

ONCE again, Derby County's goalscoring genius Steve Bloomer finished the season as the leading League scorer with 24 goals. This was the fourth time in six years the England inside-right was the country's top marksman. During his career with Derby and Middlesbrough he scored a total of 352 League goals, 291 of of them for Derby. Bloomer was the most unlikely of forwards. He was slender and pale, not really a dribbler, nor was he particularly tricky on the ball. Yet the press and the public alike took him to their hearts. It was probably because he possessed something that no other striker had — the ability to shoot suddenly and powerfully with both feet.

Bloomer seemed to adapt well to the developing phenomenon of the sophisticated passing game that was becoming fashionable in football. He had a simple philosophy: "The purpose of play is the scoring of goals." Indeed.

Bloomer: goalscoring genius

Doherty pair either blow hot or cold

REGGIE DOHERTY was not one to listen to his doctor's advice, particularly when it came to defending the Wimbledon title. An unwell Doherty was told not to play in the challenge round against Arthur Gore. But he went ahead, and even won the first set, before losing 4-6 7-5 6-4 6-4. It was the only time in 10 years either Reggie or his brother Laurie did not win the title.

FOOTBALL

25 killed at Ibrox but Scotland still play on

The wooden stand that collapsed at Ibrox in April

FOOTBALL

THE home international between Scotland and England at Ibrox on April 5 ended in disaster. Twenty-five people died and more than 500 were injured when the wooden stand on the west terrace collapsed. With heavy rain falling and a huge crowd, there was a surge of spectators into the ground. They pushed their way to the top of the stand for a better view, but the flimsy structure could not sustain their weight.

Amazingly, the match was not abandoned because the authorities thought that would have aggravated matters, and after a 20-minute delay the game was re-started. It finished 1-1, but did not count as an official international. Ironically, Ibrox was chosen as the venue because of its modern amenities, Rangers having returned to their "new" stadium only three years earlier.

GOLF

New ball wins by a distance

A DENTIST from Ohio found a way to bind an elastic thread to a hard core and changed the face of golf. Dr Coburn Haskell became the toast of hackers and professionals by inventing a ball that could be hit further than the commonly used gutta-percha ball.

Some Scottish players protested that the new ball would take the skill out of the game, but their voices were drowned by the cheers of the majority whose eternal quest for greater distance had been temporarily

satisfied. Sales of the ball soared. Courses had to be lengthened to accommodate the extra distance players could achieve, and clubmakers began to manufacture hard persimmon club heads which were better suited to the soft, resilient ball.

There was no greater advertisement for Haskell's ball than Sandy Herd's victory in the Open. The Scottish baker, the only player to use the new ball, dented the domination of the great triumvirate of James Braid, J H Taylor and Harry Vardon.

And across the Atlantic, Laurie Auchterlonie boosted sales by using the Haskell ball to became the first player to break 80 in all four rounds of the US Open.

The debate about the merits of the Haskell ball raged until 1914 when four leading players settled the argument. Braid, Taylor and Vardon were joined by George Duncan in a 36-hole competition between the two balls. The Haskell ball won by nine holes. It also won a long-driving contest by 278 yards to 240 yards.

TENNIS

Robb: Wimbledon replay

Battling Victor produces the trumps to salvage Australia's damp summer

Trumper: "All bowling came alike to him"

IT WAS a wretched summer, brightened only by the prospect of watching Joe Darling's Australians defend the Ashes. Among their number was Victor Trumper, an elegant stroke-maker and one of his country's most brilliant batsmen. He had been to England before as a late inclusion in the 1899 team on an agreed bonus of £200 while the rest of the side were awarded £700 a man. Trumper's success was such that halfway through the tour he was earning the same as his teammates. Trumper preferred style to statistics and fluency to figures. He produced his best innings in difficult conditions and conditions were never more difficult than in the wet summer of 1902.

The tour started badly for Australia. They were dismissed for 36, their lowest-ever score against England, on a damp pitch at Edgbaston in the first Test. Wilfred Rhodes took seven for 17 and Trumper scored half of Australia's runs. Three days later, Yorkshire bowled Australia out for 23. Then Trumper blossomed. He finished the summer with 2,570 runs, 956 more than his nearest rival, Clem Hill. "All bowling came alike to him and he reduced our best bowling to the level of the village green," Wisden said. He saved his best for the fourth Test at Old Trafford, when Darling won the toss and elected to bat. Just 108 minutes later Trumper was the first of four Test batsmen to hit a century before lunch on the opening day. He made 103 of Australia's 173 for one and was dismissed five balls after lunch. The others who have scored centuries before lunch are Charlie Macartney in 1926, Don Bradman in 1930 and Majid Khan in 1976.

Trumper's innings set the tone for one of cricket's most famous matches. Australia made 299 in their first innings and England recovered from 44 for five to finish 37 runs behind. Darling, attempting to rescue his team from 10 for three in the second innings, was dropped by Fred Tate and went on to top score with 37 in Australia's total of 86. England, needing 124 for victory, began well but collapsed and were eight short of their target with one wicket in hand when rain came.

When the match resumed 45 minutes later Tate struck the first ball he received from John Saunders for four. Three deliveries later Saunders bowled him. England lost by three runs and Tate had played in his only Test.

A tearful Tate said: "I've a little lad at home who'll make up for that." His name was Maurice and he became one of England's greatest fast bowlers.

Sceptre the classical actress

SCEPTRE was bought for 10,000 guineas, a record for a yearling, and she soon proved that she was worth every penny even though she had to do it the hard way. Sceptre was trained by her owner Robert Sievier, who ran her in an astonishing 12 top-flight races in the season. So it was even more remarkable that she had the strength to win four of the five classics. She opened her account by winning the 2,000 Guineas in record time. Two days later, the 1,000 Guineas was a formality. Sievier went for another double at Epsom. Sceptre was only fourth in the Derby but two days later she romped away with the Oaks.

Many of Sceptre's races came in pairs: she was unplaced in the Coronation Stakes then first in the St James's Palace Stakes at Royal Ascot; beaten in the Sussex Stakes then the winner of the Nassau Stakes at Goodwood. Sceptre's final classic was the St Leger, which she won as comfortably as the Oaks.

Sceptre: record price and record performance

BASEBALL

Americans deny game is British import

THE National League of Professional Baseball Clubs had seen off several challenges to its monopoly. But it could not withstand the American League, which declared itself a major league at the start of the 1901.

The poaching of players had been rife for many years. However, the battle in 1902 was particularly fierce. The American League, with unlimited salaries, won, with its total attendance outstripping the National League by more than half a million. A crumbling National League accepted the American League as an equal at the start of 1903, and so began the World Series between the champions of the two leagues.

As one battle ended another began. Henry Chadwick, a sports writer and promoter, was known as the "Father of the Game". He was British by birth and caused uproar when he wrote that the most American of sports was derived from rounders. A commission investigated his claim, but it was packed with baseball officials who ignored the overwhelming evidence. Not surprisingly, four years later they decided that baseball had been invented in America.

CYCLING

Editor starts race to sell his paper

Clean sweep: Maurice Garin won by three hours

HENRI DESGRANGE was a disillusioned newspaper editor at the turn of the century. His sports paper, l'Auto, was facing a difficult time. He could sell no more than 20,000 copies a day while Le Vélo, the market leader, had reached 80,000 copies. And he had been forced to drop the name Vélo (cycle) from the title of his publication after losing a lawsuit against his rivals.

But the former cyclist was determined to succeed. So, in a bid to boost circulation and to prove his paper would continue its coverage of his favourite sport, Desgrange announced that l'Auto would hold a month-long cycle race with 20,000 francs in prize-money. The event would cover two-thirds of France, twice as long as the record Paris-Brest-Paris race promoted by Le Vélo.

Despite initial interest, few cyclists entered and it was not

until Desgrange trimmed the Tour to a three-week event over six stages a month before the start that interest was rekindled.

The 2,428km Tour began at 3pm on July 1 at Montgeron and 19 days later Maurice Garin, a 32-year-old Italian chimney sweep, became the first winner, in 94hr 33min. Garin led 21 finishers home nearly three hours ahead of Louis Pothier, who took second place. Desgrange was delighted. The sales of his paper had increased and the Tour was the talk of France.

A year later the second Tour, marred by cheating and violence, was a disaster. Garin won again, but an investigation by the French authorities led to the first four finishers being disqualified for cheating. Henri Cornet was promoted to first place and, at 20, remains the youngest winner of the Tour. Desgrange announced the Tour

was finished but, no sooner had his dream died, he relaunched the race with subtle changes. He shortened the stages, cancelled night riding and saved the Tour.

His newspaper, renamed l'Equipe at the end of the Second World War, became the biggest selling daily sports newspaper in the world and the Tour de France the most prestigious cycling event on the calendar.

BOXING

Third title for veteran world champion

THE former world heavyweight champion, Bob Fitzsimmons, won the light heavyweight championship in San Francisco on November 25 when he outpointed George Gardiner over 20 rounds in the first year of the newly-created title. It was his third crown, and he was the first boxer to achieve such a feat.

Fitzsimmons was born in Cornwall but he and his family emigrated to New Zealand when he was nine. He took up professional boxing in New Zealand and Australia before arriving in the United States, where he won the world middleweight crown in 1891 and the heavyweight title in 1897 when, at the age of 34 and weighing only 167lb, he knocked out Jim Corbett with a much publicised punch to the solar plexus.

Fitzsimmons's heavyweight reign lasted only 2¼ years. In 1902 he squared up to Jim Jeffries, a mountain of a man, and mercilessly hammered him for eight rounds — breaking his nose, cutting open both cheeks, and opening up gashes above both eyes — before succumbing to a crashing left hook to the jaw.

Fighter turns actor

AFTER three years of inactivity, Gentleman Jim Corbett tried for one last time to recapture his heavyweight crown on August 14. But he was stopped in the tenth round in San Francisco by the Grizzly Bear of the West, Jim Jeffries. Corbett promptly quit the ring and turned his attention to the stage, where he had made a successful debut in the 1890s in a melodrama called Gentleman Jack.

Corbett, a former bank clerk, had first won the title in 1892 from the legendary John L Sullivan, when his scientific fighting completely outshone the out-dated slugging methods and rocked the world of boxing. It was the first heavyweight championship to be held under Queensberry rules. Corbett had been a popular champion, and had attracted a different kind of audience to the sport — the swells rather than the low-lifes. At his peak there was not a fighter who could match his mental and physical agility.

Jim Jeffries: ended the career of Gentleman Jim Corbett

Master detains the star pupil

KEN MCLEOD, a 15-year-old schoolboy at Fettes College in Edinburgh, was invited to become the youngest ever international when the Scottish selectors chose him on the wing against Wales. But his headmaster, Dr Heard, refused him permission to play. McLeod eventually made his debut in 1905, won 10 caps and gave up rugby three years later at his father's request after the death of his brother during a game.

On tour: Foster, Douglas and Warner in Australia

FOR THE RECORD

BOWLS

■ The English Bowling Association was founded. Its first president was W G Grace, who, when he was not playing cricket, encouraged the development of indoor bowls.

CRICKET

■ MCC sponsored a team to tour Australia, under P F Warner. Previously, individual cricketers had selected teams and conducted tours of the colonies.

■ Middlesex ended Yorkshire's domination by winning the county championship.

FOOTBALL

■ Bury won the FA Cup without conceding a goal in the tournament. Queen's Park unveiled Hampden, then the greatest stadium in the world, with a League game against Celtic.

GOLF

■ The Vardon brothers, Harry and Tom, finished first and second in the Open.

■ Willie Anderson became the first player to win the US Open twice. His first round of 73 was a new low and he beat David Brown in a play-off, 82 to 84.

■ The first golf club in Japan, the Kobe Golf Club, was opened. There are now more than 10 million people playing golf in Japan.

ICE HOCKEY

■ Five teams formed the first league in England.

MOTOR RACING

■ The Paris-Madrid race was abandoned after the first day at Bordeaux because of accidents. As a result, motor racing was generally taken off open roads and transferred to closed circuits.

RACING

■ The Jockey Club banned doping. It had been estimated that two owners and their trainer alone had won £2m in four or five years in bets on doped horses.

SAILING

■ Reliance was the largest yacht ever built for the America's Cup and it beat Shamrock III 3-0. Shamrock got lost in the fog and never finished the third race.

Bury 6 Derby 0: the FA Cup final at Crystal Palace

Quinn's hat-trick rallies Celtic

CELTIC won the Scottish Cup final by beating Rangers 3-2. Two goals from Finlay Speedie seemed to have given their arch-rivals a winning lead, but Celtic rallied and a brilliant hat-trick by Jimmy Quinn, normally a left-winger but playing at centre-forward, gave them the trophy. Quinn's first goal was a virtuoso performance of strength, speed, and powerful shooting. Although no colossus at 5ft 8in, he was Celtic's human dynamo.

The team, under the astute managership of the legendary Willie Maley, who held the job from 1897 to 1940, dominated the rest of decade. They won six League championships in succession and two Scottish Cups. In all League games from 1904 to 1910 they played 192 times, winning 136 and drawing 33 and were undoubtedly the first great modern Scottish team, concentrating on precision passing.

Games fiasco again

Ralph Rose: another gold medal for the United States

THE floundering Olympic Games continued to flounder. Instead of taking a lesson from the disaster in Paris, President Theodore Roosevelt decided to move the Games from Chicago to St Louis to coincide with the World Fair. Like its predecessor, the Olympics became a badly-organised sideshow. If ever gold medals were awarded for sporting fiascos this one would have been a strong contender.

Nothing epitomised the farce more than the marathon. Fred Lorz led 31 runners out of the stadium but he developed cramp after 15 kilometres, dropped out of the race and was given a lift in one of the many cars that clogged the course. When the car broke down Lorz resumed running. He overtook the eventual gold medallist, Thomas Hicks, and came into the stadium to be acclaimed the winner. Lorz said he had continued to run as a joke but was banned for a year. He returned to win the 1905 Boston Marathon. The majority of the 625 competitors was American and the Games were little more than an inter-college championship, with the United States winning 244 of the 281 medals.

Pretty Polly leaves the others standing

PRETTY POLLY was almost invincible. Her first victory in 1903 was the only time she did not start as favourite. The bookmakers soon caught on as she won eight more times, including several leading two-year-old races.

She carved a swathe through the summer of 1904 as she extended her winning streak to 15, taking the fillies Triple Crown in the process. Her triumphs were: 1,000 Guineas, 4-1 on; The Oaks, 100-8 on; Coronation Stakes, 5-1 on; Nassau Stakes, 33-1 on; St Leger, 5-2 on; Park Hill Stakes, 25-1 on. Her amazing run finally came to an end in October, when she was beaten by a 66-1 outsider in Paris.

There was no respite for the bookies in 1905 either. Pretty Polly took the Coronation Cup in record time and two of her other victories were at the prohibitive odds of 55-1 on and 1,000-35 on. In total, Pretty Polly won 22 of her 24 races. Her only other defeat was in her final race, the 1906 Ascot Gold Cup.

Pretty Polly: comfortably won 15 successive races

The master of deception

Close call for equal partners in double act

Bosanquet: turning the world upside down

BERNARD BOSANQUET started his career as a fast bowler on flat, hard pitches in the sweltering sun. But it was as the pioneer of the googly that he made his mark, helping England regain the Ashes in Australia with a devastating spell of five for 12 in the fourth Test in Sydney. Bosanquet had further success two Tests later, at Trent Bridge in 1905, taking eight for 107 to spin England to victory. But his Test career ended before the series was over.

It took an education at Eton and Oxford and the student game of "twisti-twosti" for Bosanquet to realise there was life after bowling fast. The peculiar pastime required a player to spin a tennis ball past his opponent at the other end of the table. Bosanquet became one of its finest exponents with an over-the-wrist action that made the ball move from left to right. He adapted the technique to his

bowling and came up with the googly, an off-break bowled with a leg-break action. After a few seasons of fine-tuning Bosanquet sent down his first googly for Middlesex against Leicestershire at Lord's in 1900. The ball bounced four times but Sammy Coe missed it and was stumped for 98.

> ❝ The googly is not unfair, only immoral ❞
>
> **Bernard Bosanquet**

Although Bosanquet only played in seven Tests the Australians were so impressed by his technique that they still call their googly a "Bosie". Bosanquet might have faded from view but the art of googly bowling was not lost. Reggie

Schwartz, a friend of Bosanquet's at Oxford, became its custodian and took the skill to South Africa. There, lying in wait for Plum Warner's 1906 tourists, were a googly quartet of Schwartz, Aubrey Faulkner, Ernie Vogler and Gordon White. They took 43 wickets to sweep South Africa to a 4-1 triumph.

Ironically, when the quartet faded, the two countries who had turned googly bowling into an art never again used the "wrong 'un" as a strategy to win Test matches.

Dod trounces all comers

THE 12th British women's golf championship at Troon became little more than another showpiece for Lottie Dod's sporting excellence. The five-times Wimbledon tennis champion beat May Hezlet on the final hole to add one more title to her impressive list of achievements.

Dod, who reached the semi-finals in 1898 and 1899, was a hockey international, an excellent ice skater, a fine billiards player, an Olympic archery silver medallist and the first woman to go down the Cresta Run.

Dod: consummate all-rounder

FRANK RISELEY and Sidney Smith, who were doubles partners, met in the fifth round at Wimbledon for the second successive year. Riseley had won their first match 7-5 6-3 7-9 1-6 9-7 in 1903, and their knowledge of each other's play suggested another close contest. The pair slugged it out for 50 tight games, which left them at two sets all. The exhausted duo had had enough. Rather than put themselves through more torture they tossed a coin to decide the winner. Riseley won, but lost the challenge round to Laurie Doherty, 6-1 7-5 8-6.

FOR THE RECORD

AMERICAN FOOTBALL
■ Charles W Follis signed for Shelby in exchange for a job at a hardware store and became the first verified black professional player.
■ Massillon scored 26 touchdowns to beat Marion 148-0. Marion punted on their first possession and never got the ball back, because the team conceding a score had to kick off.

BOXING
■ Joe Bowker, the British champion, took the world bantamweight title when he outpointed Frankie Neil, from San Francisco, over 20 rounds at the National Sporting Club in London.

FOOTBALL
■ Aston Villa became the first club to score 1,000 goals in the League.
■ In the Second Division, Manchester United set a record of 14 consecutive League wins.
■ FIFA was formed.

GOLF
■ Jack White became the first man with a winning total under 300 in the Open. He was also the first champion to break 70, with a first round of 69. J H Taylor went one better with 68 in the final round, a score not bettered for 30 years.

HOCKEY
■ The England men's team lost an international for the first time, 3-2 to Ireland in Dublin. They were not beaten again until 1912, and did not lose at home until 1933.

JANUARY

1905

DECEMBER

Mears invents Chelsea as an afterthought

AT THE start of the year Chelsea FC did not exist. Gus Mears and his brother began with the idea of a ground inspired by the great Scottish stadiums of Hampden, Ibrox and Celtic Park. The new venue, capable of seating 5,000 and holding perhaps 95,000 standing, came into being on the site of the London Athletic Club and was called Stamford Bridge. It was essentially an entrepreneurial venture designed to attract big matches such as the Cup final, which it did from 1920 to 1922.

The football team was an afterthought put together in months, mostly with Scottish imports brought in by the hastily appointed manager John Tait Robertson, a Scottish international from Rangers who had played in England. One of his most important acquisitions was the mountainous goalkeeper, Billy Foulke from Sheffield United, who was made the captain. At 6ft 2in and 22st 3lb Foulke was, unsurprisingly, called "Fatty", yet he was remarkably agile and adept at saving penalties. He was also extremely temperamental. If he felt that his defence had let him down when Chelsea conceded a goal, he was quite capable of refusing to make any other saves. He disliked forwards barging him and would often grab an offender with one massive hand and toss him into the back of the net. Opponents were known to have admitted that instead of keeping the ball low they often shot at his huge stomach — his most vulnerable area. Steve Bloomer is said to have knocked the giant flat twice with shots to his belly, which was no mean feat. Apparently he was denied a third strike when the ball sailed into the net because Foulke had fled.

To intimidate the opposition Chelsea used to send out two small boys to stand behind the goal to call attention to Foulke's bulk. They soon became more than ornaments and thus the ball-boy was inadvertently born.

Within a month of signing their first player Chelsea had elbowed their way past the Football League's annual meeting and were elected into the Second Division. They lost their first match to Stockport but finished the season third and were promoted the next season as runners-up.

Foulke: nicknamed "Fatty"

Common worth every penny

ALF COMMON was the first footballer transferred for £1,000. The move from Sunderland to Middlesbrough caused outrage at such a sum being paid. But Middlesbrough got value for their money. They won their first away match for two years and staved off relegation to the Second Division.

Teenager sets new fashion

MAY SUTTON was the envy of the women's locker-room at Wimbledon when she turned up for her first championship. The cheerful Californian was allowed to wear a short dress because she was only 18, while her older opponents were forced to don ankle-length creations which hindered their movement around the court. Sutton, in an almost knee-length skirt, took the tournament by storm. With the brashness of youth and a powerful top-spin forehand she did not drop a set in becoming the first overseas player to win a championship at Wimbledon.

Sutton: shocked Wimbledon

AMERICAN FOOTBALL
■ Eighteen players were killed and 149 injured during the season. President Theodore Roosevelt threatened to ban the game unless it was made less violent.

BOXING
■ Bob Fitzsimmons relinquished his light-heavyweight world title when he was stopped by Jack O'Brien, one of the fastest fighters of the day, in the 13th round in San Francisco.

CRICKET
■ Northamptonshire became the 16th county to join the championship.

GOLF
■ Willie Anderson won the US Open for a record third time. His total of four victories (1901, 1903, 1904 and 1905) was equalled 25 years later by Bobby Jones, and then by Ben Hogan and Jack Nicklaus.

RACING
■ The Jockey Club continued its clean-up of the sport by ordering that all trainers had to be licensed.

SAILING
■ The three-masted schooner Atlantic won the Kaiser's Cup transatlantic race from Sandy Hook to the Lizard in 12 days 4hr 1min 19 sec, a time not bettered for 70 years.

TENNIS
■ Britain made a clean sweep in the Davis Cup, and Australasia and Austria joined the competition.
■ The first Australian championships were staged and the event became the last of the four majors.

CRICKET

Captain calls all the shots

SIR STANLEY JACKSON couldn't get a trick wrong in the Ashes series against Australia. He was the first captain to win every toss in a five-match series, he helped England to a 2-0 victory, and he headed the averages, batting at 70.28 and bowling at 15.46.

Sir Stanley had been given a good start in life. Winston Churchill polished his shoes and carried his books at Harrow. The Prime Minister's fagmaster later became president of the MCC and chairman of the England selectors.

Referee wrong-foots the All Blacks

WHEN Dave Gallaher arrived with his New Zealand team not many Britons thought much of his chances on a gruelling 32-match tour. Scotland had so little regard for the New Zealanders that they refused to guarantee them a £200 game fee. Instead, they agreed the tourists would receive any profit from the match after expenses had been deducted.

Much to the chagrin of the Scots, Gallaher's side were a sensation. They opened the tour with a 55-4 win against Devon and by the time they reached Scotland in mid-November the All Blacks, as they became known, were a sell-out. They beat Scotland 12-7 at Inverleith and made £1,000 from the game. In the next two weeks they beat Ireland 15-0 at Lansdowne Road and England 15-0 at Crystal Palace.

Nothing, it appeared, would stop the first national team from New Zealand completing a clean sweep. They had won all 27 matches, scoring 801 points to a mere 22 against them. Then they went to Cardiff to face 40,000 singing Welshmen and the pride of the Principality.

Wales took the initiative and Teddy Morgan scored a try in the 25th minute. The All Blacks rallied and Bob Deans appeared to have levelled the score. However, the referee, John Dallas of Scotland, was wearing his street clothes and flat shoes and could not keep up with the play. He ruled that Deans had not crossed the try line and his decision was one of the most controversial in rugby history. The disappointed All Blacks lost 3-0, won their remaining four matches and returned home having conceded only seven tries and lost one match.

Gallaher and his vice-captain Billy Snead spent the voyage home writing a book, "The Complete Rugby Footballer", which described how they had

The All Blacks on their way to another easy victory over the Midland Counties

The Originals: the first team to plan their moves and give them a code

achieved success on the tour.

The Originals, as they were called, were the first to plan their moves and give them code names. They used their hooker to throw the ball into the line-out instead of the scrum-half, had extra men in back moves, used skip passes and decoys, and attacked with the blindside wing. Their thoroughness was unique. They kept a record of how they scored each try and the way tries were scored against them. For the first time they used the lineout as a platform of attack, scoring 33 tries. They also introduced the hip swing pass and, unlike their opponents, did not lie on the ball in loose scrums, preferring second and third-phase play.

Gallaher's most controversial idea was to reduce his scrum to seven men and play himself as a roving wing forward who would wait on the fringe of scrums and mauls and then harry the opposition or defend his scrum-half. The ploy proved to be so effective and so disconcerted opponents that several accused him of cheating.

JANUARY
1906
DECEMBER

President puts safety first

IN THE wake of President Theodore Roosevelt's warning about American football being too brutal, the Intercollegiate Athletic Association rewrote the rules and gave the game its modern shape. Forward passes were allowed for the first time, although they did not prove immediately popular. The rules were changed in January, but it was not until late October that the first completed pass was recorded in a professional game.

A more open style of play was created by increasing the distance that had to be made on the three downs (the fourth down was introduced in 1912) from five yards to 10. A neutral zone was introduced at the line of scrimmage, and a team had to have six players on the line. Those linemen were not allowed to drop back to form a pack with their backs, which led to a gradual elimination of the "Flying Wedge" and the other massed attacks that had caused so many of the injuries. Although the game became less violent the injuries continued, and it was not until after another six players died in 1909 that mass attacks were finally banned in 1910.

CRICKET

Woolley leads Kent to title

KENT, after years of watching Lancashire and Yorkshire dominate the county championship, finally broke the northern supremacy. A large part of their success was due to Frank Woolley, playing his maiden season in first-class cricket. Woolley became one of the game's greatest all-rounders, scoring 58,969 runs, second only to Jack Hobbs, and taking 2,068 wickets. R C Robertson-Glasgow said of Woolley: "When you bowled at him there weren't enough fielders, and when you wrote about him there weren't enough words."

Woolley: maiden season

MOTOR RACING

France change gear

Szisz at the wheel of his winning Renault

THE first Grand Prix was held near Le Mans on a triangular town-to-town closed circuit, and was effectively the beginning of what became Formula 1. It was won by the Hungarian Francois Szisz in a Renault.

The two-day race, organised by the Automobile Club de France, was run in blazing heat over 769.9 miles and won at an average speed of 73.3mph. On the first day each competitor went out at 90-second intervals, but on the second they started at intervals corresponding to the cumulative result of the first day's six 50-mile laps. A victory by a French car was almost inevitable. France entered 25 cars, and Britain and the US none.

CRICKET

Last stand wins Test

DAVE NOURSE and Percy Sherwell shared an unbroken partnership of 48, the highest for a tenth wicket to win a Test. The pair clinched South Africa's first Test victory, beating England by one wicket in Johannesburg. South Africa went on to win the series 4-1 with an unchanged team. The England side in Australia in 1884-85 was the only other unchanged team throughout a five-match series.

Nourse: beat England

Dohertys' reign draws to close

Winners at last: Smith and Riseley finally beating the Doherty brothers at Wimbledon

Smaller is better

RUGBY LEAGUE spent 11 years emulating its big brother after a momentous breakaway in 1895 when the Rugby Football Union refused northern clubs permission to pay players for the loss of their wages when playing. But the sport only came into its own with two major rules changes in the space of two years. The first change came in 1906 when the number of players in each team was reduced from 15 to 13, and the next year came the change which allowed a player who was tackled in possession to restart the game by dropping the ball at his feet; a move that became known as play-the-ball.

THE financial statement from the Wimbledon championships in 1895 made unpleasant reading. It reported a loss of £33. In a desperate attempt to increase funds the committee decided to readmit its croquet members and change the club's name to the All-England Lawn Tennis and Croquet Club. But the real saviour of their flagging fortunes was William Vernon Doherty, an Oxford University captain who had introduced the sport to his younger brothers, Reggie and Laurie.

Wimbledon was never the same after Reggie and Laurie arrived. Reggie started their reign in 1897 when he won the first of four successive singles titles. And when Big Do bowed out because of ill health Little Do took over. Laurie won the title five times and also became the first non-American to win the United States men's singles championship in 1903. The pair won the Wimbledon men's doubles eight times in 10 years and the United States title twice. In the Davis Cup, Reggie played eight matches for Britain and lost once, Laurie played 12

matches and was never beaten.

The duo were the sport's greatest asset in a lean period when the game had outlived its novelty value. The Dohertys were timely white knights, setting high standards in skill and sportsmanship to play a crucial role in reviving a sport that was quietly dying in SW19. Although they dominated the era they were never supreme and crowds flocked back to Wimbledon knowing that their matches would not be one-sided. Reggie was the more graceful, concentrating on control to win his matches. Laurie, who was three years younger, was aggressive, using his long arms at the net to perfect an awesome smash. Reggie was regarded as the more proficient despite his ill health. He won their only challenge round match in 1898.

The end of their era in 1906 was both sweet and sour. Laurie won his fifth singles title against Frank Riseley, who had lost to him twice before in the challenge round. But Riseley earned his revenge in the men's doubles with Sidney Smith. In their fifth successive final

against the Dohertys, Riseley and Smith finally triumphed 4-6 8-6 6-3 4-6 11-9. A decade of dominance was over.

Reggie died only four years later at the age of 36. Little Do died in 1919, but the brothers are still remembered. The Wimbledon club has honoured them by erecting "The Doherty Gates".

OLYMPIC GAMES ▰▰▰▰▰

Greece receive compensation

PIERRE DE COUBERTIN took a tentative step towards establishing the Olympic Games as a significant sporting event by staging an Interim Games in Athens. The Greek capital was awarded the Games as compensation for losing the right to be a permanent home for the Olympics. After the shambles of 1900 and 1904 the Games needed a fillip and the Greeks provided it with enthusiastic support which made up for their organisational faux pas. Great Britain won eight gold medals, 11 silver and six bronze.

FOR THE RECORD

■ **Sport finally gained an air of respectability when the Board of Education officially allowed sport as part of the school curriculum.**

FOOTBALL ▰▰▰▰▰

■ **Liverpool won the League championship for the second time, having won the Second Division championship the year before. They were the first club to win the two titles in consecutive years.**

■ **George Hilsdon scored five goals on his League debut for Chelsea against Glossop. In the following season he hit Worksop for six in the FA Cup.**

RACING ▰▰▰▰▰

■ **Solly Joel won the Cambridgeshire, and some large bets, with Polymelus. The horse was bought for only 4,200 guineas, but when retired to stud was champion sire five times.**

SAILING ▰▰▰▰▰

■ **Brooke Heckstall-Smith, the secretary of the Yacht Racing Association, arranged a 16-nation conference in London which was the origin of the International Yacht Racing Union.**

TENNIS ▰▰▰▰▰

■ **W J Clothier recovered from the depths of 0-40 and 2-5 down in the fifth set to beat F B Alexander 8-6 6-2 4-6 1-6 7-5 in the men's quarter-finals of the US championship. Clothier went on to win the title.**

Built for speed: Brooklands became the spiritual home of British motor racing

TENNIS

Wizard of Aussie

NORMAN BROOKES became the first model off that prolific factory-floor of tennis champions called Australia. There have been more popular, more skilful and more successful players from down under, but the left-handed Brookes will always be remembered as the father of the Australian game.

An aggressive volleyer with quick footwork and a variety of disguised services which earned him the nickname "The Wizard", Brookes became the first overseas player to win the men's singles title at Wimbledon, beating Arthur Gore 6-4 6-2 6-2. He returned in 1914 to win his second title against the New Zealander Tony Wilding, who had held the crown for four years.

Brookes founded the Australasian Lawn Tennis Association in 1904 and included New Zealand so that his friend Wilding could play in the Davis Cup. The pair dominated the event, taking the title four times and winning 35 of their 48 matches.

Brookes: overseas winner

Green light for Brooklands

BROOKLANDS, built on part of Lord Northcliffe's estate near Weybridge, was opened as the world's first specialist motor racing circuit. Because it was the first of its kind, the designer, Colonel Holden, modelled the course on a horse-racing track and it was consequently oval-shaped with the full circuit measuring 2.77 miles. Brooklands bordered the railway line 20 miles from London. Its long turns were steeply banked, and two of the bends rose to a height of 27ft and were the most striking features of the circuit. Part of the 100ft-wide track crossed the River Wey and was ingeniously supported by a ferro-concrete bridge. The actual surface was extremely flimsy, a mere six-inch layer of concrete, and the battering it took during the motor racing season required it to be repaired each winter.

Racing at Brooklands was conducted in a very gentlemanly fashion — there were no competitions on Sundays — and the track was the spiritual home of British motor sport until the Second World War. Brooklands cost £150,000 but was invaluable to British manufacturers for testing because the speed limit was 20mph at the time.

Mr Edge averaged 65mph around Brooklands for 24 hours

RUGBY UNION

Twickenham begins to take root

A 12-ACRE market garden 12 miles from the centre of London was purchased for £5,572 12s 6d as a home for English rugby. The Rugby Football Union began developing the site at Twickenham, which had become known as the "cabbage patch", and the first match was held two years later.

Messenger arrives

VICTOR TRUMPER, the Australian Test cricketer, and James Giltinan, a businessman, spent most of the night of August 16 trying to persuade Annie Messenger to allow her son Herbert to play against the New Zealand rugby league team in Sydney the next day.

£180 did the trick. "Dally" Messenger, the New South Wales rugby union captain, was the star attraction, drawing a 20,000 crowd to the first rugby league match in Australia. Although New South Wales lost 12-8 there was enough interest generated to start a Sydney premiership the next year. Australia had taken the first step towards becoming the most powerful rugby league nation in the world.

Messenger was invited to join the New Zealand All Golds on their first tour of Britain. His ability to avoid tackles and kick goals attracted scouts from

Tottenham Hotspur, who offered him £1,500 to join the club. He declined, returned to Sydney and captained Australia in two Tests on their first tour of Britain in 1908.

Messenger: star attraction

Celtic's double first

The Celtic team show off their trophies

CELTIC beat Hearts 3-0 in the Scottish Cup final and became the first Scottish side to do the Double when they romped away with the League championship seven points clear of the field. The triumph made up for several near-misses: in 1893 and 1894 they won the League and lost in the Cup final, and in 1900 they won the Cup and were runners-up in the League. Then, to prove it was no fluke, they did the Double again in 1908.

Hayward's first ball dismissal

IT WAS a rare pleasure for a bowler to dismiss Tom Hayward with the first ball he faced. The England opener was technically the most perfect batsman of the era and meticulously compiled 43,551 runs in his first-class career. However, Joe Cresswell of Warwickshire had dismissed him first ball in his first innings for Surrey in 1893. And Ernie Vogler, a South African googly bowler, repeated the feat when Hayward became the only English batsman to be dismissed with the first ball of a Test match in England, trapped lbw in the third Test at The Oval.

Hayward had his days in the sun, though. He was the second batsman after W G Grace to score 100 centuries and a father-figure for Jack Hobbs, with whom he made 40 century opening stands for Surrey.

Northants out for only 12

NORTHAMPTONSHIRE have had some grey days in their cricketing history, but none were bleaker than June 11.

The morning started well for them. They dismissed Gloucestershire for 60 on a soggy pitch early on the second day of their county championship match and were confident of overhauling the modest total. But disaster struck in the shape of E M Dennett, a fast bowler whose ability to turn the ball on the Gloucester pitch made him virtually unplayable. A mere 40 minutes later Northants were bowled out for 12 the lowest total in first-class cricket. They faced only 69 balls and their score equalled that of Oxford University against the MCC in 1877, but the students had only 10 batsmen. However, the rain which had turned the Northants innings into a nightmare did them one last favour. It washed out play on the final day and the match was drawn.

FOR THE RECORD

AMERICAN FOOTBALL
■ Six brothers named Nesser played at the same time for the Columbus Panhandles. In the early 1920s one of them played in the same side as his son, making them the only father and son to play a professional game together.

BADMINTON
■ Women's singles matches were reduced from 15-up to 11-up.

BILLIARDS
■ Tom Reece of Oldham used the anchor cannon to compile a break of 499,135. He averaged 10,000 points a session for five weeks.

EQUESTRIANISM
■ The first International Horse Show was held at London Olympia.

FOOTBALL
■ The Professional Footballers Association was formed at the Imperial Hotel, Manchester, on December 2, with Billy Meredith as chairman.
■ The idea of having numbers on shirts was mooted but rejected.

GOLF
■ Arnaud Massy, of France, became the first overseas player to win the Open. Qualifying rounds were introduced for the first time.
■ A D S Duncan won the first New Zealand Open, which was played over 36 holes. He was the leading amateur 28 years later at the age of 60.

RACING
■ Orby was the first Irish-trained horse to win the Derby.

NORTHAMPTONSHIRE

First Innings

E M Crosse c Board b Dennett	4
M Cox lbw b Dennett	2
C J T Poole c Spry b Dennett	4
W A Buswell st Board b Dennett	1
L T Driffield b Dennett	0
G J Thompson b Dennett	0
R W R Hawtin lbw b Dennett	0
W East st Board b Dennett	0
R N Beasley b Jessop	1
S King not out	0
W Wells c Parker b Jessop	0
Extras	0
Total	**12**

Bowling

Dennett 6-1-9-8;
Jessop 5.3-4-3-2

OLYMPIC GAMES
Marathon man wins in the end

Famous loser: Pietri is helped over the finish line and subsequently disqualified

FOOTBALL
Meredith the inspiration

MANCHESTER UNITED won their first League title, captained by the finest centre-half of his generation, Charlie Roberts, and inspired by the genius of the Welsh international goalscoring winger Billy Meredith.

Meredith, who was the first chairman of the fledgling Players' Union, made his debut in 1894 for Northwich Victoria and then played for Manchester City twice and Manchester United. He had a slender frame and spindly legs but he adorned the international stage until he was 45, and played in an FA Cup semi-final in his 50th year. In all, he played 1,568 matches, including 51 for Wales, and scored 470 goals. He has been described as "the Matthews, Finney and Best of his day rolled into one".

Meredith: goalscoring genius

DORANDO PIETRI was merely a face in the crowd of 56 runners when he stood in the gardens of Windsor Castle waiting for the start of the Olympic marathon on July 24. Three hours later he was the most famous marathon runner in history.

The doughty little Italian made a remarkable late burst to lead the field into the stadium but turned right instead of left and collapsed on the track. He was helped to his feet by doctors and officials and instinctively stumbled towards the tape, falling another four times before he finished in 2hr 54min 46.4sec. Johnny Hayes of America came in 32 seconds behind him.

Pietri was disqualified for receiving help, but his brave run brought him greater glory in defeat than victory. Queen Alexandra awarded him a replica of the winner's cup, Irving Berlin wrote a song about him and they held a collection for him in his hometown of Carpi. Hayes and Pietri turned professional and inspired a marathon craze in America. They re-ran their epic race in New York and Pietri won by 45 seconds.

The marathon was planned for 26 miles, but Princess Mary had the start moved to beneath the windows of the royal nursery so her children could watch. The race was extended to 26 miles 385 yards, a distance adopted for all Olympic marathons from 1924.

The fourth Olympics were the first to achieve a measure of organisational success, despite complaints from the Americans that British officials conducted illegal coaching, fixed heats and broke the rules. Their most acrimonious protests were in the 400m final. The American John Carpenter led into the home straight but ran diagonally across the track to prevent Wyndham Halswelle of Scotland overtaking him. The British judges disqualified Carpenter and decided to re-run the event the next day. William Robbins and John Taylor, the other two American finalists, refused to race and Halswelle completed the only walkover in Olympic history.

Britain dominated the Games, winning 56 gold, 50 silver and 39 bronze medals, almost as many as the combined total of the 21 other nations competing.

BOXING
Johnson cuts up roughest

THE black boxer Jack Johnson destroyed Tommy Burns to take the heavyweight title in Sydney on Boxing Day. Johnson took great delight in cutting up his opponent and the police eventually stopped the fight in the 14th round. Burns had been guaranteed $30,000 for the fight and the purse was the precursor of big pay-days to come.

Johnson: police stopped fight

W G Grace finally hangs up the bat that dominated for half a century

Grace: fine bowler and fearsome batsman

EASTER MONDAY at The Oval was so cold that a blanket of snow covered the ground before the start of Surrey's match against the Gentlemen of England. Dr William Gilbert Grace spent the day in the field, watching Jack Hobbs dismissed for a duck and Surrey scoring 390. He bowled just two overs for five runs. The 59-year-old doctor returned the next morning to score 15 in two hours, but he failed to prevent the Gentlemen following on. He fared better in the second innings until Sydney Busher, an amateur from Barnes, bowled him for 25. The Gentlemen lost by an innings and 41 runs and thus ended the first-class career of W G Grace.

It had started in 1865 when the 16-year-old Grace hit 23 and

> **'I hate defensive strokes, you can only get three off 'em '**
>
> **W G Grace**

12 not out and took seven for 125 for the Gentlemen against the Players at The Oval. In the next 43 years Grace was the catalyst who turned a Victorian pastime into a national sport. With his thick beard, immense stature and an argumentative character he became as well known as Queen Victoria. This regal cricketer was regarded as the greatest player in history. His only blemish was that he

bent the rules in the firm belief that the crowd had come only to watch him bat. He may have been right, for Grace would have made an ideal model in the MCC coaching manual. His philosophy was to keep a straight bat, never play a rash shot, treat each delivery on its merits, keep the bat and pad together, and always concentrate.

C B Fry wrote: "He revolutionised batting. He turned it from an accomplishment into a science. The theory of modern batting is, in all essentials, the result of W G's thinking and working on the game."

The sight of Grace, with his upright stance and high back-lift, was a bowler's nightmare. James Shaw of Nottinghamshire once said: "I put the ball where I likes and 'e puts the ball where 'e likes."

One of Grace's favourite shots was a push to leg, which earned him many of his 54,896 first-class runs. His other great strength was that he was quick between the wickets despite his great bulk. He had an innate ability to pierce defensive fields, regularly scoring well against teams of up to 22 fielders.

Grace was a fine slow bowler who on 17 occasions took eight or more wickets in an innings. He dismissed all 10 Oxford University players in an innings in 1886. But it was his batting that made him a cricket colossus.

The Gloucestershire opener was most prolific in the summer of 1876 when he scored 3,908 runs. He had consecutive innings of 344 against Kent, 177 against Nottinghamshire and 318 not out against Yorkshire in 10 days. In May 1895 he was the first player to reach 100 first-class centuries and later that month the first to hit 1,000 runs in May.

GRACE'S RECORD

	FIRST-CLASS	TESTS (22)
Innings	1,493	36
Not out	105	2
Runs	54,896	1,098
Highest	344	170
Average	39.55	32.29
Hundreds	126	2
Wickets	2,876	9
	at 17.92	at 26.22
Catches	877	39

FOR THE RECORD

CRICKET
■ Jack Hobbs celebrated his Test debut with 83 in 195 minutes against Australia in Melbourne. England won by one wicket but the match would have been the first tied Test had Gervys Hazlitt tossed the ball to Carter instead of hurling it at the stumps and missing when Barnes and Fielder were scampering the winning run.

FOOTBALL
■ England played their first full internationals, beating Austria 6-1 and 11-1 in Vienna.

■ The transfer fee limit was set at £350 in January but withdrawn in April because it was unworkable.

■ Sunderland recorded the biggest away win in the First Division, 9-1 including eight goals in 28 minutes, at Newcastle.

GOLF
■ C A Palmer beat Lionel Munn at the 28th hole in the longest ever match in the British amateur championship.

■ Fred McLeod, who weighed only 108lb, became the smallest winner of the US Open when he beat Willie Smith in a play-off.

■ James Braid lowered Jack White's record winning aggregate in the Open by five strokes, to 291.

ICE HOCKEY
■ England were founder members of the International Ice Hockey Federation.

RACING
■ Signorinetta, the only filly in the race, won the Derby as a 100-1 outsider. Two days later she easily won the Oaks.

Empire establishes the ruling governing body at Lord's

THE Imperial Cricket Conference was formed at a meeting at Lord's on July 15. England, Australia and South Africa were represented under the chairmanship of Lord Chesterfield of the MCC. The sport's governing body was renamed the International Cricket Conference on July 15, 1965. It changed its name to the International Cricket Council on July 12, 1989.

England dither while Australia keep faith

THE England selectors chose 25 players in a futile attempt to maintain a winning combination in the five-Test Ashes series. Among their selections were two one-Test wonders. John King top-scored with 60 in his single appearance and the 37-year-old Douglas Carr, in his maiden season in first-class cricket, had three for 19 in his opening spell, was over-bowled and dropped.

The England selectors could have learned something from their Australian counterparts who persisted with the rookie Warren Bardsley. The opener had averaged a mere 16.25 in the first four Tests before hitting form at The Oval with 136 and 130, the first batsman to score two centuries in a Test. Australia won 2-1 and Bardsley became a left-handed legend.

Bardsley: found his form at The Oval

Gore gains from sporting gesture

Gore: oldest champion

LIFE for Arthur Gore began at 40. Fast, fit and the owner of a fierce forehand, Gore was the oldest Wimbledon men's singles champion when he won the crown at 41 years and seven months.

Gore appeared to have given up any hope of successfully defending his title when M J G Ritchie swept to a 8-6 6-1 2-0 lead in their challenge round. Then a close line call was ruled against Gore and Ritchie sportingly threw the next point. The incident unsettled the challenger's concentration and

Gore grabbed his opportunity with open arms. He won the next six games to seal the set and maintained his superiority in a 6-8 1-6 6-2 6-2 6-2 victory.

Gore continued to play at Wimbledon until 1927, a year before his death, winning 121 of the 182 matches he played in a 39-year period.

BOXING

■ Jim Driscoll, the British featherweight champion, failed to officially win the world title in Cardiff on February 19 despite out-boxing the champion Abe Attell, "the Little Hebrew" from San Francisco. However, the New York newspapers gave every round to Driscoll and consequently he billed himself as the world champion and successfully defended the "title" twice.

EQUESTRIANISM

■ The first Nations Cup was held at Olympia. King Edward VII presented a gold cup, worth £500, competed for by teams of three officers riding in uniform.

FOOTBALL

■ The Football League decreed that goalkeepers should wear distinctive colours.

■ Nottingham Forest beat Leicester Fosse 12-0 in a First Division match. Three players, West, Hooper and Spouncer, all scored hat-tricks.

GOLF

■ Dave Hunter became the first player to score under 70 in the US Open, with a 68 in the opening round.

■ Robert A Gardner became the youngest-ever winner of the US amateur championship at the age of 19 years and five months.

ICE HOCKEY

■ England beat Scotland 11-1 in the first match between the two countries.

RUGBY UNION

■ Harlequins beat Richmond 14-10 in the first match staged at Twickenham on October 2. The two clubs, founder members of the Rugby Football Union, have played an influential role in the development of the sport.

Second 'slam' for the Welsh

WALES hammered France 47-5 in Paris to claim their second successive Grand Slam. However, the achievement is subject to interpretation. The Welsh win in Paris and their 36-4 victory the previous season were not Five Nations championship matches. The French only entered the championship in 1910. Welshmen, though, have added 1908 and 1909 to their Grand Slam years because the team beat England, Ireland, Wales and France.

Hampden wrecked in Cup final riot

The pay-boxes blaze during the riot at the Scottish Cup final when the replay ended all-square

HUNDREDS of people rioted after the Scottish Cup final replay between Celtic and Rangers at Hampden Park. Both games were drawn, and at the end of the second match the spectators and players were confused as to whether there would be extra time. The 60,000 crowd roared for the match to continue because it was suspected that the two draws had been stage-managed in order to secure extra gate money. However, under Scottish Football Association rules there was no provision for extra time and a further replay would be required.

When all the players finally left the pitch and it became apparent that the match was over, hundreds of spectators swarmed on to the field, uprooted the goals, cut up the turf and finally set fire to the pay-boxes and other buildings. Barricades were torn down and a bonfire was started, with whisky used to keep it blazing. At least 100 people, mostly policemen and firemen, were injured.

The Cup and the players' medals were withheld after both clubs petitioned the SFA to abandon the tie. A correspondent wrote to the Glasgow Evening Times: "I would suggest the withdrawal of all policemen from football matches, and substitute a regiment of soldiers with fixed bayonets."

Celtic at least had the consolation of winning the League. Because of fixture congestion, they played eight League games in 12 days, winning six and drawing two to pip Dundee for the title by one point.

RACING

Crowd cheers Royal winner

KING EDWARD VII was the first monarch to win the Derby, although he had two successes in the race when he was the Prince of Wales. Many of his victories were very popular with the public and Minoru, who had already won the 2,000 Guineas, received a rapturous reception when he returned to the unsaddling enclosure.

Minoru, who had been leased for the King by his racing manager, then went for the Triple Crown but was well beaten in the St Leger.

Minoru: rapturous reception

MOTOR RACING

Grands Prix halted by French threats

THE French constructors pulled out of Grand Prix racing partly because their monopoly of success on the track was no longer secure and partly because, for the first time since the dawn of the motor car, supply was beginning to exceed demand. Grand Prix cars had become big, over-engined vehicles that had little in common with touring cars, so to promote sales the French wanted to switch to the smaller, more economical voiturette class.

However, to avoid losing face and to prevent any other European constructor getting ahead in the game, they persuaded 17 constructors (12 of them French) to sign an agreement to abandon Grand Prix racing on pain of a £4,000 fine. Despite protestations, the ban worked. Only nine entries were received for the 1909 Grand Prix and the race was abandoned. There were no further European Grands Prix competitions until 1912.

1910s

The profits and losses of gambling

Ever since time began, sport and betting have been inextricably linked. So, as sport started to boom in the early years of the century it was hardly surprising that gambling on sports events also flourished.

Interestingly enough, the middle classes hardly participated in this betting boom. Gambling was largely the preserve of the upper and lower classes. The noble lords would wager vast sums that their boxer, or team of cricketers, would beat another peer's. The cricketers themselves, even in the smallest of village teams, often played for sweepstakes of a few shillings a man.

And wherever working men congregated, shillings — and very soon very many shillings — changed hands on the outcome of football matches. Just as the northern industrial urban working class proved to be the engine that drove football's expansion, they were also the cornerstone of betting on football.

This was a new phenomenon. In the past, gambling was confined to boxing and racing, although large sums of money were wagered on such cruel activities as cock fighting and badger baiting. Popular opinion caused these sports to decline or vanish, so the gamblers switched their attention to football, which was the leading sport of the day.

Before long, northern newspapers were not only publishing football fixtures and results, they were also printing their own football coupons, which bore a remarkable resemblance to the fixed odds betting of today. The Anti-Gambling League had succeeded in having many of these coupons declared illegal, but that did not stop bookmakers cashing in on the new craze.

The coupons were distributed in factories and outside grounds by workmen hoping to earn commission for taking bets from their colleagues. Just like today, they offered the poor the great hope of winning a fortune that would allow them to escape their life of drudgery. By 1907, in the Liverpool area alone, it was estimated that nearly a quarter of a million coupons were in circulation every week. And, as in racing, tipsters not being slow to miss a chance of making money were soon offering "systems" to predict results — for a fee, of course. Although gambling was illegal, it was tolerated by many people, because it was thought that it did not cause much "harm". But as the sums of money being bet grew ever larger — one football bookmaker was reckoned to be turning over tens of thousands of pounds a week, in those days an astronomical sum — the temptations to cheat grew ever greater.

Racing, mindful of the fact that there was a history of rigging races and nobbling horses, started to realise that it had to take action. There had already been crackdowns on doping, and jockeys had been warned off, but cheating was ever-present.

Peter "Ringer" Barrie painted horses in different colours to fix races. When the notorious Barrie was finally brought to trial, he was asked by the judge: "What is your definition of a good thing?" Barrie replied: "A good three-year-old in a bad two-year-old race."

And in 1919, The Panther, a red-hot favourite for the Derby, was fed an apple laced with powdered glass. He finished nowhere in the race, never ran again, and bookmakers, who were responsible for the attack, saved a fortune.

By the early part of the decade, football was also starting to be worried about the pernicious influence of betting, a concern that proved to be remarkably prescient.

Within a few years, the Football League, mindful of the pressure brought to bear on public opinion by the Anti-Gambling League and aware that the game was fast becoming too disreputable, was calling on the government to take tough action against betting on the outcome of matches. The football authorities were also aware that betting went on among players, in some cases even while matches were taking place, with players shouting bets to each other while they played. And suddenly they had a terrible scandal on their hands, one that dealt a blow to the very spirit of the game.

On Good Friday 1915, Manchester United beat Liverpool 2-0, a result vital to United, who were fighting relegation. A few weeks later, the Sporting Chronicle revealed that a number of players had laid bets on the exact score of the match.

It was unusual to bet on the score rather than the result, and particularly suspicious because large sums had been staked at odds of 7-1. The Football League investigated the allegations and eight players, four from each team, were suspended for life.

Four years later, America experienced a similar scandal which, once again, rocked the country to its foundations when it was revealed that the baseball World Series — the very symbol of the American nation — had been fixed. Even though the eight Chicago White Sox who threw the game were acquitted in dubious circumstances, the public found that their idols were tarnished and felt betrayed.

The idea that Shoeless Joe Jackson, one of the greatest and most popular players of the era, could be one of the infamous eight was unthinkable and gave rise to the plea: "Say it ain't so, Joe?" It was only the punitive action of baseball's newly appointed commissioner, who had no hesitation in banning the offenders for life, that restored confidence in the game.

Everywhere, it seemed, people were profiting from professional sport. While fortunes were being won and lost, sport not only was not benefiting financially, its image was being dented.

But no matter how much governing bodies tried to stamp it out, gambling would not go away. Any attempt to outlaw it would simply drive it underground. The uncertainty of sport, and the passion that it engendered, made it a natural vehicle for gambling.

In time, both racing and football would come to a proper relationship with betting and, ironically, come to depend on the revenues generated by the levy on bookmakers and the tax on pools companies. Unfortunately, in the same way that the urge to gamble could not be eradicated, the desire to cheat could not be prevented from casting a permanent shadow over sport. Further scandals would emerge, proving that the cost of having heroes is the existence of villains.

ATHLETICS
■ *British Olympic gold medals*
1912 *1500m* Arnold Jackson; *4x100m relay*

BASEBALL
■ *World Series*
1910 Philadelphia Athletics
1911 Philadelphia Athletics
1912 Boston Red Sox
1913 Philadelphia Athletics
1914 Boston Braves
1915 Boston Red Sox
1916 Boston Red Sox
1917 Chicago White Sox
1918 Boston Red Sox
1919 Cincinnati Reds

BOXING
■ *British world champions*
1913 *Flyweight.* Sid Smith, Bill Ladbury
1914 *Flyweight.* Percy Jones
1914 *Lightweight.* Freddie Welsh
1914 *Welterweight.* Matt Wells
1915 *Flyweight.* Joe Symonds
1915 *Welterweight.* Ted Kid Lewis

1916 *Flyweight.* Jimmy Wilde
1917 *Welterweight.* Ted Kid Lewis

CRICKET
■ *County championship*
1910 Kent
1911 Warwickshire
1912 Yorkshire
1913 Kent
1914 Surrey
1919 Yorkshire

CYCLING
■ *Tour de France*
1910 Octave Lapize
1911 Gustave Garrigou
1912 Odile Defraye
1913 Phillipe Thys
1914 Phillipe Thys
1919 Firmin Lambot

FOOTBALL
■ *Football League*
1910 Aston Villa
1911 Manchester Utd
1912 Blackburn
1913 Sunderland
1914 Blackburn
1915 Everton

■ *FA Cup*
1910 Newcastle 2 Barnsley 0 (after 1-1)
1911 Bradford City 1 Newcastle 0 (after 0-0)
1912 Barnsley 1 West Bromwich 0 (aet)
1913 Aston Villa 1 Sunderland 0
1914 Burnley 1 Liverpool 0
1915 Sheffield Utd 3 Chelsea 0

■ *Scottish League*
1910 Celtic
1911 Rangers
1912 Rangers
1913 Rangers
1914 Celtic
1915 Celtic
1916 Celtic
1917 Celtic
1918 Rangers
1919 Celtic

■ *Scottish Cup*
1910 Dundee 2 Clyde 1 (after 2-2 and 0-0)
1911 Celtic 2 Hamilton 0 (after 0-0)
1912 Celtic 2 Clyde 0
1913 Falkirk 2 Raith 0
1914 Celtic 4 Hibernian 1 (after 0-0)

GOLF
■ *The Open*
1910 James Braid
1911 Harry Vardon
1912 Ted Ray
1913 J H Taylor
1914 Harry Vardon
■ *US Open*
1910 Alex Smith
1911 John McDermott
1912 John McDermott
1913 Francis Ouimet
1914 Walter Hagen
1915 Jerry Travers
1916 Chick Evans
1919 Walter Hagen
■ *US PGA*
1916 Jim Barnes
1919 Jim Barnes

RACING
■ *The Derby*
1910 Lemberg
1911 Sunstar
1912 Tagalie
1913 Aboyeur
1914 Durbar II
1915 Pommern
1916 Fifinella
1917 Gay Crusader
1918 Gainsborough
1919 Grand Parade

■ *Grand National*
1910 Jenkinstown
1911 Glenside
1912 Jerry M
1913 Covetcoat
1914 Sunloch
1915 Ally Sloper
1916 Vermouth
1917 Ballymacad
1918 Poethlyn
1919 Poethlvn

ROWING
■ *Boat Race*
1910 Oxford
1911 Oxford
1912 Oxford
1913 Oxford
1914 Cambridge

RUGBY LEAGUE
■ *Challenge Cup*
1910 Leeds 26 Hull 12 (after 7-7)
1911 Broughton 4 Wigan 0
1912 Dewsbury 8 Oldham 5
1913 Huddersfield 9 Warrington 5
1914 Hull 6 Wakefield 0
1915 Huddersfield 37 St Helens 3

RUGBY UNION
■ *Five Nations championship*
1910 England
1911 Wales
1912 England and Ireland
1913 England
1914 England

TENNIS
■ *Wimbledon*
1910 Tony Wilding bt Arthur Gore; Dorothea Lambert Chambers bt Dora Boothby
1911 Tony Wilding bt H Roper Barrett; Dorothea Lambert Chambers bt Dora Boothby
1912 Tony Wilding bt Arthur Gore; Ethel Larcombe bt Charlotte Sterry
1913 Tony Wilding bt Maurice McLoughlin; Dorothea Lambert Chambers bt R J McNair
1914 Norman Brookes bt Tony Wilding; Dorothea Lambert Chambers bt Ethel Larcombe
1919 Gerald Patterson bt Norman Brookes; Suzanne Lenglen bt Dorothea Lambert Chambers

■ *Australian championship*
1910 Rodney Heath
1911 Norman Brookes
1912 J Cecil Parke
1913 E F Parker
1914 Pat O'Hara Wood
1915 Francis Lowe
1919 A R F Kingscote

■ *US championship*
1910 William Larned; Hazel Hotchkiss
1911 William Larned; Hazel Hotchkiss
1912 Maurice McLoughlin; Mary Browne
1913 Maurice McLoughlin; Mary Browne
1914 Richard Williams; Mary Browne
1915 Bill Johnston; Molla Bjurstedt
1916 Richard Williams; Molla Bjurstedt
1917 R L Murray; Molla Bjurstedt
1918 R L Murray; Molla Bjurstedt
1919 Bill Johnston; Hazel Wightman

The boom in racing was so great that commoners flocked to see the King at Royal Ascot

CRICKET

Hobbs has to wait for his century

IT WAS almost inevitable that Jack Hobbs, England's new batting find, would score a century in South Africa. What was surprising, though, is that it took him five Tests to do so. The Surrey opener had hit four half-centuries in eight innings when he took guard at Newlands on March 11. He passed the elusive milestone later in the day and was eventually out, hit wicket, for 187.

South Africa won the series 3-2, but had little success in their first Test series against Australia later in the year. Australia hammered 494 for six on the opening day of the first Test in Sydney. It remains the highest total for the first day of a Test. Only England have scored more runs in a day — 502 for two, again against the unfortunate South Africans, on the second day at Lord's in 1924.

RUGBY UNION

England stoop to conquer

THE Rugby Football Union's cabbage patch at Twickenham had finally been turned into a green field fit for its first rugby international after three years of hard work. While caring hands had transformed the ground, quick hands had transformed the England side from also-rans into potential champions. Adrian Stoop, an innovative fly-half, had introduced a sense of urgency into the back line with his skilful passing and running. So there was an air of expectancy in the crowd of 18,000 when Wales prepared to defend their 11-year unbeaten record against England in the first match at the new home of rugby.

The Welsh were in for a shock for, on January 15, the red Tudor rose on the white jerseys of the England team was in full bloom. Stoop fielded the kick-off from Ben Gronow, a Bridgend forward, and immediately launched a surprise attack by running to his right and putting in a punt which had the Welsh defence in disarray. Before they could recover, the England wing F E Chapman, making his international debut, had scored a try in the opening minute. The body blow left Wales breathless and England went on to win 11-6. The Welsh had to wait until 1933 for their first triumph at Twickenham.

England's win was engineered by Stoop, the captain of Harlequins, who realised that the back line would perform better if the scrum-half and fly-half specialised in their positions rather than continually swop roles. Stoop's emphasis on attack brought England rich rewards. Although they were held to a no-score draw by Ireland at Twickenham a month later, the team then slipped into top gear. They beat France 11-3 and Scotland 14-5 in the space of eight days to clinch the first Five Nations championship. England's find of the season was 20-year-old Cherry Pillman. The Blackheath loose forward was the first player to develop the tactic of quickly breaking from the scrum to harry the opposing fly-half when the opposition heeled the ball.

Stoop (*middle row, centre*) with the team that drew 0-0 against Ireland

TENNIS

Dashing ace wows girls

Wilding: heart-throb

TONY WILDING was Wimbledon's first heart-throb. The New Zealander's handsome looks and solid baseline game brought teenagers flocking to Worple Road to watch him win four successive men's singles championships. His first title was always going to be the most difficult. He won a torrid all-comer final against the American Beals C Wright 4-6 4-6 6-3 6-2 6-3 and used his good form to overpower the defending champion Arthur Gore in a four-set final.

Wilding, who raced to tournaments across Europe on a motorbike, won four Wimbledon doubles titles and helped Australasia rule the Davis Cup roost immediately before the First World War. He was killed in action soon after fighting began.

FOOTBALL

United unveil grand plan

MANCHESTER UNITED demonstrated the extent of their ambitions by moving into Old Trafford, a truly luxurious stadium, on February 19. There was a billiard room, massage rooms, a gymnasium, a laundry and a plunge bath. The ground could accommodate 80,000 spectators, with some 13,000 under cover. There were even attendants to usher the well-heeled to the new-fangled tip-up seats and show them into the tea rooms.

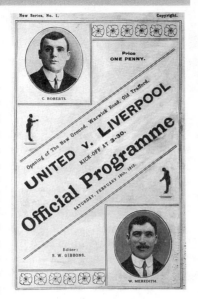

New home for United

FOR THE RECORD

CRICKET
■ Shots hit out of the playing area scored six runs. Previously, only balls that went out of the ground were sixes.

FOOTBALL
■ The first penalty was awarded in an FA Cup final. Albert Shepherd successfully converted it for Newcastle against Barnsley.

■ James Gordon made his debut for Rangers. In the next 20 years he was to play for them in all 11 positions, including goalkeeper.

GOLF
■ James Braid won his fifth Open in the golden jubilee of the championship at St Andrews. The first round was abandoned at 1.30pm because of a thunderstorm and only the leading 60 players were allowed to play the final two rounds. The prize-money was increased to £125.

■ Alex Smith won the first three-way play-off in the US Open when he beat his brother, Macdonald, and Johnny McDermott.

ICE HOCKEY
■ Princes, representing England, won the inaugural European championships in Switzerland.

RUGBY UNION
■ The fledgling French team turned up in Swansea on New Year's Day for their first-ever match in the Five Nations championship. It was a day they would prefer to forget. Wales walloped them 49-14.

BOXING

Black champion scandalises white America

THE great white hope was a great white flop when Jack Johnson, the first black man to win the world heavyweight crown, easily demolished an ageing Jim Jeffries over 15 rounds in Reno, Nevada, to retain his title on July 4. Jeffries had been tempted out of retirement six years after his last fight by the flamboyant promoter Tex Rickard and the writer Jack London to try to wrest the title from Johnson, and return it to its "rightful" home — white America. But the former champion was a hollow shell of his earlier self and he received a severe beating. After the fight there were race riots across the country.

White America, shocked by the notion that the heavyweight champion of the world was black, had been scandalised by Johnson's escapades and marriages to white women, and public sentiment demanded that a white man teach him, and his race, a lesson. The spectacular failure of Jeffries to deliver the goods meant the search for a real Great White Hope began in earnest.

Johnson went into exile in Europe and South America to avoid serving a prison sentence. He lived the good life, engaged

The great white flop: Johnson demolishes Jeffries in Reno, Nevada

in three defences of his title and squandered his fortune. In 1915 Jess Willard, an ungainly fighter — but white and 6ft 6in and 250lb — knocked out a homesick, poverty-stricken and physically ravaged 37-year-old Johnson over 26 rounds in Cuba. Johnson later sold a "confession" to Ring Magazine that he had thrown the fight to get his sentence reduced.

33

RUGBY UNION

Swansea duo hit the mark

THERE were only two names on the tongues of the miners who lived in the valleys of Wales in 1911: Dicky Owen and Billy Trew. In the land of rugby legends Owen was the organiser and Trew the captain of the Welsh team who won the first-ever Five Nations Grand Slam.

Some Welshmen in the valleys may argue that the principality won the Grand Slam in 1908 and 1909 when they added victories against France to their successive Triple Crowns. Hear nothing of it. The French officially joined the championship in 1910. Instead, the credit for the first Grand Slam must go to the class of 1911.

Owen, the inventor of the reverse pass, was a rugged little scrum-half who was the first player to combine attacks with his loose forwards. Trew, his Swansea teammate, was the versatile leader whose experience in the back line helped Wales overcome a spirited English side 15-11 in Swansea. They then scored eight tries in a 32-10 win against Scotland and shut out France 15-0. Wales won the decider 16-0 against unbeaten Ireland at Cardiff Arms Park on March 11. Trew's team scored 18 tries in their four matches and conceded only five.

The season marked the end of a golden era for the Welsh miners who celebrated six Triple Crowns and seven championships in 11 years.

TENNIS

The 22-minute rout

DOROTHEA Lambert Chambers was the daughter of a clergyman but that is where her sense of charity ended. She had no time for the genteel garden parties that passed for lawn tennis in the leafy suburbs of London. When she put on an ankle-length white dress, a white shirt buttoned at the wrists and took possession of a tennis racket she turned into a ruthless player whose game was all about winning.

A late developer, Lambert Chambers was a dogged right-hander who used her tall, athletic body to move swiftly about the court, hitting a devastating forehand which took the women's game a step closer to a fast, competitive sport. The most prominent female player in the 10 years before the war, Lambert Chambers had Lottie Dod's record of five singles titles in

her sights when she arrived at Wimbledon to defend the championship in 1911. Her opponent in the challenge round was Dora Boothby, a determined player who had won the crown in 1909 and was runner-up to Dorothea the previous year.

The match was a massacre. In a trifling 22 minutes Lambert Chambers became the only player to win a Wimbledon final 6-0 6-0. She took two more championships in 1913 and 1914 and her record of seven singles titles has been eclipsed only by Helen Wills Moody with eight and Martina Navratilova with nine. She was beaten a mere six times at Wimbledon in 13 years between 1902 and 1920 and, at the age of 46, spearheaded Britain's first Wightman Cup victory on American soil. She died in 1960.

Perfect final: Chambers did not drop a game

GOLF

Minor wins two majors

BLINK and you may miss Johnny McDermott's contribution to golfing history. The precocious Philadelphian burst into prominence at the age of 18, won two United States Open titles and retired before he was 25.

After losing a three-way play-off to Alex Smith in the US Open in 1910, McDermott had a taste for the big time when he went to the Chicago Golf Club in 1911. This time his nerve held and, at the age of 19 years 10 months and 14 days, he was the youngest winner of a major championship. McDermott retained the US Open title at Buffalo the next year, finished joint fifth in the Open and ninth in the US Open in 1913 and retired in 1915 after he had suffered a mental breakdown.

FOOTBALL

West plays last card for United

MANCHESTER UNITED, basking in the luxury of their new stadium at Old Trafford, won the League championship from Aston Villa by one point. The goalscoring feats of Enoch "Knocker" West undoubtedly clinched the title, but also crucial for United was the presence of several of the players that had secured their first championship three years earlier, in particular the centre-half Charlie Roberts and the winger Billy Meredith.

West was a storming player who was always a bundle of energy. He loved to gamble and he was subsequently banned for life for his role in a betting coup. And United did not win the title again for 41 years.

Golden Wagstaff

Bargain buy: Wagstaff leads out Huddersfield

THE Huddersfield rugby league club paid the princely sum of five gold sovereigns to the Underbank amateurs for a 15-year-old in 1906. Five years later their investment in Harold Wagstaff had paid substantial dividends. The youngest-ever professional player in Britain had matured into an astute captain who was to guide one of the greatest teams in rugby league history. Wagstaff had under him a phenomenal line-up; among them Ben Gronow, the former Welsh rugby union international who kicked 330 points in a season, Albert Rosenfeld, a centre who scored 80 tries in a season, and Edgar Wrigley, a Kiwi who was bought for a club record £200.

Huddersfield began their brilliant era in 1911 and were supreme until the First World War and in the two seasons after the conflict. The "team of all talents", as they were known, won the championship three times, the Challenge Cup three times, the Yorkshire League five times and the Yorkshire Cup on six occasions.

Wagstaff also captained the Great Britain team in Australia in 1914. He courageously led his side to a 14-6 win in the final Test in Sydney after injuries had reduced the team to 10 men for the last 30 minutes. The casualties were so high the match became known as the Rorke's Drift Test.

FOR THE RECORD

BOXING
■ England experimented with using a circular ring.

CRICKET
■ R D Burrows recorded the furthest flight of the bails — 67yd 6in. W G Grace had achieved 64yd 6in in 1901.

FOOTBALL
■ Bradford City, fielding a record eight Scots, beat Newcastle United 1-0 in the replay of the FA Cup final at Old Trafford, having drawn 0-0 five days earlier. Although the team was not exactly home-grown the brand new trophy certainly was — made in Bradford by Fattorini & Sons at a cost of 50 guineas.

French conquerors

MAX DECUGIS needed one of the biggest trophy cabinets in tennis. The Parisian with a huge smash and aggressive volley won 36 major championships between 1902 and 1920. He crossed the English Channel in 1911 with his countryman André Gobert, also an attacking net player, and the pair took the men's doubles title at Wimbledon. Decugis reached the quarter-finals in the singles. But it was at home where he was most successful, winning the French singles title eight times, the doubles 14 times in a row and the mixed doubles on seven occasions. However, Decugis did have one advantage — until 1925 the French championships were restricted to players resident in France.

French invasion: Gobert and Decugis

Larned was quick on the draw

WHEN America went to war against Spain in 1898, Bill Larned was one of the first volunteers to join Theodore Roosevelt's "rough riders". It was little wonder he rode roughshod over his opponents in the United States championships during the next 13 years. Larned's winning repertoire of a powerful backhand and a fast, attacking game paved the way to a fifth successive, and seventh overall, United States singles title in 1911. In the last challenge round of the championships he beat Maurice McLoughlin 6-4 6-4 6-2.

Under pressure: Bradford keep Newcastle at bay in the Cup final

35

FOOTBALL

Keepers kept in the box

GOALKEEPERS were restricted to handling the ball in the penalty area; previously they had been allowed to handle in their own half. The change in the rules was thought to have come about because of a game in Scotland in 1910 between Third Lanark and Motherwell, where both goalkeepers scored in the same match. This is the only known instance in first-class football of this happening.

RUGBY UNION

Springboks unstoppable

WHEN Billy Millar's South African team arrived at Twickenham for the last international of their tour they had cut a swathe through Britain, beating Scotland, Ireland and Wales. The Springboks had scored 57 points without conceding one. But their hopes of a comfortable victory against England evaporated when the English centre Ronnie Poulton went on a brilliant run from near the right-wing. He cut inside and out before scoring under the posts for one of the greatest tries at Twickenham. It was, however, not enough to stop South Africa winning 9-3. Poulton inherited a fortune from his uncle, the Rt Hon G W Palmer, on condition he change his name to Poulton-Palmer. He collected his money, but was killed in 1915.

OLYMPIC GAMES

Thorpe stripped of medals

THE small matter of $60 and a sharp sportswriter took the gloss off the fifth Olympic Games in Stockholm. Roy Johnson, a reporter for the Worcester Telegram in Massachusetts, cracked the biggest story of his life. Six months after Jim Thorpe won gold medals in the pentathlon and decathlon, Johnson reported that Thorpe had been paid for playing minor league baseball in 1909. The Amateur Athletic Union took away his amateur status and the officious International Olympic Committee jumped on the bandwagon by taking back his medals. Thorpe was nonplussed. He was unaware that he had broken the stringent amateur code and, with nowhere to run, turned his athletic ability to American football and baseball.

In October 1982, 29 years after his death, the IOC finally pardoned Thorpe and presented the medals to his family. It had taken 70 years to credit the part-Potawatome Red Indian with a place in Olympic history. Thorpe was also fifth in the high jump and seventh in the long jump. When King Gustav presented him with his medals the monarch said: "You, sir, are without doubt the greatest athlete in the world." Thorpe is said to have replied: "Thanks, King."

Another famous personality to compete in the modern pentathlon was George C Patton. He finished fifth and later made his name as a tough general in the Second World War.

The efficient Swedish hosts turned the Games into one of the most successful in history. They were the first to use electrical timing equipment, and they marked the lanes on the track with chalk instead of movable cords tied to pickets. The athletes paid back their hosts with some stirring performances. Hannes Kolehmainen, the first of the "Flying Finns", triumphed in the inaugural 5,000m and 10,000m events, winning six races in nine days over a total distance of 41km. Ted Meredith, Melvin Sheppard and Ira Davenport staged a superb finish to the 800m, which Meredith won in a world record 1min 51.9sec. Arthur Jackson of Britain won the 1500m in one of the greatest mass finishes in Olympic history. Jackson clocked 3min 56.8sec and the next six runners finished within five seconds. Britain were also successful in football, beating Denmark 4-2 in front of a crowd of 25,000 in the final. Britain won 10 gold medals, 15 silver and 16 bronze, finishing third among a record 28 countries on the medal table.

Thorpe: fateful $60

TENNIS

California comet blazes a trail

HALLEY'S COMET was the brightest comet seen on Rhode Island until Maurice McLoughlin turned up for the US singles championship. The "Californian Comet" was the first leading player to master the cannonball service, a high-kicking service so powerful that it nullified his puny backhand and bewildered most of his opponents. He spectacularly blasted the opposition off the court to win his first of two US titles. In a victory for power over precision, Halley beat Wallace Johnson, an underspin artist, 3-6 2-6 6-2 6-4 6-2 in the final of the first US championship without a challenge round.

Californian Comet: McLoughlin turns on the power

Beaten home and away: the 1912 Australians

Barnes and Foster swing the Test series

THERE was a theory that a touring team required a pair of in-form fast bowlers to succeed on the hard, true pitches of Australia. Sydney Barnes and Frank Foster, two Englishmen who were no more than fast-medium, threw that idea out of the window.

Foster had captained Warwickshire to their first county championship title the year before and his nagging left-arm, round-the-wicket deliveries earned him a place in the 16-man party. He was a pioneer of leg theory, bowling with up to six men on the leg side. Little did the Australians know that 20 years later he would be consulted by Douglas Jardine on the eve of the Bodyline series.

Foster and the 38-year-old Barnes were devastating and helped England retain the Ashes by taking 66 of the 95 wickets. Barnes captured 34 and Foster headed the averages with 32 at 21.62. After winning the opening Test, Australia's confidence was torn to shreds within the first hour of the second Test when Barnes took five for six in 11 overs. England won the match by eight wickets and took the series 4-1.

Double treble

ENGLAND, the hosts, won a nine-match triangular tournament against Australia and South Africa. The event was marred by wet weather and poor performances by the outclassed South Africans, who were twice beaten in under two days by England. Tom Matthews, a tiny leg-spinner, provided one of the rare highlights of the tournament on an incredible day. The Australian bowler achieved the hat-trick in both innings against South Africa at Old Trafford, helping his team to victory by an innings and 88 runs. They were the only wickets he took in the match.

FOR THE RECORD

FOOTBALL
■ Barnsley won the FA Cup the hard way. Half of their matches ended in goalless draws and, in total, they had to play 12 games and 20 hours in the competition.

■ Tottenham won at Anfield and then began a sequence they would rather forget. They did not win again at Liverpool until 1985.

■ Manchester City did not do too well against Newcastle, missing three penalties in the match.

GOLF
■ John Ball won the British amateur championship for a record eighth time.

■ Johnny McDermott won his second successive US Open title with a four-round total of 294 at Buffalo. It was the first time the use of par was adopted and McDermott's score was the first under-par aggregate in the tournament.

■ Cecil Leitch also started on a record sequence. She won the first of her four women's British Open amateur titles. She had one victory in each of the four home countries.

MOTOR RACING
■ France restored its Grand Prix as a two-day race over 950 miles.

RACING
■ Ernest Piggott, grandfather of Lester, won the Grand National on Jerry M.

RACKETS
■ Charles Williams, the world champion, was challenged to a match in America. He set sail on the Titanic, survived the disaster, but lost the match.

RUGBY UNION
■ Wales, who had dominated the international championship from 1900 until 1911, lost three times in five matches.

TENNIS
■ The International Lawn Tennis Federation was established in Paris.

GOLF

Winning streak: Cecil Leitch dominated the British open

C B Fry
The last of the great Corinthians

Cliff Temple

Charles Burgess Fry was one of sport's rare but genuine all-rounders at the highest levels, equally proficient whether wielding a cricket bat, defending a football goal or sprinting down the long-jump runway. His ability to excel not only in a proliferation of sporting settings but also in academic surroundings at Oxford University has never been equalled. He played cricket for England in 26 Test matches, earned an FA Cup winner's medal and held the world long jump record.

Born in Croydon on April 25, 1872, his sporting prowess became apparent during his schooldays at Repton, where he captained the football and cricket teams. At Wadham College, Oxford, he shook the athletics world in 1892 by setting a United Kingdom long jump record of 23ft 5in. And at Iffley Road, Oxford, on March 4, 1893 he equalled the world record with 23ft 6in. He could sprint 100 yards in "evens" (10 seconds) and high jump 5ft 10in. Yet his athletics talent was never fully explored because he concentrated more on other sports. He even missed the opportunity of being one of the original modern Olympic champions at Athens in 1896 simply because he was unaware of the revival of the Games. Fry would surely have won the long jump in Athens — it was won by an American with a jump of just 20ft 10in — but instead spent the afternoon on which the competition was held watching the FA Cup final between Sheffield Wednesday and Wolverhampton Wanderers.

Fry played at full-back for Southampton when they lost 2-1 to Sheffield United in the 1902 FA Cup final replay. The previous year he had been capped for England against Ireland. In rugby he played as a three-quarter for Blackheath and the Barbarians, and he was also said to be a good shot and a keen fisherman.

"He has compassed all kinds of athletic exploits, including a First Class in Classical Moderations," said a Vanity Fair profile published in 1894, while Fry was still only 21. "He is an enterprising boy who may always be relied upon to do as well as he is expected to do. He is generally ready for 'fun', being full of the strongest instincts of the young barbarian at play."

But it was cricket which drew out most of Fry's talent. His 26 Test appearances included captaining England against Australia in 1912. He scored a total of 30,886 runs at an average of 50.22 in his career, playing at county level for Sussex (1894-1908) and Hampshire (1909-21). His 94 centuries included six in consecutive innings during 1901, a record unequalled until Don Bradman's prime nearly four decades later. Fry was also a useful right-arm medium pace bowler, and although frequently called for "throwing", he took 166 wickets at an average of 29.34.

Away from the sports field, Fry became a master at Charterhouse before turning to journalism. He founded and edited Fry's Magazine, authored a number of well-regarded cricket books, and wrote effusively.

"He was the only man I ever knew who could write and talk simultaneously on two different subjects," E W Swanton recalled. Swanton reported the 1934 Australian tour of England for the London Evening Standard while Fry contributed a daily column, "C B Fry Says", for the same paper.

"He had been, of course, not only an incomparable all-round sportsman, but a top-rate scholar," Swanton said, "and some of his references were way above the heads of every Evening Standard reader. Yet they gave him his head, only jibbing, I seem to recall, at the Greek quotations. Everything about Charles was highly individual and arresting: his looks, his dress, his voice, and above all his talk. He wore, for instance, his own version of a Norfolk jacket with a belt and specially large pockets, and trousers, to conform to some pet theory, buttoned above the ankle. The brim of his hat was broad, as was the ribbon that carried his monocle."

> **❝ He is generally ready for "fun", being full of the strongest instincts of the young barbarian at play ❞**
>
> VANITY FAIR, 1894

Fry's interests continued to extend way beyond sport. He served on the League of Nations and was offered, and rejected, the Kingdom of Albania. He tried several times, unsuccessfully, to become a Liberal Member of Parliament. And, for more than 40 years from 1908 to 1950, as commandant of the training ship HMS Mercury on the River Hamble, he schooled youngsters so that they might make their careers in the Royal Navy.

"C B Fry in his younger days was,'I'm sure, too much of a good thing for some tastes," Swanton said. "He did not suffer fools gladly and always spoke his mind."

Fry was, for some reason, usually referred to by his initials, although even in 1894, according to the admiring Vanity Fair profile, "it has lately been suggested that he should be called Charles III".

Certainly one can imagine him as a prickly character. The veteran cricket broadcaster Rex Alston recounted an occasion at The Oval in 1946 when the BBC had asked Fry, then in his mid-seventies, to act as Alston's summariser on the Indian tour. "At the end of the first over I brought him in, saying, 'What do you think, Charles?' On the air, he raised his voice, 'Charles? My name is not Charles to you, sir. To you my name is Commander Fry.' Odd chap. No, we never used him again."

Fry died in Hampstead on September 7, 1956, at the age of 84. It is quite probable that men (and women) of similar multi-abilities exist today, but increasingly unlikely that the world of sport will allow them their head in the way of C B Fry. He may well have been the last great all-rounder.

Man for all seasons: Fry was a top-class cricketer, athlete, footballer and rugby player, as well as a scholar, journalist and diplomat.

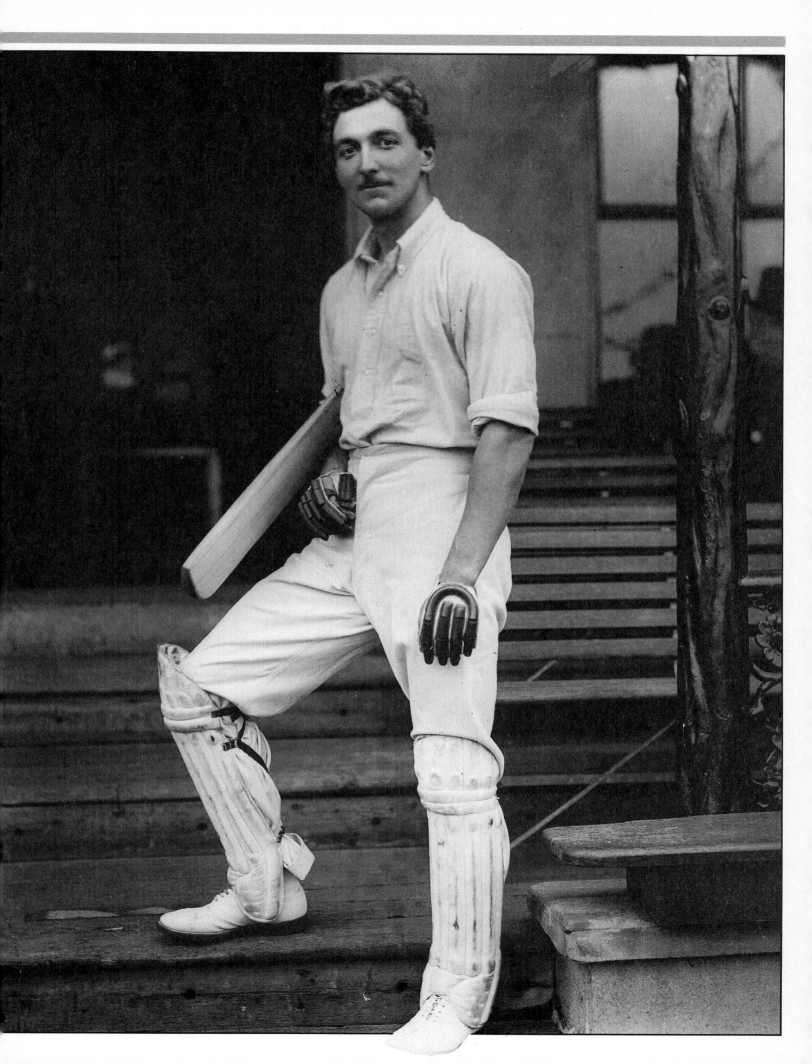

CRICKET

Barnes's record 49-wicket haul

THE 40-year-old figure of Sydney Barnes was the nemesis of South African batsmen in the winter of 1913-14. The England fast-medium bowler captured 49 wickets in four Tests as England won 3-0 in South Africa in the last series before the First World War halted Test cricket.

Barnes was at his devasta-ting best in the second Test in Johannesburg when he took 17 for 159 (8-56 and 9-103), a record which stood until Jim Laker's 19 for 90 against Australia at Old Trafford in 1956. The Staffordshire player ended his career with 83 South African scalps at the cost of a trifling 9.85 runs per wicket.

Thorpe: Olympic hero

RACING

Suffragette's fatal protest

EMILY WILDING DAVISON had been one of the most militant suffragettes since she joined the Women's Social and Political Union in 1906. She had served several prison sentences for her violent protests, one for breaking windows in the House of Commons. She had only just been released from jail again when she received a telegram. Its contents and sender have never been discovered, but on the morning of June 4, Davison visited the offices of the WSPU to collect two suffragette flags before she set out on her fateful journey to Epsom.

By the time the 15 runners in the Derby reached Tattenham Corner the field had already split into two groups with the King's horse, the little-fancied Anmer, several lengths adrift of the leading bunch. Davison dashed across the course, dodged one horse and lunged at Anmer. She managed to grab the reins and hold on for a second before the horse stumbled and crashed to the ground, rolling on his jockey, Herbert Jones. Davison, bleeding profusely, was taken to hospital. She never recovered consciousness and died of a fractured skull four days later.

The country was outraged. Even Queen Mary was driven to write to Jones that she was sorry to hear of his accident caused by "the abominable behaviour of a brutal, lunatic woman".

The race itself also had its share of controversy. The closing stages were very roughly ridden, with the hot favourite, Craganour, beating the 100-1 outsider Aboyeur by a head. Many people felt Craganour had been robbed of the 2,000 Guineas when he was placed second by the judge even though everybody else at Newmarket thought Craganour had just won. And he was to lose out again. Aboyeur's jockey said that he had been beaten fairly and that he did not intend to object to the result. But the Stewards still decided to conduct an inquiry. Major Eustace Loder, one of the Stewards who questioned the first three jockeys, was rumoured to bear a grudge against Craganour's owner. After a lengthy investigation Craganour was disqualified and placed last, giving the race to Aboyeur.

Death at the Derby: Emily Davison is crushed by the King's horse

FOR THE RECORD

AMERICAN FOOTBALL

■ Jim Thorpe, the hero of the 1912 Olympics, started his professional career when he signed for the little-known Pine Valley Pros. He also played in baseball's World Series for the losing Giants.

FOOTBALL

■ Sunderland and Aston Villa cancelled out each other's Double ambition. Sunderland won the League but lost 1-0 to Aston Villa, who had been League runners-up, in the FA Cup final.

■ The distance an opponent had to be from the ball at a free kick was increased from six yards to 10.

GOLF

■ J H Taylor's victory in the Open meant a record 19 years between his first win in 1894 and his last.

ICE HOCKEY

■ The British Ice Hockey Association was formed by five teams.

MOTOR RACING

■ The first Indianapolis 500 was run. Jules Goux won in a Peugeot.

RUGBY UNION

■ W J A Davies began a 22-cap career in England's first Grand Slam season and was never on a losing international side.

TENNIS

■ Canada, Germany, and South Africa joined the Davis Cup.

Boy next door shock

Arsenal move home

ARSENAL played their first match at Highbury on September 6, beating Leicester Fosse 2-1. It was also a victory for their ambitious and calculating chairman, Sir Henry Norris. He was a wealthy estate agent and MP for Fulham East, who channelled his energies into attempting to transform the unfashionable Arsenal into a leading club.

From 1910, although the chairman of Fulham, Norris made Arsenal his life's work. He failed to amalgamate them with Fulham when the League blocked his plans, so he decided to move the club from Plumstead to prestigious Highbury.

Despite the strong protests of residents, who were fearful of "the undesirable elements of professional foot-ball", and the objections of Tottenham Hotspur and Clapton Orient, who argued that three clubs in the vicinity was one too many, Norris won the day.

The proximity of an underground station (later renamed as Arsenal) was vital to Norris's ambitions. The bitterness between Arsenal and Spurs almost certainly stems from Norris's manoeuvrings.

Comet attracts star gazers to the Wimbledon championships

World beater: Ouimet surprised the best players

First service: mixed doubles were introduced at Wimbledon

IT WAS the stuff of which dreams are made: a 20-year-old shop assistant goes out and beats the two best players in the world in a US Open play-off. For Francis Ouimet that dream came true. Ouimet lived across the road from the Brookline Country Club in Boston, but his golfing ability appeared limited. He seldom broke 90, and he failed to qualify for the US amateur championships three years in a row. When he did qualify in 1913 he was beaten in the second round.

Ouimet only entered the US Open to have a closer look at Harry Vardon. The English professional set the early pace with Ted Ray, and although Ouimet shot a 74 in the third round few people gave him much chance of winning. His form began to fade in the final round and he needed to score two under par over the last six holes to force a three-way play-off. A 36-foot birdie putt at the 17th and a teasing three-footer on the final green enabled him to tie Vardon and Ray on 304.

In the play-off, the trio all reached the turn in 38 and, while the Englishmen fell apart over the back nine, Ouimet kept his nerve and came back in 34 to finish with 72. He was the first amateur to win the US Open, beating Vardon by five strokes and Ray by six. His storybook victory inspired the first boom in American golf, and in 1963 the US Open returned to Brookline to commemorate the 50th anniversary of his historic triumph.

MAURICE McLOUGHLIN took his cannonball service to Wimbledon and became an instant hit. The "Californian Comet" was drawn against the popular local player Roper Barrett in the first round and the match attracted so many people the gates had to be closed. McLoughlin won 8-6 in the fifth set and progressed to the challenge round, where his service failed to stop the defending champion Tony Wilding retaining the title in a thrilling match.

Women's and mixed doubles events were introduced and both finals were won by the pair who were losing when their opponents defaulted.

FOOTBALL

The King finally visits Palace

GEORGE V was the first monarch to attend the Cup final, where Burnley beat Liverpool 1-0 on April 25. With the threat of war hanging over Britain, his presence was perceived as an attempt to forge national unity. It was also the last Cup Final at Crystal Palace.

The King congratulates players at the Cup final

GOLF

The sultans of swing reign supreme

WHEN Harry Vardon strolled up the 18th fairway at Prestwick on the final afternoon of the Open, there was no doubt that he would win a record sixth title. He was three shots ahead of his great rival, John Henry Taylor, while a little way down the field was the last man to win at Prestwick, James Braid. The Great Triumvirate, three men with vastly different swings who dominated the game from 1894 to 1914, were victorious again.

Their statistical achievements were awesome. Vardon won the Open six times and Braid and Taylor five times. The trio filled the top three positions on three occasions.

But there was more to their influence than the consistency of their swings. Born 13 months apart, they promoted professional golf as a respectable occupation and, as founder members of the Professional Golfers Association, established the etiquette that is the cornerstone of the modern game.

Braid, the son of a Scottish ploughman, was unimpressive early in his career. Then he found a driver more suited to his powerful hitting, changed his shallow-faced iron putter to an aluminium head and virtually overnight turned into a champion. A quiet man, he was the first to break 70 in the Open — in the third round at Sandwich in 1904 — and he won four Opens

in six years. He also dominated the PGA matchplay championship and was a prominent figure at Walton Heath until his death in 1950. His great strength was in recovering from bad lies, and he was one of the first to use the explosive sand-shot out of bunkers. Although suffering from bad eyesight in later years, he took great delight in scoring lower than his age, especially on his birthday.

J H Taylor was a tenacious fighter who broke the supremacy of Scottish professionals in 1894 when he won the first Open in England. The victory at Sandwich was the first of 16 major titles won by the Triumvirate. His short swing and flat-footed stance stood him in good stead in poor weather, particularly in a gale at Hoylake in 1913 when he was the only player to break 80 in both rounds on the final day, winning the Open by eight shots. A sturdy man, he was the pioneer of public courses in England, a champion of the the deprived hackers.

Vardon was the most successful of the three. He won his first Open in 1896, coming from six behind to beat Taylor on the final day. His last Open title was 18 years later.

His success was built on an upright stance and a flowing swing, which proved a fine example for many to cópy. He

The big three: Taylor, Braid and Vardon

once said of those attempting to emulate him: "Golfers find it a very trying matter to turn at the waist, more particularly if they have a lot of waist to turn."

Vardon was equally popular in America, where he won the US Open in 1900 and 1903. He contracted tuberculosis and his health and putting stroke declined, but he made one lasting impression. A bronze cast of his famous Vardon grip hangs in the South Herts Golf Club, a tribute to his contribution to the interlocking grip used by the majority of modern golfers. Although others had experimented with the grip, Vardon perfected it to become what Taylor described as "the finest and most finished golfer that the game has ever produced".

FOR THE RECORD

BOXING

■ Freddie Welsh, from Pontypridd, won the world lightweight title when he outpointed Willie Ritchie from San Francisco over 20 rounds in London on July 7. Welsh had only a light punch but was one of the finest defensive boxers in the division's history.

FOOTBALL

■ Celtic conceded only 14 goals in 38 League matches, with 25 clean sheets — a Scottish record that still stands.

RACING

■ Durbar II was the first French-trained winner of the Derby since 1865.

TENNIS

■ Otto Foitzheim, the first great German player, reached the all-comers' final at Wimbledon and took Norman Brookes to five sets. Brookes beat Tony Wilding in the challenge round, ending the New Zealander's reign.

Hobbs drives Surrey to first championship

Hobbs: adventurous style

THE MASTER was at his peak. And when Jack Hobbs was in the mood for scoring runs there was little the bowlers could do. His perfect technique and peaceful temperament proved an ideal blend for the son of a Fenners groundsman to become the most proficient run scorer in history.

After providing England with a solid foundation for their 4-0 defeat of South Africa in the winter of 1913-14, with innings of 82, 23, 92, 41, 64, 97, 33 and 11 not out, he returned home to help Surrey win their first county championship of the century. They did not win it again until 1950. Hobbs hit 2,499 runs in 42 innings with an adventurous style that became more measured after the war.

He copied his batting technique from Tom Hayward, a father figure who was instru-mental in his joining Surrey soon after his father died in 1902. He was awarded his county cap after a brilliant 155 in his first championship match, against Essex who had earlier turned him down.

Hobbs plundered bowlers for 30 years, scoring 61,237 runs at an average of 50.65. He could have scored more, according to his England opening partner, Wilfred Rhodes: "He was often content to throw his wicket away when he had reached his hundred and give someone else a chance." Fifty-one of his record 197 centuries were scores between 100 and 110. When Surrey marked his retirement by erecting the wrought-iron Hobbs Gates at the entrance to The Oval the surplus money from public contributions was used to build a wall around the ground.

HOBBS'S RECORD		
	FIRST-CLASS	TESTS (61)
Innings	1,315	102
Not out	106	7
Runs	61,237	5,410
Highest	316 not out	211
Average	50.65	56.94
Hundreds	197	15
Wickets	108 at 24.89	1 for 165
Catches	332	17

> **' A snick by Jack Hobbs is a sort of disturbance of a cosmic orderliness '**
>
> **Sir Neville Cardus**

Drake goes through the card

THE WAR had lasted nearly a month when Yorkshire travelled to Weston-super-Mare in pursuit of the county championship title. While most of the talk at the ground was about the fighting, there was one short spell of brilliance from A W Drake that took everyone's mind off the conflict. Somerset went in on the second day requiring 231 for victory on their newly-laid pitch. Drake struck, taking all 10 wickets in the space of 42 deliveries for 35 runs. Somerset were bowled out for 90 and Drake finished the match with 15 wickets for 51 and the most runs, 51 and 12.

Yorkshire finished fourth in the table behind Surrey. Drake's career was curtailed by the First World War and he died before play resumed in 1919.

Successive Grand Slams lift England's spirits

ENGLISH rugby union, crippled by the breakaway of the Northern Union in 1893, took a long time to recover from the loss of the best players. Adrian Stoop, Ronnie Poulton-Palmer and Cherry Pillman, who had revived England by winning the Triple Crown in 1910, were instrumental in getting the country's second Grand Slam in two years in 1914. England beat Ireland 17-12, Scotland 16-15, Wales 10-9 and finally thumped France 39-13 in Paris on April 13.

Storming victory: Ronald leaves André trailing in Paris

Some corner of a foreign field that is forever England

For many, the Great War began as no more than a game, an extension of the physical sports played at home.

Britain's leaders had never forgotten that the Battle of Waterloo was won on the playing fields of Eton. Once again, a century later, they went to heavily populated sports stadiums for their heroes.

Thus, as early as the spring of 1914, King George V watched Burnley beat Liverpool 1-0 in the FA Cup final. He was the first monarch to go to a final, but, more significantly, there were 72,778 people in attendance. The King's presence was seen as an attempt to forge national unity and sport quickly became a key platform for extolling patriotism and recruiting soldiers.

There were military bands, speakers and posters at sports grounds. Billboards tempted the fans. "Do you want to be a Chelsea diehard? Join the 17th Battalion of the Middlesex Regiment and follow the lead given by your favourite football players." Footballers signed up in front of stands and terraces, and by early 1915 the Football Association claimed that the campaign had persuaded 500,000 people to enlist.

A Footballers' Battalion was formed with its headquarters at the Richmond Athletic Ground. They became the 17th Service Battalion of the Middlesex Regiment and saw their first action in France in late 1915. Their second-in-command, Major Frank Buckley, was wounded in the shoulder and lung the next year. He recovered to become manager of Wolverhampton Wanderers. Croydon Common were another casualty. Twelve of their men joined the colours in the first month and the club went into liquidation three years later.

Everton won the First Division title in 1915 while Sheffield United beat Chelsea 3-0 in one of the FA's most famous matches, the Khaki Cup final. Lord Derby was there to present the Cup and he did not miss his cue in front of thousands of uniformed soldiers. "You have played with one another and against one another for the Cup," he said. "It is now the duty of everyone to join with each other and play a sterner game for England."

Despite football's sterling role, it was given a rough ride. The Football Association decided to play on after war broke out on August 4, 1914, prompting vitriolic criticism in parliament and the press. A F Pollard, an historian, wrote in The Times: "We view with indignation and alarm the persistence of association football clubs in doing their best for the enemy. Every club that employs a professional football player is bribing a much-needed recruit to refrain from enlistment, and every spectator who pays his gate money is contributing so much to German victory."

The Jockey Club's decision to continue racing after the war had started also provoked much debate in the pages of The Times, and within the sport itself. Questions were asked in parliament, which the Jockey Club countered by arguing that racing was a vital industry because of the number of people it kept in work.

By May 1915, the tide of opinion had turned and the government asked the Jockey Club to halt racing, except at Newmarket. However, substitute classics were still held for the Oaks, Derby and St Leger.

Above left: Officers and men of the 17th Service Battalion.
Bottom left: Sheffield United in 1915.
Above right: Soldiers on leave were given special dispensation to attend races like the Derby (bottom right) won by triple crown winner Gainsborough in 1918.

And in 1918 Lady Jane Douglas became the first woman owner of a Derby winner with Gainsborough, who also completed the triple crown of the 2,000 Guineas and St Leger.

Cricket, seemingly immune from the pressures put on football and racing, decided to deliberate on the weightier issues of their game. They thought about banning left-handers and penalising the batting side for maiden overs. The county championship had stumbled to a conclusion a month after war had been declared. Several matches were called off and Dr W G Grace issued his command. "Every cricketer must join the colours immediately," he bellowed. Jingoism was rife but the 1915 edition of the Wisden Almanack was filled with obituaries of early casualties.

There was as much upper-class nonsense at the front as there was at home. The fighting provided an opportunity for the public schoolboys of the playing fields to show their skills as foolhardy officers of the battlefields. On July 1, 1916, the 8th Battalion of the East Surrey Regiment attacked Prussian Guards defending Montauban Ridge on the Somme. Captain W P Nevill produced four footballs for his company, which were dribbled and kicked by his men as they advanced across no-man's land. The soldiers came under heavy machine-gun and mortar fire, there were heavy casualties and Captain Nevill was killed on the enemy wire. Amazingly, the ridge was taken.

> **' On through the hail of slaughter**
> **Where gallant comrades fall**
> **Where blood is poured like water**
> **They drive the trickling ball.**
> **The fear of death before them**
> **Is but an empty name**
> **True to the land that bore them**
> **The Surreys play the game '**
>
> **Touchstone, the Daily Mail**

And the English rugby international E R Mobbs died while punting a rugby ball ahead of him when leading a charge at the enemy lines. He was honoured with the Mobbs memorial match which is still played today.

It was the conflict that was billed as the war to end all wars. Ten million people were killed and another 20 million were wounded in four years. At the Somme, Britain lost 60,000 men on the first day with no breakthrough. By the end of the four-month battle British and French fatalities had risen to 600,000, and 500,000 Germans had died.

In the bloody mess, sport provided one of the few moments of sanity. A truce was declared on Christmas Day 1914, and several British and German rank and file soldiers decided to play football in no-man's land. When the truce ended the soldiers only went back to battle after they had been dragooned by their officers into fighting again.

The contribution of sportsmen to the war was enormous. Second Lieutenant Donald Simpson Bell, a fullback for Bradford before he was killed in action, was posthumously awarded the Victoria Cross for bravery at the Somme; 26 England rugby internationals lost their lives; more than 80 well-known cricketers and thousands of footballers were killed. Sport lost the cream of its crop.

When the fighting stopped there was a feeling that rugby players had been more patriotic than footballers, and many public schools began playing rugby union exclusively. There was a decline in the number of gentlemen playing the round-ball game and football became more professional and working-class.

However, this analysis was desperately unfair on football and its followers. One Tory politician above all others grasped this. Harold Macmillan, later to become Prime Minister, said of the First World War that the working classes will never forgive us for all this.

Losers and winners . . . E R Mobbs, the England international, was killed kicking a rugby ball into battle; the Huddersfield rugby league team, one of the greatest ever sides, swept all before them in 1915; and Surrey, who won the county championship, in a truncated season, for the first time in the century.

D.J. Knight. Rushby (T.) Smith (W.C.) Fender (P.G.H.) Abel (W.J.)

M.C. Bird.

Goatly (E.G.)

Hobbs (J.B.) Hayward (T.) Hitch (J.W.)

Harrison (H.S.)

Hayes (E.G.) Strudwick (H.) Ducat (A.)

Chicago throw the World Series

BASEBALL was booming and money was pouring into the game. But many players earned low salaries so it was hardly surprising that attempts to fix matches — something that had been common for years — were rife. Two New York Giants were banned during the season for trying to bribe other players to throw games, but not even that prepared America for the scandal of the World Series.

The Cincinnati Reds reached the World Series for the first time, but were not expected to beat the Chicago White Sox. Even when there were big bets on the Reds and the White Sox made an inordinate number of elementary mistakes as they lost 5-3 hardly anybody was prepared to accept that anything was amiss. The storm broke in September 1920 when Abe Attell, a former champion boxer, named eight White Sox who had accepted money to lose the World Series. The eight, dubbed "The Black Sox", were tried for conspiracy. But some witnesses disappeared and others changed their stories. Documents vanished, a fire destroyed more key

"Shoeless" Joe Jackson: Series record suggested innocence

evidence, and all of the defendants were acquitted.

Judge Kenesaw Landis had been elected baseball's first commissioner in 1920, and had

been charged with cleaning up the sport. So, even though the eight had been found not guilty, he had no hesitation in banning them from baseball for life.

GOLF

Hagen uses mud lark to his gain

WALTER HAGEN used a large measure of gamesmanship to win his second US Open title, beating Mike Brady by one shot in an 18-hole play-off. The drama was at the 17th hole at Brae Burn Country Club. Hagen sliced into the rough and a spectator trod on his ball, pushing it into the mud. An official ruled it should be played, but Hagen protested and asked that it be identified. When Hagen was finally satisfied it was in fact his ball, most of the mud had been removed and he had a clean shot to the green.

FOR THE RECORD

BOXING
■ Jack Britton stopped Ted Kid Lewis in the ninth round to take the world middleweight title in Canton, Ohio, on March 17.

GOLF
■ The Royal and Ancient Golf Club took over the management of the Open but there was no championship until the following year.

TENNIS
■ Algernon Kingscote became the first foreign player to win the Australian championships.

RACING
■ Tetratema won all his two-year-old races, and was also the leading stakes winner ahead of older horses. He was so good that he topped the Free Handicap by 12lb and was the champion sire in 1929.

Dempsey mauls his way to title

JACK DEMPSEY, the most spectacular heavyweight since John L Sullivan, conceded 58lb but still battered the giant Jess Willard for three remorseless rounds before the world champion gave up and quit on July 4. Two years earlier Dempsey had been a small-time slugger fighting in the back rooms of saloons and dance halls, but a chance meeting with the manager Jack Kearns in a San Francisco bar transformed his career.

Kearns was a brilliant publicist and within a year Dempsey, the Manassa Mauler, was the leading contender for the championship. When he won

Manassa Mauler: Dempsey batters Willard into submission

the world title he was not immediately popular with the public because he had not served during the war, but his exciting

style — constantly attacking with savage punches — soon made him a national hero. Dempsey held the title until 1926.

Chambers falls to Lenglen's élan

WIMBLEDON was in for a shock when the All-England championships resumed after the war. Her name was Suzanne Lenglen, a flamboyant and fashion-conscious Frenchwoman

Lenglen: flamboyant style

who took the sport by storm.

She possessed a powerful game perfected on the practice courts by her father, who had her skipping, sprinting and hitting the ball at a handkerchief on the other side of the net. Lenglen had also thrown off the corsets and long dresses of the pre-war era to reveal a low-cut, one-piece outfit that allowed her to move swiftly around the court. She advanced to the challenge round where she met Dorothea Lambert Chambers, the seven-times champion and, at 40, twice her age.

It was an epic match. Chambers fought back from 1-4 down in the deciding set to hold two match points at 6-5. Lenglen came to the net, Chambers lobbed, Lenglen stretched high and tapped the ball with the top of the racket. It bounced on the net cord and fell into the champion's court. The match point was saved, Chambers cracked, and Lenglen took the title 10-8 4-6 9-7.

It was the first of her Wimbledon crowns. In six years she won all of her 32 singles matches and 64 of her 66 sets, 29 of which finished 6-0.

Lenglen took the French championships three times and between 1919 and 1926 was beaten only once, when she retired because of illness against Molla Mallory in the second round of the US championships in 1921. Add her two Olympic gold medals to the list of honours and she finished with 46 major titles before turning professional in 1926.

Lenglen had been what tennis was waiting for after the misery of the war. Her clothes were as striking as her play. She would strut on to the court in a fur coat and wore a brightly-coloured bandeau of silk chiffon around her head when playing. She mixed with high society, attending dinners and dances and attracting attention wherever she went.

Her biggest drawback was that she was highly strung and regularly threw tantrums and argued with officials until she got her way. It was a small price to pay for one of the greatest players of all time.

> *All women tennis players should go on their knees in thankfulness to Suzanne Lenglen for delivering them from the tyranny of corsets*
>
> **Bunny Ryan**

Tour chooses yellow as the prime colour for the leader

HENRI DESGRANGE, the founder of the Tour de France, introduced a yellow jersey for the leader of the race after spectators complained that they could not tell who was winning. The leader's jersey, first worn by Eugene Christophe, was the same colour as Desgrange's newspaper, l'Auto, which promoted the race.

Bigger League kicks off in buoyant mood

LEAGUE football resumed in a mood of optimism and immediately expanded from 40 clubs to 44. The First and Second Divisions were now to be made up of 22 clubs. It was assumed that the teams who finished in the last two places in the First Division in 1915, Chelsea and Tottenham, would be retained and the two teams at the top of the Second Division, Derby and Preston, would be promoted.

However, nobody had anticipated the behind-the-scenes machinations of Sir Henry Norris, the Machiavellian chairman of Arsenal. As a consequence of secret negotiations,

the Liverpool chairman and League president John McKenna gave Arsenal's application his full backing and, despite finishing fifth in the Second Division, Arsenal were promoted along with Chelsea, Derby and Preston — and Tottenham were relegated. Arsenal have been in the First Division ever since, the only club with such a record.

Norris came unstuck in the end. In 1927 he and a fellow director were suspended by the FA and the club was censured for secretly inducing players to come to Arsenal. When Norris sued for libel he lost in a blaze of publicity that was to be his downfall.

Arsenal meet Newcastle on the first day of the season

1920s

The beautiful and the damned

"They were the last generation. People who were so deliberately and determinedly cynical that they became naive." Gertrude Stein

It was the Jazz Age, a time of sparkling frivolity, fads and female emancipation. Scott Fitzgerald had coined the phrase to capture the sense of euphoria that swept the globe as the horrors of the First World War were laid to rest.

It was a time when youth was determined to have its fling. Crazes were commonplace and fashionable. The Charleston was the dance, young women were "flappers" and dresses were shorter, as was the length of women's hair. Men even shaved off their whiskers. Their parents would hardly have recognised them.

Despite Prohibition in America, alcohol was an essential ingredient in this heady cocktail of hedonism. As was smoking. Young women scandalised their elders by smoking in public and dancing the night away in the clubs and speakeasies that were all the rage. It was a fabulous time to be young and well to do.

The outrageous was not just confined to the nightclubs. Suzanne Lenglen startled stuffy Wimbledon with her daring dress. She graced the Centre Court with a flimsy cotton frock with no petticoat or corset, and the next year topped that with a colourful silk bandeau.

Her exquisite play and French chic made her a smash hit and the public flocked to see her, so much that tickets for the new, expanded Wimbledon had to be rationed. Others followed suit. In 1927 Billie Tapscott played stockingless, and two years later Lili de Alvarez pushed the frontiers of fashionfurther by wearing a trouser suit.

The Twenties were a decade when women cast off the shackles of the past. The Suffragettes, and women's crucial contribution to the war effort, had forced the establishment to relent and give them the vote — albeit only to women over the age of 30. By 1928, however, they enjoyed equal voting rights with men and had finally won a proper place in the twentieth century. Coincidentally that year also saw the first women competitors in athletics at the Olympic Games.

It seemed that everywhere innovation was in the air. Aeroplanes were crossing the Atlantic; radio was regularly broadcasting all the leading sporting events; television was just around the corner and some of the great sporting venues of the world — Wembley, Wimbledon, Monza, Yankee stadium and Roland Garros — were constructed.

In golf they added spikes to the shoes and created the Walker and Ryder Cups; in motor racing Le Mans held its first 24-hour race and boxing drew its first $1m gate. Football's changes were even more significant. In 1925 the offside rule was altered to favour the attacking side and in 1927 it was agreed to stage a World Cup. The sport was never the same again.

Herbert Chapman, a visionary manager who guided Huddersfield to a hat-trick of League championships, was the first manager to grasp the significance of the change in rules and at Arsenal in the Thirties ruthlessly exploited it. As he did the transfer market by lashing out vast sums for quality players. Britain, sadly, ignored the fledgling World Cup

— an isolation that would cost them dear. Chapman's achievements at Arsenal, previously a modest club with no track record of success, established them as a leading club.

While Chapman was transforming Arsenal, George Halas was laying the foundations of an equally mighty dynasty in America. Halas took an equally unfashionable American football team, the Decateur Staleys, turned them into the mighty Chicago Bears, tactically changed the shape of the game, and spent hundreds of thousands of dollars on signing the best college players.

It was a time when people who were prepared to think big reaped all the rewards. The owner of the New York Yankees used his financial muscle to acquire the big-hitting Babe Ruth as the cornerstone of a club that would dominate baseball for the next 40 years.

And it was not only in the professional ranks that glittering stars wrote their names indelibly into the record books. Bobby Jones got off to a slow start in golf, tearing up his card in the third round of the 1921 Open. By the end of the decade he had won the Grand Slam which in those days was thought so unlikely it was called "The Impossible Quadrilateral'.

Helen Wills, though, started in tennis with a bang. At the age of 16 she lost the final of the US Open, her only singles defeat in the competition in 12 years. And by 1927 Mrs Wills-Moody was taking England by storm as well — winning the first of her eight Wimbledon singles titles and not dropping a set for another five years.

Joe Davis's impact was even longer lasting. In the year that Wills took charge of Wimbledon he started his stranglehold on the world snooker championship, winning the inaugural event and not losing the title for another 20 years.

If that was not enough talent on display, there was still more to come. A decade that saw Hobbs and Hammond batting in their prime also brought the emergence of still more greatness. In the 1929 Ashes series, when Hobbs, "The Master", became the oldest man to score a Test century, a 20-year-old Donald Bradman was giving a hint of what was to come during his debut for Australia.

As the decade drew to a close and the old eras were being superseded by the new, two events in the final year signified the end of a romantic history and the beginning of a horrific one. In January, Wyatt Earp, the legendary marshal of Dodge City, died peacefully in his sleep, with his Colt 45 Special hanging from the bedpost.

Nine months later, the worst economic collapse in modern times occurred when the Wall Street Stock Exchange crashed. Many investors lost everything, some speculators committed suicide and the world was plunged into crisis. The economic chaos that ensued would create a recession so great that generations of people would be permanently scarred by the experience.

The fun decade had ended with a bang all right, one that was heard around the globe.

ATHLETICS
■ *British Olympic gold medals*
1920 *800m* Albert Hill; *1500m* Albert Hill; *3,000m steeplechase* Percy Hodge; *4x400m relay*
1924 *100m* Harold Abrahams; *400m* Eric Liddell; *800m* Douglas Lowe
1928 *800m* Douglas Lowe; *400m hurdles* Lord Burghley

BASEBALL
■ *World Series*
1920 Cleveland Indians
1921 New York Giants
1922 New York Giants
1923 New York Yankees
1924 Washington Senators
1925 Pittsburgh Pirates
1926 St Louis Cardinals
1927 New York Yankees
1928 New York Yankees
1929 Philadelphia Athletics

CRICKET
■ *County championship*
1920 Middlesex
1921 Middlesex
1922 Yorkshire
1923 Yorkshire
1924 Yorkshire
1925 Yorkshire
1926 Lancashire
1927 Lancashire
1928 Lancashire
1929 Nottinghamshire

CYCLING
■ *Tour de France*
1920 Phillipe Thys
1921 Leon Scieur
1922 Firmin Lambot
1923 Henri Pellissier
1924 Ottavio Bottecchia
1925 Ottavio Bottecchia
1926 Lucien Buysee
1927 Nicholas Frantz
1928 Nicholas Frantz
1929 Maurice Dewaele

FOOTBALL
■ *Football League*
1920 West Bromwich
1921 Burnley
1922 Liverpool
1923 Liverpool
1924 Huddersfield
1925 Huddersfield
1926 Huddersfield
1927 Newcastle
1928 Everton
1929 Sheffield Wed
■ *FA Cup*
1920 Aston Villa 1 Huddersfield 0 (aet)
1921 Tottenham 1 Wolverhampton 0
1922 Huddersfield 1 Preston 0
1923 Bolton 2 West Ham 0
1924 Newcastle 2 Aston Villa 0
1925 Sheffield Utd 1 Cardiff 0
1926 Bolton 1 Manchester City 0
1927 Cardiff 1 Arsenal 0
1928 Blackburn 3 Huddersfield 1
1929 Bolton 2 Portsmouth 0
■ *Scottish League*
1920 Rangers
1921 Rangers
1922 Celtic
1923 Rangers
1924 Rangers
1925 Rangers
1926 Celtic
1927 Rangers
1928 Rangers
1929 Rangers
■ *Scottish Cup*
1920 Kilmarnock 3 Albion 2
1921 Partick 1 Rangers 0
1922 Morton 1 Rangers 0
1923 Celtic 1 Hibernian 0
1924 Airdrie 2 Hibernian 0
1925 Celtic 2 Dundee 1
1926 St Mirren 2 Celtic 0
1927 Celtic 3 East Fife 1
1928 Rangers 4 Celtic 0
1929 Kilmarnock 2 Rangers 0

GOLF
■ *The Open*
1920 George Duncan
1921 Jock Hutchison
1922 Walter Hagen
1923 Arthur Havers
1924 Walter Hagen
1925 Jim Barnes
1926 Bobby Jones
1927 Bobby Jones
1928 Walter Hagen
1929 Walter Hagen
■ *US Open*
1920 Edward Ray
1921 Jim Barnes
1922 Gene Sarazen
1923 Bobby Jones
1924 Cyril Walker
1925 Willie Macfarlane
1926 Bobby Jones
1927 Tommy Armour
1928 Johnny Farrell
1929 Bobby Jones
■ *US PGA*
1920 Jock Hutchison
1921 Walter Hagen
1922 Gene Sarazen
1923 Gene Sarazen
1924 Walter Hagen
1925 Walter Hagen
1926 Walter Hagen
1927 Walter Hagen
1928 Leo Diegel
1929 Leo Diegel
■ *Ryder Cup*
1927 United States 9½–2½
1929 Great Britain & Ireland 7–5

RACING
■ *The Derby*
1920 *Spion Kop*
1921 *Humorist*
1922 *Captain Cuttle*
1923 *Papyrus*
1924 *Sansovino*
1925 *Manna*
1926 *Coronach*
1927 *Call Boy*
1928 *Fellstead*
1929 *Trigo*
■ *Grand National*
1920 *Troytown*
1921 *Shaun Spadah*
1922 *Music Hall*
1923 *Sergeant Murphy*
1924 *Master Robert*
1925 *Double Chance*
1926 *Jack Horner*
1927 *Sprig*
1928 *Tipperary Tim*
1929 *Gregalach*

ROWING
■ *Boat Race*
1920 Cambridge
1921 Cambridge
1922 Cambridge
1923 Oxford
1924 Cambridge
1925 Cambridge
1926 Cambridge
1927 Cambridge
1928 Cambridge
1929 Cambridge

RUGBY LEAGUE
■ *Challenge Cup*
1920 Huddersfield 21 Wigan 10
1921 Leigh 13 Halifax 0
1922 Rochdale 10 Hull 9
1923 Leeds 28 Hull 3
1924 Wigan 21 Oldham 4
1925 Oldham 16 Hull KR 0
1926 Swinton 9 Oldham 3
1927 Oldham 26 Swinton 7
1928 Swinton 5 Warrington 3
1929 Wigan 13 Dewsbury 2

RUGBY UNION
■ *Five Nations championship*
1920 England, Scotland and Ireland
1921 England
1922 Wales
1923 England
1924 England
1925 Scotland
1926 Scotland and Ireland
1927 Scotland and Ireland
1928 England
1929 Scotland

SAILING
■ *America's Cup*
1920 *Resolute* (US, Charles Adams)

SNOOKER
■ *World championship*
1927 Joe Davis 20 Tom Dennis 11
1928 Joe Davis 16 Fred Lawrence 13
1929 Joe Davis 19 Tom Dennis 14

TENNIS
■ *Wimbledon*
1920 Bill Tilden *bt* Gerald Patterson; Suzanne Lenglen *bt* Dorothea Lambert Chambers
1921 Bill Tilden *bt* Brian Norton; Suzanne Lenglen *bt* Elizabeth Ryan
1922 Gerald Patterson *bt* Randolph Lycett; Suzanne Lenglen *bt* Molla Mallory
1923 William Johnston *bt* Frank Hunter; Suzanne Lenglen *bt* Kathleen McKane
1924 Jean Borotra *bt* Rene Lacoste; Kathleen McKane *bt* Helen Wills
1925 Rene Lacoste *bt* Jean Borotra; Suzanne Lenglen *bt* Joan Fry
1926 Jean Borotra *bt* Howard Kinsey; Kathleen Godfree *bt* Lili d'Alvarez
1927 Henri Cochet *bt* Jean Borotra; Helen Wills *bt* Lili d'Alvarez
1928 Rene Lacoste *bt* Henri Cochet; Helen Wills *bt* Lili d'Alvarez
1929 Henri Cochet *bt* Jean Borotra; Helen Wills *bt* Helen Jacobs
■ *Australian championship*
1920 Pat O'Hara Wood
1921 Rhys Gemmell
1922 Pat O'Hara Wood; Margaret Molesworth
1923 Pat O'Hara Wood; Margaret Molesworth
1924 James Anderson; Sylvia Lance
1925 James Anderson; Daphne Akhurst
1926 John Hawkes; Daphne Akhurst
1927 Gerald Patterson; Esna Boyd
1928 Jean Borotra; Daphne Akhurst
1929 John Gregory; Daphne Akhurst
■ *French championship*
1925 Rene Lacoste; Suzanne Lenglen
1926 Henri Cochet; Suzanne Lenglen
1927 Rene Lacoste; Kea Bouman
1928 Henri Cochet; Helen Wills
1929 Rene Lacoste; Helen Wills
■ *US championship*
1920 Bill Tilden; Molla Mallory
1921 Bill Tilden; Molla Mallory
1922 Bill Tilden; Molla Mallory
1923 Bill Tilden; Helen Wills
1924 Bill Tilden; Helen Wills
1925 Bill Tilden; Helen Wills
1926 Rene Lacoste; Molla Mallory
1927 Rene Lacoste; Helen Wills
1928 Henri Cochet; Helen Wills
1929 Bill Tilden; Helen Wills

The vamp: Lenglen on the crest of the new wave

The gentleman: Hobbs stood firm for the old guard

Tilden applies service charge

BILL TILDEN, a failed actor, turned the tennis court into his stage. The script read like a fairytale and Tilden played his role to perfection. Paul Gallico wrote of him: "To opponents it was a contest; with Tilden it was an expression of his own tremendous and overwhelming ego, coupled with feminine vanity."

Tilden's biggest weapon was his powerful service, which was clocked at 151mph. He seldom followed it to the net, preferring to out-manoeuvre his opponent from the baseline with a subtle game that had been carefully analysed. Such was his thoroughness that when he lost the 1919 US championship to Bill Johnston he spent the entire winter working on his weak backhand. The reward for his hard work was the first of three men's singles titles at Wimbledon. Tilden beat the Australian Gerald Patterson 2-6 6-3 6-2 6-4 in the challenge round and took his remodelled backhand home, where he won six successive US championship titles.

He retained the Wimbledon title the next year and won it again in 1930. Tilden won his seventh US title in 1929 and turned professional in 1931. A homosexual, Tilden was twice jailed for indecency offences and was ostracised by his friends. He continued to play tennis until he died of a heart attack at the age of 60 in 1953.

Hill's whistle-stop victory role

ALBERT HILL, a 31-year-old railway guard who fought through many bitter campaigns in the war, was finally rewarded with a couple of medals at the sixth Olympic Games in Antwerp.

The talented British athlete, who spent the best years of his life in the trenches instead of on the track, took the 800m and 1500m titles. He won five races in five days.

Hill's double was enthusiastically appreciated by his hosts, who had been through four years of occupation. They did a remarkable job in organising the Games only 18 months after the enemy guns had been silenced. Many of the world's best athletes were missing, lost in action, and Austria, Germany, Hungary and Turkey were not invited.

Two days after winning the 800m, Hill beat his fellow Briton Philip Baker in the final of the 1500m, a double not achieved for another 44 years. Baker was in the British delegation at the peace conference the year before. He became a Labour MP and won the 1959 Nobel Peace Prize for his book "The Arms Race: a Programme for World Disarmament".

The Games were a stage for the intense rivalry between Paavo Nurmi, of Finland, and Joseph Guillemot. The Frenchman won the 5,000m on August 17 and three days later Nurmi pipped him in the 10,000m to add to his gold medal in the cross-country. Britain won 15 gold medals, 15 silver and 13 bronze.

Golden double: Albert Hill wins the 800m final in 1min 53.4sec in Antwerp

Almost there: Hans Kolehmainen of Finland at the end of the gruelling marathon

Chapman set for big time

HUDDERSFIELD won promotion to the first division and were beaten in the FA Cup final, but there was far better to come. Within a year Herbert Chapman became their manager and they were turned into the dominant team of the 1920s. At the time, there was no indication that Chapman was to become the most significant and successful manager of the century, or that Huddersfield, beleaguered in rugby league country, would become the most successful side in the land, winning three consecutive League championships and one FA Cup in five years.

Chapman had been an indifferent inside-forward with Tottenham, largely remembered for his odd-coloured yellow boots. When he left Spurs he was poised to resume an engineering career. However, he was unexpectedly offered the job of player-manager at Northampton Town, then in the Southern League. His success in winning the Southern League in 1909 led him to the managership of Leeds City. However, the club's directors got themselves into difficulties with illegal payments to players. Leeds City were expelled from the League and Chapman, though uninvolved, was suspended. Some of the playing assets were absorbed by Huddersfield, who appointed Chapman manager.

Chapman's secret was in the building of teams. He had a wonderful nose for talent and how to motivate it, but more importantly how to weld the side into a whole greater than the parts. He bought wisely, but also liked to take risks.

In 1925, as Huddersfield were in the middle of their championship-winning record, Chapman rocked the football world by moving to Arsenal, who had never finished higher than sixth in the League and had never reached a Cup final. He set about building a side that would dominate the 1930s.

FOR THE RECORD

AMERICAN FOOTBALL
■ Fourteen teams formed the American Professional Football Association, the forerunner of the National Football League, and elected Jim Thorpe their president.

BADMINTON
■ Sir George Thomas, the "grand old man" of badminton, won the first of four consecutive All-England singles. In all he won 21 titles at the event, the last when he was 47.

BASEBALL
■ Ray Chapman, the Cleveland shortstop, was killed by a pitch from Carl Mays of the New York Yankees.

FOOTBALL
■ The Third Division South was formed. Of the original 20 clubs, only Merthyr Town and Newport have since lost their League status.

■ Billy Meredith, at 45 years and 229 days, appeared for Wales against England on March 15, the oldest man to have played international football.

GOLF
■ Spikes were fitted to golf shoes for the first time.

RUGBY UNION
■ The French Rugby Federation was formed.

TENNIS
■ Suzanne Lenglen won all three Wimbledon titles without dropping a set.

RUGBY UNION

England's successful revolution

WAVELL WAKEFIELD was among 11 men chosen for the first time to play for England. The selectors paid the cost for wholesale changes, or so it seemed. Wales beat England 19-5 at St Helens, Swansea, on January 17.

However, Wakefield and his teammates learned quickly and England soon became a formidable force. He introduced many new concepts to forward play including the specialisation of the front row in scrums, jumping in lineouts and cover defence behind the fly-half.

Jock Wemyss, who won his first cap for Wales in 1914, was recalled to the team against France in Paris despite losing an eye in the war. He found that there were only 14 jerseys in the dressing room and his was the one missing. When he asked an official where his jersey was, he was told: "Don't be bloody stupid Wemyss, you got your jersey six years ago."

GOLF

Duncan's amazing fightback

GEORGE DUNCAN staged the greatest turnaround in Open history when he came back to beat Sandy Herd by two strokes at Deal. Duncan scored 80 in the first two rounds to be 13 off the pace, and finished with a 71 and 72 on the final day. His prize was worth £100.

Duncan: £100 prize

Fender scores the fastest ton

WHEN Percy Fender pulled a batting glove on to his right hand and walked out to the crease you knew he meant business, as he showed at Northampton on August 26. Surrey were in command against Northants when Fender joined H A Peach. Fender made that total command. He reached his 50 in 19 minutes and his century in 35 minutes, the fastest hundred in first-class cricket. He finished with 113 out of an unbroken stand of 171 in 42 minutes.

Fender: total command

GOLF

Ray conquers United States

TED RAY pipped four players by one stroke to become the second Englishman after Harry Vardon to win the US Open. Ray's victory at Inverness was the last by an Englishman for 50 years. Tony Jacklin broke the drought at Hazeltine in 1970.

GOLF

Walker goes his own way

GEORGE HERBERT WALKER had submitted a plan to the United States Golf Association suggesting international team matches between amateurs. Nobody took up the invitation, so the desperate Americans sent a team to Hoylake in 1921 and beat Britain 9-3 in an unofficial match on the eve of the amateur championship. The seeds had been sown. The first Walker Cup between Great Britain and Ireland and the United States was held the next year.

FOR THE RECORD

CRICKET
■ Glamorgan became the 17th county to join the championship. They finished last.

FOOTBALL
■ Southport were admitted to the League. They did not have a player sent off in 1,027 matches until Walter Taylor was dismissed on October 18, 1952.

■ Burnley were unbeaten in 30 matches in the First Division. They won 21, drew 9 and scored 68 goals.

■ The Third Division North was formed. Of the original 20 clubs, eight have since lost their League status.

GOLF
■ Jim Barnes won the 25th US Open by nine strokes after leading every round.

TABLE TENNIS
■ Ivor Montague organised a match between Cambridge and Oxford University which started a revival of the sport.

TENNIS
■ The Wimbledon championships were held at Worple Road for the last time.

CRICKET

England routed: Jack Gregory on the attack at Headingley

Doughty Douglas keeps on losing

THE First World War took a heavy toll on English cricket — 77 leading players were listed on the 1920 Wisden Roll of Honour and those who had survived were out of touch. So when Johnny Douglas took the England team to Australia for the first Ashes series in eight years he had little talent to choose from. Douglas, who won a boxing gold medal at the 1908 Olympics, was a fighter though, and his defensive ability was captured by the Australians interpreting his initials J W H T as "Johnny Won't Hit Today".

He was also a popular captain among the locals: he lost the series 5-0. The teams returned to England together aboard the liner Osterley and when their struggle for the Ashes was resumed at Trent Bridge — the 100th Test between the two countries — England had five new caps in their side. Little changed. The Australians won by 10 wickets and England used 30 players in the five-match series. England made six changes for the second Test and seven for the third, but lost both times. In their desperation they invited C B Fry to play in the second Test at Lord's, but the 49-year-old batsman was having none of it.

Big-hitting Gregory in run spree

JACK GREGORY did not wear batting gloves. He did not need to. He was 6ft 3½ in, 14 stone and described by R C Robertson-Glasgow as "tall, strong and raw-boned, like one of his native kangaroos". Gregory was a spectacular Australian all-rounder, a powerful left-hand batsman and a devastating fast bowler who would terrorise batsmen with his looks and pace. His most spectacular innings was in the second Test against South Africa in Johannesburg in mid-November. He took only 70 minutes to hit the fastest century in Test cricket, reaching 100 in 67 balls.

RUGBY UNION

Dave and K never out of tune

WHEREVER they went, Dave Davies and Cyril Kershaw were called "Dave and K", which made the two naval officers sound like a singing duo. Far from it. They were arguably England's greatest half-back combination. They played 14 internationals together and were never in a losing side, helping England win three Grand Slams.

Kershaw was an attacking scrum-half who linked admirably with his loose forwards Wavell Wakefield, Tom Voyce and Geoffrey Conway. He also possessed a long throw, providing Davies with time to fire his left-footed drop kicks or launch long-striding runs. England's first Grand Slam of the decade was sealed in Paris on March 28 when they beat France 10-6.

Dempsey draws $1m

MORE than 80,000 swamped Boyle's Thirty Acres in New Jersey to see Jack Dempsey retain his world heavyweight title against the dashing Frenchman, Georges Carpentier on July 2. The crowd generated the first million-dollar gate.

Dempsey won the first round, but in the second Carpentier almost knocked out the champion with a stunning right hand. Somehow Dempsey clung on. But that blow was the challenger's undoing: he damaged his right thumb and, in the next two rounds, took a fearful beating until the Manassa Mauler dispatched his lighter opponent in the fourth.

Million-dollar match: Dempsey knocks out Carpentier

Bears start to growl

THE NFL expanded to 22 teams at the start of the season, but even so some teams found the going tough. The New York Giants stopped playing after two games, and the Green Bay Packers were only kept afloat by a loan from local businessmen. George Halas, the player-coach of the Decateur Staleys, emerged from the uncertainty to become the driving force of the game.

When the Staley Manufacturing Company could no longer support its team Halas moved it to Chicago, where he won the league championship. In 1922 Halas renamed his team the Chicago Bears and the reign of "Papa Bear" began. In all, he coached for 40 years and only had six losing seasons in a record of 326 wins from 506 games.

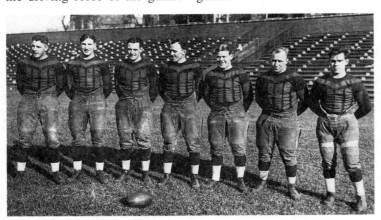

Start of a dynasty: George Halas (*centre*) and the Bears

Ace start rewarded

JOCK HUTCHISON started his challenge for the Open with a hole in one at the eighth at St Andrews. At the next hole his tee shot finished only inches from a second ace. Hutchison's Open record of three shots in two holes gave him a launching pad to a 72 in the opening round. Although the Scottish professional slumped in the latter rounds he produced a big finish to beat the amateur Roger Wethered by nine shots in the 36-hole play-off. Hutchison's accuracy prompted officials to examine his clubs and some believed that the rough faces on his irons provided him with unfair backspin. Bobby Jones found the going even harder. He gave up in the third round.

Sun shines on Segrave

SIR HENRY SEGRAVE had made a quiet debut at Brooklands the year before and had won several minor races. On the strength of that he persuaded the newly-formed Sunbeam-Talbot-Darracq Group to let him drive a works car in the French Grand Prix, where he finished last.

The group only gave him the car on the understanding that he paid for any damage. He didn't damage the car and was invited to join the team on a permanent basis. Segrave soon justified their belief in him when he came third in the Grand Prix des Voiturettes at Le Mans and won the Junior Car Club 200-mile race at Brooklands.

Greatest Yankee ever

APART from owning the Boston Red Sox, Harry Frazee also staged Broadway shows. To finance his latest production he sold the heart of his team to the New York Yankees. Babe Ruth went for $125,000 plus a $300,000 loan and it was a bargain. The Red Sox went from good to bad to worse, while Ruth took the Yankees from strength to strength.

Ruth hit a record 54 home runs for the Yankees in 1920, with an all-time record slugging percentage of .847. Then, in probably his best season ever, he hit even harder — raising his own record to 59 home runs. The Yankees reached the World Series for the first time. Although they lost to their local rivals the Giants, Ruth had established the foundations of a dynasty that saw the Yankees win 29 divisional titles and 20 World Series in 44 years.

Ruth: inspired the Yankees

1922

Hagen does it with style

Hagen: "I never wanted to be a millionaire, I just wanted to live like one"

CRICKET

Macaulay's golden debut

THE England captain, Frank Mann, tossed the ball to George Macaulay on the first day of the year and asked him to bowl the second over against South Africa in the second Test in Cape Town. The Yorkshireman dismissed George Hearne for a golden duck to become the fourth bowler in history to take a wicket with his first ball in Test cricket. And he had the last say in the match, too, scoring the winning run in England's one-wicket victory. It was England's first Test success after the war.

Macaulay: first and last

GOLF

Guest writer

BERNARD DARWIN, a sportswriter for The Times, was sent to New York to report on the first Walker Cup event between the United States and Britain. But he not only wrote about it, he also played in it. Darwin replaced Robert Harris, the unwell British captain, and won his singles match. The United States triumphed 8-4.

WHEN Walter Hagen arrived at Sandwich for the 29th Open championship he was far from happy with British protocol. As a professional he was not allowed to change or eat in the clubhouse. So Hagen hired a stretch limousine, parked it in front of the clubhouse and used it for changing and eating.

Hagen appeared to have thrown away his opportunity to win when he shot 79 in the third round. That left him two strokes behind the defending champion, Jock Hutchison. In a howling wind and driving rain Hutchison faded in the last round and, instead, Hagen had to hold off a late charge from George Duncan, who needed a four on the final hole to force a play-off. Duncan's second shot landed in a hollow on the edge of the green. He left his pitch 15 feet short and two-putted. Hagen was the first American-born player to win the Open and the little

hollow at the 18th at Sandwich became known as "Duncan's Hollow". When Hagen was presented with the prize for winning he looked at the amount

> *All the professional golfers who have a chance to go after the big money today should say a silent thanks to Walter Hagen each time they stretch a cheque between their fingers*
>
> Gene Sarazen

on the cheque . . . and handed it to his caddie. The next year officials condescended to allow him into the clubhouse to receive his second prize. Hagen

declined and invited the crowd to the local pub for a drink.

Hagen was a picture of sartorial elegance with his well-cut suits and sleek sports cars. The first man to make a million for hitting a golf ball spent his money as quickly as he earned it. "I never wanted to be a millionaire, I just wanted to live like one," he said.

Hagen's popularity did much to turn professional golfers into cult heroes. His attitude, though, was that golf was there to be enjoyed. "Never hurry, never worry and be sure to smell the flowers along the way," he said. Hagen spent a lot of time among the flowers because of an awkward and erratic swing, but his excellent ability to recover enabled him to win 10 major championships. His strength at matchplay brought him five US PGA titles, including four in a row, and he won the US Open twice and the Open four times.

Wimbledon expand their horizon

A BURGEONING interest in tennis forced the All-England Lawn Tennis and Croquet Club to move to new premises for the Wimbledon championships. The courts at Worple Road were inadequate for the crowds attracted by the charisma of Bill Tilden and Suzanne Lenglen,

and the club moved to Church Road, its present site. The new venue took two years to prepare and cost £140,000.

Leslie Godfree was quick to realise the significance of being the first man to serve on the Centre Court. Algy Kingscote hit his return into the net and

Godfree grabbed the ball, put it in his pocket and kept it as a souvenir. The Wimbledon committee decided to abolish the challenge round, which had operated since 1877. Gerald Patterson and Lenglen were the first men's and women's champions at the new Wimbledon.

Puddefoot: first £5,000 transfer

More room: the All-England Club's spacious new home at Wimbledon

MOTOR RACING
Monza draws 150,000

THE Italians hosted the first European Grand Prix at Monza on September 10. Because the Italians were able to charge for admission it made motor racing something of a commercial proposition, particularly as some 150,000 spectators turned up. The total prize money was half-a-million lire, nearly £6,000. However, the actual race was one of the dullest ever as the Fiats were completely dominant, finishing first and second. They were so far ahead of the third car that it was flagged down seven laps behind the second and nine laps behind the winner.

GOLF
Early charge for spectators and late charge by Sarazen

SPECTATORS were charged an entrance fee for the first time to watch the US Open at Skokie, Illinois. But they got their money's worth. It took a birdie on the final hole for Gene Sarazen to win by one shot from John Black and Bobby Jones. The 20-year-old Sarazen was the first winner to break 70 in the final round when he shot 68.

Two months later Sarazen emphasised his arrival as a leading player on the golfing scene by taking the US PGA crown.

TENNIS
Wills vows not to lose again

HELEN WILLS, a 16-year-old Californian, burst on to the tennis scene when she reached the finals in the United States championships. However, the power and experience of Molla Mallory proved too much and she was beaten 6-3 6-1. It was her only defeat in the US singles event until she retired against Helen Jacobs in the 1933 final.

Wills started her reign as champion when she was 17 and won the US title seven times in nine years. She did not enter in 1926 because of appendicitis and did not attend the championships in 1930.

FOR THE RECORD

BASEBALL

■ Yankee Stadium, the "house that Ruth built" opened. Most of the construction costs were paid for by the bigger crowds generated by Babe Ruth. Fittingly, Ruth hit a winning home run in the first game at the stadium .

FOOTBALL

■ Littlewoods distributed the first pools coupon outside Old Trafford.

■ Exeter City went 20 months — April 12, 1923 to November 7, 1924 — without scoring an away goal.

■ Scotland initiated a Third Division but it folded without completing its third season.

GOLF

■ Arthur Havers became the last Briton in 11 years to win the Open. Gene Sarazen made his first appearance but was caught in a storm and failed to qualify.

RACING

■ The Aga Khan, in only his second season as an owner, won several of the leading sprint races with Mumtaz Mahal, the "flying filly".

SQUASH

■ The Tennis and Racket Association formalised the sizes of courts and balls. The following year it standardised the rules.

TABLE TENNIS

■ The upsurge of interest in the game was marked by 30,000 people, including Jack Hobbs, entering the Daily Mirror tournament.

TENNIS

■ The United States beat Britain 7-0 in the first Wightman Cup.

■ Vincent Richards, a 19-year-old American, was the first player to bring an entourage to Wimbledon. "Team Richards" included a secretary, a typist and a doctor. Despite his back-up Richards lost in the quarter-finals.

FOOTBALL

White horse the star at Wembley

BOLTON beat West Ham 2-0 in the first FA Cup final held at Wembley on April 28. The match will be remembered for the size of the crowd and a brave policeman on a white horse.

The owners of the new stadium boasted that it was the finest in the world and could hold 125,000. Their claim proved to be disastrous. More than 200,000 people turned up, perhaps even 250,000, and they poured into the ground, spilling on to the pitch. The kick-off was delayed for 45 minutes as the crowd good-naturedly sang the national anthem for the arrival of the King while policemen on horses inched the crowd back to the touchline. The West Ham captain, Jack Tresarden, said the best pass he had all afternoon was from a spectator.

When the police constable on the 13-year-old white horse got home he was asked by his girlfriend what sort of day he'd had. "Oh, just ordinary, lass," he said. "Just ordinary." It became known as the White Horse Cup Final and finals have been all-ticket ever since.

Nowhere to play: the teams wait for police to clear the pitch

RUGBY UNION

Liddell turns to the track

ONE of Scotland's faint hopes of breaking England's domination of the Five Nations championship lay in Eric Liddell using his phenomenal speed to upset his opponents. But the Edinburgh University winger could not stop England clinching their fourth Grand Slam with an 8-6 win at Inverleith.

Liddell, who had scored four tries in seven internationals, retired from rugby. He decided to concentrate on athletics and the next year returned to the Stade Colombes in Paris, where he had made his international rugby debut in 1922, to win the 400m at the Olympics.

CRICKET

Rhodes from last to first

WILFRED RHODES provided a shining example for all No 11 batsmen. He started his first-class career as the last man in for Yorkshire and rose to open for England with Jack Hobbs. But it was as a slow left-arm spinner that Rhodes is best remembered. He was 46 and still a formidable force, taking 120 wickets at 11.27 for Yorkshire. He topped the championship bowling averages for the fifth time in his career and, not surprisingly, Yorkshire retained the title.

Rhodes: formidable force

Our Steve wins third Derby

Dempsey thriller

Three in a row: Donoghue returns in triumph on Papyrus in his third Derby success

"OUR STEVE" was idolised for his brilliance on the racecourse. So when he won his third successive Derby there were celebrations throughout the country. Steve Donoghue's mother hoisted a flag in Warrington to mark the event. The race was cause for double cheer. Papyrus, the winner, was owned by a farmer who started with one horse and was able to buy Papyrus from his prize-money for winning the Ascot Gold Cup with Periosteum.

Ever since the start of the war Donoghue had reigned supreme.

He was champion jockey every year from 1914 to 1923. He won his first Derby in 1915 on Pommern, who went on to win the Triple Crown. Two years later Gay Crusader was his second Triple Crown winner.

Donoghue's first Epsom Derby came in 1921. He rode a masterful race on Humorist, handling the frail horse perfectly to hold off Craig an Eran, the favourite. Captain Cuttle gave him the second leg of the hat-trick in 1922, and Papyrus rounded off a sequence that has never been equalled.

In all Donoghue won six Derbys, a total only beaten by Lester Piggott. His last victory in the race was in 1925. Donoghue's career then went into a bit of a decline although he did not finally retire until 1937.

On the track he was the perfect gentlemen — he was respected by his fellow jockeys and he was never once called before the stewards. Generous to a fault, although Donoghue earned a fortune he had virtually nothing left by the time he died of a heart attack in March 1945, aged 60.

FOR 3min 57sec Jack Dempsey and Luis Angel Firpo slugged it out in New York on September 4 for the world heavyweight title. It was quickly called the greatest fight ever.

As the bout started Dempsey threw a left hook and missed. The 6ft 3in Argentinian, appropriately called the Wild Bull of the Pampas, countered with a right that caught Dempsey flush on the chin. Dempsey fell forward, jumped up without a count and had Firpo down seven times in the first round. But Firpo still managed to land a straight right that knocked Dempsey through the ropes. If it had not been for hands illegally pushing him back into the ring he would have lost his title. But the near-unconscious Dempsey was saved by the bell.

In the second round both boxers were in a bad way, Dempsey summoned the strength from somewhere to knock Firpo down twice more. When he got up after a count of four, Firpo was defenceless and the Manassa Mauler demolished him with two hooks after 57 seconds of the round.

Segrave French hero

SIR HENRY SEGRAVE, in a two-litre six-cylinder Sunbeam, became the first Briton to win a Grand Prix when he took the blue riband event, the French GP at Tours. The crack Italian Fiats were undone by the grit and dust of the surface, the cars having been tested on the near-perfect Monza circuit. Segrave, by patient endeavour, outran his swifter, but more fragile, rivals.

It was the first major victory by a Briton for 21 years, and it put Britain firmly on the motor racing map. As Segrave said: "How can I ever forget those last few miles — every noise in the engine seemed magnified a hundredfold, every corner seemed impossible, my brain refused to work in complete co-ordination with my hands and feet. But luck was with us." Luck indeed. One of the leaders, Albert Divo, wasted 15 minutes trying to remove the filler cap before he decided to drive on his reserve tank. Another, Carlo Salamano, had a faulty gauge and thought he was out of petrol. After his mechanic cycled two miles for more fuel the car would not restart.

Best of British: Segrave after the French GP

59

Flying Finn strikes gold as regular as clockwork

WHEN the International Olympic Committee put their medals in the mail to the champions of the Paris Olympics, a postman in Finland carried the heaviest load. He arrived on Paavo Nurmi's doorstep with five gold medallions. The Phantom Finn's haul remains a record for a track and field athlete at a single Olympics.

Nurmi, who started running at nine and six years later set his sights on emulating the long-distance success of his countryman Hannes Kolehmainen, realised the best way to conserve energy was to run at an even pace and he trained and competed with a stop-watch in his hand, gauging his progress against the clock. The tactic helped him become one of the greatest runners of the century. He broke 20 world records and won 12 Olympic medals, nine gold and three silver.

He broke the 1500m and 5,000m world records on the same day in a warm-up for the Olympics. Then on July 10 he began his Olympic gold haul. He won the 1500m and 42 minutes later started his successful 5,000m run. Two days after that he won the 10,000m cross-country individual and team gold medals and

the next day he helped Finland take the 3,000m team title. He was so upset at his exclusion from the 10,000m race that he went on to the training track at the same time as the race and ran a better time than the winner, his fellow Finn Ville Ritola.

Britain achieved surprise victories in the 100m and 400m. Harold Abrahams shocked the American favourites Charles Paddock and Jackson Scholz in the short sprint, and Eric Liddell, who declined to run in the 100m because it was staged on a Sunday, won the 400m. The pair were the central characters in the Oscar-winning film Chariots of Fire, loosely based on the Games.

Johnny Weissmuller, the first man to break one minute for the 100m freestyle, won three swimming golds and a bronze medal for the United States in the water polo. He turned to the silver screen in the 1930s and became the most famous Tarzan.

The American Gertrude Ederle won a relay gold medal in the first Olympics to use lane dividers in the pool and two years later was the first woman to swim the English Channel.

Britain won nine gold medals, 13 silver and 12 bronze. Harry

Mallin had the most controversial victory. The Frenchman Roger Brousse was awarded a points victory over Mallin in their middleweight boxing contest, but a Swedish official protested that the Briton had been bitten and Brousse was disqualified. Mallin never lost an amateur fight.

The Irish, who had been members of the British team before, competed separately for the first time. They won one silver and one bronze medal.

Games go out in the cold

THE first Winter Olympics were held at Chamonix from January 25 to February 4, with 294 competitors, including 13 women, from 16 countries.

The first gold medal was won by Charles Jewtraw from the United States in the 500m speed skating. In the ice hockey, Britain finished third behind the United States and Canada.

Jumping for gold

How's that for openers

HERBERT SUTCLIFFE celebrated his Test debut with the first of 15 century opening partnerships with Jack Hobbs. The pair put on 136 in the first Test against South Africa at Edgbaston and followed up with stands of 268 and 72. England won the five-Test series 3-0.

FOR THE RECORD

CRICKET

■ John MacBryan became the only Test cricketer who has never batted, bowled or dismissed anyone in the field. The Somerset opener's Test career lasted just 165 minutes. Torrential rain washed out his sole appearance, on the first day of the fourth Test against South Africa at Old Trafford.

■ Yorkshire, needing 58 to beat Lancashire, were dismissed for 33.

FOOTBALL

■ Billy Meredith became the oldest player in the FA Cup at 49 years and 8 months when he appeared for Manchester City against Newcastle in the semi-final.

■ The rules were changed to allow goals to be scored directly from corners.

MOTOR RACING

■ The authorities decided that from 1925 it would no longer be compulsory for a mechanic to travel in the car with the driver. To accommodate the mechanics, pits were dug next to a convenient straight, usually opposite the grandstand, so that spectators could watch the work.

SNOOKER

■ Tom Dennis, a Nottingham professional, suggested holding a world championship. The idea was rejected because it was not popular enough.

TENNIS

■ The United States Open men's singles event moved from Philadelphia to Forest Hills, New York, where the women's singles had been staged since 1921.

Record haul: Paavo Nurmi (*second from the left*) at the start

Four Musketeers cut and thrust France on to the centre courts of the world's finest duellists

ON THE clay courts of France, the names of Jean Borotra, Jacques Brugnon, Henri Cochet and Rene Lacoste are a legend. Their motto might not have been one for all and all for one, but the Four Musketeers blended perfectly into a combination whose cut-throat play made France the most powerful tennis nation of the 1920s.

They started their domination of Wimbledon in 1924 when Borotra beat Lacoste 6-1 3-6 6-1 3-6 6-4 in a stirring final. It was the first of five successive titles won by the quartet. Borotra, the Bounding Basque, was the most popular and persistent of the four. He always played in a black beret and his joie de vivre and good humour delighted the crowds. Borotra once said: "The only possible regret I have is the feeling that I will die without having played enough tennis." Yet he played at Wimbledon from 1922 until 1964, winning 152 of his record 221 matches. He was the French Minister of Sport from 1940 until 1942 and was imprisoned by the Nazis.

Brugnon's strength was in doubles and a steady game earned him four Wimbledon men's doubles titles. Cochet was the fighter who made up for his lack of skill with aggression and anticipation. His finest win was at Wimbledon in 1927 when he came back from two sets down in the quarter-final, the semi-final and the final to win the title. He saved six match points in the final before beating Borotra 4-6 4-6 6-3 6-4 7-5.

Lacoste, the youngest of the four, kept copious notes on his opponents which helped him win at Wimbledon in 1925 and 1928. He turned his notes into an authoritative book, Lacoste on Tennis, but was forced to retire because of ill health in 1929 at the age of 24. He played with a crocodile mascot sewn on to his shirts. Lacoste developed one of the biggest sports clothing companies in the world after his retirement and he continued to use the distinctive logo.

WHAT THEY WON

WIMBLEDON	AUSTRALIAN CHAMPIONSHIP	FRENCH CHAMPIONSHIP
Singles	**Singles**	**Singles**
Borotra: 1924, 1926	Borotra: 1928	Borotra: 1924, 1931
Cochet: 1927, 1929	**Doubles**	Cochet: 1926, 1928, 1930, 1932
Lacoste: 1925, 1928	Borotra and Brugnon: 1928	Lacoste: 1925, 1927, 1929
Doubles	**Mixed Doubles**	**Doubles**
Borotra and Brugnon: 1932, 1933	Borotra and Akhurst: 1928	Borotra and Brugnon: 1928
Borotra and Lacoste: 1925		Borotra and Lacoste: 1924, 1925, 1929
Cochet and Brugnon: 1926, 1928	**UNITED STATES CHAMPIONSHIP**	Cochet and Brugnon: 1927, 1930, 1932
Mixed Doubles	**Singles**	**Mixed Doubles**
Borotra and Lenglen: 1925	Cochet: 1928	Borotra and Billout: 1924
	Lacoste: 1926, 1927	Borotra and Bordes: 1927
DAVIS CUP	**Mixed Doubles**	Brugnon and Lenglen: 1925, 1926
1927-1932 inclusive	Borotra and Ryan: 1926	Cochet and Bennett: 1928, 1929
	Cochet and Bennett: 1927	

Musketeers: Rene Lacoste and Jean Borotra

Bridge too far for downhearted Wales

THE Welsh team traditionally visited the Forth Bridge the day after their match against Scotland at Inverleith. So the day after the Scots had thumped them 35-10 the battered Welshmen went on their sightseeing trip. When they arrived the Welsh official with the team, T D Schofield, said: "Take a good look at it boys, it's the last time any of you will see it at the expense of the Welsh Union."

Two weeks earlier the Welsh had been beaten 17-9 by the eventual Grand Slam winners, England, their first loss to the English at Swansea since 1895.

Big winners: the Scottish team that hammered Wales

FOOTBALL

Mighty Atom bombs Dundee

CELTIC won the Scottish Cup with a thoroughly bizarre goal. They were down 1-0 to Dundee with seven minutes left when their diminutive and eccentric player Patsy Gallagher, nicknamed the Mighty Atom, started a run from his own half. Several times it seemed he was up-ended, but each time Gallagher recovered and continued on his way. Close to the Dundee goal he was finally brought down, but reacting quickly, he somersaulted into the net with the ball wedged between his feet. Gallagher was disentangled from the net, the goal stood, and five minutes later, Jimmy McGrory scored the winner.

TENNIS

Allez France

THE magnetic attraction of Wimbledon drew players and spectators alike. There were so many players the All-England club introduced a qualifying round. The increased entry was matched by an increase in spectator interest and tickets were rationed for the first time.

The primary reason for the interest was Suzanne Lenglen, the flamboyant Frenchwoman who won her sixth and last women's title, crushing Joan Fry 6-2 6-0. Rene Lacoste made it a first French double by winning the men's singles 6-3 6-3 4-6 8-6 against his countryman Jean Borotra.

FOOTBALL

Whole new game

THE most revolutionary rule change in the century came when the offside laws were altered. Previously there had to be three men between the attacker and goal (usually two and the goalkeeper), now there only needed to be two. Some radical change was necessary: professional football had become a sterile game of professional defenders and games with 40 offside decisions were commonplace.

The leading exponent of exploiting the old law was Bill McCracken, Newcastle's Irish full-back. He and Frank Hudspeth, an England international, would infuriate the attacking side by going further and further upfield. When an attack began one of them would sneak behind the forwards. This left the forward in possession with nobody to pass to lest he be given offside. It was a standing joke for teams coming to Newcastle to reply to the guard's whistle at the railway station: "Blimey, offside already."

The impact of the change was immediate. Although the law had been altered to reduce the number of irritating stoppages, the effect on goalscoring was sensational. On the opening day of the season Aston Villa scored 10 against Burnley. The number of goals scored in the Football League in the last season under the old law was 4,700, the first under the new law produced 6,373. However, the law-makers had not fully realised how they had fundamentally changed the game. But at Arsenal they did.

The problem with the old style of play was that now the two full-backs were hopelessly vulnerable to fast-breaking forwards. Herbert Chapman, prompted by his captain Charlie Buchan, moved his centre-half, then an attacking midfielder, into defence as a stopper and an inside forward back into midfield. In short, the formation changed from 2-3-5 to 3-3-4. Then, to foil other teams mounting this defence against his attackers, Chapman introduced long cross-field passes from the back to strong, direct forwards.

Tactical genius: Frank Hudspeth won the FA Cup in 1924

AMERICAN FOOTBALL

Fans flock to marvel at Grange

RED GRANGE was lionised as the best player college football had ever seen. But even though he ran for more than 1,000 yards in each of his three seasons for the University of Illinois, his father was not keen on his turning professional. Then Charles Pyle, a cinema manager and promoter, made him an offer he could not refuse: "How would you like to make a hundred thousand dollars? Maybe even a million?" So the "Galloping Ghost" signed for the Chicago Bears for $100,000. His reputation was so great that 36,000 watched his debut. Anxious to cash in on their investment, the Bears arranged a grand end of season tour.

The exhibition matches were a spectacular success. More than 70,000 paid to see Grange in New York, and the Giants' share of the gate money was enough to keep the hard-pressed club in existence. In all, the tour attracted 400,000 spectators and the NFL, which had got off to a shaky start, was firmly established in the public eye.

SAILING

Fastnet launched

SEVEN yachts left Ryde on the inaugural Fastnet race. The winner was the Le Havre pilot cutter Jolie Brise, owned by George Martin. The Royal Ocean Racing Club was formed at a party after the race and Martin was its founding Commodore. The Bermuda race, the leading event in America, had been resurrected in 1923 as a yearly competition. But it switched to a biennial format so as not to clash with the established Fastnet race.

Played 30, won 30

GEORGE NEPIA, a 19-year-old Maori, was the almost impenetrable last line of defence that made the New Zealand side The Invincibles. Nepia played fullback for the All Blacks in all 30 matches of their unbeaten tour of Britain and France. His solid tackling and skilful kicking made him the team's mainstay. However, Nepia was unable to show his skills in South Africa two years later. He was barred from touring with the All Blacks because of the colour of his skin.

Cyril Brownlie became the first player to be sent off in an international when the New Zealander was given his marching orders by the Welsh referee Albert Freethy in the eighth minute of a heated match against England.

The Invincibles beat England at Twickenham

THE INVINCIBLES' 30 VICTORIES

Devon 11-0; Cornwall 29-0; Somerset 6-0; Gloucestershire 6-0; Swansea 39-3; Newport 13-10; Leicester 27-10; North Midlands 40-3; Cheshire 18-5; Durham 43-7; Yorkshire 42-4; Lancashire 23-0; Cumberland 41-0; Ireland 6-0; Ulster 28-6; Northumberland 27-4; Cambridge University 5-0; London Counties 31-6; Oxford University 33-15; Cardiff 16-8; Wales 19-0; Llanelli 8-3; East Midlands 31-7; Warwickshire 20-0; Combined Services 25-3; Hampshire 22-0; London 18-3; England 17-11; French XV 37-8; France 30-6.

FOR THE RECORD

BASEBALL
■ Lou Gehrig started a run of 2,130 consecutive games for the New York Yankees on June 1.

FOOTBALL
■ Arthur Chandler scored in 16 consecutive matches for Leicester in the Second Division.

RUGBY UNION
■ Scotland beat England 14-11 watched by 70,000 people in the first match at Murrayfield on March 21 and went on to win the Grand Slam.

GOLF
■ Macdonald Smith needed a 78 to win the last Open at Prestwick but scored 82 and Jim Barnes took the title.

CRICKET
■ Yorkshire topped the county championship for the fourth time in succession. Eleven of their 21 victories were by an innings and they were unbeaten in 32 matches. They lost only six games in five years.

MOTOR RACING
■ The constructors established the first manufacturers' world championship, based on the four major races. It was won by Alfa-Romeo in front of cheering crowds at Monza in the Italian Grand Prix.

TENNIS
■ The French championships were opened to non-French club players for the first time.

Hobbs matches Grace

Still going strong: Hobbs (*left*) opening for Surrey

THERE was concern in cricketing circles that Jack Hobbs was losing his touch. The 43-year-old Surrey opener no longer looked as though he had been batting for an hour when he faced the first ball of an innings.

His supporters need not have feared; The Master was still in good nick. He returned from a successful Ashes series in Australia to hit 3,024 runs in the county championship, including 16 centuries. Two of his most memorable hundreds were scored against Somerset at Taunton, when he equalled W G Grace's record 126 first-class centuries on August 16 and surpassed the record the very next day with an unbeaten knock of 101 in the second innings.

GOLF

Hard work

WILLIE MACFARLANE, a Scottish professional, needed two play-offs to beat Bobby Jones in the US Open at the Worcester Country Club in Massachusetts. The pair scored 75s in the first and were still level after the 17th hole of the second. MacFarlane took four on the last for a 72 and won by one shot.

CRICKET

Fourth title: Yorkshire's winning team

Brilliant shot saves Jones

Storming finish: Jones drives off in the final round

RACING

Churchill taxes bets

WINSTON CHURCHILL'S budget could have hardly left the sporting world more divided when he announced that betting would be taxed from November 1. The establishment press followed the government line, reporting that the tax was well received and would raise about £6m a year. But the popular press, representing punters and the racing industry, was outraged. It described the tax as unjust, unfair, and unpopular. Edgar Wallace, the novelist and a racehorse owner, was quoted in the Daily Express: "A tax on turnover is simply monstrous, and is against all principles of taxation. It is designed to kill racing."

GOLF

Ryder sows the seed

SAMUEL RYDER, who made his fortune when he persuaded his father to sell flower seeds in penny packets, suggested a series of internationals between the professionals of Britain and the United States. He donated a trophy for the event and on June 4 the first Ryder Cup match was staged at Wentworth. Bill Mehlhorn was the only US player to win in Britain's 13-1 victory with one match halved. There is still controversy over whether this was the first Ryder Cup or an unofficial event.

THE Royal and Ancient club decided to introduce an entrance fee for the Open for the first time. The patrons who turned up certainly received value for their money.

The first hint that this would be a memorable tournament was in the qualifying round at Sunningdale on June 16. Bobby Jones, who had torn up his card during his first Open in 1921, was by now one of the best players in the world. Even the best, though, were forced to qualify. Jones went out and shot a record 66, three better than any previous round in the cham-

> _One might as well attempt to describe the smoothness of the wind as to paint a clear picture of his complete swing_
>
> **Grantland Rice**

pionship. His pair of 33s put him four under par in a round that included 34 putts. He scored 68 in his second round to qualify with 134, but firmly believed he had peaked too early for the

tournament proper at Royal Lytham.

His fears appeared to have been confirmed when his playing partner Al Watrous was two up with five to play in the final round. Jones, though, clawed his way back with typical tenacity to be all square at the 17th tee. Then he struck disaster, hooking his drive into sandy ground while Watrous landed on the green in two and appeared confident of winning his first Open. He was not counting on Jones taking a mashie iron and hitting one of the most famous shots in history. The ball flew 170 yards and finished on the green. Watrous was shattered. He took three putts while Jones was down in two.

When Jones made par on the final hole the challenge from Watrous had crumbled and Jones won his first of three Open titles by two shots.

BOBBY JONES'S TRIUMPHS

1923 US Open; **1924** US amateur championship;
1925 US amateur championship; **1926** US Open, The Open;
1927 The Open, US amateur championship; **1928** US amateur championship; **1929** US Open; **1930** US Open, The Open, US amateur championship, British amateur championship

CRICKET

Larwood's the man

ENGLAND finally found a partner for Maurice Tate, their leading strike bowler who had shouldered a heavy burden since 1924. Harold Larwood, a right-arm bowler from Nottinghamshire, was thrown into the attack for the decisive fifth Test against Australia at The Oval. He generated tremendous pace with a rhythmical run-up and flowing

action that helped England to a 289-run victory and their first win in a series against Australia since 1912. England's winning formula was a mix of Larwood's fire with the teasing spin of the 48-year-old Wilfred Rhodes, who had been recalled for one last effort. Larwood took three for 34 and Rhodes four for 44. Tate took a back seat for once.

Larwood: flowing action

MOTOR RACING

Campbell second in British GP

Sandbank chicanes: the first British Grand Prix at Brooklands

THE first British Grand Prix was held at Brooklands on August 7, complete with chicanes made of sandbanks. Malcolm Campbell, in a new Bugatti, was second behind Robert Senechal and Louis Wagner in a Delage. Sir Henry Segrave, who struggled with carburation and braking problems, had the consolation of winning the Stanley Cup for logging the fastest lap at 85.99mph.

Britain was now officially part of the sudden growth of Grand Prix racing, joining Italy, Belgium, Germany and Spain as host countries alongside the pioneering France. Segrave also became the fastest man on earth when he took an aero-engined V12 four-litre Sunbeam to 152.33mph for the flying kilometre along Southport sands.

BOXING

Tunney outfoxes rusty Dempsey

AGE and brain-power caught up with the fast-living Jack Dempsey on September 23 when he lost his world heavyweight crown to the highly-literate ex-marine Gene Tunney in the open air in Philadelphia. In driving rain, a crowd of 120,000, the largest in boxing history, saw Dempsey, 31, out-boxed for 10 rounds by the 28-year-old challenger.

Tunney, who was as familiar with the works of Shakespeare as with the records and styles of his fellow boxers, had studied Dempsey's methods and ruthlessly exploited the flaws he had discovered to out-point the champion. Rusty after three years of inactivity, and beset by domestic and managerial problems, Dempsey was made to look a clumsy plodder by the cleverness and sharp hitting of the younger man.

Beaten at last: Dempsey is outboxed by Tunney

FOOTBALL

Huddersfield win their third title

HUDDERSFIELD became the first club to win the League championship for the third year in succession. The team was the one largely built by their former manager Herbert Chapman, who had left them for Arsenal the year before. Ominously, the runners-up were Arsenal, who under Chapman's guidance were to emulate Huddersfield's achievement in the 1930s.

RACING

Judge's oversight

THE Cambridgeshire finished in confusion. The judge placed Medal and Niantic in a dead-heat with Insight II third, a length behind. But everybody thought that Insight II had won by at least half a length. The judge later admitted he made a mistake but only in the margin of victory, and had intended to place Insight II third by a neck. The result was amended.

Weissdorn, the favourite, trailed in near the back of the field because he was more interested in a filly alongside him at the start than running.

BOXING

Battle of the long count

GENE TUNNEY'S coolness of brain enabled him to retain his world heavyweight title in Chicago against Jack Dempsey on September 22 in one of boxing's most controversial fights.

In the seventh round, with Tunney well ahead on points, Dempsey caught the champion with a right and followed through with both hands to knock him into a daze, clutching the ropes. But in his excitement to regain the title Dempsey forgot the referee's instructions before the fight. Boxers had to retire to a neutral corner after a knockdown. Instead Dempsey, as he had always done, stood over Tunney waiting to finish him off. The referee had to grab Dempsey round the waist, haul him into the centre of the ring, and point to the neutral corner. Only then did the referee start the count. Tunney rose at nine, having gained an extra five-second respite, survived the next 2½ rounds, and easily retained his title on points.

The fight became known as "the battle of the long count".

Tunney insisted that he could have beaten the count at nine without the additional five seconds, but wrote: "The first nine seconds of a knockdown belong to the man on the floor. No boxer goes into the ring with a stopwatch, boxers go by the referee's timing; whether 25 seconds or nine had elapsed would have made no difference to me. I go by the referee's 'nine'." It was an all-time record gate with receipts of $2,658,660, of which a record $1m went to the champion.

Long count: Tunney gains a few vital seconds in the seventh round

TENNIS

Moody's winning hand

HELEN WILLS MOODY was cool, calm and calculating. Or was she? One minute she was a cheerful Californian with a chatty, charming personality. Give her a tennis racket and the next minute she became "Little Miss Pokerface", intent only on winning. No wonder she was not a Wimbledon favourite.

Helen Wills Moody collected her first of eight women's singles titles at Wimbledon when she beat Lili de Alvarez 6-2 6-4 in the final. She had dropped a set in the first round against Gwen Sterry but, such was her dominance, she did not lose another set in any match until 1932.

Seeding on merit was introduced for the first time at a wet Wimbledon which stretched into a third week. And it was the year of the comeback king, Henri Cochet. The Frenchman staged remarkable recoveries against Bill Tilden in the semi-finals and Jean Borotra in the final. Cochet came back from two sets down and 1-5 against Tilden to win 17 points in a row on his way to a five-set victory. And in the final he saved six match points and won 4-6 4-6 6-3 6-4 7-5.

The first radio broadcast was made at the tournament and a loudspeaker was attached to the umpire's chair.

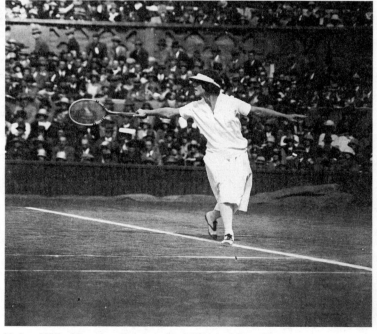

Helen Wills Moody wins her first Wimbeldon title

Hammond gets batting bug

THE England selectors had hoped to groom Wally Hammond into the man who would win back the Ashes in 1926. But their plans went awry when they sent him to the West Indies to hone his batting skills. Hammond was bitten by a mosquito and spent most of 1926 in bed with fever. His recovery in 1927, though, was spectacular. He was the first batsman to hit 1,000 runs in May since W G Grace in 1895 and by the end of the season had scored 2,969.

He was put on the boat to South Africa and made an indelible impression on his Test debut, compiling 51 and taking five for 36, including three wickets for no runs in 23 balls.

US win first Ryder Cup

THE United States beat Britain 9-2 with one match halved at Worcester, Massachusetts, in what the British and American PGAs regard as the first official Ryder Cup event. The teams had played at Wentworth in 1926 but some regard that as an unofficial international. Publicity of the clash in 1927 was overshadowed by news of the first single-handed flight across the Atlantic by Charles Lindbergh.

FOR THE RECORD

BASEBALL
■ Babe Ruth broke his own record, with 60 home runs.

BASKETBALL
■ The Harlem Globetrotters were founded.

CYCLING
■ Amateurs and professionals rode together in the world road-race championship. Jean Aerts won, and in 1935 became the first person to win both the amateur and professional titles.

GOLF
■ Bobby Jones led from start to finish to win his second Open with a record aggregate of 285 which included his only round under 70 in an Open, and an opening 68.
■ John Ball made his last appearance, aged 65, after first playing in 1878.
■ Tommy Armour made a 10-foot birdie at the 72nd hole of the US Open to force a

play-off against Harry Cooper, who took three putts on the final green. Armour won the play-off.

MOTOR RACING
■ Empty seats for mechanics were no longer compulsory, and the single-seater racing car was born.
■ Sir Henry Segrave retired to concentrate on the land speed record. He immediately took it to 203.79mph with a 1,000hp Sunbeam in Daytona, Florida.

RUGBY LEAGUE
■ The League removed a bar on signing overseas players.
■ Seven New Zealanders were sent home during an unhappy tour of Britain and were given life bans.

SNOOKER
■ Joe Davis won the first world championship and was the undefeated world champion until 1947.

Record breaker: Henry Segrave at Daytona

Back to square one as Arsenal lose Cup

Lewis fumbles Ferguson's shot to give Cardiff victory

BBC radio broadcast the first football match commentary from Highbury on January 22, when Arsenal drew 1-1 with Sheffield United. So that listeners could understand where the ball was the Radio Times printed a diagram of the pitch divided into numbered squares. The commentator placed the ball by saying it was in "square three" or "square five". This was the origin of the phrase: "Back to square one."

The FA Cup final was the first to be broadcast live, but will be better remembered for the result and how it came about than any broadcasting milestone. Arsenal lost 1-0 to Cardiff City, the only time the trophy has left England, to one of the most extraordinary goals witnessed at Wembley. Cardiff's centre-forward, Hugh Ferguson, shot weakly at the Arsenal goal. The keeper, the Welsh international Danny Lewis, went down for a perfunctory save but the ball wriggled out of his clutch and spun over the line and the Welsh club (with one Englishmen, three Scots, four Irishmen and three Welshmen) had won the FA Cup.

Gallacher's Newcastle take title

HUGHIE GALLACHER, one of the all-time great centre-forwards, led Newcastle to an impressive Football League championship. Between 1923 and 1926 Gallacher had inspired Airdrie to second place in the Scottish League four times in succession and their first Scottish Cup. Although only 5ft 5in he was brave, quick, unpredictable, good in the air and incredibly talented. Gallacher scored 387 goals in 541 League games, and 22 in 20 internationals for Scotland.

FOR THE RECORD

BASEBALL
■ Babe Ruth and Lou Gehrig virtually won the World Series single-handed for the New York Yankees, who triumphed 4-0 for the second year running. Ruth batted .625 with three home runs in one game, and Gehrig hit .545 with four home runs.

CRICKET
■ Bob Wyatt had an opening spell of 11-10-1-1 for England against South Africa in the third Test in Durban. He was not recalled until the total reached 241, when he took two wickets in his first over and finished with figures of 13-10-4-3.

■ West Indies became the fourth country to play Test cricket. They lost all three matches in England by an innings.

FOOTBALL
■ David Jack was the first five-figure transfer, from Bolton to Arsenal for £10,340.

■ Irregularities at Arsenal over inducements to players were investigated by the FA and led to the suspension of their chairman, Sir Henry Norris, and another director. Foolishly, Norris took action for libel when the FA's findings were published and lost. He was replaced as chairman by Sir Samuel Hill-Wood.

■ Ronnie Dix was the youngest scorer in the League, at 15 years and 180 days, for Bristol Rovers against Norwich in the Third Division South.

■ Jim Barrett of West Ham experienced the shortest peacetime international career on October 22, for England against Ireland. He was injured in the eighth minute and never picked again.

GOLF
■ Johnny Farrell beat Bobby Jones in the first US Open play-off over 36 holes. The entry for the tournament exceeded 1,000 for the first time.

SQUASH
■ The Squash Rackets Association was formed

Grand National chaos

Tipperary Tim wins the National at 100-1

FORTY-TWO horses started the Grand National but only two finished. The record field was reduced to almost nothing at the Canal turn. Easter Hero, a fancied runner, swerved, landed on the fence and fell into the ditch. The horses behind him had nowhere to go, and they fell or pulled up in droves. In total, some 30 horses came to grief.

By the time the last fence was reached the race was down to just two outsiders. Tipperary Tim went on to win at 100-1 when the American horse Billy Barton fell and had to be remounted before finishing. The Home Secretary faced questions about the race and the carnage led to the Canal turn ditch being filled in to make the race safer.

CRICKET

Bradman humbled

DON BRADMAN was selected for his first Test, aged 20. It was a humbling experience. He spent most of the first two days watching England amass 521 and when he batted his innings of 18 was far from shattering. His second knock was even shorter. He was dismissed for one in Australia's total of 66. England won by 675 runs — a record margin of runs in Tests — and Bradman was dropped for the only time in his career. There was no denying his genius though. When he was recalled for the third Test he grabbed the opportunity with both hands and scored 79 and 112.

TENNIS

Homeless holders

FRANCE'S victory in the 1927 Davis Cup left them without a suitable stadium in which to defend the trophy. So they built the Stade Roland Garros in western Paris and named it after the first man to fly over the Mediterranean.

Bill Tilden had been suspended by the United States and was ineligible for the challenge round. The French, wanting to fill their stadium, petitioned the United States President, and the ambassador in Paris instructed the American captain to select Tilden. France won 4-1 and there was a packed house to see Big Bill.

Dean: ahead of the field

DIXIE DEAN, at the tender age of 21, swept Everton to the championship with a record 60 League goals in 39 matches. Dean was a burly centre-forward and despite his 5ft 10in was lethal in the air. Forty of those 60 goals were headers.

Dean, like George Camsell of Middlesbrough, who the season before had scored a record 59 goals, benefited from the confusion that reigned after the offside law changed. With three matches to go Dean needed nine goals to take the record. He scored two against Aston Villa, four against Burnley and created history in true style by completing his hat-trick against Arsenal eight minutes from the end of the season.

Dixie Dean: 60 goals

WINTER OLYMPICS

Silver put on ice

THE second Winter Olympics in St Moritz from February 11 to 19 attracted 494 competitors from 25 countries. Sir Arnold Lunn persuaded the International Skiing Federation to include downhill and slalom competitions as an experiment. Williams Fiske, the driver of the American five-man bobsleigh, became the youngest male Winter Games gold medallist ever at 16 years and 260 days. In the 500m speed skating two men tied for first place and three for third, with no silver medal awarded.

Women hurdle sex barrier

ANNI HOLDMANN is by no means the most famous athlete in history. However, on July 30, the German sprinter had her moment of fame. She won the opening heat in the 100m to become the first woman to win an Olympic track race.

It took years of acrimonious debate by the IOC to break down the barriers at the ninth Olympic Games in Amsterdam and allow women a place in the track and field programme. They were restricted to the 100m, the 800m, the 4x100m relay, the high jump and the discus, and when several runners finished the 800m in distress the event was not held again until 1964.

The United States were the most dominant of the 43 countries, although they were surprisingly overshadowed on the track by the Finns. Paavo Nurmi won one gold medal and two silver. Britain had a lean Games, winning only three gold medals, 10 silver and seven bronze. Douglas Lowe retained his 800m title. Patrick O'Callaghan, Ireland's first gold medallist, won the hammer throw, and India collected their first gold medal when their powerful hockey side took the first of six successive Olympic titles.

A torch was carried from Olympus for the first time and burned throughout the successful 88-day event.

The start of the last women's 800m for 36 years

Osler kicked into touch

Benny Osler: "Mr King"

BENNY OSLER, a South African fly-half, earned the nickname "Mr King of Rugby" because of his powerful kicking. He introduced the 10-man game, with kicking for position rather than passing to the back line. Osler's unadventurous style helped South Africa draw a series with New Zealand but, perhaps not unsurprisingly, his tedious method of play was widely criticised.

Wembley Wizards cast spell over England

ENGLAND were thrashed 5-1 by Scotland at Wembley on March 31. The victors were promptly dubbed the Wembley Wizards.

It was a curious match. Both countries had performed badly in the home international championship and were playing for the wooden spoon. Scotland picked eight Anglos, which caused an outcry north of the border. The Scots prayed for rain, and were duly obliged. The English captain, Bishop, fell ill the night before the game and did not play. Within three minutes England almost scored but, with the goalkeeper beaten, the ball rebounded off the post. Then Scotland scored moments later.

For the next 42 minutes little happened, then Alex James put Scotland two up. In the second half Scotland ran riot, adding another three goals and teasing England with a leisurely and elaborate passing game of possession football. At one point the Scots were playing at a walking pace and taunting the English defence, which silenced the 80,000 crowd. It is little wonder that all Scots fans can recite the forward line that day: Jackson, Dunn, Gallacher, James and Morton.

The Wembley Wizards take the field

Joe Davis
The master of the green baize

Clive Everton

Joe Davis contributed to the death of billiards as a public entertainment and played far and away the leading role in establishing snooker in its place. This was no master plan. "All we were doing," he recalled late in life, "was scraping and scratching to get a living."

The trouble was that the leading group of billiards professionals — Walter Lindrum, Davis, Tom Newman and Clark McConachy — became so good that they made the game look too easy. The public tired of watching them churn out breaks of 1,000 or more and became receptive to snooker's more pronounced duelling element and more varied dramatic content.

Davis had seen this coming, even if Willie Smith, another billiards giant had not. "They'll fall for a lot of things but they'll never fall for this," was his reaction to Davis's vision for snooker. The Billiards Association and Control Council was no more encouraging, and rather than wait for them Davis drafted the conditions for the first world professional championship. In May 1927 he won the first final at Campkins Billiard Hall in Birmingham and pocketed £6 10s for his trouble. The event rated four paragraphs in The Billiard Player.

Davis and a few other visionaries could see snooker's popularity in the billiard halls. A frame being relatively short and easy to handicap, snooker was a better gambling game. Billiards, though, had to remain Davis's main preoccupation. It was a tough life. He made a 980 break in winning the £15 first prize for the second division championship in 1923 but he did not take up his entitlement to compete in the world championship because the entry fee was £200.

It was standard practice for matches to last a week with two sessions a day, often on handicap, thus encouraging close finishes and allowing top players to protect their reputations. In 1926 Davis at last felt ready to go for the championship, but he was swamped by the only other entry, Newman. The General Strike started during a match against Smith the next week at Northampton and he bought his first car to get home to Chesterfield, where he had moulded his game on the table in a back room of his father's pub.

Among billiards players, Davis was an outstanding potter and this gave him a head start at snooker. He also started to work out, virtually single-handedly, the shot sequences and strategies which are now taken for granted. Starting from scratch, there was an enormous amount to be learned about positional play and how to open bunches of reds. For most players the basic idea of snooker was still to pot a red and a colour and run for safety. It was not until 1928 that even Davis made a century, exactly 100, in public. It was not until 1935 that he made a century, 110, in the championship, even though he was head and shoulders the best player.

By this time Davis had won the billiards championship four times and twice lost to Lindrum for the title. In the 1930 final against Newman, Davis made a break of 2,052, and averaged 113.3 per visit to the table for the fortnight. Due to billiards politics Lindrum did not play in that championship but he successfully conceded Davis a 7,000 start in a fortnight's match. When Lindrum did eventually play in the championships in 1933 he beat Davis only by 694 over the fortnight. In 1934, when Davis challenged him for the title in Australia, he lost only by 855 but the experience was so financially disastrous that it took him six months to earn enough money to get home.

So ended the golden age of billiards. Snooker started to take over.

Horace Lindrum, a nephew of Walter, arrived from Australia for the 1936 championship and led 27-24 in the final only for Davis to take seven frames in a row for a 31-27 winning lead.

As war approached a serious rival was at last emerging, his younger brother, Fred, whom he beat only 17-14 in the 1939 semi-final and 37-35 in the 1940 final.

Joe played through the war raising money for charity and made a name for himself in music halls with an act in which he played trick shots in front of a large angled mirror. Fred went into the army and was still rusty when he lost to Lindrum in the 1945-46 semi-final. Joe's final against Lindrum brought snooker to its first peak of popularity. Crowds of 1,200 per session packed the Royal Horticultural Hall, Westminster, twice a day for a fortnight. Joe won 78-67 and promptly retired from the championship, having held it undefeated for 20 years. He wanted to have it both ways: he did not want to risk defeat but he wanted to be regarded as the best player.

As chairman of the Professional Billiard Players Association and as the most powerful partner in Leicester Square Hall, the game's main venue, he virtually ran professional snooker. When television came along in the 1950s negotiations were conducted with Joe; if an amateur wished to turn professional he knew he would be frozen out if he did not have Joe's approval.

Television snooker was invariably a meaningless five-frame exhibition between Joe and A N Other. He wished the game all the best, but ever mindful of his early struggles he shamelessly put his own interests first. Nobody seemed to expect otherwise. He remained the best player but his absence from the championship so devalued it that by 1957 it was down to four entries and from 1957 until 1964 it was defunct. Fred beat him three times on level terms; nobody else did and not many beat him even when they were receiving seven or 10. In 1955 he made the first officially recognised 147 break.

In the quality of his close control, and even more through the force of his personality, he would have been a top player in any era. He was not a potter from distance, nor did he have the cue power of some of the modern greats, but snooker in the immediate aftermath of the gentle age of billiards was played differently, with less power, a less responsive type of ball and sometimes on tables with less receptive pockets. Even uprooting him unchanged from his peak in the 1940s and 1950s he would have enjoyed considerable success in the modern game, whose plush venues and television coverage he would have loved, although he would have found the best of nine or 17 a much greater strain than the best of 37 or 73, in which tension played a relatively minor role.

Imperious and self-assured as he was, his off-table dominance at times exerted an on-table influence against certain opponents, but he played with an exquisite delicacy and design which inspired in me, as a schoolboy, an enduring fascination with the most beautiful of games. On a cold, unembroidered recital of the facts, he appears a monster. In person, he had warmth, humour and the ability to sustain innumerable friendships. He grabbed snooker by the scruff of the neck and made something of it. He became a dictator but the alternative, without any effective governing body, was anarchy.

Snooker's "dictator": Davis created the world championship, made the title his own for 20 years, and then devalued it.

FOOTBALL

Arsenal's astute buy

HERBERT CHAPMAN made one of the most astute purchases for Arsenal when he paid Preston North End £9,000 in June for Alex James, the disaffected Scottish international forward. Preston had refused to release James for an international against Wales and his bitter resentment towards the Preston directors sparked off the transfer.

James was an efficient goal-scorer, but Chapman did not want him to score goals, he wanted him to create them. Under Chapman's tutelage, James became a brilliant midfield schemer and goal-maker, and the key player for Arsenal over the next six seasons.

Alex James: midfield schemer

FOOTBALL

English flop in Madrid

ON A blazing hot May day in Madrid and on a bone-hard pitch, England lost their first international abroad, 4-3 to Spain. The Foreign Office had warned England to put out their strongest team, but the players arrived at the end of a gruelling tour where they had beaten France and Belgium and were surprised by a lively and combative Spanish national side, which included the talented goalkeeper Ricardo Zamora.

TENNIS

English shine at Wimbledon

BUNNY AUSTIN used his skilful touch game to spearhead a substantial English challenge in the men's singles at Wimbledon. Colin Gregory, who had won the Australian title, was the first Englishman to be seeded when he was ranked eighth, and five local players reached the quarter-finals. Austin went one better and took a set off the Frenchman Jean Borotra in the semi-finals. The Bounding Basque lost 6-4 6-3 6-4 to his countryman Henri Cochet in the final.

AMERICAN FOOTBALL

The greening of America

THE Green Bay Packers did not lose a game as they took the first of three successive titles. But, as the Depression bit in the United States, other American football teams found the going much tougher.

More than half a dozen sides stopped playing in quick succession. But it left the NFL a leaner and fitter organisation with franchises concentrated in the major cities, where they were able to draw big enough crowds.

GOLF

Some of the American team that lost the Ryder Cup

FOR THE RECORD

CRICKET

■ Les Ames, who had a record 128 dismissals in the season, made a duck in his Test debut but took two catches in the fifth Test against South Africa at The Oval. England won the series 2-0.

■ Teams in the county championship played an equal number of games for the first time. Their 28-match programme was decided on the team with the most points instead of a percentage of points.

■ The first public women's match was staged at Beckenham between London and District and the Rest of England.

FOOTBALL

■ Rangers won 38 League matches in a row and were unbeaten for more than a year. Jock Buchanan of Rangers was the first player sent off in a Scottish Cup final, on April 6.

■ Alex Cheyne of Aberdeen was the first player to score direct from a corner in an international on April 13. It was the only goal of the game and came two minutes from time as Scotland beat England at Hampden.

■ Albert Whitehurst scored seven goals for Bradford against Tranmere. In total, Bradford scored 128 times in 42 Third Division North matches.

■ Andy Cunningham, of Newcastle, became their first player-manager. He

was also the oldest player to make his Football League debut, at 38 years and 2 days against Leicester.

GOLF

■ George Duncan crushed Walter Hagen 10 & 8 to help Britain win the Ryder Cup 7-5 at Moortown, Leeds.

■ Bobby Jones beat Al Espinosa in the third successive play-off to decide the US Open championship. Jones had two sevens in his final round and holed a 12-foot putt to tie. Jones pocketed $1,000 out of a total prize-money of $5,000.

ICE HOCKEY

■ The Scottish Ice Hockey Association was formed. All its teams were based at the new rink at Crossmyloof, Glasgow.

MOTOR SPORT

■ Sir Henry Segrave recaptured the world land speed record in the Golden Arrow at 231.21mph in Daytona.

RUGBY LEAGUE

■ Wigan beat Dewsbury 13-2 in the first Challenge Cup final held at Wembley. A crowd of 41,500 attended the match on May 4.

TABLE TENNIS

■ Fred Perry won the world title.

FOOTBALL

English consternation as Scotland's corner-kick goes in

Hammond the pillar of Ashes victory

Wally Hammond: cricketing colossus

WALLY HAMMOND would tuck a blue handkerchief in his right pocket before striding to the wicket. It was his mascot in 1,005 first-class innings. But there was more to Hammond than a handkerchief. He prompted Colin Cowdrey to remark: "Every career has an ignition point somewhere, and in my case, it was not watching a giant batting, but merely watching a giant walking out to bat."

Hammond started his career as a flamboyant batsman for Gloucestershire in 1920. By the end of the Ashes series in Australia in 1929 he had replaced his flamboyance with finesse, to emerge as one of the world's finest batsmen. The tour of Australia was his watershed. Hammond thrived in the five Tests played to a conclusion on hard, true pitches. He was content to stay on the back foot and limit his range of strokes to solid drives between mid-wicket and extra cover. His disciplined approach yielded a scoring sequence of 44, 28, 251, 200, 32, 119 not out, 177, 38 and 16. When the statistics of England's 4-1 victory were tallied, Hammond had hit 905 runs at an average of 113.12.

The ubiquitous Hammond, who scored centuries in both innings of the fourth Test in Adelaide, was on the field for 26½ hours. Yet the Australians had an opportunity to win the match when they started the seventh day needing 89 for victory with four wickets remaining. They lost by 12 runs.

Jack Hobbs had his moment in the sun. The England opener was the oldest player to score a Test century when he made 142 in the fifth Test in Melbourne. Hobbs was 46 years and 82 days old. And while The Master was carving out his last of 15 Test centuries, a 20-year-old Australian provided the first glimpse of his genius. Don Bradman, after an inauspicious start to his Test career, hit a century in his second match. The Don's innings of 18, 1, 79, 112, 40, 58, 123 and 37 not out were a harbinger of things to come.

> **'Whenever I saw Wally Hammond batting, I felt sorry for the ball'**
>
> **Sir Len Hutton**

HAMMOND'S RECORD

	FIRST-CLASS	TESTS (85)
Innings	1,005	140
Not out	104	16
Runs	50,551	7,249
Highest	336 not out	336 not out
Average	56.10	58.45
Hundreds	167	22
Wickets	732 at 30.58	83 at 37.80
Catches	819	110

Slow start for the Tote in very first outing

THE Tote finally made its debut at Newmarket in July. After Winston Churchill had introduced betting tax there was a growing feeling that the profits from racing should, at least in part, go back into the sport rather than straight into the bookmakers' pockets. The Jockey Club favoured the idea of a Tote, which was championed by its senior steward, Lord Hamilton.

The original proposal debated by parliament was that the Jockey Club should run the Tote. But the legislation was badly drafted and MPs objected to racing controlling the body. So the upshot was the establishment of a Racecourse Betting Control Board. Business was not brisk on the first day, although several bookies were quick to inspect the workings of their new rival in a wooden building they dubbed the "hen coop". One feature of the Tote was quick to emerge — it often returned longer odds on outsiders. The tote paid 40-1 for the winner of the first race while the bookmakers' starting price was only 33-1.

1930s

The shadow of Depression and fascism

The Thirties were the catastrophic decade of the century. They began with a deep recession and ended with a war so terrible that more than 50 million people perished. Its legacy was to haunt the world for the rest of the century.

In Britain, the aftermath of the Wall Street crash of 1929 was high unemployment, devaluation of the pound and the collapse of the Labour government. The urban working class inevitably bore the brunt of the Depression. In 14 months at the start of the decade the number of Britain's unemployed doubled. Yet still they managed to flock to football and cricket matches.

Cruelly, the pain was not spread evenly throughout the country. In Jarrow, in the north-east and the worst hit, unemployment reached 70%, while in London it was only 6%. As a consequence, London football clubs were deeply unpopular outside of the south-east. Arsenal, the product of Herbert Chapman's astute managership, were the team of the Thirties, winning the League championship five times and the FA Cup twice. So when Walsall, of the Third Division North, knocked mighty Arsenal out of the FA Cup in 1933 there was national rejoicing at the downfall of the privileged Londoners.

But as the world was being tortured by its economic ills, sport, apparently, was largely immune. Perhaps it was a valuable distraction, an escape from a world gone mad. The economy might have been ailing, but British tennis was in a very healthy state, led by the son of a Labour MP and a former table tennis world champion, Fred Perry. In 1933 he took Britain to their first Davis Cup victory in 21 years, and his team retained the title for the next three years as Perry won 45 of his 52 matches.

Perry crowned his career in 1934 when he won Wimbledon and went on to become the first man to have held all four Grand Slam singles titles. He successfully defended his Wimbledon crown twice in succession, a feat never before accomplished, before turning professional and making his fortune.

Cricket, though, was not in such a healthy state. Australia won the Ashes in 1930, with Don Bradman plundering nearly 1,000 runs in the five Tests at an average of almost 140. His domination sowed the seeds of a controversy that was to severely strain diplomatic relations between Australia and Great Britain.

England, under Douglas Jardine's captaincy, had a seemingly impossible task on their 1932-33 tour to Australia. Stop Bradman. But Jardine had noticed that Bradman was uncomfortable when he had to face fast rising balls. Not only was the Australian not keen to counter-attack by taking risks and putting the ball in the air, there was also a doubt about his resolve.

Jardine decided to use his fast bowlers to attack the Australian batting with short-pitched balls on the leg-side and deploy a cordon of close fielders. The strategy became known as Bodyline and the result was extraordinary as England regained the Ashes winning four tests to Australia's one and Bradman only averaged 56.

However, there was a public outcry in Australia at these intimidatory tactics and terse telegrams were exchanged between London and Sydney. Although Jardine had accomplished his mission it was felt on both sides of the world that he had not been "playing the game". The cricket authorities agreed and changed the rules to prevent the use of such tactics again. But history may have judged Jardine prematurely and too harshly.

Soon, sport was to be sucked even deeper into politics. Fascism was on the march in Europe: at home in the guise of Sir Oswald Mosley, who had defected from the Labour Party; in Germany with Adolf Hitler and the Nazis; in Italy with Mussolini and in Spain with Franco. Stalin had taken an iron grip on the Soviet Union and he used show trials and executions to purge any dissent. The continent was being ripped asunder.

There were fears that the Depression would hit the 1932 Olympics hard, but the Games, in Los Angeles, turned out to be a great success, making a profit of $1m. The celebrations did not last long. Four short years later Hitler attempted to turn the Berlin Olympics into a Nazi festival.

He hoped the competition would prove his theory of Aryan supremacy but was upstaged by Jesse Owens and 10 black American athletes, who won seven gold medals. Hitler, though, was merely carrying on where Mussolini had left off with the 1934 World Cup, where he successfully used Italy's triumph to legitimise his regime. The president of the Italian football federation said at the time: "The ultimate purpose of the tournament was to show that fascist sport partakes of a great quality of the ideal with one unique inspiration, Il Duce."

By 1938 the looming war overshadowed everything. Somehow football staged the third World Cup in France despite the turmoil in Europe. Hitler had overrun Austria in the Anschluss and Germany had snapped up all of Austria's best players. Spain, still beset by civil war, were unable to participate. Italy retained the gold trophy, but they did not take it home with them. Instead, Jules Rimet, the French football leader, kept it under his bed, fearing that the occupying German forces would confiscate it and melt it down.

The 1939 football season began on August 26. Seven days later Germany invaded Poland and the world was at war. The government decided that sport could be allowed to continue, at least for the moment, although crowds had to take gas masks with them to matches. The visiting New Zealand rugby league team, though, did not stop long.

They arrived in England on August 29, played two matches and left for home on September 7, ending probably the shortest tour of all time.

Sport would now make an incalculable contribution to the war effort as thousands of sportsmen and women would abandon the playing fields for the battlefields and fight for their country. For many that summer they would have played their last game.

ATHLETICS

■ *British Olympic gold medals*

1932 *800m* Thomas Hampson; *50km walk* Thomas Green

1936 *4x400m relay; 50km walk* Harold Whitlock

BASEBALL

■ *World Series*

1930 Philadelphia Athletics
1931 St Louis Cardinals
1932 New York Yankees
1933 New York Giants
1934 St Louis Cardinals
1935 Detroit Tigers
1936 New York Yankees
1937 New York Yankees
1938 New York Yankees
1939 New York Yankees

BOXING

■ *British world champions*

1930 *Junior welterweight.* Jack Kid Berg
1935 *Flyweight.* Benny Lynch
1938 *Flyweight.* Peter Kane

CRICKET

■ *County championship*

1930 Lancashire
1931 Yorkshire
1932 Yorkshire
1933 Yorkshire
1934 Lancashire
1935 Yorkshire
1936 Derbyshire
1937 Yorkshire
1938 Yorkshire
1939 Yorkshire

CYCLING

■ *Tour de France*

1930 Andre Leducq
1931 Antonin Magne
1932 Andre Leducq
1933 Georges Speicher
1934 Antonin Magne
1935 Romain Maes
1936 Sylvere Maes
1937 Roger Lapebie
1938 Gino Bartali
1939 Sylvere Maes

FOOTBALL

■ *World Cup*

1930 Uruguay 4 Argentina 2
1934 Italy 2 Czechoslovakia 1 (aet)
1938 Italy 4 Hungary 2

■ *Football League*

1930 Sheffield Wed
1931 Arsenal
1932 Everton
1933 Arsenal
1934 Arsenal
1935 Arsenal
1936 Sunderland
1937 Manchester City
1938 Arsenal
1939 Everton

■ *FA Cup*

1930 Arsenal 2 Huddersfield 0
1931 West Bromwich 2 Birmingham 1
1932 Newcastle 2 Arsenal 1
1933 Everton 3 Manchester City 0
1934 Manchester City 2 Portsmouth 1
1935 Sheffield Wed 4 West Bromwich 2
1936 Arsenal 1 Sheffield Utd 0
1937 Sunderland 3 Preston 1
1938 Preston 1 Huddersfield 0 (aet)
1939 Portsmouth 4 Wolverhampton 1

■ *Scottish League*

1930 Rangers
1931 Rangers
1932 Motherwell
1933 Rangers
1934 Rangers
1935 Rangers
1936 Celtic
1937 Rangers
1938 Celtic
1939 Rangers

■ *Scottish Cup*

1930 Rangers 2 Partick 1 (after 0-0)
1931 Celtic 4 Motherwell 2 (after 2-2)
1932 Rangers 3 Kilmarnock 0 (after 1-1)
1933 Celtic 1 Motherwell 0
1934 Rangers 5 St Mirren 0
1935 Rangers 2 Hamilton 1
1936 Rangers 1 Third Lanark 0
1937 Celtic 2 Aberdeen 1
1938 East Fife 4 Kilmarnock 2 (after 1-1)
1939 Clyde 4 Motherwell 0

GOLF

■ *The Open*

1930 Bobby Jones
1931 Tommy Armour
1932 Gene Sarazen
1933 Denny Shute
1934 Henry Cotton
1935 Alf Perry
1936 Alf Padgham
1937 Henry Cotton
1938 Reg Whitcombe
1939 Dick Burton

■ *US Open*

1930 Bobby Jones
1931 Billy Burke
1932 Gene Sarazen
1933 John Goodman
1934 Olin Dutra
1935 Sam Parks Jnr
1936 Tony Manero
1937 Ralph Guldahl
1938 Ralph Guldahl
1939 Byron Nelson

■ *US PGA*

1930 Tommy Armour
1931 Tom Creavy
1932 Olin Dutra
1933 Gene Sarazen
1934 Paul Runyan
1935 Johnny Revolta
1936 Denny Shute
1937 Denny Shute
1938 Paul Runyan
1939 Henry Picard

■ *US Masters*

1934 Horton Smith
1935 Gene Sarazen
1936 Horton Smith
1937 Byron Nelson
1938 Henry Picard
1939 Ralph Guldahl

■ *Ryder Cup*

1931 United States 9-3
1933 Great Britain & Ireland 6½ -5½
1935 United States 9-3
1937 United States 8-4

RACING

■ *The Derby*

1930 *Blenheim*
1931 *Cameronian*
1932 *April the Fifth*
1933 *Hyperion*
1934 *Windsor Lad*
1935 *Bahram*
1936 *Mahmoud*
1937 *Mid-day Sun*
1938 *Bois Roussel*
1939 *Blue Peter*

■ *Grand National*

1930 *Shaun Goilin*
1931 *Grakle*
1932 *Forbra*
1933 *Kellsboro Jack*
1934 *Golden Miller*
1935 *Reynoldstown*
1936 *Reynoldstown*
1937 *Royal Mail*
1938 *Battleship*
1939 *Workman*

ROWING

■ *Boat Race*

1930 Cambridge
1931 Cambridge
1932 Cambridge
1933 Cambridge
1934 Cambridge
1935 Cambridge
1936 Cambridge
1937 Oxford
1938 Oxford
1939 Cambridge

RUGBY LEAGUE

■ *Challenge Cup*

1930 Widnes 10 St Helens 3
1931 Halifax 22 York 8
1932 Leeds 11 Swinton 8
1933 Huddersfield 21 Warrington 17
1934 Hunslet 11 Widnes 5
1935 Castleford 11 Huddersfield 8
1936 Leeds 18 Warrington 2
1937 Widnes 18 Keighley 5
1938 Salford 7 Barrow 4
1939 Halifax 20 Salford 3

RUGBY UNION

■ *Five Nations championship*

1930 England
1931 Wales
1932 England, Wales and Ireland
1933 Scotland
1934 England
1935 Ireland
1936 Wales
1937 England
1938 Scotland
1939 England, Wales and Ireland

SAILING

■ *America's Cup*

1930 *Enterprise* (US, Harold Vanderbilt)
1934 *Rainbow* (US, Harold Vanderbilt)
1937 *Ranger* (US, Harold Vanderbilt)

SNOOKER

■ *World championship*

1930 Joe Davis 25 Tom Dennis 12
1931 Joe Davis 25 Tom Dennis 21
1932 Joe Davis 30 Clark McConachy 19
1933 Joe Davis 25 Willie Smith 18
1934 Joe Davis 25 Tom Newman 23
1935 Joe Davis 25 Willie Smith 20
1936 Joe Davis 34 Horace Lindrum 27
1937 Joe Davis 32 Horace Lindrum 29
1938 Joe Davis 37 Sidney Smith 24
1939 Joe Davis 47 Sidney Smith 30

TENNIS

■ *Wimbledon*

1930 Bill Tilden *bt* Wilmer Alison; Helen Wills Moody *bt* Elizabeth Ryan
1931 Sidney Wood *bt* Francis Shields; Cilly Aussem *bt* Hilde Krahwinkel
1932 Ellsworth Vines *bt* Henry Austin; Helen Wills Moody *bt* Helen Jacobs
1933 Jack Crawford *bt* Ellsworth Vines; Helen Wills Moody *bt* Dorothy Round
1934 Fred Perry *bt* Jack Crawford; Dorothy Round *bt* Helen Jacobs
1935 Fred Perry *bt* Gottfried von Cramm; Helen Wills Moody *bt* Helen Jacobs
1936 Fred Perry *bt* Gottfried von Cramm; Helen Jacobs *bt* Hilde Sperling
1937 Don Budge *bt* Gottfried von Cramm; Dorothy Round *bt* Jadwiga Jedrzeiowska
1938 Don Budge *bt* Henry Austin; Helen Wills Moody *bt* Helen Jacobs
1939 Bobby Riggs *bt* Elwood Cooke; Alice Marble *bt* Kay Stammers

■ *Australian championship*

1930 Gar Moon; Daphne Akhurst
1931 Jack Crawford; Coral Buttsworth
1932 Jack Crawford; Coral Buttsworth
1933 Jack Crawford; Joan Hartigan
1934 Fred Perry; Joan Hartigan
1935 Jack Crawford; Dorothy Round
1936 Adrian Quist; Joan Hartigan
1937 Vivian McGrath; Nancye Wynne
1938 Don Budge; Dorothy Bundy
1939 John Bromwich; Emily Westacott

■ *French championship*

1930 Henri Cochet; Helen Wills Moody
1931 Jean Borotra; Cilly Aussem
1932 Henri Cochet; Helen Wills Moody
1933 Jack Crawford; Margaret Scriven
1934 Gottfried von Cramm; Margaret Scriven
1935 Fred Perry; Hilde Sperling
1936 Gottfried von Cramm; Hilde Sperling
1937 Henner Henkel; Hilde Sperling
1938 Don Budge; Simone Mathieu
1939 Don McNeill; Simone Mathieu

■ *US championship*

1930 John Doeg; Betty Nuthall
1931 Ellsworth Vines; Helen Wills Moody
1932 Ellsworth Vines; Helen Jacobs
1933 Fred Perry; Helen Jacobs
1934 Fred Perry; Helen Jacobs
1935 Wilmer Allison; Helen Jacobs
1936 Fred Perry; Alice Marble
1937 Don Budge; Anita Lizane
1938 Don Budge; Alice Marble
1939 Bobby Riggs; Alice Marble

Driving force: Bradman swept all before him in the 1930s

Golden service: Perry swept all before him around the world

JANUARY

1930

DECEMBER

FOR THE RECORD

CRICKET

■ West Indies won their first match, against England in the third Test in Georgetown. Wilfred Rhodes ended the world's longest Test career (31 years, 315 days) in the fourth Test, and at 52 years and 165 days was the world's oldest Test cricketer.

■ Donald Bradman took his first Test wicket in the first match played between Australia and West Indies in Adelaide. Australia won by 10 wickets.

COMMONWEALTH GAMES

■ The first meeting was held in Hamilton, Ontario.

FOOTBALL

■ On April 21, the Monday before the Cup final, Leicester and Arsenal drew 6-6 in the League. Arsenal were 3-1 down at half-time until David Halliday scored four goals to level the scores. He was not picked for the final, where Arsenal beat Huddersfield 2-0.

■ Rangers swept all before them, winning the Cup, the League, the Glasgow Cup, the Scottish Second XI Cup and, after two hours battling with Celtic, the Scottish Charity Cup on the toss of a coin.

■ Brentford won all 21 home games in the Third Division South.

RACING

■ A bookmaker was killed by lightning when a storm hit the second day of Royal Ascot.

RUGBY LEAGUE

■ The Australian Chimpy Busch was denied a try two minutes from the end of the only scoreless Test, against Britain at Swinton. The Australians demanded a fourth Test to decide the series and lost 3-0.

TENNIS

■ Wilmer Allison became the first non-seeded player to reach a Wimbledon singles final, but he lost to his fellow American Bill Tilden 6-3 9-7 6-4.

■ Tilden added the United States championship to his third Wimbledon crown and then turned professional.

GOLF

Grand Slam for Jones

Jones wins the British amateur championship at St Andrews

TO SOME it was the Impregnable Quadrilateral, to others the Grand Slam of golf. Never had a player won the four major events on the calendar: the Open, the United States Open and the British and United States amateur championships. Until Bobby Jones.

The Atlanta amateur with the easy swing started his bid to conquer the mountain at the home of the sport, St Andrews, in late May. In many ways, the British amateur championship was the toughest of the four legs of the Grand Slam, requiring a player to be on top form against some of the world's best players in the matchplay event.

Jones struggled through several difficult matches in the early rounds, including a 19th-hole win against Cyril Tolley and a victory at the 18th against George Voigt. The final, though, was one-sided against Roger

Wethered as Jones hit top form.

He then went to the Open at Hoylake, led for two rounds and held off his countrymen Leo Diegel and Macdonald Smith over the last 18 holes to win by two shots. Jones swung the US Open in his favour with a third-round 68. He led the 1,177 entries home with an unimpressive 75 in the final round after going into a water hazard at the 17th. And so to the last leg of the Grand Slam, the United States amateur championship at Merion, where Jones had won his first amateur title in 1924. He was in excellent form against his first four opponents and easily qualified for the 36-hole final against Eugene Homans.

That was where the legend of Bobby Jones was born. He led by three holes at the turn and was seven up after 18. He finally sealed the Grand Slam at the 29th hole.

THE GRAND SLAM

May 26-31 British amateur championship, St Andrews
Bobby Jones beat Roger Wethered 7&6

June 18-20 The Open, Hoylake
291: Bobby Jones 293: Leo Diegel, Macdonald Smith

July 10-12 United States Open, Interlachen
287: Bobby Jones 289: Macdonald Smith 292: Horton Smith

Sep 24-27 United States amateur championship, Merion
Bobby Jones beat Eugene Homans 8&7

BOXING

The Whirlwind storms world

THE Whitechapel Whirlwind, Jack Kid Berg, won the world light-welterweight title on February 18 by stopping Mushy Callahan of America in the 10th round at the National Sporting Club in London in only the fifth title fight since the weight was invented in November 1922. There was some confusion about the new division, and Callahan had been stripped of his title in America. Britain did not seem to recognise the weight, and as the two fighters were introduced Lord Lonsdale stood up at the ringside and protested that there was no such weight.

Berg, known as the Whirlwind because of his all-action style, had been a sensation in America the year before, when he was unbeaten in 15 fights. After beating Callahan, Berg returned to America to claim his title, which he did in 1931 when he outpointed Goldie Hess in Chicago. But Berg lost the crown when he fought Tony Canzoneri for the lightweight title and was knocked out in three rounds. Because they both scaled inside the light-welterweight division the two titles were at stake.

One of the most dramatic achievements of Jack Kid Berg's career also occurred in 1930, when he ended the 160-fight unbeaten run of the brilliant super-featherweight Kid Chocolate in the Bronx.

Kid Berg: sensation Stateside

Britain boycott first World Cup

Uruguay beat Argentina to win first World Cup

THE first World Cup was held in Uruguay and proved an indifferent success. Only 13 countries took part, and powerful European nations such as Italy, Germany, Austria and Spain, who had supported the idea of a World Cup, refused to go, angry at the choice of host country but citing a three-week boat journey and lack of funds as their excuse. None of the British countries took part because they had withdrawn from Fifa over "shamateurism" two years earlier and were not eligible.

Only France, the initiators of the tournament, Belgium, Yugoslavia and Romania crossed the Atlantic. Romania were organised by King Carol, who selected the squad and threatened to close the British oil company employing most of the country's leading players unless they were given paid leave.

There were seven South American countries, Mexico and the United States, which was composed mostly of expatriate Scots and English. Not only were the entries mediocre — apart from the finalists, Uruguay and Argentina — the refereeing was abysmal. Argentina were awarded five penalties in their 6-3 defeat of Mexico.

Uruguay, the Olympic champions, took the event very seriously. They even banished their goalkeeper, Masali, from the tournament for breaking a curfew. The final, Uruguay versus Argentina, was a repeat of the 1928 Olympic final, pitting bitter rivals against each other.

Thousands of Argentinians came by boat, and were cheered ashore by crowds chanting: "Victory or death!" Surprisingly it was a good-tempered game and Uruguay won 4-2, having been 2-1 down at half-time.

Montevideo went mad, and the next day was proclaimed a national holiday. In Argentina the Uruguayan embassy in Buenos Aires was stoned by angry crowds and police had to open fire to disperse the mob. Football relations between the two countries were broken off. The World Cup had truly begun.

Schmeling wins on low blow

GERMANY'S Max Schmeling became world heavyweight champion at Yankee Stadium on June 11 when awarded the fight because of a low blow from Jack Sharkey. It was the first time a challenger had won the title when he was on the canvas.

Speed king killed

Sir Henry Segrave on "Miss England II"

SIR HENRY SEGRAVE died on Friday June 13 at the age of 34 when his boat hit a log on Lake Windermere having set a world water speed record of 98.76mph. He had, in his short life, been a Great War flying ace, the fastest man in the world on land and water, and helped establish Britain in GP racing.

Bradman runs wild

Australia's Don Bradman in full flow at Leeds

DON BRADMAN signalled his emergence as the game's greatest batsman when he hit a record 974 runs, including a record 334 at Headingley, in the five-Test series in England. The 22-year-old right-handed batsman had an average of 139.14.

RUGBY UNION

French outlawed

PROFESSIONALISM, the dirtiest word in rugby union, was on everybody's lips in the late 1920s. And the accusations were levelled at the French, who were in the dock for paying players to move from club to club in a no-holds barred quest to win the club championship.

The French simply shrugged their shoulders and in February the four Home Unions announced that all fixtures at club and international level against France would be abandoned at the end of the season. They were banished until 1947. With France out of the Five Nations championship, rugby league in the country flourished. In the first rugby league match in France, Australia beat England 63-13 in Paris on December 31, 1933 and the professional code took off.

CRICKET

Yorkshire's attrition

YORKSHIRE'S aim in the 1930s was to amass a huge score on the first day and give themselves the best part of two days to dismiss the opposition. While the ploy did not make them popular it did make them mightily successful. They won the county championship, the first of seven in the nine years preceding the First World War.

GREYHOUND RACING

Mick the Miller: a runt who became a real colossus

MICK THE MILLER was bred by Father Martin Brophy, a parish priest in Ireland, in June 1926 and named after the village handyman. He was one of the weakest pups in the litter and was lucky to survive a bad attack of distemper.

When Father Brophy came to England for a crack at the 1929 Derby, Mick the Miller immediately caused a stir. He ran a blistering trial at White City and was auctioned on the terraces for 800 guineas, an enormous price for a novice. He was 7-4 on for the Derby but Palatinus crossed the line first. However, it was declared a "no race" and Mick the Miller beat Palatinus by three lengths in the re-run. The victory sent his value soaring and he was sold for a record 2,000 guineas.

Mick the Miller did not have the raw speed of a sprinter. He preferred galloping tracks where he could use his stamina, and White City, with its sweeping turns, was tailor-made for him. He romped away with the 1930 Derby, again by three lengths.

By now Mick the Miller was almost five, an exceptional age for a racing greyhound. But that did not stop him "winning" an unprecedented third Derby. Unfortunately, there was fighting among the other runners and, as in 1929, there was a "no race" ruling. With the years catching up with him, Mick the Miller found the re-run too much and could only finish fourth. Everybody expected him to be retired, especially after he was beaten in the first round of the Welsh Derby. But he was raced one last time, in the St Leger at Wembley on October 3.

The 700-yard trip was further than Mick the Miller had ever raced before, but in a gutsy performance that had the crowd cheering he bravely clung on to win by one length for his fifth Classic triumph.

Mick the Miller: won five classics

FOR THE RECORD

BADMINTON

■ Jack Purcell, the Canadian champion, was the first foreign entrant to the All-England championships.

CRICKET

■ South Africa won 1-0 in their first series victory against England since 1909-10. The start of the fifth Test in Durban was delayed 20 minutes because the correct size of bails were unavailable.

FOOTBALL

■ Manchester United got off to the worst possible start to the season, losing 12 First Division matches in a row, a record that still stands.

■ Rochdale fared little better in the Third Division North. They did not win a match from November 7 until September 3, 1932.

■ Aston Villa scored 128 goals in 42 First Division matches.

GOLF

■ Tommy Armour won the first Open held at Carnoustie.

ICE HOCKEY

■ The Streatham rink opened in February. An English League was formed and was won by Oxford University.

RUGBY UNION

■ The weight of the ball was increased from 13½ oz to 15oz.

TENNIS

■ The men's final at Wimbledon never took place. Frank Shields injured his ankle when leading 4-3 in the fourth set of his semi-final against Jean Borotra. Although he won the match he withdrew from the final against fellow American Sidney Wood because of impending Davis Cup matches.

South Africans were all at sea

The Springboks were virtually unbeatable in Britain, except in the Midlands

THE Windsor Castle liner from South Africa to England was no place to train for a rugby tour. The roll of the ship made keeping one's balance difficult and the sun decks were not an ideal surface on which to throw rugby balls. The Springboks, however, needed the occasional run around to relieve the rigours of travel, but they paid the price. They lost three balls overboard and, in an heroic bid to stop another ball plunging into the Atlantic, Jock van Niekerk injured his knee.

The South African winger recovered sufficiently to be chosen for the first match of the tour against Midland Counties but he injured the knee again, this time so badly that he was carried off and never played rugby again.

There was further anguish for the South Africans. George Beamish, an Irish forward, led Midland Counties to a 30-21 win against the Springboks. Then the tide turned. The South Africans did not lose another game, beating Wales 8-3, Ireland 8-3, England 7-0 and Scotland 6-3.

The Springbok selectors had plucked Danie Craven from obscurity for the tour and the South African press greeted his selection with such disdain that Craven's father cancelled his subscription to the local paper. Craven, though, mastered the dive pass, which had been devised by his countryman Dauncey Devine. He played 16 Tests for the Boks before becoming a coach and then one of rugby's most controversial rulers.

Scot free Albion

WEST BROMWICH Albion won the FA Cup, beating Birmingham City 2-1, and gained promotion from the Second Division in the same season, the first club to do so. Because of the youth of their side they were known as "the team of boys". Unusually for the time, there was not a single Scot in the side — and a Scot had not played for the club since 1907.

Richardson wins the FA Cup for West Bromwich Albion

AMES catches selectors' eye

LES AMES was competing with George Duckworth for the wicketkeeping berth in the England team when New Zealand arrived for their first Test in England. The England selectors chose Ames for the match at Lord's. It appeared that their selection had been swayed by the superior batting of the Kent player. And they certainly needed all his batting prowess to save losing their first Test on home soil against the unfancied New Zealanders.

The visitors had been restricted to 224 in their first innings but immediately struck back on the opening day to have England at a precarious 190 for seven at stumps. Ames was joined by Gubby Allen, a dependable partner who could play with the straightest of bats when needed. The pair put on a record 246 for the eighth wicket, a partnership that changed the game. Allen scored 122, his highest score in Test cricket, and Ames cemented his place in the side until the Second World War with a brilliant 137.

The New Zealanders managed to draw the match and impressed their hosts so much with the display that a further two Tests were hastily arranged. Both were marred by rain, although England saved face by winning the second Test by an innings and 26 runs.

Gubby Allen and Les Ames

79

Games bonanza in Depression

JANUARY
1932
DECEMBER

FOR THE RECORD

BADMINTON
■ Seeding was introduced at the All-England championships. The names of the seeds were not announced to avoid offending the unseeded.

BILLIARDS
■ Walter Lindrum compiled a world record break of 4,137.

CRICKET
■ India became the sixth country to play Test cricket. They lost by 158 runs against England at Lord's on June 25 in their only Test of the series.

FOOTBALL
■ Stanley Matthews made his debut for Stoke City.
■ Everton won the championship having won the Second Division the previous year.

GOLF
■ The United States beat Britain 5½ to 3½ in the first Curtis Cup at Wentworth.

RACING
■ The Aga Khan owned the first, second, fourth and fifth placed horses in the St Leger.

TENNIS
■ Helen Wills Moody lost only 13 games in her six matches in the women's singles at Wimbledon. The attendance at the championships topped 200,000 for the first time.

Eddie Tolan wins the 100m in Los Angeles

> *' The most important thing in the Olympic Games is not to win but to take part, just as the most important thing in life is not the triumph but the struggle. The essential thing is not to have conquered but to have fought well '*
>
> **Ethelbert Talbot**
> **Bishop of Central Pennsylvania**

WITH the world in a deep financial depression the 10th Olympic Games in Los Angeles looked doomed. There were fears that because of the travelling involved and the lack of money few Europeans would attend. Instead, the Olympics enjoyed one of its finest hours. There were 1,408 competitors from 37 countries, and more than a million spectators. The organising committee were able to make $1m profit despite providing accommodation, food, entertainment and transport for every competitor.

Their solution to housing the male athletes was to build the first Olympic village, with 550 cottages, 10 minutes from the Los Angeles Coliseum. The women were booked into the Chapman Park Hotel on Wilshire Boulevard. After initial reservations about the village, the idea proved a success and all subsequent Games have housed athletes in Olympic villages.

The Games were also the first to use photo-finish equipment, the three-tiered victory stand and the raising of national flags during the medal ceremonies.

Most of the medals went to the host country. One of the rare exceptions to the United States' domination was their hockey team, who were thumped 24-1 by the champions India.

Britain won four gold medals, seven silver and five bronze. There were 16 world records broken, two equalled and 33 Olympic records bettered.

Mildred Didrikson was one of the stars of the Games. The 18-year-old Texan was restricted to only three events, but broke world records in the 80m hurdles and the javelin. In the high jump she cleared the same height in the jump-off as her teammate Jean Shiley, but officials ruled that her "Western Roll" style was illegal because her head went over the bar before her body. She had to be content with the silver medal but later became one of the best golfers in the world under her married name Zaharias.

Lauri Lehtinen was fortunate not to be disqualified when winning the men's 5,000m. The Finn twice blocked the American Ralph Hill in the final straight. The American crowd booed but were silenced by the announcer Bill Henry, who said: "Remember please, these people are our guests."

BILLIARDS

Lindrum sets world record

WINTER OLYMPICS

British women fly the flag in America

THE British team achieved a first at the Winter Olympics in Lake Placid, New York, when their flag was carried by a woman, the skater Mollie Phillips. Her teammate Cecilia Colledge was Britain's youngest competitor in any sport when she took part in the skating aged 11 years and 73 days. Eddie Eagan joined the US four-man bobsleigh team at the last moment and became the only man to win a gold medal at the summer and Winter Games — he was a boxing champion in 1920.

CRICKET

S Africa skittled

SOUTH AFRICA were out for 36 and 45 in the fifth Test against Australia in Melbourne. Their aggregate of 81 was the lowest by a Test side losing all 20 wickets. The total playing time was 5hr 53min, the shortest completed Test in history.

Bodyline defeats Bradman

WHEN the England team boarded the liner Orontes on September 17 for their tour of Australia they had one question on their minds: How do we stop Don Bradman? He had hammered 974 runs in five matches against England in the previous series and Douglas Jardine was not prepared to put his players through similar purgatory. Jardine, the England captain, had come up with a brilliant and controversial tactic which became known as Bodyline. He kept his plan under wraps until the tourists met an Australian XI in Melbourne in mid-November and then unleashed his fast bowling trio of Harold Larwood, Bill Voce and Bill Bowes on the unsuspecting Australians.

The tactic was to reinforce the leg-side with a cordon of players around the batsman and bowl a barrage of fast, short-pitched balls on or outside leg stump. The batsman could either attempt a defensive shot, risking a catch to the cluster of fielders around his legs, or duck out of the way. The ploy met with disapproval from the Australian crowds who watched their bruised batting heroes succumb to some of the most intimidatory bowling in cricket.

The series degenerated into a slanging match between the Australian Board of Control and the MCC, who exchanged tersely-worded telegrams after the bitter third Test in Adelaide. The controversy reached its climax when the Australian captain, Bill Woodfull, was hit on the heart and Bert Oldfield sustained a fractured skull from short-pitched balls from Larwood.

The Australian attitude to Bodyline was epitomised when the England manager, Plum Warner, went into the Australians' room to ask after Woodfull's health. The captain replied: "I don't want to speak to you Mr Warner. Of two teams out there one is playing cricket, the other is making no effort to play the game of cricket."

While the two controlling bodies continued their exchange of telegrams Larwood finished the series with 33 wickets at 19.51 as England swept to victory. Jardine's attitude was that he had found a successful method to curb Bradman by simply changing the attack from the traditional off-side to the leg-side. Bradman had failed, averaging only 56.

Jack Fingleton, an Australian batsman, later described Jardine as "the most efficient, scientific and shrewdest Test captain ever". But popular opinion viewed Jardine's tactics differently and the MCC were forced to restrict teams to only two leg-side fielders behind square. It sounded the death-knell of Bodyline, but not the end of intimidatory bowling.

THE BODYLINE SERIES

First Test: Australia 360 & 164; England 524 & 1-0 (England won by 10 wickets)
Second Test: Australia 228 & 191; England 169 & 139 (Australia won by 111 runs)
Third Test: England 341 & 412; Australia 222 & 193 (England won by 338 runs)
Fourth Test: Australia 340 & 175; England 356 & 162-4 (England won by six wickets)
Fifth Test: Australia 435 & 182; England 454 and 168-2 (England won by eight wickets)
England regained the Ashes by winning the series 4-1

Larwood strikes, the leg cordon is poised, but Woodfull takes evasive action

New club tames sand

Sarazen: record score

GENE Sarazen had been frustrated with his attempts to hit balls out of bunkers with a club not specially made for the purpose. The American wanted a club head that floated through the sand rather than stuck in it. So he soldered lead to the leading edge of an iron to make a deep-flanged sand iron.

Within weeks Sarazen had mastered his new club and he enjoyed one of the finest spells in his career. He won the Open for the first time, leading from start to finish in the only championship held at Princes. He won by five strokes with a record low aggregate of 283, a total that was not beaten until Bobby Locke's 279 in 1950.

Then, 10 years after winning the United States Open, his first major victory, Sarazen put together one of the greatest finishes to repeat his American triumph at Fresh Meadow on June 25. Sarazen played cautiously at first and was six shots behind midway through the third round. Then he threw caution to the wind. He hit a four-under-par 34 for the back nine and a 66 in the final round to beat Bobby Cruickshank by three shots. His last 28 holes were played in only 100 strokes.

TENNIS

Crawford leaves baseline to eventually win title

JACK CRAWFORD was the epitome of a classical player. The Australian wore a long-sleeved white shirt which he buttoned at the wrists, had immaculately combed hair and played with a square-topped racket. His opponent in one of the finest matches on the Centre Court at Wimbledon was the American Ellsworth Vines, a complete contrast, who possessed the biggest serve in the game at the time.

Vines had blasted Bunny Austin off the court in the 1932 final and Austin had said of the service ace he faced at match point: "I did not know which side of me it had gone."

Crawford and Vines matched each other blow for blow on the baseline for 100 minutes in the first four sets of the final and were locked at 4-4 in the deciding set. Then Crawford followed his serve to the net for the first time, won a decisive point and went on to clinch the match 4-6 11-9 6-2 2-6 6-4.

RACING

Richards overhauls Archer's record

THE Wavertree Selling Plate at Liverpool was not normally the sort of race that would generate any excitement. But on November 8 it produced a monumentous result. On the 47th anniversary of Fred Archer's death, Gordon Richards overtook his record of 246 winners in a season. Richards, who received a congratulatory telegram from the King, admitted that he was relieved to reach the milestone. "I can relax a bit now. Sausages and mash tonight, and a good feed to celebrate," he said. Not that Richards had difficulty in keeping his weight down. He rode at less than 8 stone for most of his career — and it was a career without equal.

In 1925, in his first full season, he was champion jockey. Tuberculosis then laid him low, but he fought off the illness and regained his crown in 1927. From then on Richards held the title every year until he retired in July 1954, except in 1930 and 1941, when he broke a leg. Richards owed much of his success to Fred Darling, who was as brilliant a trainer as Richards was a jockey. Richards started his 16-year partnership with Darling in 1932, a year that brought him 190 winners and first gave him the idea that Archer's record could be broken.

It was a close run thing and only a few days remained when Golden King obliged. Richards was undoubtedly helped to his goal by one purple patch when he rode a record 12 winners in succession, 11 of them at Chepstow. Richards ended the season with 259 winners and, apart from the war years when racing was curtailed, he topped the 200 mark 11 more times.

Richards on his 200th winner, Nevertheless, a 20-1 shot

TENNIS

French fall to British

BRITAIN, inspired by the formidable Fred Perry, won the Davis Cup for the first time in 21 years, beating France 3-2 in Paris. Britain retained the title for the next three years and the redoubtable Perry won 45 of his 52 Davis Cup matches between 1931 and 1936.

Briton beats French again

PEGGY SCRIVEN had such an awful style she was given little chance of winning and was not included in the British team for the French championships in Paris. Instead, she paid her own way and became the first Briton to win the title, beating Simone Mathieu 6-2 4-6 6-4.

Peggy Scriven (*right*) on Centre Court at Wimbledon

Strongman Carnera imitation ring master

Crude giant Primo Carnera was known as the Ambling Alp

PRIMO CARNERA, a one-time circus strongman and the dullest and crudest boxer to become the world heavyweight champion, stunned the world when he knocked out Jack Sharkey, the holder, in six rounds at Long Island on June 29.

Because of his size, 6ft 5¾ and 18st 8lb, Carnera had been carefully groomed with hand-picked opponents for this opportunity, and it was generally believed that many of the fights had been fixed. The public were not fooled by this imitation champion and they bayed for a bout with Max Baer, a real fighter. Within two years they had their wish and Baer humiliated Carnera into appealing for the fight to be stopped in the 11th.

Baer had floored Carnera 11 times, cracked jokes, plucked at the hairs on his chest and, at the start of the tenth, walked over to the Italian's corner and shuffled in his resin. Unsurprisingly, the so-called championship bout was dubbed the Comedy of Errors by the scribes.

Lord Derby wins Derby

HYPERION was a lazy horse but George Lambton was a shrewd trainer who was expert in getting the best out of his charges. The elderly trainer was in poor health and was not able to travel to Epsom to watch his horse make all the running to win the Derby by three lengths for Lord Derby.

At just over 15 hands Hyperion was a tiny horse — the smallest to win the Derby since 1840 — but he was tough enough to go on to take the St Leger by leading from the start again. Hyperion was retired to stud in 1934, and it was there that he really made his mark as the champion sire for an un-equalled six times after the war.

FOR THE RECORD

CRICKET
■ Clifford Roach became the only Test player to be bowled first ball in both innings for the West Indies in the opening Test against England at Lord's.
■ India played their first official home Test at the Gymkhana Ground, Bombay, in December. It was the first Test to include Sunday play and England won by nine wickets.

CYCLING
■ The King of the Mountains classification was introduced in the Tour de France.

FOOTBALL
■ The players in the Everton versus Manchester City Cup final were numbered for the first time but, unusually, from 1 to 22.

GOLF
■ Densmore Shute won the first all-American play-off for the Open. He had four rounds of 73, the only time an Open winner has shot identical scores in every round. But Shute did not do so well in the Ryder Cup. He missed two putts on the final green in the last match to give Britain a 6½ to 5½ victory at Southport and Ainsdale.

RUGBY LEAGUE
■ London Highfield became the first club in the capital but after losing £8,000 were moved to Liverpool in 1935.

RUGBY UNION
■ Wales won at Twickenham for the first time.

TENNIS
■ Bunny Austin was the first man to wear short trousers on the Centre Court at Wimbledon.

Hammond's run feast

TED BADCOCK, a New Zealand medium pace bowler, had a rare moment of glory against the English tourists. He bowled Wally Hammond. The mainstay of the English batting had, however, scored 227 before he heard the rattle of his stumps in the first Test in Christchurch.

Hammond was determined not to make the same mistake in the second Test at Eden Park, Auckland. He came to the crease with England 56 for one and did not leave until Bob Wyatt declared at 548 for seven. Hammond finished with a then-record 336 not out, going from strength to strength against a six-man New Zealand attack which had little to threaten the great Gloucesterman.

The 318-minute innings provided a feast for statisticians. He hit 10 sixes, 34 fours and reached 300 in only 288 minutes, the fastest Test triple hundred in history. His last 100 runs were scored in a mere 47 minutes and left him with a tour average of 563.00. Not surprisingly, it has not been beaten.

Hammond: statisticians' joy

FOOTBALL

Italy's win delights Mussolini

THE second World Cup, in Italy, was a different affair from the first. Now it was to be a European-dominated tournament — without any British involvement, of course — and with only two South American nations, Brazil and Argentina, qualifying. The holders, Uruguay, refused to participate, still piqued by the European "boycott" in 1930. The Argentinians pointedly sent a weakened team because the Italians had lured away many of their best players on the pretext that they were of Italian descent. But what gave the tournament its distinctively sour taste was the spectre of fascism hanging over the event and the desperate need for Italy to win to legitimise Benito Mussolini.

The two strongest sides in Europe were Italy and Austria,

both guided by brilliant managers, Vittorio Pozzo and Hugo Meisl. The natural final would have been between these two sides, with Austria narrow favourites as they had beaten Italy 4-2 in Turin only months before. However, they met in the semi-final in Milan on a rain-sodden pitch that made the Austrians' delicate ball skills impossible to deploy. Italy won 1-0 to meet Czechoslovakia in the final.

This was a strange affair in Rome, which had not really taken to the tournament, and the stadium was less than full. Italy were trailing 1-0 with eight minutes left when Raimondo Orsi, one of the Argentine-Italians, scored a goal so freakish that he could not repeat it the next day for the photographers, even without a goalkeeper. Italy wrapped up the game 2-1 in extra time and Il Duce was happy.

FOOTBALL

Italy's Ceresoli saved a penalty but the world champions lost to England 3-2

Battle of Highbury

IN NOVEMBER, Italy, the newly-crowned world champions, played an international at Arsenal that was so ferocious it was instantly known as the Battle of Highbury. For England the World Cup meant nothing, it was a foreign novelty; for Italy to beat England would prove their global credentials.

Injuries sustained at League matches the previous weekend meant the England team kept changing until, surprisingly, seven Arsenal players were in the side. But if the match was meant to be a showpiece between the two best teams in the world that died in the first 90 seconds, when a fierce challenge from Ted Drake on Luisito Monti, who had played for Argentina in the 1930 World Cup, led to the centre-half leaving the field with a broken toe saying: "He kicked me." Inevitably, the 10-man Italian side spent the rest of the half retaliating. Despite this, England played sublimely for 20 minutes, scored three goals and had a penalty saved.

Eddie Hapgood, the England captain and left-back had his nose broken, and there were many other injuries. One journalist wrote: "There were so many bodies lying all over the field that our selectors must have wondered if they had

picked more than 11 players." Strangely, the Italians abandoned their vendetta in the second half and played sweet football. Peppino Meazza, their elegant inside-right, scored two excellent goals, and if it had not been for the inspired saves of the Arsenal goalkeeper Frank Moss they would surely have equalised.

CRICKET

The Australians easily take their revenge

THE bitterness of the Bodyline series was still festering when Australia came to England. Douglas Jardine decided to write rather than play and Harold Larwood refused to play, accusing the Australians of interfering with the selection of the England team.

Without the pace of Larwood to contend with, the Australians made run scoring easy. Don Bradman was back to his best and, with Bill Ponsford, put on 451 in 316 minutes in the fifth Test, which clinched the series for Australia 2-1. Their record stand was beaten by the New Zealanders Andrew Jones and Martin Crowe, with 467 against Sri Lanka in 1991.

Fascist salutes from Italy at the World Cup Final

Perry and Round crowned king and queen of SW19

WIMBLEDON was no place for the fainthearted. A mysterious virus swept through the All-England club forcing 63 players to withdraw from the championships with "Wimbledon Throat". But it was clear that nothing was going to stop Fred Perry reviving British tennis. The son of a Labour MP, Perry's enthusiasm for the sport was matched by his determination to succeed.

He had not started playing the game until 19. His famous forehand was hit on the rise and off the wrong foot, a skill he mastered while winning the world table-tennis championship in 1928 and 1929. By the time Perry arrived at Wimbledon his collection of trophies had increased rapidly, and he had the Australian and United States titles under his belt. He had to battle through several tough early rounds to reach the final against Jack Crawford, an Australian who had more trouble overcoming the virus than many of his opponents.

Perry made a slow start and was 3-1 down before he hit top form. Then it became a rout. With an ecstatic crowd behind him, Perry went on to win 6-3 6-0 7-5 and become the first Briton in 25 years to win the men's singles. Dorothy Round added to the British euphoria by winning the women's singles 6-2 5-7 6-3 against the top seed, Helen Jacobs. Round had refused to play in the French championship because it was held on a Sunday, and she was known as "the Sunday school mistress".

Perry, though, had become the master. He retained his United States title and the next year beat Baron Gottfried von

Perry: England's ace

Cramm in the French championships to become the first player to win all four Grand Slam titles, although he did not hold them simultaneously.

He retained his Wimbledon title in 1935 by beating von Cramm, and completed his hat-trick the next year when the

injured German succumbed 6-1 6-1 6-0 in only 45 minutes. He was the first player since the challenge round had been abolished to win three successive men's singles titles.

Perry beat the 20-year-old Don Budge in the final of the United States championships in 1936. He then turned professional and pocketed $91,335 for a series of 61 matches against Ellsworth Vines.

GOLF

Cotton near to perfection

HENRY COTTON was the first Briton in 11 years to win the Open. The foundations for his five-stroke victory lay in a second-round 65, consisting solely of threes and fours. His only blemish was a dropped shot at the eighth, where his tee shot was plugged in a bunker.

Cotton's shot in million: from bunker to six yards from the flag

FOR THE RECORD

AMERICAN FOOBALL

■ Bert Bell, of the struggling Philiadelphia Eagles, persuaded his fellow owners to adopt the draft system on May 19, with the weakest NFL team getting the first pick of college players.

CRICKET

■ England beat West Indies by four wickets in Bridgetown, the first time a Test was won against a second-innings declaration.

■ Clarrie Grimmett became the first bowler to take 200 Test wickets.

FOOTBALL

■ Ted Drake scored seven goals for Arsenal against Aston Villa, a First Division record. The first six came from his first six shots.

■ Tranmere beat Oldham 13-4 in the Third Division North.

GOLF

■ A Scottish professional started 7, 10, 5, 10 and took 65 to reach the turn in the Open. He had another 10 at the 11th and retired at the 12th.

RACING

■ Bahram was the first Triple Crown winner since 1903, and retired unbeaten.

TENNIS

■ Helen Wills Moody equalled Dorothea Lambert Chambers's record of seven Wimbledon wins when she beat Helen Jacobs 6-3 3-6 7-5.

RACING

Freddy Fox on Bahram

FOOTBALL

Chapman's amazing Arsenal

ARSENAL equalled Huddersfield's record of three consecutive League championships to give Herbert Chapman a unique place in history as the first manager to produce two such winning clubs. Unfortunately he was with neither club when they completed the hattrick. He missed Huddersfield's feat because he had left to transform Arsenal. And his untimely death from pneumonia in 1934 denied him again.

Arsenal's dominance of the era was almost total and Chapman was responsible for their unrivalled supremacy. It was very much the club he had built, both in its steely professionalism and the players he had either bought or discovered. They were nearly all famous names: Alex James, David Jack, Joe Hulme, Cliff Bastin, Herbie Roberts, Tom Parker, George Male, Eddie Hapgood.

Arsenal's success and professionalism were bitterly resented. When Walsall knocked them out of the Cup in 1933 there was widespread celebration. Their results were often greeted with "Lucky Arsenal". Not that they were lucky as such, but misunderstood. Arsenal played in a style that was completely alien to the rest of the League. Infuriatingly, they were happy to absorb pressure

Ted Drake: household name

ARSENAL'S RECORD IN THE 1930s

1929-30	FA Cup winners
1930-31	League champions
1931-32	Runners-up in League and Cup
1932-33	League champions
1933-34	League champions
1934-35	League champions
1935-36	FA Cup winners
1936-37	Third in League
1937-38	League champions
1938-39	Fifth in League

from less talented sides and then win with a breakaway goal.

Arsenal were always the team to beat. Not just because of their style, but also because of what they represented: the wealth and affluence that London enjoyed while the rest of the country had to contend with the misery of the depression. The club that Chapman built put a lot of noses out of joint. First, Chapman acquired his players in the transfer market with an almost cavalier attitude to money. Second, not only did Chapman's teams ruthlessly exploit the change in the offside law, they were never afraid to experiment with different formations. Not for them the cosy idea that a centre-forward was there to head the ball and wingers to hug the touchline.

Chapman changed things. He changed the strip. He changed the name of the club from "The Arsenal" to Arsenal. He even persuaded the transport authorities to change the name of the nearby underground station to Arsenal. Chapman also introduced a trainer, Tom Whittaker, as a physiotherapist complete with modern medical equipment, individual treatment and training routines. All of this was unheard of, and most of it unthinkable in the boardrooms of the other clubs.

BOXING

Cinderella man upsets Baer

JAMES BRADDOCK caused one of the greatest upsets in the history of the heavyweight division on June 23 when he out-pointed a clowning Max Baer over 15 rounds to lift the world title in the Garden Bowl. Braddock had virtually retired two years earlier because of an injured right hand. Unable to box or work because of the Depression, he had to live on hand-outs until he forced his way up the heavyweight division.

Despite his heart-warming story the public had little faith in him and he was written off as the Cinderella Man. Braddock began the fight at the outrageous odds of 10-1. Although Baer was a popular, charismatic and talented boxer he never took the game seriously enough, and was often erratic. This time he was physically unprepared as well. Braddock out-boxed the young champion, who frittered away his title in his first defence.

Braddock outpoints Baer

Sutcliffe limps out as England lose first Test to South Africa

HERBERT SUTCLIFFE'S last innings in Test cricket was tinged with irony. The Yorkshire opener who had turned running between wickets into an art required a runner during his final visit to the crease at Lord's. Sutcliffe's innings, though, was laced with the firm strokes that had made him one of his country's finest cricketers. His 38 was the top score in England's second innings, but could not prevent South Africa winning their first Test in Eng-

land on July 2. Sutcliffe, however, had preserved the highest average in Test cricket by an Englishman — 60.73.

His finest hours were with Jack Hobbs in the greatest opening partnership to represent England. Sutcliffe also had a successful association with Percy Holmes. They made 74 century stands for Yorkshire, the best of which was their 555 against Essex at Leyton in June 1932, when Sutcliffe hit 313, his highest first-class score.

SUTCLIFFE'S RECORD

	FIRST-CLASS	TESTS (54)
Innings	1,088	84
Not out	123	9
Runs	50,138	4,555
Highest	313	194
Average	51.95	60.73
Hundreds	149	16
Wickets	14 at 40.21	–
Catches	473	23

Herbert Sutcliffe: highest average in Tests by an Englishman

He often had to live above his technical income. He had, remember, to keep up with the Hobbses and Hammonds. His wasn't a triumph of skill only. It was a finer triumph of character, application and willpower

Sir Neville Cardus

RACING

Carthorse turns into champion

GOLDEN MILLER did not look much of a prospect when he was bought from Ireland. His trainer described him as a carthorse. But he was sold to Dorothy Paget and she was rewarded when Golden Miller completed a hat-trick of Gold Cups from 1932 to 1934. For good measure he won the 1934 Grand National as well, a double that has not been repeated.

Golden Miller faced his greatest rival, Thomond II, in

the 1935 Gold Cup and they produced one of the most stirring finishes ever seen at Cheltenham. Golden Miller and Thomond cleared the last two flights together and attacked the run-in up the hill at a furious pace. Golden Miller, though, inexorably inched ahead to win by three-quarters of a length.

That was nothing compared with the drama at Aintree. Golden Miller only got as far as the first fence in the Grand National, where he half-refused and unseated his jockey, Gerry Wilson. Golden Miller was run in the Champion Chase the next day. The crowd were incredulous when the same thing happened again — Golden Miller baulked at the first and Wilson went flying.

GOLF

Sarazen rewrites history

THE fledgling Masters had been no more than an informal gathering place for Bobby Jones and his friends until Gene Sarazen stepped on to the 15th tee at Augusta National. It required something special to catapult the event into prominence. The 5ft 5in Sarazen provided that something.

Craig Wood led by three shots with four holes to play but Sarazen hit his tee shot on the par-five 15th to within 232 yards of the hole and then struck his second shot as sweetly as he could ever have hoped. The ball cleared the pond protecting the green, skidded along the putting surface and rolled into the hole.

Sarazen's double eagle closed the gap on Wood. He played the last three holes in par to finish tied on 282. Wood had finished his round earlier and the Masters committee had prepared the winner's cheque in Wood's name. The cheque had to be torn up when Sarazen won the 36-hole play-off by five strokes.

TABLE TENNIS

And the game went on for ever

TABLE TENNIS was fast getting a reputation for being ridiculously slow. Matters came to a head during the world championships in Prague when Alex Ehrlich of Poland met Fareas Paneth of Romania. They started their match and went on, and on, and on . . . The two players were still playing the first point more than two hours later.

Driven to distraction, a committee meeting was held during the rally to discuss ways of stopping ultra-defensive play strangling the sport.

Michael Haguaneur of France and another Romanian, Dvoboj Marin, did even worse. Their match lasted seven hours.

GOLF

Shut and then Open

ALF PADGHAM faced a crisis shortly before the start of the final two rounds of the Open. His clubs were locked in the professional's shop at Hoylake and his caddie had disappeared. So Padgham threw a brick through the shop window, rescued his clubs, employed a new caddie and won the Open by one shot.

Padgham: locked out

RUGBY UNION

Russian prince's crowning glory

Prince Obolensky and England demoralise the All Blacks at Twickenham

PRINCE Alexander Obolensky fled the Russian Revolution in 1917. Nineteen years later he fled the New Zealanders' clutches to score one of the greatest tries at Twickenham.

The All Blacks were hoping to wrap up their tour with a win against England after beating Scotland and Ireland and losing narrowly to Wales 13-12. There was nothing to shake their confidence in the first 20 minutes of the match against the English on January 4. But they had not taken into account Obolensky playing a blinder on his debut. He outpaced the defence to open the scoring and then came up with his pièce de résistance two minutes before the interval.

England won a scrum on the half-way line on the left and, with the ball being passed to the right, the New Zealanders ran across the field to prevent Obolensky beating them to the corner flag again. But he moved inside to receive the ball, zig-zagged his way diagonally through the wrong-footed defenders and scored in the left-hand corner. England won 17-0.

Obolensky played three more games for England but did not score another point in internationals. Sadly, the 24-year-old was the first rugby international to lose his life in the war when his Hurricane crash-landed in Norfolk on March 29, 1940.

FOR THE RECORD

CRICKET

■ A record 588 runs (England 398-6 and India 190-0) were scored on the second day of the second Test at Old Trafford on July 27 — the most runs scored in a day in Tests.

■ Derbyshire won the county championship for the only time in their history.

FOOTBALL

■ Jimmy McGrory, of Celtic and Clydebank, retired having scored 410 goals in League football with a career average of 1.0049 per game.

■ Joe Payne scored 10 goals for Luton in their 12-0 defeat of Bristol Rovers in the Third Division South on Easter Monday, April 13.

■ Britain's first televised match was on August 29, a film of Arsenal v Everton shown by the BBC.

■ December 25 saw the fastest sending-off: Ambrose Brown of Wrexham in 20 seconds at Hull in the Third Division North.

■ Charlton became the first side to advance from the Third Division to the First in consecutive seasons.

RACING

■ The Aga Khan owned the winner and runner-up in the Derby. Mahmoud was only the third grey to win the race, and did so in a record time.

BOXING

Schmeling knockout of Louis shocks fight fans

THE irresistible rise of Joe Louis came to a halt on June 19 when he was knocked out by Max Schmeling in the 12th round in Yankee Stadium. The 40,000 who had turned up to see the "Brown Bomber" put yet another opponent to sleep were flabbergasted. But it was only a hiccup in his career. Schmeling was Louis's only setback on his world title quest.

Nazis upstaged by American blacks

THE eleventh Olympics in Berlin became the platform for Adolf Hitler to legitimise his Nazi regime in the eyes of the world. Hitler spared no expense in portraying his Third Reich in a favourable light. The Germans built a magnificent new stadium, removed anti-Jewish posters, staged lavish parties for politicians, and turned the Games into a military-style ceremony.

Nothing Hitler did, though, could dilute the influence of 10 black American athletes, led by the 22-year-old Jesse Owens. The magnificent 10 took seven gold medals, three silver and three bronze. Owens won the 100m, 200m and long jump and spearheaded a United States victory in the 4x100m relay. Their success shattered Hitler's illusion of Aryan supremacy.

Legend has it that Hitler snubbed Owens. The truth is that Hitler congratulated only some of the winners on the first day and was told by the president of the IOC to meet all the winners or none. He complied and received no other winners. Owens, who was not one of the winners on the first day, said: "We lost no sleep over not being greeted by Adolf Hitler."

Hitler might have lost sleep over the sight of two tall, black Americans, Cornelius Johnson and Dave Albritton, shooting craps in the middle of the stadium while their high jump rivals were being eliminated. The pair eventually removed their tracksuits and Johnson cleared 2.03m to win the gold medal. Albritton won the silver and only they know who won the game of craps.

Britain won four gold medals, seven silver and three bronze. Among their successes was the ride by Captain Richard Fanshawe, who won the bronze medal for his team in the three-day event despite chasing his horse for 2½ miles before remounting. The men's 4x400m relay team broke the American domination thanks to a brilliant effort by Godfrey Rampling, the father of the actress Charlotte, who took Britain from last to first in the second leg. Peter Scott, the son of the Antarctic explorer, won the bronze medal in the Olympia class yachting.

Jack Lovelock provided New Zealand with their sole success in one of the highlights of the Games. He broke the 1500m world record with 3min 47.8sec.

The first five home all beat the Olympic record.

When the curtains were drawn on the event, Leni Riefenstahl produced a film of the Games, "Olympische Spiele". It was both criticised as propaganda and hailed by film buffs as an outstanding cinematic achievement.

Opening ceremony of Hitler's Olympics in Berlin

THE TALE OF THE TAPE

100m: 1 Jesse Owens (US) 10.3sec; 2 Ralph Metcalfe (US) 10.4; 3 Martinus Osendarp (Holl) 10.5

200m: 1 Jesse Owens (US) 20.7sec; 2 Mack Robinson (US) 21.1; Martinus Osendarp (Holl) 21.3

4x100m: 1 United States (Jesse Owens, Ralph Metcalfe, Foy Draper, Frank Wykoff) 39.8sec; 2 Italy 41.1; 3 Germany 41.2

Long jump: 1 Jesse Owens (US) 8.06m; 2 Luz Long (Ger) 7.87m; 3 Naota Tajima (Jap) 7.74m

Mahmoud wins Derby in record time of 2min 33.8sec

Rejects' last laugh

AN INFLUX of Canadians had helped to raise the popularity of ice hockey in Britain. Two of them, Sandy Archer and the goalminder Jimmy Foster, were not picked by Canada for the Winter Olympics in Garmisch-Partenkirchen in February. So they were selected for the British squad instead.

The International Ice Hockey Federation declared them ineligible, but Britain ignored the ban. Although there were mutterings about the rules, no action was taken, because nobody gave Britain a chance. But victories over Sweden, Hungary, Austria and Czechoslovakia, and a draw with Germany guaranteed Britain a medal. Canada were the favourites for gold but, amazingly, the cast-off players inspired Britain to a 2-1 win, with Foster keeping his countrymen at bay in a frantic last six minutes.

Foster was even more brilliant against the United States, who attacked throughout. He saved shot after shot, and after three periods of extra time the match finished 0-0. Everything rested on the final match of the tournament, with the United States having an outside chance of snatching the gold medal if they beat Canada. But the Americans had lost their captain, injured against Great Britain, and they were beaten, handing the Olympic, World and European titles to Great Britain.

Jesse Owens
The man who left Hitler speechless

Cliff Temple

For most people, the name of Jesse Owens awakens two instant associations. Primarily, of course, his excellence as a sprinter and long jumper which yielded an unprecedented six world records in a single afternoon in 1935, and four gold medals in the 1936 Berlin Olympics. But almost as well known is the alleged public snub, long perpetrated as fact, which he supposedly received at those Games from Adolf Hitler.

The snub, although totally feasible in the circumstances which surrounded success on a world stage by an American negro in the middle of a Nazi Germany preparing for war, did not occur quite the way legend has it. Instead, Owens recalled many years later, if there was a snub to any American negro it happened on the first day of the athletics competition: "That day four gold medal winners were crowned: two Germans, one Finn, and Cornelius Johnson, the American high jump winner. Johnson is a negro. Hitler personally congratulated the two Germans and the Finn in his box. Just as Johnson was to receive his medal, Hitler left the stadium. There was no question of his intent."

The next day Count Henri de Baillet-Latour, president of the International Olympic Committee, pointed out to Hitler that as patron of the Games he should either congratulate every winner or none. Hitler complied, and subsequently received no other winners. "We lost no sleep over not being greeted by Adolf Hitler", Owens added. But although he did not publicly snub Owens, Hitler's grim attitude to his success was recorded by Baldur von Schirach, the Reich Youth Leader, who was in the box of honour when Owens won. According to von Schirach, Hitler said: "The Americans should be ashamed of themselves, letting negroes win their medals for them." When he was put under pressure from several colleagues to meet Owens "in the interests of sport", Hitler lost his temper and shouted: "Do you really think that I will allow myself to be photographed shaking hands with a negro?"

Owens was born James Cleveland Owens in Oakville, Alabama, on September 12, 1913, the thirteenth and last child of impoverished sharecroppers. When he was nine the family moved to Cleveland, Ohio, and it was there that his Christian name became transformed. On his first day at Bolton Elementary School a teacher asked his name, and inadvertently misinterpreted his shy Southern drawl reply of "J C Owens" into Jesse. And Jesse it remained.

His athletic talent surfaced at high school, and he became one of America's fastest sprinters while still a teenager. While attending Ohio State University he created athletics history at Ann Arbor, Michigan, on May 25, 1935. Competing for Ohio State in the Big Ten championships, despite a back injury which required his teammates to help him dress, at 3.15pm Owens set a 100 yards world record of 9.4sec. Then he went immediately to the long jump, where his only attempt measured 26ft 8¼in, the first eight-metre jump (8.13m) and a world record which was to survive for the next 25 years. At 3.45pm he won the straight 220 yards sprint in 20.3sec, a world record which counted for both 220 and the slightly shorter 200 metres. And at 4pm he picked up his fifth and sixth world records in under an hour by running 22.6sec for the straight 220 yards

(and 200m) hurdles. "When the meeting was over," he said later, "the pain returned to my back, and I had to be practically carried to the dressing room."

His nickname was the Ebony Antelope, yet he ran with a noticeably short, if deceptively fast, stride. At the Berlin Olympics he dominated the explosive events, winning the 100m, 200m and long jump, and running the first leg for the victorious United States 4x100m relay team which set a world record of 39.8sec.

His long jump duel with Lutz Long of Germany was a classic. Long drew level with Owens at 7.87m midway through the contest, only for Owens to respond with winning jumps of 7.94m and 8.06m. Their friendship forged at those Games cut through the political situation, and to the great regret of Owens he never met Long again; the German was killed fighting in Sicily in 1944.

For Owens, the Berlin Olympics were virtually the end of his athletics career, at just 22 years of age. His last competitive appearance was at White City in London, running in the sprint relay for the United States a few days after the Olympics ended. But he declined to travel with the rest of the American team to a meeting in Stockholm, preferring instead to return home to discuss the many lucrative offers made after his Games success. He was suspended by the AAU of America and sadly, considering the cost of his amateur status, few of the offers proved to carry much substance. He had abandoned his degree and was reduced to racing dogs, cars and horses to earn money to support his wife and children. A business venture failed and he was thrown into debt for $114,000.

> **❢ We lost no sleep over not being greeted by Hitler ❣**

He eventually resolved his financial predicament, founding his own public relations company, and through the 1960s and 1970s finally achieved a degree of status and respect which was much harder to attain, even as a successful sportsman, as a black in the 1930s.

"I came back to my native country after winning in Berlin to all those stories about Hitler and his snub," he was to say years later. "But I couldn't ride in the front of the bus. I couldn't live where I wanted. I wasn't invited to shake hands with Hitler — but I wasn't invited to the White House to shake hands with the President either."

In 1979, at the age of 66, Owens, a successful businessman and widely admired ambassador for American sport, was diagnosed as having inoperable lung cancer. He had long been a heavy smoker. He died on March 31, 1980. Even while undergoing chemotherapy he maintained a watch on Olympic affairs. One of his last stands, early in 1980, was against the proposed American boycott of the Moscow Olympics because of the Soviet invasion of Afghanistan.

"The road to the Olympics doesn't lead to Moscow," he wrote. "It leads to no city, no country. It goes far beyond Lake Placid or Moscow, ancient Greece or Nazi Germany. The road to the Olympics leads, in the end, to the best within us."

The first superstar: Owens's talent as a sprinter and long jumper knew no equal. He broke six world records in a day in 1935 and won four golds at the Berlin Olympics.

AMERICAN FOOTBALL

The Washington swells embrace the Redskins

GEORGE Preston Marshall wanted to be an actor. He never made it on the stage, so he brought a theatrical approach to his American football team. Marshall was a co-owner of the Boston Braves in 1932 and when he took sole charge the next year he renamed them the Redskins. But Boston was predominantly a baseball and ice hockey city, and Marshall, fed up with lack of support, moved his team to Washington.

Then the fun started. His team had its own marching band, dressed in full Red Indian garb, and his wife, a former movie star, wrote the words for its anthem, Hail to the Redskins. Marshall skilfully mixed the razzmatazz with the idea that his stadium was the ideal place for Washington's high society to spend an afternoon dressed in their Sunday best.

Marshall was also an innovator within the game, introducing the season tickets that are now treated as valuable family heirlooms, and creating the post-season all-star game that became the Pro Bowl.

BOXING

America applauds the Brown Bomber

JOE LOUIS came off the floor in the first round to take James Braddock's title by knocking him out in the eighth round of their world heavyweight title fight in Chicago on June 22. Although Louis was clearly hurt from the right uppercut, he proceeded to take Braddock apart. Braddock did not give up his crown lightly, although it was later discovered that he was to receive $300,000 and 10% of the net profits of Louis's heavyweight title promotions for the next decade should Louis win.

At the end of the seventh Braddock's manager wanted to call it a day, but Braddock, with a split lip, a bad cut over his left eye, and his right eye swollen, said: "If you do, I'll never speak to you again." A little over a minute later it was all over when Louis caught him with an overhead right that landed on the jaw.

Louis achieved what Jack Johnson, the first black world heavyweight champion, had failed to do — acceptance by the American public. To be sure, he was appreciated for his athletic ability rather than accepted for his colour. And it is true that Louis went out of his way not to offend whites and not speak out against racism. But he did make mild appeals for equal opportunity and he opposed segregation in the army during and after the war. His spectacular talent, a vicious left jab and a knock-out punch in either hand, made him the idol of the ghettoes and a role model for young blacks.

Joe Louis: black idol

Farr's heroic battle

Tommy Farr: went the full distance with Joe Louis

THE nation held its breath on August 31 as it listened in the small hours of the morning to the live BBC radio broadcast of Tommy Farr's impossible tilt at Joe Louis's world title. The one-time coalminer from Tonypandy battled bravely but Louis won comfortably on points. But Farr's game and stubborn performance against the best fighter of the age turned him into a national hero. Farr was not convinced. Years afterwards he told Henry Cooper: "I wish you wouldn't talk about that fight. Just the mention of the name Louis makes my nose bleed."

FOR THE RECORD

CRICKET
■ The lbw law was changed to prevent excessive use of the pads. A batsman could be out to a ball pitched outside the off stump instead of only between wicket and wicket.

FOOTBALL
■ Brechin City suffered the first of three 10-0 defeats in the season at Cowdenbeath on November 20. The others, also away, were at Albion Rovers on January 15 and Airdrie on February 12. They conceded 139 goals in their 34 Second Division games.

■ The highest number of paying spectators, 149,547, saw Scotland beat England 3-1 at Hampden on April 17.

GOLF
■ Reg Whitcombe survived gales on the final day to win the last Open in which the first three were British.

ICE HOCKEY
■ Britain retained the European title in London.

TABLE TENNIS
■ In an attempt to speed things up, the International Table Tennis Federation ruled that both players would be scratched if any game lasted more than 20 minutes. Ruth Aarons of the United States and Trudi Pritzi of Austria fell foul of the new rule in their world singles final clash.

Hutton survives poor debut

Len Hutton: became the permanent mainstay of England's batting line-up

HUTTON'S RECORD

	FIRST-CLASS	TESTS (79)
Innings	814	138
Not out	91	15
Runs	40,140	6,971
Highest	364	364
Average	55.51	56.67
Hundreds	129	19
Wickets	173 at 29.42	3 at 77.33
Catches	396	57

❝Yorkshire were 232 all out. Hutton ill. No, I'm sorry, Hutton 111❞

John Snagge
radio commentator

WHEN Len Hutton made his way from Yorkshire to Lord's for the first Test against New Zealand he was being touted as the successor to Herbert Sutcliffe. Much was expected from him on his Test debut. The new England opener, though, was far from impressive. He was bowled for a duck by Jack Cowie in his first innings and scored only one run in his second innings before he again fell to the New Zealand fast bowler they called The Bull.

Fortunately, the England selectors decided to retain Hutton for the next Test. Their faith in the young man was vindicated at Old Trafford.

Walter Robins won the toss for England, opted to bat and Hutton never looked back. He hit 100 in 210 minutes to set up England's 130-run victory.

Although he had a wide range of strokes, Hutton generally curbed his repertoire, cutting out the risky shots that would have put a solid opening innings for England in jeopardy. A shy man, Hutton was forced to hold together many England innings after the war in a side that lacked depth in batting. Most of his support came from Denis Compton, the Arsenal and England footballer, who earned his debut in the third Test against New Zealand at The Oval.

Unmoveable Budge

IT WAS left to Don Budge to carry the flag for amateur tennis after Fred Perry and Ellsworth Vines had turned professional. And he accomplished it with poise and power.

Budge, the son of a Glasgow Rangers footballer, preferred baseball and basketball as a schoolboy. When he was 15 his brother Hugh persuaded him to play in the 1930 California boy's championships. He trained in secret and surprised even himself by winning the title. He then acquired a strong service, solid ground strokes and his most devastating weapon: a topspin backhand drive, which was especially effective against a less-than-perfect service.

Budge came to prominence in 1935 when he beat Jack Crawford, the world's No 2, in 4hr 10min in a Davis Cup preliminary round. But it was at Wimbledon where he will be best remembered. He beat the Australian Vivian McGrath, the first two-handed player of note, in the quarter-finals. In the semi-finals, against Frank Parker, he dropped his only set in the championships. The ubiquitous Gottfried von Cramm, in his third successive final, was no match for Budge who won 6-3 6-4 6-2. Budge also took the men's doubles with Gene Mako and the mixed doubles with Alice Marble to become the first triple champion at Wimbledon.

Don Budge: assumed Fred Perry's amateur mantle

MOTOR RACING

Triumph of the maestro

BRITAIN hosted its third Grand Prix at Donington Park in front of 60,000 spectators including the Duke of Kent. It was a dramatic race eventually won by the greatest driver of the decade, Il Maestro, the Italian Tazio Nuvolari in an Auto-Union. Nuvolari negotiated his car off the track and back on again when oil was spilt on the descent to the hairpin bend. Then, with 10 laps to go and in third place, he produced one the greatest attacking drives and eventually finished 1min 38sec ahead of the second-placed car.

Much of what he achieved from 1933 to 1939 was done with inferior cars pitted against drivers of the very highest skill. It was said of Nuvolari: "To see him in his heyday, chin out, sitting well back in the driving seat, his outstretched hairy arms flashing in the sun as he made his car perform seemingly impossible antics not once, but corner after corner, lap after lap, the tyres screaming . . . was quite fantastic."

BOXING

Farr robbed

TOMMY FARR boxed four more times in America after failing to take the world title from Joe Louis the year before and lost all four contests, although by popular consensus he was robbed against James Braddock and Max Baer in New York.

TENNIS

Budge wins first Grand Slam, Moody wins eighth Wimbledon

A BOAT trip to Australia in the 1930s was beyond the call of duty for most amateur tennis players. But most did not include Don Budge, who had set his sights on adding the Australian championships to his growing list of titles. He cruised past John Bromwich in the final and then turned his attention to the French championship. Roderick Menzel provided little opposition in the final and by this stage Allison Danzig, a sportswriter on the New York Times, began to write about Budge possibly achieving the Grand Slam by winning the four major tournaments.

The pressure began to grow on Budge, but he did not show it when he became the first player to win the men's singles title at Wimbledon without dropping a set. Bunny Austin was the cannon fodder for Budge in the final, winning only four games. And so to New York and Forest Hills where Budge was well aware he was only one step away from history. His opponent in the final was Gene Mako, his friend and doubles partner.

Budge was tentative at first and after winning the first set 6-3 he lost the second 8-6. He then moved up a gear in the third set and eventually wrapped up the Grand Slam in convincing style.

It was a year for records. Helen Wills Moody won her record eighth Wimbledon singles title with a 6-4 6-0 victory against Helen Jacobs.

DON BUDGE'S GRAND SLAM FINALS

Australia: John Bromwich 6-4 6-2 6-1
France: Roderick Menzel 6-3 6-2 6-4
Wimbledon: Bunny Austin 6-1 6-0 6-3
United States: Gene Mako 6-3 6-8 6-2 6-1

CRICKET

Australia massacred by Hutton

ANYBODY watching Len Hutton push and prod his way to one run in two innings against New Zealand on his Test debut in 1937 would never have believed that only five matches later he would hit the then highest score in Test cricket. But the 22-year-old Yorkshireman was in complete command in his marathon innings of 364 in the fifth Test against Australia. He batted for 13 hours and 17 minutes and struck 35 fours on a placid pitch at The Oval.

Later he was dismissive of his achievement, saying the pitch was too true and he had scored the runs against an Australian attack that included only three regular bowlers. England won the most one-sided Test in history by an innings and 579 runs. Their first-innings total of 903 for seven declared remains a Test record for the highest total.

Bradman congratulates Hutton on beating his record

Italy retain Cup

THE third World Cup, in France, was plagued by politics. Europe was in turmoil: Austria had been overrun by Germany in the Anschluss and their best players had been snapped up by the Fatherland, and there was civil war in Spain. Despite being begged by the French organisers, Britain still refused to send even one competing nation; Uruguay stayed at home beset with problems of professionalism and still sulking about 1930; Argentina would not forgive Fifa for not awarding them the tournament, so they stayed at home as well — provoking a riot outside the Argentine football federation's offices in Buenos Aires that police had to break up. Interestingly, new faces appeared: Cuba, the Dutch East Indies and Poland.

Italy had rebuilt their side in the four years since winning the 1934 World Cup; only Meazza and Ferrari were retained. But Vittorio Pozzo, their genius of a manager, brought them perfectly to their peak. The other two great sides in the competition were Brazil, fiery and brilliant, and Hungary, cool and precise.

Italy, organised and masterful, dispatched each of them in the semi-final and final respectively and retained the World Cup.

Vittorio Pozzo's Italy triumphant again

Italy's Foni executes a black-flip against Hungary

Armstrong triple crown

Henry Armstrong: a Yank known as Homicide Hank

HENRY ARMSTRONG became the first man to hold three world titles simultaneously when he won the lightweight championship in August by beating Lou Ambers in a split decision. Armstrong was also the feather and welter champion.

FOR THE RECORD

AMERICAN FOOTBALL

■ Mel Hein of the New York Giants was named the NFL's first Most Valuable Player.

BADMINTON

■ Thirteen Danes entered the All-England championships. They did not win any of the titles, but it heralded the impending foreign domination of the sport.

BOXING

■ Benny Lynch of Scotland was stripped of his world title on June 29 for failing to make the weight in a world flyweight title fight in Paisley against Jackie Jurich of California. The two met later that afternoon as catch-weights and Lynch floored Jurich six times and knocked him out in the 12th round. England's Peter Kane captured the flyweight crown left vacant by Lynch's retirement when he beat Jurich in Liverpool on September 22.

FOOTBALL

■ Manchester City, the champions the previous season, were relegated. Yet they scored 80 goals, three more than Arsenal who took their title.

■ The English team were instructed to give the Nazi salute in Berlin..

■ The FA celebrated its 75th anniversary with a match in which England beat the Rest of World at Wembley.

■ When Stanley Matthews asked for a transfer the people of Stoke demonstrated by hanging out banners saying: "Matthews must not go". He stayed until 1947.

■ East Fife were the first Second Division side to win the Scottish Cup.

■ The laws of the game were re-written by Stanley Rous.

GOLF

■ Britain won the Walker Cup for the first time, beating the US 7½ to 4½ at St Andrews after 16 years of trying.

■ The number of clubs a golfer could carry in his bag were limited to 14 from January 1, and tee pegs became popular.

ICE HOCKEY

■ Britain won the European title for the third year running.

RACING

■ Bruce Hobbs, at 17, was the youngest jockey to win the Grand National. He rode Battleship, a 40-1 outsider.

RUGBY UNION

■ Wilson Shaw scored a try to give Scotland victory over England on March 19. They did not win at Twickenham again for 33 years.

TABLE TENNIS

■ Richard Bergmann, who won the world title for Austria the year before, took British nationality. He retained his crown, the first of three times he won the title as an Englishman.

TELEVISION

■ It was a year of firsts with the FA Cup final, the Derby, the first rugby union international (England v Scotland), and the first ice hockey match (Harringay v Streatham) all shown live.

BASEBALL

Sad Gehrig struck out

AN INCURABLE wasting disease finally ended Lou Gehrig's enormous contribution to the New York Yankees. Gehrig hit almost as far and as hard as Babe Ruth in an era when sluggers dominated the American League. His illness finally forced him to retire on May 2, after he had played an incomparable 2,130 consecutive games for the Yankees in a sequence that stretched back to June 1, 1925. But despite losing Gehrig, there was still no stopping the Yankees. Inspired by the recently-discovered Joe Di-Maggio, who was voted the American League's MVP, they won their fourth consecutive World Series.

FOR THE RECORD

AMERICAN FOOBALL
■ The NFL attracted 1m spectators for the first time.

CRICKET
■ England experimented with eight-ball overs.

■ Wally Hammond became the first fielder to hold 100 catches in Tests in the second Test against West Indies at Old Trafford.

FOOTBALL
■ A crowd of 118,567 watched Rangers play Celtic at Ibrox on January 2. It was a League record for the British Isles and the first six-figure attendance for a League match in Britain.

■ Numbered shirts were finally applied to League football.

■ Johnny Cochrane was appointed manager of Reading. He lasted exactly 13 days.

TENNIS

Riggs lands lucrative coup

AT LEAST one London bookmaker would attest to Bobby Riggs being one of the best hustlers in tennis. The naive bagman substantially lengthened the odds on the 21-year-old Californian winning the Wimbledon title when Riggs lost 6-0 6-1 to Gottfried von Cramm in the semi-finals of the London grasscourt championships at Queen's Club on the Friday before Wimbledon.

Little did the bookmaker know that Riggs had audaciously thrown the match and promptly backed himself heavily to win the All-England title. It was with a wry smile that Riggs duly collected his winnings after a 2-6 8-6 3-6 6-3 6-2 victory against his doubles partner Ellwood Cooke in the final. Riggs completed his perfect record in his only Wimbledon appearance by winning the men's and mixed doubles titles. And while Riggs was winning the triple crown another Californian, Alice Marble, was making her mark in a T-shirt and short trousers.

Doctors gave Marble little hope of playing again when they diagnosed tuberculosis after she collapsed on court in the French championships in 1934. But she returned to the sport two years later a fitter and faster player and brought with her a serve-volley game that, until then, had been the exclusive privilege of the men's game. Marble's fight-back reached its zenith when she won the triple crown at Wimbledon. She crushed the German Hilde Sperling 6-0 6-0 in the singles semi-final and beat the left-handed Kay Stammers 6-1 6-1 in the final. She won the doubles crown with Sarah Fabyan and the mixed doubles with Riggs.

When Riggs played against two women 34 years later the matches earned even greater publicity. He beat Margaret Court 6-2 6-1 and lost to Billie Jean King 6-4 6-3 6-3 in "Battle of the Sexes" matches, the latter attracting an estimated television audience of 50 million people.

Alice Marble: the triple Wimbledon champion

RUGBY LEAGUE

War quickly sends New Zealand packing

A POWERFUL New Zealand side arrived in Britain on August 29 full of optimism. Little did they know what was in store. Three days after they had landed, Germany invaded Poland. And the day after they opened their tour with a 19-3 win against St Helens, Britain and France declared war on Germany.

The government decided sport could continue but a crowd of 6,200 people were required to take gas masks to the New Zealanders' second game, against Dewsbury on September 7. The tourists won 22-10 and a week later had packed their bags and were on the boat home with a 100 per cent record: played two, won two. It was the shortest tour in history.

Last hurrah: the Kiwis trouncing Dewsbury in September

Constantine still just as quick off the mark

TIME had started to catch up with Learie Constantine. The once fiery West Indian fast bowler had slowed to little more than medium pace on the tour of England in his 38th year. And when he moved in the field was there not a slight hesitation in those reactions that had made him one of the greatest fielders of all time? Morris Nichols certainly thought so when batting in the third Test at The Oval.

Constantine was trundling in to deliver his medium pacers interspersed with the occasional quicker ball. A loose delivery was despatched into the covers and Nichols saw no danger as he set off for a quick single. Suddenly Constantine bounded after the ball. He swooped cat-like to gather it and in a spectacular, flowing movement threw at the stumps. A stunned Nichols was short of his crease when the ball shattered its target. Constantine had struck. And he had not finished. With an extra spring in his step he took five for 75 and then went out and hit 78 out of 103 in a

CONSTANTINE'S RECORD

	FIRST-CLASS	TESTS (18)
Innings	197	33
Not out	11	0
Runs	4,475	635
Highest	133	90
Average	24.06	19.24
Hundreds	5	None
Wickets	439 at 20.67	58 at 30.10
Catches	162	28

❛ Learie Constantine wanted to field all the time, everywhere, and there were many moments when he appeared to be doing just that ❜

J M Kilburn

mere 55 minutes on the last morning of his Test career.

When the sun finally set on a drawn game he was remembered as a dynamic cricketer whose

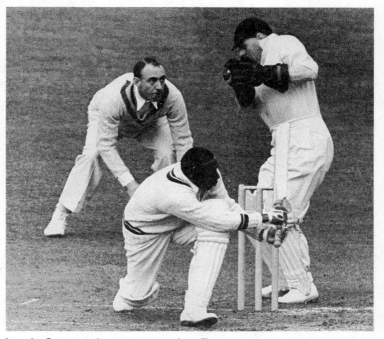

Learie Constantine: never made a Test century

philosophy was epitomised in his comment: "I never wanted to make a hundred. Who wants to make a hundred anyway? When I first went in my immediate objective was to hit the ball to each of the four corners of the field. After that, I tried not to be repetitive."

Constantine was never repetitive. With an unlimited energy and zest for the game, he was a magnet whose penchant for the unorthodox attracted thousands to watch him. For he played in the days when the West Indians were lovely to watch, but seldom won.

Edrich slow to get into his run-making stride

Edrich: magnificent comeback

THE England selectors were a patient breed. They had watched Bill Edrich begin his Test career with innings of 5, 0, 10, 12, 28, 12, 4, 10, 0 and 6. And still they persisted with him. And still he failed them.

He had been provided with yet another opportunity to succeed when he was chosen for the fifth Test against South Africa in Durban. However, while almost everyone else took full advantage of the flattest strip ever prepared for a Test, Edrich scored only one in England's first innings and his average dipped to 8.00. The Middlesex right-hander was given a lot of time to contemplate his predicament. The teams had decided the final

match would be a timeless Test and they certainly took their time about scoring runs. A week after the start they were still nowhere near finishing, with England needing 696 to win.

Edrich, though, took his cue and with a superb 219 rescued his floundering Test career and helped England to within 42 runs of victory. But when rain began to fall during the tea interval on the tenth day, after 43 hours and 16 minutes of play, the match was abandoned. The England team had to begin their two-day train journey to Cape Town to catch their ship home.

With six years to reflect on the state of the game, when play resumed after the war the cricket world decided it did not want

timeless Tests. While some might have relished the prospect of watching 10 days of Test cricket, the majority had had more than enough.

BOXING

Louis rattled by oddball challenger

TONY GALENTO, who was nick-named the "fat freak" and who reputedly trained on cigars and beer, stunned Joe Louis, himself and fight fans when he put the world champion on the floor on June 8. It made no difference. Galento was knocked out in the fourth round.

Sport helped to keep the home fires burning

The world pitched into battle 21 summers after Britain had won the war to end all wars. But this time there were no foolhardy officers kicking footballs on the battlefield and no romantics believing that it was a glorious game. The spectre of Adolf Hitler and his Third Reich made sure of that.

In a conflict that touched everyone, an estimated 55 million people lost their lives. And British sport was one of the first casualties, dealt a knockout blow within days of war being declared on September 3, 1939.

Two days before, Hedley Verity had taken seven for nine in six overs for Yorkshire at Hove, and then Blackpool had moved to the top of the First Division with three wins. But the war brought an immediate blanket ban on sport. The mood was sombre and many people wondered if they would ever play again. Verity did not. He was killed in action in Italy.

The draconian edicts were gradually repealed and as the country came out of its shell so, too, did sport, which eventually played an important role in lifting the morale of battered Britain.

The Phoney War, seven months in early 1940 when the two adversaries were entrenched behind defensive lines, helped sport emerge from the blackout. But not before table tennis had experimented with phosphorescent balls to allow play under decreased light, and Wembley Arena had spent £300 painting its glass roof black so events could be staged at night.

However, when people began playing and watching sport again the anti-sport lobby launched their usual vociferous attack. It held lit-

Cricket playing on in 1940 . . . Second Lieutenant Hedley Verity, Sergeant Maurice Leyland and Sergeant Len Hutton at a Red Cross fund-raising match at Headingley; and L F Parslow scores 101 for the British Empire XI at Lord's.

tle water. The tone of the argument was exemplified by Sir Stafford Cripps, the leader of the House of Commons. "All wastage, all unnecessary expenditure is to be ended," he said. "Our motto can neither be 'business as usual' nor 'pleasure as usual'."

It was open season on sport, which was accused of wasting petrol, money and manpower. There was a demand for a total war effort. It was a call that did not go unheeded by sportsmen. When the world speedway championships at Wembley were cancelled soon after the outbreak of war many of the stars enlisted as dispatch riders.

And what the critics ignored was that an afternoon at the cinema or a day in the country used up as much money, petrol and manpower as sport. They also neglected to mention that sport provided relaxation for tired war workers and entertainment for soldiers on leave. It took people's minds off the horrors and provided a glimpse of normality. Above all, it lifted morale.

Sir Pelham Warner, the mastermind behind many war-time cricket matches, suggested in his book about the history of Lord's that sport provided a healthy and restful antidote to the strain of war. "I had the feeling that if Goebbels had been able to broadcast that the war had stopped cricket at Lord's it would have been valuable propaganda for the Germans," he wrote.

Cricket's flag was flown by two ever-changing teams, London Counties XI and the British Empire XI, who travelled the country raising money for charity and cheering the locals by playing mainly one-day matches. Ernest Bevin, the Minister of Labour, encouraged the game, even if it meant lying low on the turf at Lord's when flying bombs started falling on London in the summer of 1944.

The campaign against sport really ran aground when Winston Churchill, the Prime Minister, attended football matches and the government spent £50,000 on a poster campaign urging cheerfulness. Sport, they said, nurtured cheerfulness.

Football was organised into regional leagues and international

West Ham beat Blackburn 1-0 in the 1940 Cup final at Wembley, watched by survivors of Dunkirk; and the England team continued with Britton, Cullis and Mercer as half-backs; and Tommy Lawton was still scoring goals, whoever he played for.

matches attracted large crowds. Nearly 40,000 watched Wales beat England 1-0 at Wembley in April 1940 and 75,000 turned up at Hampden Park to see Scotland draw 1-1 with England a month later.

West Ham won a War Cup in the spring of 1940, beating Blackburn 1-0 at Wembley in front of a crowd of 42,399, which included survivors of the previous week's retreat from Dunkirk. The 137 matches were condensed into seven weeks.

The football authorities were determined to keep their sport going, even in unusual circumstances. Many stars earned extra money as guests for clubs. Tommy Lawton played two games on Christmas Day in 1940, helping Everton beat Liverpool 3-1 in the morning and scoring both Tranmere's goals in a 2-2 draw at Crewe in the afternoon. He then played a game for Morton in January 1941 while he was in Scotland on honeymoon. Several clubs found it difficult to muster 11 men for matches and some even appealed to the crowd to help make up the numbers.

Racing and greyhounds continued, mainly due to gambling. There were four race meetings a week and the Derby was moved to Newmarket in 1940. Many racecourses, with their open tracts of land, were used for the war effort and 16 did not reopen when the fighting finished, including Gatwick, which became a commercial airport. Greyhound racing thrived as an afternoon entertainment for night workers and the sport became so popular that some meetings became all-ticket events.

Sport also provided the stage prop for one of the great escapes from Germany. Prisoners of war used a Red Cross crate as a gymnastic vault in the famous "wooden horse" escape from the Stalag Luft III camp. While prisoners dug a tunnel under the vault, others leapt over it above the ground to create a diversion. But all did not end well. The rank and file soldiers complained that they had dug the tunnel while the officers had escaped. And the reaction by the German guards was to flatten the budding golf course.

While the rest of the world went to war in 1939, America sat on the fence, watching, waiting and playing sport. George Halas and his "Monsters of the Midway" produced the most spectacular performance the NFL has ever seen. The Chicago Bears demolished the Washington Redskins 73-0 in the 1940 championship game. By the third quarter Chicago were so far ahead that the referee asked them to stop kicking extra points. So many balls had disappeared into the crowd that there were only just enough left to complete the game.

Sugar Ray Robinson was doing his own demolition job. Unbeaten in 85 fights as an amateur, he turned professional in 1940. His dazzling hand and foot speed, with a potent mixture of grace and power, brought him another 40 straight victories. And they were far from pushovers. Robinson beat three world champions in his first three months to become the unofficial welterweight champion.

When the United States joined the war after the attack on Pearl Harbour the same questions about whether sport should continue were asked as in Britain. And the answer was the same. Franklin Roosevelt was determined that the show should go on.

But many players joined the battle. Halas joined the navy, and Joe DiMaggio and a host of other baseball superstars also enlisted. Sport, like the rest of the world, struggled on, mainly with players who were not fit for active service.

Top left: Pont l'Eveque wins the Derby at Newmarket
Bottom left: The Welsh XV who played England in 1942
Right: Dunkirk survivors watch the 1940 Cup Final

BASEBALL
■ World Series
1940 Cincinnati Reds
1941 New York Yankees
1942 St Louis Cardinals
1943 New York Yankees
1944 St Louis Cardinals
1945 Detroit Tigers
1946 St Louis Cardinals
1947 New York Yankees
1948 Cleveland Indians
1949 New York Yankees

BOXING
■ British world champions
1943 *Flyweight.* Jackie Paterson
1948 *Flyweight.* Rinty Monaghan
1948 *Light-heavyweight.* Freddie Mills

CRICKET
■ County championship
1946 Yorkshire
1947 Middlesex
1948 Glamorgan
1949 Middlesex and Yorkshire

CYCLING
■ Tour de France
1947 Jean Robic
1948 Gino Bartali
1949 Fausto Coppi

FOOTBALL
■ Football League
1947 Liverpool
1948 Arsenal
1949 Portsmouth
■ FA Cup
1946 Derby 4 Charlton 1 (aet)
1947 Charlton 1 Burnley 0 (aet)
1948 Manchester Utd 4 Blackpool 2
1949 Wolverhampton 3 Leicester 1
■ Scottish League
1947 Rangers
1948 Hibernian
1949 Rangers
■ Scottish Cup
1947 Aberdeen 2 Hibernian 1
1948 Rangers 1 Morton 0 (after 1-1)
1949 Rangers 4 Clyde 1
■ Scottish League Cup
1947 Rangers 4 Aberdeen 0
1948 East Fife 4 Falkirk 1 (after 1-1)
1949 Rangers 2 Raith 0

GOLF
The Open
1946 Sam Snead
1947 Fred Daly
1948 Henry Cotton
1949 Bobby Locke
■ US Open
1940 Lawson Little

1941 Craig Wood
1946 Lloyd Mangrum
1947 Lew Worsham
1948 Ben Hogan
1949 Cary Middlecoff
■ US PGA
1940 Byron Nelson
1941 Vic Ghezzi
1942 Sam Snead
1944 Bob Hamilton
1945 Byron Nelson
1946 Ben Hogan
1947 Jim Ferrier
1948 Ben Hogan
1949 Sam Snead
■ US Masters
1940 Jimmy Demaret
1941 Craig Wood
1942 Byron Nelson
1946 Herman Keiser
1947 Jimmy Demaret
1948 Claude Harmon
1949 Sam Snead
■ Ryder Cup
1947 United States 11-1
1949 United States 7-5

RACING
■ The Derby
1940 Pont l'Eveque
1941 Owen Tudor
1942 Watling Street
1943 Straight Deal
1944 Ocean Swell
1945 Dante
1946 Airborne
1947 Pearl Diver
1948 My Love
1949 Nimbus
■ Grand National
1940 Bogskar
1946 Lovely Cottage
1947 Caughoo
1948 Sheila's Cottage
1949 Russian Hero

ROWING
■ Boat Race
1946 Oxford
1947 Cambridge
1948 Cambridge
1949 Cambridge

RUGBY LEAGUE
■ Challenge Cup
1941 Leeds 19 Halifax 2
1942 Leeds 15 Halifax 10
1943 Dewsbury *bt* Leeds 16-9 0-6
1944 Bradford *bt* Wigan 0-3 8-0
1945 Huddersfield *bt* Bradford 7-4 6-5
1946 Wakefield 13 Wigan 12
1947 Bradford 8 Leeds 4
1948 Wigan 8 Bradford 3
1949 Bradford 12 Halifax 0

RUGBY UNION
■ Five Nations championship
1947 Wales and England

1948 Ireland
1949 Ireland

SNOOKER
■ World championship
1940 Joe Davis 37 Fred Davis 36
1946 Joe Davis 78 Horace Lindrum 67
1947 Walter Donaldson 82 Joe Davis 63
1948 Fred Davis 84 Walter Donaldson 61
1949 Fred Davis 80 Walter Donaldson 65

TENNIS
■ Wimbledon
1946 Yvon Petra *bt* Geoff Brown; Pauline Betz *bt* Louise Brough
1947 Jack Kramer *bt* Tom Brown; Margaret Osborne *bt* Doris Hart
1948 Bob Falkenburg *bt* John Bromwich; Louise Brough *bt* Doris Hart
1949 Ted Schroeder *bt* Jaroslav Drobny; Louise Brough *bt* Margaret du Pont
■ Australian championship
1940 Adrian Quist; Nancye Wynne
1946 John Bromwich; Nancye Wynne
1947 Dinny Pails; Nancye Wynne
1948 Adrian Quist; Nancye Wynne
1949 Frank Sedgman; Doris Hart
■ French championship
1946 Marcel Bernard; Margaret Osborne
1947 Joseph Asboth; Patricia Todd
1948 Frank Parker; Nelly Landry
1949 Frank Parker; Margaret du Pont
■ US championship
1940 Don McNeill; Alice Marble
1941 Bobby Riggs; Sarah Cooke
1942 Ted Schroeder; Pauline Betz
1943 Joseph Hunt; Pauline Betz
1944 Frank Parker; Pauline Betz
1945 Frank Parker; Sarah Cooke
1946 Jack Kramer; Pauline Betz
1947 Jack Kramer; Louise Brough
1948 Pancho Gonzales; Margaret duPont
1949 Pancho Gonzales; Margaret duPont

Fiery Miller disturbs peace

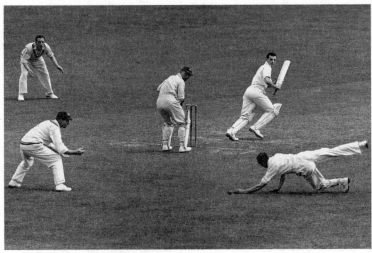

England v. Australia 2nd day w./o. An Australian batsman gets one past the slips on a ball from Lieut. D V P Wright, 21 May 1945

JANUARY

1945

DECEMBER

MILLER'S RECORD

	FIRST-CLASS	TESTS (55)
Innings	326	87
Not out	36	7
Runs	14,183	2,958
Highest	281 not out	147
Average	48.90	36.97
Hundreds	41	7
Wickets	497 wickets at 22.30	170 wickets at 22.97
Catches	136	38

Miller: extrovert all-rounder

BOMB-SCARRED Britain was looking for an ideal way to celebrate V-Day in the summer. So five three-day victory matches between an England XI and their Australian counterparts were hastily arranged.

There was no better player to help the spectators forget the woes of the war than the extrovert Australian all-rounder Keith Miller. He became one of the most popular players of the series and laid the foundations for a 10-year career as one of the finest all-rounders in the game.

Miller burst onto the world stage with a solid century in the first match at Lord's in mid-May. He was the only batsman to reach three figures as the Australians won by six wickets. He then scored another century in the fourth match at Lord's on August 6, in the only drawn fixture of the series which the sides shared two-all.

But Miller's finest performance came in the three-day match between England and The Dominions at Lord's in late August. Major Martin Donnelly, a left-handed New Zealander, set the pace for The Dominions with a blazing 133 which included two sixes and 18 fours. It took a century from Wally Hammond to rescue England before Miller took control.

He hit a dazzling 185 in better than even time, striking seven sixes and 13 fours. One of his sixes off Eric Hollies lodged in the roof of the broadcasting box above the England players' dressing-room. It remains one of the biggest hits at cricket's headquarters. The Dominions won the match by 45 runs with eight minutes to spare after Hammond hit his second century of the match. Miller scored 568 runs at an average of 94.68 in four first-class matches in the summer, but was dropped down the batting order by Don Bradman when Test cricket resumed. The Don preferred to use Miller as a strike bowler rather than as a batsman who could strike the ball more fluently than most.

Toothless reject turns into fearsome scorer

BRIAN BEVAN began the most prolific try-scoring career in the code's history. The Sydney-born wing earned his first-class debut in the winter after the war and went on to score a record 796 tries from 1945 until 1964. But he had an inauspicious start. Both Leeds and Hunslet turned him down when he approached them for trials after being posted to Portsmouth as a stoker in the Royal Australian Navy. Warrington, though, snapped him up. He played one match in the reserves and earned his first-team debut against Oldham on November 17. It was the start of a 17-year love-affair with the club. He scored 740 tries in 620 matches and helped Warrington win the championship three times and the Challenge Cup twice. Bevan then finished his career with two seasons at Blackpool Borough.

Bald, without teeth and a heavy smoker, Bevan was often patched together with bandages and did not look like a rugby league wing. But once he had the ball in his hands there were few who could stop him, as Leeds and Hunslet were soon to learn.

Bevan: 796 tries

FOR THE RECORD

AMERICAN FOOTBALL
■ The NFL finally spanned all of America when the Cleveland Rams announced that they were moving to Los Angeles.

BASEBALL
■ Pete Gray, who only had one arm, played 77 games for the St Louis Browns.

RACING
■ The Flat lost two of its great characters with the deaths of Steve Donoghue and George Lambton, the greatest jockey and trainer of their day.

Russians invade Britain and bow out unbeaten

THE RUSSIANS arrived in October in the shape of Moscow Dynamo and embarked on one of the most curious tours hosted by Britain. Their demands were extraordinary: they would only play club sides; they would provide their own referee who had to be in charge of at least one match; they had to eat all their meals in the Soviet embassy, and so on. Britain starved of top flight football for six years, and happy to accommodate their allies, acceded to everything.

Dynamo's first match, against Chelsea at Stamford Bridge, was packed to the rafters. Nobody knew what to make of the Russians – the press had already written them off as slow amateurs – particularly when they took to the field with each player bearing a bouquet of flowers which they solemnly handed over to each Chelsea player.

When the match began Dynamo simply overran Chelsea with fast, fluent football, but against the run of play found themselves two down. Undeterred the Russians attacked unceasingly and deservedly gained a 3-3 draw.

Chelsea flower show: the home players were perplexed by Russians bearing gifts

Cardiff City were trounced 10-1 before Dynamo met an Arsenal team strengthened by the presence of three England players, Stanley Matthews, Stan Mortensen and Joe Bacuzzi, at White Hart Lane.

The fog was so thick that visibility was down to 10 yards.

Accounts vary as to who refused to call off the match, and both sides blamed the other. The game was played with, at the Russian referee's request, the two English linesman on one touchline and him on the other. The Russians took an early lead, fell behind and, after a host of dubious decisions, won 4-3.

Their final match was at Ibrox against Rangers, where 90,000 saw the Russians take a 2-0 lead that evaporated into a 2-2 draw. And then they flew home, unbeaten.

Busby marshals United into a fighting force

MANCHESTER UNITED were in much the same condition as the rest of the country, ravaged by war, heavily in debt but prepared to tackle their problems with optimism and vision.

In February, they turned to Matt Busby and offered him the manager's job. It was an astute move. Busby had been a player for Manchester City for eight seasons from 1928, where he had won an FA Cup winner's medal, and then a player at struggling Liverpool until the outbreak of the war. Military service had given him great opportunities to work with footballers such as Joe Mercer, Tommy Lawton and Arthur Rowe in the Army PE corps and Busby's managerial skills were born.

Sergeant-major Busby demanded, and got, a five-year contract and complete control of the team.

Busby: complete control

He had much to do. Old Trafford had been destroyed in the bombings and there would be no home matches played there in the foreseeable future. The club had a £15,000 overdraft and there would be no money for players.

Busby would have to develop what he had. And he did that by analysing his players' skills and redeploying people in his teams. Johnny Carey, for example, was moved from centre forward to wing half to full back – and became one of the greatest players of the decade.

Busby also grasped the opportunity of a new start that the war offered. At 45 he was young enough to mix with, and play with, his own players. He became the first track-suited manager, recreating his Army days, engendering esprit de corps and the notion that he and his players were a family unit.

Carey: positional switches

GOLF

Easy Open for Snead

SAM SNEAD certainly did not put Britain at the top of his list of travel destinations. Instead, the Virginian compared a stay in Britain to "camping out". He had pitched up for the Open at Carnoustie in 1937 and finished a disappointing 11th. So it was with trepidation that he ventured across the Atlantic a second time for the Open at St Andrews.

German prisoners of war had cleared some of the rough at the course in preparation for the championship and Snead started with a 71, two shots off the pace set by Bobby Locke, who needed only one putt on seven greens. Dai Rees made his charge in the second round when he hit a record 67 and, with Henry Cotton also in the running, it was shaping up as a classic finish. Six players were in contention at the start of the final round.

Rees took seven at the first and three-putted the second and third. He never recovered from 17 shots in three holes, turned in 40 and finished with an 80. Slammin' Sam, though, found his rhythm and with a near-flawless swing sealed the title with a closing 75 that left him four shots clear. However, he regarded the Open as "just another tournament" and criticised the course and the prize-money which totalled £1,000.

Snead's ambition was to win the US Open. He tried 25 times

> **❛ Any guy who would pass up a chance to see Sam Snead play golf would pull the shades driving past the Taj Mahal ❜**
>
> **Jim Murray**

but cruel luck robbed him. The greatest player never to win the US Open was runner-up on four occasions. His success at St Andrews, three Masters titles, three victories in the US PGA and 135 tournament victories worldwide were testimony to his stature as one of the finest ever golfers. Snead's classic swing and strong all-round game stood the test of time for 40 years at the top.

> **❛ Sam was born with a natural ability to keep his bar bills as low as his golf scores ❜**
>
> **Jimmy Demaret**

"Just another tournament"

FOOTBALL

Carter lifts Derby to FA Cup triumph

Carter: inspired his team in extra time

RAICH CARTER's Derby County beat Charlton 4-1 after extra time in extraordinary fashion to win the first post-war FA Cup final. At full-time the teams were level at one goal apiece, both of them having been scored by Charlton's Bert Turner, the first man to achieve the dubious distinction of scoring for both sides in a Cup final. But in extra time Derby ran amok with two goals from Jack Stamps and one from Peter Doherty, who with Carter formed the most formidable inside-forward partnership in the League.

The Cup was also remarkable for other bizarre firsts. For once, the four rounds were played over two legs with the aggregate scores determining which club progressed. In the third round Charlton lost 2-1 to Fulham yet went through, becoming the first team to reach a Cup final having been beaten en route. Then, in the match at Wembley, the ball burst for the first time in a Cup final. Coincidentally, BBC radio speculated on this happening.

The final will be remembered for the silky skills of the veteran Carter. The silver-haired Carter had been an astute purchase from Sunderland the year before, and in his first season had led Derby to their first FA Cup. His full name was Horatio Stratton "Raich" Carter and he was revered throughout the country as the greatest inside-forward of the day. He had helped Sunderland win the championship in 1936 and captained them to the FA Cup in 1937 at the age of 23. His wondrous, and effortless, skills and masterful strategy easily transferred to the international stage where, with Stanley Matthews, England had a right-sided partnership of mind-boggling dimensions.

A colleague once said of Carter: "I never know for sure how good he is. You can only judge a player when you've seen him under pressure. And I've never seen him under pressure. He carries space around with him like an umbrella."

Bedser turns India upside down

THE first post-war Test in England drew capacity crowds to Lord's to watch Wally Hammond's side beat India by 10 wickets in late June; the only result in a three-match series.

England's success was masterminded by Alec Bedser who, on his Test debut, took 11 for 145. His right-arm medium-pace bowling yielded seven for 49 in the first innings, the harbinger of many successful performances by the Surrey professional. Bedser, the twin brother of Eric, had a well-balanced bowling action that produced a vicious leg-cutter and a useful stock in-swinger. He concentrated on making batsmen play the ball, and achieved a strike rate of more than 4½ wickets per match in 51 Tests.

Big Al was England's first post-war find. He dominated the bowling and had 14 opening partners in an era when talent was in short supply. The game had swung in favour of medium-pacers and the laws and pitches were suited to Bedser and his kin. A new ball could be taken after 55 overs and the full effects of a change in the lbw law in 1937 had begun to take effect. Bedser adapted to the changes more quickly than most batsmen, and when he had finished wreaking havoc among their ranks he became an England selector in 1962. He resigned in the mid-1980s.

Bedser: 11 wickets on his debut for England

BEDSER'S RECORD

	FIRST-CLASS	TESTS (51)
Innings	576	71
Not out	181	15
Runs	5,735	714
Highest	126	79
Average	14.51	12.75
Hundreds	1	None
Wickets	1,924 at 20.41	236 at 24.89
Catches	290	26

RUGBY LEAGUE

Record breaker Sullivan retires

JIM SULLIVAN called it a day after one of the most illustrious careers in rugby league. He had joined Wigan as a strapping 17-year-old full-back from the Cardiff rugby union club in 1921, and his build of 14st and 6ft 2in influenced the club to pay a record-equalling fee of £750.

Sully, as he became popularly known, scored a record 2,867 goals in his 25-year career and played in 60 internationals and 928 first-class matches. He took over as coach of Wigan when he retired and in the next seven years the club won the Challenge Cup twice, the championship four times, the Lancashire Cup six times and the Lancashire league four times.

GOLF

Berg shrugs off shattered knee in US Open

PATTY BERG had been through agony when she arrived at Spokane for the qualifying round of the first US women's Open. The 5ft 2in American had her knee smashed in an accident in 1942 and it was so badly set that the bones had to be broken again and reset three times.

Her golf swing, though, remained as sweet as ever and with rounds of 73 and 72 she led the qualifiers. Berg beat Betty Jameson 5 and 4 in the match-play final of the leading championship in women's golf.

FOR THE RECORD

ATHLETICS
■ Lord Burghley, the Marquis of Exeter, was elected president of the IAAF.

CRICKET
■ Jim Laker took his first wicket in first-class cricket, but it was a shade lucky. Alf Gover caught the ball between his legs while he was putting on a sweater.

■ New Zealand scored 42 and 54 on March 29-30 and lost to Australia by an innings and 103 runs in the first official Test between the two countries and the last until 1973.

FOOTBALL
■ Crush barriers collapsed at Burnden Park on March 9 during a Cup tie between Bolton and Stoke. Thirty-three people were killed and more than 400 injured.

■ Walter Winterbottom was appointed the FA's chief coach. Shortly afterwards Stanley Rous, the FA secretary, was able to manoeuvre his way past the various FA committees and have Winterbottom installed as the first England manager.

■ The British associations joined Fifa.

GOLF
■ Lloyd Mangrum won the US Open, but he had to play a lot of golf. He beat Byron Nelson and Vic Ghezzi in a second play-off after they all shot 72 in the first play-off.

■ Herman Keiser started the last round of the Masters five strokes ahead of Ben Hogan. But he thought he had thrown it all away with three putts on the final green. Fortunately for Keiser, Hogan also took three putts at the same hole and blew his chance of winning.

TENNIS
■ The United States crushed Great Britain 7-0 in the Wightman Cup in June. They did not even drop a set.

TENNIS

Part-time Petra wins Wimbledon

YVON PETRA was fortunate to be playing at Wimbledon. The Frenchman had been seriously wounded during the war and was taken prisoner. He seemed likely to lose his leg but for the skill of a German surgeon who saved the limb.

Petra, born in Indo-China, learned to hit a powerful service when playing barefoot in the French colony. He moved to France, where he became a barman and part-time tennis player. His service won him the first post-war men's singles title at Wimbledon when he beat the Australian Geoff Brown 6-2 6-4 7-9 5-7 6-4.

The American Pauline Betz won the women's title without dropping a set in the tournament, but she later dared to discuss a professional contract. The US Lawn Tennis Association banned her, so she immediately turned professional.

Petra and Brown

FOOTBALL

Jittery Arsenal sign the veteran Mercer

Mercer in action for Arsenal against Leeds

ARSENAL surprised everyone in football and Joe Mercer himself when they signed the veteran midfielder from Everton. Herbert Chapman's brilliant Arsenal of the Thirties were fading by the time the war had begun and the seven-year hiatus only compounded matters. By December Arsenal were in debt and in danger of being relegated. So in desperation they signed Mercer and made him captain, hoping to get a couple of good seasons out of the former England player.

Mercer was a stylish wing-half with a robust tackle that belied his spindly legs, but to most observers it seemed a move born of panic rather than shrewdness. Mercer, after all, had joined Everton in the days of the legendary Dixie Dean and, as the right-half, had been a key member of the Everton side that had won the championship in 1939. But the gamble paid off, Arsenal avoided relegation and Mercer played on for eight years, having just one season

more each year, until a broken leg forced him to retire. The grateful has-been inspired the Gunners to two League championships and two Cup finals, winning one, in the twilight of his career.

FOR THE RECORD

BOXING
■ Sugar Ray Robinson won the vacant world welterweight title when he outpointed the stubborn, but limited Tommy Bell at Madison Square Garden on December 20.

FOOTBALL
■ The first Scottish League Cup competition was held. It was won by Rangers.

KORFBALL
■ This Dutch sport was introduced to London.

RACING
■ Harry Wragg bowed out in some style. He rode a hat-trick in his last three races before he retired.

TENNIS
■ Marcel Bernard was the last Frenchman to win the men's singles at the French championship for 37 years.

Fans flock to opening games

FOOTBALL League returned to England as the first season for seven years got under way on August 31. Although the fixtures were familiar — they were identical to those of the aborted 1939 season — many of the faces were not. Some players were absent because age had caught up with them; others were casualties of the war, notably Tom Cooper, the Liverpool and England full-back, and Harry Goslin, Bolton's captain; others were still scattered worldwide waiting to be demobbed.

Fans who were demobbed had money burning in their pockets and flocked in their hundreds of thousands to watch football. As too did those who had been working in industry where, though the wages were good, rationing meant that there was little to spend the money on. Consequently, when the gates were opened at noon there were huge queues outside virtually every football ground.

The return of football was also a symbol of hope, as if everything could return to the way it had been. The illusion that life could pick up where it had left off was heightened by the repetition of 1939's fixtures.

TENNIS

US dominates the Davis Cup

THE powerful United States team dropped only four sets on their way to beating Australia 5-0 in the Davis Cup challenge round in Melbourne.

The Americans beat the Philippines, Mexico and Sweden 5-0 and then became the first cup squad to fly to Australia, island-hopping across the Pacific Ocean in four days. Their win was the first of four successive victories and they played against Australia in every challenge round until 1960.

Bradman sours Ashes series

Hammond is caught behind by Tallon in the second Test in Sydney

THE first post-war Ashes series was more acrimonious than most. The conflict centred on the bitter rivalry between the two captains, Wally Hammond and Don Bradman. The feud flared on the first day of the series when Bradman chopped a ball waist high to Jack Ikin in the gully. The Don, who had struggled to 28, refused to walk and was given not out. At the end of the over Hammond said: "This is a bloody fine way to begin a Test series". Bradman hit 187 that day and Australia won by an innings and 332 runs.

The match in Brisbane provided Keith Miller with a platform to launch his Test career as one of the game's most talented all-rounders. He hit 79 and then took seven for 60.

There was no respite for the tourists in the second Test in Sydney a fortnight later. Bradman and Sid Barnes hammered 405 at more than a run a minute against a weak England attack. They both scored 234 and their mammoth fifth-wicket partnership led to an Australian victory by an innings and 33 runs.

Sad Lynch found dead in gutter

BENNY LYNCH, Scotland's greatest boxer, was found dead in a Glasgow gutter at the age of 33. Lynch captured the world flyweight title and the public's affection in 1935. Although he was a brilliant fighter he led a wildly undisciplined life outside the ring. After his final fight in 1938 he was a pathetic figure drowning in a sea of whisky, pawning his boxing trophies and fighting in booths to support his drinking habit. When his mother died he was homeless, destitute and on the inevitable road to self-destruction.

Lynch: Scotland's greatest

Triumphant tourists win the hard way

THE Great Britain rugby league team were keen to tour Australia but their biggest stumbling block was trying to find a way to get there. Eventually they settled for a 26-day voyage aboard the aircraft carrier HMS Indomitable, which was carrying Australian servicemen home.

The tourists then had to endure a five-day rail journey from Perth to the east coast. Their marathon ordeal fused the side into a powerful combination and they won 21 of their 27 matches.

The Indomitables drew the first Test 8-8 in Sydney and then won 14-5 in Brisbane and 20-7 in Sydney in matches that attracted more than 140,000 people. One of the side's rare losses was a 13-8 defeat against New Zealand.

Great Britain en route for Australia on HMS *Indomitable*

FOR THE RECORD

BADMINTON
■ Snow blew in through the ventilators at the All-England championships and restricted play to six matches on the first day. All of the titles were won by Danes or Danish-born players, who were of a higher standard because they were allowed to play throughout the war.

FOOTBALL
■ Neil McBain, New Brighton's player-manager, appeared as a stand-in goalkeeper against Hartlepools aged 52 years and four months in a Third Division North match. He became the oldest player to turn out in the League but New Brighton still lost 3-0.
■ The season's attendances totalled 35,604,606.
■ Italy beat Hungary 3-2 on May 11 with 10 players from Torino.

SQUASH
■ Mahmoud Kerim of Egypt won the British Open the first time he entered, and kept the title for three years.

TENNIS
■ England's women became the first team from this country to win a world title at the world championships in Paris.

SQUASH

Kerim: first-time winner

FOOTBALL

Mortensen makes spectacular start

STAN MORTENSEN, the Blackpool forward, made a spectacular debut for England in Lisbon on May 27, when he helped himself to four goals in a 10-0 drubbing of Portugal. Tommy Lawton also scored four, with Tom Finney — playing in only his second international — and Stanley Matthews completing the rout.

Mortensen had replaced Raich Carter, the darling of the man on the terraces, after England had embarrassingly lost 1-0 to Switzerland in Zurich nine days earlier. Mortensen kept the No 8 shirt for the other four internationals of that year. And at Highbury, in November, he turned a difficult game for England against Sweden with a hat-trick in a 4-2 victory that could easily have been a defeat.

Mortensen's goalscoring abilities were uncanny: utilising his wonderful acceleration he always seemed to find the quickest, shortest and most unexpected route to goal, and he was appropriately called the "Electric Eel". Mortensen was always a battler. He had had to fight back from a terrible injury he received when his RAF bomber crashed in training during the Second World War.

Although England won five internationals and drew two that year, the unexpected loss to Switzerland, compounded by Scotland losing to Belgium in Brussels, caused the Football Association to reconsider their attitude to the national team. The depressing England performances must have also greatly concerned Walter Winterbottom in his first term in charge.

Record signing works wonders for Liverpool

LIVERPOOL won their fifth championship in June when Stoke failed to beat Sheffield United in the last match of a season that had to be extended because of the disruption caused by the ferocious winter.

Liverpool started the season promisingly, but a 5-0 hammering by Manchester United frightened them into lashing out a record £12,500 for Newcastle's goalscorer Albert Stubbins.

The gamble proved worthwhile. The combination of Stubbins and Billy Liddell, who had had to wait eight years for his League debut, up front and Bob Paisley at the centre of their defence, took them through a difficult campaign where only two points finally separated the top four teams.

Mannion conquers Europeans

Da Rui, of France, in the Rest of Europe's goal, punches clear

GREAT BRITAIN cruised past the Rest of Europe 6-1 at Hampden Park in May in a match to celebrate the return of the four British associations to Fifa.

It was an easy victory for Britain with Wilf Mannion, the Middlesbrough inside-forward, outstanding as he tore Europe's defence to shreds and scored twice.

Johnny Carey, Manchester United's versatile double Irish international, captained a Rest of Europe side that was made up of players from 10 different countries. Although out-thought, the Europeans were disadvantaged by neither sharing a common language nor being acquainted with one another. The big Swedish centre-forward Gunnar Nordahl, who equalised the first goal, left a strong impression.

Tail-enders rescue England

AUSTRALIA and England played out the first drawn Test in Australia in 65 years in Melbourne on January 7. The Australian Cricket Board had decided to abandon timeless Tests, but it took a rearguard action from Norman Yardley and Alec Bedser to save England on the sixth day. The fourth Test in the series in Adelaide a month later was also drawn, thanks partly to Godfrey Evans, the England wicketkeeper, who took a record 97 minutes to score his first run.

Hammond is bowled by Toshack at Adelaide

France celebrate their return

FRANCE, barred from the Five Nations championship since 1931, celebrated their return by beating Scotland 8-3 in Paris on New Year's Day and Ireland 12-8 at Lansdowne Road on January 25. They tied for third place with Ireland behind England and Wales, the joint winners of the first championship in 15 years.

Pebeyre attacks for France against England

Tudor Minstrel flops in Derby

FRED DARLING's health was failing and he was in his final season before retirement. But he had charge of Tudor Minstrel, who was being labelled the "horse of the century".

Tudor Minstrel gave Gordon Richards an armchair ride in the 2,000 Guineas, and it was little surprise that he was the shortest-priced favourite in the Derby for years. Richards, still searching for his first victory in the race, was drawn 13, and it proved unlucky. Tudor Minstrel was a distant fourth and the crowd blamed Richards for the defeat.

But Richards was vindicated when subsequent races proved that Tudor Minstrel could not stay and had been over-hyped.

Gordon Richards on his dubious mount, Tudor Minstrel

Stylish finale for Hammond

WALLY HAMMOND bowed out of Test cricket with a standing ovation and three cheers from the New Zealand fielders after his walk to the crease in Christchurch on March 22. Hammond rose to the occasion by top scoring for England with 79 in a drawn match marred by rain.

Demaret makes a splash to sink his rivals

JIMMY DEMARET, a wise-cracking Texan and one of golf's nattiest dressers, made a confident start to his quest for a second Masters title. Then he reached the 520-yard 15th hole.

He hit a bold second shot and although the ball carried the pond protecting the green it hit the bank and rolled back into the water. Undeterred, Demaret took off his shoes and socks and waded into the water. With one foot in the pond he splashed his wedge into the water and the ball landed four feet from the hole. He sunk the putt for a birdie, finished the opening round in 69 and won the tournament by two strokes.

Snead misses out yet again

SAM SNEAD holed an 18-foot putt to force a play-off in the US Open and was tied with Lew Worsham at the 18th green. The pair needed putts of less than a yard to remain level.

Snead was settling to putt when Worsham interrupted him to ask for measurement. Snead was further from the hole and had to putt first. He missed and Worsham holed out for the championship. It was the closest Snead came to achieving his dearest ambition.

Fruit packer keeps Britain well stocked

BOB HUDSON, an Oregon fruit packer, was determined to see the Ryder Cup continue so he sponsored the first post-war match at Portland in November.

The match was a humiliating experience for Henry Cotton's British team — Sam King was the only visitor to win, beating Herman Keiser 4 and 3 in the 11-1 defeat. Hudson believed that food rationing was the major reason for Britain's failure and sent the entire team food hampers for Christmas every year until 1957.

FOR THE RECORD

CRICKET
■ The first ever Test between Australia and India started in Brisbane on November 28. Australia won by an innings and 226 runs.

FOOTBALL
■ William Sharp was quick off the mark on December 20. He scored for Partick Thistle against Queen of the South seven seconds after the kick-off.

GOLF
■ The US women's Open became a strokeplay tournament. It was staged as a matchplay event in its first year in 1946.

MOTOR RACING
■ John Cobb became the first man to drive a car at more than 400mph on Bonneville Salt Flats on September 16.

RACING
■ The first evening meeting was held at Hamilton Park on July 18.

Rusty Louis jeered after split decision

FOR the first time in his career Joe Louis left the ring to boos when he controversially retained his world heavyweight title against the 34-year-old Jersey Joe Walcott in December.

The challenger, who had an indifferent record before facing Louis, knocked the champion down twice — in the first and fourth rounds. At the end of the fight both boxers were convinced that the title had changed hands. Louis had left the ring and had to be called back to hear he had won on a split decision.

Louis, at 32, may well have been past his prime, but the setback was put down to the ring rust he had accumulated during the war, when he had relentlessly given exhibitions to boost the morale of the troops.

Walcott and Louis sign for their title fight

Robinson overcomes the black barrier

A WEEK before the start of the season the Brooklyn Dodgers bought Jackie Robinson from one of their farm clubs. There was uproar. Some of the team demanded to be traded. And several clubs said they would go on strike rather than play against Robinson, the first black player signed by a Major League team.

The National League president, Ford Frick, was unmoved: "I do not care if half of the league strikes. They will all be suspended, and I do not care if it wrecks the National League for five years. This is the United States of America and one citizen has as much right to play as another."

Neither of the Major Leagues had ever formally barred black players but they had been excluded none the less. But Branch Rickey, the Dodgers president, realised there was an enormous pool of talent in semi-professional black leagues.

Even then he had to move carefully. When he first signed Robinson and two other black players in 1945 he placed them with minor league clubs and told his scouts he was forming a team to play in the black leagues. Rickey waited nearly two years until he was sure that Robinson could handle the pressure of playing in the National League. His patience was rewarded. Robinson had to endure constant abuse and being intentionally spiked, but he refused to be cowed. He hit .297 and stole 29 bases to secure his place on the team.

Kramer's grand plan rewarded

JACK KRAMER mapped out his career while doing duty for the United States Coast Guard during the war. He would win Wimbledon and the United States Open, turn professional and earn a lucrative salary playing tennis. There was one problem. He aggravated a blister on his hand during a fourth-round match against Jaroslav Drobny at Wimbledon in 1946 and lost.

With the US title in his pocket he was determined to put his plans back on track. So Big Jake honed his powerful service and volley game during the winter until his relentless percentage game was at its peak. He dropped only 37 games on his way to winning the men's singles title at Wimbledon and in the final took a mere 45 minutes to crush Tom Brown 6-1 6-3 6-2. He added a second US singles title and then joined the paid ranks.

Kramer's first professional match made a lasting impression on him. A crowd of 15,000 ploughed through thick snow to watch him lose to Bobby Riggs at Madison Square Garden. They brought with them $250,000 and the astute Kramer knew then that the professional tour would become a goldmine. He took control of it in 1951.

Kramer: lucrative career

Middlesex pair in full flow

Monaghan claims the world title

NEVER in the history of cricketing conflict have so few scored so many. Denis Compton hit 3,816 runs and Bill Edrich scored 3,539. The phenomenal strokeplay of the Middlesex and England pair brought crowds flocking to cricket. Compton's record aggregate was scored at an average of 90.85 and included 18 centuries. Edrich averaged 80.43 and hit 12 centuries. The next highest ever aggregate was 3,518 by Tom Hayward in 1906.

When they were not scoring runs they were taking wickets. Compton took 73 and Edrich 67 before he strained his shoulder in late July. When they were finished Middlesex had won the championship and England had beaten South Africa 3-0.

Such was Compton's form that in a match against Worcestershire he began to charge

Watching Bill Edrich face a fast bowler was like watching some tough little kid walking up to the school bully and kicking him smartly in the shins

Barry Norman

down the pitch before the leg-spinner Roly Jenkins reached the crease to bowl. Jenkins stopped and said: "I don't mind you giving me the charge Denis, but am I expected to shake you by the hand?"

Denis Compton was the only player to call his partner for a run and wish him good luck at the same time

John Ward

Compton loved to attack and his favourite shot was the sweep, while his offside repertoire included a majestic cover drive. His only flaw was running between the wickets. Leslie Compton paid for his younger brother's indecision when he was run out in his own benefit match. They had more success

together on the football field in 1947-8 when they won League champion's medals with Arsenal.

Edrich was a less unorthodox batsman than Compton with a high backlift and straight bat. He was a courageous player who loved to score runs in adverse conditions. He captained Middlesex from 1953 until 1957 after two years of sharing the job with Compton, and a year later returned to Norfolk, where he played until he was 55.

COMPTON'S RECORD

	FIRST-CLASS	TESTS (78)
Innings	839	131
Not out	88	15
Runs	38,942	5,807
Highest	300	278
Average	51.85	50.06
Hundreds	123	17
Wickets	622 at 32.27	25 at 56.40
Catches	415	49

EDRICH'S RECORD

	FIRST-CLASS	TESTS (39)
Innings	964	63
Not out	92	2
Runs	36,965	2,440
Highest	267 not out	219
Average	42.39	40.00
Hundreds	86	6
Wickets	479 at 33.31	41 at 41.29
Catches	529	39

Compton, Edrich at the Oval

THE colourful Irishman Rinty Monaghan, who used to croon When Irish Eyes Are Smiling on the ring microphone, claimed the world flyweight title when he outpointed Dado Marino of the Philippines at the Harringay Arena in London on October 20. Because the previous champion, the Scot Jackie Paterson, had been denied the opportunity to defend his title, forfeiting it when failing to make the weight for a defence against Marino, the two had to box off for the title a year later. Monaghan ended the argument by knocking Paterson out in the seventh round in the King's Hall, Belfast.

Overseas players thrive on rule change

ONE of the worst winters on record failed to dampen the spirits of rugby league supporters who thronged to matches in record numbers to watch a galaxy of overseas stars.

Brian Bevan, Harry Bath, Arthur Clues, Lionel Cooper and Cec Mountfield thrived on an alteration to the play-the-ball law which had opened up the game. The acting half-back had to be two yards behind the tackled player and everyone else at least five yards behind.

After taking two steps forward, the sport took one step back in August when Australia imposed a five-year ban on importing players between the two countries. Four months later New Zealand introduced a similar two-year ban.

Notts County cash in by signing Lawton

NOTTS COUNTY, of the Third Division North, became the first club to break the £20,000 transfer barrier when Tommy Lawton signed for them from Chelsea in November.

It was an amazing coup. Lawton was England's established leader in attack, had successfully stepped into Dixie Dean's boots at Everton, and was the classic centre-forward — fast, brave and a lethal finisher, particularly in the air. The gates at Meadow Lane immediately tripled to 30,000.

Lawton: £20,000 transfer coup

Laker's stormy debut

JIM LAKER endured two weeks of gales aboard a boat to the West Indies. Then he took Test cricket by storm. The off-spinner grabbed seven for 103 on his debut in Bridgetown, including a spell of six for 25 on the second morning.

Billy Griffith made his mark in the second Test in Port of Spain. The England reserve wicketkeeper, selected as a makeshift opener because of injuries, compiled 140 in 354 minutes. It was his maiden first-class century, but after that he scored only 17 runs in his remaining four Test innings.

Laker: seven for 103

United stun mighty Blackpool

Rowley heads United's equalizer past the stranded Robinson

IN ONE of the most dramatic Cup finals ever staged Matt Busby's Manchester United twice came from behind to beat Blackpool boasting Stanley Matthews and Stan Mortensen.

Blackpool had taken the lead with a controversial Mortensen penalty in the 15th minute, Jack Rowley equalised but Mortensen scored five minutes later and Blackpool were 2-1 ahead at half-time. During the interval Busby was utterly composed. He and Irish captain Johnny Carey told the players to keep playing and the goals would come.

The second-half was a drama of attack and counter-attack with United never abandoning their neat passing game. But with 21 minutes to play Blackpool were still ahead. Then Johnny Morris took a quick free kick and Rowley headed the equaliser.

United's tails were up and Johnny Anderson, who until recently had only been a reserve team player, set up a goal for Stan Pearson. The fourth goal distorted the result. Anderson scored with a 35-yard punt.

The run that had taken United to Wembley was almost as impressive as the final. In every round they had to eliminate quality First Division teams: Aston Villa, Liverpool, Charlton, Preston and Derby. And because Old Trafford was under repair every game was an away game. Even Maine Road, which United were sharing with Manchester City, was only available once because of City's Cup commitments. As a consequence the other matches were played at Goodison and Huddersfield. None of this seemed to bother Busby's teams. Every tie was won by at least two goals and without a single replay.

The Manchester United that won the Cup so thrillingly was very much a Matt Busby creation. Only two of the team had cost transfer fees, and seven were local players. A Manchester United of Mancunians.

Jockey Club's grand old man dies, aged 82

THE 17th Earl of Derby died in February, aged 82. He had been a member of the Jockey Club for more than half a century and was recognised as the elder statesman of racing. The Daily Telegraph reported that "nothing of importance was done without his being consulted" and Lord Rosebery, Senior Steward of the Jockey Club, said: "Lord Derby was by far the greatest influence in racing history."

But Lord Derby was more than just a member of the great and the good. He was one of the most successful owners in English racing with 20 Classics, including three Derbys, to his credit. He was also heavily involved in racing in France, Argentina and America.

Hibs just grab first title from Rangers

HIBS won the Scottish championship for first time since 1903. But it was a close thing. Rangers finished two points behind them and the destiny of the title was probably settled in January when Hibs narrowly beat Rangers 1-0.

It was an exceptional side captained by the Scottish international full-back Davie Shaw, and it included Gordon Smith, Alec Linwood, Willie Ormond, Eddie Turnbull and Bobby Coombe, an Englishman.

The foundations were laid by Willie McCartney, who had arrived in 1936 having managed Hearts for many years. McCartney never saw the fruits of his work for he died in January.

Frank Swift: down but not out

Irish gamble pays off against England

Kyle scores Ireland's first try at Twickenham

FOR THE RECORD

FOOTBALL
■ Frank Swift became the first goalkeeper to captain England on May 16. He had a good first match in charge, with a 4-0 victory against Italy in Turin.

■ Lightning struck the Army Cup final replay at Aldershot, and two players were killed. The referee was also hit, but survived.

■ Inspired by Joe Mercer, Arsenal coasted to their sixth League title with almost a month to spare.

■ Huddersfield were embarrassed in the FA Cup third round when beaten 1-0 by Colchester of the Southern League.

GOLF
■ Claude Harmon hit a hot streak in the US Masters. He shot 2, 3 and 3 at the 6th, 7th and 8th holes in the final round and went on to win the tournament by five strokes.

■ Bobby Locke won the Chicago Victory National championship by 16 strokes, a record for a US PGA Tour event.

■ Fred Corcoran started the first women's tour and signed up the leading trio of Patty Berg, Betty Johnson and Babe Zaharias.

RUGBY LEAGUE
■ Australia, Britain, France and New Zealand formed the International Rugby League Board in Bordeaux on January 25.

RACING
■ Fifty-eight runners started the Lincoln, the biggest-ever field in British flat racing.

TABLE TENNIS
■ 10,000 people watched England's women retain their world title at Wembley.

Louis gets the better of Walcott

THE tide seemed to have turned for Joe Louis on June 25. Once again the veteran Jersey Joe Walcott embarrassed the world champion, knocking him down in the third round. True, Louis did better than six months ago, when he was floored twice and saved by the judges. This time Louis found the strength to knock out Walcott in the eleventh.

Louis: 11th round victory

THE Irish selectors took a gamble by dropping their captain Ernie Strathdee after a 13-6 victory against France in Paris on New Year's Day. They chose Karl Mullen, a 21-year-old hooker, to lead the team against England at Twickenham.

It proved an inspired choice. Mullen kicked the decisive conversion in Ireland's 11-10 win. A fortnight later he scored a try against the Scottish in a 6-0 triumph, and he crossed the Welsh tryline in a 6-3 victory on March 13 to seal Ireland's only Grand Slam.

Mullen was a superb tactician who could spot the strengths and weaknesses in both his own side and the opposition. One of the strengths under his command was Jackie Kyle, a brilliant fly-half who is regarded as one of the greatest Irish backline players of all time.

113

Don Bradman
The heart-breaking run-machine

Robin Marlar

Sir Donald Bradman was the towering cricketing figure of the twentieth century. Occasionally you hear him called, formally, Bradman, sometimes Braddles, but even his greatest friends and contemporaries are likely to refer to him as The Don, the definitive article adding appropriate respect to one whose massive achievements in cricket, and notably a Test average of 99.94, are unlikely ever to be bettered.

A fifth child of country people whose ultimate sire left Withersfield in Suffolk during the agricultural slump of the 1850s in search of gold in the hills of New South Wales, the 18-year-old Bradman arrived in Sydney from a healthy little town in the ranges 80 miles to the south-west and was soon known as the Bowral Boy. In the competitive Sydney cricket of the time he was in a big pack of promising youngsters, but two retirements and a boil on Archie Jackson's knee meant that Don Bradman as well as the great bowler Bill O'Reilly became big-time cricketers in the same season, 1927. Perhaps inevitably, he hit a century in his first game which was in Adelaide, a city which became his home but was then somewhere he had never even visited. Young players today see more of the world.

In the next season, as a 20-year-old, he played four Tests against England, hitting two centuries even though Australia were well beaten. Such vertical progress would not then, or now, have been possible in England. It is all the more remarkable in that Bradman had also to cope with the transition from matting on concrete to turf pitches. As a little fellow, 5ft 6¾ in, there was only one way he could play on the concrete — off the back foot. His runs came from cutting, hooking and pulling, all dependent on the lightning footwork that a flyweight batsman had to develop. For him these were never risky strokes but bread-and-butter shots which kept the scoreboard ticking on its unspectacular way towards three figures.

He was, too, a quick mover, the master of the short single as well as a devastating fielder at cover point. After years of practice in the back yard he had perfected his throwing, aiming at a single stump and being prepared to run after the ones that escaped. Anybody whose memories of boyhood are sharp will recognise this as a form of self-flagellation only undertaken by the highly motivated.

When he hit almost a thousand runs on his first tour of England a phenomenon was recognised and furthermore one that aroused hostility. Many pillars of English cricket at the time were tall upstanding fellows to whom the straight drive was the only authentic stroke, singles, whether short or long, a boring substitute for boundaries and little men, particularly successful ones, nothing but potential upstarts.

If that was the romanticised view of what was being talked about as the Bradman menace, the professionals concentrated on trying to discover some weakness, any weakness, that might be played upon, a nerve for the dentist's drill. Fast bowling pitched at leg stump had been seen to ruffle Bradman by several senior England players. Douglas Jardine,

England's captain on the Bodyline tour of 1932-33 which all but destroyed the British Empire, has taken most of the literary stick for not only picking a bunch of fast bowlers but also for packing the legside field. Those who knew and admired Herbert Sutcliffe, the great Yorkshire opener, for his cricketing cunning will not be surprised that Bill O'Reilly thought that Sutcliffe's was the mind which shaped the strategy.

In the previous winter Bradman had averaged over 200 against the hapless South Africans. Now he was cut to 56 as England repeated the 4-1 drubbing of Australia they had achieved four years before, but this time amid a welter of controversy as batsmen ducked and dived, not always successfully. Such results are unthinkable now. To some extent the feeling that what had been done to Bradman was ungentlemanly, unsporting and unfair, probably in that order, created a situation of shame which has deeply affected English cricket ever since.

Immediately, Bodyline bowling was effectively outlawed. Harold Larwood, the greatest of the England fast bowlers, went into decline and what he imagined to be unappreciated exile. Losing a national institution like Larwood meant that fast bowling itself was to suffer and England have mostly been short of it ever since.

There were already signs that run-making was not the only motivation for Bradman. Money-making also mattered. There were disputes with the Australian authorities over his off-the-field commitments, particularly with newspapers. To be fair to Bradman, not only has he been the best technical writer about cricket but he was also following a well-trodden path because money has always been a source of conflict in Australian cricket.

In 1934 Australia won again in England and these external issues diminished when Bradman, now established in Adelaide as a stockbroker, took on the Australian captaincy which he held until 1948 without losing the Ashes and without any diminution in his run-making.

If only his eyes had remained clear when The Oval rose and the England team gave three cheers as he arrived at the crease for his last innings he might not have missed the second, and straight ball from Eric Hollies: just one more boundary would have given him a Test average of 100.

Ever afterwards Bradman exerted an immense influence on Australian cricket as the shrewdest of selectors and a towering administrator. Indeed, his was the most influential voice in world cricket for 50 years. He it was, for instance, who destroyed a fundamental principle of the game, namely that captains should be able to put fieldsmen where they like, by successfully campaigning for restrictions to the legside field, the direct result of his own experience. That was unsupportable, in my opinion. He it was who also ignored the deep dissatisfaction with conditions among the Australian players which led to Packerism, and also to the vile habits like sledging which originated in his own state.

Years ago I asked a contemporary in the Australian side what he thought of Bradman. "As a batsman, the greatest ever. As a man I wouldn't give you that for him," and so saying he picked a spent match out of the ashtray and snapped it in his fingers. There are many who feel like that about him. To be fair, there are others in this country and in Australia who put all that down to jealousy. They could be right. Certainly, there have long been respected figures in English cricket — the late Sir Gubby Allen, once his opponent, Jim Swanton and the Bedsers — who revere Bradman.

BRADMAN'S RECORD

	FIRST-CLASS	TESTS (52)
Innings	338	80
Not out	43	10
Runs	28,067	6,996
Highest	452 not out	334
Average	95.14	99.94
Hundreds	117	29
Wickets	36 at 37.97	2 at 36.00
Catches	131	32

The greatest batsman of all time: from his earliest days, Bradman's technique was without equal, and he was as fast in the field as he was between the wickets.

JULY

1948

DECEMBER

CRICKET

England win off last ball

ENGLAND and South Africa produced one of the most exciting finishes in Test cricket. England won the first Test in Durban by two wickets when Cliff Gladwin and Alec Bedser scrambled a leg-bye off the final ball.

Len Hutton and Cyril Washbrook dominated the drawn second Test with a record opening stand of 359 in 310 minutes for England.

The South African selectors operated a quaint procedure of naming their next team midway through a Test. It backfired when they dropped Eric Rowan during the second Test. He responded by hitting a match-saving century, but their decision was irreversible.

Washbrook: record stand

FOR THE RECORD

EQUESTRIANISM

■ Officers and gentlemen were abolished. The rules were changed to leave only two showjumping categories.

RUGBY UNION

■ The value of a drop goal was reduced from four points to three.

TENNIS

■ Bob Falkenburg played an all-or-nothing point at Wimbledon. The American was 2-5 and 15-40 down to John Bromwich in the fifth set when he gambled on a daring cross-court shot. It paid off and he took the next five games and the title.

Falkenburg: great recovery

RUGBY LEAGUE

Churchill has finest hour in England

AUSTRALIANS called him The Little Master. Clive Churchill was 5ft 7in tall and weighed a mere 12 stone, but his tactical awareness, prodigious kicking and crushing tackles made him Australia's greatest rugby league full-back.

One of Churchill's finest hours was in the first Test against Great Britain at Leeds on October 9 when his performance was described as being head and shoulders above everyone else despite Great Britain's 23-21 victory.

CRICKET

Bradman's farewell spoilt by Hollies

The England team lead the cheers for Bradman

IT WAS about six o'clock on August 16 at The Oval when Australia lost their first wicket. That was the cue for the crowd to rise as one.

It was one of those sporting moments which leave a lump in the throat. Don Bradman, the batting colossus, walked to the crease for the 80th and last time in his Test career. The crowd cheered him all the way to the middle, and then some more.

Norman Yardley, the England captain, shook his hand and asked the players for three cheers. The crowd joined in and there were tears in the eyes of the Australian captain.

When everybody had settled Bradman took guard and played the first ball from Eric Hollies with familiar confidence. The Warwickshire leg-spinner kept his second ball straight. It beat the bat and dislodged the bails. Bradman turned to see his stumps shattered and quickly left the scene with a Test average of 99.94. Another boundary and he would have compiled 7,000 runs and been able to tell his grandchildren that on average he had scored a century for each time he had been out.

Thus ended the most one-sided contest in cricket. The last 508 of Bradman's Test runs were scored in a brilliant

> **❝ It's hard to bat with tears in your eyes ❞**
>
> **Don Bradman, b Hollies 0**

summer when the Australians plundered England, winning 25 of their 34 matches, 17 by an innings. Their batting was led by the peerless Bradman and supplemented by the likes of Lindsay Hassett and Arthur Morris, a left-handed opener who added 304 with his captain for the second wicket in Leeds as Australia raced to 404 in less than a day to win by seven wickets. And then there was the talented young Victorian Neil Harvey, on his first tour, the all-rounder Keith Miller and his fast bowling partner Ray Lindwall.

Miller was his enigmatic self, mixing brilliance with boredom. There was a day at Southend when Australia scored 721 against Essex and Miller, wanting no part of the massacre, threw his wicket away and went to the beach.

Lindwall bowled with fire and fury. He left his best until last when he took six for 20 at The Oval to dismiss England for 52, their lowest total this century.

Dutch star wins four golds

Blankers-Koen wins the 4x100m relay gold in 47.5sec

FRANCINA BLANKERS-KOEN found an escape from the rigours of raising two young children by going to the local track to run and jump. By the time athletes gathered in London for the 14th Olympic Games the unassuming Dutchwoman had run and jumped to world records in the 100m, 80m hurdles, high jump and long jump.

Surprisingly, she did not enter either of the jumping events at the Olympics. Instead, Fanny concentrated on the track events and won 11 races during the 17-day Olympiad from July 29 to August 14.

The 30-year-old became arguably the greatest woman athlete of the century, taking home four gold medals from the 100m, 200m, 80m hurdles and 4x100m relay. Her closest race was in the hurdles where she was a shade faster than her British rival Maureen Gardner. They were both credited with an Olympic record of 11.2sec.

She was the darling of the Dutch when she arrived home and was treated to a parade at which she simply said: "All I did was win some foot races."

Emil Zatopek also showed his talent for foot races. The Czech won the 10,000m by more than 45sec and staged a brilliant finish in the 5,000m, but was narrowly beaten by Gaston Reiff of Belgium.

Another Belgian, Etienne Gailly, was involved in a stirring finish to the marathon. The 21-year-old paratrooper led the field into the stadium only to watch Delfo Cabrera of Argentina and the Briton Tom Richards pass him on the track.

Jamaica, in their first Olympics, started with a bang. Arthur Wint, a 6ft 4in medical student with a stride of nearly 10ft, won the 400m and was second in the 800m. His teammate Herb McKenley was the runner-up in the 400m on the makeshift cinder track at Wembley Stadium.

The London Olympics were bereft of the cream of a generation who had fallen on the battlefields of the Second World War. So thin was the talent that no world records were broken in the track and field programme. They were known as the Austerity Games. Food and clothing were rationed and because of a housing shortage the athletes were accommodated in RAF barracks. The total expenditure on the Games was about £600,000.

There were 4,099 athletes from 59 countries at the opening ceremony which was broadcast by television and radio for the first time. Half a million Britons tuned in to watch. Not surprisingly, Germany and Japan were not invited.

The swimming was held indoors for the first time and the Wembley pool produced one of the greatest galas in Olympic history. One world record and eight Olympic records were broken. Britain won three gold medals, 13 silver and six bronze.

GOLF

Straight forward for Cotton

HENRY COTTON loved to play golf. He would play every day given the chance. It probably helped that he was one of the straightest hitters in the game. Cotton, though, was not a naturally gifted player. Instead, he achieved his accuracy by practising. When his fellow professionals went to the 19th hole Cotton returned to the course to master the game he loved. He was the first player to practise between tournaments and between rounds, and his hard work paid rich dividends.

Cotton won the Open at Sandwich in 1934 with a second round of 65 that gave the name to a ball, the Dunlop 65. Three years later he weathered a storm on the final day at Carnoustie to win his second Open title. And in 1948 he was at Muirfield seeking a third title.

The war had taken its toll on Cotton and he was released from the RAF with ulcers and a burst appendix. Nothing, though, was able to could keep him off the golf course for long and he returned to his best on the narrow fairways.

There was little doubt Cotton would win once he had taken his driver out of the bag and hit the ball straight down the middle of the first fairway. Cotton hit 56 drives in 72 holes and missed the fairway only four times. His accuracy prompted Bob Toski, a fellow professional, to say: "You couldn't tell whether Cotton was in the right or left side of the fairway because his ball was so close to the middle."

The 41-year-old's most majestic golf was played in the second round when he scored 66 in the presence of the King. The round provided the foundation for his five-shot win and a third Open title.

The most dominant British player since the First World War donated the bag of clubs he used to the PGA. But after his victory he began to struggle with his putting and several years later he reclaimed his putter.

Cotton: third Open title

FOOTBALL

Swift swaps gloves for a pen

FRANK SWIFT, who for two decades had been Manchester City's goalkeeper and one of the country's finest men between the posts, finally took off his jersey, hung up his gloves and turned his attention instead to writing about the game for the Manchester Evening News.

Swift, born in Blackpool on Boxing Day in 1913, had enjoyed great success at City, the only League club he ever played for. He helped them win the FA Cup in 1934, their first League championship in 1937 and the Second Division in 1947.

After the war he automatically became England's goalkeeper and won 19 caps, two of them as captain, and conceded only 18 goals. His last international was in May in Norway when England won 4-1.

Swift was a genial giant with huge hands frequently referred to as frying pans. He was also hugely popular as a goalkeeper and was a great crowd puller. Big Swifty also delighted in being a mischievous showman. He could be a wicked humorist as he was blessed with a wonderful talent for mimicry.

During the war he had been a special constable in Manchester. He was fond of telling the tale of his first day of traffic duty: "I got everything so muddled that, on the advice of a colleague, I walked away leaving the traffic to sort itself out. I felt at that moment how many full-backs must have felt when playing against Stanley Matthews."

RACING

Nimbus always in the frame

RACING had suffered many arguments about close finishes down the years, so photo-finish equipment had been introduced.

The first two classics to be decided by a photo were both won by the same horse, Nimbus — who just got the verdict in the 2,000 Guineas and the Derby.

One man went to his grave thinking otherwise. Leon Volterra owned Amour Drake, who was beaten by a head in the Derby. Volterra was on his deathbed in France, so his wife told him that Amour Drake had won. He died of a heart attack the next day, a happy man.

Nimbus just gets the verdict in the Derby

FOOTBALL

Rangers win the first Treble

RANGERS won the Scottish League and Cup and achieved the first Treble by winning the fledgling League Cup as well. They won the championship by one point from Dundee; beat Clyde 4-1 in the Scottish Cup and Raith Rovers 2-0 in the Scottish League Cup.

Rangers' success stemmed from their impenetrable defence, called in Cold War rhetoric the "Iron Curtain". The club had two formidable centre-halves, Willie Woodburn and George

Young, and also ferocious tacklers like Sammy Cox and Jock Shaw.

Understandably most opposing teams did not relish playing Rangers. But there was a creative dimension to this historic side that was not always given the credit it was due. In Willie Waddell they possessed a skilful and entertaining winger who also scored goals, and in tandem with Willie Thornton, the two wreaked havoc on opposing defences.

Shaw clutches the Scottish Cup

RUGBY LEAGUE

Bradford beat local rivals

A RECORD crowd of 95,050 turned up at Wembley to watch Bradford Northern beat their local rivals Halifax 12-0 in the Challenge Cup final. Bradford Northern were the first team to reach Wembley on three successive occasions.

One of their biggest assets was the 18 stone prop Frank Whitcombe, whose excellent speed had helped him earn the Man of the Match award the previous year despite his team's 8-3 loss to Wigan. Most of their inspiration, however, came from Eric Batten who played in eight Challenge Cup finals and was the third highest all-time tryscorer behind Brian Bevan and Billy Boston with 446 tries.

FOR THE RECORD

BADMINTON
■ The first Thomas Cup was won by Malaya.
■ Bill Carlton produced plastic shuttles to replace feathered ones.

CRICKET
■ Don Bradman was knighted.

FOOTBALL
■ Hull City, inspired by their player-manager Raich Carter, won the Third Division North.
■ Stanley Rous, the FA secretary, was knighted for services to football.

GOLF
■ Cary Middlecoff and Lloyd Mangrum were declared co-winners after 11 holes of a sudden-death play-off for the Motor City Open. It was the longest sudden-death play-off in the history of the US PGA tour.

Locke opens up whole new ball game

FOR 76 years the silver claret jug presented to the winner of the Open had been the exclusive property of British and American golfers. In 1949 tenure was transferred to two colonials for the next decade. Bobby Locke of South Africa and Peter Thomson of Australia won the championship eight times in 10 years.

Locke was the first to get his hands on the trophy with a victory at Sandwich that was achieved with one of the most inelegant swings in golf. His long, lazy swing with floppy wrists was no advertisement for a golf manual. The result was that he had to aim well to the right, and with a mixture of a hook and a draw he uncannily landed the ball on the fairway.

Locke's forte, though, was his short game, including his brilliance with a discoloured putting blade that he had acquired at the age of 18 and played with throughout his career.

> **'That son of a bitch Locke was able to hole a putt over 60 feet of peanut brittle'**
>
> **Lloyd Mangrum**

Sam Snead learned about Locke's putting ability during a 16-match series in South Africa in 1946-47. The American was surprised that Locke never seemed concerned where the flag had been positioned. He simply landed on the green, holed the putt and won the series 12-2.

Locke, like most of the players of his era, had his career interrupted by the war. He spent his war years flying Liberator bombers in more than 100 missions over the Mediterranean, did not touch a golf club for 2½ years and added four stone to his 10-stone frame. He adapted his game to his greater bulk after the war and made two successful and lucrative raids into America, where his impassive expression earned him the nickname Muffin Face.

He needed all his guile and patience to win his first Open. His charge in the final round appeared to be over when he uncharacteristically three-putted at the 16th. But a three at the 17th and a four at the 18th forced a play-off against the Irishman Harry Bradshaw, and with rounds of 67 and 68 Locke won by 12 strokes.

Golfing lore has it that Bradshaw lost the Open because

> **' Bobby Locke was a golfer with an amazingly even temperament. He did everything quietly and in slow motion '**
>
> **Peter Thomson**

he had to hit his ball out of a beer bottle. In fact, he had the misfortune of landing next to a piece of broken glass at the fifth hole during the second round. He believed he was entitled to a free drop but was unsure so he hit the ball where it lay. A piece of glass hit his eye but did not hurt him and the ball flew only 15 yards. Bradshaw dropped two shots at the hole and his round of 77 was the rotten apple in scores of 68, 77, 68 and 70.

Locke: brilliant short game

Louis retires at the top

JOE LOUIS, the heavyweight champion of the world, and a man who graced his sport with excellence and dignity for 15 years, finally decided to quit the ring on March 1.

17 killed in Torino crash

AN AEROPLANE carrying the Italian champions, Torino, which included eight current Italian internationals, crashed on a hill above the town of Superga in May and all 17 players perished. Torino, who were returning from a tour in Portugal, were in the process of winning their fifth successive League championship.

Secret diet sinks Sunderland

SOUTHERN League Yeovil became the giantkillers of all time when the First Division Sunderland — including England internationals Len Shackleton and Willie Watson — were felled on the famous sloping pitch in Somerset in the Fourth Round of the FA Cup on January 29.

The 2-1 victory was masterminded by their player-manager Alec Stock, who, to add spice to the occasion, scored Yeovil's first goal. Stock's, and Yeovil's, secret was their training diet: glucose, eggs and sherry.

This had taken them through one qualifying round and four others. But the Fifth Round draw threw up not another sweet home tie but a sour visit to Maine Road and a match against the Cup-holders, Manchester United.

Dyke saves for Yeovil under pressure from Sunderland

More than 81,000 spectators crammed into the stadium, with thousands left outside, hoping to see the impossible happen. West Country dreams died in the fifth minute as Jack Rowley scored the first of his five goals as Manchester United won 8-0.

MOTOR CYCLING

Graham: 500c champion

FOR THE RECORD

MODERN PENTATHLON
■ Sweden won the first world championship. Tage Bjurefelt won the individual title.

MOTOR CYCLING
■ Leslie Graham of Britain, riding an AJS, won the first world 500cc championship. His countryman Freddie Frith won the 350cc title and the Italians Bruno Ruffo and Nello Pagani won the 250cc and 125cc classes respectively. Eric Oliver of Britain was crowned the sidecar champion.

RUGBY UNION
■ Australia beat New Zealand 16-9 in Auckland on September 24 to take home the Bledisloe Cup for the first time. Three weeks before they had beaten the All Blacks 11-6 in Wellington.

VOLLEYBALL
■ The Soviet Union won the first world championship, which was held in Prague.

WATER-SKIING
■ Christian Jourdan of France and Guy de Clercq of Belgium shared the title in the first world championship, held at Juan Les Pins in France.

TENNIS

Moran catches world's eye

LOUISE BROUGH epitomised the superiority of American women in tennis in the post-war era.

The tall, blonde right-hander possessed a powerful serve and superb volley which won her the triple crown at Wimbledon in 1948. She seemed likely to repeat the feat the following year when she beat Margaret duPont 10-8 1-6 10-8 in the singles final and then teamed up with duPont to win the doubles 8-6 7-5. But in the dusk on the last Saturday of the championships Brough and John Bromwich lost the mixed final to Eric Sturgess and Sheila Summers 9-7 9-11 7-5.

Brough had played 117 games in 5hr 20min, but she failed to capture the headlines. Instead, a petite, pretty Californian called Gussy Moran put on a pair of lace panties under a short ballerina skirt and distracted the attention of the world's press. Gorgeous Gussy's outfit had been created by Ted Tinling, an assistant in the referee's office at Wimbledon, and it certainly blew up a storm.

Photographers scrambled to shoot a picture of the barely visible panties under Moran's dress and the All-England Club committee accused Tinling of "drawing attention to the sexual area". He resigned after 35 years at the club and became the best-known designer of women's tennis wear.

Tinling and Gorgeous Gussy had brought into focus the ever-widening rift between the amateur establishment and the players, who were seeking a more professional approach to their sport.

THE WIMBLEDON CATWALK

1905 May Sutton wore a short skirt, permitted because she was still in her teens.

1919 Suzanne Lenglen wore a one-piece, flimsy cotton frock with no petticoat or corset.

1920 Suzanne Lenglen wore a colourful silk chiffon bandeau.

1927 Billie Tapscott did not wear stockings.

1929 Lili de Alvarez wore a trouser dress.

1931 Joan Lycett played on Centre Court without stockings.

1932 Helen Jacobs wore a short-sleeved shirt and Bermuda shorts.

1939 Alice Marble wore a T-shirt and shorts.

1947 Joy Gannon and Betty Hilton wore coloured trims.

1949 Gussy Moran wore lace panties.

1950 Maria Weiss wore a lace dress and Pat Ward a nylon dress.

1963 The committee ruled that dress should be "predominantly white throughout". Maria Bueno wore purple and green panties, the colours of the All-England Club.

1985 Anne White wore an all-white catsuit because she claimed it was too cold for normal attire. She was asked not to wear it again.

Moran: ballerina skirt

CRICKET

Youth has his fling but fails the test

ENGLAND'S selectors opted for youth in their bid to achieve a result against New Zealand in the third Test at Old Trafford.

So Brian Close was called up at the age of 18 years and 149 days. But England's youngest-ever Test player had a disappointing debut. He was dismissed for a duck in his only innings and took just one wicket. Not unexpectedly, he was discarded for the next Test.

All four matches were drawn despite the efforts of the England captain George Mann to force a result in the second Test at Lord's. He declared on the opening day after England had scored 313 for nine. They were the last three-day Tests played in England.

Close: only one wicket

Lucky Ted leads charmed life

Schroeder beats Jaroslav Drobny in five sets in the final

TED SCHROEDER, a pipe-smoking Californian, lived a charmed fortnight at Wimbledon. He lost eight sets and 119 games and still won the men's singles title in his only appearance at the All-England Club.

Schroeder was called Lucky Ted because of his penchant for coming out on top when all seemed lost. His luckiest escape was when he was match point down against Frank Sedgman in the quarter-finals. The ball hit the frame of his racket and scraped over the net for a winning volley. He was not as fortunate in a marathon United States Open final against Pancho Gonzales later in the year, losing 16-18 2-6 6-1 6-2 6-4.

Fangio makes a mark in Europe

Fangio: invited to join Alfa Romeo next season

A STAR was born. The Argentinian driver Juan Manuel Fangio took the European circuit by storm in his first season.

Some European drivers had raced against him in South America and were impressed. But most knew next to nothing of his ability, and others were sceptical that he would be able to adapt to the different demands of European tracks and European cars.

Fangio soon showed his South American success was no flash in the pan. Driving a Maserati he won races in San Remo, Pau, Perpignan, Marseilles, Autodrome and Albi. On the strength of these victories Fangio was invited to join Alfa Romeo for the next season.

Beef survives a Yorkshire pudding

BOB HUDSON, the benevolent Oregon fruit packer who had sent the British Ryder Cup team Christmas food hampers in 1947, arrived at Southampton with a strong American team and $1,349 of prime beef.

The team had an easier time getting to Ganton in Yorkshire than the meat. Customs officials demanded an import licence from Hudson and it took a great deal of persuasion before the British team could tuck into their latest gift.

The hosts won the foursomes 3-1 but could not sustain their form in the singles against a determined comeback by the American team led by Dutch Harrison. He started with five threes in a row and beat Max Faulkner 8 and 7. The Americans won 7-5.

Cleveland success puts paid to league

THE National Football League became even stronger when it merged with the All America Football Conference. The AAFC started as a rival organisation in 1946, when the end of the war created a surfeit of players. Many cities were keen to have their own teams, and at first the AAFC prospered because it offered much higher pay.

But it suffered because the Cleveland Browns were too good — in four seasons they won 47 of their 54 games. Attendances declined because the AAFC was so one-sided, and rising costs forced the merger. The only teams that survived were the Browns, the San Francisco 49ers, the Baltimore Colts and the New York Yankees who, as the Brooklyn Dodgers, had defected from the NFL in 1946.

England dismiss home rule

ENGLAND lost their first home international to non-British opposition on September 21 when they were beaten 2-0 by Eire at Goodison Park. It was something of a shock as England had won all of their previous 14 home internationals against foreign opposition.

It was, coincidentally, the first time that Eire had played in the United Kingdom. However, as nine of the Eire team played in the Football League, they were not regarded as "foreign" opponents and this setback was not widely recognised as ending England's unbeaten record.

1950s

Paradise Lost, and Partially Regained

The second half of the century opened in a mood of complacent optimism. The post-war euphoria had produced a boom in attendances at sports events that dwarfed all previous records. In the football season of 1949-50 over 40 million spectators poured through the turnstiles, more than twice today's figure. All spectator sports enjoyed similar popularity, as did the cinema, the theatre, dance halls and restaurants. But the boom was a false dawn: never again would the 40 million peak ever be scaled by football, and never again would the entertainment industry enjoy such easy pickings.

The British public, starved of opportunities to go out and enjoy themselves for the long, hard years of the Second World War, initially flocked to anything that was put on. But as the 1950s wore on the novelty of live entertainment, and their patience, grew thin. The fare they were offered was the same as in the 1930s, and in the same decrepit halls and stadiums.

This was not what they had fought a world war for. It did not live up to the Labour party slogan, A Home Fit for Heroes, that had so staggeringly won them the 1945 election. The Labour government had overseen major social reforms, notably in health, housing and education, but sports bodies seemed to have done little, if anything.

It was a marvellous opportunity that was not grasped, a chance to build from the ashes and for the future. Instead, sport stayed firmly rooted in the past and paid the price. By the middle of the decade all sports were in crisis as attendances plummeted. Complacency had allowed them to fritter away their brief boom. Dogmatism now prevented them from dealing with the crisis. Far from adapting to the changing times, they dug in their heels and rejected all new thinking.

Thus, football opposed floodlighting at grounds, English clubs entering the newly-created European Cup and the scrapping of the regionalised Third Divisions for a straightforward Third and Fourth Division. Cricket set up a committee which recommended a form of one-day game. The proposal was shelved. Sport sat on its hands.

In time, all these changes would come, but not because of the men that ran sport in Britain. Manchester United, under the far-sighted Matt Busby, did defy the Football League and enter the European Cup. Television, still a novelty, would change cricket, and other sports, irrevocably. Apparently minor decisions would also play their part in ringing in the new. As the 1950s ended a quiet revolution was happening at Second Division Liverpool as they gambled on a new manager and appointed Bill Shankly. Some, it seemed, instinctively knew what was needed.

Essentially, though, it was a decade of opportunities missed, a decade when inaction would inevitably lead to sport losing power over its own destiny. Men of the past ruled and only survived because the men of the present delivered in the sporting arena. Their prowess, in turn, laid the basis for a renaissance.

There were some glorious achievements by those who seized their time. Juan Manuel Fangio took motor racing's newly created Formula One world championship by the scruff of the neck and won it five times. Rocky Marciano became the first, and only, world heavyweight champion to retire undefeated after 49 bouts. Emil Zatopek, the greatest distance runner of any generation, achieved a unique treble at the 1952 Olympics, winning gold medals at the 5,000m, the 10,000m and the marathon. That will almost certainly never be equalled.

The West Indies arrived in 1950 without ever having won a Test in England, and with two untried 20-year-old spinners, Sonny Ramadhin and Alfred Valentine. They shattered England 3-1. Three West Indian batsmen, all from Barbados, all Ws, Frank Worrell, Clyde Walcott and Everton Weekes scored nearly 6,000 runs between them on the tour and delighted those who watched. West Indian cricket had come of age.

Two precocious talents made dramatic entrances on to their respective world sporting stages, and to this day they can still steal the show. In 1951 a 15-year-old Lester Piggott was second in the Derby, having ridden his first winner when he was 12. In 1958 Edson Arantes do Nascimento, the 17-year-old Pele, helped Brazil to a World Cup final victory in Sweden that was marked by his virtuosity and Brazil's exhilarating attacking flair. Not to mention Pele's six goals in the last three games, including two in the final.

So even as sport's administrators were first frittering away a golden opportunity, and then twiddling their thumbs as the roof was caving in, the foundations for the future were being built by the people who make sport one of the most powerful cultural forces in the world: the practitioners.

When Roger Bannister broke four minutes for the mile in Oxford in 1954 he set down a marker that said there is no barrier to human achievement. But, also, he sparked off a belief in British athletics that eventually spawned the golden age of British middle distance running a generation later with Sebastian Coe, Steve Ovett and Steve Cram.

Another who profoundly influenced the direction of his sport was Stirling Moss. He won a record 16 Grands Prix but never motor racing's world championship. Heartbreakingly, Moss was second four times, but his bravery and determination to succeed, despite living in the shadow of Fangio, captured the imagination of everybody.

To this day, taxi drivers on British roads still crack the old chestnut: "Who do you think you are, Stirling Moss?" Television even cashed in by making an advert based on the joke, complete with Moss as the recipient of the question. Was it a coincidence that the world championship was then won six times by Britons in the 1960s?

If the 1950s were Paradise Lost, they were also Paradise Partially Regained. Because brilliant champions emerged, and there were sterling victories to enjoy and dismal defeats to mull over, sport hung on to its status and its audience by a fingernail. But there was much to be done to halt the slide, and no evidence that there was anybody prepared, or able, to do anything about it. However, other social forces were gathering, and in the next decade they would be unleashed.

ATHLETICS

British Olympic gold medals
1956 *3,000m steeplechase* Chris Brasher

BASEBALL

World Series
1950 New York Yankees
1951 New York Yankees
1952 New York Yankees
1953 New York Yankees
1954 New York Giants
1955 Brooklyn Dodgers
1956 New York Yankees
1957 Milwaukee Braves
1958 New York Yankees
1959 Los Angeles Dodgers

BOXING

British world champions
1950 *Flyweight.* Terry Allen
1951 *Middleweight.*
Randolph Turpin

CRICKET

County championship
1950 Lancashire and Surrey
1951 Warwickshire
1952 Surrey
1953 Surrey
1954 Surrey
1955 Surrey
1956 Surrey
1957 Surrey
1958 Surrey
1959 Yorkshire

CYCLING

Tour de France
1950 Ferdinand Kubler
1951 Hugo Koblet
1952 Fausto Coppi
1953 Louison Bobet
1954 Louison Bobet
1955 Louison Bobet
1956 Roger Walkowiak
1957 Jacques Anquetil
1958 Charly Gaul
1959 Federico Bahamontes

FOOTBALL

World Cup
1950 Uruguay 2 Brazil 1

1954 West Germany 3 Hungary 2
1958 Brazil 5 Sweden 2
European Cup
1956 Real Madrid 4 Reims 3
1957 Real Madrid 2 Fiorentina 0
1958 Real Madrid 3 AC Milan 2 (aet)
1959 Real Madrid 2 Reims 0
Fairs Cup
1958 Barcelona *bt* London 2-2 6-0
Football League
1950 Portsmouth
1951 Tottenham
1952 Manchester Utd
1953 Arsenal
1954 Wolverhampton
1955 Chelsea
1956 Manchester Utd
1957 Manchester Utd
1958 Wolverhampton
1959 Wolverhampton
FA Cup
1950 Arsenal 2 Liverpool 0
1951 Newcastle 2 Blackpool 0
1952 Newcastle 1 Arsenal 0
1953 Blackpool 4 Bolton 3
1954 West Bromwich 3 Preston 2
1955 Newcastle 3 Manchester City 1
1956 Manchester City 3 Birmingham 1
1957 Aston Villa 2 Manchester Utd 1
1958 Bolton 2 Manchester Utd 0
1959 Nottingham Forest 2 Luton 1
Scottish League
1950 Rangers
1951 Hibernian
1952 Hibernian
1953 Rangers
1954 Celtic
1955 Aberdeen
1956 Rangers
1957 Rangers
1958 Hearts
1959 Rangers
Scottish Cup
1950 Rangers 3 East Fife 0

1951 Celtic 1 Motherwell 0
1952 Motherwell 4 Dundee 0
1953 Rangers 1 Aberdeen 0 (after 1-1)
1954 Celtic 2 Aberdeen 1
1955 Clyde 1 Celtic 0 (after 1-1)
1956 Hearts 3 Celtic 1
1957 Falkirk 2 Kilmarnock 1 (after 1-1)
1958 Clyde 1 Hibernian 0
1959 St Mirren 3 Aberdeen 1
Scottish League Cup
1950 East Fife 3 Dunfermline 0
1951 Motherwell 3 Hibernian 0
1952 Dundee 3 Rangers 2
1953 Dundee 2 Kilmarnock 0
1954 East Fife 3 Partrick 2
1955 Hearts 4 Motherwell 2
1956 Aberdeen 2 St Mirren 1
1957 Celtic 3 Partrick 0 (after 0-0)
1958 Celtic 7 Rangers 1
1959 Hearts 5 Partick 1

GOLF

The Open
1950 Bobby Locke
1951 Max Faulkner
1952 Bobby Locke
1953 Ben Hogan
1954 Peter Thomson
1955 Peter Thomson
1956 Peter Thomson
1957 Bobby Locke
1958 Peter Thomson
1959 Gary Player
US Open
1950 Ben Hogan
1951 Ben Hogan
1952 Julius Boros
1953 Ben Hogan
1954 Ed Furgol
1955 Jack Fleck
1956 Cary Middlecoff
1957 Dick Mayer
1958 Tommy Bolt
1959 Billy Casper
US PGA
1950 Chandler Harper
1951 Sam Snead
1952 Jim Turnesa
1953 Walter Burkemo
1954 Chick Harbert

1955 Doug Ford
1956 Jack Burke Jnr
1957 Lionel Herbert
1958 Dow Finsterwald
1959 Bob Rosburg
US Masters
1950 Jimmy Demaret
1951 Ben Hogan
1952 Sam Snead
1953 Ben Hogan
1954 Sam Snead
1955 Cary Middlecoff
1956 Jack Burke Jnr
1957 Doug Ford
1958 Arnold Palmer
1959 Art Wall Jnr
Ryder Cup
1951 United States 9½-2½
1953 United States 6½-5½
1955 United States 8½-4½
1957 Great Britain & Ireland 7½-4½
1959 United States 8½-3½

MOTOR RACING

World championship
1950 Giuseppe Farina (Alfa Romeo)
1951 Juan Manuel Fangio (Alfa Romeo)
1952 Alberto Ascari (Ferrari)
1953 Alberto Ascari (Ferrari)
1954 Juan Manuel Fangio (Maserati/Mercedes)
1955 Juan Manuel Fangio (Mercedes-Benz)
1956 Juan Manuel Fangio (Lancia-Ferrari)
1957 Juan Manuel Fangio (Maserati)
1958 Mike Hawthorn (Ferrari)
1959 Jack Brabham (Cooper-Climax)

RACING

The Derby
1950 Galcador
1951 Arctic Prince
1952 Tulyar
1953 Pinza
1954 Never Say Die
1955 Phil Drake
1956 Lavandin
1957 Crepello
1958 Hard Ridden

1959 Parthia
Grand National
1950 Freebooter
1951 Nickel Coin
1952 Teal
1953 Early Mist
1954 Royal Tan
1955 Quare Times
1956 E.S.B.
1957 Sundew
1958 Mr What
1959 Oxo

ROWING

Boat Race
1950 Cambridge
1951 Cambridge
1952 Oxford
1953 Cambridge
1954 Cambridge
1955 Cambridge
1956 Cambridge
1957 Cambridge
1958 Cambridge
1959 Oxford

RUGBY LEAGUE

Challenge Cup
1950 Warrington 19 Widnes 0
1951 Wigan 10 Barrow 0
1952 Workington 18 Featherstone 10
1953 Huddersfield 15 St Helens 10
1954 Warrington 8 Halifax 4 (after 4-4)
1955 Barrow 21 Workington 12
1956 St Helens 13 Halifax 2
1957 Leeds 9 Barrow 7
1958 Wigan 13 Workington 9
1959 Wigan 30 Hull 13

RUGBY UNION

Five Nations championship
1950 Wales
1951 Ireland
1952 Wales
1953 England
1954 England, Wales and France
1955 Wales and France
1956 Wales
1957 England
1958 England
1959 France

SAILING

America's Cup
1958 Columbia (US, Briggs Cunningham)
Admiral's Cup
1957 Great Britain
1959 Great Britain

SNOOKER

World championship
1950 Walter Donaldson 51 Fred Davis 46
1951 Fred Davis 58 Walter Donaldson 39
1952 Horace Lindrum 94 Clark McConachy 49; Fred Davis 38 Walter Donaldson 35
1953 Fred Davis 37 Walter Donaldson 34
1954 Fred Davis 39 Walter Donaldson 21
1955 Fred Davis 37 John Pulman 34
1956 Fred Davis 38 John Pulman 35
1957 John Pulman 39 Jackie Rea 34

TENNIS

Wimbledon
1950 Budge Patty *bt* Frank Sedgman; Louise Brough *bt* Margaret du Pont
1951 Dick Savitt *bt* Ken McGregor; Doris Hart *bt* Shirley Fry
1952 Frank Sedgman *bt* Jaroslav Drobny; Maureen Connolly *bt* Doris Hart
1953 Vic Seixas *bt* Kurt Nielsen; Maureen Connolly *bt* Doris Hart
1954 Jaroslav Drobny *bt* Ken Rosewall; Maureen Connolly *bt* Louise Brough
1955 Tony Trabert *bt* Kurt Nielsen; Louise Brough *bt* Beverly Fleitz
1956 Lew Hoad *bt* Ken Rosewall; Shirley Fry *bt* Angela Buxton
1957 Lew Hoad *bt* Ashley Cooper; Althea Gibson *bt* Darlene Hard
1958 Ashley Cooper *bt* Neale Fraser; Althea Gibson *bt* Angela Mortimer
1959 Alex Olmedo *bt* Rod Laver; Maria Bueno *bt* Sandra Reynolds

Australian championship
1950 Frank Sedgman; Louise Brough
1951 Richard Savitt; Nancye Wynne
1952 Ken McGregor; Thelma Long
1953 Ken Rosewall; Maureen Connolly
1954 Mervyn Rose; Thelma Long
1955 Ken Rosewall; Beryl Pemrose
1956 Lew Hoad; Mary Carter
1957 Ashley Cooper; Shirley Fry
1958 Ashley Cooper; Angela Mortimer
1959 Alex Olmedo; Mary Reitano
French championship
1950 Budge Patty; Doris Hart
1951 Jaroslav Drobny; Shirley Fry
1952 Jaroslav Drobny; Doris Hart
1953 Ken Rosewall; Maureen Connolly
1954 Tony Trabert; Maureen Connolly
1955 Tony Trabert; Angela Mortimer
1956 Lew Hoad; Althea Gibson
1957 Sven Davidson; Shirley Bloomer
1958 Mervyn Rose; Zsuzsi Kormoczy
1959 Nicola Pietrangeli; Christine Truman
US championship
1950 Arthur Larsen; Margaret du Pont
1951 Frank Sedgman; Maureen Connolly
1952 Frank Sedgman; Maureen Connolly
1953 Tony Trabert; Maureen Connolly
1954 Vic Seixas; Doris Hart
1955 Tony Trabert; Doris Hart
1956 Ken Rosewall; Shirley Fry
1957 Mal Anderson; Althea Gibson
1958 Ashley Cooper; Althea Gibson
1959 Neale Fraser; Maria Bueno

Young pretender: Piggott won his first race at 12

Old master: Fangio was the world champion five times

Hogan makes an amazing recovery

BEN HOGAN, riding on a wave of emotion, won the 50th US Open after a play-off at Merion, near Philadelphia. Hogan had nearly been killed on February 2 the previous year when a bus hit his new Cadillac. Many thought he would never walk again, but he made a remarkable recovery and within a year had returned, losing a play-off to Sam Snead in the Los Angeles Open.

Hogan struggled to stay on his feet in the final round at Merion but returned the next day to shoot 69 and beat Lloyd Mangrum and George Fazio in the 18-hole play-off. Mangrum, who scored 73, was penalised two strokes at the 15th for illegally cleaning his ball when he blew a fly off it.

Hogan: wins play-off

FOOTBALL

Americans shame England

The victorious United States team

ENGLAND experienced one of the most humiliating defeats in their history when they were beaten 1-0 by the United States on June 29 in the fourth World Cup in Brazil.

England had begun the tournament as one of the favourites, and with Stanley Matthews, Stan Mortensen, Tom Finney, Alf Ramsey, Wilf Mannion and Billy Wright in their team the expectations seemed justified.

England were so confident of victory at Belo Horizonte that they did not even bother picking Matthews and treated the game as a practice match. For the first 40 minutes England spent most of the time in the American half, hitting the post and shooting over the bar. It seemed that a deluge of goals was inevitable.

But with eight minutes to go before half-time Walter Bahr shot from the left. Bert

> **Bloody ridiculous. Can't we play them again tomorrow?**
>
> **Wilf Mannion**

Williams, the England goalkeeper, appeared to have the ball covered when the Haitian Larry Gaetjens deflected it with his head into the net. It has never been resolved whether he headed it or whether the ball hit him. But a goal it was and no matter how hard England fought for the equaliser (they hit the bar or post 11 times, should have had a penalty, and had 90% of the play) it was the only goal of the game.

Perhaps England should have imitated Scotland and stayed at

home. Fifa had designated the Home championship as a World Cup qualifying group with the top two teams going to Brazil. But the Scottish said they would only compete if they won the championship. When they came second to England they stubbornly refused to participate.

Brazil, the hosts, were convinced they would win the World Cup and, given their fanatical supporters and a competition structure that overwhelmingly favoured them, few doubted they would be the holders of the Jules Rimet trophy.

For the first time a World Cup was organised in pools with no actual final scheduled. As luck would have it, the last match became, in effect, the final — Brazil versus their arch-rivals and neighbours Uruguay.

On July 16 a world record 199,854 spectators poured into the Maracana convinced of victory. But Brazil paid dearly for their over-confidence. Despite facing a constant barrage on their goal the Uruguayan defence held with majestic composure.

Two minutes into the second half Brazil did score, but Friaca's goal was too late. The Uruguayans had realised their opponents were mortal. After 20 minutes Schiaffino equalised with a thunderous shot, and with 16 minutes left Ghiggia grabbed the goal that brought the World Cup back to Montevideo after 20 years.

RUGBY UNION

Transformed Lions switch on the style

THE Five Nations championship had become a staid, unattractive competition with an emphasis on winning. So when the British Lions toured Australasia they proved a revelation. They shed the win at all costs policy and became an attractive and popular side.

Karl Mullen's squad of 30 players and one late replacement

was the first fully representative Lions team and their entire cast were international players. They were also the first Lions party not dominated by Englishmen; there were 13 Welshmen from the Grand Slam team.

However, the tourists had little answer to the New Zealand forwards and the hosts won three of the four Tests after

drawing the first 9-9 in Dunedin on May 27.

The running skills of Jackie Kyle, Ken Jones and Bleddyn Williams made the Lions a spectacular side. They averaged 18 points a game in New Zealand and 25 points a game in Australia. The highlights of the tour were 19-6 and 24-3 victories against the Wallabies.

Spirited Compton bows out with Cup

DENIS COMPTON ended his career as an Arsenal footballer with the perfect send-off: an FA Cup winner's medal. The England cricketer and left-winger also laid on the decisive goal in the 63rd minute with an accurate and long centre for Reg Lewis. The 32-year-old Compton had appeared to be thoroughly exhausted by half-time, but a stiff brandy during the interval worked wonders.

A heavy shower just before the kick-off made conditions difficult and Liverpool seemed to be the team best adapting to the pitch. But in the 17th minute a wonderfully measured pass from Peter Goring split their defence to give Lewis a perfunctory goal.

Although Liverpool hit the bar, from then on Arsenal out-played and out-thought them in a runaway 2-0 victory. Liverpool had made one change from the team that thrillingly beat Everton in the semi-final, and one they may have regretted. Bob Paisley, who had scored the second goal in their 2-0 triumph over their Merseyside rivals, was dropped for Laurie Hughes.

For Compton, who first played for Arsenal in 1932, it was another footballing triumph to add to his exploits on the cricket field. During the war Compton played 12 times for the England football team, including the 8-0 destruction of Scotland in 1943. How sad it was that the war interrupted the full flowering of this talented all-rounder and that a serious knee injury, received when playing football, curtailed both his careers.

Compton (front, far right) and the victorious team

Pompey just take second title thanks to Dickinson and Scoular

PORTSMOUTH, who had won the League the previous year without a single home defeat and had finished five points ahead of the field, captured the title again — but on goal average from Wolves. Once again the famous Fratton Park chant "Play up Pompey, play up" inspired a team not obviously blessed with outstanding talents to play above themselves match after match.

The midfield pair of Jimmy Dickinson at left-half and Jimmy Scoular at right-half was a formidable combination. Dickinson, a loyal one-club man, provided guile and artistry with Scoular adding power and passion.

Wales learn art of winning Grand Slam

Wales score the decisive try at Twickenham

HAYDN TANNER had given the Welsh selectors five months to find his successor as captain when he announced his retirement as one of the principality's greatest scrum-halves in August 1949. They settled on Bleddyn Williams to lead the side against England at Twickenham on January 21.

But the day before the match Williams withdrew with an injury and the captaincy was handed to John Gwilliam, a schoolmaster who was irritating rather than inspirational, treating his players in the same manner as his pupils.

Wales dominated the match and their 11-5 victory in front of a crowd of 75,532 was only the second Welsh win at Twickenham. Gwilliam gave his teammates scant praise for their performance and a fortnight later they were determined to impress him, beating Scotland 12-0. It was to no avail. But the captain did show his approval when Malcolm Thomas scored a try with two minutes remaining in a 6-3 victory against Ireland in Belfast.

Sadly, the celebrations of Wales's first Triple Crown since 1911 were tempered with the news that nearly 80 supporters died when the plane carrying them back from the match crashed.

Two weeks later Wales wrapped up the Grand Slam by thumping France 21-0 in Cardiff. It was the start of a remarkable decade. Their record in the championship was first, third, first, second, first, first, first, second, second and second.

FOR THE RECORD

BASKETBALL
■ The first men's world championship was won by Argentina in Buenos Aires.

CRICKET
■ Australia, needing 336 in 435 minutes to beat South Africa, won by five wickets thanks to Neil Harvey, who scored an unbeaten 151 in 5½ hours.

CYCLOCROSS
■ The Frenchman Jean Robic, the first post-war winner of the Tour de France in 1947, won the inaugural world championship.

FOOTBALL
■ John Charles, the Leeds United centre-half, became the youngest international for Wales when he played against Northern Ireland at the age of 18 years and 71 days.

ICE HOCKEY
■ The World and European championships were held in London. Britain, without the benefit of dual national players, were the European runners-up.

FOR THE RECORD

CYCLING
■ The Swiss rider Hugo Koblet became the first non-Italian to win the Giro d'Italia.

FOOTBALL
■ Scotland were beaten 1-0 by Austria at Hampden, the first time they lost at home to opponents from outside of the British Isles.

■ Two clubs were added to each of the regionalised Third Divisions.

■ The pools produced the first £100,000 winner.

GOLF
■ Bobby Locke lowered the record aggregate for the Open to 279 at Troon.

RACING
■ Lord Mildmay of Flete, the leading amateur rider who introduced the Queen and Princess Elizabeth to National Hunt racing, vanished while swimming in the River Yealm near his home in Devon.

MOTOR RACING

Farina wins his first world title

Alberto Ascari (Ferrari) finished fifth in the championship

THE first world championship began on May 13 at Silverstone when the Turin doctor Giuseppe Farina swept home to take the inaugural Formula One Grand Prix in an Alfa Romeo. The two other Alfa Romeos were second and third.

Farina, aged 44, went on to win the Swiss and Italian GPs and the world title in the seven-race championship. Close behind him though, was the new star on the horizon: the incredible Argentinian Juan Manuel Fangio, who although 39 also won three GPs to finish second.

Farina had been in motor racing for some 17 years, starting as a hill-climber in 1933. His courage was noted by the eagle-eyed Enzo Ferrari, who signed him to race Alfa Romeos for him in 1938. After the war Farina, unhappy at his treatment at Alfa Romeo, retired. Two years later he changed his mind and in 1948 he was racing for Maserati. Fortunately for him and Alfa Romeo, their differences were patched up in time for the beginning of a new chapter in motor racing: the world championship.

TENNIS

Hopman spawns champions

Hopman: Sedgman's mentor

HARRY HOPMAN, a sandy-haired Melbourne coach, was a disciplinarian who took tennis training into a new era. The Fox was determined to get the best out his players, organising training schedules, supervising their lifestyles and fining them for throwing rackets or being late. But his revolutionary regimen did not meet with everybody's approval.

Hopman was appointed non-playing captain of the Australian Davis Cup team in 1950. The 44-year-old former doubles champion took the game by the scruff of the neck and the team blossomed, winning 15 of the next 18 titles. The list of his protégés read like a Who's Who of Australian tennis: Mal Anderson, Ashley Cooper, Roy Emerson, Neale Fraser, Rex Hartwig, Lew Hoad, Rod Laver, Ken McGregor, John Newcombe, Tony Roche, Mervyn Rose, Ken Rosewall, Frank Sedgman and Fred Stolle.

Such was Hopman's dedication that he once flew his team from Sydney to Brisbane to escape the rain on the eve of a tie and get in two days' extra practice.

RACING

French run away with Classics

ATTENDANCES were in decline at racecourses and matters were not helped by the French winning every Classic apart from the 2,000 Guineas. They had the first and second in both The Oaks and the St Leger, and ran away with many of the other leading races as well. Marcel Boussac was the leading owner and breeder and his trainer was the most successful in England, without even once visiting the country.

What little the home crowds had to celebrate was thanks to Winston Churchill and Colonist II. The grey won six times in succession, finishing the season by out-staying two French horses in the Jockey Club Cup.

Marcel Boussac wins the Derby with Galcador

Young spin twins tie England in knots

ALFRED VALENTINE, a 20-year-old Jamaican leg-break bowler, had done little to impress the West Indian selectors. He bowled 78 overs with little success in two trial matches against Trinidad. Instead, the sensation was the Trinidadian right-arm off-spin bowler Sonny Ramadhin, who took 12 wickets. The selectors wanted a left-arm bowler to accompany Ramadhin, and because of his ability to turn the ball they chose Valentine, who only realised he needed glasses when he could not see the scoreboard.

So the West Indies began their 33-match tour of England with two 20-year-old spinners who had each played only two first-class games.

Although the spin pair regularly troubled county batsmen it was the batting that ignited interest in the tourists. At the hub of the attack were the three Ws: Frank Worrell, Clyde Walcott and Everton Weekes. The trio from Barbados hit spectacular form, particularly Weekes, who scored an unbeaten 304 against Cambridge University sandwiched between four double centuries against the counties.

The first Test at Old Trafford was played on a crumbling pitch and it proved a memorable debut for Valentine. He took the first eight wickets, including five for 34 before lunch when England lost half their team for 88. They recovered, though, and won by 202 runs.

The second Test at Lord's was a watershed. Ramadhin, with 11 for 152, and Valentine, with seven for 127, bowled the West Indians to victory by 326 runs on June 29. The first win by a West Indian team in England sparked a spontaneous reaction from the small crowd of Caribbean supporters. They danced and sang calypso songs on the turf, much to the chagrin of MCC members.

The West Indians continued their success in the third Test at Trent Bridge, and they secured a 3-1 victory in the series at The Oval. The England selectors used 25 players in the series but only Len Hutton and Cyril Washbrook had any success. Hutton carried his bat with an unbeaten 202 at The Oval and Washbrook hit two of the four centuries by the England side. The rest had no answer to Valentine and Ramadhin who took 33 and 26 wickets respectively and received honourable mention in a calypso tune with the words "those little pals of mine, Ramadhin and Valentine".

The three Ws were also on song. Worrell hit 261 in the third Test, Walcott made 168 not out in the second Test and Weekes scored three half centuries and a fine 129 in his six visits to the crease. The West Indies had come of age.

TOUR AVERAGES

BATTING	M	I	NO	Runs	HS	Avge
E D Weekes	23	33	4	2310	304no	79.65
F M Worrell	22	31	5	1775	261	68.26
C L Walcott	25	36	6	1674	168no	55.80
R J Christiani	24	34	10	1094	131no	45.58
G E Gomez	27	30	4	1116	149	42.92
R E Marshall	20	28	0	1117	188	39.89
A F Rae	26	38	4	1330	179	39.11
J B Stollmeyer	25	37	1	1334	198	37.05
K B Trestrail	19	28	5	629	94	27.34
J D Goddard	22	21	5	309	58no	19.31
H H Johnson	17	16	4	184	39no	15.33
C B Williams	20	18	4	152	33no	10.85
P E Jones	17	16	4	83	20	6.91
S Ramadhin	21	15	8	36	7no	5.14
A L Valentine	21	19	3	49	9no	3.06
L R Pierre	12	7	1	2	1	0.33

BOWLING	O	M	Runs	Wkts	Avge
S Ramadhin	1043.4	398	2009	135	14.88
A L Valentine	1185.2	475	2207	123	17.94
J D Goddard	295.2	96	618	33	18.72
L R Pierre	204	39	557	24	23.20
F M Worrell	480.1	170	970	39	24.87
G E Gomez	680.3	221	1407	55	25.58
C B Williams	301.2	57	856	31	27.61
H H Johnson	435.5	102	954	34	28.05
P E Jones	388.3	82	980	33	29.69
R E Marshall	120.5	36	336	7	48.00
J B Stollmeyer	27	3	117	2	58.50

Also bowled K B Trestrail 3-0-17-0, C L Walcott 12-6-22-0, E D Weekes 9-0-41-2

Ramadhin: inspired West Indies' first victory in England

Valentine: could not see the scoreboard

GOLF

Hogan tames the monster

BEN HOGAN scored 67 in the last round to win successive US Open titles. The American described his final round over the tough Oakland Hills course in Detroit as the finest of his career. It was one of only two rounds under par in the championship and elicited the comment: "I vowed I'd bring this monster to its knees". He also tamed Augusta to win the Masters with a last round of 68.

RACING

Young genius in top flight

LESTER PIGGOTT rode his first winner when he was 12, and it wasn't long before the boy jockey was being talked about. He fast developed a reputation for being in the thick of tight finishes, and the press were quick to call him a prodigy.

Piggott did nothing to dispel the idea. Indeed, when the 15-year-old apprentice was beaten into second place in the Derby he was convinced that he was robbed of the race.

Piggott got the acclaim he wanted when he won the Eclipse Stakes, the biggest triumph of his career so far, on Mystery IX. But if he was hard done by in the Derby he was fortunate here, only picking up the ride when the great Scobie Breasley had to pull out at the last moment because he was unwell.

Tottenham's sweet success

Tottenham's championship side: the arch exponents of push and run

ARTHUR ROWE'S fabulous Tottenham won the First Division title for the first time in their history, a year after being promoted as Second Division champions. They had a match to spare on April 28 when they dispatched the hapless Sheffield Wednesday 1-0 at White Hart Lane. Tottenham were worthy champions playing a neat form of football that hushed opponents but sent crowds into a noisy delirium. No championship is won in a single match, and it was two devastating bursts that brought Spurs their first title. From September to mid-November in 1950 they

won eight straight games, then in March they faced a hectic programme including four matches in nine days. Tottenham serenely amassed 12 points out of the possible 14 and were set fair for their first title.

Tottenham's style of play which had confounded teams the length and breadth of the land was called "push and run", although Rowe, its architect, disliked the term. It was based on short, accurate passing with three-man triangles and was finally formulated on a table in the dining car of a train returning to London.

To illustrate why their last-

minute winning goal was so brilliant and what could be learnt from it Rowe used sugar cubes. "I spread the sugar around trying to map out the moves," Rowe recalled. "It was one to savour because there were about seven passes starting out from our own penalty area. I argued that if we could play like that, instead of just hoping for it to happen, we would score more often."

The players heeded Rowe's words and Bill Nicholson, Alf Ramsey, Sonny Walters, Les Bennett, Len Duquemin, Ron Burgess, Eddie Baily and the rest executed the theory magnificently.

CRICKET

Hutton sweet, Compton sour

IT WAS a sweet and sour winter for two of England's leading cricketers in Australia: sweet for the prolific Len Hutton, sour for the out-of-form Denis Compton. Hutton anchored England's batting with 533 runs in the five-Test series at an average of 88.83, 50 runs an innings better than the next best England batsman, Reg Simpson.

Compton scratched together a meagre 53 runs at an average of 7.57. It was a far cry from the man who had scored nearly 4,000 runs in 1947. His most significant contribution was a 33-run partnership with Hutton to steer England to their first win over Australia in 12½ years.

The two-wicket victory in the fifth and final Test in Melbourne

on February 28 halted Australia's run of 25 Tests without defeat. Australia won the series 4-1 but Hutton had fond memories. He hit a courageous 62 not out from a total 122 on a vicious pitch in the first Test in Brisbane. Then, with an unbeaten 156, he carried his bat in England's total of 272 in the fourth Test in Adelaide.

Awkward start for Statham

BRIAN STATHAM spent three months in Australia watching Ray Lindwall devastate England with his immaculate length and direction. It was a performance which left an indelible impression on the 20-year-old Lancastrian, who set his mind on emulating the Australian fast bowler.

Statham was let loose on the New Zealanders in his Test debut in Christchurch on March 17. But far from cutting a swathe through the home side, his sole success on a lifeless pitch was bowling the New Zealand opener Bert Sutcliffe for 116.

Statham, though, soon earned a reputation for his unrelenting accuracy and had a philosophy that "if they miss, I hit".

> **❝ I always used to say about Brian Statham that I'd throw a cocktail party every time he bowled a half volley ❞**
>
> **Jim Laker**

Statham: only one wicket

St Valentine's day massacre in Chicago

Sugar Ray pounds La Motta in the third

SUGAR RAY ROBINSON fought Jake LaMotta, the first professional to have beaten him, for the world middleweight championship in Chicago on February 14. When it was over the fight was inevitably called the St Valentine Day's Massacre, and for once this was not some headline writer's fantasy.

LaMotta met Robinson six times, but this was the most one-sided of their contests. For 10 rounds Sugar Ray drew the sting from the champion, who had struggled to make the weight. Then Sugar Ray upped the ante and LaMotta was in trouble. In the 13th round he was punched to a complete standstill and the fight was halted by the referee with a still proud and stubborn LaMotta upright against the ropes, refusing to go down.

Wor Jackie captures the Cup

The triumphant team that beat Blackpool 2-0

JACKIE MILBURN won the Cup final for Newcastle with one of the most spectacular goals ever seen at Wembley. Blackpool were behind 1-0, to another goal from Milburn, but the Lancashire side, with Stanley Matthews and Stan Mortensen in the team, were threatening to equalise. Then Milburn let fly with a thunderbolt from his left foot which rocketed, unstoppably, into the net.

Wor Jackie, as he was known to his adoring fans on Tyneside, had shown once again that, as for England, Wembley was his own personal showcase.

ASIAN GAMES
■ The first Asian Games were held in New Delhi from March 8-11. Eleven nations took part. The first Pan-American Games were also held in Buenos Aires, and Alexandria hosted the first Mediterranean Games.

CRICKET
■ An experiment was introduced allowing teams to declare at any time.

FOOTBALL
■ Scunthorpe, in their first season in the League, conceded only nine goals in 23 home matches.

ICE SKATING
■ Jeannette Altwegg won the world and European titles for Britain.

ROWING
■ Oxford sunk in the Boat Race.

RUGBY UNION
■ France beat England at Twickenham for the first time. Ireland also beat England for the first time in 10 years, but England won the Calcutta Cup and held it until 1964.

SQUASH
■ Hashim Khan of Pakistan won the first of seven British Open championships. He was said to be 35, but was probably 42 when he won the Open for the last time. It was the first of 13 successive years when the title was won by one of the four members of the Khan family.

TABLE TENNIS
■ Johnny Leach won the world singles title for the second time. It turned out to be the last ever singles world title that England won.

TABLE TENNIS

Leach: second world title

Louis finally founders on the rock of young Marciano

Marciano: sheer power

TWO legends collided in October in New York, one in the making and one on the way out. After eight punishing rounds Rocky Marciano finally shattered the comeback hopes of Joe Louis, the former champion.

Louis had acquitted himself creditably since his disastrous return to the ring in September the previous year, when Ezzard Charles had spared the great man further punishment by refusing to knock him out and cruising to an easy points victory to keep the world heavyweight title. Louis had won eight fights in a row since then. But the fading 37-year-old was never a real match for the younger Marciano.

For five rounds Louis's splendid left jab kept him in the fight, even splitting Marciano's eyebrow. But the sheer power and relentless pressure of Marciano was always going to be too much for Louis. By the end of the seventh round Marciano was clearly ahead on all cards. In the eighth Marciano went in for the kill and put Louis on the floor, and then Marciano knocked him through the ropes. Louis was out, sprawled on the mat with one leg under the bottom rope. The referee began the count, but then waved his arms at three to signal the end of the contest, and Joe Louis.

There were many tears shed for the demise of boxing's first genius that night, not least from the man would now wear his mantle. But Louis would have none of it when a tearful Marciano visited his dressing room. "What's the point in crying," the dignified Louis said. "The better man won, that's all. Marciano is a good puncher and is hard to hit. I'm not looking for sympathy."

Marciano, the son of an immigrant shoemaker from Naples, was now the hottest property in boxing, although he relied on power and passion to overcome his numerous technical shortcomings. Efforts by his connections to inject some skill into his savagery proved fruitless. Marciano was just the Rock.

As his trainer Charlie Goldman recalled the first time he saw Marciano in the sparring ring with an experienced professional: "He was so awkward we just stood there and laughed. He didn't stand right, he didn't throw a punch right, he didn't do anything right. Then all of a sudden, he throws a roundhouse right and the big guy is out like a mackerel."

Fangio sees off challenge

JUAN MANUEL FANGIO won the second world championship in an Alfa Romeo when he added the Spanish Grand Prix on October 28 to his victories in the Swiss and French GPs earlier in the season. Fangio saw off the late challenge of Alberto Ascari, who had captured the previous GPs in Germany and Italy and menacingly started in pole position at Pedralbes in Barcelona — a circuit with which he was very familiar. But a typically aggressive drive by Fangio wore down Ascari and when his Ferrari developed its usual tyre troubles in the eighth lap the Italian could only manage fourth place.

Turpin dethrones Robinson

Turpin: outpointed Robinson to win middleweight title

RANDOLPH TURPIN enthralled a capacity crowd at Earl's Court when he convincingly outpointed boxing's golden boy, Sugar Ray Robinson, to lift the world middleweight crown on July 10. Robinson, having won the title four months earlier, was concluding a seven-fight whirlwind defence of his title in Europe and had under-rated the British champion.

Robinson could never come to grips with Turpin's unorthodox, crouching style and was always vulnerable to his left jab. A cut over Robinson's eyebrow in the seventh round made a successful defence virtually impossible.

Turpin's reign was short-lived however, as 64 days later he made history as the shortest serving world middleweight champion when he lost the crown to Robinson in New York. The referee stepped in to save Turpin in the tenth round.

Pros set to call the shots

THE battle lines for the longest conflict in tennis were drawn at Madison Square Garden in New York on October 9, 1926, with the first professional tennis match between Suzanne Lenglen and Mary Browne. After 25 years the dividing line was as wide as ever. The amateurs might have controlled the sport's most important tournaments and venues, but they did not control the best players.

The professionals, barred from Grand Slam events, played exhibitions for a variety of promoters and by the late 1940s had banded together to form a tour run by Bobby Riggs, the triple champion at Wimbledon in 1939. The biggest draw was Jack Kramer, the 1947 Wimbledon champion whose personality dominated the tour.

Kramer realised that the rebels needed new blood to sustain interest, so he took control in 1951 and systematically signed up every Wimbledon champion. Kramer made his first significant coup when he coaxed the Australian Frank Sedgman to sign on the dotted line for $75,000 or 30 per cent of the gate. Australian fans raised money to persuade Sedgman to remain an amateur, and gave him a petrol station. But Kramer had the last say. Ken McGregor, Tony Trabert, Pancho Gonzales, Ken Rosewall, Lew Hoad, Ashley Cooper and Mal Anderson soon followed.

Kramer's playing career was ended by back problems, but this enabled him to fine-tune the first tennis Grand Prix, a professional tour with his troupe of

Sedgman signed for $75,000

leading players. The tour was such a success that chinks in the establishment's resistance to professional tennis began to show in 1960.

Springboks swiftly bounce back

THE all-conquering South Africans had been stopped in their tracks by London Counties, who scraped home 11-9 at Twickenham. It proved an ill omen for Scotland. Three matches later the Springboks trounced the Scots 44-0 at Murrayfield on November 24, a massacre which produced the phrase "we were lucky to get nothing".

Seven of the nine tries were converted by the prodigious goal-kicker Aaron Geffin, whose nickname Okey came from his habit of saying "okay" when called up to kick.

Scotland lost 44-0. "We were lucky to get nothing."

AMERICAN FOOTBALL

■ Norm van Brocklin passed for 554 yards for the Los Angeles Rams against the New York Yankees on September 28. The record yardage has never been beaten.

BASEBALL

■ The 86-year-old Connie Mack retired as the owner-manager of the Philadelphia Athletics after 50 years in charge.

CRICKET

■ Peter May scored a century on his debut for England against South Africa.

■ Len Hutton was the first batsman out obstructing a fielder in a Test. He also scored his hundredth hundred against Surrey at The Oval in July.

CYCLING

■ The first Tour of Britain was won by Ian Steel.

GOLF

■ The United States won the Ryder Cup 9-2 with one match halved at Pinehurst. Arthur Lees was the first Briton to win both his foursomes and singles matches in America.

■ A team of American women beat a men's team that included four Walker Cup players 6½ -2½ at Wentworth.

RACING

■ The King George VI and Queen Elizabeth Stakes was run for the first time at Ascot in July to mark the Festival of Britain. It was the richest race ever staged in England.

WRESTLING

■ The first freestyle world championships were held in Helsinki.

GOLF

Faulkner gets script right in advance

MAX FAULKNER was so confident of winning the Open after two rounds that when asked for his autograph he began to sign his name "Max Faulkner, Open champion, 1951". Despite tempting fate, the eccentric Briton, who brightened up the post-war golf scene with his bright clothing, held his lead with some superb putting to win by two shots from Antonio Cerda of Argentina in the only Open staged at Royal Portrush.

131

JANUARY
1952
JUNE

Lofthouse the lion of Vienna

Lofthouse: two goals

NAT LOFTHOUSE was dubbed The Lion of Vienna for his dramatic breakaway goal that shattered the Austrians and gave England a morale-boosting 3-2 victory in Vienna on May 25. The Bolton centre-forward was in his typical "never say die" mood and his two goals turned a difficult game against a team regarded as the finest in Europe.

It was a match reminiscent of the hard-fought 2-2 draw at Wembley the previous season, where the bulldog tenacity of Lofthouse and Ramsey had to contend with the deceptive subtleties of a ball-playing team.

Lofthouse's performance in Vienna made him the obvious first pick for the England No 9 shirt and he rewarded that faith in him by scoring seven more goals in the remaining four internationals of the year.

Hibs's famous five triumph again

Famous Five: (*left to right*) Smith, Johnstone, Reilly, Turnbull, Ormond

HIB'S Famous Five led them to a second successive Scottish championship, although by a four-point margin over Rangers rather than the previous 10.

Under Hugh Shaw's management Hibs were clearly the best team in Scotland, if not Britain. The Five: Eddie Turnbull, Bobby Johnstone, Gordon Smith, Lawrie Reilly and Willie Ormond, made up one of the most formidable attacks ever to come together on a football field. What pleased crowds and devastated opponents was not just their individual abilities, stunning as they were, but the way their skills and temperaments complemented each other.

This was not the whole story of Hibs's success. In Bobby Coombe they possessed one of Britain's most versatile players, who played in five different positions during the season.

Their goalkeeper, Tommy Younger, was solid and invaluable. So much so that while he was doing his national service in West Germany Hibs persuaded the Royal Scots to let him fly back each weekend to keep goal.

With Hibs winning the championship, Motherwell the Scottish Cup and Dundee the League Cup, it was the first time since 1895 that neither Celtic nor Rangers won a major trophy.

Celtic pluck Stein from obscurity

CELTIC, in disgrace for their defeat in the first round of the Scottish Cup at the hands of Third Lanark, delved into the obscurity of the Welsh Leagues to bring Jock Stein from Llanelli to bolster their defence.

It was a timely call for Stein as he was about to quit the club, but an unusual move for Celtic. Stein had played Second Division football for Albion Rovers but then drifted into the wilderness. Also, he was an unusual centre-half, a sound defender but capable of the unorthodox, such as clearing the ball with his knee.

However, it proved inspired. Stein captained Celtic to the Double two years later.

Stein: from Llanelli to the double in two years

Wales and Morgan get a lucky break

Morgan: 29 internationals for Wales

ROY BURNETT was a fine fly-half destined for great things when he played for Newport against Cardiff in front of the Welsh selectors in 1951. But he broke his collarbone late in the match, so instead the selectors chose his opposite number Cliff Morgan to play against Ireland. The 5ft 7in Morgan, a half-back from the Rhondda, played in 29 internationals for Wales. Burnett played in only one.

Morgan established an excellent partnership with his scrum-half Rex Willis, and with a penchant for seeking an extra yard of space provided Wales with the scoring opportunities to win the Grand Slam in 1952.

The team opened their campaign with an 8-6 win against England at Twickenham on January 19. They beat Scotland 11-0 in Cardiff a fortnight later, went to Dublin to beat Ireland 14-3 and won the Grand Slam with a 9-5 victory against France in Swansea on March 22.

Morgan inspired Cardiff and Wales to victories against New Zealand the next year, played a key role in the British Lions squaring a series in South Africa in 1955 and then became a leading commentator for the BBC.

He had the pleasure of describing a try by Gareth Edwards for the Barbarians against New Zealand at Cardiff in 1973, rated as arguably the finest try in rugby history.

Yorkshire tearaway lets rip

ENGLAND'S six-year search for a fast bowler to partner Alec Bedser ended in Leeds on June 5. Fred Trueman, a young Yorkshire tearaway, burst on to the arena against India with seven wickets on his home ground.

Fiery Fred took 29 wickets in four Tests as England won 3-0. He captured eight for 31 in the third Test in Manchester when India made only 58, their opener Vinoo Mankad falling to a brilliant catch by Tony Lock at short leg. It was the first time Lock had touched the ball in Test cricket.

Trueman: 29 wickets

Slamming Sam gets his second wind

SAM SNEAD mastered high winds for the second time in four years to win the green jacket at Augusta. The American repeated his Masters victory of 1949 with closing rounds of 77 and 72. Jack Burke, the only player to break 70 on the last day, finished four shots adrift.

United on top in topsy-turvy battle for championship

MANCHESTER UNITED won their first League championship under the managership of Matt Busby when they trounced their nearest rivals Arsenal 6-1 at Old Trafford. It had been a see-saw season with six different clubs topping the table at one time or another, and from the turn of the year, when they were not beaten until the end of April, Arsenal had looked the most likely to end the season on top. But the ageing core of Busby's 1948 Cup-winning side, seven in all, held on to secure United's first League title since 1911.

Newcastle first to be the second

NEWCASTLE became the first club this century to retain the FA Cup when they beat Arsenal 1-0 with a goal from the Chilean international George Robledo. The final was a scrappy affair as Arsenal's dour defence fought to stave off Jackie Milburn and his men. By the end of the match Arsenal were down to only eight fit players.

FOR THE RECORD

CRICKET

■ India recorded their first Test victory, in their 25th Test, when they beat England by an innings and eight runs on February 10.

■ West Indies beat New Zealand by five wickets in Christchurch on February 12, in the first Test between the two countries.

■ Nazar Mohammad was the first player to be on the field for an entire Test match during the second Test between India and Pakistan.

TABLE TENNIS

■ Hiroji Satoh began the Japanese domination of the sport when he won the world title using a thick sponge bat, whose spin baffled his opponents.

Magnificent Zatopek runs opposition into the ground

JUNE

1952

DECEMBER

Zatopek: three golds

FOR THE RECORD

ATHLETICS
■ A post-Olympic match between the British Empire and the United States drew a capacity crowd of 45,000 to the White City, with another 20,000 people unable to get into the stadium. Despite being held in heavy rain, the meeting produced three world records.

RACING
■ Tulyar broke the 1895 record for stakes won, with £76,417.

SNOOKER
■ A rift between professionals and the Billiards Association and Control Club led to a boycott of the world championship. Only two players took part and Horace Lindrum beat Clark McConachy 94-49.

TENNIS
■ Britain recorded their first win in the Curtis Cup, beating the United States 5-4 at Muirfield.

■ Pancho Gonzales won the world professional championships at Wembley and his third successive London professional championships.

THERE was no lonelier long distance runner than Emil Zatopek. When others were satisfied that they had done enough training he would still be out pounding the roads. The brilliant Czech spent 1,000 hours running each year. He ran more than 100 miles a week, more than half a marathon a day.

Zatopek believed that if he trained hard enough then competitive running would be easy. The pay-off was three gold medals at the 15th Olympic Games in Helsinki.

The Finns had a tradition for producing legendary long distance runners. They gave the 55-year-old Paavo Nurmi a standing ovation when he carried the torch into the stadium and cheered again when he handed it to another of their greats, Hannes Kolehmainen, to light the flame. So it was with appreciation that they watched Zatopek achieve a unique triple. It was no surprise that he retained the 10,000m title in 29min 17sec on the first day of the Games, July 20.

Two days later he won his 5,000m heat and in the final on July 24 was the victor in one of the great Olympic finishes. Four men — Zatopek, the Frenchman Alain Mimoun, the German Herbert Schade and Chris Chataway of Britain — were in front at the bell. Chataway stepped on the kerb at the last corner and fell while Zatopek opened up a lead and fought to the finish in 14min 6.6sec. Mimoun was second and Schade third. Within an hour Zatopek's wife Dana had added to the family heirlooms by winning the women's javelin.

But Zatopek was not finished. Three days later he joined 67 other runners for his first marathon. He did not know what pace to run and when he was

> ❛ **Emil Zatopek isn't human in his achievement. While he goes out for a 20-mile run on his only free day, we lie here panting and moaning that the gods are unkind to us** ❜
>
> **Roger Bannister**

sharing the lead with the Briton Jim Peters and the Swede Gustaf Jansson he said: "I know virtually nothing about marathon running, but don't you think we ought to go a little faster?" They did not reply, so he increased his pace, ran away from his rivals and won in 2hr 23min 3.2sec.

The Australian sprinter Marjorie Jackson nearly matched Zatopek's gold medal haul after breaking world records in the 100m and 200m. But she had the baton knocked from her hand in the relay when leading at the final exchange.

There was also disappointment for the Swedish heavyweight boxer Ingemar Johan-

sson. He was disqualified in the final for not trying, but seven years later redeemed himself by winning the professional world heavyweight title against Floyd Patterson. The 17-year-old American won the middleweight title in Helsinki.

The French swimmer Jean Boiteux, who won the men's 400m freestyle, was joined in the pool by his father who jumped in, fully clothed, to congratulate his son.

The Soviet Union made a successful return to the Games after 40 years and finished second in the medal table behind the United States.

Foxhunter, a horse bred in Norfolk for hunting, and Harry Llewellyn, a lieutenant-colonel who had finished second in the Grand National at Aintree in 1936, spared Britain's blushes. The country had not won a gold medal when Llewellyn mounted Foxhunter for the last event, the team showjumping. Officials were already preparing the closing ceremony. The pair needed a clear second round to win. They were faultless and added Britain's only gold medal to two silver and eight bronze.

Llewellyn and Foxhunter: won Britain's only gold

Stop-gap Surridge transforms Surrey into dominant force

Surrey celebrate their first title in 38 years

SURREY had been juggling captains ever since the war. So when their committee appointed Stuart Surridge the next leader few people believed that the mediocre all-rounder would be more than a stop-gap.

Surridge had other ideas. He was an eternal optimist who moulded his men into a team which reflected his positive philosophy.

His tactics were simple. When his team batted they scored runs as quickly as possible. When they bowled he set attacking fields and would position himself, with two others, as close as possible to the batsman. The policy worked wonders. Surrey won 20 of their 28 matches and took their first title

after a long wait of 38 years.

Surridge retained the captaincy for another four years and when he bowed out with a fifth title in 1956 Surrey had played 170 matches, won 101, drawn 42 and lost only 27. They were the first county in 44 years to beat Australia. Peter May took over the captaincy and led them to a seventh successive title in 1958.

With the swing bowling of Alec Bedser, the spin of Jim Laker and Tony Lock and the pace of Peter Loader, Surrey had the best attack in the land. And although their batting was not as strong, they possessed in Ken Barrington and the brilliant May the core capable of scoring runs quickly.

Their positive play brought crowds flocking to The Oval. Repairs to the ground after the war had changed the character of the pitch from a batsman's paradise to a green top. It certainly suited the Surrey attack, taking swing on the first day and spin on the last.

One of Surridge's most remarkable matches was against Worcestershire at The Oval in August 1954. Worcestershire were dismissed for 25 and when Surridge heard from the Meteorological Office that rain was forecast he declared an hour before the close at 92 for three. Worcestershire were bowled out for 40 before lunch the next day and Surrey had sealed the title. It then rained for a day and a half.

Daly lets huge lead slip from his grasp

THERE was an Irishman, an Australian and a South African at Royal Lytham. They concentrated on accuracy rather than length off the tee and the joke was on the long hitters in the 81st Open championship.

Fred Daly, Peter Thomson and Bobby Locke set the early pace with the Irishman, Daly, scoring 67 and 69 to lie four shots ahead of Locke going into the final day. Thomson was a further shot behind.

Daly, who had won the Open in 1947, fell apart with a 77 and a 76, and Locke produced the steady golf to win his third Open title. The South African had to hold off a late charge from Thomson. The Australian picked up three shots in the last round to finish one back in a tournament he was to dominate for the rest of the decade. Ill-health robbed Daly of another opportunity to challenge for the title.

Sedgman nets three titles at Wimbledon

FRANK SEDGMAN became the first player since Bobby Riggs in 1939 to win the men's triple crown at Wimbledon. The Australian used his powerful forehand and superior play at the net to beat the Czechoslovak exile Jaroslav Drobny 4-6 6-2 6-3 6-2 in the men's singles final. He won the men's doubles with Ken McGregor and the mixed doubles with Doris Hart.

The women's singles title was won by the 17-year-old Maureen Connolly. Little Mo, named after the American battleship Mighty Mo, beat Louise Brough in the final.

Ascari and Ferrari utterly unbeatable

THE third world championship, run under Formula Two rules, was utterly dominated by Alberto Ascari and Ferrari. Ascari scorched to the world championship by winning six of the seven Grands Prix in a Ferrari 500F2, and his team-mates Giuseppe Farina, Piero

Taruffi and Rudi Fischer finished second, third and fourth.

Ferrari's team and the 500 car were unbeatable in 1952 and 1953, winning 14 of the 15 Grands Prix, and with Ascari as their No 1 driver they dominated in a way that no driver or manufacturer had done before.

Ascari wins the British Grand Prix at Silverstone

> **When it was all over, I felt it couldn't have gone to a better man. There were no recriminations in our dressing room. I don't think a bullet would have stopped Stan in the last 17 minutes**
>
> **Nat Lofthouse**

FOOTBALL

Matthews casts magic spell

MAGIC was in the air — a young queen was crowned; Hillary and Tensing conquered Everest; England captured the Ashes; Sir Gordon Richards finally won the Derby; Arsenal won a seventh League title and the Hungarians took football on to a different planet at Wembley. But the FA Cup final on May 2 reached romantic heights that nobody would have dared script.

With 20 minutes to play Blackpool were 3-1 down to Nat Lofthouse's Bolton and it appeared that the 38-year-old Stanley Matthews was going to be denied a winner's medal for the third time. Then the maestro turned the game on its head.

Matthews, who had had a poor first half, went haring down the right wing to the goal-line and sent a high, curling cross to the far post. The goal-keeper, Stan Hanson, took his eye off the ball and just got a fingernail to it, but the ball spun away and Mortensen slid in behind him with an outstretched boot to pull a goal back.

The 100,000 crowd sensed a miracle was on. The Matthews the nation adored was now in his element, he mesmerised the Bolton left flank and defenders went spinning like skittles, but with only three minutes left it was still 3-2.

Then Blackpool won a free-kick on the edge of the Bolton penalty area. Mortensen, the man with the hardest shot in football, managed to find a narrow gap in the wall and the ball screamed into the net by the left-hand post. It was 3-3. There was less than a minute of injury time left before the ref's whistle.

As the Blackpool players scurried back for the re-start Matthews looked at his team and clapped his hands three times. From the kick-off Bolton were like men condemned. Immediately, they lost possession and the ball was arrowed to Matthews on the wing.

He swayed, he swerved and as he cut towards goal with the entire defence attempting to cover him and Mortensen, he passed the ball back towards the penalty spot and directly to Bill Perry who shot straight into the left-hand corner of the net. 4-3.

The Cup final was over, and the nation, overwhelmed by the drama of it all, wept tears of joy. Mortensen may have scored a hat-trick, but it was Matthews's final.

GOLF

Fixture clash costs Hogan Grand Slam

WHEN Ben Hogan went out to practise his fellow professionals would follow him to watch. At Carnoustie, on the bleak Scottish east coast, he drew huge galleries who gasped at his ability to drop ball after ball, hour after hour at the feet of his caddie Cecil Timms.

Hogan had control over the ball few could emulate, and an unmatched skill of placing the ball precisely on the fairway with his next shot in mind. His most successful year was 1953 and he played what he regarded as his finest golf over four

rounds in winning the Masters. Opening with a 70, Hogan then strung together three scores under 70 — the first player to do so at Augusta — for a five-shot victory over Porky Oliver.

The next stop was the US Open at the tough Oakmont course. He started with a 67 and when Sam Snead faded Hogan cruised to his fourth title by six shots.

The pressure grew on Hogan to round off his achievements in the Open at Carnoustie. He spent a week acclimatising but disliked the long grass on the greens. "I've got a lawn mower back in Texas, I'll send it over," he quipped. Hogan, in inimitable fashion, mastered the unfamiliar conditions and the small 1.62in British ball, and with scores of 73, 71 and 70 was tied for the lead with Roberto de Vicenzo.

In the final round the Wee Ice Mon, as the Scots dubbed the expressionless Hogan, played an exquisite chip from the fringe of

the bunker at the fifth hole which bounced off the back of the cup and dropped in for a birdie. It was the impetus he needed for a round of 67. He won his only Open by four shots.

The first prize of a mere £500 was small change for a man who had won three of the four Majors in the same year. The missing link was the US PGA, but a clash of dates with the Open prevented Hogan completing the Grand Slam. Walter Burkemo won the US PGA title.

> **All I know is that Nicklaus watches Hogan practise and I never heard of Hogan watching Nicklaus practise**
>
> **Tommy Bolt**

> **If I miss one day's practice I know it, if I miss two days the spectators know it, and if I miss three days the world knows it**
>
> **Ben Hogan**

Hogan: three majors

Sir Gordon celebrates with his first Derby

IT TOOK a long time, but Sir Gordon Richards finally captured the one prize that had eluded him. And although it took him 28 attempts to win his first Derby he could not have picked a finer occasion. The 49-year-old jockey had just been awarded a knighthood for his services to racing, and the Queen had been crowned just a few days before.

The crowd at Epsom was close to half a million and their loyalties were divided. Should they back Sir Gordon on Pinza, the 5-1 joint favourite, or the

Queen's runner Aureole, who was well supported at 9-1.

In the end, the race was clear-cut. Sir Gordon took the lead two furlongs out and he did not have any difficulty in coming in four lengths ahead of Aureole. The headline writers had a field day with the result: "Yes Sir! Gordon's First Derby" and "Half a million groaned for Elizabeth the SECOND".

Not that the new Queen was a bad loser. She responded to the cheers that greeted Sir Gordon's victory by summoning him to receive her congratulations.

Sir Gordon returns triumphant on Pinza

FOR THE RECORD

BASEBALL
■ It was the year of the big hitters. Mickey Mantle blasted a 565-feet home run out of Griffith Stadium, Washington, on April 17, and the Boston Red Sox blasted 17 runs in a single inning against Detroit on June 18.

BASKETBALL
■ The United States won the first women's world championship.

FOOTBALL
■ Pegasus, composed entirely of Oxford and Cambridge University players and representing the last great hurrah of the Corinthian ideal, won the FA Amateur Cup in front of 100,000 spectators at Wembley. The club was founded in 1948 by Sir Harold Thompson and disbanded in 1960.

MOTOR RACING
■ Jaguars finished first, second and fourth in the Le Mans 24-hour race. The winners, Tony Rolt and Duncan Hamilton, were the first to average more than 100mph, with 105.6mph. Stirling Moss and Peter Walker were second at 104.3mph.

TABLE TENNIS
■ England's men's team, including the former Austrian Richard Bergmann, won the world title for the only time in Bucharest.

TENNIS
■ Jaroslav Drobny beat Budge Patty 8-6 16-18 3-6 8-6 12-10 after 4hr 20min in the third round of the men's singles at Wimbledon. It was the longest match in the championships until 1969.

Little Mo powers to a full set of titles

Connolly narrowly beats Doris Hart at Wimbledon

THERE was never any doubt in the mind of Wilbur Folson that he had spotted a potential champion when he saw an 11-year-old left-hander training at the Balboa municipal courts in San Diego in 1945.

Folson, a local coach, persuaded Maureen Connolly to play with her right hand and within five years she was the US champion. Little Mo's meteoric rise reached its peak in 1953 when she became the first woman to win the Grand Slam. She used her solid baseline game and powerful drives to win

the Australian, French, Wimbledon and US titles. Her closest call was in a classic final at Wimbledon, where she beat her great rival Doris Hart 8-6 7-5.

The people of San Diego presented her with a horse named Colonel Merryboy. But while she was riding him in 1954 he bolted and ran into a truck. Connolly smashed her right leg and when it failed to heal properly she gave up tennis. "If I can't play like I used to there is no point in playing at all," she said. She died of cancer in 1969 at the age of 34.

Bergmann: wins for England

Scots mourn their great playmaker

ALEX JAMES of Raith, Preston, Arsenal and Scotland, and one of the greatest footballers this century died on June 1 after a long illness at the age of 51.

Although James was capped only eight times for Scotland, he was the most influential inside forward of his day, leading Herbert Chapman's Arsenal to four League titles and three Cup finals. Unusually, The Times carried an obituary of a footballer.

Stanley Matthews
The magic went on for ever

Brian Glanville

When the 19-year-old Stanley Matthews played in the notorious Battle of Highbury against Italy in November 1934, a match in which boots flew and bones were broken, the Daily Mail columnist Geoffrey Simpson was dismissive. Matthews, he wrote, had displayed the same faults of slowness and hesitation as in a recent inter-League match. Perhaps he did not have the big match temperament. Twenty-two years later at Wembley, by then aged 41, Matthews demolished Nilton Santos of Brazil, then known as the best left-back in the world, and inspired an easy English victory. He would go on playing League football, ultimately for his original club, Stoke City, till over 50.

He was, of course, a classical outside-right, but attempts to minimise his fame by comparing him with supposedly more versatile wingers ignore his feats elsewhere on the field. Thus, in 1937, when England played Czechoslovakia at Tottenham, were down to 10 men and looked as if they might lose their unbeaten home record against foreign teams, Matthews moved to inside-right and scored three goals with his weaker left foot. In the 1954 World Cup in Switzerland, when England began against Belgium, they retrieved the game only when Matthews moved to inside-left. During that tournament he was nicknamed "Der Zaberer", The Magician. In England he was called "The Wizard of Dribble".

His swerve was unique, inexplicable even by himself. "Don't ask me how I do it," he once pleaded. "It just comes out of me under pressure." Most left-backs he played against knew what he was going to do, but could still do nothing to stop it. Matthews, a pale, slight, seemingly unathletic figure, would take the ball up to them and sway towards his left, as though he were going to move inside. The full-back, watching closely, would inevitably lean that way himself. At which point Matthews, with a sudden, sharp movement, would flick the ball up the touchline with the outside of his right foot and be away, leaving the full-back hopelessly off-balance. As often as not, Matthews would go to the goal-line and pull the ball back into the middle, the most dangerous pass in the game.

He was born in the Potteries, the son of Jack Matthews, a boxer known as "The Fighting Barber of Hanley". His father's insistence on physical fitness would serve his son well: deep breathing exercises at an open window, even on the coldest winter morning, were de rigueur. In his subsequent career Matthews would live an abstemious, even monastic, life. His light was said to be out by 9 o'clock at night. After he joined Blackpool, where he and his first wife kept a boarding house, he would go for long runs across the sands. It was Blackpool he played for as a guest in the war, joining them when it was over after bitter quarrels with the Stoke City manager Bob McGrory. He had served in the air force and his career almost came to an end after a dreadful injury caused in physical training by a sadistic instructor.

Eventually he would return to Stoke and help them back into the First Division. Before each match, even at that age, he would admit: "You must have butterflies." In the dressing room he would seem remote, almost in a trance, waiting for the kick-off. Few players have ever been such an attraction. When Blackpool came to London it was reckoned that Matthews would put 10,000 spectators on the gates. The longer he played the more anxious they were to see him, fearing he must soon retire, little guessing that would not happen until he passed his half-century. His longevity became a minor miracle.

Yet for all his elusive brilliance, his technique complemented by the devastating 10-yard burst, Matthews was never persona grata with the England selectors. Traditionally mistrusting brilliance, they were forever leaving him out of the team, and as often having to recall him. He was not even picked originally for the 1950 World Cup in Brazil, the first that England ever entered. Instead, he went on tour with a Football Association party in North America, during which they defeated the United States team which would eventually beat an England without Matthews in Belo Horizonte. At the very last moment the selectors called him up, but he would play only one game, the last, in Rio, against Spain.

With Tom Finney, another immensely gifted outside-right returned from the war, the selectors were only too eager to prefer him to Matthews. Not until May 1947, in Lisbon, did they appreciate that the two could co-exist. Matthews played on the right, Finney on the left, and Portugal were beaten 10-0. The following year, in Turin, Matthews tormented Eliani, Italy's reserve left-back, once even stopping with the ball and casually smoothing his hair. Finney played on the left again, scoring two goals. Italy were beaten 4-0.

Five years later came the so-called Matthews final, his third for Blackpool. Defeated in 1948 and 1951, it was taken for granted that this was the last chance for Matthews's Blackpool to win at Wembley. In a game of many mistakes in which Bolton were reduced to 10 fit men it seemed for a long time that the Cup would be dashed from Matthews's lips once more. But in the dying moments he swerved and sped his way to the line as only he could do, passed the ball back into the goal-mouth and Bill Perry scored the goal whereby Blackpool won 4-3. Outside Bolton, the nation exulted.

Partners sometimes found it hard to play with Matthews. Though he made so many goals for other players with perfectly delivered high crosses and balls pulled back from the line he was essentially a soloist. It was said that an inside-right who gave him the ball had to resign himself to not getting it back for quite some time. He found a perfect foil in the gifted Sunderland inside-right Raich Carter. Later, he would strike up a famous partnership for Blackpool and England with a very different type of player, the direct and dashing Stanley Mortensen. A joke went round that Mortensen, playing for England, headed in a couple of crosses from Tom Finney and each time returned to the centre circle rubbing his head. When it happened a third time Finney asked him why. "It's just that when Stan Matthews plays," Mortensen supposedly replied, "he puts the balls over with the lace facing the other way."

When he retired Matthews for a time became general manager of another Potteries club, Port Vale. But it was never really the metier of so private a person and it ended unhappily when Port Vale were fined by the FA for allegedly improper payments. For some years Matthews roamed the world, coaching in Africa, living in Canada and Malta, finally returning to England in his middle seventies. Football did not make him rich, he came too early for that, but few other British players have become such an international legend. Speculation over how he might have fared in the modern game seems otiose. Such talents would have allowed Matthews to flourish anywhere at any time.

BORN
February 1, 1915 (Hanley, Staffs.)

PLAYING CAREER

Stoke 1930-1947
Debut: v Bury, 1932
203 pre-war appearances, 11 goals in 1933-34
Honours: 1933, Second Division champions
Guested for Morton, Blackpool and others during the war
1946: 23 appearances, 4 goals

Blackpool 1947-1961
379 appearances, 17 goals
Honours: First Division runners-up, 1956; FA Cup winners 1953; FA Cup finalists 1948 and 1951

Stoke 1961-1965
59 appearances, 3 goals
Honours: Second Division champions, 1963
Last game: v Fulham, Feb 6, 1965 (the oldest player in the First Division at 50 years and 5 days)

Internationals
Debut v Wales, 1934; 84 appearances (including 2 for Great Britain), 11 goals

MANAGERIAL CAREER

Port Vale 1965-1968; Hibernian (Malta) 1970

OTHER HONOURS

European Footballer of the Year, 1956
Footballer of the Year, 1948 and 1963
CBE, 1957; Knighted, 1965

The wizard of dribble: Matthews continued to weave his spell on defences until he was over 50. He made 84 appearances for England, single-handedly won the FA Cup for Blackpool in 1953, and was knighted in 1965.

FOR THE RECORD

FOOTBALL

■ The Football Association celebrated its 90th year with a match between England and the Rest of the World at Wembley on October 26. England were fortunate to escape with a 4-4 draw when Alf Ramsey scored a penalty in the last minute.

GOLF

■ The first World Cup was won by Argentina.

MOTOR SPORT

■ The first Safari rally was held in Kenya, Tanzania and Uganda.

RACING

■ Bookmakers refused to pay out on the winner of the first race at Bath on July 16. Francasal, a 10-1 outsider, was the subject of some large bets after the telephone line to the course failed. The bookmakers suspected that an inch-think wire had been cut deliberately, but although there was a clean break in the cable the police decided that it was not sabotage.

GOLF

The shot that everyone saw

LEW WORSHAM chipped in for an eagle at the final hole for a one-shot victory in the World Championship of Golf in Chicago. Worsham's 110-yard shot earned him $65,000 and sparked a boom in the United States after millions saw it on television.

Jimmy Demaret, describing the shot, said: "He's hit it fat . . . It will probably be short . . . It just hit the front edge of the green . . . It's got no chance . . . It's rolling but it will stop . . . It's rolled toward the cup . . . Well I'll be damned!"

RUGBY UNION

Williams out-thinks All Blacks

Cardiff shocked a 53,000 crowd with an 8-3 defeat of New Zealand

BLEDDYN WILLIAMS grew up on plenty of beef stew and rugby talk. The recipe turned the Welsh centre and his seven brothers into proud Cardiff players.

Williams possessed an astute rugby brain, as New Zealand found out. The Cardiff captain instructed his team to play to their strengths at the back of the lineout, and with their fly-half Cliff Morgan weaving his way through the All Black backline Cardiff delighted 53,000 Welshmen with a shock 8-3 win.

The New Zealanders had a second taste of the brilliance of Morgan and Williams against Wales in Cardiff on December 19. The teams were level with five minutes remaining. Clem Thomas launched an attack down the left and, when he was hemmed in, spotted Ken Jones on the far side. "I just hoofed it across," Thomas said. Jones took the ball on the bounce, rounded his opponent and scored the decisive try under the posts. Wales won 13-8.

CRICKET

Bedser helps England to Ashes

ENGLAND wrested the Ashes from Australia for the first time in nearly 19 years. The 1-0 victory was achieved with fine bowling by Alec Bedser and solid strokeplay by Len Hutton. It also required the patience of Trevor Bailey and Willie Watson, who saved the second Test at Lord's with resolute batting. Watson was at the crease for 346 minutes and Bailey 275 minutes.

Bedser took 39 wickets in the series, including 14 for 99 in the first Test in Nottingham when the rain which dogged the series denied England a certain victory. Hutton had more success with the bat than the coin, scor-

Compton wins the Ashes at The Oval

ing 443 runs but losing the toss on all five occasions. It did not matter in the fifth Test when Australia yielded to the combination of Jim Laker and Tony Lock to lose by eight wickets.

Baffled, bemused and beaten

Youngsters' mistakes prove costly

Marching to disaster: Billy Wright leads England into the unexpected

BRITISH football was turned upside down on November 25 when Hungary came to Wembley, displayed the most exquisite skills and routed England 6-3. The headlines the next day told the whole story: "The New Wembley Wizards"; "Now It's Back to School for England — With Hungary the Soccer Masters"; "Make 'em run? — We couldn't".

For the first time in their history, England had been beaten on home soil by continental opposition. But that was the least of it. For the first time they were made to look posi-

tively second-rate by Ferenc Puskas and his magnificent Magyars.

Within 60 seconds Hungary, including Nandor Hidegkuti, Sandor Kocsis and the incomparable Puskas, were ahead when Hidegkuti skilfully drew the centre-half out of position with a swerve and then hit the ball through the gap. The Hungarians went on to play football that combined the individualistic skills of continental artistry with British enterprise and vigour. By half-time they were 4-2 ahead.

England, by contrast, were

leaden-footed and panic-stricken. In the second half Alf Ramsey converted a penalty and Hidegkuti completed his hat-trick to leave the score 6-3. Even defeat at the hands of Eire in 1949, and humiliation by the USA in the World Cup in 1950, had not prepared England for this.

The speed of thought and movement, and the sudden striking power of the Hungarians shocked England. Six months later, despite much soul-searching and seven changes to their team, England could still not cope with Puskas's side as they lost the return match 7-1.

PETER ALLISS and Bernard Hunt, the youngest members of the British Ryder Cup team, missed short putts on the final green at Wentworth to deny the hosts their first victory in 20 years.

The Americans won 6-5 with one match halved but collapsed after clinching the foursomes 3-1. The most spectacular fall from grace was by Sam Snead who lost to Harry Weetman on the last after leading by four shots with six to play.

Allis: missed short putt

Rosewall the outstanding prospect

KEN ROSEWALL, a tenacious right-hander with an excellent backhand and fine ground strokes, signalled his emergence as one of the world's greatest players by winning the Australian and French titles.

As a result, the 18-year-old Australian was awarded the top seeding at Wimbledon. But his charge to the Grand Slam ended in the quarter-finals when he lost to Kurt Nielsen, the sensation of the tournament. The unseeded Dane reached the final but was beaten in straight sets by Vic Seixas. Rosewall recovered from his surprise defeat but lost to Tony Trabert in the final of the US championship.

Hawthorn just makes it home for Britain

MIKE HAWTHORN triumphed in one of the most thrilling races when he finished a mere 45 yards ahead of Juan Fangio in the French Grand Prix in Rheims on July 5.

As they began the last lap, after 306 miles of fiercely competitive racing, Hawthorn, in a Ferrari, and Fangio, for Maserati, were neck and neck. Breathing down their necks, a

second behind, were Alberto Ascari and Froilan Gonzalez, also Ferrari and Maserati.

As they approached the final hairpin the 24-year-old Englishman was just in front. Then Fangio made a mistake and Hawthorn used the Ferrari's power to become the first Briton to win a world championship Grand Prix in one of motor racing's closest races.

Hawthorn: first British winner

Bowlers made to do hard labour

PORT OF SPAIN in March was no place for a bowler. The jute matting pitch at the Queen's Park Oval was a batting paradise. West Indies had first use of the featherbed and after the three Ws — Frank Worrell, Clyde Walcott and Everton Weekes — scored centuries they declared at 681 for eight.

England replied with 537 and when the captains called it a day the batsmen had averaged nearly 64 runs a wicket. Fred Trueman suggested that "serving a term of hard labour would have been a lot more fun".

The match was the only draw in a squared five-match series in which Garry Sobers took four for 75 on his debut in the fifth.

Bannister breaks four-minute mile

Bannister: beat Landy to the record by 46 days

THERE was a strong wind whipping across the track at Iffley Road, Oxford in the early afternoon of May 6. It appeared that Roger Bannister's dream had been blown away.

The 24-year-old Oxford student wanted to be the first man to run the mile in under four minutes. He had planned everything to the last detail. His training had gone well and he had invited Chris Chataway and Chris Brasher, two of his teammates at the Achilles club, to help him achieve the elusive mark.

But time was running out. Somebody was bound to break the barrier. The great Swede Gunder Hägg had come within two seconds. So had John Landy in Australia, and the American Wes Santee was also close. Just when Bannister had given up hope the wind died with only minutes to spare before the start at 6pm. The race was on.

Brasher took the lead as agreed, with Bannister and Chataway on his tail. They were through the first lap in a fast 57.5sec and reached the halfway mark in under two minutes. Brasher had done his job, now it was Chataway's turn. The pace slowed and when Bannister went through the bell in 3min 0.5sec his hopes appeared to be fading. He took the lead 200m out and surged down the final straight.

"I leapt at the tape," he wrote later, "like a man taking his last spring to save himself from the chasm that threatens to engulf him. My effort was over and I collapsed almost unconscious with an arm on either side of me. It was only then that the real pain overtook me. I felt like an exploded lightbulb with no will to live."

Bannister's time was 3min 59.4sec. Forty-six days later Landy clocked 3min 58sec in Turka, Finland. The stage was set for what was billed as the Mile of the Century. The great rivals lined up at the British Empire Games in Vancouver on August 7.

Landy, as always, set the pace while Bannister was content to wait. But when Landy glanced over his left shoulder as he entered the final straight Bannister burst past on the right and sprinted to the finish.

Later that sweltering day Jim Peters led the marathon into the stadium. The Englishman was so tired that he fell 11 times on the last lap and when the manager of the England team could take no more he helped Peters off the track 200 yards from the finish. The race was won by Joe McGhee of Scotland.

THE MIRACLE MILE

	Lap Time	Cumulative time
1	57.5sec	57.5sec
2	60.7sec	1min 58.2sec
3	62.3sec	3min 00.5sec
4	58.9sec	3min 59.4sec

Bad boy Piggott taught a lesson

Piggott's Derby on 33-1 outsider Never Say Die

LESTER PIGGOTT still had not learnt to curb the excesses of youth. His problem was that he tried too hard for his own good; the desire to win drove him to do things that were unwise, or even dangerous.

Piggott won his first Derby on Never Say Die but a fortnight later, at Royal Ascot on June 17, that triumph was overshadowed by the lowest point in his career. The King Edward VII Stakes was a rough race and Piggott, on Never Say Die again, was involved in a clash with Rashleigh on the final bend. The Stewards suspended Piggott for the rest of the meeting and ordered him to appear before the

Stewards of the Jockey Club.

Their verdict left Piggott stunned. They said that because of his continual "dangerous and erratic riding", and "complete disregard for the rules of racing and for the safety of other jockeys" his licence was being withdrawn. He could only ride again if he spent at least six months working for a trainer other than his father.

Piggott insisted that he had been unfairly treated but wiser heads thought otherwise. They felt that Piggott had to be taught a lesson and the only way to do it was by removing him from the influence of his ambitious father.

Marciano survives two bloody battles

EZZARD CHARLES, the 33-year-old former champion, gave Rocky Marciano the toughest fight of his career in June in Yankee Stadium, New York. The heavyweight champion was badly cut in the fourth round, with a two-inch long and one-inch deep wound by his left eye. Only Marciano's immense strength sustained him, and by the eighth Charles was cut too, on the right eyelid. Although Charles hung on he was at Marciano's mercy in the 15th round. Marciano no longer had the power to dispatch the challenger and he retained his title on a unanimous points decision.

It was one of the decade's great contests, and to many it signalled the decline of the impregnable champion. The rematch was three months later. Once again it was a bloodbath. In the sixth round Charles caught Marciano's nose with an elbow, splitting it wide open. The cut was so bad that Marciano's corner had to beg the doctor not to stop the fight with Marciano miles ahead on points.

Marciano furiously went for a knock-out, and in the process received another bad cut in the corner of his left eye in the eighth round. He ignored the blood pouring from his face, smashed Charles to the floor, and when he got up at four put him down for good.

Marciano rocks Charles with a straight left

FOR THE RECORD

CRICKET
■ Jack Hobbs was knighted.

■ New Zealand enforced a follow-on for the first time in a Test, but South Africa managed to draw the match.

FOOTBALL
■ Scot Symon, who played cricket and football for Scotland, was appointed the manager of Rangers with a mission to rebuild the team.

■ Jock Stein captained Celtic to the Double.

■ Uefa was formed.

RACKETS
■ G W T Atkins, an amateur, won the world championship and held it for a record 17 years.

TABLE TENNIS
■ Di and Ros Rowe, twins from Middlesex, won the women's world doubles title for the second time. Their triumph at Wembley was the last time England won a world title of any kind.

Twin peaks: Di and Ros Rowe's second title

Wolves climb to top of the world

WERE Wolves the greatest side in the world? The manner in which the English champions dismissed Honved, the Hungarian champions, at Molineux on December 13 suggested that this was no idle boast by their manager Stan Cullis.

A full house had turned up to see how Wolves would cope with Ferenc Puskas and Honved's five other players from the Hungarian national side that seemed able to dismember England at will. They did not have long to wait. Within 14 minutes Honved had galloped into a 2-0 lead and the script seemed depressingly familiar. But the resilient English champions held on until half-time, came out fired up, scored from a penalty, equalised in the 76th minute and then stormed to the winning goal two minutes later.

The victory capped a marvellous year of international conquests for Wolves. They had beaten Racing Club of Buenos Aires 3-1, Maccabi Tel Aviv 10-0 and Russian champions Spartak Moscow 4-0 with three goals in the last three minutes.

TENNIS

Wimbledon finally falls to Drobny

Drobny: oldest champion

CHALK one up to the left-handers. Jaroslav Drobny broke a 40-year drought when he became the first left-handed men's singles champion at Wimbledon since Norman Brookes in 1914.

The 33-year-old Czech exile triumphed at his 11th attempt. He used his powerful serve and smash to take a popular win against the 19-year-old Australian Ken Rosewall 13-11 4-6 6-2 9-7. Drobny was the oldest post-war men's champion.

Maureen Connolly retained the women's title with the loss of only 19 games. But the biggest achievement of the year was by Doris Hart, who won the triple crown at the US championships. She had clinched the triple crown at Wimbledon in 1951 and at the French championships in 1952.

Union prodigy joins pro league for £3,000

RUGBY LEAGUE scouts cast covetous eyes on Billy Boston when he scored 126 tries in a season for the Royal Signals rugby union side in 1953. It was Wigan who persuaded the 18-year-old to sign for £3,000.

Boston made such an impression that he was drafted into the Great Britain team to tour Australia, and he scored 36 tries on the wing. Australia won the series 2-1 but the tour was marred by a brawl in the match against New South Wales in Sydney on July 10.

Britain's Ray Price was sent off for arguing with the referee, Aub Oxford. The game degenerated into an all-out brawl and when Oxford realised that he could not regain control he walked off the field to the applause of the crowd, and quit the sport for good. The match was abandoned in the 56th minute with New South Wales leading 17-6.

Boston (*right*) scored 36 tries in Australia

Thomson the nearly man just made it

Thomson: spectacular recovery

PETER THOMSON appeared destined to become the nearly-man for the third time in succession when the Open made its debut at Royal Birkdale.

The Australian, who was the runner-up to Bobby Locke and Ben Hogan the previous two years, was one of four in contention over the closing holes. Then disaster struck. He lodged his second shot in soft sand under the lip of a bunker at the 16th hole and the elusive title had begun to slip away again.

But Thomson's 75-foot recovery shot was spectacular, flying 30 feet into the air and landing inches from the hole. He tapped in for par and with a 71 won his first Open by one shot from Bobby Locke, Syd Scott and Dai Rees.

Germans steal Cup from Hungary

HUNGARY, the hot favourites for the fifth World Cup, held in Switzerland, lost the tournament in their second game when Ferenc Puskas, the greatest player on the world stage, was kicked by West Germany's centre-half, Werner Liebrich, and spent an hour off the field with an injured ankle.

Hungary won 8-3 in Basle, but only against a West Germany that had deliberately put out a weakened side, and the injury to Puskas dogged them throughout the tournament.

England had Stanley Matthews, Tom Finney and Nat Lofthouse, but they could not lift a makeshift side who did creditably well to reach the quarter-finals, where poor keeping by Gil Merrick cost them the tie against holders Uruguay.

Scotland, who deigned to participate this time despite once again coming second in the Home championships which doubled as a World Cup qualifying group, were eliminated without a goal or a point. Not that it seemed to bother them. As a selector put it: "Never mind lads, just so long as we beat the English next April."

The quarter-final between Brazil and Hungary was so unruly it became known as the Battle of Berne. Two Brazilians and a Hungarian were sent off, the match was littered with fouls and squabbles, and after Hungary won 4-2 the dressing rooms resembled a war zone with boots and bottles flying. The Brazilian centre-half Pinheiro was struck in the face with a bottle (possibly by Puskas who had not played because of his ankle) and had to leave the ground swathed in bandages.

The final, against West Germany, was a pulsating match that almost certainly turned on Puskas. He played with his badly-injured ankle and was desperately slow and leaden-footed. Without a fully fit Puskas the Hungarian machine could not run smoothly.

True, they began in their usual thrilling fashion, 2-0 up inside eight minutes, but the Germans soon hit back and were level by the 16th minute. The match see-sawed as each side had periods of full-out attack. In the second half Hidegkuti missed a simple chance with 12 minutes left. Five minutes later, the West Germans delivered the killing goal.

Frenetically, the Hungarians sought an equaliser, and with two minutes to go they thought they had it, but Puskas's goal was controversially ruled offside. The West Germans had snatched the World Cup from the world's best team.

Pakistan defy English elements

RAIN robbed Pakistan of nearly four days of their first Test in England and then they ran into a Typhoon in the fourth Test. But neither the elements nor Frank Tyson could stop the Pakistanis becoming the first team to square a series on their debut in England.

Tyson took five for 57 in his first match but Pakistan recovered to win by 24 runs at The Oval on August 17. A swashbuckling 278 by Denis Compton gave England their victory in the second Test.

Compton could not stop Pakistan at The Oval

Chataway's neat revenge

CHRIS CHATAWAY was seeking revenge when he clashed with the Ukrainian Vladimir Kuts in a 5,000m race under floodlights at White City in London on October 13. The Englishman had watched Kuts slip away to win the European title earlier in the year and was determined not to repeat his mistake. So Chataway kept in touch and in a stirring finish beat Kuts in the final stride. Chataway clocked 13min 51.6sec in front of an enthralled full house of 50,000.

FOR THE RECORD

ATHLETICS
■ Sandor Rozsnyoi, of Hungary, became the first world record holder in the 3,000m steeplechase with a time of 8min 49.6sec at the European championships in Berne. The rules of the event had only been clarified earlier in the year.

MOTOR RACING
■ Mercedes returned to top-flight competition in the French Grand Prix at Rheims in July. Juan Fangio and Karl Kling led throughout the race and celebrated the comeback by crossing the finishing line side by side.

GOLF
■ Arnold Palmer won the US amateur championship at Detroit Country Club. He beat Robert Sweeney at the 36th hole and turned professional soon after.

ROWING
■ Crews from the Soviet Union entered the Henley regatta for the first time, and won the Grand Challenge Cup, the Stewards Cup and the Silver Goblets. The Daily Telegraph's correspondent was far from impressed, and said: "I suppose we shall see Cossacks riding in the Grand National next year."

The Russian eight breaks the Thames barrier

FOOTBALL

Robertson corners TV and Celtic

THE first Scottish Cup final televised live had plenty of surprises for the viewers and for Celtic, who had imagined they would coast home against the unfancied Clyde. And so it appeared as Celtic led 1-0 with two minutes left.

Then Clyde won a corner on the right and Archie Robertson's inswinger curled over the fingers of Celtic's goalkeeper. It was the first goal direct from a corner in the Scottish Cup final.

Robertson admitted that not only had he no intention of trying to score, he had not even intended to play the ball so close to the goal. Clyde's luck held. In the replay a buoyant Clyde won 1-0 to bring the Cup to Shawfield for the second time.

GOLF

Slowcoach races away to Masters

CARY MIDDLECOFF had a reputation for taking so long to play his shots that his fellow American Dick Mayer once took a camping stool around the course. But there was nothing to hold up the slowcoach of the US Tour at Augusta when he won the Masters by seven strokes from Ben Hogan.

BOXING

Marciano's world title saved by disgraceful decisions

ROCKY MARCIANO was extremely fortunate to end the year as the world heavyweight champion. First he fought England's Don Cockell in San Francisco in May in one of the dirtiest fights ever seen. The list of fouls the champion perpetrated on the challenger was disgraceful and stricter refereeing would have see him disqualified.

In the first round Marciano kidney-punched Cockell; in the third he hit him after the bell; in the fourth he head-butted Cockell and split his forehead open; Cockell was hit low in the fifth and the sixth; in the seventh he was hit low and butted again; in the ninth Cockell was hit while on the deck and counted out.

Then, in September in Yankee Stadium, Marciano met the light-heavyweight champion, Archie Moore. In the second round Marciano missed with a right and Moore stepped inside Marciano's left and put him down with a short right. The standing eight count had been waived for this fight, but the referee apparently forgot.

Marciano rose at two, but the referee prevented Moore, the most devastating finisher in the game, from finishing Marciano off. The champion was in serious trouble. He was unsteady and clinging on to the ropes while staring into the crowd. The referee continued the count to four, and wiped Marciano's gloves. This eight-second delay cost Moore the title as a recovered Marciano went on to knock out a tired Moore in the ninth.

> *I was so furious with the referee I thought I'd hit him first and get the obstacle out of the way. But as it was, I turned to fight Rocky and I was stupid with rage. I felt I now had to fight two men*
>
> **Archie Moore**

> *Marciano played a different sport from Cockell. He butted unmercifully, he hit with his elbows, he hit low. A British referee would have sent him to his corner after three rounds*
>
> **Eamonn Andrews**

Marciano and Cockell

CRICKET

Hutton almost has a perfect swansong

LEN HUTTON could not have asked for a better way to bow out of Test cricket. The only thing he did wrong in the second Test against New Zealand in Auckland was to lose the toss.

New Zealand were dismissed for 200, and then the England captain steadied the batting when he came in with his side 112 for three which soon became 112 for four. Hutton had the top-score of 53 in England's total of 246.

After that everything ran England's way. The pace pair of Frank Tyson and Brian Statham started the rout of New Zealand, and when Bob Appleyard and Johnny Wardle took over the home side were on their way to the lowest total in Test history.

New Zealand were bowled out for 26 in 106 minutes, to give England victory by an innings and 20 runs. The previous lowest totals in Tests were 30 by South Africa against England in 1896 and 1924.

Hutton had hoped to captain England in the home series against South Africa in the summer but was troubled by lumbago and retired from Tests.

Australians indulge in run feast in Caribbean

FIVE batsmen scored centuries in the same innings when Australia declared at 758 for eight in their fifth Test in the West Indies. Colin McDonald (127), Neil Harvey (207), Keith Miller (109), Ron Archer (128) and Richie Benaud (121) were the centurions in Kingston, Jamaica. Australia won by an innings and 82 runs on June 17 to secure a 3-0 victory in the high-scoring series on their first visit to the Caribbean.

83 killed at Le Mans but the race goes on

THE Le Mans 24-hour race witnessed the worst disaster in the history of motor racing when 83 people died and more than 100 were injured on June 11. Pierre Levegh's Mercedes was travelling at 150mph when it hit the rear of another car, somersaulted over the safety barrier, caught fire and broke into pieces, killing Levegh and sending debris flying into the crowd.

Incredibly the race continued to the finish and the drivers were not told about the extent of the tragedy. Eight hours after the accident the other two Mercedes, driven by Juan Fangio and Stirling Moss, were pulled out of the race at the express command of the German manufacturers.

The organisers believed that cancelling the race would have started a panic and a mass exodus of spectators would have impeded rescue operations. However, many thought that the race should have been cancelled immediately and Spain, Switzerland and Mexico banned motor racing completely. In France it was suspended until the rules were revised.

The disaster starts when Levegh's Mercedes explodes

Fate deals cruel hand again to Ascari family

ALBERTO ASCARI, a genius of a driver and second only to Juan Fangio as the greatest since the war, crashed while testing a borrowed Ferrari sports car and died instantly at Monza on May 26.

The accident was inexplicable since he was not travelling very fast when he skidded and the car turned over several times. Nor was he wearing a crash helmet. Strangely, Ascari had escaped unscathed from a potentially more dangerous accident four days earlier at the Monaco Grand Prix when he made an error at the chicane, slid across the wall and tumbled into the harbour. Ascari swam to the rescue boat and suffered only a broken nose.

His father, Antonio Ascari, was a racing driver who also lost his life on the track, in the French Grand Prix in 1925 at Montlhery. Coincidentally both Ascaris died at the age of 36, and both left a widow with two young children.

Typhoon Tyson ties the Australians down

Gotcha: Keith Miller and Australia lose third Test

ENGLAND won their first series in Australia in 22 years on a tour dominated by Frank Tyson and a small contribution from Admiral Horatio Nelson.

Tyson captured 28 wickets in England's 3-1 victory, their first down under since the Bodyline tour in 1932-33. And Nelson struck when Australia were twice dismissed for 111 in their second innings.

The home side's only victory was in the first Test in Brisbane, when Len Hutton won the toss and elected to field. It was the first time an English captain had done so in Australia since Johnny Douglas in 1912. Hutton was left to rue his contribution to the history books. Australia made 601 for eight declared, the highest Test score by a side put in to bat.

FOR THE RECORD

ATHLETICS
■ There were a pair of firsts on June 29. Glenn Davis broke the 50sec barrier in the 400m hurdles and Charles Dumas became the first man to clear 7ft in the high jump.

FOOTBALL
■ Because of falling attendances, the Football League reported a deficit of £10,489. To cover the loss they decided to raise the minimum admission charge from 1s 9d to 2s. The management committee also proposed the creation of a national Third Division and Fourth Division to replace the two regionalised Third Divisions and stimulate spectator interest. The clubs threw the proposal out.

■ Duncan Edwards, of Manchester United, became England's youngest international when, at the age of 18 years and six months, he played against Scotland.

TABLE TENNIS
■ Angelica Rozeanu of Romania won a record sixth world singles title in Utrecht.

CYCLING

Bobet: third successive Tour

FOR THE RECORD

CYCLING
■ The Frenchman Louison Bobet became the first man to win three successive Tours de France.

FOOTBALL
■ Accrington Stanley fielded a team composed entirely of Scottish-born players.

■ The Fairs Cup competition was started, but the first tournament dragged on for three years.

GOLF
■ Peter Thomson won his second Open at St Andrews. The tournament was shown live on television for the first time on July 7, and also had a £1,000 first prize for the first time.

■ The United States won the Ryder Cup 8-4 at Palm Springs.

RACING
■ Meld won the fillies' Triple Crown, making Captain Boyd Rochfort the first trainer to win £1m in total.

SPEED
■ Donald Campbell became the first man to exceed 200mph in a boat on November 16.

CRICKET

May leads in exemplary style to usher in glorious summer

PETER MAY celebrated his appointment as England captain by hammering 582 runs off South Africa in a typically prolific season. He took over the leadership when Len Hutton stood down because of lumbago. May, who had hit a century against South Africa on his Test debut in 1951, enjoyed another productive innings against the Springboks on the first day of his captaincy. He made the top score of 83 in the first Test at Trent Bridge to steer England to victory by an innings and five runs. Ken Barrington, his Surrey teammate, had a less auspicious debut and was dismissed for a duck.

May also dominated proceedings in the second Test at Lord's. He scored a classic century full of characteristic drives, particularly on the leg-side, to rescue England who were 171 runs behind on the first innings. May then called on Brian Statham to bowl for nearly four hours, and his heroic spell of 29-12-39-7 took England to a 71-run victory.

The Springboks won the next two Tests and when their off-spinner Hugh Tayfield had a spell of 52 overs for 54 runs and four wickets, South Africa appeared on the brink of winning the series in the fifth Test at The Oval. However, Jim Laker, with five for 56, and Tony Lock, with four for 62, struck back on their home ground and England's 92-run victory ended the first series in England to produce five outright results.

> *'Peter May is a cavalier batsman and a roundhead captain'*

May: Surrey and England star

MAY'S RECORD

	FIRST-CLASS	TESTS (66)
Innings	618	106
Not out	77	9
Runs	27,592	4,537
Highest	285no	285no
Average	51.00	46.77
Hundreds	85	13
Wickets	None	Did not bowl
Catches	282	42

FOOTBALL

Wolves provoke European Cup

THE proud boast by Stan Cullis that Wolves were the greatest side in the world stirred Uefa and Fifa into action. Spurred on by the editor of L'Equipe, Gabriel Hanot, who had long campaigned for such a tournament, and stung by Cullis's remarks after Wolves had stunned Honved the previous December, they gave their formal blessing to a European Cup, contested by the champions of Uefa's member countries.

Sadly for Wolves, they were not eligible as Chelsea were the League champions. And sadly for Chelsea, and English football, Chelsea declined the invitation at the behest of the Football League, whose reasons were pitiful: "The additional fixtures might be difficult to fulfil."

In Scotland there was no hesitancy about the infant competition, and the Scottish Football Association approved Hibs's participation. This was a little

hard on Aberdeen, who had actually won the championship, but Hibs had been invited because of their performances throughout the early 1950s, when they were unquestionably the best team in Scotland, and because their chairman had shown himself to be committed to European football.

Hibs had little problem fulfilling the additional fixtures, progressed to the semi-final, and made a profit of £25,000.

Flawless Trabert puts opponents in a spin

TONY TRABERT, the all-American college boy, tormented his opponents with backhand and forehand topspin lobs on his way to winning three of the four Grand Slam events. Trabert, one of the few players to use a topspin lob in his armoury, did not drop a set at Wimbledon or the US championships. He won the All-England title with a 6-3 7-5 6-1 victory against the Dane Kurt Nielsen in the final.

Trabert's only blemish in the major events was a semi-final defeat against Ken Rosewall in the Australian championships. Rosewall beat his fellow Australian Lew Hoad 9-7 6-4 6-4 in the final.

Trabert: only player with topspin lob

Morgan inspires Lions to stop Springboks

CLIFF MORGAN had been given the runaround by three big South African loose forwards in his first season as fly-half for Wales in 1951. Four years later the little Welshman returned the compliment in kind when he inspired the British Lions in South Africa.

In the first Test, played in Johannesburg, the tourists, trailing 11-8 at half-time, lost Reg Higgins with an injury soon after the restart of play. Morgan responded immediately with a brilliant try which sparked a scoring spree. The Lions raced to a 23-11 lead before the Springboks could draw breath.

The home side, spurred on by 95,000 supporters, fought back gallantly but with the last kick of the game their full-back, Jack van der Schyff, missed a relatively easy conversion. The Lions won 23-22 and van der Schyff was dropped from the team. He received such bad publicity that he sought refuge in the bush and became a crocodile hunter.

Morgan led the Lions to a 9-6 victory in the third Test to ensure their record as the first touring team to square a series in South Africa this century.

Lightning strikes twice after delayed Ascot endures heatwave

ROYAL ASCOT had been postponed in June because of a rail strike, and when the meeting was finally held it ended in tragedy. Gold Cup day was July 14, and the temperature had been stifling all week. The weather finally broke late in the afternoon when a storm swept over the course. The crowds were running to find shelter from the downpour when lightning struck near the Royal box. Hundreds of people on the Heath were knocked over and a pregnant woman was killed.

Racing was abandoned for the day, only the second time that had happened at Royal Ascot. The other occasion was in 1930 when lightning had also struck the course, killing a bookmaker.

Imports leave Britain skating on thin ice

BRITAIN'S triumph at the 1936 Winter Olympics probably brought about the steady decline in ice hockey after the Second World War. Inspired by the success of the dual nationals in the 1936 team, Canadians flocked to Britain. At one point it was even estimated that 90 per cent of the players in Britain were of Canadian descent.

But as spectators were drawn away by rival attractions clubs found it ever more difficult to pay their spiralling wage bills. Harringay Greyhounds had folded in 1949, Wembley Monarchs gave up in 1950, Earls Court announced that it was withdrawing from ice hockey in 1953, and Streatham pulled out in 1954.

Things had got so bad that in 1954 the four remaining English sides had to join forces with Scotland to form a 12-team British League. Even that was not enough to halt the slide, and in 1955 the British League had shrunk to a mere five teams: Nottingham, Wembley, Paisley, Brighton and Harringay.

Bert Oig of Harringay Racers scores against the Russians

GOLF

Britain scrape a Curtis Cup win

FRANCES SMITH sunk a 15-foot putt on the final hole to beat Polly Riley in the decisive match, earning Britain their last Curtis Cup victory against the United States for 30 years. Smith's one-shot win gave Britain a 5-4 triumph at Sandwich.

FOR THE RECORD

ATHLETICS
■ **Gordon Pirie broke the world 5,000m record, beating his great Russian rival Vladimir Kuts in a memorable race in Bergen. Pirie, who broke five world records and 22 British marks in his career, clocked 13 min 36.8 sec.**

■ **Jim Bailey ran the first four-minute mile in the United States on May 5.**

CRICKET
■ **After 26 years and 45 matches New Zealand won their first Test when they beat West Indies by 190 runs in Auckland on March 13. Captain John Reid top-scored with 84 and Henry Cave took eight for 43 in the match. West Indies made 77 in the second innings.**

FOOTBALL
■ **The first floodlit League match was held on February 22. But the game between Portsmouth and Newcastle was held up for 30 minutes because of problems with the lights' fuses. Portsmouth lost 2-0.**

■ **The first official floodlit League match in Scotland was played on March 7 at Ibrox, where Rangers hammered Queen of the South 8-0.**

■ **Hearts beat Celtic to win the Scottish Cup. It was their first Cup or League Trophy for 50 years.**

NETBALL
■ **England staged their first overseas tour, to South Africa.**

RACING

Devon Loch slips in race mystery

NOBODY knew what befell Devon Loch in the Grand National on March 24, but there were as many theories as there were runners in the race to explain what one newspaper described as the "greatest hard luck story in the history of racing".

The Queen Mother's horse was well clear of the field, on the way to breaking Reynoldstown's record time set in 1935 and had about 50 yards to go to the finishing line. Suddenly, inexplicably, the Queen Mother's horse crumpled to the turf in the space of a few strides, leaving ESB to win the race by 10 lengths. The crowd that had been roaring the royal horse home was stunned into silence. But soon there was a buzz of speculation and everybody had their own, wildly conflicting, explanation.

One vet said that Devon Loch could have been struck down by a cramp. Another said that a blood clot in one of his hind legs was to blame. A trainer even suggested that Devon Loch had been electrocuted by an underground cable. Many people believed that Devon Loch had been startled by the noise of the crowd and still more thought that he had been misled by water alongside the course and had tried to jump an obstacle that was not there.

The Queen Mother very nobly congratulated the owners of ESB, but her words of sympathy were not able to console Dick Francis, Devon Loch's jockey, or Peter Cazalet his trainer.

The debate raged in the newspapers for days but Francis, at least, was sure he knew what happened: "I am convinced the horse just slipped," he said. "It's as simple as that."

> **❛ In one stride he was bounding smoothly along; in the next, his hind legs stiffened and refused to function. He fell flat on his belly and when he stood up he could hardly move . . . the dream was over and the race was lost ❜**
>
> **Dick Francis**

Devon Loch belly flops 50 yards from the finish

TENNIS

Rosewall and Hoad square up

Hoad: trading shots

LEW HOAD and Ken Rosewall had been trading shots on the tennis court since they were schoolboys in Sydney during the war. Little did they know that 15 years later they would be staging some of the greatest battles in Grand Slam history.

Hoad, three weeks the younger, won his first Australian title by beating Rosewall 6-4 3-6 6-4 7-5 in 1956. He then added the French trophy to his cabinet with a victory against the Swede Sven Davidson. The Australian said of his fortnight in the French capital: "Every year you say you'll never play Paris again. Your arm nearly falls off. The balls are heavy. They water the courts. You're always playing some guy you've never heard of and he keeps you out there for well over 3½ hours. But it's a great tournament."

Back on the familiar grass at Wimbledon he beat Rosewall 6-2 4-6 7-5 6-4 in an entertaining final. But with the Grand Slam in his sights at the US championships at Forest Hills, who should pop up and beat him in the final: his old school chum and nemesis Rosewall, 4-6 6-2 6-3 6-3.

Wily Revie and brave Trautmann lead Manchester City to the Cup

Marciano quits with no losses

ROCKY MARCIANO retired from the ring on April 21 as the only man to have held the undisputed heavyweight championship of the world without ever being beaten. He had fought 49 times and won all 49, with 43 inside the distance. The fight with Archie Moore the previous September had finished the champion and he intelligently decided to quit with his perfect record intact.

Marciano's retirement also ended the iron grip Jim Norris and his International Boxing Club had enjoyed over the world heavyweight championship since Ezzard Charles became the champion on the retirement of Louis in 1949.

Two days before Marciano's announcement the government started proceedings against Norris and the IBC for anti-trust violations relating to the monopoly.

Lucky to be alive: Bert Trautmann unknowingly sustained a broken neck saving at Murphy's feet

DON REVIE provided the guile and Bert Trautmann the guts that brought Manchester City the FA Cup after the disappointment of losing the final the previous year. Revie's "deep lying centre-forward", a strategy he had adopted from Ferenc Puskas's Hungarians, proved masterly as Birmingham toiled to overcome Revie's tactical acumen. Revie set up City's

first goal with a neat back-heel. And despite Birmingham's equaliser, Revie and the heavily-strapped Bobby Johnstone did the rest in a 3-1 romp, with Johnstone becoming the first man to score in consecutive Cup finals.

Three days after the final the Manchester City team discovered how brave their giant German goalkeeper had been, when X-rays

revealed that Trautmann had a broken neck. The former PoW had dived courageously at the feet of Birmingham's Peter Murphy and lain on the ground stunned. Five minutes later Trautmann was in another collision and again fell to the ground. Eventually he got up, rubbed his painful neck and played on. Trautmann was voted Footballer of the Year.

Open hat-trick for Thomson

Thomson: orthodox swing

PETER THOMSON'S penchant for playing simple golf paid off for the third year in a row. The Australian with an orthodox swing and straight putting stroke thrived on the links courses of Britain.

He had won at Royal Birkdale and St Andrews the previous two years and wrapped up his hat-trick at Hoylake with a five-shot victory over the Belgian Flory van Donck. Bobby Locke, Thomson's great rival, surprisingly did not qualify.

Manchester United defy League to enter fledgling European Cup

MANCHESTER UNITED won the championship in glittering fashion. They were unbeaten at Old Trafford (winning 18 and drawing three), they clinched the title in the first week in April and the average age of the side was 23. The FA invited the club to participate in the European Cup, now in its

second year. The League, who had dissuaded Chelsea from taking part the previous year, tried to block United. To no avail. Matt Busby was adamant: "Prestige alone demanded that the continental challenge be met, not avoided."

United's first home match was against Anderlecht, the Belgian

champions seven times in the previous 10 years, and the Manchester club won 10-0 in one of the most scintillating team displays ever produced by a British side. More than 75,000 turned up for the next round, against Borussia Dortmund. England's love affair with the European Cup was born.

Games marred by political rows

Betty Cuthbert of Australia wins the 100m

1956

DECEMBER

BOXING

Patterson KOs Moore for title

Patterson: youngest champion

FLOYD PATTERSON stepped into Rocky Marciano's shoes in Chicago on November 30 when he knocked out Archie Moore in the fifth round to claim the vacant world heavyweight title. At 21 years and 10 months, Patterson, the 1952 Olympic middleweight gold medallist, became the youngest man ever to hold the heavyweight world title.

FOR THE RECORD

BASEBALL
■ Don Larsen of the New York Yankees pitched the only perfect game in the history of the World Series during the fifth game on October 8. The Yankees beat the Brooklyn Dodgers 4-3 in the series.

CRICKET
■ Lancashire beat Leicestershire without losing a wicket.
■ Len Hutton was knighted.

JUDO
■ The first world championship was won by Shokichi Natsui of Japan.

MOTOR RACING
■ Juan Fangio won his fourth World championship in a Ferrari.

THE ONLY Olympic Games staged in the southern hemisphere opened to a backdrop of conflict and controversy.

The XVI Games in Melbourne were marred by the Soviet invasion of Hungary and the intervention of Britain and France in the Suez Canal dispute. Egypt, Lebanon, Holland, Spain and Switzerland withdrew, and China pulled out because of the presence of Taiwan. The Games were also in doubt when the Australian government imposed its strict animal quarantine laws, forcing the equestrian events to be held in Stockholm.

The conflict between the Soviets and Hungarians spilled into the pool when the water polo semifinal turned into a battle. In a game described as a boxing match under water the Hungarians won 4-0 and then beat Yugoslavia in the final.

The buoyant Australians dominated the swimming in front of crowds who had queued for days to buy tickets. The hosts won all the men's and women's freestyle events, which lifted their medal tally to third place behind the Soviet Union and the United States.

The Americans were supreme on the track, where their sprinter Bobby-Joe Morrow won three gold medals. The Australian Betty Cuthbert emulated him in the women's events.

India won their sixth successive gold medal in hockey and Ireland their first gold medal since 1932 when Ron Delaney won the 1500m. And Alain Mimoun, a Frenchman who had won three silver medals in the 1948 and 1952 Games, finally came home first. Mimoun, a month short of his 36th birthday, won the marathon and then waited to embrace the sixth-placed Emil Zatopek, who had beaten him each time on the track.

Britain won six gold medals, seven silver and 11 bronze, but nearly had one gold medal taken away when Chris Brasher was briefly disqualified in the 3,000m steeplechase for interference.

RACING

Perfect finish to perfect career

RIBOT'S last race was the Arc de Triomphe on October 7. He bowed out in the only way he knew — with a runaway victory. It was a second triumph in the race for the best horse in Europe.

Ribot was bred in Italy and he won seven races there as a two-year-old. Despite that, he started at 9-1 for the 1955 Arc, which he duly won by three lengths.

His final season was even more ambitious and he came to Britain for the King George VI and Queen Elizabeth Stakes. He was reckoned not to have run a good race, but he still charged home by five lengths in heavy going. After the Arc Ribot was retired to stud, and with a perfect record of 16 wins from 16 starts he proved himself a fine sire as well.

Ribot: twice a runaway winner of the Arc de Triomphe

Surrey pair wreak havoc on Australians

"ASHES to Ashes, dust to dust, if Laker don't get you, Locky must." That was the catchphrase doing the rounds on the county circuit when Ian Johnson's Australians arrived, hoping to win back the most treasured urn in cricket.

The Surrey spin twins, Jim Laker and Tony Lock, had been mesmerising batsmen summer after summer. Now Johnson's men were about to fall into their web. Their first acquaintance with the Surrey pair was at The Oval on May 16. Laker had spent most of the previous night caring for his sick daughters, Fiona and Angela, and was looking forward to a day in the dressing room.

Stuart Surridge, the Surrey captain, had other ideas. He put Australia in and shortly before noon threw the ball to Laker. The off-spinner, with his high action and ability to flight the ball tantalisingly, bowled for 4¼ hours and when he eventually put his feet up he had figures of 46-18-88-10. Lock did not get a look-in until the second innings, when he took seven for 49. Surrey's victory was the first by a county side against Australia since 1912.

Laker became a hero overnight. The News Chronicle signed him up for a series of instructional articles, he was the flavour of the month for cartoonists and photographers, and the manufacturers of Lucozade proclaimed in one of their advertisements: "Jim Laker takes 10 wickets for 88 runs. How's that for sustained energy?"

The start of the Test series was an anti-climax for Laker. The first Test at Trent Bridge was drawn and the Australians won the second. That defeat brought about the recall of the 41-year-old Cyril Washbrook, who had not played in a Test for nearly six years and was by then an England selector. It was a controversial choice but it worked as he scored 98 and Laker, with 11 for 113, and Lock, with seven for 81, helped England win by an innings and 42 runs at Headingley. And so to Old

Trafford and the fourth Test. Praise on the first day for England's score of 307 for three was drowned out by complaints from the Australians about the pitch. They said it was breaking up unusually early.

By the second day their criticism had reached a crescendo. Laker's spell from the Stretford End had accounted for nine of their men, including the last seven for eight runs off only 22 balls.

Australia recovered momentarily and enjoyed lunch on the final day at 112 for two with a draw in sight. But the sun came out, the pitch stirred again and when Len Maddocks was trapped leg before an hour before the end Laker had taken all 10 wickets. The Ashes were still in England.

His analysis of 19 for 90 was the greatest feat by a bowler and the ink was still drying in the history books when the telegrams from around the world started to land on his doorstep. One said: "Congratulations. Why not 20?" Amid all the trumpeting one man was nearly forgotten. Lock had bowled 55 overs in the second innings and conceded only 69 runs. While he was walking off the field Peter May, the England captain, quietly said to him: "Well bowled Tony. Forget the scoreboard. You played your part too."

Three weeks earlier, Lock had taken all 10 Kent wickets in an innings . . . and 16 in the match. "Ashes to Ashes, dust to dust, if Laker don't get you, Locky must."

Laker leaves the field having taking 10 for 88.

CAREER STATISTICS

	Jim Laker		Tony Lock	
	FIRST-CLASS	TESTS (46)	FIRST-CLASS	TESTS (49)
Innings	548	63	812	63
Not out	108	15	161	9
Runs	7,304	676	10,342	742
Highest	113	63	89	89
Average	16.60	14.08	15.88	13.74
Hundreds	2	0	0	0
Wickets	1,944 at 18.40	193 at 21.24	2,844 at 19.32	174 at 25.58
Catches	271	12	831	59

Bowlers have a field day in slow Test

AUSTRALIA and Pakistan plodded their way through the slowest day in Test cricket in Karachi on October 11. In 5½ hours' play, Australia struggled to 80 all out and Pakistan replied with 15 for two. Fortunately there was only one Test in the series, which Pakistan won by nine wickets.

CRICKET

England finally discover how to tame Ramadhin

SONNY RAMADHIN arrived in England seven years after he had bamboozled the English batsmen. Now he was back for more of the same. Few batsmen could read whether he was sending down an off-break or a leg-break because he disguised his grip by keeping his sleeves buttoned at the wrists.

When Peter May won the toss and elected to bat in the first Test at Edgbaston Ramadhin went to work. He took seven for 49 as England were bowled out for 186 on a perfect pitch. England's worst nightmare had come back to haunt them.

The West Indies were nearly 200 runs ahead when Ramadhin struck in the second innings to have England reeling at 113 for three. Colin Cowdrey then joined May and by padding the ball away for eight hours and 20 minutes they destroyed Ramadhin's effectiveness. "They kicked me to bloody death," was the spinner's curt summary.

The England captain and his lieutenant made 411, an England record, with May hitting an unbeaten 285 and Cowdrey 154. Ramadhin bowled 588 balls in the innings, a first-class record. His 774 deliveries in the match was a Test record.

The jaded West Indians collapsed to 72 for seven. Although the Test was drawn, England had the measure of Ramadhin. He took only five more wickets and England won the series 3-0.

BOXING

Sugar Ray as sweet as ever

Robinson beats Fullmer to become the champion again

You could have set him to music when he was performing in the ring with a grace and style that was almost ballet. Until he let fly with his ferocious combinations that owed more to ballistics than ballet

Henry Cooper

SUGAR RAY ROBINSON, pound for pound the best fighter of the century, was back to his old ways, losing the world middleweight crown and winning it back again.

Sugar Ray retired in 1955, but his financial straits caused him to return to the ring and he regained his title by knocking out Bobo Olson in two rounds that year. In January 1957 Sugar Ray defended the title against Gene Fullmer and lost it on a unanimous points decision. But four months later a brilliant left hook in the fifth round meant Sugar Ray was the world middleweight champion for the fourth time.

Although, at 36, he was past his prime, he was still capable of exhibiting the skills that made him such an exquisite boxer and the biggest draw outside of the heavyweight division. He was the welterweight champion from 1946 to 1951, when he moved up to middleweight to take that title away from Jake LaMotta.

If it had not been for the 100-plus degrees temperature he would also have captured the light-heavyweight title from Joey Maxim in June 1952. The heat was so great that the referee collapsed at the end of the 10th round and had to be replaced. Sugar Ray, despite being well ahead on points, was so dehydrated and exhausted that he was unable to come out for the

14th. It was the only time he was stopped, and it was the conditions not the opponent that beat him.

In September 1957 Sugar Ray lost his middleweight title to Carmen Basilio, who, like Robinson, had been the welterweight champion but moved up to the heavier division, when the New Yorker won a close decision.

But Sugar Ray wasn't finished with titles yet. In March 1958 the remarkable Robinson became the world middleweight champion for the fifth time when he outpointed Basilio in Chicago. In his career Sugar Ray contested 25 title fights in 25 years, fought 19 world champions, never took the count in 202 contests and lost only 19 times.

RACING

Piggott and Crepello's double hit

IT WAS a classic season for Noel Murless and Lester Piggott. They had high hopes for Crepello and their confidence was rewarded.

Crepello missed his warm-up race because the going was too hard, but Piggott rode a well-timed finish to take the Two Thousand Guineas by half a length. The going remained firm for the Derby but Crepello was not bothered, winning by 1½ lengths.

Two days later, on June 7, Piggott and Murless made it a sparkling summer when they gave the Queen her first Classic winner, Carrozza in the Oaks.

Piggott returns after winning the Derby by 1½ lengths

Jackson cuts through dominant defences to set up Grand Slam

Eric Evans, the England captain, scores a try in the corner against France

THE Five Nations championship was on the road to nowhere. The emphasis was on defence and a flaw in the laws enabled the three-quarters to line up so close to each other that no sooner had the attacking team gained possession then the opposition would be in position to tackle the fly-half. As a result, the game had become bogged down in a midfield morass.

There was one sparkling gem in the mire, though. Peter Jackson, a nimble winger from Coventry, took England to their first Grand Slam in 29 years by scoring three of his country's seven tries.

A large slice of Jackson's success was due to England's fine lock combination of John Currie and David Marques, whose excellent lineout jumping provided Jackson with plenty of possession. And the centre pairing of Jeff Butterfield and Phil Davies formed a formidable partnership and did a good job under trying circumstances.

England's victory roll consisted of a bruising 3-0 win against Wales, a 6-0 victory against Ireland, a 9-5 win against France and a 16-3 romp against Scotland.

Two cups are dashed from United's grasp

MANCHESTER UNITED'S first foray into Europe had proved highly successful on and off the field. Attendances were high and they had progressed to the semi-finals. United had an impossible dream in their sights: the Treble of the League, FA Cup and European Cup. However, their European opposition in the semi-final were the formidable Real Madrid, the Cup-holders.

The dream turned to ashes. The inexperienced United fell to Real Madrid, won the League in a can-ter and then had the FA Cup, and the Double, snatched from their grasp. Their goalkeeper, Ray Wood, was charged by Aston Villa's Peter MacParland and had to leave the field with a broken jaw. Jackie Blanchflower took over in goal but a 10-man United succumbed 2-1.

Only 24 hours before the final the FA rejected a Fifa proposal that substitutes be used. So once again a Wembley Cup final was virtually reduced to farce when 10 men had to battle against 11.

Italians in record deal for Charles

JUVENTUS doubled the British transfer record when they paid £70,000 for John Charles, the Wales and Leeds centre-forward on April 19. Charles received a £10,000 signing-on fee and £60 a week basic wages, more than four times the wage permissible in the Football League. Charles, who became known as the Gentle Giant in Italy, had been a formidable goalscorer for Leeds with 151 goals in 297 games. In Italy he was equally successful, and also adept at playing at centre-half. While he played for Juventus they won three championships and two Italian Cups.

Magic Finney honoured as England's best

Finney: always great

TOM FINNEY of Preston and England was chosen as the Footballer of the Year for the second time. Bill Shankly once said of the winger and occasional centre-forward: "Finney would have been great in any team, in any match, in any age — even if he had been wearing an overcoat."

FOR THE RECORD

CRICKET

■ Hugh Tayfield, the South African spinner, bowled a record 137 consecutive balls without conceding a run to England on the first day of the third Test in Durban in January.

■ Declarations were allowed at any time.

FOOTBALL

■ Stanley Matthews played his last game for England, winning his 54th cap aged 42.

■ The pools produced their first £200,000 winner.

■ Alan Hardaker was appointed secretary of Football League on January 1.

RACING

■ The Whitbread Gold Cup became the first sponsored race.

GOLF

Caddy's error hands Rawls hollow victory

BETSY RAWLS won her third women's US Open title at Winged Foot, New York, but it was a hollow victory.

Her great rival Jacqueline Pung had finished one shot ahead but when the scorecards were checked, Pung's caddie had correctly tallied up her round as 72 but inadvertently written down a six instead of a five for the fourth hole. Pung was disqualified and the members of the club collected a consolation prize of $3,000, $1,200 more than Rawls received for her victory.

FOR THE RECORD

BOXING

■ Pete Rademacher's first professional fight in August was for the world heavyweight title. The bout with Floyd Patterson in Seattle was thought to be a mismatch, but the Olympic heavyweight champion put Patterson down in the second round before being knocked out in the sixth.

CYCLING

■ Jacques Anquetil won his first Tour de France. The Frenchman went on to win a further four Tours in the 1960s.

FOOTBALL

■ The entertainment tax on football, introduced during the First World War, was withdrawn.

■ Arsenal appointed Ron Greenwood, the manager of Eastbourne United, their senior coach in December.

GOLF

■ Peter Thomson won the Yorkshire Evening News tournament by 15 strokes at Sand Moor, a record margin for a European Tour event.

MOTOR RACING

Fangio outwits Ferrari for fifth world title

A FIFTH world championship for Juan Fangio was extremely sweet. And the German Grand Prix at Nurburgring gave Fangio especial pleasure.

Although Fangio won the world championship the previous year with Ferrari he was never happy with the Maranello regime so he quit and returned to Maserati for the 1957 season. When Ferrari and Maserati lined up for the race in Germany the powerful Ferrari team had decided to run the race on full fuel without pit stops or tyre changes. But Maserati and Fangio planned to run on half fuel. Both teams were planning a tactical duel.

At half-way Fangio, using the weight advantage of a lighter fuel load, had built a 30-second lead over the two Ferraris and then had to stop for fuel and tyres. A bad pit stop meant that his lead became a 50-second deficit.

With 10 laps to go Fangio broke the lap record lap after lap. The 200,000 crowd roared in anticipation. With two laps to go the deficit was down to two seconds. On the last lap but one he overhauled one Ferrari and then the other to roar home 3.6sec ahead of his nearest challenger.

It was Fangio's 23rd victory in a Grand Prix, his fourth consecutive world championship, and his fifth in all. This was a collection of triumphs made all the sweeter by the magnificent way he had outwitted Ferrari in one of the greatest displays of individual driving ever witnessed.

Fangio wins the European Grand Prix at Rheims

GOLF

Britain win Cup at an odd course

SIR STUART GOODWIN, a member of the Lindrick Golf Club, wanted the Ryder Cup staged on his home course. So he sent the PGA £10,000 and got his wish.

The choice of the venue was controversial. Many believed it would favour the Americans because their superior short game would suit its 6,541-yard layout, with many holes requiring only a drive and a pitch.

The fifth hole was shortened by 18 yards because the tee was on land owned by Janet Sidda, who demanded what the organisers thought was an exorbitant fee for its use. She was upset because members of the club had occasionaly ordered her off the land.

The Americans won the foursomes 3-1 on October 4. The tide turned on the second day when Britain won all but one of the singles, Peter Alliss losing to Fred Hawkins 2 and 1. The 7-4 triumph with one match halved was Britain's first victory in 23 years.

SAILING

Admiral's Cup launched by Cowes admiral

SIR MYLES WYATT, admiral of the Royal Ocean Racing Club, was keen to attract more overseas entries to Cowes Week. So he presented a £300 Cup for four races between teams of three boats and the Admiral's Cup was born, although only Britain and the US entered the first competition.

The Fastnet Race set off into the teeth of a gale and was hit by a second storm, with 29 of the 41 yachts forced to retire. The United States won the race but only just, Carina crossing the line with several leaks. But Britain took second and third place and the Cup by two points, 70-68.

Gibson comes from ghetto to greatness

THE ivy-covered walls of the All-England Lawn Tennis Club were a far cry from the seedy streets of Harlem. Althea Gibson had an affinity with both.

The daughter of a poor sharecropper in South Carolina, Gibson grew up in the ghetto where she learned to box and play basketball and tennis. She took to tennis and 20 years later the walls of Wimbledon echoed to the acclaim of the first black singles champion when Gibson swept aside Darlene Hard 6-3 6-2 in the final.

All week Britain had watched the spectacular rise of the 16-year-old Christine Truman. Gibson ended the euphoria with a 6-1 6-1 victory in the semi-finals and later joined Hard to retain the doubles title she had won with Angela Buxton.

Gibson needed to be thick-skinned and street-wise to succeed in a sport seen as an exclusive preserve for middle-class whites. She could not gain entry to the top events and after a mediocre career she was on the point of giving up in 1953 when Sydney Llewellyn, a part-time professional, changed her mind and her grip. Gibson developed a strong serve and volley game and made her first breakthrough when she won the French championships in 1956.

After her victory at Wimbledon there was no holding her back. She beat Louise Brough in straight sets for the US championships, retained her Wimbledon and US titles the next year and then turned professional as the best woman player in the world.

Gibson took up golf in the 1960s and became the first black member of the US LPGA in 1963. She had won $25,000 by the time she was appointed Athletic Commissioner for New Jersey in 1975.

> ❝ I don't want to be put on a pedestal. I've always wanted to have an identity. I'm Althea Gibson, the tennis champion. I hope that makes me happy ❞
>
> **Althea Gibson**

Locke puts a stop to Thomson's procession

Locke: won his fourth Open at St Andrews

BOBBY LOCKE finally ended Peter Thomson's run of Open victories when he won by three shots at St Andrews. Thomson had won the previous three Opens. The tournament had been moved from Muirfield at short notice because of a petrol shortage during the Suez crisis.

Locke nearly had a crisis of his own. He marked his ball a putter's head length from the spot on the final green but replaced it on the marker instead of a length away. The R&A decided to let the result stand.

Quick-fire Summers Charlton's 7-6 hero

CHARLTON, reduced to 10 men when their captain went off injured, beat Huddersfield 7-6 on December 21. Huddersfield led 5-1 seven minutes into the second half, but Johnny Summers scored a hat-trick in six minutes, another goal six minutes later, and then netted again to put Charlton ahead at 6-5.

Huddersfield equalised in the 88th minute but Summers, wearing a new pair of boots that had not been broken in, set up the winning goal for John Ryan with almost the last kick of the match.

Moss sensibly switches cars

STIRLING MOSS began the year driving for Maserati alongside Juan Fangio but met with indifferent success despite setting the fastest lap in the Argentine Grand Prix.

He switched to Vanwell and won three of the last four GPs, including the British, to finish second in the world championship for the second successive year.

Gibson: Wimbledon's first black singles champion

FOR THE RECORD

FOOTBALL
■ Albert Quixall became the first £45,000 transfer when he moved from Sheffield Wednesday to Manchester United.

GOLF
■ Sam Snead failed to qualify for the last 36 holes of the US Open for the first time in his 18 appearances at the tournament

■ Arnold Palmer won the Masters for the first time, aged 28.

HOCKEY
■ Lincolnshire won the first men's county championships. It was their only title.

RACING
■ Airmile IV made his National Hunt debut at the extreme age of 15, and won the race at Warwick.

SQUASH
■ Janet Morgan retired after winning a record tenth successive British Open.

SQUASH

Morgan: tenth title

CRICKET

Sobers arrives with a big bang

Sobers: 365 not out to break Len Hutton's record

GARRY SOBERS was the brightest star in a twinkling galaxy of young West Indian cricketers when Pakistan arrived for their first tour of the Caribbean. However, it was the little Pakistani opener Hanif Mohammad who dominated the first Test in Bridgetown by scoring 337 runs in 16hr 10min, the longest innings in a Test.

Sobers had to wait until the third Test at Sabina Park to reach his century. The pitch was true and fast and Pakistani bowlers were in short supply. Mahmood Hussain pulled a thigh muscle in his fifth delivery and the 16-year-old Nasim-ul-Ghani had an unmemorable debut cut short by a fractured thumb.

Sobers and Conrad Hunte put on 446 for the second wicket and when Hunte was run out for 260 Sobers was joined by Everton Weekes. Soon after he had settled, Weekes played a shot to midwicket and Sobers set off for a run. To his horror his partner had not moved and he was fortunate to regain his ground. It was the only chance he gave. On and on he batted . . . 250 . . . 300 . . . 350.

When he had reached 363 Hanif was called up to bowl. Sobers struck the ball to long off and his single took him level with Len Hutton's record. Hanif asked the umpire if he could bowl left-handed. "You can bowl with both hands if you like," Sobers suggested. The next ball was pushed into the covers, Sobers took a single to reach 365 not out and the crowd invaded the field to congratulate their hero.

WEST INDIES

First Innings		
C C Hunte run out		260
R B Kanhai c Imtiaz b Fazal		25
G S Sobers not out		365
E C Weekes c Hanif b Fazal		39
C L Walcott not out		88
Extras (2b, 7lb, 4w)		13
Total (3 wkts, declared)		**790**
Fall: 1-87 2-533 3-602		

Bowling	O	M	R W
Mahmood Hussain	0.5	0	2 0
Fazal Mahmood	85.2	20	247 2
Khan Mohammad	54	5	259 0
Nasim-ul-Ghani	15	3	39 0
A H Kardar	37	2	141 0
W Mathias	4	0	20 0
Alimuddin	4	0	34 0
Hanif Mohammad	2	0	11 0
Saeed Ahmed	6	0	24 0

Sobers had batted for 10hr 14min and had hit 38 fours in his record innings. The West Indies declared at 790 for three and although nearly an hour was lost to repair the damaged pitch the hosts sealed victory by an innings and 174 runs.

FOOTBALL

Trio push Hearts to easy title

HEARTS cruised to the Scottish championship and finished 13 points ahead of Rangers. They had seemed almost unbeatable with Dave Mackay at wing-half and the Terrible Trio of Willie Bauld, Alfie Conn and Jimmy Wardhaugh in attack.

The trio struck terror into the opposition because although individually talented, each complemented the other two. Bauld was strong in the air, Conn was prepared to do the fetching and carrying, and Wardhaugh could outsprint a greyhound.

Tommy Walker, the Hearts manager, had built well, adding steel to the traditional Edinburgh artistry and this team (minus Mackay who had gone to Spurs) captured the title again in 1960.

RACING

Hot favourite's mystery injury

ALCIDE attracted a welter of bets when he won the Derby trial at Lingfield by 12 lengths. But a lot of money was lost on the hot favourite for the Derby when he had to be pulled out of the race.

Nothing was ever proved, but everybody thought that he had been nobbled. Alcide was found badly bruised one morning and it was suspected that somebody hit him so hard that he suffered a broken rib.

Manchester United devastated by 23 deaths in air disaster

THE Busby Babes, the great Manchester United side created by Matt Busby, perished in the snow at Munich airport on February 6.

The team was returning from Yugoslavia where they had negotiated their way past Red Star Belgrade to reach the semi-finals of the European Cup. Their plane had stopped in Munich to refuel before returning to Manchester. The weather was appalling, and twice the craft had been unable to get enough height to take off.

The British pilots, unwilling to take the prudent step and stop over for a night to have the engines checked and re-tuned, tried a third time. The plane hit a house at the end of the runway and 23 died.

The heart was ripped out of Manchester and of England's greatest club team that afternoon. Roger Byrne, David Pegg, Tommy Taylor, Eddie Colman, Mark Jones, Billy Whelan and Geoff Bent were players who all lost their lives in the crash. Duncan Edwards, perhaps the most talented Englishman to pull on a pair of football boots, died a fortnight later. The club's trainer, coach and secretary also perished. Eight journalists, including the former Manchester City and England goalkeeper Frank Swift, also died.

After a terrific battle, where his chances were only rated as 50-50, Matt Busby recovered. Two players who survived, Jackie Blanchflower and Johnny Berry, were injured so badly they never played again.

While Manchester and the country went into mourning, United had a season to complete. They slumped in the League to finish ninth, but they swept to the Cup final on a tide of emotion. By the time of the match, however, the spell had been broken. Although everybody in the country outside of Bolton wanted them to win, Nat Lofthouse's team easily carried the day. Lofthouse scored both goals, the second when he barged Harry Gregg into the net.

The most damning postscript to the disaster was perpetrated by the Football League. Uefa invited Manchester United to enter the 1958-59 European Cup along with Wolves, the League champions. It was an appropriate way to mark United's terrible loss.

The League, however, had not forgotten how Busby snubbed them and entered the competition against their advice in 1956. They took their revenge and refused permission on the spurious grounds that it was against the competition's rules, ignoring the fact that the organisers had already waived their own rules.

The wreckage of the fateful flight that crashed on take-off from a snowbound Munich

Goodbye Shackleton

Shackleton: clown prince

LEN SHACKLETON, the Clown Prince of football, retired with an old ankle injury. Shackleton's view of the game — that it was fun — delighted crowds but infuriated officials and in particular selectors and almost certainly curtailed his international career with England, for whom he only won five caps.

Discarded by Arsenal during the war, Shackleton ended up at Sunderland via Bradford Park Avenue and Newcastle. The Roker crowds loved him as a "box of tricks" entertainer.

RUGBY UNION

Jackson sprints to late victory

PETER JACKSON had an ability to score tries out of nothing. His finest was a 30-yard sprint at Twickenham which gave England a last-minute victory against Australia on February 1.

With the score level at 6-6 England won a lineout 30 yards from the Australian line. The ball moved swiftly down the line, Jackson collected the final pass, swerved past his opposite number and, with a change of pace, outsprinted the fullback to score in the corner. The try gave England a 9-6 victory and the Coventry wing his fondest memory in 25 internationals.

Pele
Beauty beyond belief

Brian Glanville

Yes, of course, Pele was incomparable. No footballer ever did so much so young, nor for so many years. He was still only 17 when he excelled on the most difficult and demanding stage of all: the World Cup, the competition which is football's Olympics separating the men from the boys, the good from the genuinely great.

I can still see him in his first final. The Rasunda Stadium, Stockholm, on a wet summer afternoon in 1958. I can still see the two amazing goals he scored. For one of them, surrounded by hefty Swedish defenders in the penalty box, among them Parling, a left-half known for his delicate attentions as "The Iron Stove", Pele, impervious, simply and coolly hooked the ball over his head, spun, and volleyed it into the net. Right-footed, of course. It was almost always his right foot, especially with his lethal free kicks, though he could use the left when he had to.

The second goal was one of his typical, extraordinary headers. He was only 5ft 8in, though powerfully muscled in the thighs, yet his vertical take-off made him the equal, often the superior, of any six-footer. Sweden's defenders did not get near him as he rose splendidly among them to head Zagalo's cross inexorably home. That meant five goals for him in Brazil's last two World Cup games in the Rasunda, three others having come against France, though largely a 10-man France, in the semi-final.

Seventeen and a World Cup hero. What did you do for an encore? Pele, in fact, had been a Brazilian international at 16.

He was born in an obscure little town called Tres Coraçes — Three Hearts — in the huge state of Minas Geras. Later the family would move to Bauru. Pele's father, Don Dinho, was a promising footballer whose career was ruined when his knee was smashed in a collision with Augusto, who would captain Brazil in the 1950 World Cup. Edson Arantes Do Nascimento picked up the nickname of Pele as a child in Bauru, but he has never known why. At first he detested it. Kicking around with balls made of old newspapers or rags stuffed in socks, he graduated to the boys' team of the local club, and there another Brazilian World Cup man would play his role: the coach Waldemar DeBrito who had played in the 1944 World Cup in Italy. A bit of a "shouter", Pele has always paid tribute to his teaching.

Pele's fame spread swiftly to Rio, whence yet another Brazilian World Cup star, Tim of 1938 vintage, later to manage the 1982 World Cup team in Spain, arrived. He wanted Pele for the Bangu Club, but Pele's mother would not have it. She didn't object, however, to his joining Santos, much nearer home. It would be the only major club of his career.

Perhaps as a player, one of total versatility, acrobatic capability, astounding reflexes and flawless technique, Pele may best be defined by the goals he scored — more than 1,000. And by the goals he made, for he was utterly unselfish. In the 1970 World Cup final in Mexico City he put Brazil ahead against Italy with another of his majestic headers, soaring high, high above his marker, Tacisio Burgnich, to thump the ball irresistibly into the goal. Late in the second half he created two goals, one for the winger Jairzinho and one for the right-back Carlos Alberto, with two exquisite lay-offs to the right, which his colleagues thundered in.

BORN
October 23, 1940 (Tres Coraçes)
PLAYING CAREER
Santos (São Paulo) 1955-74
Debut: v Corinthians 1956
1959 scored 126 goals
Honours: 1962 & 1963, World Club Cup winners; 1962 & 1963, South American Club Cup winners; 1968, National champions
New York Cosmos (signed for $4m) 1975-1977
105 appearances, 55 goals
Internationals
Debut v Argentina, 1957; 111 appearances (95 "A" Internationals), 97 goals
Honours: 1958, World Cup winner; 1962, World Cup winner; appeared in 1966 World Cup; 1970, World Cup winner.
OTHER HONOURS
FIFA ambassador
Became first player to score 1,000 goals (in 909 games) in 1969
Scored 1,283 goals in total (1,365 games)

That, too, was the World Cup in which two goals that he did not quite score are equally well remembered. Both incidents occurred in Guadalajara. The first was in the game against Czechoslovakia. Pele, always a sharp student of the opposition, had noticed that the Czech goalkeeper, Victor, tended to drift off his line. Seeing this happen, he let fly a shot from just inside his own half, an extraordinary compound of power and impudence. The ball sailed over the stranded Victor, but bounced just wide of a post.

So did the sudden shot when, playing against Uruguay, he exploited the habit of their excellent keeper, Mazurkiewicz, of rolling the ball short to a defender. More remarkable still was Pele's attempt, when he had broken through alone, to sell the goalkeeper a dummy, pushing the ball to one side of him while racing past him on the other. He could not quite catch it in time.

Pele's two intermediate World Cups were both star-crossed. In Vina del Mar, Chile, in 1962, he pulled a muscle in the second game and dropped out of a tournament Brazil still won. "Con Pele o sin Pele tomaremos Nescafé" read the boastful slogans on Santiago's buses before Chile lost to Brazil in the semi-final. With Pele, or without Pele, we shall drink the Nescafé.

In 1966, Pele arrived for the World Cup in England with an ageing Brazilian team, his own physical condition in doubt. He was disgracefully fouled, first by the Bulgarians, then by the Portuguese, who put him out of a second game. It was, he later said, only when he saw the film of the World Cup that he realised just how brutally he had been treated. He swore he would never play in another World Cup, but ultimately changed his mind.

Not that Pele himself was any kind of martyr. He had always insisted that an opponent who maltreated him must forcefully be shown it did not pay. In 1964, during an international tournament in São Paulo he was close marked and consistently fouled by an Argentine called Mesiano. Eventually Pele could take no more. He butted his tormentor in the face, breaking his nose. Mesiano had to leave the field and Pele was so remorseful that he faded from the game, which Brazil lost.

Cheerful, charming and courteous off the field, Pele, alas, was twice "turned over", once by his plump Spanish business advisor, known as Pepe Gordo, once when Zito, his team-mate for club and country, who had recommended Pepe Gordo, persuaded him to join a company called Filolax. Not only did the company go bust, ruining Pele for the second time, he also found himself obliged to pay huge fees when it turned out to have infringed import restrictions.

So it was that, having eschewed the 1974 World Cup to the bitter dismay of his fans in Brazil he began, per force, a new career in the United States with the New York Cosmos. "Love! Love!" he would chant in the Giants Stadium, New Jersey, in his eventual, farewell game. But he's still to be seen, immaculate in his white suit, all around the world. Applause is terribly addictive when you have had so much of it.

All the world's his stage: in 1957 Pele embarked upon his glittering international career and, in his finest moment in 1970, he scored one goal and made two in the World Cup final.

Bailey's go-slow is a big turn-off for television

CRICKET officials had thoughts of promoting the sport on their minds when they agreed to allow the first Test between Australia and England to be broadcast on television. It was not much of a promotion. The viewers were forced to sit through the slowest half-century in Test cricket. Trevor Bailey took 357 minutes to reach 50 and 101 minutes later was dismissed for 68. He scored fewer than nine runs an hour.

The series began to liven up when the Australian left-arm fast bowler Ian Meckiff started to take wickets with his suspect bowling action. The British press accused Meckiff, Jim Burke, Gordon Rorke and Keith Slater of throwing and their Australian counterparts began casting aspersions about the actions of Tony Lock, Brian Statham and Fred Trueman.

Meckiff captured 17 English wickets in the first two Tests and was hounded for the rest of a bitter tour. He had, however, sparked Australia to win the Ashes for the first time in 5½ years.

FOOTBALL

Pele explodes on to the world's stage

THE sixth World Cup in Sweden saw the explosion on to the world stage of the greatest talent that has ever graced a football field, a 17-year-old Brazilian called Pele.

For the first time four British teams qualified: England, Scotland, Northern Ireland and Wales. Before the Munich air-crash great things had been expected of England, but the loss of Duncan Edwards, Roger Byrne and Tommy Taylor, then the omission of Stanley Matthews and Nat Lofthouse, an injury to Tom Finney in the first match and the refusal to pick Bobby Charlton saw England eliminated, without winning a game, in the play-offs for the quarter-finals. Scotland also did not win a game and finished bottom of their group, but they did get their first World Cup point, a 1-1 draw with Yugoslavia.

Northern Ireland and Wales did much better, both going through to the quarter-finals, with Wales, with the indomitable John Charles out with an injury, only losing 1-0 to a goal by Pele. Pele scored three more goals in Brazil's 5-2 defeat of France to take them to the final against Sweden.

Sweden, without doubt the slowest team in the tournament, had been a European power for a decade. To reach the final they had overcome Hungary, the Soviet Union and West Germany. And they were at home. When the tournament started their supporters had given them little chance, but as the team progressed a national orgy of chauvinism had been whipped up, which even threatened to prevent the semi-final against West Germany being played at all.

Before the final, Sweden's manager predicted that "Brazil would panic all over the show if they conceded an early goal". He got the Swedish goal he wanted in just four minutes, the first time Brazil had been behind in the tournament, but not the panic.

Within six minutes Brazil had equalised, and raised the tempo. Pele hit the post, then Brazil went ahead just after the half hour. Ten minutes after half-time Pele killed off the Swedes with a wickedly cheeky goal. In the midst of the penalty box he caught the ball on his thigh, hooked it over his head, spun round and crashed it into the net. Brazil got a fourth, Sweden a second, then Pele crowned the event with a majestic header and Brazil had their first World Cup, the first to be won by a country outside the host's continent.

Pele puts Svensson, the Swedish goalkeeper, under pressure

Brazil celebrate their 5-2 victory, in which Pele scored twice

Hawthorn edges out Moss by one point

THIS was surely Britain's annus mirabilis in motor racing. Four British drivers won all but one of the 10 Grands Prix and three of them finished in the first three places in the world championship. But which one would capture the title?

It all boiled down to the last race in Casablanca on October 19. Mike Hawthorn, for Ferrari, was in a commanding position in the table with 40 points to Stirling Moss's 32. Moss had to win and set the fastest lap, which was worth an extra point. However, if Hawthorn won or came second, or third and set the fastest lap, he would be the champion.

Hawthorn was in pole position yet it was Moss's Vanwall that set a furious pace. By the 13th lap Moss was leading with Hawthorn fourth. If the race finished in those positions Moss would finally have captured the championship that had eluded him for so long.

Moss's intense desire for the title almost undid him when he clipped a Maserati in the 16th lap, but fortunately for him it was the other car that dropped out of the race.

Two-thirds of the way through the race Moss held a commanding lead over Phil Hill, Hawthorn's teammate with Hawthorn in third place. Ferrari instructed Hill from the pits to let Hawthorn through, which he did.

Moss was powerless to do anything himself and Hawthorn had the championship in his sights. It was up to Moss's teammate, Stuart Lewis-Evans, to attack Hawthorn and deprive him of the second place he needed. But with 11 laps remaining Lewis-Evans's engine blew up and he died from the burns six days later.

So although Moss won the race by more than a minute and set the fastest lap Hawthorn snatched the title by a single point, the first Briton to become world champion. Even more galling for Moss was that Hawthorn had won only one GP whereas Moss had taken five.

After the race Hawthorn announced his retirement. His decision had been prompted by the death in August of his Ferrari teammate and friend Peter Collins in the German GP at Nurburgring. Two weeks before his death Collins had won the British GP at Silverstone.

Moss wins the Dutch Grand Prix at Zandvoort

Robinson: Tour success

FOR THE RECORD

ATHLETICS
■ Herb Elliott broke the world mile record when he won what was described as "The Mile of the Millenium" in Dublin on August 6. He clocked 3min 54.5sec and four other runners broke the four-minute barrier.

■ The built-up shoe was banned from high jumping.

CYCLING
■ Brian Robinson became the first Briton to win a stage in the Tour de France.

FOOTBALL
■ The Fourth Division was created from the bottom 12 from the two regionalised Third Divisions. The top 12 from each division were amalgamated into a national Third Division.

■ Denis Law became Scotland's youngest international when, aged 18 years and 256 days, he played against Wales on October 18.

■ Everton were the first club to install underground heating at a cost of £70,000. The experiment was not successful.

■ Jimmy Greaves scored five goals for Chelsea against Wolves in August. Greaves, at 18, was the youngest player to score five in a First Division match.

ICE HOCKEY
■ Harringay Arena closed after 22 years.

MOTOR RACING
■ Juan Fangio retired after the French Grand Prix, where he finished fourth in a Maserati.

French surprise South Africans

LUCIEN MIAS transformed France from whipping boys into a powerful combination which drew 3-3 with South Africa and then shocked the Springboks 9-5 in Johannesburg on August 16. They were the first team to win a series in South Africa in 60 years.

The legendary French lock was described by the French writer Georges Duthen as: "Four musketeers in one: Porthos for size and appetite, d'Artagnan for enthusiasm and fighting spirit, Athos for stubbornness and Aramis for his thoughtful nature."

Truman in Wightman Cup upset

CHRISTINE TRUMAN, a 17-year-old Essex girl, shocked the Wimbledon champion Althea Gibson in the Wightman Cup. Truman, who had won only two games against Gibson in the semi-finals at Wimbledon, won 2-6 6-3 6-4 to set up Britain's first victory in the Cup since 1930.

Truman: beat Gibson

MOTOR RACING

Track champion Hawthorn dies on the road

THREE months after becoming world champion and retiring from motor racing, Mike Hawthorn was killed on the Guildford bypass when his Jaguar skidded on the wet road, caught the back of a lorry and crashed into a tree. Hawthorn was dead before the ambulance arrived.

In the short time since he had retired Hawthorn had already started a new career. While continuing to manage the family garage he was also writing about motor racing. His father, Leslie, had also died in a car accident five years earlier when he crashed while returning from the racing at Goodwood.

FOR THE RECORD

BOBSLEIGH
■ Flight-Lieutenant Colin Mitchell won the world championship.

FOOTBALL
■ Dave Mackay was transferred from Hearts to Tottenham.

■ Ted Murphy was involved in three of the four goals in Tooting and Mitcham's 2-2 draw with Nottingham Forest in the third round of the FA Cup in January. He scored Tooting's second but then conceded an own goal and a penalty. Nottingham Forest scored the equaliser from the spot and went on to win the Cup.

TABLE TENNIS
■ The design of the sandwich bat was subjected to strict limits, but that did not stop the Japanese continuing to win world titles.

BOXING

Patterson humiliated by Swedish playboy

Down and on his way out: Patterson in the third round

INGEMAR JOHANSSON staggered his critics, American boxing circles and, most importantly, Floyd Patterson by destroying the world heavyweight champion in New York on June 26 in front of a paltry 18,000 fans.

Nobody went because the Swede was not given a cat in hell's chance. He had disgraced himself in the 1952 Olympics when he had been disqualified in the heavyweight final for not trying, having spent two rounds running away and not landing a single blow. To add to this bizarre reputation, his training before the Patterson title fight was eccentric to say the least. He had his sultry girlfriend with him in his training camp, hardly trained, and the couple would spend the evenings dancing in the adjacent hotel.

By contrast, Patterson had lived the traditional life of a hermit working out every day in the gym. Patterson was supposed to make easy meat of the playboy.

The first two rounds matched the predictions. The third was somewhat different as Johansson caught the champion with a left hook and followed through with a right on to Patterson's mouth. Patterson was down for a nine count. When he got up he was so bewildered he went to a neutral corner believing he had scored the knockdown and waited for the referee to start the count.

That right-hand punch immediately became famous as Ingo's Bingo. Johansson floored him six more times in the round before the referee called a halt and announced a European playboy as the world heavyweight champion.

Patterson's mistake, and the experts', was to have ignored the Swede's record. He had won 20 fights out of 20, with only seven lasting the distance. Johansson had incredible one-punch hitting power, and he had demolished some good opponents, admittedly most of them European, which the Americans disdainfully disregarded. But he had also knocked out the American Eddie Machen in the first round, and Machen was an opponent Patterson had carefully avoided.

CRICKET

Innings closed for Evans

THE curtain came down on one of the longest running shows in Test cricket when Godfrey Evans hung up his gloves. The acrobatic Kent wicketkeeper retired after helping England to an eight-wicket victory against India in the second Test at Lord's on June 20.

His 91-Test career was characterised by his superb agility, fast reflexes and a lively personality which helped to lift the spirits of the England team during long days in the field. Evans, the finest keeper in his era, was comfortable standing up to the likes of even Alec Bedser, the England medium pacer. He earned a reputation for taking spectacular diving catches which few of his contemporaries would have attempted.

EVANS'S RECORD

	FIRST-CLASS	TESTS (91)
Innings	753	133
Not out	52	14
Runs	14,882	2,439
Highest	144	104
Average	21.22	20.49
Hundreds	7	2
Catches	816	173
Stumpings	250	46
Total wickets	1,066	219

BASEBALL

Perfect game all for naught

THERE was no stopping Harvey Haddix, the Pittsburgh Pirates pitcher, on May 26. Haddix pitched only the eighth perfect game since records were first kept in 1876. With the Pirates unable to score the game went into extra innings and Haddix kept going. He pitched a perfect 12-inning game, but it all came to nothing as he lost 1-0 to the Milwaukee Braves in the 13th.

St Helens gain from Wigan's misfortune

Von Vollenhoven scores a try against Halifax

WIGAN believed their big-money offer to Tom von Vollenhoven in July 1957 would secure the services of the brilliant South African wing. But the boy carrying the telegram was delayed fixing a punctured bicycle tyre while von Vollenhoven was accepting £4,000 to play for St Helens.

Wigan were left to regret their missed opportunity. Von Vollenhoven inspired St Helens to the league title in 1959 by scoring 62 tries in the season. The team, coached by the legendary Jim Sullivan, were the first side to score 1,000 points in a season and they capped their winter by beating Hunslet 44-22 in the championship play-off in Bradford. Von Vollenhoven scored three tries, including a 70-yard solo effort.

Another player to score a hat-trick of tries in a big match was the Australian centre Reg Gasnier, who helped the Kangaroos beat Great Britain 22-14 in the first Test in Swinton. Britain won the remaining two Tests 11-10 in Leeds and 18-15 in Wigan to record their last series victory at home against Australia.

Hanif just misses a record 500

HANIF MOHAMMAD was a patient man. He had batted for 640 minutes to steer Karachi to an imposing total against Bahawalpur in the semi-final of the Quaid-e-Azam Trophy. But on the last ball of the third day the little Pakistan opener had a rare rush of blood to the head. He attempted an impossible second run and was run out for 499, the highest score in first-class cricket.

Hanif's partner was Abdul Aziz, a 19-year-old wicketkeeper whose career ended tragically in the final against Combined Services. Aziz was struck on the chest by a ball from the off-spinner Dildar Awan and died on his way to hospital. Play was suspended for a day.

Wright becomes world's first centurion

BILLY WRIGHT, the Wolves and England centre-half, became the first footballer in the world to win a century of international caps when he led England to a 1-0 victory over Scotland at Wembley on April 4.

Ten-man Forest defy Wembley Cup jinx

Forest celebrate after their 2-1 defeat of Luton

THE Wembley jinx struck again when Nottingham Forest's Roy Dwight was carried off with a broken leg. But for once, the loss of a player did not automatically mean defeat and Forest became the first team reduced to 10 men by injury to win the FA Cup.

Brabham engineers his way to the world title

Brabham receives his trophy for winning the British Grand Prix

JACK BRABHAM, the son of a Sydney greengrocer, won the world championship in a Cooper-Climax with victories in the British and Monaco Grands Prix. Brabham had been an engineer in the Royal Australian Air Force during the war, and his engineering expertise was to prove immensely valuable to Cooper with their revolutionary rear-engined car. Cooper-Climax easily won the Constructors' Cup with five GP victories out of the possible eight.

Player has to wait for title

Player: tenacious charge

GARY PLAYER started the final day eight shots off the pace in the Open at Muirfield. He cut the lead by four strokes after the third round and then launched a typically tenacious charge over the final 18 holes. However, he came unstuck at the last where he took a six and had to sweat for nearly two hours waiting for the leaders to come home. It was well worth the wait. Player's final round of 68 gave him the first of his nine Majors.

Spurs swoop for Scots ace

BILL NICHOLSON, Tottenham's manager, swooped to purchase Scotland's rising young genius John White from Falkirk for £20,000. The only hitch in the deal was White's reluctance to join Spurs. "I'm not good enough for here. I'll never fit in with these players," he told Tommy Younger, the Falkirk manager.

Clarke's kicks give Lions a trying time

DON CLARKE had a right boot which could accurately propel a rugby ball more than 50 yards. The biggest full-back in Test history was in top form when the British Lions arrived in New Zealand full of the joys of running rugby. Alas, the Lions learned that tries do not always win matches.

In the first Test in Dunedin on July 18 the tourists roared to a 17-9 lead with 13 minutes remaining. Then The Boot struck. Clarke kicked two penalties of more than 45 yards in three minutes and, with two minutes remaining, slotted home his sixth penalty to give New Zealand an 18-17 victory. The Lions were peeved: they had scored four tries.

The All Blacks won the second and third Tests 11-8 and 22-8, but tries by the Lions wings Peter Jackson and Tony O'Reilly helped the tourists to a 9-6 win in the fourth Test in Auckland on September 19. It was the least they deserved.

Clarke's right foot, though, dominated the series. He scored more than two-thirds of New Zealand's points, with 39 out of the team's 57.

Clarke: 18 points

Shankly given task of rebuilding Liverpool

LIVERPOOL were humbled 2-1 by Worcester City of the Southern League in the third round of the FA Cup and failed to win promotion from the Second Division at the end of the season so, on December 1, Bill Shankly, the manager of Huddersfield Town, was appointed manager on an annual salary of £2,500.

Liverpool were beaten 4-0 by Cardiff in his first match in charge. Afterwards he wrote down the names of 24 of the club's long list of players. Within a year all 24 had moved on.

Shankly: new manager

First title for young Nicklaus

JACK NICKLAUS sank an eight-foot birdie putt at the final hole to win the US amateur championship at Broadmoor, Colorado. Nicklaus, who was 19 years eight months and 29 days old, became the second-youngest champion after Robert Gardner in 1909.

Australia win amateur trophy

AUSTRALIA won the first Eisenhower Trophy when they beat the United States 222-224 in a play-off at St Andrews. The teams had finished level on 918 in the first world amateur team championship. It remains the closest finish to the event. Britain were third with 919.

Paupers beaten by millionaires

THE British team virtually lost the Ryder Cup before they had even arrived in Palm Desert, California. They had decided to travel by boat instead of fly so they could foster team spirit. But the voyage on the Queen Mary was a rough one and many of the players were sea-sick. And the last leg of their journey nearly ended in disaster. Their 40-minute flight in a twin-engined Convair plane across the San Jacinto mountains turned into a nightmare when the aircraft ran into a storm and plunged 5,000 feet. The airport was closed, the plane returned to Los Angeles and the players caught a bus to the salubrious Eldorado Country Club.

The team were overawed when they arrived at the rich venue. Dai Rees, the British captain, said: "We were paupers in a millionaire's playground."

However, they did well to trail only 2-1 in the foursomes. But on the second day the Americans, inspired by the in-form Sam Snead, dominated the singles and won 7-2 with three matches halved.

Bueno puts her stamp on Wimbledon

ELVIS PRESLEY was The King, strutting his stuff on the stage. Maria Bueno was The Queen, strutting her stuff on the court.

The 19-year-old Brazilian swept all before her at Wimbledon with grace, charm and unmatched talent. She stumbled only twice on the way to the title but quickly regained her poise.

Bueno had reached the quarter-finals the year before in her first appearance at Wimbledon but lost to the unseeded Anne Haydon. She returned as the sixth seed in the summer of 1959 and although she dropped the first set against Margot Dittmeyer in the second round and Mimi Arnold in the next round there was no stopping her once she was into her stride. She won her remaining matches in straight sets, including a 6-4 6-3

win against Darlene Hard in the final.

Bueno's strength was her powerful service, which she used to win three Wimbledon titles and four US championships, the first of which was in 1959. She had grown up opposite the São Paulo tennis club and her one-month training schedule before her first world tour in 1958 was so intense that she lost 17 pounds in weight. However, Bueno won the Italian title and took the women's doubles crown at Wimbledon with Althea Gibson. It was with this grounding that she became the world's leading player and a heroine in her homeland. When she retained the Wimbledon title in 1960 a stamp bearing her picture was issued in Brazil and her statue was erected in São Paulo. It was the least Bueno deserved.

Bueno: no stopping her once she was in her stride

Mercer killed by wild horse

Mercer: died instantly

ASCOT seemed to be fated and the course claimed another victim during the final day of the September meeting. The widely respected Manny Mercer, the brother of Joe, was riding down to the start when his horse, Priddy Fair, reared up. He was thrown against the rails, kicked in the head by the horse and died instantly. Racing was abandoned for the day as a mark of respect.

FOR THE RECORD

CRICKET
■ Dwight D Eisenhower became the first American president to see Test cricket, when he watched Pakistan draw with Australia on December 8.

FOOTBALL
■ The Football League moved its headquarters from Preston to Lytham St Annes. The building was acquired for £11,000. Previously, it was a small private hotel and the modifications took six months to complete and cost a further £40,000.

■ The first £300,000 pools winner coincided with the Football League establishing in the High Court in July their copyright over the League fixtures and thus receiving one-half of a per cent of the gross takings (less betting duty) from the Pools Promoters and a guarantee of at least £245,000 per annum for 10 years.

■ Joe Baker, of Hibs, became the first registered player at a Scottish club to play for England. Baker, born in Liverpool but brought up Scotland, scored in England's 2-1 defeat of Northern Ireland on November 18.

■ Brian Clough, of Second Division Middlesbrough, made his debut for England in a scrappy game against Wales in Cardiff where he hardly got a kick in a 1-1 draw.

■ Jimmy Greaves scored five goals for Chelsea against Preston in December.

Marathon match takes toll of hot-shot Laver

THE summer of 1959 was hot and if anybody knew about heat it was Rod Laver, who had learned to play tennis in tropical Queensland.

Laver thrived under the scorching sun at Wimbledon, becoming only the third unseeded player to reach the men's singles final. But he took 87 games to get past Barry Mackay in the semi-finals, winning 11-13 11-9 10-8 7-9 6-3. The marathon sapped Laver for the final, which he lost 6-4 6-3 6-4 to the top seed Alex Olmedo.

Laver: lost 6-4 6-3 6-4 to the No1 seed Alex Olmedo

1960s

The Golden Dawn of the Superstar

MUCH OF what we take to be modern sport was conceived in the giddy, glorious Sixties. The world was changing fast and the spearhead of the social and cultural revolution that engulfed the globe was youth. The baby boomers were not hidebound by the fears and doubts generated by the horrors of the Second World War as their parents had been. They saw the world as rich in possibilities and ripe for change. Optimism and a blind faith in their own energies and creativity were the hallmarks of the decade.

Football was the sport that most benefited from this tidal wave of change. The arrogant insularity of English football in the first half of the century had been rudely shattered in the 1950s. First by the humiliating defeat by the United States, and then the painful lesson by the Hungarians at Wembley. The country that had given the game to the world, and therefore assumed a divine right to be the masters of the universe, had suddenly discovered it was a second-class power. The shock to the national psyche was so devastating that English football went into a coma.

But other horizons were opening up. The brave, new world of European club football had dawned. And it was in these new competitions that British football first regained its confidence. Tottenham, who had so gloriously won the Double in 1961, were the first team to breach the European citadel in 1963. West Ham, Celtic and Manchester United quickly followed. But in 1966 England finally cast off the shackles of the past and regained its pride by winning the World Cup. At last it could look the rest of the world in the eye and say: "We are world-beaters, after all." And England did it at just the right time, because for once the world was paying attention.

It was the first World Cup to be televised globally by satellite and two billion watched the 32 matches. And it was won in London, the world capital of the Swinging Sixties. The Beatles, the Rolling Stones, Bob Dylan, Carnaby Street, flower power — these were the icons of the age. A new type of hero was emerging: young, male, long-haired, outrageously talented, hedonistic and rebellious.

Enter George Best. The adulation that Manchester United's young Irishman received was comparable to any rock star. Football, and its stars, had joined the glitzy world of show business. The cloth cap, the short back-and-sides haircut and the £20 a week wage were forever consigned to the dustbins of bygone eras.

Cricket, too, was not immune to the revolution. The absurd distinction between "Players" and "Gentlemen", a relic of a class-obsessed age, was quietly dropped. Yet the changes that were to transform cricket, and that probably secured its future into the 21st century, were almost accidental. The game's administrators, facing awesome financial difficulties with attendances at county championship matches dwindling to the level of three men and a dog, took the plunge and created the Gillette one-day Cup in 1963. Despite the misgivings of many counties it was a brilliant success.

However, the mushrooming of one-day cricket was effectively brought about by the BBC. In 1965 they put together an irresistible package. International Test players drawn from all over the world playing against county sides in competitive 40-over games, sponsored by Rothmans, and live on BBC2 on a Sunday afternoon. It is impossible to believe that they realised what they had done, but, magically, they had brought together the holy trinity of modern cricket. Live television, sponsorship, and the one-day game.

The 1960s were the television age. Everybody could afford a television set and, with global communications possible, sport from all over the world was beamed into our living rooms, and vice-versa. The global village was established. The advent of colour television meant that viewers could stay up after midnight and watch David Hemery win the 400m hurdles at the Mexico Olympics live. As if you were there. Nothing would ever be the same, the world had shrunk, and our vision had broadened.

Radical was chic. Cassius Clay righteously declared himself Muhammad Ali, disdainfully flattened every heavyweight in sight, unpatriotically refused to fight in Vietnam, and was everybody's hero. Black power graced the Olympic Games in 1968 when Tommie Smith and John Carlos raised their black leather-clad fists in clenched salutes on the winner's rostrum and sent a political message round the world.

When Jack Nicklaus displaced Arnold Palmer diehard golf fans hated it — everywhere the old order was being overturned by upstarts. It was the best of times: an age when everything seemed possible, when talent alone was a wave of such force it would sweep anybody to the top. The Superstar was born. Stars even greater than the stars their parents had worshipped on the silver screen. But perhaps it was the beginning of the worst of times for, like all Golden Ages, the very energy that created it — the unfulfilled passions and desires of previous eras — was essentially uncontrollable. It happened too fast. One minute it was the grey, austere 1950s, the next mini-skirts, sex, drugs and rock 'n roll.

The legacy of the 1960s was looming as the decade was closing. In 1967 Tommy Simpson, a reckless and brave cyclist who had successfully conquered the European circuit, died at the age of 29 from a drug overdose in the middle of the Tour de France.

But not from a recreational drug, now commonplace wherever young people congregated socially, but a performance-enhancing drug. The tangible rewards of success in sport had become so great that any risk was worth it. After all, taking risks, defying the establishment, was now the name of the game.

Tennis, that bastion of stuffiness in private clubs from Paris to New York, had steadfastly refused to move with the times. As a consequence wonderful champions such as Rod Laver had defected to the professional circuit as blazered administrators refused to countenance anything other than the amateur.

Their comeuppance came in 1968 when they were forced to declare Open championships and pay prize money. Superstars were now what it was all about. Without them there would be little television or spectator interest. The tail now had the dog firmly by the throat.

AMERICAN FOOTBALL
■ *Super Bowl*
1967 Green Bay Packers
1968 Green Bay Packers
1969 New York Jets

ATHLETICS
■ *British Olympic gold medals*
1960 *50km walk* Donald Thompson
1964 *800m* Ann Packer; *20km walk* Kenneth Matthews; *long jump* Lynn Davies, Mary Rand
1968 *400m hurdles* David Hemery

BASEBALL
■ *World Series*
1960 Pittsburgh Pirates
1961 New York Yankees
1962 New York Yankees
1963 Los Angeles Dodgers
1964 St Louis Cardinals
1965 Los Angeles Dodgers
1966 Baltimore Orioles
1967 St Louis Cardinals
1968 Detroit Tigers
1969 New York Mets

BOXING
■ *British world champions*
1961 *Middleweight.* Terry Downes
1966 *Flyweight.* Walter McGowan (WBC)
1968 *Featherweight.* Howard Winstone (WBC)

CRICKET
■ *County championship*
1960 Yorkshire
1961 Hampshire
1962 Yorkshire
1963 Yorkshire
1964 Worcestershire
1965 Worcestershire
1966 Yorkshire
1967 Yorkshire
1968 Yorkshire
1969 Glamorgan
■ *Gillette Cup*
1963 Sussex bt Worcestershire by 14 runs
1964 Sussex bt Warwickshire by 8 wickets
1965 Yorkshire bt Surrey by 175 runs
1966 Warwickshire bt Worcestershire by 5 wickets
1967 Kent bt Somerset by 32 runs
1968 Warwickshire bt Sussex by 4 wickets
1969 Yorkshire bt Derbyshire by 69 runs
■ *Sunday League*
1969 Lancashire

CYCLING
■ *Tour de France*
1960 Gastone Nencini
1961 Jacques Anquetil
1962 Jacques Anquetil
1963 Jacques Anquetil
1964 Jacques Anquetil
1965 Felice Gimondi
1966 Lucien Almar
1967 Roger Pingeon
1968 Jan Janssen
1969 Eddy Merckx

FOOTBALL
■ *World Cup*
1962 Brazil 3 Czechoslovakia 1
1966 England 4 West Germany 2 (aet)
■ *European championship*
1960 USSR 2 Yugoslavia 1 (aet)
1964 Spain 2 USSR 1
1968 Italy 2 Yugoslavia 0 (after 1-1)
■ *European Cup*
1960 Real Madrid 7 Eintracht Frankfurt 3
1961 Benfica 3 Barcelona 2
1962 Benfica 5 Real Madrid 3
1963 AC Milan 2 Benfica 1

1964 Inter Milan 3 Real Madrid 1
1965 Inter Milan 1 Benfica 0
1966 Real Madrid 2 Partizan Belgrade 1
1967 Celtic 2 Inter Milan 1
1968 Manchester Utd 4 Benfica 1 (aet)
1969 AC Milan 4 Ajax 1
■ *European Cup Winners' Cup*
1961 Fiorentina bt Rangers 2-0 2-1
1962 Atletico Madrid 3 Fiorentina 0 (after 1-1)
1963 Tottenham 5 Atletico Madrid 1
1964 Sporting Lisbon 1 MTK Budapest 0 (after 3-3)
1965 West Ham 2 Munich 1860 0
1966 Borussia Dortmund 2 Liverpool 1
1967 Bayern Munich 2 Rangers 1
1968 AC Milan 2 SV Hamburg 0
1969 Slovan Bratislava 3 Barcelona 2
■ *Fairs Cup*
1960 Barcelona bt Birmingham 0-0 4-1
1961 AS Roma bt Birmingham 2-2 2-0
1962 Valencia bt Barcelona 6-2 1-1
1963 Valencia bt Dynamo Zagreb 2-1 2-0
1964 Real Zaragoza 2 Valencia 1
1965 Ferencvaros 1 Juventus 0
1966 Barcelona bt Real Zaragoza 0-1 4-2 (aet)
1967 Dynamo Zagreb bt Leeds 2-0 0-0
1968 Leeds bt Ferencvaros 1-0 0-0
1969 Newcastle bt Ujpest Dozsa 3-0 3-2
■ *Football League*
1960 Burnley
1961 Tottenham
1962 Ipswich
1963 Everton
1964 Liverpool
1965 Manchester Utd
1966 Liverpool
1967 Manchester Utd
1968 Manchester City
1969 Leeds
■ *FA Cup*
1960 Wolverhampton 3 Blackburn 0
1961 Tottenham 2 Leicester 0
1962 Tottenham 3 Burnley 1
1963 Manchester Utd 3 Leicester 1
1964 West Ham 3 Preston 2
1965 Liverpool 2 Leeds 1 (aet)
1966 Everton 3 Sheffield Wed 2
1967 Tottenham 2 Chelsea 1
1968 West Bromwich 1 Everton 0 (aet)
1969 Manchester City 1 Leicester 0
■ *League Cup*
1961 Aston Villa bt Rotherham 0-2 3-0 (aet)
1962 Norwich bt Rochdale 3-0 1-0
1963 Birmingham bt Aston Villa 3-1 0-0
1964 Leicester bt Stoke 1-1 3-2
1965 Chelsea bt Leicester 3-2 0-0
1966 West Bromwich bt West Ham 1-2 4-1
1967 QPR 3 West Bromwich 2
1968 Leeds 1 Arsenal 0
1969 Swindon 3 Arsenal 1 (aet)
■ *Scottish League*
1960 Hearts
1961 Rangers
1962 Dundee
1963 Rangers
1964 Rangers
1965 Kilmarnock
1966 Celtic

1967 Celtic
1968 Celtic
1969 Celtic
■ *Scottish Cup*
1960 Rangers 2 Kilmarnock 0
1961 Dunfermline 2 Celtic 0 (after 0-0)
1962 Rangers 2 St Mirren 0
1963 Rangers 3 Celtic 0 (after 1-1)
1964 Rangers 3 Dundee 1
1965 Celtic 3 Dunfermline 2
1966 Rangers 1 Celtic 0 (after 0-0)
1967 Celtic 2 Aberdeen 0
1968 Dunfermline 3 Hearts 1
1969 Celtic 4 Rangers 0
■ *Scottish League Cup*
1960 Hearts 2 Third Lanark 1
1961 Rangers 2 Kilmarnock 0
1962 Rangers 3 Hearts 1 (after 1-1)
1963 Hearts 1 Kilmarnock 0
1964 Rangers 5 Morton 0
1965 Rangers 2 Celtic 1
1966 Celtic 2 Rangers 1
1967 Celtic 1 Rangers 0
1968 Celtic 5 Dundee 3
1969 Celtic 6 Hibernian 2

GOLF
■ *The Open*
1960 Kel Nagle
1961 Arnold Palmer
1962 Arnold Palmer
1963 Bob Charles
1964 Tony Lema
1965 Peter Thomson
1966 Jack Nicklaus
1967 Roberto de Vicenzo
1968 Gary Player
1969 Tony Jacklin
■ *US Open*
1960 Arnold Palmer
1961 Gene Littler
1962 Jack Nicklaus
1963 Julius Boros
1964 Ken Venturi
1965 Gary Player
1966 Billy Casper
1967 Jack Nicklaus
1968 Lee Trevino
1969 Orville Moody
■ *US PGA*
1960 Jay Herbert
1961 Jerry Barber
1962 Gary Player
1963 Jack Nicklaus
1964 Bobby Nichols
1965 Dave Marr
1966 Al Geiberger
1967 Don January
1968 Julius Boros
1969 Raymond Floyd
■ *US Masters*
1960 Arnold Palmer
1961 Gary Player
1962 Arnold Palmer
1963 Jack Nicklaus
1964 Arnold Palmer
1965 Jack Nicklaus
1966 Jack Nicklaus
1967 Gary Brewer
1968 Bob Goalby
1969 George Archer
■ *Ryder Cup*
1961 United States 14½-9½
1963 United States 23-9
1965 United States 19½-12½
1967 United States 23½-8½
1969 Drawn 16-16

MOTOR RACING
■ *World championship*
1960 Jack Brabham (Cooper-Climax)
1961 Phil Hill (Ferrari)
1962 Graham Hill (BRM)
1963 Jim Clark (Lotus-Climax)
1964 John Surtees (Ferrari)
1965 Jim Clark (Lotus-Climax)
1966 Jack Brabham (Brabham-Repco)
1967 Denny Hulme (Brabham-Repco)
1968 Graham Hill (Lotus-Ford)
1969 Jackie Stewart (Matra-Ford)

RACING
■ *The Derby*
1960 St Paddy
1961 Psidium
1962 Larkspur
1963 Relko
1964 Santa Claus
1965 Sea Bird II
1966 Charlottown
1967 Royal Palace
1968 Sir Ivor
1969 Blakeney
■ *Grand National*
1960 Merryman II
1961 Nicolaus Silver
1962 Kilmore
1963 Ayala
1964 Team Spirit
1965 Jay Trump
1966 Anglo
1967 Foinavon
1968 Red Alligator
1969 Highland Wedding

ROWING
■ *Boat Race*
1960 Oxford
1961 Cambridge
1962 Cambridge
1963 Oxford
1964 Cambridge
1965 Oxford
1966 Oxford
1967 Oxford
1968 Cambridge
1969 Cambridge

RUGBY LEAGUE
■ *Challenge Cup*
1960 Wakefield 38 Hull 5
1961 St Helens 12 Wigan 6
1962 Wakefield 12 Huddersfield 6
1963 Wakefield 25 Wigan 10
1964 Widnes 13 Hull KR 5
1965 Wigan 20 Hunslet 16
1966 St Helens 21 Wigan 2
1967 Featherstone 17 Barrow 12
1968 Leeds 11 Wakefield 10
1969 Castleford 11 Salford 6

RUGBY UNION
■ *Five Nations championship*
1960 France and England
1961 France
1962 France
1963 England
1964 Scotland and Wales
1965 Wales
1966 Wales
1967 France
1968 France
1969 Wales

SAILING
■ *America's Cup*
1962 *Weatherly* (US, Emil Mosbacher Jnr)
1964 *Constellation* (US, Bob Bavier Jnr)
1967 *Intrepid* (US, Emil Mosbacher Jnr)
■ *Admiral's Cup*
1961 United States
1963 Great Britain
1965 Great Britain
1967 Australia
1969 Team: United States. Individual: Red Rooster (US)

SNOOKER
■ *World championship*
1964 John Pulman 19 Fred Davis 16; John Pulman 40 Rex Williams 33
1965 John Pulman 37 Fred Davis 36; John Pulman 25 Rex Williams 22; John Pulman 39 Freddie van Rensburg 12
1966 John Pulman 5 Fred Davis 2
1968 John Pulman 39 Eddie Charlton 34
1969 John Spencer 37 Gary Owen 34

TENNIS
■ *Wimbledon*
1960 Neale Fraser bt Rod Laver; Maria Bueno bt Sandra Reynolds
1961 Rod Laver bt Chuck McKinley; Angela Mortimer bt Christine Truman
1962 Rod Laver bt Martin Mulligan; Karen Susman bt Vera Sukova
1963 Chuck McKinley bt Fred Stolle; Margaret Smith bt Billie Jean Moffitt
1964 Roy Emerson bt Fred Stolle; Maria Bueno bt Margaret Smith
1965 Roy Emerson bt Fred Stolle; Margaret Smith bt Maria Bueno
1966 Manuel Santana bt Dennis Ralston; Billie Jean King bt Maria Bueno
1967 John Newcombe bt Wilhelm Bungert; Billie Jean King bt Ann Jones
1968 Rod Laver bt Tony Roche; Billie Jean King bt Judy Tegart
1969 Rod Laver bt John Newcombe; Ann Jones bt Billie Jean King
■ *Australian championship*
1960 Rod Laver; Margaret Smith
1961 Roy Emerson; Margaret Smith
1962 Rod Laver; Margaret Smith
1963 Roy Emerson; Margaret Smith
1964 Roy Emerson; Margaret Smith
1965 Roy Emerson; Margaret Smith
1966 Roy Emerson; Margaret Smith
1967 Roy Emerson; Nancy Richey
1968 Bill Bowrey; Billie Jean King
■ *Australian Open*
1969 Rod Laver; Margaret Court
■ *French championship*
1960 Nicola Pietrangeli; Darlene Hard
1961 Manuel Santana; Ann Haydon
1962 Rod Laver; Margaret Smith
1963 Roy Emerson; Lesley Turner
1964 Manuel Santana; Margaret Smith
1965 Fred Stolle; Lesley Turner
1966 Tony Roche; Ann Jones
1967 Roy Emerson; Francoise Durr
■ *French Open*
1968 Ken Rosewall; Nancy Richey
1969 Rod Laver; Margaret Court
■ *US Open*
1960 Neale Fraser; Darlene Hard
1961 Roy Emerson; Darlene Hard
1962 Rod Laver; Margaret Smith
1963 Rafael Osuna; Maria Bueno
1964 Roy Emerson; Maria Bueno
1965 Manuel Santana; Margaret Smith
1966 Fred Stolle; Maria Bueno
1967 John Newcombe; Billie Jean King
1968 Arthur Ashe (*amateur & open*); Margaret Court (*amateur*), Virginia Wade (*open*)
1969 Stan Smith (*amateur*), Rod Laver (*open*); Margaret Court (*amateur & open*)

Jacklin: British and US win

Best: new-style hero

Wolves denied rightful destiny

FOR THE RECORD

BOXING

■ Dave Charnley failed on points to capture the world lightweight title from the holder, Joe "Old Bones" Brown at Earls Court on April 18. The referee's decision was universally condemned, and the crowd booed for 30 minutes after the bout had finished.

FOOTBALL

■ Jock Stein made his managerial debut in charge of the relegation-stricken Dunfermline in March. Nobody, least of all Stein, thought it was possible to escape the drop as maximum points were needed from six matches. Dunfermline began by beating Celtic, Stein's former club, won the next five games and duly stayed up.

■ Kilmarnock had a disheartening season, missing out on the League title to Hearts by four points and losing the Cup final to Rangers 2-0.

■ Cliff Holton scored a hat-trick for Watford against Chester on April 15. The next day he scored another hat-trick against Gateshead.

■ Birmingham lost to Barcelona in the final of the Fairs Cup.

■ Denis Law became the first player to be transferred for over £50,000 between British clubs when he joined Manchester City from Huddersfield in March.

■ Fifa, meeting in Rome, chose England to host the 1966 World Cup.

ICE HOCKEY

■ The British League folded at the end of the 1959-60 season.

MOTOR RACING

■ Colin Chapman's Lotus recorded their first Grand Prix victory at Monaco on May 29. The race was not won by a member of the Lotus team, but by Stirling Moss who had privately entered the car.

RUGBY LEAGUE

■ Wakefield Trinity beat Hull by a record 38-5 in the Challenge Cup final at Wembley. Neil Fox scored 20 points.

One moment of glory: Wolves flatten Blackburn 3-0 in the Cup final

POOR Wolves! On the very last day of the football season, Monday May 2, their dreams of immortality vanished when Burnley beat Manchester City at Maine Road. Wolves had been poised to become the first club this century to achieve the Double of League championship and FA Cup in the same season, and, in one fell swoop, to complete a hat-trick of successive League titles to emulate Herbert Chapman's Huddersfield and Arsenal.

If they had done so, they would have gone down as the greatest club side ever in English football. Instead, Burnley went top for the only time in the season, snatched the championship, and dashed a singular place in history from the grasp of the holders.

On March 30 Wolves appeared to be coasting to the championship, and into the record books, having thrashed Burnley 6-0. On April 24 Wolves entertained Spurs at Molineux in their penultimate League match where a victory would virtually clinch the title. For Spurs the match was just as important. They were already thinking about the Double next season — their Double — and a resounding win would confirm their aspirations. Tottenham held their team talk on the pitch and, fired up, convincingly beat Wolves 3-1 in one of their greatest performances. Burnley collected maximum points in their last two games and, by a single point, occupied the top spot for the first, and last, time in the season.

Wolves steamrollered their way past Blackburn in the FA Cup final as expected. But the moment was gone — a side that had been so predominant in the 1950s had missed their crowning glory by losing one match to the team that would, briefly, inherit their mantle, Tottenham of the early 1960s.

Danny Blanchflower said of that match: "We had beaten the best of the rest, and done it in style. It was difficult to see who would stop us the following season." Wolves have not won the League or FA Cup since.

Posh arrive in the quality street

AFTER 20 years of applying for election to the Football League, Peterborough finally succeeded on May 28. Peterborough, nicknamed "The Posh" because of their marvellous ground and facilities, were almost certainly elected for their success in the FA Cup.

They knocked out Second Division Ipswich at Portman Road in the third round and then lost to First Division Sheffield Wednesday in the fourth round; in 1957 they reached the fourth round by eliminating Second Division Lincoln; in 1954 they battled to the third round and lost to First Division Cardiff.

Gateshead were the unfortunate club to lose their Football League status.

CRICKET

Lindwall bowls his final ball

RAY LINDWALL, one of the fastest and most furious of Australia's bowlers, called it a day at Eden Gardens in Calcutta on January 28. Lindwall, who had formed a devastating opening combination with Keith Miller in the decade after the war, took 228 wickets at 23.03 in his 61 Tests.

His ability to move the ball prompted one colleague to suggest: "I was brought up to believe that Louis Armstrong was the king of swing. But I'm no longer so sure after seeing Lindy bowl today."

Lindwall: king of swing

Marathon men defy England

GARRY SOBERS and Frank Worrell defied England for nearly 10 hours in the longest partnership in Test cricket. The West Indians were 102 for three when Sobers joined Worrell at the crease at 4.50pm on Friday, January 7. Their 399-run stand ended at 11.40am the next Tuesday when Fred Trueman bowled Sobers for 226. It lasted for 579 minutes.

The West Indians remain the only pair to bat throughout two consecutive days, although their partnership was broken by an hour of rain and a rest day.

RACING

Off-course bookmakers allowed to set up shop

THE face of racing was changed by Sir Leslie Peppiatt, whose report provided the foundations for the Betting Levy Bill which received its third reading in parliament in the winter.

Attendances had been falling at racecourses and the Jockey Club was looking for ways to make up the lost money. It argued that punters should put money back into the sport through a £3m-a-year levy. Sir Leslie accepted the principle but decided that the levy should be half of what the Jockey Club wanted.

The result was a reformation of off-course betting. At long last bookmaking would be legal and licensed rather than the preserve of people with credit accounts or contacts with underground bookmakers.

RUGBY UNION

Risman is left out in the cold as England scorch to Triple Crown

The England team that beat Ireland for the Triple Crown

BEV RISMAN could not have chosen a worse moment to catch flu than on the eve of his Five Nations match against Wales. While the England fly-half was recuperating his replacement was playing a blinder at Twickenham on January 16.

Richard Sharp had the Welsh defence in tatters and inspired England to a 14-6 victory. Then he kicked drop goals against Scotland and Ireland to give England the Triple Crown and a share of the championship with France. The selectors moved Risman to inside centre the next season, but he soon turned to rugby league.

WINTER OLYMPICS

Disney Games a smash hit as postman delivers goods

GEORG THOMA would regularly don his skis to deliver mail to snowbound homes in Germany's Black Forest. The job stood him in good stead at the VII winter Olympic Games in Squaw Valley, 200 miles east of San Francisco, when he became the first non-Scandinavian to win the Nordic Combination.

Thoma's victory was the upset of a Games which had defied the odds. Alexander Cushing persuaded the IOC to hold the Games at his tourist hostel more than 6,500 feet above sea level. He ignored protests about the altitude, decided not to build a bobsled track for only nine teams, had Walt Disney direct the opening and staged a relatively successful Olympics.

171

BOXING

Patterson first to regain title

FLOYD PATTERSON and Ingemar Johansson had occupied themselves in different ways since Patterson had surrendered his world heavyweight crown in 1959. The former champion, deeply ashamed, had spent 12 months training for the re-match. The new champion, by contrast, had explored the outer limits of life as a playboy. By the time they met again, on June 20 in New York, there was only one outcome.

Patterson knocked the Swede out in the fifth round with two shattering left hooks to exact his revenge and become the first man to win back the world heavyweight championship.

Patterson: sweet revenge

172

FOOTBALL

Real Madrid stage a command performance

SEVEN years after Ferenc Puskas and the Hungarians shattered the cosy confidence of British football, Puskas returned and demonstrated in mesmerising style that, even at the age of 33, genius is still genius. In tandem with Alfredo di Stefano, also 33, the pair scored seven goals as Real Madrid retained the European Cup and dazzled Eintracht Frankfurt in the final at Hampden.

On May 18, 127,000 spectators, and millions more watching on television, saw for themselves why Real Madrid had won five consecutive European finals and were the undoubted masters of Europe.

Eintracht, who had beaten Rangers in the semi-final 12-4 on aggregate, started well, taking the lead in the 19th minute. But they were completely swept away as Puskas and di Stefano ran riot. Within 11 minutes di Stefano had put the Spanish champions 2-1 up. Puskas added two more either side of the break, then a fifth.

If that were not enough, there were four more goals in the space of four minutes. Puskas got his fourth in the 70th minute, Stein pulled one back for Eintracht, but straight from the re-start di Stefano completed his hat-trick. Two minutes later Stein scored the Germans' third: 7-3.

The Germans had been overwhelmed and Glasgow had enjoyed a football feast. Not a soul left the stadium until the victors had completed their lap of honour with a trophy that will forever be associated with Real Madrid.

Puskas scores Real Madrid's fifth goal at Hampden

CRICKET

Suspicion blights Griffin's career

GEOFF GRIFFIN was unable to straighten his right arm after an accident at school and his suspect bowling action brought him nothing but heartache on South Africa's tour of England. He was no-balled 17 times in three matches before the second Test at Lord's.

Griffin achieved the first Test hat-trick at cricket's headquarters when he bowled Mike Smith for 99 and then dismissed Peter Walker and Fred Trueman. But the umpire, Frank Lee, called him for throwing 11 times during the innings. He never played Test cricket again and retired the next season.

ATHLETICS

■ Armin Hary, a German sprinter, became the first man to run 100m in 10 seconds in Zurich on June 21.

CRICKET

■ The Gentlemen and Players drew their match at Lord's when Ted Dexter hit the middle stump from long-on as the Players were scampering for what would have been the winning run off the last ball.

GOLF

■ The United States, spearheaded by Jack Nicklaus, won the second Eisenhower Trophy by a record 42 shots.

■ Betsy Rawls became the first four-time winner of the US women's Open with a score of 292 at the Worcester Country Club in Massachusetts.

RUGBY UNION

■ Anti-apartheid protesters launched an unsuccessful campaign to prevent New Zealand touring South Africa.

SAILING

■ Francis Chichester won the first single-handed Transatlantic race from Plymouth to Newport, Rhode Island, in Gypsy Moth III. Colonel Blondie Hasler, who thought up the idea of the race, was second.

TENNIS

■ Darlene Hard, a former waitress from Los Angeles, was denied an elusive Wimbledon title when she lost to Sandra Reynolds in the quarter-finals. Hard, who won the French and US titles, was also the runner-up at Wimbledon in 1957 and 1959.

RACING

Piggott blamed for leaving it too late

FOR once, Lester Piggott's tactics failed him. He had won his fourth Classic in five years on Petite Etoile in the 1959 Oaks, and the grey filly was expected to make a mere formality of the King George VI and Queen Elizabeth Stakes on July 17. But Piggott was criticised for leaving her in last place as the field entered the straight and, with too much ground to make up, the 5-2 on favourite was beaten by half a length.

Palmer's cavalry charge astounds world

A HUGE army had mustered on both sides of the Atlantic. It had no uniforms, no sergeant-majors and awarded no medals. But Arnie's Army were the most loyal foot soldiers in the world.

Their field marshal was Arnold Palmer, the most popular golfer in history. The tough, blond American, who grimaced and joked his way around the course, had a magnetic appeal which catapulted the sport into a multi-million pound business.

Palmer's charisma brought people flocking to the game. He would hit every shot as hard as he could

Palmer: extraordinary round

> *If ever I needed an eight-foot putt, and everything I owned depended on it, I would want Arnold Palmer to putt for me*
>
> **Bobby Jones**

and when he landed in the rough he would blast his way out of trouble. His putter was as accurate as any in the game. Palmer was at his peak in 1960. He birdied the last two holes in the Masters at Augusta to beat Ken Venturi by one shot and won four other tournaments in the build-up to the US Open in Denver.

But the man from Latrobe had a bad start at the Cherry Hills Country Club. He drove into a creek at the first hole and when a young boy picked his ball out of the water, officials penalised the tournament favourite one stroke. Things went from bad to worse and, by the start of the final round, Palmer was seven shots off the pace set by Mike Souchak.

What unfolded on Saturday, June 18 was one of the greatest rounds in history. There were 14 men in front of Palmer when he began with a blaze of birdie threes on the first four holes. The opposition faltered while Palmer flourished and when he reached the turn in 30, Arnie's Army were on the march.

There was no stopping Palmer, who stormed home with a 65 to beat the young amateur Jack Nicklaus by two shots. Arnie ruled the world.

ARNOLD PALMER'S MAJOR HONOURS

1958 The Masters
1960 The Masters; US Open
1961 The Open
1962 The Masters; The Open
1964 The Masters

. . . and the missing US PGA

1964 Colombus, Ohio
    271 Bobby Nichols
    274 Arnold Palmer,
    Jack Nicklaus

1968 Pecan Valley, Texas
    281 Julius Boros
    282 Arnold Palmer,
    Bob Charles

1970 Southern Hills, Oklahoma
    279 Dave Stockton
    281 Arnold Palmer,
    Bob Murphy

> *If Arnold asked all of those people to go and jump into the river for him, they would march straight to the river and jump*
>
> **Gary Player**
> on Arnie's Army

Grand Slam dream dies at Open

ARNOLD PALMER was on the road to the Grand Slam when he arrived at St Andrews for the Centenary Open. He had won the Masters and the US Open and needed victories in his first Open and the US PGA to complete a clean sweep. In front of an adoring gallery, Palmer kept alive his faint hopes when he birdied the last hole. Alas, it was not enough. Kel Nagle, a genial Australian, sank a testing six-foot birdie putt at the notorious Road Hole and kept his nerve up the final fairway to deny Palmer victory.

Leading clubs put boot into the League Cup

THE new League Cup, the brainchild of the Football League and in particular their secretary, Alan Hardaker, began in the worst possible way. Within days of the announcement of the competition in June five leading First Division clubs refused to have anything to do with it. Wolves, Tottenham, West Bromwich, Arsenal and Sheffield Wednesday announced they would not play.

Bill Nicholson, Tottenham's manager, was especially incensed with the creation of another competition. Nicholson said the League was demanding too much from players. Instead, the First Division should be smaller and there should be fewer games.

Match-point specialist excels at Wimbledon

NEALE FRASER had a reputation for saving match points when he reached the men's singles final at Wimbledon. The Australian saved six match points against his countryman Rod Laver before losing 5-7 3-6 6-3 8-6 8-6 in the Australian final. And he saved another half-dozen match points against Butch Buchholz in the quarter-final at Wimbledon before the American retired with cramp at 15 games all in the fourth set.

Fraser left nothing to chance in the first Wimbledon final between two left-handers and, with his big serve on song, he triumphed over Laver 6-4 3-6 9-7 7-5.

He then won a second successive United States title, beating Laver 6-4 6-4 10-8.

Fraser: beat Laver

Barefoot Ethiopian promoted to new heights in marathon

AUGUST
1960
DECEMBER

Liston brawls into contention

AS Floyd Patterson was having his troubles with a tiresome Swede a new force was working his way up the heavyweight rankings — Sonny Liston. He was a brute of a fighter with a record to match, in the ring and with the courts. Liston, a product of a broken home and terrible poverty, had been imprisoned for armed robbery, and he had discovered boxing in jail. By the end of 1961 he had won 33 of his 34 professional fights.

Liston: former prisoner

ABEBE BIKILA was a private in Emperor Haile Selassie's Imperial Guard before the Olympic Games in Rome on August 25. When the 27-year-old Ethiopian returned home a month later with a marathon gold medal around his neck he was promoted to sergeant.

Private Bikila had been an unknown among the 69 starters in the marathon on September 10. He had sweated through only two marathons before, clocking an impressive 2hr 21min 23sec in his second race in Addis Ababa, more than 2,000 feet above sea level.

The favourite in Rome was the European champion Sergey Popov, who had run a world best 2hr 15min 17sec. Few people gave the African in the No 11 vest much chance. But the bare-footed Bikila's fast pace destroyed the field and he came home in 2hr 15min 16.2sec, pipping Popov's best time. The Soviet was fifth.

There was also cause for celebration in New Zealand. The country woke on September 3 to the news that Murray Halberg and

Peter Snell had won gold medals on the track. Halberg held off a late surge from the German Hans Grodotzki to win the 5,000m and Snell outsprinted a quality field in the 800m. Herb Elliott completed an Antipodean treble in the 1500m. The Australian won by 20 yards in 3min 35.6sec, a world record which stood for seven years.

Wilma Rudolph, a 20-year-old American who had overcome polio as a child, was the most successful athlete of the Games. She won the sprint double and a relay gold medal. The boxing was marred by poor judging, but not even the most biased official could have ignored the skill of Cassius Clay. The 18-year-old American outboxed Zbigniew Pietrzykowski in the final of the light-heavyweight division with all the artistry that later made him one of the sport's greats.

The Danish cyclist Knud Jenson died from a drug overdose during the road race, prompting the International Cycling Federation to become the first international body to introduce drug tests.

Britain took two gold medals, six silver and 12 bronze. The gold medals were won in the swimming pool and the bathroom. Anita Lonsbrough won the 200m breaststroke and Don Thompson triumphed in the 50km walk after he had acclimatised to the Italian heat with steam kettles and heaters in his sealed bathroom.

Bikila: killing pace

Dorothy Hyman wins silver for Britain in the 100m

Thompson: Olympic record

West Indians tie dramatic Test

Perfect Spurs look certainties

Solomon runs out Meckiff as he fails to make the winning run for Australia

TEST matches had become a tedious ritual in the late 1950s with the emphasis on defensive tactics and slow scoring. Richie Benaud and Frank Worrell provided a contrast with adventurous captaincy during a five-match series between Australia and West Indies.

They were prepared to gamble on attacking fields and flamboyant batting in their quest for victory, and they produced one of cricket's most dramatic final innings in the first Test in Brisbane on December 14.

Australia needed 233 for victory

at 45 runs an hour. But Wes Hall soon had the home side struggling at 92 for six before Benaud and Alan Davidson took their team to seven runs from victory with four wickets and five minutes left.

The pair had taken sharp singles all afternoon. They took one too many. Joe Solomon struck from 25 yards to run out Davidson and when the last eight-ball over from Hall began Australia needed six runs to win. They scored a single off the first ball. Benaud was dismissed with the second ball. A bye and a single left Australia needing

three runs off three balls.

The sixth delivery was hit to the leg side and when Grout scrambled for the third and seemingly winning run, Conrad Hunte's throw was hard and low. Grout's desperate dive was not enough.

Lindsay Kline came in and struck the seventh ball to square-leg. Ian Meckiff set off for the winning run but never made it. Solomon had only one stump at which to aim and was spot on with a magnificent throw. The West Indians danced for joy; cricket had produced its first tied Test.

TOTTENHAM began the season in record-breaking fashion. They won their first 11 League games before dropping a point at home to Manchester City, then won their next four. Only a defeat by Sheffield Wednesday at Hillsborough, and another dropped point at home to Burnley in a 4-4 draw having led 4-0, marred their perfect start.

Spurs went into 1961 with 46 points from 25 games, having scored a colossal 82 goals and conceded 27. It was little wonder that the bookmakers would not accept any money on Tottenham winning the League title.

Britain squelch to World Cup

GREAT BRITAIN ploughed through the mud at Odsal on October 8 to win the third World Cup with a 10-3 victory against Australia.

Billy Boston and Mick Sullivan scored the winning tries in a match which provided little sparkling rugby for the crowd of 32,773. The hosts had beaten New Zealand 23-8 and France 33-7 to set up the decider against a surprisingly out-of-form Australian team.

FOR THE RECORD

■ Ralph Boston leapt 8.21m at Walnut, California, on August 12 to beat the 23-year-old world long jump record of 8.13m set by Jesse Owens at the 1936 Olympic Games.

■ Bill Bradley became the only rider to win successive Tours of Britain.

■ The 20-year-old Jimmy Greaves scored five goals for Chelsea against West Brom in December and became the first player to score five goals, or more, three times in any division since the war.

■ The Football League experimented with a live television broadcast but when the game finished scoreless decided to abandon the idea.

■ The European Cup Winners Cup, modelled along the lines of the European Cup, was established.

■ Arnold Palmer and Sam Snead won the first of five successive World Cup titles for the United States.

■ Jack Brabham won five consecutive Grands Prix from June 6 to September 4 to take his second world championship in a Cooper-Climax.

■ Maria Bueno won the women's doubles Grand Slam.

■ Italy broke the domination of the United States in the Davis Cup by winning 3-2 in Perth but lost to Australia in the Challenge Round.

Brabham: won second world championship in a Cooper-Climax

CRICKET

Australian Test Drama

Worrell: charismatic leader

FRANK WORRELL inspired his West Indians to play dynamic cricket on their tour of Australia. And with the host captain, Richie Benaud, following suit, the teams produced an enthralling series. The theme was set in the first Test in Brisbane which ended in a tie and the drama continued for the next two months with each side winning a Test.

So popular was the cricket they were playing that the second day of the final Test in Melbourne drew a record crowd of 90,800. On the final day Australia were four runs short of victory with two wickets in hand when Wally Grout late-cut a delivery from Alf Valentine. The off-bail fell to the ground but the umpires ruled in favour of the Australian wicketkeeper and the hosts won by two wickets. The charismatic Worrell and his men were given a ticker-tape send-off.

GOLF

Gary Player: he beat Palmer in sand trap shoot-out

FOOTBALL

Dunfermline show character in Cup win

Dunfermline's hands are on the Cup after gritty replay victory

UNDER the canny management of Jock Stein, Dunfermline shocked Celtic and won the Scottish Cup for the first time when they triumphed 2-0 in the replay on April 26. The platform for Dunfermline's victory had been established four days earlier when, with 10 men, they had held the 17-time winners to a 0-0 draw in the final.

Player masters Palmer

GARY PLAYER needed all his expertise at the final hole in the Masters at Augusta. After landing in a bunker, Player got down in two. Moments later Arnold Palmer's ball settled in the same hazard. The American, needing three to tie, took four and Player became the first foreign winner of the Masters. The South African maintained his momentum to finish the leading money-winner on the US PGA Tour with $64,540.

RUGBY UNION

Springboks beaten at the last

SOUTH AFRICA'S rugby players preferred to win at any cost and they made few friends with their dour style of play in Britain. And win they did. They beat Wales 3-0, Ireland 8-3, England 5-0 and Scotland 12-5.

But when they were expected to play yet another tight game against the Barbarians the Springboks came out to throw the ball around. The Barbarians were having none of it. They broke tradition by keeping the ball among their forwards and ended South Africa's 29-match unbeaten record with a 6-0 victory in Cardiff.

Kicking pays off for France

A CHANGE in tactics from running to kicking rugby brought France their first outright Five Nations championship and extended their unbeaten run to 18 matches. The French embarked on a tour of New Zealand with great hope, only to lose all three Tests, including a 32-3 thumping in Christchurch.

176

Football enters the modern world

FOOTBALL entered the modern era of industrial relations when the players' union forced the League to abandon the maximum-wage ceiling and give players the right to be transferred from their clubs at the end of their contracts.

The League only caved in 48 hours before the players were to go on strike for the first time in the League's 73-year existence. The threat of a strike, and the attendant publicity about the draconian conditions and earning power of footballers, effectively swung the country behind the players.

Before the climbdown in January, professionals could earn no more than £20 a week in the season and £17 in the summer, and were contractually tied to their clubs for life. The union, led by Jimmy Hill, called this a "slave contract" and George Eastham was challenging the "retain and transfer" clause in his contract in the High Court.

But as well as the militancy of the players, there was the fear of many star players going to Italian clubs, who could, and would, pay fabulous salaries. The transfer of John Charles to Juventus in 1957 for £65,000 had shown that the Italians were prepared to pay through the nose to get the man they wanted as well.

It was not until March 1960 that a fee in excess of £50,000 was paid by an English club. And Jimmy Greaves, Denis Law and Gerry Hitchens did follow Charles to Italy in the summer of 1961.

The first player to benefit from the abolition of the restrictions was Fulham's England international Johnny Haynes. Tommy Trinder, the Fulham chairman, immediately made him England's first £100 a week footballer, and made certain he did not join the exodus to the continent.

Johnny Haynes: England's first £100 a week player

CRICKET

Youngest Test centurion at 18: Mushtaq Mohammad

FOR THE RECORD

BASEBALL
■ Warren Spahn of Milwaukee pitched the second no-hitter of his career at the age of 40 against the San Francisco Giants on April 28.

BOXING
■ Floyd Patterson retained his world heavyweight title in a brawl, rather than a boxing match, in March. Patterson was knocked down twice in the first round, but knocked out Ingemar Johansson in the sixth.

CRICKET
■ Mushtaq Mohammad became the youngest century maker in Test cricket when he hit 101 for Pakistan in their last Test against India for more than 17 years.

FOOTBALL
■ Kilmarnock's impossible tilt at the Old Firm's stranglehold on trophies was once again dashed as they lost the League to Rangers by a single point and the League Cup final to the same team 2-0.

■ Ipswich, with Alf Ramsey as manager, scored exactly 100 goals and won the Second Division championship.

■ Peterborough, only elected to the Fourth Division the previous year, stormed to the Fourth Division championship with a record-breaking 134 goals, of which Terry Bly scored 52.

■ Scotland were slaughtered by England 9-3 at Wembley on April 15. Jimmy Greaves scored a hat-trick.

■ Sir Stanley Rous was elected president of Fifa.

MOTORCYCLING
■ John Surtees, who had won seven world motor cycling titles between 1956 and 1960, abandoned his two-wheel exploits to concentrate on four-wheels full-time in a Cooper-Climax.

RUGBY LEAGUE
■ Tom von Vollenhoven ran the length of the field to score a try which helped St Helens beat Wigan 12-6 in the Challenge Cup final at Wembley in front of a capacity crowd of 94,672.

■ Leeds won their first championship title by beating Warrington 25-10.

SQUASH
■ The Pakistani Azam Khan won his fourth successive British Open title.

ATHLETICS

Fibreglass heralds a leap into the future

GEORGE DAVIES took pole vaulting into a new era at Boulder, Colorado, on May 20. The American was the first to break the world record with a revolutionary fibreglass pole. Davies cleared 4.83m. Within two years Brian Sternberg had smashed the five-metre barrier and in 20 years the record was broken more than 40 times.

The fibreglass poles provided greater upward momentum than the bamboo and metal poles used previously, their flexibility enabling athletes to improve the world record by nearly a metre in 20 years. The vault is the most progressive discipline in athletics.

POLES APART	
How the world record for pole vault has improved	
1960	4.80m
1961	4.83m
1962	4.94m
1963	5.20m
1964	5.28m
1965	5.28m
1970	5.49m
1975	5.65m
1980	5.78m
1985	6.00m
1990	6.06m
1991	6.10m

FOOTBALL

Spurs capture elusive Double

ON THE plane back from the 1958 World Cup the only topic of conversation that interested Danny Blanchflower was the Double. "It is going to be done," he told Stan Cullis and Joe Mercer. "And Spurs will be the ones to do it."

Before the start of the 1960-1 season Blanchflower told the Tottenham chairman that this was the year they would do it. The Double was the impossible feat, achieved by Preston in 1889 and Aston Villa in 1897, but missed throughout the century by the greatest of club sides, recently by Manchester United in 1957 and Wolves the previous season.

The Double had proved elusive because every team had cracked eventually, frequently as the prize was just in their grip. Thus, while bookmakers would not take bets on Tottenham winning the League from halfway through the season the smart men predicted Tottenham would go the way of the others.

The reason they didn't was probably down to one man: Danny Blanchflower. Not because of his unshakeable faith that the impossible was possible, but because in a team of all the talents he could control a game in a way that football would not understand for more than a decade. Blanchflower dictated the flow in a way no other player had before. As he said: "I could change the rhythm, change the pace, slow it down if necessary, speed it up when we needed to. I also had the ball much more often than anyone else — so I should have done something with it, shouldn't I?"

For Spurs, as they pursued their dream, every game became a Cup tie, every team wanted to beat them and raised their game accordingly. With Blanchflower at the helm Tottenham were never out-thought, out-played or out-hustled, no matter how inspired the opposition.

But Spurs were not just Blanchflower. As Bill Nicholson, the manager put it: "In a poor side Danny was a luxury." And the side that Nicholson had built was anything but poor (or cheap). Bill Brown in goal; full-backs Peter Baker and Ron Henry; centre-half Maurice Norman; wing-halves Blanchflower and Dave Mackay; inside-forwards John White and Les Allen; centre-forward Bobby Smith and wingers Cliff Jones and Terry Dyson.

Tottenham equalled or broke most records (games won, goals scored, points accumulated) as they cantered to the title with three games remaining by beating their nearest rivals, Sheffield Wednesday. By the time of the FA Cup final against Leicester on May 6 the expectation was extraordinary, and for once neutrals were not supporting the underdog.

It was a largely disappointing match, weighed down by the enormity of the occasion and a Leicester City who sensed that the Wembley crowd were not behind them. Spurs won 2-0, but without the swagger that everybody had hoped to see. Yet they had done it, achieved what Chapman's Huddersfield and Arsenal couldn't, and what had eluded two of Matt Busby's Manchester United teams and Stan Cullis's Wolves: the impossible Double. The glory days had arrived at White Hart Lane.

TENNIS

Wimbledon divides all England

IT WAS a momentous year, with two Britons in a singles final at Wimbledon. Not since Dorothea Lambert Chambers had beaten Ethel Larcombe in 1914 had Britain been guaranteed a champion. Forty-seven years was a long time to wait and the nation did not let the occasion go unnoticed.

Their dilemma was who to support: Christine Truman, an exuberant player with a powerful forehand, or Angela Mortimer, a fighter who made up for her lack of skill with determination. The nation chose Truman with her girl-next-door charm.

Truman came storming back from 4-2 down in the opening set to win 6-4. She was poised to take a 5-3 lead in the second set when she fell awkwardly when charging to the net on break point. She hurt her left thigh and although she continued to play, her movement around the court had slowed.

Mortimer won the set and broke in the first game of the deciding set. Truman fought back bravely with the crowd behind her but, after six games had gone against serve, Mortimer held on to win 4-6 6-4 7-5.

Four Britons reached the last 16 in the men's singles but it was Rod Laver's year. The Australian, with the experience of two finals under his belt, was too strong for Chuck McKinley in the final, beating the American 6-3 6-1 6-4.

Truman and Mortimer make it a 1-2 for Britain

178

Downes: briefly took Paul Pender's world middleweight title

FOR THE RECORD

BOXING

■ Terry Downes won the world middleweight crown from Paul Pender in July. The holder stayed on his stool at the end of the ninth round and quit. Pender, a Boston fireman, had already beaten Downes six months earlier, and reclaimed the championship in April 1962.

CRICKET

■ The follow-on law was suspended in county championship matches. It was reintroduced two seasons later. The new ball could be taken after 85 overs. Previously the law had allowed a new ball after 75 overs or 200 runs.

FOOTBALL

■ Rangers lost the first European Cup Winners' Cup final to Fiorentina 4-1 on aggregate. Afterwards the final became a single match.

■ Italian clubs made two raids into the English transfer market: Inter Milan pounced for Aston Villa's Gerry Hitchens, and Torino paid £100,000 for Manchester City's Denis Law in July.

MOTORCYCLING

■ Mike Hailwood won the 250cc world championship title on a Honda. He also took the Isle of Man senior Tourist Trophy race on a Norton. He won a record 14 TT races until 1979.

TABLE TENNIS

■ China took over from Japan as the dominant force when Chuang Tse-tung and Chiu Chung-hui won the world singles titles in Peking, and the Chinese men took their first world team title.

MOTORCYCLING

Hailwood: world 250cc and Isle of Man champion

Racing staggered by two doping scandals

DOPING horses to stop them was becoming common again and matters were not helped by the Jockey Club's rules which were, strangely, too strict. If any horse was found to have been doped its trainer automatically lost his licence, whether he was to blame or not.

Not surprisingly, many trainers were scared to admit that a horse had been got at by somebody for fear that they would lose their jobs. Local stewards, too, were often loathe to order tests for fear of depriving an innocent man of his livelihood.

The Duke of Norfolk recommended on May 4 that stewards should have the option of a fine or a ban depending on the circumstances, and soon afterwards two disturbing cases emerged.

Pinturischio was shaping up nicely for the Derby but the day before the Dante Stakes on May 16 he was got at. A few days later, a second attack was made and Pinturischio was so badly damaged that he never ran again. It was estimated that £250,000 of ante-post bets were lost as a result.

Then, in July, Pandofell, an overnight favourite, was found dazed and bleeding in his box. Tests confirmed he had been drugged, but fortunately he recovered to win at Doncaster in September.

Palmer whips up a storm as he blasts to a first Open victory

JULY 13 was no day to venture along the Lancashire coast. A storm had whipped up off the Irish Sea and the driving rain and howling wind turned the second round of the Open at Royal Birkdale into purgatory for the players and spectators.

There was one player who thrived in the conditions. Arnold Palmer. The popular American had finished second to Kel Nagle in his first Open the year before and after an opening round of 70 was clearly in contention. Palmer put on several sweaters and a dark cap to protect himself from the elements, turned up his collar and went out to conquer the course.

The wind was so strong that he needed a one-iron to reach the 212-yard fourth and a driver and a six-iron at the 315-yard fifth. He putted only six times on the opening six holes and collected five birdies.

Palmer turned in a three-under-par 34 and with two more birdies and a few blemishes scored 73 in what he rated as one of his finest-ever rounds. The storm was even fiercer the next day, blowing down tents and flooding the course. When it partially cleared on the Saturday Palmer held on to beat the Welshman Dai Rees by one stroke for his first Open victory.

Palmer: one stroke win

179

FOOTBALL

Shankly in swoop for Scots pair

BILL SHANKLY, Liverpool's manager, swooped into Scotland and made two astute and expensive signings for his Second Division club. In April he paid Motherwell £37,500 for their centre forward Ian St John. Then in June Shankly went raiding again and £30,000 persuaded Dundee United to part with their giant centre-half Ron Yeats.

The new recruits settled in well. Yeats was made captain within three months and Liverpool made a cracking start to the season, dropping only one point in their first 11 League matches and scoring 31 goals.

St John: cost £37,500

FOOTBALL

Spurs save a pound and spend a fortune

JIMMY GREAVES joined Spurs from Milan in December for £99,999, having been transferred from Chelsea in June for £80,000. The fee was deliberately £1 short of six figures because Bill Nicholson, the Tottenham manager, did not want his latest acquisition saddled with the burden of being England's first £100,000 player.

Greaves scored on both debuts in 1961, something he had made a habit of throughout his career.

Greaves: moved from Milan to Tottenham for £99,999

WHAT JIMMY DID ON HIS DEBUTS

1957, August 23, Tottenham v CHELSEA. *Scored*

1957, September 25, ENGLAND U-23 v Bulgaria. *Scored twice*

1959, May 17, Peru v ENGLAND. *Scored*

1961, June 7, MILAN v Botafogo. *Scored*

1961, December 16, TOTTENHAM v Blackpool. *Scored a hat-trick*

1962, May 4, First Cup final. TOTTENHAM v Burnley. *Scored*

1970, March 20, Manchester City v WEST HAM. *Scored twice*

MOTOR RACING

Hill wins title in tragic fashion

PHIL HILL won the world championship in tragic fashion. He and his teammate Wolfgang von Trips were Ferrari's top drivers and first and second in the world championship. In the penultimate Italian Grand Prix at Monza victory would have given von Trips the title.

But von Trips hit Jim Clark's Lotus and the German lost his life. Hill went on to win the race, and the title by a single point from von Trips. Hill was the first American to become world champion.

GOLF

Lady luck smiles on Barber

JERRY BARBER was short-sighted and had the worst swing on the US PGA Tour. His saving grace was his short game, which kept him within striking distance of Don January in the final round of the US PGA championship at Olympic Fields. He pitched in from 40 yards at the third to save par after driving into a tree, and holed a chip from long grass at the 10th for another par after topping his drive.

January, who played accurately all day, went to the par-three 11th with a five-shot lead. But his tee shot hit the flagstick and rebounded into a bunker. Barber stepped up and pulled his ball into a tree. It struck a branch and bounced to within three feet of the hole. "I'm four or five shots ahead of him all day and he keeps pulling stuff like that," January said.

Worse was to come. Barber sank a 25-foot birdie putt at the 16th and coaxed the ball in from 40 feet at the 17th. Then came a miracle. Barber needed a 60-foot putt at the last to force a play-off. He struck the ball sweetly and when it disappeared into the hole, January was stunned. "I couldn't believe it," he said. "And in the play-off I shot 68 and the little so-and-so beat me by a stroke."

Barber: freak bounce

Wily Benaud bowls himself out of hole

RICHIE BENAUD was living a captain's nightmare for the second time in a month. He won the toss in the fourth Test against England at Old Trafford, decided to bat and saw his team crumble.

Three weeks earlier he called correctly at Headingley, only to see Fred Trueman take 11 for 88 to give England an eight-wicket win. Now Benaud was in the soup again. Australia were 157 runs ahead in their second innings when Garth McKenzie joined Alan Davidson for the last wicket. They put on 98 to save their captain some embarrassment, leaving England to make 256 runs in 230 minutes to take a 2-1 lead in the series.

Ted Dexter hit a masterly 76 in 84 minutes as England reached 150 for one, so Benaud decided to go for broke. He set an attacking field, shrewdly bowling his leg spinners from around the wicket so that the ball pitched in the scuff marks created by Trueman and Brian Statham. The England batsmen had no answer.

Dexter gave a catch to Wally Grout at the wicket and Peter May was bowled second ball round his legs. Brian Close and Raman Subba Row were dismissed before tea and when Benaud took a

breather he had taken four for nine off 19 balls.

The tailenders fell under his spell after the break and Davidson bowled Statham 20 minutes from the end to give Australia victory by 54 runs — Benaud six for 70.

Australia retained the Ashes by drawing the fifth Test at The Oval, the last of May's 41 Tests as England captain.

> **'The hallmark of a great captain is to win the toss, at the right time'**
>
> **Richie Benaud**

BENAUD'S RECORD

	FIRST-CLASS	TESTS (63)
Innings	365	97
Not out	44	7
Runs	11,719	2,201
Highest	187	122
Average	36.50	24.45
Hundreds	23	3
Wickets	945 at 24.73	248 at 27.03
Catches	249	65

Benaud removes Dexter to start the England collapse

Shackleton the old warhorse

Shackleton: 153 wickets

DEREK SHACKLETON, a right-arm medium pacer, would earn his keep for Hampshire by sending down 1,500 overs a season. His ability to contain batsmen enabled his captain Colin Ingleby-Mackenzie to make 10 well-timed declarations and earn Hampshire their first county championship in 66 years.

They won 19 of their 32 matches and turned a three-horse race with Middlesex and Yorkshire into a solo gallop by winning five games running near the end of the summer. The greying Shackleton, in his 13th year with the county, took 153 of his career-record 2,857 wickets for the champions.

Ingleby-Mackenzie's success as a captain was founded on one premise: "I always insist that my team be in bed before breakfast."

FOR THE RECORD

FOOTBALL

■ The two legs of the League Cup final of the 1960-61 season were staged on August 22 and September 5, the first final of a major domestic competition to be held in the following season. Aston Villa beat Rotherham 3-2 on aggregate.

SAILING

■ The Admiral's Cup left Britain for the first time when it was won by the United States by 10 points.

TENNIS

■ Britain, with the Wimbledon singles finalists and the French champion, lost 6-1 against a team of inexperienced American teenagers in the Wightman Cup.

White heat for openers

BUTCH WHITE, the Hampshire fast bowler, after years of trying was eventually given an opportunity in England's first-ever Test in Pakistan and in an inspired spell of bowling dismissed the openers Hanif Mohammad and Imtiaz Ahmed in his first three overs.

White played only one more match but his breakthrough on his debut enabled England to win by five wickets in Lahore on October 26. It was 22 years before the two countries produced another outright result in Pakistan.

Alliss tie not enough for Britain

PETER ALLISS halved a tense singles match with Arnold Palmer and beat Bill Collins 3 and 2 on the final day of the Ryder Cup at Royal Lytham on October 14. It was not enough to stop the United States winning 13-8 with three matches halved.

Hammond fails to stop the rot for struggling New Zealand

DON HAMMOND enjoyed his finest 80 minutes at Headingley on September 30. The New Zealand captain lifted his struggling side to new heights in their 29-11 victory against Great Britain.

Then it was downhill. Great Britain won the next two Tests 23-10 and 35-19 and the New Zealanders went home with their worst tour record in history. They won only eight of their 20 fixtures.

Double heartbreak for Spurs

JANUARY

1962

MAY

RACING

Betting shop boom lures punters from racecourses

THE Betting and Gaming Act came into force and there was a boom in betting shops throughout the country. Many more opened than expected and the change in the law appeared to be a success. When the first levy was distributed the total amount of prize money available to the Jockey Club was in excess of £2m. However, the spread of betting shops and televised racing meant that attendances at racecourses continued to decline.

THIS was to be Tottenham's crowning glory. The season when they would repeat the Double and cap that by winning the European Cup. With the prolific goalscoring of Jimmy Greaves added to the historic side of the previous year confidence was sky high. Then in three short weeks two-thirds of the dream died.

On March 14 Spurs were at home to Ipswich, the newcomers who were setting the pace in the title race. Bill Nicholson proposed that they adjust their tactics to counter the deep-lying threat of Jimmy Leadbetter. The players disagreed and Nicholson gave way as he thought it imprudent to force his team to change their style if they were unhappy with it. Spurs lost 3-1. If that result had been reversed Spurs would have won the title instead of Ipswich.

In Lisbon a week later Spurs lost 3-1 to Benfica in the semi-final of the European Cup. Spurs had two goals that they thought were perfectly fair disallowed for offside. As Greaves said: "I reckon to this day the Swiss ref refereed us out of the final."

Tottenham beat Benfica 2-1 but lose 4-3 on aggregate

In the return at White Hart Lane on April 5 Tottenham's task became a mountain when they conceded an early goal and had one disallowed. But with 40 minutes left they were only one goal behind on aggregate. In a frantic finish they hit both posts and Dave Mackay hit the crossbar, but to no avail. Spurs won 2-1 but lost 4-3.

The Cup final a month later was a muted occasion for Spurs and although they beat Burnley 3-1, to Tottenham fans it was merely a consolation prize. Nicholson made his point in the Charity Shield match in August. Tottenham played to the tactics he had outlined in March, and Ipswich were walloped 5-1. But too late.

FOOTBALL

Ipswich bamboozle big clubs

IPSWICH, the previous year's Second Division champions, won the League championship under the astute managership of Alf Ramsey. They were largely a nondescript side and as newcomers to the First Division an unknown quantity. Ramsey played to his side's strengths: a fearsome pair of centre-forwards in Ted Phillips and Ray Crawford, with the slippery Jimmy Leadbetter firing the bullets from a withdrawn left-wing position. Nobody could fathom them as Ipswich became the fourth club to win consecutive Second and First Division championships.

Leadbetter, Ipswich's key player, scores against West Ham at Upton Park

Prolific Hanif torments England

THERE had been celebrations in the Mohammad household when Hanif was included in the first Pakistani Test team in 1952. His older brother Wazir earned his first cap two Tests later and there were more celebrations when Mushtaq and Sadiq were called up.

HANIF'S RECORD

	FIRST-CLASS	TESTS (55)
Innings	370	97
Not out	44	8
Runs	17,059	3,915
Highest	499	337
Average	52.32	43.98
Hundreds	55	12
Wickets	53 at 28.58	1 at 95
Catches	178	40
Stumpings	12	–

Mushtaq earned his first-class debut at the age of 13 years and 41 days, but it was Hanif who was always the master in the most famous dynasty in cricket. His phenomenal concentration made him one of the most difficult batsmen to dislodge, as England found out on their first visit to Pakistan.

Hanif had scored 337 against West Indies and a world record 499 in a first-class match in Pakistan when Ted Dexter's team arrived. England won the first Test in late 1961 and travelled to India, where Nari Contractor led the home side to their first series victory against England.

There was no respite for England. They returned to Pakistan to complete their remaining two Tests and ran into Hanif in top form. The Pakistani opener, who had made only 19 and 17 in the first Test, tormented England with innings of 111, 104, 67 and 89. The matches were drawn, but after bowling to Hanif for 893 minutes in the second Test Dexter's team had seen enough of him.

Hanif: scored freely

Collins saves Revie's bacon

JUST before the transfer deadline, Don Revie, battling against relegation, brought the 31-year-old former Scottish inside-forward Bobby Collins to Leeds from Everton for £25,000. Within a fortnight Collins asked for a transfer but Revie talked him out of it. Under Collins's leadership Leeds lost only one of their last 10 League matches but still only avoided relegation to the Third Division by winning the last game of the season 3-0 at Newcastle.

Collins: wanted transfer

France lose perfect record and miss Grand Slam once again

France, unbeaten in 20 matches, lose 3-0 to Wales

FRANCE were having a feast. They had won 18 matches in a row on the way to three successive Five Nations titles and were confident of winning a record fourth crown. They opened their campaign with a fine 11-3 win against Scotland and Michel Crauste, their brilliant loose forward, scored three tries in a 13-0 win against England. Pierre Albaladejo — known as Monsieur le Drop because of his ability to kick drop goals — was in great form and it seemed France would win their first Grand Slam.

But they lost 3-0 to Wales in Cardiff on March 24, ruining their perfect record. It was cold comfort that they beat Ireland 11-0 in Paris three weeks later to seal the title. The Grand Slam had eluded them again.

CRICKET

■ Sidney Burke was made a scapegoat by the South African selectors when New Zealand registered their second victory in Test cricket. Burke, who took 11 for 196 in 81 overs, was dropped for three years.

FOOTBALL

■ Faced with insurmountable financial problems, Accrington Stanley, who joined in 1921, resigned from the Football League. Oxford United were elected in their stead.

■ The England international forward Johnny Byrne was transferred from Third Division Crystal Palace to West Ham in March for British record of £65,000.

■ Dundee were the surprise League champions in Scotland, three points ahead of Rangers, who, with the Cup and League Cup under their belts, were denied a Treble. It was Dundee's first, and only, League title.

■ Liverpool beat Southampton 2-0 on April 21 to return to the First Division eight years after being relegated.

■ Wrexham's Ron Barnes, Roy Ambler and Wyn Davies all scored hat-tricks in a 10-1 trouncing of Hartlepools on March 3.

MOTOR RACING

■ Stirling Moss was almost killed in a crash at Goodwood on Easter Monday. The greatest driver never to have won the world championship had to retire from Formula 1.

SAILING

■ Prince Philip sent the Australians a good luck telegram before they challenged for the America's Cup. Unfortunately it was delayed and arrived a day after the Australians were beaten.

SQUASH

■ Heather Blundell (later McKay) was beaten for the last time in her career. Then, in February, she won the first of 16 successive British Open titles.

SQUASH

Blundell: last defeat

Smith's clean sweep in majors marred by early Wimbledon exit

Margaret Smith adds the French title to her collection by beating Lesley Turner 6-3 3-6 7-5

MARGARET SMITH, a 20-year-old Australian, took women's tennis by storm. She had already shown signs of greatness by winning three successive Australian titles and had lost in the quarter-finals at Wimbledon the year before. Her hard work in the gym and on the practice courts finally paid off. She added the French title to her Australian success with a 6-3 3-6 7-5 victory against Lesley Turner and then took her third major title of the year by beating Darlene Hard 9-7 6-4 in the US championships.

Smith's only blemish was at Wimbledon, where she was bundled out in the first round by the promising Billie Jean Moffitt. Smith's defeat left the way open for Karen Susman to win the title, beating the unseeded Czech Vera Sukova 6-4 6-4.

RUGBY UNION

Springboks blunt Lions' sharp edge

RICHARD SHARP was an excellent advertisement for the training techniques of the Commandos. The England fly-half was fast, fit and resilient. He needed all those attributes on the Lions' tour of South Africa.

Sharp was displaying his skills against Northern Transvaal in Pretoria on the eve of the Test series. But his performance was cut short by Mannetjies Roux, who was reputed to have practised his defence by tackling sheep on his farm. Roux's tackle broke Sharp's jaw and the Cornishman missed most of the tour.

The first Test was drawn 3-3 and the Springboks won the second 3-0 after a controversial decision against the visitors. Sharp signalled his return with a drop goal in the third Test, but a handling error cost the Lions the match 8-3. The South Africans completed the series with a 34-14 victory.

Sharp: broken jaw

GOLF

Unstoppable Palmer wins by a distance

THE Arnold Palmer legend lived on. His army of supporters had grown larger each year and he had inspired an American invasion of the Open championship. Palmer's only flaw was that in his quest for greater distance he played low, punching shots which had a tendency to run on once the ball hit the green. When he arrived at Troon for the Open he had developed a higher trajectory, which worked wonders.

The Scottish links were dry and fast as Palmer started the defence of his title with a 71. He settled in well, taking a grip of the tournament and turning the event into a one-man show with some of the finest golf of his career. He scored 69 in the second round and wrapped up the title with a brilliant 67 in the third and a closing 69.

Palmer beat the Australian Kel Nagle by six shots while Brian Huggett, who finished third, was 13 shots behind. The margin of victory was the biggest since Walter Hagan in 1929 and Palmer's aggregate of 276 was a record which lasted 15 years.

RACING

Derby donkeys wreak havoc

BIG pile-ups are features normally associated with the Grand National, not the Derby. Yet on June 6 seven horses came to grief at Epsom.

The 26 runners were coming down the hill to Tattenham Corner and at a point where it is difficult to see the track from the stands. So nobody was ever able to find out exactly what happened in the few fateful seconds. Seven horses came down, including the favourite Hethersett, and one broke a leg and had to be destroyed. The jockeys fared little better with six riders being taken to hospital, two of them seriously injured.

The stewards conducted a lengthy investigation and decided that nobody was to blame. It appeared that as the leaders were overhauled by the rest of the field one horse stumbled. This set off a chain reaction in the jostling pack with none of the other runners able to take avoiding action.

The stewards did, however, make the point that they thought many of the horses in the race were simply not good enough to be running in the Derby and this contributed to the accident.

Brazil unveil perfect understudy to Pele

BRAZIL had arrived in Chile for the seventh World Cup as holders and clear favourites. In Pele they had unquestionably the greatest player in the world, and many of the stars of 1958, although ageing, were still world-beaters.

Pele limped out of the tournament with a torn thigh muscle in Brazil's 0-0 draw with Czechoslovakia in the opening rounds. Brazil immediately produced, seemingly out of nowhere, a quicksilver replacement Amarildo, who, with Garrincha and Zagalo, was to win the trophy for them.

Of the home nations only England qualified. They appeared to be a strong side with Johnny Haynes, Jimmy Greaves, Bryan Douglas and Gerry Hitchens in attack and the two robust centre-halves Maurice Norman and Peter Swan. However, Ron Springett was suspect in goal and neither Greaves nor Haynes ever reproduced their club form for their country. As a consequence England stumbled to the quarter-finals where they were dispatched 3-1 by Brazil. Czechoslovakia surprised everybody by reaching the final, beating Spain, Hungary and Yugoslavia on the way, and then taking the lead against Brazil. Amarildo,

however, proved the perfect understudy to Pele. He scored the equaliser and made Brazil's second.

Schroiff, the Czech goalkeeper who had such an outstanding tournament, had a wretched final. If he had been in top form perhaps the Czechs might have astounded the world. But with 13 minutes to go Schroiff, unable to see a high ball in the glare of the sun, dropped it and Brazil had retained the World Cup, 3-1.

It was Walter Winterbottom's fourth World Cup as the manager of England, and his last. He resigned having been passed over for the job of FA secretary when Stanley Rous became the Fifa president. The post of England manager was advertised, but although there were 59 applications the FA were not satisfied that the man they required was among them. So they went head-hunting.

Alf Ramsey, the England and Tottenham full-back who had transformed Ipswich into First Division swans from Third Division ducklings, was not their first choice but he got the job. And for once the England manager would select the team himself, not the selection committee. A new era had begun.

Despite losing Pele, Brazil easily retained the World Cup

Lame horse clings on with helpless jockey

Winter: managed a stirring finish on Mandarin

FRED WINTER was one of the country's leading National Hunt jockeys and he needed all of his skill on Mandarin in the Grand Steeplechase de Paris on June 17.

Before the race Winter was so unwell that he had to be helped to get dressed. Then, after only three fences, the bit broke leaving Winter with precious little control over his mount. Somehow he managed to stay on for more than three miles, guiding Mandarin by using his knees and heels and tugging at the horse's neck. To make matters worse, Mandarin went lame in the final straight.

Somehow, Winter produced a stirring finish to get Mandarin up by a head. He received a hero's reception from the crowd but he had to admit that the triumph owed more to horse than jockey: "What could I do? I couldn't steer him, I couldn't stop and I was too frightened to jump off."

FOR THE RECORD

CRICKET

■ The last match between the Gentlemen and Players was held at Lord's. The fixture was discontinued because the distinction between amateurs and professionals was abolished.

■ Alec Bedser became an England Test selector and served for a record 23 years.

■ Joseph Filliston umpired the Lord's Taverners match against Old England at Lord's. He was 100 years old.

FOOTBALL

■ Billy Wright was appointed manager of Arsenal in the summer.

RACING

■ The Irish Sweeps Derby was run for the first time. With a prize of more than £50,000 it was the richest three-year-old race ever run in Europe.

RUGBY LEAGUE

■ Britain won 18 of their 21 matches in Australia, including the first two Tests, but they lost the third 18-17.

Laver takes on lobs and climbs upwards to Grand Slam heights

Three up, one to go: Laver accepts the Wimbledon trophy

ROD LAVER'S MAJOR SINGLES TITLES

1960 Australian
1961 Wimbledon
1962 Australian, French, Wimbledon, United States
1968 Wimbledon
1969 Australian, French, Wimbledon, United States

County change puts Graveney to the Test

TOM GRAVENEY, who had been dropped after the tour of Australasia in 1958-59, returned with a vengeance against Pakistan in the summer. Graveney had found a new lease of life when he moved from Gloucestershire to Worcestershire the previous season, and he carried his form into the Test series. He hit 97 in his first match back, 153 in the second Test and 114 in the fourth.

With Peter Parfitt also in good form Pakistan were put to the sword, losing 4-0 in the five-match series. Hanif Mohammad, who had frustrated England in the winter, failed miserably with an average of only 17.7. Instead, it was his younger brother Mushtaq who provided the most resistance, scoring 401 runs including an unbeaten century and three half-centuries.

ROD LAVER needed an answer to the superb lob volleys from Manuel Santana if he wanted to win the Grand Slam. Laver had won the Australian and French titles but was being given the runaround in the quarter-finals at Wimbledon. Santana won the first set 16-14 and moved to a commanding 5-1 lead in the second set. Laver's dream of becoming the first player since Don Budge in 1938 to win the four major titles was turning into a nightmare.

Suddenly, Laver snapped out his trance. He won the next four games and never looked back, sweeping past Santana and then Neale Fraser in the semi-finals. The final against the unseeded Martin Mulligan was an anticlimax. Laver retained his title with a 6-2 6-2 6-1 victory in his fourth successive final.

Laver had beaten his great rival and countryman Roy Emerson in the final of the Australian championship and repeated his success against Emerson in the Italian championships in Rome. But he struggled to find top form in the French championships on the clay courts of Roland Garros in Paris. He saved a match point against Mulligan in the quarter-finals and had to come back from two sets down to beat Emerson in the final.

With a victory in the German championships in Hamburg, Laver was in top form for the last leg of the Grand Slam, the United States championships in New York. With his excellent mix of spinning serves, sliced drives and crisp volleys, the unassuming Australian progressed to the final where he met the ubiquitous Emerson. Laver had lost the two previous finals at Forest Hills in straight sets. This time there was no stopping him as he wrapped up the match 6-2 6-4 5-7 6-4.

Laver had come a long way from the little lad with bandy legs who had grown up on his father's cattle ranch on the outskirts of Rockhampton in Queensland. There was nothing more for him to win so he signed a $100,000 contract with the International Professional Tennis Association early the next year.

Graveney: back in form

RUGBY LEAGUE

Weather freezes Second Division

ONE of the most severe winters on record helped to scuttle an experiment to divide British rugby league clubs into two divisions. The administrators were concerned about the dramatic decline in attendances and concluded that one of the main reasons was too many meaningless fixtures.

So the inaugural season with a First and Second Division started in the autumn of 1962. But by the following March nearly 200 matches had been postponed because of bad weather and attendances plunged. The season dragged on until June 1 when Swinton won the First Division.

Swinton retained their title the next season but with Bradford Northern folding because of poor crowds the clubs decided on February 14, 1964 to scrap the two-division experiment.

Patterson cannot disguise beastly appropriation of his world title

Floyd Patterson (*left*) signs up to meet big bad Liston (*right*)

IT WAS billed as "Beauty versus the Beast", and the public lapped up the idea that Floyd Patterson represented all that was good in the new, thrusting modern America, and that Sonny Liston, the ex-con, represented all that was bad. Then the bad guy won.

On September 25 in Chicago, Patterson surrendered his world heavyweight crown in craven fashion, a mere 126 seconds after the fight began. Despite the hype that Beauty was going to slay the Beast, Patterson did not fall for it. He came prepared for the outcome, brought a false beard and spectacles, and slipped out of the stadium in disguise after his humiliation.

With Liston installed as the world heavyweight champion, could they take the next phenomenon: Cassius Clay? Nicknamed the Louisville Lip because of his boasting and outspoken cheekiness, Clay had been the wonder of the 1960 Olympic Games when he took the light-heavyweight gold medal. As a professional he had surged up the rankings with a series of shattering wins, many of them predicted in advance.

In November, Clay, the outrageous youngster, met Archie Moore, the legendary veteran, now nearly 50. The kid predicted that Moore would fall in four and duly delivered. Moore never boxed again and the world waited for another Beauty v the Beast title fight, but this time with the bombastic Clay, rather than the wimpish Patterson, cast as the Beauty.

GOLF

Arnie and lawyer join gold rush

WHEN Arnold Palmer won a golf scholarship to Wake Forest University he teamed up with Mark McCormack, a sharp graduate who went on to earn a law degree at Princeton. Their friendship changed the face of golf.

McCormack struck a goldmine as his old school pal's agent. He secured lucrative contracts for Palmer and was so successful that he soon signed up Jack Nicklaus and Gary Player. They became known as the Big Three and had their most successful year in 1962, sharing the four major titles for the only time.

THE BIG THREE'S MONOPOLY				
	Masters	Open	US Open	US PGA
Champion	Palmer	Palmer	Nicklaus	Player
Runner-up	Player	Nagle	Palmer	Goalby

FOR THE RECORD

BOXING
■ Dick Tiger, the Liverpool-based Nigerian boxer, outpointed Gene Fullmer in San Francisco on October 23 to capture the world middleweight crown.

FOOTBALL
■ Denis Law followed in Jimmy Greaves's footsteps and returned from Italy. Like Greaves, he returned to the same city, but not the same club. In August Law was transferred from Torino for £115,000 to Manchester, but United, not City.

■ Don Revie brought back John Charles from Juventus for £53,000 in August. But Charles was unable to re-adjust to English football, only played 11 games for Leeds and returned to Italy in November, to Roma for £65,000.

■ Jock Stein's Dunfermline amazed Scotland and shocked Everton by knocking them out of the Fairs Cup 2-1 in the first round. And Bangor, the Welsh Cup holders from the Cheshire League, took Napoli to a play-off in the European Cup Winners' Cup before being eliminated.

MOTORCYCLING
■ Mike Hailwood won the first of four 500cc world championships, riding an MV.

MOTOR RACING
■ Graham Hill won his first world title and became Britain's second world champion in a BRM. Jim Clark was second, 12 points behind in a Lotus-Climax. The two Britons won seven of the nine Grands Prix.

TENNIS
■ Australia won their fourth successive Davis Cup title, beating Mexico 5-0. The Mexicans inflicted the first defeat of the United States in the American Zone since 1936.

CRICKET

Worcs cupboard stays bare

THE Worcestershire trophy cupboard had been bare for 97 years. Now their time had surely come. Don Kenyon, their captain, hit an unbeaten 103 in 2½ hours to give them a thrilling victory against Nottinghamshire and a 10-point lead at the top of the table in their final match of the season.

But Yorkshire caught Glamorgan on a rain-affected pitch at Harrogate on the last day of the season and won their second title in three years.

Moore and Paret die after bouts

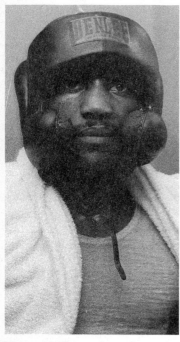

Moore: collapsed

ON MARCH 21 Davey Moore, defending his world featherweight title, retired at the end of the tenth round and in his dressing room collapsed into a coma, dying two days afterwards.

The following evening Emile Griffith, in a grudge match for the world welterweight title where the holder had taunted him with jibes of homosexuality, savagely defeated Benny Paret. He too collapsed into a coma and died 10 days later. The Paret fight was shown live on American television, and there was universal outrage.

CRICKET

Davidson thwarts English hopes

TED DEXTER'S team saw the last of two distinguished Australians who had tormented England for 10 years. Alan Davidson and Neil Harvey ensured that the Ashes stayed Down Under and then called it a day.

Davidson frustrated England until the end when he captured his 186th wicket with his last ball in Test cricket, dismissing Alan Smith in the final Test in Sydney in mid-February. Harvey took six catches in the match. He failed to make an impression with the bat in his swansong but did enough to finish with 6,149 runs at an average of 48.41.

Australia levelled the series in the third Test and drew the remaining matches after England had looked like wresting back the Ashes when the Rev David Sheppard won them an eventful second Test in Melbourne.

Davidson: 186th wicket from last ball in Test cricket

Sheppard began badly when he was trapped leg before by Davidson for a duck in the first innings. He then dropped two catches as Australia set England a target of 234 in slightly more than a day. But the Reverend turned from sinner to saint with his third Test century. He was run out when attempting the winning single but had given England their first victory in Australia since 1955.

FOR THE RECORD

CRICKET

■ New South Wales's record run of nine successive Sheffield Shield titles was ended by Victoria.

■ The Wisden Cricketers' Almanack celebrated its centenary.

FOOTBALL

■ Dundee reached the semi-final of the European Cup only to go down 5-1 to Milan in the first leg in the San Siro stadium. Dundee's goalkeeper, Bert Slater, complained that he couldn't see crosses coming over because he was dazzled by the flashbulbs of the photographers. In the return Dundee won 1-0, Alan Gilzean scoring and then being sent off shortly before the end.

■ The players' revolution was complete when George Eastham took Newcastle to the High Court and they ruled that the "retain and transfer" system was "an unreasonable restraint of trade".

■ Rangers achieved the Double in Scotland, but although the League title was won at a canter the Cup proved more difficult with Celtic forcing a replay before Rangers eventually triumphed 3-0.

TENNIS

■ Roy Emerson won the first of five successive Australian men's singles titles. He also won the French championship.

FOOTBALL

Pools plan warms up punters in big freeze

IT WAS one of the worst winters for football on record with more than 400 League and Cup games called off during a six-week period of snow, ice and freezing cold in January and February. Although the clubs were hit hard, the Pools companies were hit harder.

With three weeks' coupons void and the fourth certain to be void again they hit on the bright idea of a panel of experts forecasting the results. So on January 26, Tom Finney, Ted Drake, Tommy Lawton, George Young and Arthur Ellis became the first Pools Panel and gave seven draws, eight aways and 23 homes. With the unpaid dividends being carried over from the void weeks they made somebody very rich that weekend.

On February 9, the number of games played in a full fixture list in England and Scotland dropped to an all-time low of seven — 57 were postponed. Because of the large number of cancellations the season had to be extended.

CRICKET

Trueman overhauls Statham

FRED TRUEMAN became the first man to take 250 Test wickets when he bowled England to a 3-0 victory in their series in New Zealand. He took seven for 75 in New Zealand's first innings in Christ-church to overtake Brian Statham's world record haul of 242 Test wickets. Fiery Fred then grabbed two more scalps in the second innings to take his tally to 250 wickets in 56 Tests. New Zealand, who had been beaten by an innings in the first two Tests, lost by seven wickets.

Spurs pave the way in Europe

TOTTENHAM cast aside their disappointment of the previous season and went out and boldly captured the European Cup Winners Cup. They thus became the first British side to win a European trophy.

They did it in true Spurs style with a dazzling display in Rotterdam when the holders, Atletico Madrid, were thrashed 5-1 on May 15. But there were some anxious moments along the way.

In an earlier tie against Rangers, Danny Blanchflower had been sandwiched by two defenders, his knee was badly damaged and he missed 22 games. The 37-year-old captain played in the European final effectively on one leg.

Dave Mackay, whom Billy Nicholson the manager called "the heart of the team", was unfit to play with a stomach injury. The loss of Mackay terrified Nicholson, and his team talk before the match intimidated his own players. Nicholson went through the opposition player by player and made them all out to be world-beaters.

Nicholson left the dressing room, and Blanchflower took over. Blanchflower went through the Spurs team. By the time he had finished he had them convinced they were the world-beaters, and nobody appeared to be more convinced than little Terry Dyson. The left-winger played the game of his life, scoring twice.

The first was a teasing cross that eluded the keeper and found the net; the second was a winger's goal as he ran 30 yards with the ball, dummying this way and then that before thundering the ball into the net from outside the penalty area. As the Spurs players left the field Bobby Smith told Dyson: "You'd better retire now, you'll never play better."

They were prophetic words, as this was to be the last hurrah for Nicholson's Double side. But as history was made and a great side began to disintegrate something else, equally interesting, had happened. Nicholson had won a European trophy with a 16-man squad, not an 11-man team.

Cup salvages United's season

Crerand and Law combined brilliantly for Law to score the first goal in the Cup

DESPITE spending most of the season battling against relegation and the fixture backlog caused by the terrible winter, Manchester United won their first trophy since the Munich air disaster when they beat the favourites Leicester City 3-1 to win the FA Cup.

It had been a transitional season for United: Denis Law had arrived just before the season began and then Pat Crerand was bought from Celtic in February. The two Scots did not immediately fit into the team, but on the day of the final Crerand and Law combined bril-liantly for Law to score the opening goal. David Herd scored two more.

It had been a hard road from Munich 1958 to Wembley 1963 for Matt Busby. His legendary Babes had been largely home-grown — by contrast the 1963 side included six players who had been brought to Old Trafford by the power of the cheque book: Noel Cantwell, Pat Crerand, David Herd, Denis Law, Maurice Setters and Albert Quixall.

As United struggled through the season Busby mollified his team by saying that they would win the Cup. Then three home wins in 15 days against Huddersfield, Aston Villa and Chelsea saw them into the quarter-finals.

Even with the Cup on the agenda United had to survive their relegation derby with Manchester City. A draw was good enough for United because City needed the two points. In the second half United were 1-0 behind when Law was brought down in the area and Quixall scored. United stayed up, and City, Law's previous English club, were relegated.

Sharp's try stuns Scotland

RICHARD SHARP inspired England to a 10-8 victory against Scotland with a brilliant solo try at Twickenham on March 16 to seal the Five Nations championship. The England captain had led his team to a 13-6 win against Wales in Cardiff and a 6-5 triumph against France after a scoreless draw against Ireland.

But Sharp and four other key players were unavailable for England's first-ever tour and after a win against Wellington everything went downhill on their visit to Australasia. Don Clarke, the New Zealand full-back, kicked 15 points in the first Test, and then landed a 60-yard penalty in the final minute of the second Test to give the All Blacks a 9-6 victory.

ENGLAND'S FIRST TOUR

Opposition	Result	Score
Wellington	won	14-9
Otago	lost	9-14
New Zealand	lost	11-21
Hawke's Bay	lost	5-20
New Zealand	lost	6-9
Australia	lost	9-18

Nicklaus in his element at Augusta

THE supreme test provided by the Augusta National in Georgia was just the challenge the most talented player in golf had been waiting for. Jack Nicklaus began his love affair with one of the world's finest courses by beating Tony Lema by one shot in foul weather. Nicklaus, who had beaten Arnold Palmer in the US Open the previous year, added a third major title to his honours list by winning the US PGA championship.

Seconds out Patterson the fall guy

THE much expected re-match between Sonny Liston and Floyd Patterson lived up to all expectations. This time Liston took four seconds longer to dispatch the former champion on July 22 in Las Vegas. In 130 seconds Liston knocked him down three times and then knocked him out. Liston, aware of his unpopularity, said that the public would have to put up with him "until somebody else comes along."

FOR THE RECORD

CRICKET
■ A controversial experiment was introduced to the no-ball law whereby the bowler was judged on the position of his front foot, which had to be grounded within the popping crease.

FOOTBALL
■ Alf Ramsey officially took over as the England manager on May 1 and declared: "England will win the World Cup in 1966."

MOTORCYCLING
■ Mike Hailwood started his five-year spell as the Isle of Man senior Tourist Trophy champion when he roared to his second win in the event.

NETBALL
■ Australia won the inaugural world championship.

RUGBY LEAGUE
■ Australia thumped Britain 28-2 and 50-12 in the first two Tests of their tour, but lost 16-5 against a new-look home side in the third Test.

BOXING

Split glove saves Clay from Cooper

Clay rocks Cooper with a straight left at Wembley

WHILE Sonny Liston was dealing with Floyd Patterson, the young pretender Cassius Clay was waiting in the wings and racking up victories to confirm his status as the No 1 contender. One of the fall guys in this campaign of terror was supposed to be Henry Cooper. However, Cooper did not exactly follow the script.

On July 19, 30,000 turned up at Wembley to see the outrageous 21-year-old. For the first three rounds it was as expected, with the clowning American making a monkey out of Cooper. Then in the dying seconds of the fourth an arrogant Clay got careless and was caught with a left hook that could have changed boxing history.

The bell stopped Cooper from hitting him again, but Clay's trainer, Angelo Dundee, almost certainly saved him. In the third round there had been a minor tear in Clay's left glove and during the interval between the fourth and the fifth rounds Dundee used his expertise to turn this into a major tear.

The referee was summoned to inspect the glove. By the time this performance was finished Clay had gained sufficient breathing space to recover from Cooper's punch. And 75 seconds after the fifth round began Clay had inflicted so much damage around Cooper's left eye that the referee was forced to stop the fight.

GOLF

Right-handers left behind by Charles

BOB CHARLES was an anomaly. The New Zealander was the only left-handed player to be recognised among the leading golfers in a sport dominated by right-handers. Charles, who was right-handed in everything else he did, concentrated on accuracy and made up for his lack of distance with one of the most reliable putters in the business. He was the first to take the wrist out of the putting stroke and he seldom missed putts from under 10 feet.

It was his skill on the green which put his name in the history books as the only left-handed player to win a major championship. He averaged just 30 putts a round in his Open victory at Royal Lytham.

A course record 66 in the third round helped Charles force a play-off against the American Phil Rodgers. Charles took a three-shot lead in the morning of the last 36-hole play-off in the Open. He needed only 26 putts in 18 holes and with his putter still hot in the afternoon, he cruised home by eight shots.

Charles: southpaw winner

Flawless McKinley weathers Wimbledon

McKinley: did not drop a set at Wimbledon

IT WAS the year of upsets at Wimbledon as a fortnight of persistent rain played havoc with the programme.

Chuck McKinley, an American who was seeded fourth, used his strength as a great retriever to dominate the men's singles. He was one of only four seeded players to reach the quarter-finals, and he beat the unseeded Australian Fred Stolle in the final. In fact McKinley won the title without dropping a set.

Margaret Smith, who had been bundled out in the first round by Billie Jean Moffitt the year before, gained her revenge with a 6-3 6-4 victory in the final. She had to wait until the Monday for her win because rain forced the postponement of the final on Saturday. Smith joined Ken Fletcher to become the first pair to win the mixed doubles Grand Slam.

Jockey Club's rulings cause embarrassment

THE 1963 season was not a good one for the Jockey Club's image. Their discomfiture started when the public took great delight at Paddy Prendergast's raids from Ireland. Ten years before, Prendergast had been banned by the Jockey Club in a decision that was widely condemned. The ban was lifted a year later, and there was a feeling that Prendergast got his revenge in 1963 when he made off with the Oaks, the Eclipse, and the St Leger to become the leading trainer in England.

The affair of Relko's victory for France in the Derby was even less pleasant. Several weeks after the race the Jockey Club announced that seven horses had shown evidence of being doped. Speculation mounted and the stewards finally confirmed that Relko was one of the horses under investigation, but one set of tests had been negative while another positive.

The French were outraged at what they saw as a slur on their horse and they were not further pleased when the Jockey Club took until October to announce that there was no evidence of wrongdoing by Relko's connections and the result would stand.

Relko wins the Derby in controversial circumstances

Wounded Cowdrey holds off West Indies

Cowdrey: brave innings

IT WAS shortly before six o'clock on June 25 when Colin Cowdrey walked down the pavilion steps at Lord's. His broken left arm was protected by a plaster cast and England needed six runs off two balls to beat West Indies with one wicket remaining in the second Test. Cowdrey's arm had been fractured the previous day by a rising delivery from Wes Hall. He was given a warm reception but did not have to face a ball. Instead,

David Allen blocked the last two deliveries from Hall and one of the most dramatic Test matches in history ended in a draw.

Rain delayed the start on the final day when England resumed their innings at 116 for three. They needed another 118 runs in 200 minutes and immediately fell behind the clock when Ken Barrington scored only five runs in nearly an hour.

Then Brian Close stood firm

while Hall and Charlie Griffith battered him. The West Indian pair bowled throughout the day with the exception of one over when Griffith changed a damaged boot.

They appeared to have won the game when Frank Titmus and Fred Trueman were dismissed in successive balls. But the West Indians were not counting on Cowdrey's last stand. Trueman, who took 11 wickets in the match, described it as "one hell of a game".

GOLF

Wright the women's pathfinder

MICKEY WRIGHT won a record fourth US LPGA title in her most successful season as one of golf's greatest woman players. Wright won a record 13 tournaments on the US Tour and prompted her fellow professional Judy Rankin to suggest: "Mickey got the outside world to take a second hard look at women's golf and when they looked they discovered the rest of us."

CRICKET

Close and Yorkshire march on

YORKSHIRE celebrated their centenary by winning their fourth county championship in five summers. It was the first season without amateur players and the forthright Brian Close achieved immediate success in his tempestuous eight-year reign as captain.

Geoff Boycott, who had made his debut for Yorkshire the previous summer, scored 1,446 runs to finish second in the averages behind Ken Barrington. Another man who made an early impression was the 18-year-old Derek Underwood. The Kent slow-medium bowler became the youngest player to capture 100 wickets in a season.

ATHLETICS

Record breaker lacks Midas touch

RON CLARKE, an Australian who had lost interest in running since he carried the torch in the 1956 Olympic Games in Melbourne, began to run again. The gifted 26-year-old trained twice a day before and after his work as an accountant and his improvement was spectacular. In five years he broke 18 world records from two miles to the one-hour run. He started with the 10,000m and six-mile records on December 18 and finished with the two-mile record in London on August 24, 1968. Clarke, the fastest long distance runner in the 1960s, had one regret — he never won a gold medal.

Clarke: 18 world records

RON CLARKE'S ELUSIVE GOLD		
1962 Commonwealth Games	Three miles	Second
	Six miles	Retired
1964 Olympic Games	5,000m	Ninth
	10,000m	Third
	Marathon	Ninth
1966 Commonwealth Games	Three miles	Second
	Six miles	Second
1968 Olympic Games	5,000m	Fifth
	10,000m	Sixth

MOTOR RACING

Precocious Clark blasts to first world title in innovative Lotus

JIM CLARK and Lotus blasted every other car off the track on their way to the world and constructors championship. Clark, the rising star in motor racing and the youngest-ever world champion at 27, had a revolutionary car in the Lotus 25, the first modern car with a monocoque, a single-shell fibre-glass body.

The car had been driven by Clark the previous year, when he had finished second in the championship, but now driver and car were virtually unbeatable as Clark won seven of the 10 Grands Prix. Title-holder Graham Hill finished a distant second in his BRM.

Clark wins the European Grand Prix at Brands Hatch in his Lotus 25

Deadly Dexter and Sussex save cricket in only one day

CRICKET was in decline and few people could afford to spend three or more days watching a match. Attendances at county matches had slumped from nearly two million in 1950 to 700,000 in 1962; there was a dearth of talent and too many Test matches were ending in boring draws.

The MCC had set up a committee under the chairmanship of Harry Altham in 1956 to look into ways of reviving interest. The committee suggested a knockout competition. It took six years for the establishment to react but when Derbyshire, Leicestershire, Northamptonshire and Nottinghamshire played in a successful trial one-day competition in May 1962 the seeds had been planted for a limited-over cup the next summer.

The major stumbling block would be the expense if matches were interrupted by poor weather. Henry Garnett, the managing director of the Gillette Safety Razor Company, agreed to underwrite the event for £6,500, providing the counties with insurance against bad weather.

And the rain did disrupt the first match between Lancashire and Leicestershire at Old Trafford on May 1, forcing the game to be extended by a day. But by the first weekend in September the Gillette Cup had proved a resounding success. Cricket was saved in a day.

Many players believed that to

> **❝In full flow it was not too much to claim that Dexter was worth at least double the admission price❞**
>
> **Trevor Bailey**

win 65-over matches required only good batting and bowling. Ted Dexter thought otherwise. The Sussex captain set a funnel-shaped field stretching outwards from the batsmen and instructed his bowlers to pitch the ball up, forcing the opposition to drive the ball into the funnel.

Dexter used his tactical awareness to earn Sussex their first trophy in the county's 124-year history. They beat Worcestershire by 14 runs in front of a full house at Lord's in the September final.

The limited-over game brought about a decline in spin bowling and an emphasis on containing batsmen rather than getting them out. But it forced batsmen to attack and fielders to improve their skills and, most importantly, it brought money and youth back to the sport.

DEXTER'S RECORD

	FIRST-CLASS	TESTS (62)
Innings	567	102
Not out	48	8
Runs	21,150	4,502
Highest	205	205
Average	40.75	47.89
Hundreds	51	9
Wickets	419 at 29.93	66 at 34.93
Catches	234	29

Dexter: beat Worcestershire by 14 runs in the final

Meckiff finally thrown out

IAN MECKIFF, a left-arm Australian pace bowler, had been dogged for five years by accusations that his bowling action was illegal. He had gone 17 Tests without being called for throwing when he was selected for the first Test against South Africa in Brisbane.

The umpire Col Egar no-balled Meckiff four times in his first over for throwing. Richie Benaud, the Australian captain, said to him: "I'm afraid this is the end, Dad." He bowled only one over and retired from cricket.

FOR THE RECORD

FOOTBALL

■ Borough United, of the Northern Welsh League, became the first non-League side to win a European tie when they eliminated Sliema Wanderers 2-0 in the Cup Winners' Cup.

■ Don Revie prised the Eire international forward John Giles away from Manchester United for £35,000 in August. Giles had played for Manchester United in their winning Cup team but he and Matt Busby did not see eye to eye. When he was dropped for the first League game of the season he demanded a transfer and within days he was playing for Second Division Leeds United.

■ An Irish waif called George Best made his League debut for Manchester United at the age of 17 years and four months in September.

■ Spurs had a record seven players on duty in home internationals on October 12.

GOLF

■ The United States beat Britain 20-6 with six matches halved in the Ryder Cup in Atlanta. Fourballs were introduced for the first time and Britain won only one out of eight.

■ Arnold Palmer became the first player to win more than $100,000 in a single season on the US PGA Tour. The total prize money for 43 events broke the $2 million barrier.

■ The United States broke the domination of Australia in the Davis Cup. It was the only time in nine years that Australia lost. The American women also beat Australia in the first Federation Cup, staged at Queen's Club in London.

193

BOXING

Clay is as good as his word

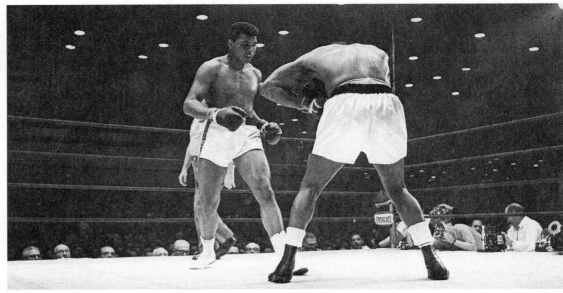

Double shock: Clay beats Liston and changes his name to Muhammad Ali

RUGBY UNION

Scotland run into top form at long last

SCOTLAND won their first Five Nations championship since 1929, sharing the crown with Wales. Earlier in the winter Scotland had denied New Zealand an historic first clean sweep of the home countries by holding Wilson Whineray's team to a scoreless draw at Murrayfield on January 18.

The All Blacks had beaten Ireland 6-5, Wales 6-0 and England 14-0 thanks to Don Clarke, who kicked 15 of their 26 points. Newport ruined their unbeaten tour with a 3-0 victory.

CRICKET

Smith has no appetite for India

MIKE SMITH took over the England captaincy from Ted Dexter for the tour of India and spent two months trying to gather 11 fit souls. The tourists were plagued with stomach disorders soon after they arrived on the subcontinent.

England were reduced to 10 men in the second Test when Micky Stewart went down with dysentery at tea on the opening day. Peter Parfitt and Colin Cowdrey joined the tour for the third Test and were the most successful batsmen in a side that did well to draw all five Tests.

WHEN the swaggering braggart met the world champion in Miami on February 25 the only person in America, it seemed, who gave Cassius Clay a prayer was himself.

In an amazing turnaround Sonny Liston, the ex-con, was perceived by America as the good guy who was going to button that Louisville Lip. But Clay had completely out-psyched Liston, convincing the champion that he was stepping into the ring with a lunatic.

Some lunatic. Clay danced round the ring picking off a plodding, leaden-footed Liston at will. By the fourth round Liston had a serious cut under his left eye, and at the end of the sixth Liston was beaten. Thoroughly demoralised, he refused to come out for the seventh and the 7-1 on favourite had given way to the brash upstart with a fancy way with words. America could not believe that Liston, of all people, had quit on his stool.

The day after the fight America had another bombshell to contend with. Their new world heavyweight champion was not Cassius Clay, but Muhammad Ali. Clay embraced the Muslim religion, became a follower of the much reviled Malcolm X, and decided to renounce his "slave name".

The most important athlete in the world, in his moment of triumph, had turned his back on his homeland in the most hurtful fashion. It cost Ali millions of dollars in endorsements, but certainly endeared him to millions of young blacks worldwide.

> ❛ King Liston will stay
> Only until he meets
> Cassius Clay
> Moore fell in four
> Liston in eight ❜

FOOTBALL

Three jailed for fixing matches

A BOMBSHELL dropped on to the breakfast tables of the nation on Sunday April 12 when the People published allegations that three players, two of them England internationals, were part of a betting ring that had fixed matches.

Two of the three, Peter Swan and David "Bronco" Layne, were with Sheffield Wednesday, and the third, Tony Kay, had moved from Wednesday to Everton for a record fee of £55,000 and had won a championship medal.

The trio were accused of fixing the match on December 1, 1962 between Sheffield Wednesday and Ipswich, which Wednesday lost 2-0, and to have each won £100 on the outcome of that match and two others that Saturday.

The allegation came at a time when there were widespread rumours in the game about players conspiring to fix matches to land a betting coup. For this to be profitable it required several matches to be rigged at the same time and therefore a ring of players at different clubs, with go-betweens to organise the coup. The scale of such an operation meant that the truth would eventually surface.

The League acted swiftly, as it had to when more allegations and more names tumbled out of the woodwork in the ensuing weeks. Most of the players named were suspended for life. Kay, Swan and Layne received prison sentences, their promising careers, and lives, in tatters.

Rivals help win gold for Nash and Dixon

TONY NASH and Robin Dixon were one of the world's leading two-man bobsled teams despite having no practice facilities in Britain. They finished third in the world championship in Innsbruck in 1963 and returned to the Austrian town for the IX Winter Olympics hoping to break the domination of the crack Italians.

The axle bolt on their sled broke after their first of two runs on the opening day. Just when it appeared that they would have to withdraw their Italian rival Eugenio Monti came to the rescue. Monti and his brakeman Sergio Siorpaes had completed their second run and were at the bottom of the mountain. Monti removed his axle bolt and made sure it reached Nash. The British team completed their run and the next day won the gold medal. The Italians took bronze.

The Games also provided a stage for the Soviet husband and wife skating pair of Ludmila Belousova and Oleg Protopopov, whose background in ballet enabled them to win the gold medal with their trademark, a spectacular death spiral.

Nash and Dixon triumph in Innsbruck

FOR THE RECORD

CRICKET

■ Frank Worrell, the West Indian captain, was knighted.

■ Anti-apartheid demonstrators damaged the pitch at Wellington on February 21 but failed to prevent the start of the first Test between New Zealand and South Africa. It was the last series between the two countries.

FOOTBALL

■ Jim Fryatt of Bradford Park Avenue scored the fastest goal in football, in four seconds, against Tranmere on April 25.

■ Rangers saw off everybody in Scotland when they completed a wonderful Treble of League championship, Cup and League Cup.

■ Jimmy Dickinson finally hung up his boots with a record 764 League appearances for his only club, Portsmouth. Dickinson won two consecutive championship medals in 1949 and 1950, and had been England's left-half for several years until Portsmouth switched him to centre-half. Loyal and industrious, Dickinson was awarded the MBE.

■ Oxford became the first Fourth Division side to reach the quarter-finals of the FA Cup when they knocked out Blackburn Rovers in the fifth round.

■ Denis Law was voted the European Footballer of the Year.

TRAMPOLINING

■ Danny Millman was crowned the first world champion. His fellow American Judy Wills won the women's title which she held for five years.

Amazing Arkle runs Mill House ragged

Arkle beats Mill House in the Gold Cup

ALL OF the great racing duels of the past had been the preserve of the Flat until two Irish-born horses engaged in a battle for supremacy that set National Hunt racing alight.

Mill House looked to have the upper hand when he won the Hennessy Gold Cup at Newbury in November 1963. The People's racing correspondent rashly wrote: ". . . the massive Gold Cup winner will never be beaten." He must have overlooked Arkle, who finished third after slipping near the end of the race.

Mill House was odds-on for the Cheltenham Gold Cup on March 7. He ran a scorching race but Arkle treated him with contempt. Three fences out Arkle was coasting. When he turned on the power he roared away to break the course record and win by five lengths.

With the score at one each the decider was held at Newbury for the 1964 Hennessy. Arkle absolutely slammed Mill House, doubling the winning margin to 10 lengths. Both horses went back to Cheltenham for the 1965 Gold Cup and Arkle doubled the distance again, beating Mill House by 20 lengths.

> **❝ I can't believe that any horse could have done what Arkle did ❞**
>
> **Fulke Walwyn**
> Mill House's trainer, after the 1964 Cheltenham Gold Cup

Everton spur Liverpool to title

LIVERPOOL became League champions for the first time since 1947. Although they had started the season shakily, only taking nine points from the first nine games, a 2-1 defeat of their bitter rivals, and the champions, Everton seemed to inspire them.

Liverpool went on to accrue 47 points from 30 games, and they finished the season four points ahead of Manchester United. The purchase of Peter Thompson, Preston's left-winger, for £40,000 the previous August enabled Shankly to achieve his lifelong ambition. Thompson would burst down the wing and send over devastating crosses for Roger Hunt or Ian St John to convert into goals.

1964

GOLF

Doctor helps Venturi pass his physical

KEN VENTURI appeared to have lost all hope of winning a major title before his late qualification for the US Open at Congressional in Washington. A dramatic slump in form left him in 94th place on the US Tour in 1963.

A brilliant 66 on the morning of the hot and humid final day brought Venturi back into contention, but many feared he would be unable to complete his afternoon round. Venturi was dehydrated and a doctor accompanied him over the last 18 holes. He fought off exhaustion and his rivals to win by four shots from Tommy Jacobs in a dramatic finish. It was the last time two rounds were played on the final day.

Venturi: dehydrated

TENNIS

Grand Slam escapes Emerson at his peak

Emerson: beat Stolle in four sets at Wimbledon

ROY EMERSON confirmed his status as the world's leading amateur when he won three of the four Grand Slam titles. Only the French title eluded him in his most successful year.

Emerson's game centred around his strong serve and a sizzling forehand, his strength coming from the powerful wrists he was said to have developed milking cows on his father's farm in Queensland. He was one of the fastest players around the court, a legacy of his brilliance as a schoolboy athlete who ran 100 yards in 10.6sec when he was 14.

Emerson beat his countryman

Fred Stolle in the finals of the Australian, Wimbledon and United States championships. The closest final was at Wimbledon, where Emerson won 6-4 12-10 4-6 6-3. He went on to win 39 major singles and doubles titles, more than any other man in tennis.

FOOTBALL

Tottenham's White killed by lightning on golf course

JOHN WHITE of Tottenham was killed by lightning in July while sheltering under a tree on a golf course at Crews Hill, Middlesex. It was a devastating blow to his young wife and family and to Spurs.

The 26-year-old inside forward had been one of the key components of the fabulous Double side. With Danny Blanchflower retired, White had been destined for the role of midfield general, a role he had filled with aplomb during Blanchflower's previous absences.

ROY EMERSON'S MAJOR SINGLES TITLES

1961 Australian, United States
1963 Australian, French
1964 Australian, Wimbledon, United States
1965 Australian, Wimbledon
1966 Australian
1967 Australian, French

FOR THE RECORD

BOXING

■ Sugar Ray Robinson retired at 44 having won 174 of 201 fights and having been world champion at two weights.

FOOTBALL

■ Howard Kendall, at 17 years and 346 days, became the youngest player to appear in a Cup final. He only played because Ian Davidson misled Preston about his reasons for a sudden trip home to Scotland and was disciplined by the club.

GOLF

■ Mickey Wright won her fourth US women's Open title at her home club in San Diego. She tied Betsy Rawls's record.

MOTOR RACING

■ Dan Gurney won the French Grand Prix, the first to be captured by a Brabham-designed car. Jack Brabham, the designer, finished third.

■ Jackie Stewart joined forces with Ken Tyrell to race Coopers in Formula 3.

RACING

■ Scobie Breasley won his first Derby at the age of 50.

SURFING

■ Bernard Farrelly became the first world amateur champion. His fellow Australian Phyllis O'Donnell was the first women's champion.

TENNIS

■ Dorothy Cavis-Brown, a lineswoman at Wimbledon, made front-page news when she fell asleep in her chair during the championships.

White: devastating blow

Shoemaker chooses the wrong partner

RARELY can Bill Shoemaker have made such a bad choice. Northern Dancer was being talked about as a Triple Crown winner when Shoemaker partnered him to victory in two races before the Kentucky Derby. But on May 2 at Churchill Downs Shoemaker opted to ride Hill Rise. It looked like he had made the right choice as Hill Rise cut down Northern Dancer's lead with every stride in the finishing straight. But Northern Dancer stayed on to win by ¾ of a length in record time.

Many people thought Northern Dancer had been fortunate and Hill Rise was favourite for the second leg of the Triple Crown, the Preakness. Hill Rise was pressing hard, but this time Northern Dancer had no difficulty in pulling away.

The Triple Crown eluded Northern Dancer when his stamina gave out and he could only finish third in the Belmont Stakes. Even so, when an injury forced him to retire he had proved he was no slouch on the track with a total of 14 wins from 18 starts.

Anquetil's successful formula

JACQUES ANQUETIL loved la dolce vita. He would often sit down after a gruelling stage in the Tour de France and eat lobster and drink champagne, usually in female company.

But there was no denying Anquetil's skill when he won the Giro D'Italia and then added a record fifth Tour victory in 1964. Anquetil, a brilliant time triallist, suggested after winning one race by 12 seconds that "it was 11 seconds more than necessary".

Lema gets the right direction

Lema: late arrival

TONY LEMA was on a hot streak when he arrived at St Andrews a day before the Open championship. He had won four of the last five events in the United States, but he had such a busy schedule that there was scarcely more than a day to prepare for his first tournament on a links course.

Lema, relying on his caddie Tip Anderson to show him the way, took the lead with rounds of 73 and 68. But he faltered in the first of two rounds on the final day and Jack Nicklaus, who had been nine shots behind, picked up eight strokes in six holes. Lema snapped out of his slump just in time and went to lunch with a 68. Nicklaus had fired a 66 but was too far off the pace and Lema finished with a 70 for a five-shot victory.

Lacklustre West Ham come from behind to win their first trophy

Hurst scores West Ham's second goal at Wembley

WEST HAM won their first trophy when they beat Second Division Preston 3-2 in the FA Cup final. West Ham displayed their characteristic traits, flashes of brilliance laced with erratic moments. Preston, the obvious underdogs, led twice and were anticipating extra time when Ronnie Boyce beat the injured Preston goalkeeper Alan Kelly.

For West Ham the victory had been an anti-climax. Their real triumph came in the semi-final when they thumped Cup-holders Manchester United 3-1 and Ron Greenwood cried on the train home.

When it came to the final, West Ham seemed to have left their football in the semi. As Bobby Moore said: "We'd been magic against Manchester United. Wembley should have belonged to West Ham. We simply played badly. We were lucky to beat Preston, and bloody lucky Preston were no better than they were."

RUGBY LEAGUE

Subs given half a chance

RUGBY LEAGUE made the first tentative step towards ensuring that matches were not decided by injuries by allowing the use of two substitutes for injured players, but only until half-time. Substitutes were allowed irrespective of injuries until half-time the following season and in 1969 at any time throughout a match.

CRICKET

Dexter repeats Cup strategy

TED DEXTER inspired Sussex to their second successive Gillette Cup with an eight-wicket victory in the final against Warwickshire at Lord's. Dexter's tactic of loading the boundary with fielders frustrated Warwickshire who were dismissed for 127. The competition had proved so popular the previous season that five Minor Counties were admitted.

BOXING

Downes looks for better bet

THE former world middleweight champion Terry Downes, ahead on points at the time, walked into a straight right from Willie Pastrano and out of the world light heavyweight championship in Manchester on November 30. Downes, having failed to win his second world crown, retired and invested in a chain of betting shops.

Packer and Rand lead bumper medal hunt for Great Britain

BRITISH women athletes had never made much impression at the Olympic Games, but the XVIII Olympics in Tokyo in October proved a watershed. Ann Packer and her room-mate Mary Rand had a small celebration with a haul of two gold medals, two silver and one bronze.

Rand became the first British woman to win a field event when she leapt 6.76m to break the world long jump record. She added a silver medal in the pentathlon and a bronze medal in the 4x100m relay to her collection.

Packer showed her ability as one of the nation's most versatile athletes when she shocked the world in only her eighth 800m. Packer, who had finished second to Betty Cuthbert in the 400m, produced a spectacular sprint in the 800m to win by five metres and break the Olympic record with a time of 2min 1.1sec.

Lynn Davies gave Britain the long jump double by winning the men's event with 8.07m, and Ken Matthews grabbed the nation's fourth gold medal with a victory in the 20km walk. Matthews was the only British gold medallist not awarded an MBE at the end of the year, but after a 14-year campaign he was eventually honoured. Britain won 12 silver medals and two bronze.

Joe Frazier was crowned heavy-

Ann Packer wins the 800m in record time

weight boxing king and Abebe Bikila, the bare-footed Ethiopian who had won the marathon in Rome four years before, came back with a pair of shoes to retain his title only five weeks after an appendicitis operation.

The New Zealander Peter Snell retained the 800m title and won the 1500m and the American Bob Hayes won the 100m, equalling the world record of 10.0sec. Hayes sealed victory for the United States in the 4x100m relay which prompted one rival to suggest that Hayes was all the United States team had. One American athlete replied: "Man, that's all we needed."

MOTOR RACING

Surtees just a double champion

JOHN SURTEES became the first man to win the world championship on four wheels having already won the equivalent title on two wheels seven times. However, his achievement of a unique double was completely overshadowed by the thrilling last Grand Prix of the season in Mexico on October 25.

The world championship was wide open. Graham Hill had 39 points, John Surtees 34 and Jim Clark 30. For Surtees to win he had to stop Hill or Clark finishing first or second, and preferably win the race.

With seven laps left Clark had the title in his sights. He was well ahead of Dan Gurney, Lorenzo Bandini, Surtees's Ferrari teammate, and Surtees. Then fate struck

when an oil pipe split and he had to conserve the car. Worse, on the last lap his engine seized.

Gurney was now first, Bandini second and Surtees third, which was not enough for Surtees to secure the title. Bandini waved his teammate through into second position, six valuable points, and the world championship by a single point.

Trueman makes hard work of Test record

FRED TRUEMAN began with a curving, long run-up. When he reached the wicket he took one long final stride and slung the ball towards Neil Hawke. The Australian batsman pushed his bat nervously towards the ball and only succeeded in edging it to Colin Cowdrey who took the catch cleanly. Frederick Sewards Trueman had become the first man to take 300 wickets in Test cricket.

Hawke grinned and said: "Well done, mate. I should be all right for champagne now, eh?" When the celebrations were over Trueman was asked if he thought his feat

> **" They set me up as an untameable northern savage who ate broken glass and infant batsmen for breakfast "**
>
> **Fred Trueman**

would be repeated. "Aye," he replied, "but whoever does it will be bloody tired."

Trueman was unable to prevent Australia regaining the Ashes but his record at The Oval on August 15 was just reward for one of the most colourful characters in cricket. "Fiery Fred" was forthright with a sharp sense of humour, maturing from a young tearaway who always answered a boundary with a bouncer into a formidable opponent.

While Trueman was in full flight Geoff Boycott celebrated his debut in the first Test at Trent Bridge by scoring 48. The first of his 22 centuries came two days after Trueman's celebration.

TRUEMAN'S RECORD

	FIRST-CLASS	TESTS (67)
Innings	713	85
Not out	120	14
Runs	9,231	981
Highest	104	39 not out
Average	15.56	13.81
Hundreds	3	–
Wickets	2,304 at 18.29	307 at 21.57
Catches	439	64

Trueman is applauded from the field at The Oval

Barrington completes full set of centuries

KEN BARRINGTON completed his metamorphosis from a promising bowler into one of England's finest batsmen with a unique record. The Surrey stalwart, who had shown more potential as a bowler than batsman when he joined the county, became the first to score a century in each of the seven Test-playing countries.

Barrington got his record in the nick of time. He scored an unbeaten 148 in England's last series in South Africa. England won the first Test by an innings and 104 runs and drew the remaining four matches.

Barrington was the most successful batsman on the tour, scoring 508 runs in five Tests at an average of 101.60. He had continued his good form from the English summer, when he hit a career-beat 256 against Australia and led the domestic averages.

> **" Whenever I see Ken coming to the wicket I imagine the Union Jack fluttering behind him "**
>
> **Wally Grout**

Barrington: good form

BARRINGTON'S RECORD

	FIRST-CLASS	TESTS (82)
Innings	831	131
Not out	136	15
Runs	31,714	6,806
Highest	256	256
Average	45.63	58.67
Hundreds	76	20
Wickets	273 at 32.61	29 at 44.82
Catches	515	58

All-rounder Standen two times a winner

JIM STANDEN enjoyed the finest year in his versatile sporting career. The West Ham goalkeeper helped his club win the FA Cup then donned his cricket flannels to spearhead Worcestershire to their first county championship title. Standen topped the first-class bowling averages, taking 64 wickets at an average of 13.00 with his medium pace deliveries.

Basil d'Oliveira, a coloured cricketer from South Africa, was unable to play in the championship because he was still serving his residential qualification period.

FOOTBALL

Leeds lose two trophies by slender margins

LEEDS did not arrive in the First Division, they exploded into it. The new boys from the Second Division won their first three League matches, nearly lost their manager to Sunderland, were officially branded the dirtiest team in football and were involved in a fracas so serious that the referee halted play for 10 minutes so the players and spectators could cool down. That was merely in the first three months of the season.

By January Leeds were two points clear at the top of the table, but they faltered in the run-in and lost the championship to Manchester United on goal average. And Wembley provided no solace for Don Revie's team when they lost the FA Cup final to Liverpool.

After the match the Liverpool manager, Bill Shankly, was asked if Leeds had failed that season. "Failed?" Shankly screeched. "Second in the championship. FA Cup finalists. Ninety per cent of the managers in the Football League pray every night for 'failures' like this."

FOOTBALL

Shankly's European venture turns sour

Hunt scores the first goal to beat Inter 3-1

BILL SHANKLY relished Liverpool's first foray into Europe. After two goalless draws, a 2-2 draw and extra time on a neutral ground, Cologne finally succumbed to the toss of a coin and Liverpool were in the European Cup semi-final.

Their opponents were Inter Milan, the holders managed by the legendary Helenio Herrera. In the first leg at Anfield the devious Shankly sent Inter on to the pitch first, then the FA Cup they had won the previous Saturday carried by the two injured players, Gordon Milne and Gerry Byrne, and finally his team.

The psychology worked brilliantly. The excitement in the Kop, with Shankly orchestrating the jubilation, unsettled the Italians and they lost 3-1. However, a packed San Siro was equally unsettling for Liverpool as bottles, smoke bombs, abuse and two dubious goals greeted them.

Tommy Lawrence, the goalkeeper, was charged by an Inter player and the ball was knocked from his hands and kicked into the goal. The second goal came from an indirect free kick, and was allowed to stand. A Liverpool goal was disallowed and Tommy Smith threatened to punch the referee. Inevitably, Milan scored a third time and Liverpool were out.

Shankly told his players that they were still the greatest team in the world, but the experience soured him. Although he embraced the challenge from across the Channel he would always distrust continentals.

. . . but Liverpool break their 73-year Cup jinx

LIVERPOOL had won the League six times but never the FA Cup in their 73-year history, although they had reached two finals, and there was a feeling in the city that they never would. It was even said that if they did the Liver birds would fly away from Pier Head. Their opponents, Leeds United, newly promoted and managed by Don Revie, had narrowly lost the League title on goal average to Manchester United.

As a spectacle, the final was inevitably disappointing as the country's two best defences killed the game and neither side had scored by the end of 90 minutes. Liverpool's Gerry Byrne had broken his collar bone, though, in the fifth minute and manfully played on as if nothing had happened. Leeds did not discover the extent of their opponent's injury until after the match.

In extra time it was Byrne who crossed for Roger Hunt to score. But Liverpool's joy was short-lived when Billy Bremner equalised eight minutes later. With five minutes remaining Ian St John's diving header settled the match; Liverpool had broken their duck but the Liver birds stayed put.

Jackie Charlton clears the ball for Leeds

Barrington and Boycott excel as Test bowlers

Allen dismisses Pithey at Cape Town

JIM PARKS and Denis Lindsay were the odd men out in the third Test between England and South Africa in Cape Town. The two wicketkeepers were the only players who did not bowl.

Twenty others turned their arms over as the match ground to an inevitable draw. Even occasional bowlers Ken Barrington and Geoff Boycott had their chance, Barring-ton taking three for four and Boycott three of his seven Test wickets.

England, who had won the first Test, were content to draw the remaining four matches. The only highlight was a sparkling century by Graeme Pollock, whose 137 in the fifth Test on his home ground in Port Elizabeth was his third Test ton before he was 21.

United bounce back to win championship

MANCHESTER UNITED began the season with 15 internationals on their books and ended it by winning the League championship by 0.66 of a goal from Leeds on goal average. Everything was in the balance until the spring, with Leeds and United tussling for the League and the Cup. However, United lost the FA Cup semi-final to Leeds after a replay. The first match was simply a goalless brawl with both teams and both managers blamed for allowing things to get out of hand. Leeds won the replay, also ill-tempered, 1-0.

This setback demoralised and inspired United. "We were gut-ted," Nobby Stiles said, "but Bobby Charlton was the best. In the next game, against Blackburn, he played them on his own and scored three. His spirit lifted us."

Manchester United won six of the seven League matches after the Cup semi-final, including one at Elland Road a fortnight after their infamous defeat. The only match they lost was at Villa Park on the last day of the season when the championship was already secure.

CRICKET
■ The Imperial Cricket Conference was renamed the International Cricket Conference.

■ Barbados won the first Shell Shield competition.

FOOTBALL
■ West Ham became the second British club to win a European trophy when they beat Munich 1860 2-0 at Wembley in the European Cup Winners' Cup final on May 19. Wembley witnessed the importance of Martin Peters to Ron Greenwood's team. "In Europe you needed more skill," Bobby Moore said, "and Martin added an extra quality to our game."

■ Kilmarnock finally landed the Scottish League championship, but only by 0.04 of a goal. If they had conceded one more goal then Hearts would have been champions. And if goal difference, rather than goal average, had applied then Hearts would easily have taken the title.

■ Stanley Matthews retired and was knighted, the first player to be so honoured.

■ Gillingham lost their first home game for two years on April 10 when they went down 1-0 to Exeter.

■ Northampton Town were promoted to the First Division, having been promoted from the Fourth in the course of five seasons.

■ Wolves were relegated and had to play in the Second Division for the first time since 1932.

■ In March, Jock Stein was made an offer impossible to refuse by Celtic and he left Hibs to take over at Parkhead. Within months Celtic won the Scottish Cup.

GOLF
■ Sam Snead won the Greater Greensboro Open for the eighth time, a record for a single tournament on the US PGA Tour. Snead, who first won the event in 1938, was 52 years and 10 months old.

RALLYING
■ Timo Makinen wanted to race British cars and had to have a British licence. So the winner of the Monte Carlo Rally the previous year came to Oxford, had one lesson on the Highway Code and promptly passed his test.

SOFTBALL
■ Australia won the first women's world championship.

RALLYING

Makinen: passed his test after only one lesson

GOLF

Nicklaus storms past his rivals

THE Big Three were poised to strike. Jack Nicklaus, Arnold Palmer and Gary Player, the leading golfers in the world, were at the top of the leaderboard on 138 after the second round of the Masters.

Eighteen holes later what was shaping up as a close tournament had become a one-man show. Nicklaus went blazing around Augusta National in 64 to equal Lloyd Mangrum's record score. His eight birdies left Player five shots behind in second place and put him on course for his second Masters victory.

Nicklaus scored a 69 in the last round for a record aggregate of 271 which bettered Ben Hogan's 274 in 1953. Palmer and Player were tied for second nine shots behind in the only major in which the Big Three finished 1-2-3. The effort by Nicklaus led Bobby Jones to say: "Jack is playing an entirely different game — a game I'm not even familiar with."

MOTOR RACING

Indy 500 conquered by Clark

Clark: first European

JIM CLARK became the first European for 45 years to win the Indianapolis 500 and $150,000. Clark and Colin Chapman had been pursuing this victory for two years and Chapman had designed a Lotus specifically for the race. It was extremely efficient and would require one less pit stop for fuel than was normally required. Moreover, because Clark was the Formula 1 champion Ford chose to put their engine and financial clout into Chapman's car rather than back an American designer.

In 1963 Clark was unfortunate not to win when officials refused to call in the leading car when it was leaking oil all over the track. In 1964 Clark's tyres could not handle the track. But in 1965 Clark went into the lead on the third lap and from then on was unbeatable.

BOXING

Liston falls to Ali and phantom punch

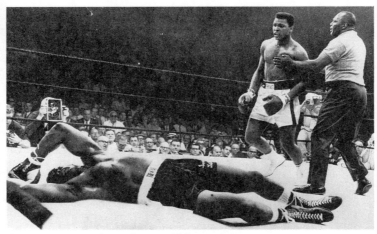

Ali hovers over the pole-axed Liston

MUHAMMAD ALI retained the heavyweight title he had won as Cassius Clay in bizarre fashion. The rematch against Sonny Liston in May never went beyond the first round and Liston was knocked out by a "phantom" punch that nobody really noticed.

Liston went down as if pole-axed, then confusion reigned. The referee had trouble forcing Ali into a neutral corner and tried to begin the count. At that point the time-keeper told the referee that Liston had already been down for 22 seconds and therefore had been "counted out" twice.

While the officials were haggling Liston got off the floor and Ali was already setting about him when the referee jumped between them and stopped the fight. Liston's excuses for this farce were that he was waiting for Ali to be pushed away before he got up, and anyway how could he be counted out when there was no official count? Inevitably, Ali claimed the "phantom" punch as a kind of secret weapon: a "corkscrew" punch to the head. Whatever, Ali was the crowned heavyweight king of the world.

He set about proving his status with a whirlwind number of defences across the globe. He fought six times in a year, and battered into submission Floyd Patterson, George Chuvalo, Henry Cooper, Brian London, Karl Mildenburger and Cleveland Williams.

Former world champion Mills found dead in gunshot mystery

FREDDIE MILLS died from gunshot wounds in mysterious circumstances in Soho. It was officially described as suicide, but others attempted to give Mills's death a more sinister ring and suggested he was a victim of a gangland "hit". However, there were persistent rumours that Mills was a homosexual and the balance of evidence favours suicide as the likely explanation of his death.

Miles: suicide speculation

RACING

Sea Bird II leaves Derby field gasping

BRITISH stables suffered a coughing epidemic for much of the summer so it was hardly surprising that a home horse did not feature in the Derby. Even so, it was very unlikely that anything could have beaten Sea Bird II. Lester Piggott had Meadow Court two lengths away in second but the margin was flattering to the Irish horse. Sea Bird II was being eased up because once he had taken the lead there was never any doubt about the outcome.

CRICKET

Slowcoach Barrington dropped

KEN BARRINGTON came up with a cure for insomniacs. The England batsman pushed and prodded for more than seven hours to reach 137 against New Zealand in the first Test at Edgbaston.

Barrington's score had remained on 85 for more than an hour while he saw off 20 overs from the New Zealand attack. The England selectors were not amused and dropped him from the team for the next Test as a disciplinary measure. Mike Smith's side were on their way to comfortable victories in all three Tests in the series and the selectors did not want anybody holding them up.

The second Test at Lord's in mid-June marked the changing of the English fast bowling guard. Fred Trueman ended his career with 307 wickets and his role as the country's leading bowler was taken over by John Snow, who took four wickets on his debut.

John Edrich played in only the third Test at Headingley, but remained on the field throughout the match and hit England's first triple century since 1938 with an unbeaten 310.

Cultured Thomson captures fifth Open

WHEN Peter Thomson was steeling himself for a final charge in the Open championship at Royal Birkdale, the Great Train Robber Ronald Biggs was escaping the clutches of the law. They were both on the front pages of the newspapers the next day.

Thomson won his fifth Open title at the Southport course where in 1955 he had become the first recipient of a £1,000 winner's cheque in the Open. This time he collected £1,750.

The Australian came back from six strokes off the pace set by the defending champion Tony Lema in the first round to win by two shots from the Irishman Christy O'Connor. It was his last major victory.

Thomson continued to play in the Open until 1984 when his interests in art, classical music, opera and golf architecture became more important than his thirst for the claret jug.

Thomson: last major

PETER THOMSON'S FIVE OF THE BEST

1954 Royal Birkdale					1958 Royal Lytham				
283 Peter Thomson	72	71	69	71	278 Peter Thomson	66	72	67	73
284 Sid Scott	76	67	69	72	278 David Thomas	70	68	69	71
284 Dai Rees	72	71	69	72	279 Eric Brown	73	70	65	71
284 Bobby Locke	74	71	69	70	279 Christy O'Connor	67	68	73	71
1955 St Andrews					*(Thomson won play-off 139-143)*				
281 Peter Thomson	71	68	70	72					
283 Johnny Fallon	73	67	73	70	1965 Royal Birkdale				
284 Frank Jowle	70	71	69	74	285 Peter Thomson	74	68	72	71
1956 Hoylake					287 Christy O'Connor	69	73	74	71
286 Peter Thomson	70	70	72	74	287 Brian Huggett	73	68	76	70
289 Flory von Donck	71	74	70	74					
290 Roberto de Vicenzo	71	70	79	70					

FOR THE RECORD

RACING
■ Starting stalls were introduced at Newmarket in July.

Turner stops Smith's charge to Grand Slam

ALTHOUGH Lesley Turner grew up on the grass courts of Australia, her brilliance was as a baseliner on the clay courts of Europe. Turner used her fine groundstrokes and superb footwork on clay to thwart Margaret Smith's attempt to win the Grand Slam.

Four years earlier Smith was denied the four major titles when Billie Jean Moffitt beat her in the first round at Wimbledon. This time Turner outplayed her in the final of the French championships in Paris, winning 6-3 6-4. Her Grand Slam would have to wait.

Smith had beaten Maria Bueno in the Australian championships when the Brazilian retired. Her defeat in France was only a hiccup in her relentless pursuit of trophies. She beat Bueno in the final at Wimbledon and outlasted Moffitt in the final of the United States championships to add two more Cups to her trophy cupboard.

Smith: beaten by Turner in the French final

Stolle's losing streak ends in French final

FRED STOLLE swapped the quiet life of a bank clerk in Sydney for the excitement of the tennis circuit and never looked back. With an excellent backhand he took on the world and won two major singles titles and 16 doubles championships.

The road to fame was never an easy one. Stolle had lost six major finals when he arrived for the French championships on the clay of Roland Garros, and his strong serve and volley game was better suited to grass. However, he made good progress to the final where he met his countryman Tony Roche. Again nerves got the better of Stolle and he lost the first set 6-3. But he clicked back into form in the second set and made his major breakthrough by winning 3-6 6-0 6-2 6-3.

It was the cue to launch an assault on Wimbledon and for the third year in a row Stolle reached the final. Alas, it was not third time lucky. Roy Emerson, who had beaten him the previous year, won 6-2 6-4 6-4. Stolle had emulated Gottfried von Cramm by losing three successive finals.

Stolle: beat Roche

Jack Nicklaus
King of the fairways par excellence

Robert Green

Jack Nicklaus the greatest golfer ever? Maybe, maybe not. But it could not be advocated with any authority that anybody else has a stronger claim to the accolade. The genuine experts and prudent historians rank Nicklaus as one of the four greatest players the game has known — along with Harry Vardon, Bobby Jones and Ben Hogan. That is not an unequivocal endorsement of supremacy but it is pretty impressive company.

While comparing sportsmen from one era with those of another is ineluctably an invidious exercise, a brief resume of Nicklaus's record provides eloquent testimony to his immense talent, and ample evidence to substantiate the argument that there has never been a better golfer. He has won three Opens, six Masters (a record), four US Opens (a joint record) and five USPGA championships (another joint record). Apart from Nicklaus, only Hogan, Gene Sarazen and Gary Player have completed professional golf's career Grand Slam, and none of them has managed to claim all four titles more than once. From 1962 to 1981, his first 20 years as a professional, Nicklaus competed in 80 major championships, of which he won 17. He was 60 times in the top 10 and 42 times in the top three. The record low 72-hole totals he set for the US Open in 1980 and the Masters in 1965 (since matched by Raymond Floyd) still stand.

Nicklaus won that 1965 Masters by nine strokes. Bobby Jones, the founder of the tournament, said afterwards: "Jack is playing an entirely different game — a game I'm not even familiar with." Twenty-one years later Nicklaus emphatically demonstrated that he could span the generations when he defied the likes of Ballesteros, Norman, Watson and Kite to triumph in the Masters once more.

Nicklaus was born on January 21, 1940. He learned the game at the Scioto Country Club in Columbus, Ohio, in the spring of 1950 under the tuition of the club's new pro, Jack Grout. Contrary to contemporary orthodoxy, Grout told Nicklaus to hit the ball as hard as he could (which was fearsomely hard); control would come later. He also permitted his eager pupil to retain his interlocking, as opposed to the more conventional overlapping, grip and he encouraged him to perfect a left-to-right flight on all his shots because if his swing got out of kilter a fade was less ruinous than a hook. Throughout his career Nicklaus's awesome power and his ability to hit that high fade into well-protected pin positions have given him an inestimable advantage over his rivals.

Armed with Grout's advice, Nicklaus first broke 70 at the age of 13. At 16 he won the Ohio State Open. At 19 he won the first of two US Amateurs. At 20 he was second in the US Open. It was no wonder that at 21 he joined the professionals in November 1961.

Nicklaus had relished being "the greatest amateur since Bobby Jones", but ultimately he felt he could not fulfil his potential as an amateur. Nor could he ignore the money he could command as a professional. He had been making $6,000 a year selling insurance, which was pitiful compared to the $100,000-plus prize money that an energetic lawyer called Mark McCormack, who handled the business affairs of Player and Palmer, had promised him if he turned pro. Nicklaus's decision was the genesis of the Big Three for McCormack, who formed his organisation, IMG.

> **❛ Jack is playing an entirely different game – a game I'm not even familiar with ❜**
>
> **Bobby Jones**

Nicklaus left IMG long ago to establish his own company, Golden Bear, that is estimated to be worth around $50 million, including his interests in golf course architecture, clothing and equipment. According to Forbes magazine in the United States, Nicklaus himself now makes $8.5 million a year and that may be a severe understatement. Certainly the $5.2 million he has earned from winning 70 tournaments on the regular tour in the United States is a small percentage of his overall career income.

Back in the early 1960s Nicklaus was not so much the Golden Bear as the Fat Pig, the usurper who ousted Palmer in his prime, especially by out-gunning him for the US Open in 1962 (which was Nicklaus's first victory as a professional) and 1967. The overweight, Teutonic, crew-cut kid was scorned by some unruly fans but subsequently his invariably gracious attitude in both triumph and adversity, and the sheer brilliance of his golf, have converted even reluctant proselytes.

Nicklaus's legacy to the game has not been entirely flawless — for example, his meticulous attention to detail has helped to perpetuate the myth that good golf is only possible if played slowly — but nor will his reputation endure simply because of his vast accumulation of titles.

He epitomised the best traditions of sportsmanship when he conceded a short putt to Tony Jacklin in 1969 that ensured the Ryder Cup match would be tied, and his demeanour in the face of potentially devastating defeats at the hands of Tom Watson in the 1977 Open and the 1982 US Open were emblematic of a generosity of spirit that future generations will seek to emulate.

Since Nicklaus turned 50 he has won five of the nine tournaments he has entered on the US senior tour. But he finds the competitive fires do not burn so intensely against that sort of opposition, and his chief goal is to establish the kind of enviable credentials as a golf course architect that he has as a player. At any time he has between 30 and 40 projects in hand. Several of his designs have received lavish praise, and seldom are they prosaic.

Behind many great men is a strong woman, and Nicklaus is no exception. "Most people have said that the best part about me is Barbara. I think they are probably right," he said. As much as he has accomplished in golf, his family — Barbara and he have four sons and a daughter — has always remained of paramount importance. Just how tolerant his wife has been of the demands put on her husband by his extraordinary career in the limelight is exemplified by perhaps their first marital confrontation over golf. In his autobiography, The Greatest Game of All, Nicklaus recalled that he and Barbara were about to leave New York after their honeymoon when he passed the remark: "Wouldn't it be terrific if on our way home I stopped off and played Pine Valley?" He added: "A heavy silence followed."

Since that inauspicious, unromantic proposal which, incidentally, his new bride indulged, Jack Nicklaus's career has mostly been followed by heavy applause.

Still winning after all these years: the Golden Bear with some of the host of major trophies he has accumulated during his illustrious career.

Player completes full set of titles

AUGUST
1965
DECEMBER

CRICKET

Flavell speeds to the top

JACK FLAVELL, one of the fastest bowlers in England in the 1950s, had slowed a little but was still too quick for many batsmen. He took 144 wickets in the summer as Worcestershire won their second successive championship title.

Bolstering their middle order was Basil d'Oliveira, who celebrated his first season with the county by hitting six centuries and 1,523 runs.

RACING

Arkle proves the master of Mill House

THERE was no stopping Arkle. No matter how much weight the handicapper forced him to carry he just kept on winning. Mill House was his nearest rival, but after Arkle won the Cheltenham Gold Cup he had to concede 16lb to Mill House in the Gallaher Gold Cup on November 6.

Not even that burden could stop Arkle and he tracked Mill House round Sandown Park as the pair produced a near-faultless display of jumping. Mill House did open up a small lead but not for long. Arkle just seemed to sprout wings and fly away.

In the end, it was yet another 20 lengths victory. And as if Arkle's mastery needed any confirmation he broke the course record, previously held by Mill House, by more than 10 seconds.

GARY PLAYER became the third man after Ben Hogan and Gene Sarazen to win the four major championships when he triumphed in the US Open at Bellerive, Missouri. Player beat the Australian Kel Nagle 71-74 in a tense play-off to become the first non-American to win the tournament since Ted Ray in 1920. He then donated $25,000 of his $26,000 prize to charity and junior golf.

But Player made his biggest impression at Wentworth. He was seven down with 17 holes to play against Tony Lema in the semi-final of the World Matchplay. His hopes of winning the second most

> **'** Were he to land in hell, his critics said, he would probably immediately start talking about what a wonderful place it is **'**
>
> **Dan Gleason**

popular tournament in Britain would require the greatest comeback in golf.

Player, displaying all the fighting qualities that had made him one of the world's leading competitors, clawed his way back to two down with three to play. He won the next hole, sank a 10-foot putt at the 17th to stay in the match, birdied the last to draw level and won at the 37th hole. The man who wore black to absorb the strength of the sun was red hot. He beat Peter Thomson three and two in the final.

> **'** It's funny, but the more I practise, the luckier I become **'**
>
> **Gary Player**

GARY PLAYER'S MAJOR HONOURS

1959 The Open
1961 The Masters
1962 US PGA
1965 US Open
1968 The Open
1972 US PGA
1974 The Masters, The Open
1978 The Masters

Player: won at Wentworth

Venturi dashes Britain's Ryder Cup ambitions

BRITAIN harboured fresh hopes of ending the American domination of the Ryder Cup when they finished all square on the first day at Royal Birkdale on October 7.

That all changed on the second day when Ken Venturi chipped the ball 40 yards over a bunker at the final hole to give his fourball partner Tony Lema a tap-in for victory. The Americans won the crucial match, took an 8-6 lead into the last day, dominated the singles and won 18-11 with three matches halved.

The American team ran away with the Ryder Cup on the final day

Pollock beats England all on his own

THE skies over Trent Bridge were dark when Graeme Pollock went out to bat on the first morning of the second Test against England on August 5. Before Pollock had time to settle the Springboks had slumped to 43 for four. The tall left-hander had to bat cautiously in the 70 minutes before lunch.

After the interval he came out and played one of the most brilliant innings in Test cricket. He began to stroke the ball fluently, nonchalantly driving with such force that the fielders barely had an opportunity to move before the ball reached the boundary.

Pollock scored 92 of the next 102 runs. His innings ended all too soon for the connoisseurs. He hit 125 in 2hr 20min and provided the platform for South Africa to win by 94 runs.

The South Africans had begun to put together a world-beating team. Apart from the Pollock brothers, they had Colin Bland, one of the few players to be selected in a Test side primarily for his fielding skills, and Eddie Barlow, a determined allrounder. Bland, nicknamed The Golden Eagle, displayed his brilliance by swooping on the ball and running out Ken Barrington and Jim Parks with direct hits from square of the stumps in the first Test at Lord's.

England recalled Brian Statham after a two-year interval for the final Test at The Oval and although he took seven wickets, England were unable to level the last series between the two countries. They were 91 runs away from victory with 70 minutes remaining when rain stopped play.

> **Fielding was not Graeme Pollock's pleasure. He would not lower himself to bowl and appeared bored unless a bat was in his hand**
>
> **Eddie Barlow**

POLLOCK'S TEST RECORD

Matches	23
Innings	41
Not out	4
Runs	2,256
Highest	274
Average	60.97
Hundreds	7
Wickets	4 at 51.00
Catches	17

Pollock: brilliant innings

Castleford step into limelight

THERE had been little for Castleford to cheer about in the 39-year history of their rugby league club. An 11-8 victory in the Challenge Cup final in 1934 had been their only major success. But on Tuesday nights in 1965 the lights came on in the West Yorkshire town and shone brightly for three winters. The players thrived under the spotlight of the BBC2 Floodlit Trophy.

They outplayed their seven opponents in the inaugural competition, beating St Helens 4-0 in the final, and then retained the trophy for two years as it grew in popularity. Castleford's success in the midweek competition provided the groundwork for greater achievements. The club went on to win the Challenge Cup in 1969 and 1970.

Castleford: triumphant

Boycott piles on the runs to dominate one-day final

GEOFF BOYCOTT played an uncharacteristically aggressive innings of 146 to help Yorkshire win the Gillette Cup final by 175 runs against Surrey at Lord's on September 4. The competition had been reduced to matches of 60-over innings.

Clark, Hill and Stewart make it a glorious 1-2-3 for Britain

BRITONS completely dominated the Formula 1 season, winning nine of the 10 Grands Prix. Jim Clark, in a Lotus-Climax, won his second world championship in commanding style, winning six GPs. Clark was clearly a winner — either he won a race or he did not finish in the points.

The former world champion Graham Hill was second. But there was another flying Scot on the horizon, Jackie Stewart, who had joined BRM and was Hill's stablemate. Stewart was sixth on his debut in the South African GP, won the Italian GP and finished third in the championship.

FOOTBALL
■ Substitutes were allowed for the first time in the Football League, but only for injured players. Keith Peacock, of Charlton, was the first to be used in a Second Division match at Bolton. Substitutes were allowed for any reason the following season.

GOLF
■ Britain and the United States played the only tied match in the history of the Walker Cup, finishing 12-12 in Baltimore.

■ Robert Mitera had the longest hole in one on a straight hole. He hit an ace at the 447-yard 10th hole at the Miracle Hills of Gold Club in Omaha on October 7.

Luck runs out for Liverpool

RUGBY UNION

Watkins only lion to roar

DAVID WATKINS, the Welshman who had admirably stepped into the fly-half void left by Cliff Morgan in 1958, continued to grow in stature. The nimble halfback, who inspired Newport to a 3-0 victory against the All Blacks in 1964, was one of the few players to emerge from a disastrous British Lions tour of Australasia with some pride.

Although the Lions beat Australia 11-8 and 31-0 they were outplayed by the All Blacks, losing 20-3, 16-12, 19-6 and 24-11. In 62 years the best of Britain had only twice beaten New Zealand, drawn once and lost 14 times.

Watkins: pride of Lions

Merseyside disappointment as Borussia Dortmund players wave to fans

ALTHOUGH the English football season was overshadowed by the forthcoming World Cup, Merseyside did not quite see it that way. Not content with being the musical capital of the world at the height of Beatlemania, they carried off both domestic trophies, Liverpool winning the League and Everton the FA Cup. And Liverpool went one better than the previous year and reached a European final — the European Cup Winners Cup.

To get there they had to edge past their semi-final opponents, the Scottish Cup winners Celtic, a fine side just being brought to the boil by Jock Stein. In the first leg at Parkhead Liverpool were without their prodigious goalscorer Roger Hunt, who finished the season with 30 League goals. Liverpool were fortunate to withstand the barrage on their goal and suffer only a single goal deficit.

At Anfield it was Liverpool's turn to be frustrated. Despite constant pressure they failed to score by half-time. A thundering free-kick from Tommy Smith got them back in the game, then Geoff Strong, who had ripped a cartilage and spent the second half limping, rose to head home an unstoppable goal. With a minute remaining, Bobby Lennox and the Celtic fans thought he had equalised, but he was given offside. Bottles rained on to the pitch.

The final was, coincidentally, at Hampden, where heavy rain the day before had virtually flooded the ground. This time Liverpool's luck in Scotland ran out. Borussia Dortmund's famed striker Siggy Held put the Germans ahead just after half-time, and after Hunt had equalised he missed a sitter with only seconds remaining. In extra time Libuda pounced on a Lawrence clearance and Borussia Dortmund, who had earlier beaten West Ham and Atletico Madrid took the trophy.

Best disobeys orders to run riot

GEORGE BEST dazzled Benfica when Manchester United defeated the holders 5-1 in Lisbon in the European Cup quarter-final.

United had won the first leg 3-2 and with such a slim lead were destined to be knocked out. Matt Busby decided the only option was all-out attack, but first United should contain Benfica for 15 minutes. Best relished the policy, but could not quite get the timing right.

Within 12 minutes he had scored twice. As United became ever more imperious the home crowd chanted "El Beatle" every time Best had the ball. At the end of the game Busby nearly had a heart attack when a spectator dashed on to the pitch and raced after Best with a knife. Best's and Busby's lives were saved when the invader cut off a lock of the hero's hair. Bestmania had reached Portugal.

Patient Lawry leads Australia to victory

Untypical aggression from the dogged Bill Lawry

BILL LAWRY, a dogged batsman whose finest attribute was his concentration, frustrated England's bowlers for nearly 42 hours on their tour of Australia. The tall opener scored 979 runs at an average of 97.90, but it was his scoring rate which was equally telling. He averaged only 23 runs an hour.

Lawry's patience was enough to give Australia victory in the fourth Test, when he and his captain Bob Simpson passed England's first innings total with an opening partnership of 244. It enabled the home side to retain the Ashes.

England's sole success was in the third Test in Sydney, where Geoff Boycott and Bob Barber provided the foundation for victory with an opening stand of 234. The left-handed Barber scored 185, his only century for his country. Simpson was out with chickenpox, Lawry was out for a duck and England won by an innings.

John makes unspectacular start

BARRY JOHN pulled on the red and white No 10 jersey for the first of 25 internationals for Wales. But the 21-year-old Llanelli fly-half lacked the experience to prevent Australia recording their first-ever victory against Wales. The Wallabies won 14-11 in Cardiff, lost 11-5 to Scotland and 9-6 to Ireland and beat England 23-11.

Unfortunate Richey the perennial also-ran

MARGARET SMITH won her seventh successive Australian title without hitting a ball in the final. She collected the trophy when Nancy Richey was injured while winning her semi-final. It was not Richey's year. The Texan lost the French final 6-3 6-1 to Ann Jones and the US final 6-3 6-1 to Maria Bueno.

Religious Ali refuses to go to war in Vietnam

MUHAMMAD ALI lost one of the most important fights of his career when the Army Draft Board re-classified him. Originally his local board had failed him because he had not passed their intelligence test but in February he was passed as 1A by the national board. Ali immediately asked to be exempted as a conscientious objector on religious grounds as he was an Islamic minister.

Wales carry on after Rowlands

WALES, without the undoubted talents of Clive Rowlands, won their third successive Five Nations championship. The scrum-half had retired the previous season to play out his career with Swansea after a successful 14-match Test career.

He had captained Wales to two championship titles and many thought the team would lose its edge without him. But the only blemish in another successful winter was a 9-6 loss to Ireland in Dublin.

Rowlands: retired Dragon

FOR THE RECORD

ATHLETICS
■ Roberta Gibb became the first woman to run in the Boston Marathon. She joined a group of male runners and finished in an unofficial time of 3hr 21min 40 sec.

CRICKET
■ England drew all three Tests in their series in New Zealand.

FOOTBALL
■ Jock Stein's Celtic completed the Double of League and League Cup, and then Stein predicted they would go on to win the European Cup. As no British team had even reached the final this was dismissed by many as an idle fantasy.

■ The chemistry of Joe Mercer and Malcolm Allison worked first time out when Manchester City were Second Division champions with five points to spare.

■ Chester lost both their full-backs with broken legs on January 1 when they beat Aldershot 3-2.

RACING
■ The Jockey Club, facing a court case, finally gave way and allowed women to hold a trainer's licence.

SQUASH
■ Jonah Barrington won the first of his six British Open titles and became the world No 1.

FOR THE RECORD

ATHLETICS
■ The American team of Bob Frey, Lee Evans, Tommie Smith and Theron Lewis broke the three-minute barrier in the 4x400m relay with 2:59.6 in Los Angeles on July 24.

BOXING
■ Randolph Turpin, the former world middleweight champion, shot himself on May 17.

■ Walter McGowan won the world flyweight title in London on June 14 by out-pointing Salvatore Burruni of Italy.

COMMONWEALTH GAMES
■ Imperial measures were used for the last time at the British Empire and Commonwealth Games in Kingston, Jamaica.

CYCLING
■ Riders in the Tour de France protested against the first drug tests in their race by walking with their bicycles during the next stage. Jacques Anquetil said: "Dope tests are an interference with individual liberty."

GOLF
■ Tony Lema, one of the top four players in the world, and his wife were killed in an air crash on July 24 while on their way to a pro-am event after the US PGA championship.

MOTOR RACING
■ Graham Hill won the Indianapolis 500 in a Lola-Ford.

RACING
■ The Tote introduced the Jackpot. The first winner, during the Royal Ascot meeting, collected more than £60,000 for a five-shilling stake.

RUGBY LEAGUE
■ Australia retained the Ashes by beating Great Britain 6-4 and 19-14 after losing the first Test 17-13 in Australia.

SOFTBALL
■ The United States won the first men's world championship.

TENNIS

King is crowned the Queen of Wimbledon

Billie Jean: beat Maria Bueno 6-3 3-6 6-1

BILLIE JEAN MOFFITT brought her new husband Larry King to London in the summer. But unlike most other American couples, the Kings avoided the sights of the capital. Instead they spent a happy fortnight at Wimbledon.

Marital bliss did not help the Californian's concentration in the early rounds. She struggled against lesser opponents and only picked up the pace in her semi-final against the top-seed Margaret Smith, whom she beat 6-3 6-3.

The other semi-final was an enthralling two-hour match which had the Centre Court crowd on their feet. Maria Bueno beat Ann Jones 6-3 9-11 7-5, but only after a struggle. Jones saved eight match points, including two in the second set when she came back from 3-1 down. The Brazilian was 5-0 ahead in the deciding set before Jones fought back again in a tense encounter which took the bounce out of Bueno.

She had none of her usual fighting qualities left for the final and King swept to a 6-3 3-6 6-1 victory, taking the first set in only 17 minutes. It was the brash and tomboyish American's first of six titles. The honeymoon was over. King had become queen of Wimbledon.

GOLF

Palmer throws title away on the last nine

ARNOLD PALMER, who had once lived by the sword, died by the sword. The amiable American had won the US Open in 1960 when he came back from seven behind to triumph at Cherry Hills in Denver. Now he was to lose the US Open, only in even more spectacular fashion.

Palmer virtually had a second title in his pocket when he reached the turn in the final round seven shots ahead of Billy Casper at the Olympic Country Club in San Francisco. Then he went off the rails. While Casper marked birdie scores on his card, Palmer bogeyed almost every hole. He hit a tree at the 16th, took two to get out the rough, went into a bunker and had to par the 18th to force a play-off. Casper won the play-off 69 to 73.

When Palmer was asked how this play-off defeat compared with his play-off defeats in 1962 and 1963, he replied: "It was pretty damned similar ... I lost all three!"

Palmer: seven up and lost

Grand master Ramsey confounds world

ALF RAMSEY won the World Cup for England. Not a Russian linesman, not Hurst's hat-trick, nor Rattin's dismissal. In the four years since he had been appointed, and had become the first England manager to enjoy sole discretion over team selection, Ramsey had toiled mercilessly in his preparation for the 1966 World Cup. When the tournament kicked off on July 11 Ramsey had the most flexible squad and the most tactically acute strategy of any of the competing nations.

Ramsey had been a fullback for England and Spurs who took penalties and scored crucial goals. He had cut his manager's teeth in the playground of the school of hard knocks, the Second Division, where Bill Shankly and Don Revie had honed their skills. Ramsey's best days as a club player were under Arthur Rowe when elegant, scientific football brought Spurs successive Second and First Division titles.

He had learnt well. Ramsey emulated the feat with Ipswich, he made bricks without straw. He understood the modern manager's role: be tactically alert and, unlike the previous era, be thoroughly independent and dismissive of interference from the board, and other non-professionals.

Ramsey, the England manager, experimented with formations and players throughout the run-up to the World Cup to such an extent that players, press and public were utterly bemused. But not Alf, he was trying to produce a world championship side in a changing world. The formation that was to win the World Cup, and to influence world football for a decade, came together in Spain in December the previous year, 4-3-3. England won 2-0 and Martin Peters and Geoff Hurst were the only changes in the team that lined up for the World Cup final.

Alf was not clubbable. His most informal team talk was during the break before extra time in the final. He pointed out that the West Germans had their socks round their ankles and said: "You've beaten them once, now do it again." After the 4-2 victory he refused to join in the lap of honour, and in the dressing room he shook hands with the players, but there were no hugs, no kisses of joy. The master tactician had won his game of human chess, confounding the critics and the world.

For Ramsey, that was the end of his main assignment.

Ramsey was the most misunderstood of managers. By football's standards he was a successful revolutionary. By the standards of the swinging sixties he was an old-fashioned fuddy-duddy. History should eventually get it right.

Ramsey: revolutionary

Santana applies clay ruthlessness to grass

Santana: tough battle with Ralston

MANUEL SANTANA brought his Spanish charm and a radiant but ruthless touch game to Wimbledon. The popular right-hander used heavy top spin and teasing lobs to carve up opponents as delicately as a surgeon. It was a game mastered on clay and successfully adapted to grass.

Santana's path to the title was given a boost when Roy Emerson, seeking his third successive crown, slipped while chasing a wide ball in his quarter-final against Owen Davidson. He crashed into the umpire's chair, injured his shoulder and lost the match.

Santana had to come back from 4-1 down in the second set of the final against Dennis Ralston to win 6-4 11-9 6-4. He was awarded the highest honour in Spain, the Cross of Isabel la Catolica.

Spending war gives birth to Super Bowl

THE battle for supremacy between the National Football League and the American Football League reached its peak, with both leagues spending millions of dollars to persuade draft choices to sign for their clubs.

Neither side could afford the sums that they were having to pay to secure top players so they started a series of secret talks that culminated on June 8 with the announcement that the two leagues had agreed to merge. Part of the deal was the staging of a World championship game between the two leagues, and so Super Bowl was born.

Road accident claims Farina

GIUSEPPE FARINA, the legendary Italian driver, the first world champion in 1950 and a man who had miraculously survived numerous crashes on the race track in a 22-year career, died at the age of 60, ironically in a car accident in June in the French Alps while he was making his way to the French Grand Prix in Rheims.

England's finest two hours

Brian Glanville

"They think it's all over," Kenneth Wolstenholme said as fans ran on to the field from behind the England goal. "It is now!" he added as a left-footed shot by Geoff Hurst screamed under the West German crossbar and put England's victory in the 1966 World Cup final beyond all doubt. Well, almost. The debate continues over whether the third English goal, also scored by Hurst, was valid or not. England probably deserved their World Cup win if only for their performances in the last two matches. Until then they had been scratching and scraping and it needed all the inspiration provided by their indomitable manager Alf Ramsey to see them through to the semi-final.

Ramsey, uncharacteristically, promised when he got the England managerial job in 1962: "We will win the World Cup." But when he was asked if he still thought so a day before the final there was a long, strangulated moment before, at last, he was able to say: "Yes."

Ramsey, his critics claim, had set a bad example with football which put a premium on hard work and hard running, scorning those wingers who for so many years had been the pride of English football. With the passing of still more time, lending still better perspective, it is clear that although England had no specialised wingers and the players did, indeed, run long and hard, there was probably more talent in that team than at any time since.

Bobby Moore very properly became the player of the tournament, a defensive left-half who, with a remarkable effort of will, had risen above his early limitations to make himself into a superb, if specialised, defender. He was forever in the right place at the right time, a perfect foil for his centre-half, and a fine tackler with a composure which embraced the teams he led.

Gordon Banks, in goal, had taken aboard Ramsey's advice, "me mind's not got to wander," and alertness was complementing courage and gymnastic agility.

Bobby Charlton, by turns an inside-forward and elegant left winger, had become a "deep" centre-forward. His pace, his skill, and his tremendous shot in either foot were still there. His strategic sense might be limited, but his ability to glide past opponents in midfield was priceless.

Martin Peters, a colleague of Moore at West Ham, had come late into the team, a "false" winger who was essentially an attacking wing-half. Praised as being "10 years ahead of his time", he was another fine technician, a splendid passer of the ball with a great knack of popping up to score in the penalty box.

Geoff Hurst, the third West Ham man in the team, who had learned what Ron Greenwood, his manager at Upton Park, called "good habits", would come in still later, at the quarter-final stage, majestically heading the only goal against Argentina when none seemed possible against a 10-man team. Tall and muscular, Hurst had once been an indifferent wing-half whom Greenwood had been ready to sell but a move into attack transformed him. He would score a record three goals in the final, one of them perhaps the most controversial in World Cup history. His choice would keep out Jimmy Greaves, who had scored so many goals for Chelsea, Tottenham and England, and nine in no time for Milan.

Ramsey, that strange sphinx, with his Sar'nt-Major posh accent, his

The final encounter at Wembley: Tilkowski, the West German goalkeeper, cannot stop England's controversial third goal, but, with seconds remaining in extra time, Hurst made sure that the game really was over.

The heroes of the moment: Moore and Banks parade the World Cup.

stubborn integrity and his contempt for the uninitiated, had played for Spurs himself, but Greaves was hardly his man. Rather, he would go for a player like Roger Hunt of Liverpool, diligent if uninspired, an adept runner of the ball, selfless where Greaves could be sublime. Greaves would surely have put away the ball Hurst nodded down to Hunt three minutes from half-time, making the game sure. Hunt, on his weaker foot, shot straight at Tilkowski, the suspect German goalkeeper, and the chance had gone. Another, to set Bobby Charlton free a few minutes from regular time, went begging too.

Nobby Stiles was also Ramsey's kind of player. "You did it, Alf," he cried, tears running down his cheeks, at the end of the final. "We'd have been nothing without you." Short, thin, gap-toothed, socks swirling round his ankles, Stiles looked anything but what he was, an implacable marker, who played a sinuous Eusebio out of the semi-final against Portugal. And he was right. Without Ramsey, and perhaps without home advantage, England would scarcely have won the World Cup.

They began clumsily against Uruguay, unable to break through a packed, powerful defence. Mexico were beaten 2-0, Bobby Charlton at last obliging a crowd chanting "we want goals" with a stupendous right-footed angled long shot. France were beaten by the same score. Greaves was injured, Stiles fouled Jacky Simon in front of the Royal Box, and Ramsey threatened to resign when told by his officials to drop Stiles.

Brazil, with a team of relics, fell to Hungary, then Portugal. Italy, incredibly, were beaten by the unknown North Koreans at Middlesbrough, with a goal by an army dentist, Pak Doo Ik. In the quarter-finals the quick little Koreans gave Portugal a dreadful fright, going three goals up in 20 minutes until Eusebio got hold of the game and scored four times. Eusebio would finish top scorer of the tournament.

England, meanwhile, faced a sour and surly Argentine team which might have won had it come to play, rather than spoil. Antonio Rattin, their towering captain, was sent off by the tiny German referee Kreitlein, "for the look on his face" when he would not stop protesting. Ramsey said he hoped that in the semi-final England would meet a team "interested in playing football, and not acting as animals." They were words which would reverberate for years.

West Germany, launching the graceful 21-year-old Franz Beckenbauer in midfield, met England, whom they had never beaten, in the final. Their decision to put Beckenbauer on Bobby Charlton nullified both of them. Ray Wilson, England's quick left-back, untypically headed straight to Helmut Haller, who put West Germany ahead. But a free kick swiftly taken by Moore and perfectly anticipated by Hurst made it 1-1. Peters gave England the lead in the second half and that seemed to be that, but, at the very death, a free kick doubtfully given against Bobby's brother, the impressive centre-half Jackie Charlton, allowed Germany to equalise. Emmerich's free kick hit Schnellinger in the back, Held crossed, the ball came off George Cohen's knee, and Weber put it in at the far post.

"You've beaten them once," Ramsey told his weary men as they sprawled on the grass, "now you've got to do it again. Look at them. They're finished!" England responded. Little Alan Ball, an inside-forward running the right flank that day as well as any winger, told himself as Stiles passed to him: "I can't get that one, I'm finished." But get it he did, speeding by Schnellinger and crossing a ball which Hurst, at the near post, smashed against the underside of the bar. Hunt, in the goalmouth, turned instantly away, exulting. The Germans protested. Dienst, the referee, went over to his linesman, Backhramov. The Russian nodded vigorously, his flag pointed to the middle of the goal. 3-2.

In the last minute Moore sent Hurst through a scattered German defence. Hurst hit the ball as hard as he could, untroubled where it went. It went into the top corner of the German goal.

THE 1966 WORLD CUP

GROUP 1

England	0	Uruguay	0
England	2	Mexico	0
England	2	France	0

	P	W	D	L	F	A	Pts
England	3	2	1	0	4	0	5
Uruguay	3	1	2	0	2	1	4
Mexico	3	0	2	1	1	3	2
France	3	0	1	2	2	5	1

GROUP 3

	P	W	D	L	F	A	Pts
Portugal	3	3	0	0	9	2	6
Hungary	3	2	0	1	7	5	4
Brazil	3	1	0	2	4	6	2
Bulgaria	3	0	0	3	1	8	0

QUARTER-FINALS

England	1	Argentina	0
West Germany	4	Uruguay	0
Portugal	5	North Korea	3
Soviet Union	2	Hungary	1

SEMI-FINALS

| West Germany | 2 | Soviet Union | 1 |
| England | 2 | Portugal | 1 |

GROUP 2

	P	W	D	L	F	A	Pts
West Germany	3	2	1	0	7	1	5
Argentina	3	2	1	0	4	1	5
Spain	3	1	0	2	4	5	2
Switzerland	3	0	0	3	1	9	0

GROUP 4

	P	W	D	L	F	A	Pts
Soviet Union	3	3	0	0	6	1	6
North Korea	3	1	1	1	2	4	3
Italy	3	1	0	2	2	2	2
Chile	3	0	1	2	2	5	1

THIRD PLACE

| Portugal | 2 | Soviet Union | 1 |

FINAL

ENGLAND (1)(2)4   W. GERMANY (1)(2)2

England: Banks, Cohen, Wilson, Stiles, J. Charlton, Moore, Ball, Hurst, Hunt, R. Charlton, Peters.

West Germany: Tilkowski, Hottges, Schulz, Weber, Schnellinger, Haller, Beckenbauer, Overath, Seeler, Held, Emmerich.

GOLF

Nicklaus finally collects Open

Nicklaus ruled at Muirfield after the referee showed him the rules

CRICKET

Underwood not able to prevent Yorkshire title

DEREK UNDERWOOD, the 21-year-old sensation of the season, stood between Yorkshire and the county championship title when Brian Close's team started their final fixture of the season at Harrogate on August 31.

The Kent slow-medium bowler had baffled batsmen throughout the land and it took the obstinacy of Geoff Boycott to steady Yorkshire on a rain-affected pitch. The England opener scored a valuable 80, and although Underwood took seven for 30 in the second innings Yorkshire won by 24 runs.

Underwood's left arm had worked overtime in the summer. He took 143 wickets at an average of 12.20 to top the bowling averages. His best effort was nine for 37 against Essex, who had become the first county to stage championship cricket on a Sunday.

JACK NICKLAUS, the king of golf, was missing only one jewel in his crown. It happened to be the most prestigious, the Open title.

The big-hitting American could not claim to be the greatest player until he had won the old claret jug. He had come close in 1963 at Royal Lytham and in 1964 at St Andrews. But still he had not won.

There was no denying the pedigree of Nicklaus in America. He had claimed the US Open, the US PGA championship and three Masters titles. Earlier in the year Nicklaus had become the first player to retain the green jacket at

Augusta when he held off challenges from Tommy Jacobs and Gay Brewer to win a play-off after the sun had set. Now he wanted the Open so badly he looked like a bear heading for a honey tree.

The rough at Muirfield had been left to grow so high that Nicklaus likened it to wheat swaying in the wind. So he abandoned his emphasis on hitting the ball as far as he could and concentrated on his iron play to post a first round of 70 for a share of the lead. He moved clear of the field with a 67 in the second round.

Five disastrous holes at the end

of the third round brought the Golden Bear back to the field with a 75, while Phil Rodgers took a two-shot lead.

It was the first time play was held over four days and Nicklaus began his charge early, moving to a three-shot lead by the 10th only to be pegged back by David Thomas and Doug Sanders. Nicklaus, though, had one last trick up his sleeve. He birdied the penultimate hole to win by one shot.

The Golden Bear had joined Walter Hagen, Gene Sarazen and Gary Player as the only men to win all four major titles.

MOTOR RACING

Brabham goes it alone to the top

JACK BRABHAM'S amazing gamble paid off in spectacular style when he won the world championship in a car manufactured by himself, and at the age of 40.

Five years earlier he had quit the Cooper outfit, where he had been successful on the driving and engineering fronts, to set up his own company and develop a Formula 1 car. And now the son of a Sydney greengrocer who had already been awarded an OBE had his third world title and a car he had created to win its own world title, the constructors championship.

Underwood: spinning sensation

Brabham wins at Brands Hatch in a Brabham

Summer when Sobers could do no wrong

IT TOOK a lot to keep Garry Sobers out of the spotlight. In the summer of 1966 it was the England football team rather than the England cricket team under Mike Smith, Colin Cowdrey and Brian Close.

While Alf Ramsey's team were beating the world, Sobers was taking full advantage of an England team in transition. The brilliant Barbadian scored 722 runs at an average of 103.14, finished second in the bowling averages with 20 wickets and took more catches than any other fielder in the series. For good measure he also called heads correctly on all five occasions the coin was tossed on his first overseas tour as the West Indian captain.

The 30-year-old genius was in tune from the start. He elected to bat in the first Test in Manchester, scored 161 and helped bowl the visitors to victory with second-innings figures of 42-11-87-3.

England's answer was to take the captaincy away from Smith, hand it to Cowdrey and select Basil D'Oliveira for his debut at Lord's. The plan worked. The West Indians lost their way and it took an unbroken partnership of 274 from Sobers and his cousin David Holford to save the match.

Derek Underwood earned his debut in the third Test and although he took a fine catch to dismiss Sobers the West Indian all-rounder had the last say. He took five catches, five wickets and scored nearly 100 runs to earn his team a comfortable victory.

Headingley was the next stop, and Sobers treated the Yorkshire crowd to one of his finest all-round displays. He smashed 174 in four hours and returned figures of five for 41 and three for 39 as his side sealed the series.

England bit back in the final Test. Brian Close was appointed their leader and they recovered from 166 for seven to 527 all out. It gave them victory by an innings. Sobers, for once, was not in the headlines.

Sobers: 161 despite giving a chance to Cowdrey

Bryant: singles title at first world championship

FOR THE RECORD

BOWLS
■ David Bryant won the singles title at the first world championships. Australia won the pairs and triples and New Zealand the fours.

BOXING
■ Dick Tiger, the former world middleweight champion, stunned Jose Torres to take the world light heavyweight title at the age of 37 with an unanimous decision on December 16.

CRICKET
■ South Africa got their first home victory against Australia in their 45th match after 64 years.
■ Clive Lloyd began his Test career for West Indies by hitting 82 and 78 not out against India.

FOOTBALL
■ Alan Ball, England's dynamo during the World Cup, was transferred to Everton from Blackpool for £100,000, the first six-figure transfer between English clubs.

■ Third Division Workington Town increased their board to 13 directors in October — more than their full-time playing staff. At the end of the season they were relegated.
■ Alf Ramsey was knighted.

GOLF
■ Gary Player won his second successive World Matchplay title when he beat Jack Nicklaus six and four.
■ Al Geiberger won the US PGA title by a then record four shots from Dudley Wysong, a runner-up to Jack Nicklaus in the 1961 US amateur championship.

ICE HOCKEY
■ The sport started to climb out of the doldrums when teams in north-east England and Scotland formed the Northern League.

ORIENTEERING
■ Age Hadler of Norway won the men's section of the first world championships. The Swede Ulla Lindkvist won the women's section.

Leeds successfully tackle rules change

RUGBY LEAGUE was dying a slow death. The laws allowed negative teams to kick and scrum their way to victory in front of diminishing crowds. The administrators had unsuccessfully tampered with the fixtures to reverse the trend. Now they rewrote the laws.

They removed the law permitting teams to retain unlimited possession and pencilled in a clause allowing sides possession for only four tackles. Players caught with the ball in the fourth tackle would concede a scrum. The revolutionary change caused panic. The result was a glut of kicking, particularly drop goal attempts.

Leeds were the first club to come to terms with the law, and they finished top of the league in the next four seasons. But the crowds still stayed away. The administrators finally achieved the right mix in 1972 when the law was extended to six tackles.

JANUARY
1967
MAY

Ali teaches Terrell the name of the game

Ernie Terrell cannot hide from a vengeful Ali

BOXING politics and the backlash from Muhammad Ali's religious politics had fragmented the world heavyweight title, so when Ali met Ernie Terrell on February 6 in Houston they were both world champions. By the end of 15 brutal rounds Terrell was no longer a champion, and was humiliated.

Terrell had refused to recognise Ali's change of name, so the champion viciously set about the pretender. Ali cruelly destroyed Terrell but refused to finish him off. Throughout the fight Ali kept asking him: "What's my name? What's my name?"

But if Ali, now the undisputed heavyweight king, thought he could do as he pleased in the ring the outraged American establishment soon put a stop to that. On April 28 Ali, the loud and outspoken rebel, was stripped of his title for refusing to join the army and fight in Vietnam.

AMERICAN FOOTBALL

Lombardi plots Packers' first Super Bowl

THE first "Super Bowl" was held at the Los Angeles Coliseum on January 15, although the game did not officially become titled Super Bowl for several years. The Green Bay Packers represented the old guard as champions of the National Football League against the upstart Kansas City Chiefs of the American Football League.

The Packers were widely expected to win, but they were far from convincing as they took a 14-0 lead at half-time. But Vince Lombardi, the Packers head coach, made good use of the blitz later and the Chiefs were beaten 35-10.

FOOTBALL

Berwick start Rangers crisis

RANGERS suffered the most humiliating defeat of their history when they were knocked out of the Scottish Cup in the first round by Berwick Rangers on January 28.

Completely overshadowed by Celtic, who won every trophy in Scotland and the European Cup, the manager, Scot Symon, was made the scapegoat and sacked in September. His replacement, Dave White, was sacked two years later. Willie Waddell took over and subsequently appointed Jock Wallace as coach. Coincidentally, Wallace had been the Berwick goalkeeper who had precipitated the crisis in the first place.

FOOTBALL

United target Europe

MANCHESTER UNITED were girding their loins for another assault on the European Cup, but first they had to win the League championship. Throughout the season Matt Busby's team had been focused on that one objective.

Since the beginning of the year they had won all their home matches, and drawn all their away matches with a single-minded conviction. Then in May, at Upton Park, United broke the habit and destroyed a West Ham that included three World Cup winners — Bobby Moore, Geoff Hurst and Martin Peters — 6-1. It was a stupendous performance. United were 3-0 up after 10 minutes, and a ticket to Europe was theirs.

FOR THE RECORD

CRICKET
■ Mike Procter took seven wickets on his Test debut as South Africa triumphed in a series against Australia for the first time, winning 3-1 in their five-match rubber.

FOOTBALL
■ Scotland, inspired by the mercurial Jim Baxter, embarrassed England, the world champions, on April 15 at Wembley, by beating them 3-2.

■ Liverpool signed the promising teenager Emlyn Hughes from Blackpool in March for £65,000. Then in the summer they bought the centre-forward Tony Hateley from Chelsea for £95,000, a club record, and a young goalkeeper from Scunthorpe, Ray Clemence for £18,000.

■ Tottenham captured the FA Cup for the fifth time when they beat Chelsea 2-1 in the first all-London final.

■ Howard Kendall moved to Everton from Preston for £80,000 in March.

RUGBY UNION
■ Gareth Edwards, a 19-year-old scrum half, made his debut for Wales against France in Paris on April Fool's Day. Within a year he became the youngest-ever Welsh captain at the age of 20 years and seven months.

SKIING
■ Jean-Claude Killy of France won the men's overall title in the first World Cup. The women's championship went to Nancy Greene of Canada.

SQUASH
■ Jonah Barrington of England won the first of six British Open titles, and became the first person since the war to win both the British Open and the British Amateur title.

■ The Australian Geoff Hunt won the inaugural world amateur title.

RUGBY UNION

Gareth Edwards: youngest

No-hoper Foinavon confounds the field

THE Grand National was brought to a virtual standstill for the second time in its history by an enormous pile-up. As in 1928, the last time there had been similar chaos, the result was that the race was won by a 100-1 "no hoper".

In 1928 it was the fearsome Canal turn that brought the field to grief, but this time it was a loose horse and one of the more innocuous obstacles that did the damage. The 23rd, the fence after Becher's on the second circuit, was one of the smallest in the race, but it sent Popham Down, who had lost his jockey at the very first fence, swerving into another runner.

Within moments most of the rest of the field were sent sprawling, with jockeys and horses scattered all over the course. As the snarl-up got ever worse runners arriving at the fence had nowhere to go and were brought to a halt.

Foinavon, though, was so far behind and travelling so slowly that he was able to pick his way around the devastation almost at walking pace, scramble over the fence and take a lead of a good 30 lengths.

The other jockeys frantically scrambled to remount their horses and set off in pursuit. But by then there was no way that they could catch John Buckingham, who was having his first ride in the National only because Foinavon's regular jockey opted to ride at lowly Worcester instead. Buckingham plodded on on Foinavon, and the 17 other finishers out of the 44 starters were beaten by 15 lengths.

And Foinavon hardly had anybody to cheer him home apart from a goat, his constant travelling companion. His owner thought so little of his prospects that he did not even bother going to the race.

Foinavon and his constant companion are feted at home

League Cup hits big time after QPR shock

Langley and Marsh are overcome by the comeback victory

THE revamped League Cup became an overnight success when Queen's Park Rangers came back from the dead to slay the First Division giants West Brom in the first Wembley final on March 4.

Rangers, champions-elect of the Third Division, were supposed to be no more than cannon-fodder, and when their former player Clive Clark scored twice for the Albion it seemed the pundits had got it right. However, goals from Roger Morgan, Rodney Marsh and Mark Lazarus turned the match on its head, thrilling 98,000 spectators and millions more on television.

Unfortunately, QPR were unable to take up the automatic place in the Fairs Cup that now went to the League Cup winners as they were not a First Division club.

The carrot of a place in Europe was just one of the changes made to the competition. The other was the abandonment of the two-legged final, with a single match at Wembley instead. The twin carrots worked. Previous dissenters such as Arsenal, Tottenham and Wolves relented and finally participated in the competition. Only the champions, Liverpool, and Cup-holders, Everton, were absent.

Woman gatecrashes the all-male marathon

THE Boston Marathon had been a male preserve and Roberta Gibb had been the only interloper in 70 years, unofficially joining the race in 1966. Her run inspired Kathy Switzer to challenge the status quo. The American entered as K Switzer, was awarded vest number 261 and failed to turn up at the pre-race medical tests.

It was only during the event that officials realised something was amiss. One organiser attempted to push Switzer off the road, but her boyfriend intervened and she was able to finish among the also-rans in 4hr 20min.

The incident was widely publicised, but it took five years of campaigning before women were finally accepted in the world's oldest annual foot race.

GOLF

Nicklaus bags Open record

JACK NICKLAUS went hunting for a US Open record at Baltusrol, New York. He strung together five birdies in six holes in the final round to have Ben Hogan's 1948 record aggregate of 276 firmly in his sights.

Nicklaus turned in 31 to leave Arnold Palmer four behind over the closing nine. But Baltusrol bit back. A missed putt at the 17th appeared to have cost Nicklaus his place in the records. He needed a birdie on the par-five last.

His tee shot was wayward and his recovery was still 230 yards from the pin. But a superb one-iron shot left Nicklaus 60 feet from the hole. He took out his putter and when the ball disappeared into the hole Hogan's record went with it. Nicklaus, with a final round of 65, had won his second US Open. Hogan was in the clubhouse, tied for 34th in his final US Open.

FOR THE RECORD

BADMINTON
■ Malaysia were leading Indonesia in the match that would have won them the Thomas Cup when, because of intense barracking from Indonesian supporters, the referee abandoned the tie.

BOXING
■ Jackie Turpin, a nephew of Randolph Turpin, was beaten by Brian Hudspeth in the ABA light welterweight final in May.

GOLF
■ Catherine Lacoste, the daughter of Rene, one of the Four Musketeers of French tennis in the 1920s, was the first amateur to win the US Open.

FOOTBALL

Celtic thunder to Europe's top prize

JOCK STEIN'S preparations for the European Cup final against Inter Milan in Lisbon were eccentric to say the least. While the Italians were cloistered like clerics the Scots ran an open house in a plush hotel with Stein the chief cheerleader.

Stein, mindful that his team were raw novices compared to the sophisticates under Helenio Herrera's tutelage, ensured that Celtic were not overawed by the occasion or Inter. When they left the dressing room for the final the Celtic players were raucously singing the Celtic song. The Italians could not fathom what was going on.

Then Stein pulled one of his traditional tricks of one-upmanship. He deliberately sat on the bench earmarked for Herrera, and would not budge. The most famous coach in the world was furious and the Celtic players thought it was hilarious. It let everybody know that Celtic were not going to be pushed around.

Inter went ahead from a penalty after seven minutes and promptly closed down the game. Herrera, the master of containment and counter attack, fully expected Inter's third European Cup in four years to be his. Stein and Celtic stuck to their guns and continued an unceasing barrage on the Inter goal. The pressure eventually paid off in the 63rd minute when Tommy Gemmell blasted an equaliser into the top right-hand corner from 20 yards.

With five minutes to go and extra time looming Celtic got a fortunate winner when a shot from Bobby Murdoch cannoned off Steve Chalmers. And so on May 25 Celtic were the European champions, the first British club to lift Europe's most important trophy. And Jock Stein had been Celtic's manager for only two seasons.

They had also performed creditably on the home front, winning the championship, Cup, League Cup and the Glasgow Cup to boot. Rangers took Celtic's triumph as well as could be expected, although their former player Willie Waddell said that Celtic had done Scottish football proud. "This was the greatest day in our history," he said graciously.

The European Cup completed a set of five for Celtic in 1967

TENNIS

Newcombe only seed to make it

Pasarell: shocked Santana

MANUEL SANTANA'S defence of the men's singles title at Wimbledon lasted less than two hours. The Spaniard who had thrilled the Centre Court the previous year became the first champion and top seed to lose in the first round.

A slippery court and attacking play from Charlie Pasarell accounted for Santana in four sets on the opening day. It was a bad omen for the favourites.

Cliff Richey beat the fourth-seeded Tony Roche in the second round and Roy Emerson, the second seed, lost in five sets to Nikki Pilic in the quarter-finals. John Newcombe was the only seeded player to steer clear of trouble, and he swept aside Pilic in the semi-finals.

The third-ranked Australian's opponent in the final was Wilhelm Bungert, the sixth unseeded men's singles finalist. But the unfancied German had no answer to Newcombe's power game. Newcombe maintained his awesome form at Forest Hills and became the last amateur to win at Wimbledon and the US championships.

Boycott quick to pay for go-slow

Wicketkeeper Engineer has seen it all before as Boycott accumulates another run

GEOFF BOYCOTT was never one to risk losing his wicket to a rash shot. His philosophy was that "if I bat for a day and a half and make a big score that is half the battle". Half the battle against India in the first Test at Headingley was won when Boycott scored an unbeaten 246 against a nine-man bowling attack.

Unfortunately, his highest score in Test cricket was controversial. Boycott faced 555 deliveries in his 9½-hour occupation of the crease. The selectors had grown tired of his slow batting and they dropped him for the second Test.

Boycott was replaced by Ken Barrington, who had been sacked in 1965 for slow batting. Barrington's gesture of thanks was to hit a laboured 97 in four hours as England plodded to victories in all three Tests.

Hailwood enjoys best year

Hailwood wins the Ulster Grand Prix

MIKE HAILWOOD powered his 500cc Honda around the 37-mile Isle of Man circuit to a record fifth successive senior TT title in his most rewarding year. The British rider, who had won the lightweight 250 and junior classes in the same week, beat his great Italian rival Giacomo Agostini who snapped a drive chain on the fifth lap.

Hailwood also won the 250cc and 350cc world championships while Agostini triumphed in the 500cc class. It was the Italian's second of a record seven titles in a row.

Perennial loser wins at last

ROBERTO DE VICENZO'S errant putting had cost him at least six Open titles in 19 years. He finished runner-up in 1950 and third in 1948, 1949, 1956, 1960 and 1964. The Argentinian went away to mend his action and returned to tackle Hoylake with renewed vigour and without the wristy action that had proved his undoing on the greens.

He had rounds of 70, 71 and 67 to lead the defending champion Jack Nicklaus by three. But there was still a nagging doubt until he steered his last putt into the final hole for a popular two-shot victory. De Vicenzo was the oldest winner this century at 44 years, 93 days.

Perennial loser fails yet again

Ann Jones: final loss

ANN JONES had been the runner-up in the world table tennis championships five times before she turned her attention to tennis. Now the Wimbledon title was proving equally elusive. Five attempts to win had ended in the semi-finals.

But Jones had improved her backhand, Margaret Smith had retired and Maria Bueno had been knocked out in the fourth round. The last hurdle, though, proved too high.

Billie Jean King used her superior power to retain the title with a 6-3 6-4 victory, and then beat Jones 11-9 6-4 in the US final.

RUGBY UNION

All-Blacks cancel tour over banned Maoris

NEW ZEALANDERS were tired of being told that the All Blacks had to be all white in South Africa. Their intransigent hosts had barred Maoris since 1919. After yet another snub the New Zealanders cancelled a proposed visit and, instead, enjoyed a successful tour of Britain and France. The only blemish was a fortunate 3-3 draw with an East Wales side led by Gareth Edwards and inspired by Barry John.

New Zealand beat England 23-11, Wales 13-6, France 21-15 and Scotland 14-3. The match against the Scots at Murrayfield on December 2 caused a storm when the famous New Zealand forward Colin Meads was sent off four minutes from the end for attempting to kick the ball as it bounced near an opponent. He was the second player after Cyril Brownlie in 1925 to be dismissed in an international.

New Zealand beat Wales 13-6 on their alternative tour

RUGBY LEAGUE

Sunday proves best

BRADFORD NORTHERN, resurrected after folding in 1964, continued their recovery by staging one of the first two matches held on a Sunday. They beat York 33-8 in a game which attracted 10,377 people on December 17. Leigh beat Dewsbury 15-10 before 6,000 on the same day.

Police threatened to prosecute clubs under the Sunday Observance Act of 1870 and grounds were picketed by Sabbatarians. Their efforts were in vain, and by 1977 the Rugby League decided Sunday would be match day.

CYCLING

Excess speed kills Simpson

BRITISH hopes in the Tour de France rested with Tommy Simpson. The talented 29-year-old had led the Tour in 1962, when he became the first Briton to wear the yellow jersey. Unfortunately, he held the lead for only one day. But victories in the Tour of Lombardy and the world professional road race championship in 1965 made Simpson a leading rider in the field. His weakness was climbing mountains, and the combination of the heat and a steep climb up Mount Ventoux in the 13th stage proved too much. He toppled from his bike 3km from the summit, remounted and collapsed again a kilometre later. He was rushed to hospital in Avignon but he was dead on arrival.

Although an autopsy revealed traces of an amphetamine stimulant a memorial was erected on Mount Ventoux in his honour.

Simpson: fatal collapse

CRICKET

Kent finally break their duck

WHEN Kent went to Lord's for the Gillette Cup final against Somerset they had not won a trophy since the 1913 championship. A 33-run victory ended their fruitless spell.

Kent missed the big one, though.

Yorkshire pipped them in the championship race with an outright win against Gloucestershire at Harrogate on September 7. Ray Illingworth's 14 wickets included a second-innings 13-9-6-7.

EQUESTRIANSIM

Smythe: took charge

FOR THE RECORD

EQUESTRIANISM
■ Pat Smythe became the first woman chef d'equipe.

FOOTBALL
■ Brian Clough and Peter Taylor joined Derby from Hartlepool.

■ The Second Division match between Cardiff and Millwall in November was abandoned after 31 minutes when a Millwall fan burst into the Cardiff offices to demand a refund and punched the Cardiff manager Jimmy Scoular on the jaw.

GOLF
■ The United States thrashed Britain 21-6 with five matches halved in Houston on October 22. It was the most one-sided contest in Ryder Cup history.

RACING
■ Vaguely Noble was sold for 136,000 guineas at Tattersall's December sales, surpassing the previous record price paid for a horse, 47,000 guineas for Solario in 1932.

■ The Government banned horse racing for more than a month as an epidemic of foot and mouth disease spread throughout the country in the winter. The ban remained until early the next year.

RUGBY LEAGUE
■ Australia beat Great Britain 17-11 and 11-3 after losing the first Test 16-11 in Britain.

■ David Watkins, a Welsh rugby union fly half who had captained the British Lions in two Tests in New Zealand the previous year, joined Salford for a record £16,000.

TABLE TENNIS
■ Ivor Montague, the founder president of the International Table Tennis Federation, resigned after 40 years.

TENNIS
■ Rod Laver won an all-professional tournament at Wimbledon.

Knott carries on the tradition

WHEN the English selectors wanted a wicketkeeper they needed only to pluck the latest talent from Kent. The county had provided Les Ames and Godfrey Evans and now it was the turn of Alan Knott. With seven catches in his first Test, the selectors knew they had made a good choice.

> **❛ Mr Consistent – has he ever had an off day? ❜**
>
> **Jim Laker**

Knott replaced Jim Murray after the drawn first Test against Pakistan at Lord's in late July and his agility, anticipation and keenness immediately inspired Eng-

land. They moved up a gear, and when Derek Underwood took five for 52 in the second innings, England ended Hanif Mohammad's run of 10 Tests without defeat as captain of Pakistan.

Knott would bend and stretch between each delivery, keeping supple and active. But Asif Iqbal took some of the bounce out of his step in the third Test at The Oval with a swashbuckling 146 off 244 deliveries. Pakistan were 53 for seven when Asif arrived at the crease. He hit two sixes and 21 fours before being tempted down the pitch by a slow ball from Brian Close. Knott whipped off the bails for the first of his 19 stumpings in Test cricket and England went on to win by eight wickets.

The aggressive captaincy of Close gave England five victories in six Tests during the summer. But

the day after England had won at The Oval Close was accused of slowing down a county game to avoid Yorkshire losing against Warwickshire. The sanctimonious Test selectors appointed Colin Cowdrey to lead England on the winter tour of the West Indies.

KNOTT'S RECORD

	FIRST-CLASS	TESTS (95)
Innings	745	149
Not out	134	15
Runs	18,105	4,389
Highest	156	135
Average	29.63	32.75
Hundreds	17	5
Catches	1,207	250
Stumpings	133	19
Total wickets	1,340	269

Knott: seven catches

Clark poised to challenge dominant Brabham

BRABHAM proved that the successes of the previous season were no flash in the pan when they ran away with both championships. Denny Hulme won the drivers' title and Brabham-Repco the constructors'. And Jack, driver, manufacturer and 41, was runner-up to Hulme.

But the outstanding figure of the season was Jim Clark, who

finished third in the drivers' championship even though he had won four of the 11 Grands Prix. Even more extraordinary was that the season will be remembered for a drive by Clark in a race he lost.

Clark was leading at the Italian GP on September 10 when, in the 13th lap, he was forced to make a pit stop to change a wheel. Over a minute later he rejoined the race

a lap behind the leaders and 15th out of 16. Then began a charge reminiscent of Juan Fangio at his most magnificent. A dozen laps later Clark had pulled back the lap disadvantage. By half-way he was seventh. Nine laps from the finish Clark was third and when his teammate Graham Hill retired with engine problems, Clark was in second place and fast catching up the

race leader, Jack Brabham.

With seven laps remaining Clark had overtaken Brabham and was poised to record one of the greatest of victories. But then Clark's Lotus developed fuel problems. In the last lap Clark was in the lead, but fading, and Brabham and Surtees overtook the brilliant, but luckless, Scot to leave him in third place.

Denny Hulme (left) gets away in the German Grand Prix, another win for him and the Brabham car

MOTOR RACING

Clark killed in bizarre crash

Clark: inexplicable disaster

JIM CLARK, the most accomplished driver since Juan Fangio, died on April 7 at Hockenheim in a Formula 2 race. Clark had no need to be there — Ford wanted him to race at Brands Hatch but the Lotus chief, Colin Chapman, insisted Clark go to Germany.

Clark had never driven at Hockenheim and after six laps he was struggling. Then, inexplicably, he lost control of the car as it came out of an easy bend at 170mph, careered down the track, overturned several times, hit the trees, and blew into bits.

The sport had lost one of its finest and best. Clark was a winner through and through. He was not interested in second or third places. In 72 Grands Prix he was on pole 33 times, won 25 races and finished second only once.

At the age of 31 Clark had won one more GP than Fangio. If there had been barriers at Hockenheim; if Clark had gone to Brands Hatch instead; if . . . who knows what Jim Clark would have achieved.

FOOTBALL

Revie's men finally end trophy famine

AT LAST! Leeds won a trophy. For four years, one of the most consistent sides in the country had to put up with a barrage of criticism for their barren sideboard.

Before their League Cup final against Arsenal in March, Don Revie was going to goad his team by opening out an empty trophy case, but he thought better of it when he saw their anxiety.

Unfortunately, the other criticisms of Revie's Leeds — boring, ultra-cautious and physical — were if, anything, reinforced by their display at Wembley in one of the poorest finals ever played there. Only Terry Cooper rose to the occasion when, in the 20th minute, the ball broke loose in the penalty area and he kept his nerve to blast it into the roof of the net. And that was that. When the final whistle sounded the Leeds players were not elated, they were relieved.

Five months after the League Cup final, Leeds had the opportunity to double their silverware in the delayed Inter Cities Fairs Cup final against Ferencvaros. In an extraordinary match at Elland Road, the Hungarians pulled eight or nine men behind the ball, pulled shirts, and kicked ankles.

Mick Jones pounced on a loose ball to put Leeds ahead just before half-time. After the break the Hungarians were so physical that John Giles had to leave the field with concussion and Jones joined him when he was kicked in the groin.

Leeds went to Budapest a month later for the second leg with a slender 1-0 advantage, but were not going to be undone by a team playing their game. Ferencvaros threw everything at them, roared on by a 70,000 crowd. But the masters of defence stood disdainfully firm.

Jack Charlton helps disrupt the Gunners' final defence

GOLF

Partner's error robs de Vicenzo

ROBERTO DE VICENZO started the final round of the Masters with an eagle two at the first, and after a string of birdies his final round of 65 appeared enough to put him in a play-off with Bob Goalby.

But de Vicenzo's playing partner, Tommy Aaron, had marked him down for a four instead of three at the 17th. Rule 6-6(d) declared the higher score would have to stand; 65 became 66 and Goalby became the Masters champion. De Vicenzo took his defeat bravely. "What a stupid I am," he said. His loss, though, and the way in which he took it, earned him many admirers.

AMERICAN FOOTBALL

Lombardi retires on high note

THE second Super Bowl in Miami on January 14 was widely expected to be the last game for Vince Lombardi, the head coach of the Green Bay Packers. Lombardi's formula for success was simple: work hard and keep the plays simple. When he arrived in Green Bay he simply announced: "I'm in complete command here."

His other legendary saying, and there were many, was: "Winning isn't everything — it's the only thing." That spirit soon suffused his team and from 1959, Lombardi's first full year in charge, Green Bay never had a losing season.

The Packers made sure he bowed out in style, beating the Oakland Raiders 33-14 and Lombardi announced his retirement after the game.

Camberabero propels France to Grand Slam

Line-out ball and a Grand Slam for France against Wales

GUY CAMBERABERO kept his kicking boots in trim as France launched their campaign for the Grand Slam they had never won. After an 8-6 victory against Scotland, a 16-6 win against Ireland and a 14-9 triumph against England they were on the brink of history.

Their last hurdle was Wales in Cardiff on March 23, where Camberabero at fly-half, scored a dropped goal, a penalty and a conversion. His brother Lilian scored one of two tries and France won 14-9 to claim the Grand Slam. Neither played for France again.

Killy stars on his home slopes as controversy dogs the Games

JEAN-CLAUDE KILLY won all three Alpine skiing events at the 10th Winter Olympics in Grenoble, but his achievement was marred by controversy.

Killy, who won the downhill and giant slalom, appeared to have triumphed in the slalom in thick fog until Karl Schranz protested that a policeman had crossed the course in front of him. Schranz was allowed a rerun, but the French protested and the medal went to Killy.

Three East Germans were disqualified for heating the runners of their sledge on a fire to obtain greater speed in the toboggan, and several leading skiers threatened to withdraw when the International Olympic Committee banned advertising on skis and clothing.

Jean-Claude Killy flies on his way to triple gold

Declaration backfires on Sobers

GARRY SOBERS loved to gamble so when the fourth Test against England in Port of Spain was heading for an inevitable draw on March 19 he made a generous declaration. England reached their target of 215 with seven wickets and three minutes to spare. It was the only outright result in the five-match series and Sobers was castigated in the Caribbean.

Knott steers the ball past Sobers in Port of Spain

MAY

1968

JUNE

TENNIS

Britain forces the game to go open

THE modern world of money and sponsorship was anathema to amateur tennis officials. They had done their best to keep the sport in the dark ages of strict amateurism, but the walls came tumbling down.

The British Lawn Tennis Association, who had once disciplined a player for exchanging his prize voucher for food instead of a trinket, were prime movers towards open tennis. They took the plunge at their annual meeting in December 1967 when they agreed to abolish the distinction between amateurs and professionals.

The International Lawn Tennis Federation expelled the British body, but at an emergency meeting in Paris on March 30 agreed to open tennis in principle. Sponsors and crowds began flocking to the sport.

Ken Rosewall won the first major open men's title when he beat Rod Laver in four sets in the French championships. But Laver ruled at Wimbledon where he won his third title, taking only 67 minutes to beat Tony Roche. Roche had more success in the men's doubles, teaming up with John Newcombe to beat Rosewall and Fred Stolle 3-6 8-6 5-7 14-12 6-3 in the longest final in Wimbledon history. Billie Jean King won her third successive women's singles title, beating Judy Tegart.

Laver, the first open champion at Wimbledon, consoles Roche

FOOTBALL

City sprinters accelerate to title

MANCHESTER CITY won the League championship for only the second time in their history on the playing fields of Wythenshawe Park. There, under the tutelage of Joe Lancaster, a former athlete, the players were subjected to an intensive and painful regime of training, the like of which had never been seen in football.

The end result was a squad of superbly fit and explosively fast players. And after the first three games of the season City, with a solitary point, needed all the sprinting power they could muster.

The new super-fit City only got motoring when Mike Summerbee was moved from the wing to centre forward and Francis Lee was bought from Bolton for £60,000. Two matches swung the championship their way. First, their sell-out derby with Manchester United, the champions, at Old Trafford, when City drew on all their resources to gain a deserved 3-1 victory. The second was on the

Summerbee scores City's first goal on the last day

last day of the season, when City had to win at Newcastle to stop Manchester United taking the title. City took the lead but Newcastle were level 2-2 at half-time.

Malcolm Allison gave no team talk at the interval. There was no need. City played like men on a mission and raced to two more goals. A late Newcastle goal made no difference. The sprinters had finally crossed the finishing line.

Best's solo effort seals European Cup

TEN YEARS after the Munich air disaster the ghosts were exorcised at Wembley when Matt Busby and Manchester United at last reached the summit of their ambition and conquered the European Cup.

The final ascent had been anything but smooth. Although the result was 4-1 after extra time, only a rush of blood to the head of Benfica's brilliant striker Eusebio denied them the trophy. In the dying minutes of normal time he only had Alex Stepney to beat, but instead of placing the ball he chose to blast it at the keeper. "He went for the glory," Nobby Stiles said. "He tried to break the net." Busby had turned away in despair as Eusebio shot — once again it seemed his European dreams were to become the depressingly familiar nightmare.

Fittingly, it had been Bobby Charlton, one of the two Munich survivors playing, who had given United the lead with a glancing header in the 65th minute before the Portuguese equalised 15 minutes later. After Eusebio's gaffe, and as they were waiting for extra time to start, Stiles thought of the World Cup final. "They were like the Germans," he said, "knackered. And Busby said the same as Alf, 'If you pass the ball to each other, you'll beat them'."

In the second minute of extra time Stepney's long kick was nodded on to George Best 25 yards from goal. Best beat one man, weaved past another, rounded the keeper and cheekily glided the ball into an empty goal. "It was like something from Roy of the Rovers," Best said.

Suddenly it all seemed so easy for United. Within eight minutes they scored two more. Brian Kidd celebrated his 19th birthday with the first, and Charlton rounded off the perfect night with the second.

Busby wept with his players on the pitch. "The moment when Bobby took the Cup," Busby said, "it cleansed me. It eased the pain of the guilt of going into Europe. It was my justification."

Matt Busby rallies his players before extra time

Piggott unleashes Sir Ivor in final strides to capture Derby

LESTER PIGGOTT had ridden many stirring races but none received more acclaim than his victory on Sir Ivor in the Derby. Even the normally restrained Sporting Life was moved to describe it as dazzling jockeyship on a superlative colt.

Sir Ivor started the odds-on favourite on the strength of his victory in the 2,000 Guineas, but there were doubts about whether he would stay the mile and a half. Piggott made sure that his mount got the trip by keeping Sir Ivor on a tight rein until the final furlong. By then he was three lengths behind the leader, Connaught.

Piggott moved out, asked Sir Ivor to go, and the horse simply exploded into the lead. Connaught looked like he was standing still as his three-length advantage rapidly turned into a length-and-a-half defeat.

After such a great race the rest of Sir Ivor's career was something of an anticlimax. He was second in the Irish Derby, third in the Eclipse Stakes and then lost to Vaguely Noble in the Arc de Triomphe.

Piggott: brilliant ride

FOR THE RECORD

AMERICAN FOOTBALL
■ George Halas retired for the fourth, and last, time as head coach of the Chicago Bears on May 27.

ATHLETICS
■ Jim Hines was the first to run 100m in under 10 seconds in Sacramento on June 30 with 9.9sec in the American Athletic Union championships.

CRICKET
■ It was ruled that a minimum of 20 overs had to be bowled in the last hour of county championship matches.

FOOTBALL
■ Jeff Astle gave West Bromwich Albion their fifth FA Cup when they defeated Everton 1-0 in extra time. West Brom's Derek Clarke became the first substitute used in a Cup final.
■ Dunfermline beat Hearts 3-1 to take the Scottish Cup for the second time in their history. Both teams used substitutes for the first time in a Cup final. The Hearts substitute, Maller, was booked and thus achieved another first he would probably have wished to forget.
■ Alan Mullery became the first English player sent off in an international when he retaliated against a Yugoslav who fouled him in the European

championship semi-final in Florence. England lost 1-0 in the final minutes.
■ Dave Mackay left Spurs for Derby in July. "I could do nothing more for them, nor they for me. If I had stayed I would have got a share of the blame. It meant a new challenge."

GOLF
■ Lee Trevino became the first player to post four rounds under 70 in the US Open. He beat Jack Nicklaus by four shots.

RUGBY LEAGUE
■ Australia won the fourth World Cup by beating France 20-2 in Sydney. It was the first time Britain had not finished in the first two.
■ Don Fox failed with a last-minute conversion for Wakefield Trinity in the Challenge Cup final in atrocious conditions at Wembley on May 11 to give Leeds an 11-10 victory in what became known as "The Watersplash Final".

RUGBY UNION
■ The British Lions, hampered by injuries, lost 25-20, 11-6 and 19-6 and drew 6-6 in a Test series against South Africa, scoring 35 of their 38 points with penalty kicks.

Garry Sobers
The one man who could do it all

Trevor McDonald

When Garry Sobers wrote his name into cricket immortality by making the highest ever score in Tests, 365 against Pakistan in Jamaica in 1958, he received a congratulatory telephone call from Len Hutton, the Yorkshire and England legend and the man whose record he had just eclipsed. Hutton was gracious. He praised the 22-year-old West Indian and said that he was always aware that his record, established 19 years earlier against Australia, would one day be broken. But Hutton went on to say that he never thought Sobers would be the man to do it.

Hutton's surprise, shared by the West Indies cricket fans and by experts from Kingston to Bombay, expressed a central truth about the greatest all-round player of the time: his brilliance was enhanced by glorious unpredictability, his genius was so extravagant that few ever acquired the measure of it. He was above the fray. And to a degree which might be considered criminal by many of his modern counterparts, Sobers believed that cricket is never more than a game. He was serious about it, and proud to lead the West Indies. But seriousness about a game had its well-defined limits.

There is a story told of the West Indies in Australia one year, and under the hammer. During an unscheduled break for rain, peals of laughter were heard coming from the West Indian dressing room. A cricket correspondent, incredulous at the thought that the West Indies could have anything to laugh about, set out to investigate. There, in the dressing room, on a pitch marked out only by the imagination of the players, was Sobers leading a game of "pass out" pretend cricket and loudly appealing against a fellow West Indian player, who Sobers claimed had "touched" one delivery on its way to the keeper. That scene, so redolent of innocence and charm, is a metaphor of its time, and says a great deal about Sobers.

And if that sounds incredible then think for a moment about what Sobers the batsman has to say about waiting for the umpires' decision. He says: "I walk, because, when you know you have hit the ball, if you don't, it's cheating." How dated it all sounds. Sobers made his debut in a West Indies side brimming with talent. Just past his seventeenth birthday he had sneaked into the company of the famous Ws – Worrell, Weekes and Walcott. He had batted at No 5 for his island, Barbados, against India, the year before, 1953. For his first Test Match, he was sent in at No 9. For the first and only time in his career he had gained his place solely as a slow left-arm bowler. After that cricket, in all its infinite variety, was to be Sobers's stage. He did everything . . . exceptionally well.

He was a born master of every department of the game. He was three bowlers in one. He added wrist spin to the natural control and deceptive flight of his orthodox finger-spin bowling. And to that was added seam bowling with a perfect body action, a full follow-through and devastating speed. On occasions he would open the bowling, pick up a couple of wickets in the middle order and return later to polish off the tailenders with his slow spin. To confound opposing batsmen he would, at will, change his style and the length of his run-up to the wicket.

He fielded magnificently close to the wicket, and was totally reliable in the outfield. But beyond all that, he was the most destructive and brilliant batsman to grace the game. He timed the ball beautifully. Sobers is a tall man; in his day he was well built and he had wrists of steel. No other player hit the ball with such power or speed. Writing about Sobers, Don Bradman said: "With his long grip of the bat, his high backlift and free swing . . . Sobers consistently hits the ball harder than anyone I can remember. This helps to make him such an exciting player to watch because the emphasis is on power and aggression rather than technique – the latter being the servant not the master. The uncoiling of those wrists as he flicks the ball . . . is a joy to watch because it is unique."

Sobers amassed more than 8,000 runs in Tests, a world record at the time. And yet he never set his mind on the accumulation of runs. He was an entertainer, the last of cricket's great gamblers. He loved hitting sixes, especially if the field had been spread out with catching hands eagerly held out on the boundary fence. Sobers never flinched from a challenge and in 1966 he hit Malcolm Nash of Glamorgan for six sixes in an over.

Sobers was never reckless about defence. He was thoroughly equipped to keep out the good ball and could, when the game demanded, play with exaggerated care. But defensive play was not his style. In one of the finest innings ever seen in Australia, Sobers scored 254 for the 1971 Rest of the World team and turned disaster into match-winning triumph. The Don called it "one of the historic events of cricket".

Sobers was given the West Indies captaincy after it was vacated by the inspirational Frank Worrell. He accepted the job with trepidation, and he was right. Worrell's was an impossible act to follow. Under Sobers, the West Indies beat Australia for the first time, defeated England and then India. But Sobers's stewardship is remembered almost solely for his declaration against England in Port of Spain in 1968, which handed Colin Cowdrey a Test match and a series on a platter. Sobers was roundly condemned for squandering a region's sporting pride on a gambler's whim. His retort, that he wanted to enliven a game of cricket heading for the doldrums, was regarded with contempt by West Indians.

Sobers was strangely innocent about the pressures surrounding a high profile West Indies player. In 1970 he took part in a double-wicket cricket competition in Ian Smith's Rhodesia, then a political pariah. When the noise of protest broke all around him he said he couldn't quite understand. Only a cleverly-worded apology to the leading political lights in the Caribbean enabled him to resume his career.

Sobers was never as politically aware as Clive Lloyd or Viv Richards, and never saw himself as the bearer of people's aspirations. He would never have addressed the United Nations as Lloyd has done, and never taken up the cause of the Rastafarians as Richards has. But he was the master of cricket. And for the gifts of a big-hearted, uncomplicated, fallible genius we should all be eternally grateful.

SOBERS'S RECORD

	FIRST-CLASS	TESTS (93)
Innings	609	160
Not out	93	21
Runs	28,315	8,032
Highest	365 not out	365 not out
Average	54.87	57.78
Hundreds	86	26
Wickets	1,043 at 27.74	235 at 34.03
Catches	407	109

The all-rounder par excellence: as a destructive force, Sobers hit the ball harder than anybody else and was three bowlers rolled into one.

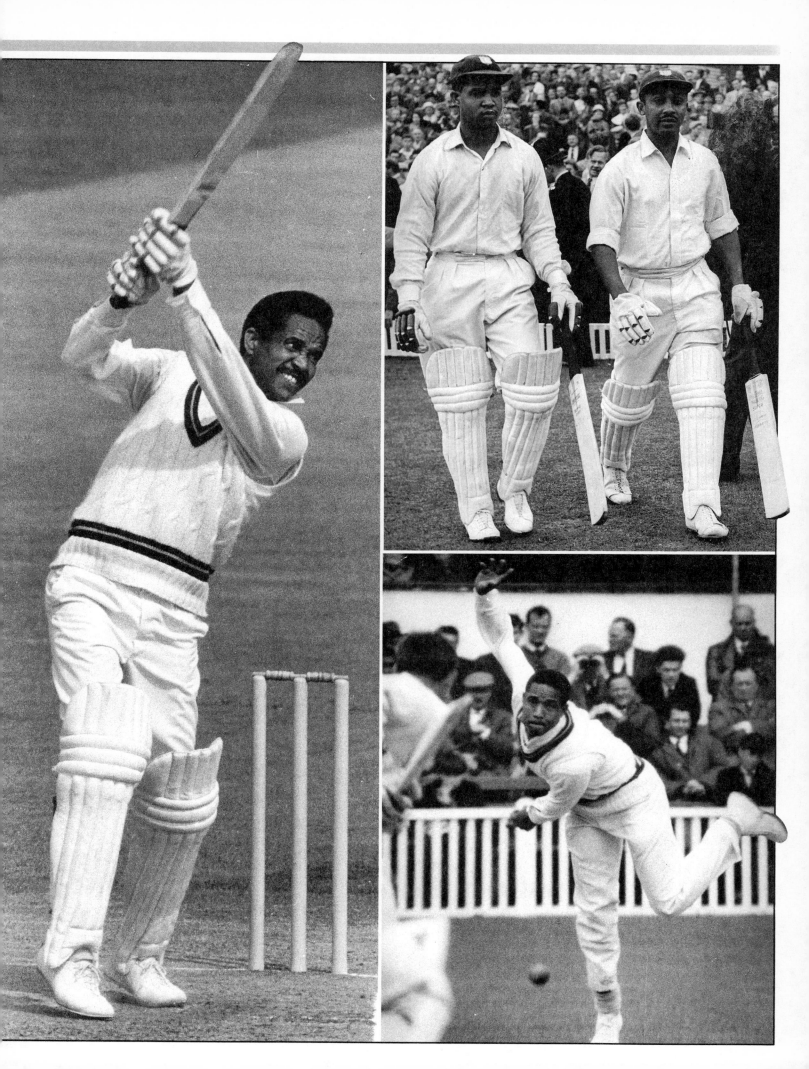

CRICKET

Tour scrapped over D'Oliveira

BASIL D'OLIVEIRA, a coloured from Cape Town, could never play first-class cricket in South Africa. So his friends paid his fare to Britain and soon Worcestershire had him on their books. When he hit six centuries in his first season to help the county retain the championship the English selectors showed an interest.

A brilliant 158 against Australia put him in contention for the tour to South Africa, despite suggestions he would be unwelcome. Surprisingly, d'Oliveira was not chosen, a decision some suggested had been made to pander to South Africa's policies. But three weeks later Tom Cartwright failed a fitness test and d'Oliveira was named as a replacement.

The South Africans were livid and their Prime Minister, John Vorster, said the tourists would not be welcome and the MCC called off the visit. D'Oliveira displayed a dignity that was to earn him an OBE in the Queen's Birthday Honours. South Africa for their part earned the wrath of the rest of the world.

❝It is not the MCC team. It is the team of the anti-apartheid movement. We are not prepared to have a team thrust upon us❞

John Vorster

Beamon leaps into unknown

BOB BEAMON was in a world of his own as he prepared for his first leap in the long jump final of the Olympic Games in Mexico City on October 17. A shower had taken the sting out of the afternoon heat and the conditions were perfect.

When he landed in the sand there was a hush and then a cheer from the crowd. Beamon's jump was too long for officials to measure with their Cantabrian device. So they used a conventional steel tape which was stretched to a phenomenal 8.90m.

Beamon had beaten the world record by 55cm. When he realised what he had done he said: "Tell me I am not dreaming." He knew he would never repeat his jump and retired soon after the Olympics.

The thin air 2,250m above sea level not only helped Beamon achieve what became known as "the jump into the 21st Century". It helped triple jumpers break five world records and Kenyans and Ethiopians dominate the long distance events. The Africans, who had lived and trained at high altitude, thrived, while Australian Ron Clarke collapsed after the 10,000m and had to be revived with oxygen.

Three days after Beamon's jump the rarefied atmosphere inspired four Americans to smash the 4x400m relay record. Lee Evans, Ron Freeman, Larry James and Vince Matthews clocked a brilliant 2min 56.16sec. Evans and his fellow black sprinter John Carlos wore black gloves, socks and no shoes on the victory dais after the 200m and raised their fists in support of Black Power during the playing of the American anthem. They were immediately banned from the Olympic village

Beamon beats the world record by 55cm

for their political demonstration.

Britain won five gold medals, five silver and three bronze. The finest performance was by David Hemery who had Britons glued to their television sets in the middle of the night for the 400m hurdles. Hemery led from the second hur-

dle and won in a world record 48.1sec.

Not everything in Mexico was golden and glorious. Ten days before the Games police ruthlessly suppressed a student protest against conditions in the country by killing 260 people and injuring 1,200.

Fosbury flops to greater heights

DICK FOSBURY began a revolution in high jumping. He started his career, like most others, using the scissors style, and at the age of 15 cleared 1.625m. But Fosbury was not satisfied. He believed he

could jump higher if he lowered his centre of gravity by lying down.

He approached the bar with a curved run-up, turned his body, jumped head first, landed on his shoulders and his progress was

meteoric. He broke the Olympic record with a leap of 2.24m.

High jumpers soon adopted the "Fosbury Flop" and when Dwight Stones flopped to a world record in 1973 other styles were history.

Crash costs Stewart his first world title

JACKIE STEWART was unlucky not to win his first world championship. Having teamed up again with Ken Tyrrell and practising for a Formula 2 race in Madrid, Stewart crashed and cracked a bone in his wrist. He missed two world championship races and had to drive the rest of the season with plastic strapping. Despite this handicap, Stewart won three Grands Prix and was runner-up in the world championship.

One of those victories, the German GP, was unbelievable. The race probably should not have taken place given the conditions. At least that was Stewart's opin-

ion, and he refused to participate. The track was waterlogged, heavy rain was falling, and mist made it impossible to see. But Tyrrell talked him into joining the starting grid. After all, his Matra had special Dunlop tyres designed for wet-weather racing. At so it proved. Stewart simply left everybody else standing. His lead after the first lap was nine seconds, then a minute, then a minute and a half. By the finish, Stewart had won by an incredible four minutes.

Despite Stewart's heroics, Graham Hill won his second world championship in his Lotus-Ford with three GPs to his credit.

Jackie Stewart and his Matra – an unlucky combination

Richards leads foreign invasion

COUNTIES were allowed to sign one overseas player without residential qualification and soon the sport's greatest stars were drawing large crowds and dominating the averages.

The South African opener Barry Richards scored more than 2,000 runs in his first summer with Hampshire, Rohan Kanhai hit the season's highest score of 253 for Warwickshire, and Garry Sobers lifted Nottinghamshire from 16th in the table the previous year to fourth.

Many criticised the decision to allow foreigners to hone their skills on the county circuit and then use their experience to thrash England.

Others were against them taking employment away from young local players.

Barry Richards: 2,000 runs

Cowdrey celebrates centenary with century

COLIN COWDREY led England against Australia in the third Test at Edgbaston on July 12 and became the first cricketer to play in 100 Tests. To mark the occasion, he scored his 21st century. But the Australians ruined a perfect script by forcing a draw, thanks mainly to the poor weather which ruined the Ashes series.

Cowdrey had reached his peak in a long and fruitful career as one of the world's finest batsmen. But his captaincy was marred by the policy of the selectors to shuffle skippers like playing cards. He was in for one Test, out the next.

Some of their other decisions were equally baffling. Pat Pocock took six for 79 and Basil d'Oliveira top-scored with an unbeaten 87 in the first Test, which the Australians won by 159 runs. But both were dropped.

D'Oliveira was only recalled for the fifth Test at The Oval and his 158 helped England level the series although Australia retained the Ashes.

COWDREY'S RECORD

FIRST-CLASS TESTS (114)		
Innings	1,130	188
Not out	134	15
Runs	42,719	7,624
Highest	307	182
Average	42.89	44.06
Hundreds	107	22
Wickets	65 at 51.21	0
Catches	638	120

> *The cover drive is the most beautiful stroke in batsmanship. Does that throw any light on why I am a self-admitted lover of all things British and traditional*
>
> **Colin Cowdrey**

FOR THE RECORD

ATHLETICS
■ Performances were boosted by the use of synthetic tracks for major events, most notably at the Olympic Games.

CRICKET
■ Garry Sobers became the first batsman to hit six sixes off an over in a first-class match. Sobers, batting for Nottinghamshire, was facing Malcolm Nash of Glamorgan in Swansea on August 31.

FOOTBALL
■ The main Nottingham Forest stand was destroyed by fire on August 24. Forest had to play their matches at Notts County for the rest of season.

GOLF
■ Michael Bonallack won the English amateur championship final by beating David Kelley 12 and 11. Bonallack shot 61 at Ganton.

RUGBY UNION
■ Argentina beat Wales 9-5 in the first Test between the two countries in Buenos Aires on August 14.

TENNIS
■ Arthur Ashe became the first black player to win a major men's singles title when he beat Tom Okker in the US Open.

Colin Cowdrey: centurion

FOOTBALL

Leicester lose out yet again

MANCHESTER CITY, who had performed so disastrously in the European Cup when they were eliminated in the first round despite the outrageous boasts of their assistant manager Malcolm Allison, redeemed their sorry season by winning the FA Cup 1-0 at the expense of Leicester City.

If it was a happy consolation for one City, it was yet another heartbreak for Leicester. This was the fourth time in 20 years they had lost a Cup final, and the third this decade. A flying dive from Peter Shilton was unable to reach Neil Young's unstoppable volley and prevent another defeat at Wembley.

A TALE OF TWO CITIES

Lancashire's two-city dominance in the swinging sixties

The League title

1963 Everton
1964 Liverpool
1965 Manchester United
1966 Liverpool
1967 Manchester United
1968 Manchester City
1970 Everton

And the FA Cup

1963 Manchester United
1965 Liverpool
1966 Everton
1968 Everton runners-up
1969 Manchester City

AMERICAN FOOTBALL

Wild Broadway Joe's boast bang on target

Namath: llama-fur carpets in his penthouse

WITH the merger between the National Football League and the American Football League almost complete the AFL badly needed something to lift their fortunes. The NFL also needed to revive interest in Super Bowl, which was getting a one-sided contest.

The only problem was that the Baltimore Colts were 18-point favourites to make it three wins in a row for the NFL. But Joe Namath, the New York Jets quarterback, thought otherwise. On the Thursday night before the game he stood up at a dinner and announced to the assembled throng: "We'll win Super Bowl III, I guarantee it." It was what the public had come to expect of "Broadway Joe". He lived the high life in New York: dating leading actresses, appearing in a movie, and living in a penthouse with llama fur carpets.

Namath duly delivered. The Colts brought their veteran quarterback Johnny Unitas off the bench in desperation in the fourth quarter, but not even he could stop the Jets winning 16-7.

CRICKET

Karachi riot denies Knott first century for England

ALAN KNOTT was only four runs short of his maiden century in Test cricket when the gates to the National Stadium in Karachi were broken down. A rioting mob invaded the field, forcing the third Test between England and Pakistan to be abandoned on the third day. Knott had to wait another 13 Tests for his first century.

Colin Milburn had time to hit a century which sadly proved to be his last for England. Soon after returning home he lost his left eye in a motor accident in Northampton and was forced to retire.

Australia put pressure on captain Sobers

THE reputation of Garry Sobers as West Indian captain took another nasty knock less than a year after he had lost a series against England with a generous declaration. Australia totalled 619 — the highest score by a Test side put in to bat — on their way to winning the fifth Test by 382 runs in Sydney. Three weeks earlier Australia settled for a draw when their last pair faced the final 26 balls to finish 20 runs short of victory.

RUGBY UNION

Wales embark on winning ways

THE Welsh jigsaw was beginning to fit together. The last two members of the great quintet, JPR Williams and Mervyn Davies, joined the clan. Gareth Edwards and Barry John had honed their half-back skills to near perfection and Gerald Davies was preparing to move from centre stage to the wing.

Scotland were the first to melt under the fire of the Welsh dragon, losing 17-3 at Murrayfield. Ireland fell 24-11 in Cardiff and France held Wales to an 8-8 draw in Paris. England, though, had no answer and when Maurice Richards ran in four tries Wales were on their way to a 30-9 victory and the first of four successive Five Nations titles.

Their world came apart in New Zealand later in the year when the All Blacks beat them 19-0 and 33-12, but a stirring 19-16 win against Australia in the Sydney mud gave them hope for the future.

J. P. R. Williams

Rogers proves extra special

Indomitable Leeds win first title

Rogers scores Swindon's second goal from a corner in their 3-1 victory over Arsenal

THE League Cup final was once again the Cinderella final when Swindon emulated QPR's feat of 1967 by winning the Cup and promotion to the Second Division. This time the fall guys were mighty Arsenal and in particular Frank McLintock, who had now played at Wembley in four Cup finals (two for Leicester) and finished on the losing side every time.

Arsenal had their excuses. The pitch was a disgrace, never having fully recovered from the disastrous decision to stage the International Horse of the Year show at Wembley the previous autumn, and was made worse by heavy rain. Many of their players had not recovered from the influenza that had invaded the Highbury dressing room. And who would have expected Don Rogers, who had been a virtual spectator, to turn into an unstoppable match winner in extra time?

Arsenal were fortunate that there was extra time. Marvellous goal-keeping by Peter Downsborough had protected Swindon's one goal lead until four minutes from time, when he made an uncharacteristic error and Bobby Gould gained a fortuitous equaliser.

Cometh the extra half hour, cometh the man. Rogers, the only player on the mudheap of a pitch still to be sporting a pristine shirt, slotted home from a corner and then ran half the length of Wembley to score a singular solo goal, and bury Arsenal's hopes.

WITH two trophies under their belts from the previous season Leeds came out like champions-elect from the start of the season, taking 16 points from their first nine fixtures. But, what was more, they played open attacking football — instead of simply trying to draw away games they tried to win them.

Don Revie said he had changed the Leeds style because of the way Manchester City won the title the previous season attacking teams home and away. Leeds were also fortunate with their bad luck. Early defeats in the FA Cup, League Cup and Fairs Cup concentrated their minds on the weekly diet of League matches.

Whenever Leeds experienced the odd setback they immediately bounced back. When they were beaten 5-1 by Burnley their critics pounced. Leeds promptly reeled off 28 matches without defeat and clinched the title with a 0-0 draw at Anfield. It was Leeds' first championship in their 69-year history. They only lost two matches and amassed a record-breaking 67 points yet, curiously, they accumulated more points than the 66 goals they scored.

FOR THE RECORD

BOXING
■ José Napoles, a Cuban emigre who was nicknamed "mantequilla" (smooth as butter), won the world welterweight title on April 18 in California from Curtis Cokes.

FOOTBALL
■ Derby, under Brian Clough and Peter Taylor, won the Second Division championship seven points clear of Crystal Palace.

■ Unstoppable Celtic completed their second Treble of League, Cup, and League Cup.

■ It was a return trip for Northampton. In 1961 they were in the Fourth Division. In 1965 the First. And four seasons later they were back from whence they came: the Fourth.

■ Matt Busby retired as the Manchester United manager in January. Three months elapsed before Wilf McGuinness was named as his successor.

CRICKET
■ Ireland dismissed the West Indies for 25 on their way to a sensational victory.

SAILING
■ Edward Heath, sailing Morning Cloud, won the Sydney-Hobart race.

SQUASH
■ Geoff Hunt of Australia won the first of eight British Open titles.

SQUASH

Hunt beats Barrington on the way to his first title

CRICKET

Turner opens his account

NEW ZEALAND had spent four years yearning for an opener of the calibre of Bert Sutcliffe to hold together their batting. They found their saviour in Glenn Turner, a talented 22-year-old.

Turner made an inauspicious start to his Test career when he was dismissed for a duck against West Indies in February. But by the time New Zealand arrived at Lord's for the first Test of their short series against England Turner was looking more comfortable in the Test arena.

In the second innings Turner displayed the concentration and flawless technique that made him one of New Zealand's most successful batsmen. He became the youngest cricketer, at 22 years and 63 days, to carry his bat with an unbeaten 43 in New Zealand's total of 131. But he could not save his side from a 230-run defeat.

Turner: carried bat

GOLF

Jacklin finally puts Britain in the frame

British hands on the claret jug at long last

AVIATORS had just broken the sound barrier when Max Faulkner became the last Briton to win the Open in 1951. Now Neil Armstrong was about to become the first man on the moon. And while the American astronaut was preparing to take one giant leap for mankind, Tony Jacklin was taking one giant step for British golf.

For 18 years, Antipodeans, Americans, South Africans and even an Argentinian had won the Open. The Americans might as well have pawned the Ryder Cup because Britain had forgotten what it looked like. British golf was in the doldrums.

Then came Jacklin, the son of a Scunthorpe steelworker. He had good looks, personality and a good driver. He had become the first British player to win in the United States since Ted Ray in 1920.

The Open at Royal Lytham beckoned and Britain expected.

Jacklin had the weight of the nation on his shoulders when he began with a birdie at the first. By the sixth he was four under and with an opening round of 68 was well placed behind Bob Charles, who shot a course record 66. A second round of 70 kept Britain's hope in contention.

Then some superb bunker play and a series of 10-foot putts helped Jacklin to a two-shot lead over Charles with a 70 in the third round. He extended his lead over the outward nine in the final round and when he reached the last tee Jacklin needed a bogey on the tight par-four 389-yard final hole to win.

A mighty roar greeted his drive down the middle of the fairway, to within 130 yards of the hole. It took a seven iron and two putts for the man in the mauve sweater to lift the claret jug. At last Britain had a world-class golfer again.

CYCLING

Merckx: first victory

Illingworth makes a late move to the top

MIKE TURNER, a sharp executive who had been appointed secretary-manager at Leicestershire, saw Ray Illingworth as the man to lift the county. So he persuaded him to move to Grace Road and thus began one of the most successful partnerships in cricket.

But Illingworth had other fish to fry first. England needed a captain when Colin Cowdrey tore his left Achilles tendon while batting in a Sunday League match. Surprisingly the selectors turned to the 37-year-old Illingworth and he began his 31-match spell as skipper by winning the toss against the West Indies at Old Trafford. England triumphed by 10 wickets.

Illingworth, who had been no more than a useful off-spinner, then rescued the team at Lord's with his maiden Test century. When Derek Underwood struck in the third Test at Headingley England had won two Tests against the West Indies for the first time in 12 years.

> *If he can get 100 per cent performance out of the other 10, a captain is worth his place*
>
> **Ray Illingworth**

ILLINGWORTH'S RECORD

	FIRST-CLASS	TESTS (61)
Innings	1,073	90
Not out	213	11
Runs	24,134	1,836
Highest	162	113
Average	28.06	23.24
Hundreds	22	2
Wickets	2,072 at 20.28	122 at 31.20
Catches	446	45

Brave Jones tames Wimbledon

Jones: came from behind after the first set

ANN JONES had been on the verge of storming the Wimbledon castle for 14 years. But each time the left-handed Briton appeared certain to win the title she fell.

This time, the top-seeded Margaret Court had the better of her in the first set of the semi-finals, winning it 12-10. But Jones changed from her usual baseline game to an aggressive style and took the next two sets 6-3 6-2.

She had the support of the crowd in the final against Billie Jean King, but lost the opening set by playing too cautiously. She again abandoned her defensive approach and won 3-6 6-3 6-2. It was a deserved victory for the tenacious Jones, who had won the French title in 1961 and 1966 and finished runner-up in six other major finals.

Ageing Gonzales wins a 112-game marathon

THE advent of open tennis gave the 41-year-old Pancho Gonzales a second crack at the Wimbledon crown. And he was not going to let it pass without a fight. The 1949 doubles champion had missed a succession of Wimbledon championships since becoming the leading professional in the 1950s.

Gonzales drew Charlie Pasarell in the first round and when they finished after 5hr 12min, their names were in the record books after the longest singles match in Wimbledon history.

Gonzales won 22-24 1-6 16-14 6-3 11-9 after 112 games. He saved 11 set points against the 35-year-old Puerto Rican in the opening set, appealed angrily about the bad light when losing the second set and was booed off court when play was finally halted.

Gonzales returned as a hero the next day and after saving seven match points in the final set sealed the marathon with his serve. Gonzales amazingly won two more matches in straight sets, but age and Arthur Ashe caught up with him in the fourth round.

Backward Lord's has to adopt cavalier style

THE reactionary officialdom at Lord's had never been fast movers. While the rest of Britain switched on their television sets on Sunday afternoons to watch English counties take on some of the world's finest players, the hierarchy sat around doing nothing.

The Cavaliers, a collection of overseas cricketers, were filling county coffers in exciting 40-over-a-side matches.

It took the Advisory County Committee three years to persuade Lord's there was potential in the abbreviated form of cricket and the Sunday League was finally launched with misgivings from several quarters.

Matches could not start before 2pm because of the Sunday Observance Act and although the players found the afternoon frolics demanding the matches soon became the lifeblood of the sport. The Cavaliers, who had provided the catalyst, were disbanded the following season.

Lancashire, under the astute leadership of Jackie Bond, won the first Sunday League and collected £1,000 for their efforts in the first summer of their golden era in one-day cricket.

LANCASHIRE: THE ONE-DAY WONDERS

1969 Sunday League
1 Lancashire 49pts
2 Hampshire 49

1970 Gillette Cup
Lancashire beat Sussex by six wickets

1970 Sunday League
1 Lancashire 53pts
2 Kent 48

1971 Gillette Cup
Lancashire beat Kent by 24 runs

1972 Gillette Cup
Lancashire beat Warwickshire by four wickets

1974 Gillette Cup
Kent beat Lancashire by four wickets

1975 Gillette Cup
Lancashire beat Middlesex by seven wickets

1976 Gillette Cup
Northamptonshire beat Lancashire by four wickets

FOR THE RECORD

AMERICAN FOOTBALL
■ John Madden became the youngest head coach in the NFL when he took over the Oakland Raiders at the age of 32.

CRICKET
■ Ken Suttle, a left-handed batsman, retired after 423 consecutive county championship matches for Sussex.

■ Mr William Frietag, who lived alongside Trent Bridge, won an injunction in November preventing cricketers hitting the ball out of the ground and on to his property. After the case was heard he said: "I am not a killjoy."

FOOTBALL
■ Bobby Robson was appointed the manager of Ipswich.

GOLF
■ Ray Floyd won the US PGA championship by one stroke after holding a five-shot lead at the start of final round.

■ Bob Charles beat Gene Littler at the 37th hole in the World Matchplay championship at Wentworth.

MOTOR RACING
■ Jackie Stewart fulfilled all his promise and rewarded Ken Tyrell's faith in him when he swept to the world championship in a Tyrrell-entered Matra-Ford, winning six Grands Prix out of the 11.

CRICKET

Trueman and Statham quit

WITH Fred Trueman and Brian Statham put out to grass, Yorkshire and Lancashire slumped dramatically in a county programme reduced to 24 matches. Yorkshire, the defending champions, finished 13th and Lancashire dropped from sixth to 15th. The title went to the unbeaten Glamorgan for the second time in their history.

Britain prove equal to America

The British took 18 matches to the final green to share the Ryder Cup

BRITAIN approached the Ryder Cup at Royal Birkdale on September 18 with new optimism. Tony Jacklin had won the Open and the team was well-balanced.

Their hopes were not unfounded. They won three foursomes on the first morning and were 4-3 ahead by the end of the day. The Americans came back on the second day and, although Jacklin had won three of his four matches and halved the other, the teams were all square.

In the end it came down to the result of the singles match between Jack Nicklaus, making his debut for the United States, and Jacklin. The Englishman sank a 60-foot putt at the 17th for an eagle to stay in contention. Then Nicklaus holed a 4-foot effort at the last and to the surprise of all walked over to Jacklin and conceded a putt of 2½ feet. Nicklaus said: "I don't think you would have missed that putt but in these circumstances I would never give you the opportunity."

The match was tied. Eighteen of the 32 matches finished on the last green and for the first time in history the cup was shared 13-13 with six matches halved.

Protests dog South African tour

THE Springboks, surrounded by policemen and barbed-wire, became easy targets for players and protesters alike. The anti-tour lobby regularly halted play, invading the field and throwing smoke flares and tacks. And while the protesters dogged the South Africans from ground to ground, the constant threat of trouble affected their concentration.

Oxford University began the rout of the tourists at Twickenham in the opening match. Then Scotland beat them 6-3, England won 11-8, Ireland drew 8-8 and Wales 6-6. Even the protesters won: it was the last tour by the South Africans until the 1990s.

A demonstrator is dragged from the pitch at Aldershot

Laver repeats perfect season

Miraculous Mets take advantage of batters' paradise

Laver: struggled in the early rounds at Wimbledon before recapturing his title

ROD LAVER brought a touch of perfection to tennis. He mastered every shot in the coaching manual, was agile and did not mind spending more time on the court than his opponent. The mixture produced the greatest player in the game.

The left-handed Australian confirmed his standing by winning his second Grand Slam seven years after first sweeping aside his rivals in the four major championships. Only Donald Budge in 1938 had won the men's Grand Slam before Laver ruled the court.

His achievement in 1969 is regarded as more worthy than his first Grand Slam. The sport had abandoned the distinction between amateurs and professionals and open tennis became a cut-throat business.

Laver began the road to the Grand Slam in the first and last Australian Open in Brisbane, beating the Spaniard Andres Gimeno in a one-sided final. He then reversed his loss the previous year to Ken Rosewall in the French Open, but had lost form before

seeking a second Wimbledon title.

The defending champion dropped the first two sets against the Indian Premjit Lall in the second round and battled through five sets to beat Stan Smith in the fourth round. But with superb displays against Arthur Ashe in the semifinals and John Newcombe in the final, Laver won comfortably.

The US Open at Forest Hills was his last hurdle. Laver dropped the first set 9-7 in the final, but then overpowered Tony Roche to claim his 11th and last major singles title.

PITCHERS had been getting the upper hand for several years so baseball reduced the strike zone from the distance between the shoulder to the knee to the distance from the armpit to the top of the knee. It had the desired effect, with almost three times as many players hitting .300 in the season.

Another four teams were also added to the two major leagues, with the Montreal Expos becoming the first franchise outside of America. But the expansion teams were not expected to do well, as evidenced by the New York Mets. They had joined the National League in 1962 and their only claim to fame so far had been losing a record 120 games in their first season.

It looked like they were going have another indifferent year, with their batters unable to exploit the new rule. In mid August they were 9½ games back, but then everything clicked. They won 38 of their last 49 games, beat the powerful Atlanta Braves in the play-offs, and, totally unexpectedly, reached the World Series.

There, the team earned their label the Miracle Mets. They faced the Baltimore Orioles, who had been dominating the American League for several years, and were given little chance, and even less so when they lost the opening game.

But the Mets had a knack of coming up with something special. They did not have any individual stars, but everybody seemed to be able make a vital hit or a key play just when it mattered. Baltimore were beaten four times in a row. It truly was a miracle — the young Mets had come from nowhere to be the first expansion team to win a World Series.

ROD LAVER'S GRAND SLAM DOUBLE

Australian championship
1962 Roy Emerson 8-6 0-6 6-4 6-4
1969 Andres Gimeno 6-3 6-4 7-5

French championship
1962 Roy Emerson 3-6 2-6 6-3 9-7 6-2
1969 Ken Rosewall 6-4 6-3 6-4

Wimbledon championship
1962 Marty Mulligan 6-2 6-2 6-1
1969 John Newcombe 6-4 5-7 6-4 6-4

United States championship
1962 Roy Emerson 6-2 6-4 5-7 6-4
1969 Tony Roche 7-9 6-1 6-3 6-2

1970s

The first cracks appear in the edifice

When the Beatles were legally dissolved in 1970 it marked the end of an era. But while the younger generation was searching for a new direction sport was carrying on much as before, pretending that very little had happened in the world at large. However, it was soon under pressure from every direction — politics, money, drugs, and death and destruction — and it did not know which way to turn.

The first shock to sport's system was South Africa. The Swinging Sixties brought a heightened awareness of global politics and the abhorrence of apartheid. But sport continued to turn a blind eye to the evils of South Africa — complacently kidding itself that sport was above the bickerings of politicians.

Despite the D'Oliveira affair in 1968 and the protest against the Springboks' rugby tour in 1969, the MCC naively planned to host the South Africans in 1970. They were rudely awakened when protestors damaged 12 county grounds and the government demanded that the tour be cancelled. It was, and cricket entered the real world the hard way.

But cricket still did not learn the entire lesson. Its own, internal politics were still living in the past. So when Kerry Packer came along to challenge the old order nobody thought he could ever succeed.

Cricket's rulers refused to contemplate his vision of cricket in the television age and retreated to their Long Rooms secure in belief that their hegemony was unassailable. The High Court soon put a stop to that nonsense and Packer won the day. The reverberations went round the world. Packer's successful mix of razzmatazz and one-day tournaments with the world's leading players proved a smash hit. So complete was Packer's victory that he virtually took control of cricket in Australia and eventually the establishment had to go cap in hand and ask for its players back.

Packer's revolution could never have succeeded, though, if the players had not been paid a pittance in the first place. Cricket was experiencing what other professional sports had, or were about to experience, the pulling power of money. Gone were the days when sportsmen simply played for the love of the game. To be sure, affection was the basis of their commitment but, with the birth of the superstar, players began to demand a fairer slice of the cake.

It was little wonder that money was an issue in cricket when the financial rewards available in other professional sports were immense. Prize money was escalating in golf and tennis; multi-million pound fortunes were commonplace and football was forking out fortunes for star players. The decade opened with Martin Peters moving to Tottenham for £200,000 plus Jimmy Greaves. It ended with Brian Clough splashing out £1m for Trevor Francis, which started a spiralling transfer market that would leave Britain gasping.

The emergence of sponsorship allied to burgeoning television coverage of sport now meant there was big money flying about. And this was the decade that Tom Wolfe called the Me decade, when being interested in yourself and your well-being was chic. Winners could scoop the pool. The down side of the demand for success was that some sportsmen would go to any lengths to win, including cheating. Some cheats were easy to catch — a Russian was found to be using a rigged épée at the 1976 Olympics — but the prevalent form of cheating, the use of drugs, went largely undetected.

The 1970s saw the unpublicised spread of performance-enhancing drugs, especially steroids. Although the evidence was there, little was done to stem the tide of abuse. From the standpoint of the 1990s this is almost impossible to understand. A kindly view would be that those in charge of sport were blissfully unaware that the use of recreational drugs was accepted among the modern generation. So the idea of taking a drug to improve your performance was only a small step on from a Saturday night party. After all, youth's cultural heroes indulged themselves. And even when two world-famous rock stars, Jimi Hendrix and Janis Joplin, died from overdoses in 1970, the alarm bells were not heard.

A harsher view, now borne out by our knowledge of how sport was manipulated in Eastern Europe, would be that blind eyes were commonplace and that certain officials connived in the use of drugs to produce winners. The full horror of what had been going on would not be revealed until the 1988 Olympics, when drug-cheating would make headlines worldwide. Whichever viewpoint is accurate — ignorance or connivance — sport, for the umpteenth time this century, was proven to be out of touch. The failure to deal with what was in front of their noses was not confined to athletics and Olympic sports. British football in the 1970s presided over the twin evils that were to beset it for the rest of the century: hooligans and unsafe stadiums.

The writing had been on the wall right from the start of the decade. In April 1971 Leeds supporters invaded the pitch and attacked the referee at Elland Road. This was interpreted as fans over-reacting to a bad decision by the official in a crucial match. And when, the following year, riot police clashed with Rangers fans in Barcelona it was seen as the enforcers of Franco's regime over-reacting to Scottish celebrations.

The clubs involved received heavy punishments for the transgressions of their supporters. But no concrete attempt was made to root out hooligans from the game. Even when, on the opening day of the season in 1973, 180 people were arrested football still did not realise that hooliganism was becoming endemic. By the spring of the following year, when Tottenham exported the English disease to Holland with a concerted onslaught on the town of Rotterdam, the seriousness of the problem was still not grasped. The usual punishments were handed out, but the fundamental cause was not tackled.

The disaster at Ibrox in 1971, where 66 people died and 140 were injured in the Old Firm derby because a stairway could not cope with an animated crowd, did not fully alert football's leaders to the need for modern, safe stadiums. But if football did not understand the need for change, the country did. Britain in the 1970s had undergone spiralling inflation, wave after wave of strikes and huge wage settlements. By 1979 the country had had enough and took a leap into the unknown by electing Margaret Thatcher. Football would look into its own abyss in the 1980s.

AMERICAN FOOTBALL
■ *Super Bowl*
1970 Kansas City Chiefs
1971 Baltimore Colts
1972 Dallas Cowboys
1973 Miami Dolphins
1974 Miami Dolphins
1975 Pittsburgh Steelers
1976 Pittsburgh Steelers
1977 Oakland Raiders
1978 Dallas Cowboys
1979 Pittsburgh Steelers

ATHLETICS
■ *British Olympic gold medals*
1972 *Pentathlon* Mary Peters

BASEBALL
■ *World Series*
1970 Baltimore Orioles
1971 Pittsburgh Pirates
1972 Oakland As
1973 Oakland As
1974 Oakland As
1975 Cincinnati Reds
1976 Cincinnati Reds
1977 New York Yankees
1978 New York Yankees
1979 Pittsburgh Pirates

BOXING
■ *British world champions*
1970 *Lightweight.* Ken Buchanan (WBA)
1974 *Light-heavyweight.* John Conteh (WBC)
1975 *Welterweight.* John H. Stracey (WBC)
1979 *Lightweight.* Jim Watt (WBC)
1979 *Junior middleweight.* Maurice Hope (WBC)
1979 *Cruiserweight.* Glenn McCrory (IBF)

CRICKET
■ *World Cup*
1975 West Indies *bt* Australia by 17 runs
1979 West Indies *bt* England by 92 runs
■ *County championship*
1970 Kent
1971 Surrey
1972 Warwickshire
1973 Hampshire
1974 Worcestershire
1975 Leicestershire
1976 Middlesex
1977 Middlesex and Kent
1978 Kent
1979 Essex
■ *Gillette Cup*
1970 Lancashire *bt* Sussex by 6 wickets
1971 Lancashire *bt* Kent by 24 runs
1972 Lancashire *bt* Warwickshire by 4 wickets
1973 Gloucestershire *bt* Sussex by 40 runs
1974 Kent *bt* Lancashire by 4 wickets
1975 Lancashire *bt* Middlesex by 7 wickets
1976 Northamptonshire *bt* Lancashire by 4 wickets
1977 Middlesex *bt* Glamorgan by 5 wickets
1978 Sussex *bt* Somerset by 5 wickets
1979 Somerset *bt* Northants by 45 runs
■ *B&H Trophy*
1972 Leicestershire *bt* Yorkshire by 5 wickets
1973 Kent *bt* Worcestershire by 39 runs
1974 Surrey *bt* Leicestershire by 27 runs
1975 Leicestershire *bt* Middlesex by 5 wickets
1976 Kent *bt* Worcestershire by 43 runs
1977 Gloucestershire *bt* Kent by 64 runs

1978 Kent *bt* Derbyshire by 6 wickets
1979 Essex *bt* Surrey by 35 runs
■ *Sunday League*
1970 Lancashire
1971 Worcestershire
1972 Kent
1973 Kent
1974 Leicestershire
1975 Hampshire
1976 Kent
1977 Leicestershire
1978 Hampshire
1979 Somerset

CYCLING
■ *Tour de France*
1970 Eddy Merckx
1971 Eddy Merckx
1972 Eddy Merckx
1973 Luis Ocana
1974 Eddy Merckx
1975 Bernard Thevenet
1976 Lucien van Impe
1977 Bernard Thevenet
1978 Bernard Hinault
1979 Bernard Hinault

FOOTBALL
■ *World Cup*
1970 Brazil 4 Italy 1
1974 West Germany 2 Holland 1
1978 Argentina 3 Holland 1 (aet)
■ *European championship*
1972 West Germany 3 USSR 0
1976 Czechoslovakia 2 West Germany 2 (Czechoslovakia won 5-3 on penalties)
■ *European Cup*
1970 Feyenoord 2 Celtic 1 (aet)
1971 Ajax 2 Panathinaikos 0
1972 Ajax 2 Inter Milan 0
1973 Ajax 1 Juventus 0
1974 Bayern Munich 4 Atletico Madrid 0 (after 1-1)
1975 Bayern Munich 2 Leeds 0
1976 Bayern Munich 1 St Etienne 0
1977 Liverpool 3 Borussia Moenchengladbach 1
1978 Liverpool 1 Bruges 0
1979 Nottingham Forest 1 Malmo 0
■ *European Cup Winners' Cup*
1970 Manchester City 2 Gornik Zabrze 1
1971 Chelsea 2 Real Madrid 1 (after 1-1)
1972 Rangers 3 Moscow Dynamo 2
1973 AC Milan 1 Leeds 0
1974 Magdeburg 2 AC Milan 0
1975 Dynamo Kiev 3 Ferencvaros 0
1976 Anderlecht 4 West Ham 2
1977 SV Hamburg 2 Anderlecht 0
1978 Anderlecht 4 FK Austria 0
1979 Barcelona 4 Fortuna Dusseldorf 3
■ *Fairs Cup*
1970 Arsenal *bt* Anderlecht 1-3 3-0
1971 Leeds *bt* Juventus 2-2 1-1 (Leeds won on away goals)
■ *Uefa Cup*
1972 Tottenham *bt* Wolverhampton 2-1 1-1
1973 Liverpool *bt* Borussia Moenchengladbach 3-0 0-2
1974 Feyenoord *bt* Tottenham 2-2 2-0
1975 Borussia Moenchengladbach *bt* Twente Enschede 0-0 5-1
1976 Liverpool *bt* Bruges 3-2 1-1
1977 Juventus *bt* Athletic Bilbao 1-0 1-2 (Juventus won on away goals)
1978 PSV Eindhoven *bt* Bastia 0-0 3-0

1979 Borussia Moenchengladbach *bt* Red Star Belgrade 1-1 1-0
■ *Football League*
1970 Everton
1971 Arsenal
1972 Derby
1973 Liverpool
1974 Leeds
1975 Derby
1976 Liverpool
1977 Liverpool
1978 Nottingham Forest
1979 Liverpool
■ *FA Cup*
1970 Chelsea 2 Leeds 1 (aet, after 2-2)
1971 Arsenal 2 Liverpool 1 (aet)
1972 Leeds 1 Arsenal 0
1973 Sunderland 1 Leeds 0
1974 Liverpool 3 Newcastle 0
1975 West Ham 2 Fulham 0
1976 Southampton 1 Manchester Utd 0
1977 Manchester Utd 2 Liverpool 1
1978 Ipswich 1 Arsenal 0
1979 Arsenal 3 Manchester Utd 2
■ *League Cup*
1970 Manchester City 2 West Bromwich 1 (aet)
1971 Tottenham 2 Aston Villa 0
1972 Stoke 2 Chelsea 1
1973 Tottenham 1 Norwich 0
1974 Wolverhampton 2 Manchester City 1
1975 Aston Villa 1 Norwich 0
1976 Manchester City 2 Newcastle 1
1977 Aston Villa 3 Everton 2 (aet, after 0-1 and 1-1)
1978 Nottingham Forest 1 Liverpool 0 (after 0-0)
1979 Nottingham Forest 3 Southampton 2
■ *Scottish League*
1970 Celtic
1971 Celtic
1972 Celtic
1973 Celtic
1974 Celtic

1975 Rangers
1976 Rangers
1977 Celtic
1978 Rangers
1979 Celtic
■ *Scottish Cup*
1970 Aberdeen 3 Celtic 1
1971 Celtic 2 Rangers 1 (after 1-1)
1972 Celtic 6 Hibernian 1
1973 Rangers 3 Celtic 2
1974 Celtic 3 Dundee Utd 0
1975 Celtic 3 Airdrie 1
1976 Rangers 3 Hearts 1
1977 Celtic 1 Rangers 0
1978 Rangers 2 Aberdeen 1
1979 Rangers 3 Hibernian 2 (after 0-0 and 0-0)
■ *Scottish League Cup*
1970 Celtic 1 St Johnstone 0
1971 Rangers 1 Celtic 0
1972 Partick 4 Celtic 1
1973 Hibernian 2 Celtic 1
1974 Dundee Utd 1 Celtic 0
1975 Celtic 6 Hibernian 3
1976 Rangers 1 Celtic 0
1977 Aberdeen 2 Celtic 1
1978 Rangers 2 Celtic 1
1979 Rangers 2 Aberdeen 1

GOLF
■ *The Open*
1970 Jack Nicklaus
1971 Lee Trevino
1972 Lee Trevino
1973 Tom Weiskopf
1974 Gary Player
1975 Tom Watson
1976 Johnny Miller
1977 Tom Watson
1978 Jack Nicklaus
1979 Severiano Ballesteros
■ *US Open*
1970 Tony Jacklin
1971 Lee Trevino
1972 Jack Nicklaus
1973 Johnny Miller
1974 Hale Irwin
1975 Lou Graham
1976 Jerry Pate
1977 Hubert Green
1978 Andy North
1979 Hale Irwin

■ *US PGA*
1970 Dave Stockton
1971 Jack Nicklaus
1972 Gary Player
1973 Jack Nicklaus
1974 Lee Trevino
1975 Jack Nicklaus
1976 Dave Stockton
1977 Lanny Wadkins
1978 John Mahaffey
1979 David Graham
■ *US Masters*
1970 Billy Casper
1971 Charles Coody
1972 Jack Nicklaus
1973 Tommy Aaron
1974 Gary Player
1975 Jack Nicklaus
1976 Raymond Floyd
1977 Tom Watson
1978 Gary Player
1979 Fuzzy Zoeller
■ *Ryder Cup*
1971 United States 18½-13½
1973 United States 19-13
1975 United States 21-11
1977 United States 12½-7½
1979 United States 17-11

MOTOR RACING
■ *World championship*
1970 Jochen Rindt (Lotus-Ford)
1971 Jackie Stewart (Tyrell-Ford)
1972 Emerson Fittipaldi (Lotus-Ford)
1973 Jackie Stewart (Tyrell-Ford)
1974 Emerson Fittipaldi (McLaren-Ford)
1975 Niki Lauda (Ferrari)
1976 James Hunt (McLaren-Ford)
1977 Niki Lauda (Ferrari)
1978 Mario Andretti (Lotus-Ford)
1979 Jody Scheckter (Ferrari)

RACING
■ *The Derby*
1970 Nijinsky
1971 Mill Reef

1972 *Roberto*
1973 *Morston*
1974 *Snow Knight*
1975 *Grundy*
1976 *Empery*
1977 *The Minstrel*
1978 *Shirley Heights*
1979 *Troy*
■ *Grand National*
1970 *Gay Trip*
1971 *Specify*
1972 *Well To Do*
1973 *Red Rum*
1974 *Red Rum*
1975 *L'Escargot*
1976 *Rag Trade*
1977 *Red Rum*
1978 *Lucius*
1979 *Rubstic*

ROWING
■ *Boat Race*
1970 Cambridge
1971 Cambridge
1972 Cambridge
1973 Cambridge
1974 Oxford
1975 Cambridge
1976 Oxford
1977 Oxford
1978 Oxford
1979 Oxford

RUGBY LEAGUE
■ *Challenge Cup*
1970 Castleford 7 Wigan 2
1971 Leigh 24 Leeds 7
1972 St Helens 16 Leeds 13
1973 Featherstone 33 Bradford 14
1974 Warrington 24 Featherstone 9
1975 Widnes 14 Warrington 7
1976 St Helens 20 Widnes 5
1977 Leeds 16 Widnes 7
1978 Leeds 14 St Helens 12
1979 Widnes 12 Wakefield 3

RUGBY UNION
■ *Five Nations championships*
1970 Wales and France
1971 Wales
1972 Not completed
1973 Five-way tie
1974 Ireland
1975 Wales
1976 Wales
1977 France
1978 Wales
1979 Wales

SAILING
■ *America's Cup*
1970 *Intrepid* (US, Bill Ficker)
1974 *Courageous* (US, Ted Hodd)
1977 *Courageous* (US, Ted Turner)
■ *Admiral's Cup*
1971 Team: Great Britain. Individual: *Ragamuffin* (Aus)
1973 Team: West Germany. Individual: *Saudale* (WG)
1975 Team: Great Britain. Individual: *Noryema* (GB)
1977 Team: Great Britain. Individual: *Imp* (US)
1979 Team: Australia. Individual: *Eclipse* (GB)

SNOOKER
■ *World championship*
1970 Ray Reardon 37 John Pulman 33
1971 John Spencer 37 Warren Simpson 29
1972 Alex Higgins 37 John Spencer 32
1973 Ray Reardon 38 Eddie Charlton 32
1974 Ray Reardon 22 Graham Miles 12
1975 Ray Reardon 31 Eddie Charlton 30
1976 Ray Reardon 27 Alex Higgins 16
1977 John Spencer 25 Cliff Thorburn 21

1978 Ray Reardon 25 Perrie Mans 18
1979 Terry Griffiths 24 Dennis Taylor 16

TENNIS
■ *Wimbledon*
1970 John Newcombe *bt* Ken Rosewall; Margaret Court *bt* Billie Jean King
1971 John Newcombe *bt* Stan Smith; Evonne Goolagong *bt* Margaret Court
1972 Stan Smith *bt* Ilie Nastase; Billie Jean King *bt* Evonne Goolagong
1973 Jan Kodes *bt* Alex Metreveli; Billie Jean King *bt* Chris Evert
1974 Jimmy Connors *bt* Ken Rosewall; Chris Evert *bt* Olga Morozova
1975 Arthur Ashe *bt* Jimmy Connors; Billie Jean King *bt* Evonne Cawley
1976 Bjorn Borg *bt* Ilie Nastase; Chris Evert *bt* Evonne Cawley
1977 Bjorn Borg *bt* Jimmy Connors; Virginia Wade *bt* Betty Stove
1978 Bjorn Borg *bt* Jimmy Connors; Martina Navratilova *bt* Chris Evert
1979 Bjorn Borg *bt* Roscoe Tanner; Martina Navratilova *bt* Chris Evert Lloyd
■ *Australian Open*
1970 Arthur Ashe; Margaret Court
1971 Ken Rosewall; Margaret Court
1972 Ken Rosewall; Virginia Wade
1973 John Newcombe; Margaret Court
1974 Jimmy Connors; Evonne Goolagong
1975 John Newcombe; Evonne Goolagong
1976 Mark Edmondson; Evonne Cawley
1977 Roscoe Tanner, Vitas Gerulaitis; Kerry Melville, Evonne Cawley
1978 Guillermo Vilas; Chris O'Neill
1979 Guillermo Vilas; Barbara Jordan
■ *French Open*
1970 Jan Kodes; Margaret Court
1971 Jan Kodes; Evonne Goolagong
1972 Andres Gimeno; Billie Jean King
1973 Ilie Nastase; Margaret Court
1974 Bjorn Borg; Chris Evert
1975 Bjorn Borg; Chris Evert
1976 Adriano Panatta; Sue Barker
1977 Guillermo Vilas; Mima Jausovec
1978 Bjorn Borg; Virginia Ruzici
1979 Bjorn Borg; Chris Evert Lloyd
■ *USOpen*
1970 Ken Rosewall; Margaret Court
1971 Stan Smith; Billie Jean King
1972 Ilie Nastase; Billie Jean King
1973 John Newcombe; Margaret Court
1974 Jimmy Connors; Billie Jean King
1975 Manuel Orantes; Chris Evert
1976 Jimmy Connors; Chris Evert
1977 Guillermo Vilas; Chris Evert
1978 Jimmy Connors; Chris Evert
1979 John McEnroe; Tracy Austin

Comaneci: perfection at the 1976 Olympics

RUGBY LEAGUE

Millward leads the Lions to record triumph

ROGER MILLWARD, a 5ft 4in scrum-half in the touring party to Australasia, thrived behind a powerful Lions pack which included Mal Reilly, a forward who so impressed his hosts he was signed by Manly for £16,000, a record fee for an overseas player.

Britain started their tour badly, losing 37-15 in the first Test and drawing with New South Wales. But they clicked into gear when Millward scored 20 points in a 28-7 victory in the second Test. Another nine points from the half-back in a 21-17 triumph in the third Test gave Britain the Ashes for the last time. They went home as the most successful Lions team ever with 22 wins in 24 matches.

CRICKET

South African tour cancelled

SOUTH AFRICA had the best cricket team in the world but nowhere to play. They were about to tour England when protesters opposing the visit damaged 12 county grounds on the night of January 20.

The Cricket Council said the tour would go ahead, and a fund was launched to raise £200,000 to protect the grounds. But on May 21 James Callaghan, the Home Secretary, requested that the tour be called off and the next day the Council bowed to the pressure.

FOOTBALL

Fabulous treble eludes Leeds

The Leeds team that, in 33 days, let slip the League title, FA Cup and European Cup

WHEN Leeds kicked off against Southampton on March 28 they had played 52 matches and lost three. A fabulous treble was in their sights: the League championship, FA Cup and European Cup. By April 29, 33 days later, they had played 10 more matches and won only one. Every trophy had slipped from their grasp.

Because of the World Cup the season had been shortened by a month. This, if you can put your finger on any one thing, was to prove their undoing. The inevitable fixture congestion led to injuries and fatigue.

The tie that probably wrecked Leeds's hopes was the FA Cup semi-final against Manchester United. It took Leeds three stamina-sapping matches to dispatch Matt Busby's team just days before they began their Easter programme. So drained were the Leeds players

that Don Revie fielded a host of reserves over that weekend and virtually handed the League title to Everton.

In the European Cup semi-final against Celtic at Elland Road on April 1 Leeds were a goal down in the first minute and never recovered. It was Leeds's eighth fixture in 22 days.

The players had a week's rest before the FA Cup final against Chelsea. Yet despite dominating the game and twice taking the lead — the second goal coming seven minutes from time — Chelsea forced the game into extra time and a replay.

Leeds were really suffering now. Three days later came the European Cup semi-final second leg at Hampden. This time it was Leeds's turn to get an early goal but, uncharacteristically, they were unable to close down the game,

conceded two more goals and were eliminated 3-1 on aggregate.

So Leeds went to Old Trafford for the FA Cup replay and the end of their tiring season, and left empty-handed. Once again Leeds began the scoring with a superb goal from Mick Jones nine minutes before half-time, and kept the lead until 15 minutes from the end. Peter Osgood took the final into extra time again. Leeds were finished, physically and emotionally, and David Webb executed the coup de grace.

> *There is no doubt in my mind that they would have done that treble had it been a normal season*
>
> **Bill Shankly**

Springbok duo devastate Aussies

MIKE PROCTER and Barry Richards devastated Bill Lawry's experienced Australians in South Africa's last Test series before apartheid was lifted. Procter's pace bowling ripped the heart out of the Australian batting, taking 26 wickets with a unique action which looked as though he delivered the ball off the wrong foot.

Richards was perfection personified, scoring 508 runs in the four-match series. Graeme Pollock hit 274 in the second Test

and even the wicketkeeper Denis Lindsay was flawless. He did not concede a bye as the Springbooks completed a clean sweep.

RICHARDS'S RECORD

	FIRST-CLASS	TESTS (4)
Innings	576	7
Not out	58	0
Runs	28,358	508
Highest	356	140
Average	54.74	72.57
Hundreds	80	2
Wickets	77 at 37.38	1 at 26.00
Catches	361	3

PROCTER'S RECORD

	FIRST-CLASS	TESTS (7)
Innings	663	10
Not out	57	1
Runs	21,904	226
Highest	254	48
Average	36.14	25.11
Hundreds	48	–
Wickets	1,407 at 19.37	41 at 15.02
Catches	324	4

> *Mike Procter bowls at a hundred miles an hour, from extra cover, off the wrong foot*
>
> **David Green**

> *Barry Richards strolls where others must hustle*
>
> **John Arlott**

Procter: 26 wickets

Hill: marathon man

FOR THE RECORD

AMERICAN FOOTBALL
■ The Kansas City Chiefs made it two victories in a row for the AFL when they defeated the Minnesota Vikings 23-7 in Super Bowl IV in New Orleans on January 11.

ATHLETICS
■ Ron Hill had his most successful year, winning the Commonwealth Games and Boston marathons. He was one of the first runners to use carbohydrate loading before events.

■ The first New York marathon was held in Central Park.

FOOTBALL
■ Manchester City completed a unique double of European Cup Winner's Cup and League Cup, and Arsenal made it a European double by capturing the Fairs Cup. However, Celtic lost the European Cup final to Feyenoord 2-1 after extra time. They also missed the Scottish treble by losing the Cup final to Aberdeen.

■ Martin Peters became Britain's first £200,000 footballer in March when he moved from West Ham to Tottenham. West Ham received Jimmy Greaves in part exchange.

■ George Best scored six goals for Manchester United as they beat Fourth Division Northampton Town 8-2 away in the fifth round of the FA Cup.

■ Bradford Park Avenue dropped out of the Football League.

GOLF
■ Jack Nicklaus became the first million-dollar golfer on the US PGA Tour when he finished second in the Bing Crosby tournament on January 25.

MOTOR SPORT
■ Sir Alf Ramsey started the World Cup rally to Mexico City in April. The first car away broke down after less than 200 yards.

TENNIS
■ The tie break scoring system, invented by James van Alen, was first used in a tournament in Philadelphia in February. It was initially declared illegal by the International Lawn Tennis Federation. Five months later they changed their decision.

■ Arthur Thomas, an umpire at the Dunlop tournament in March, got fed up with Illie Nastase challenging his decisions, so he suspended the Romanian's match with John Cooper.

Sad success by absent Rindt

Rindt: posthumous champion

JOCHEN RINDT had not begun the new season in championship-winning form, but at Monaco on May 10 he drove the race of his career and proved his mettle as a winner.

With four laps left Jack Brabham held a nine-second lead over Rindt, but difficulty overtaking a back marker reduced it to five seconds. Rindt pushed his Lotus-Ford to the limit and as the two drivers entered the tunnel for the last time there was barely a second between them. Brabham committed an uncharacteristic error, braked too late and drove into the straw. Rindt swept past to the chequered flag.

By September Rindt had confirmed his early season form by winning four more Grands Prix in succession, and he had a near-unassailable 20 points lead over Brabham in the championship.

But in the practice session for the Italian GP at Monza, Rindt braked from full speed going into the parabolic curve, something failed in the car and he ploughed into the barrier and was killed. Rindt became the only driver to win the title posthumously.

The young Brazilian driver Emerson Fittipaldi replaced Rindt as the Lotus team leader, and in only his third drive won the United States GP on October 4.

FOOTBALL

England captain accused of theft

A WEEK before England began their defence of the World Cup Bobby Moore, their captain, was arrested for the theft of a £600 emerald and diamond bracelet in Bogotá , Colombia. England had been acclimatising by playing in Colombia and Ecuador and Moore was accused by a shopgirl, Clara Padilla, who worked in a small jewellery boutique in the England hotel, of stealing the bracelet within two hours of booking in.

Moore made a statement to the police and thought nothing more of it. However, as the England team returned to Bogotá from Ecuador before going on to Mexico, Moore was detained because another "witness" had emerged. The England team left without him. For four days the controversy raged.

Gradually, the accusations began to disintegrate and it transpired that other visiting celebrities had been similarly accused and had paid up to avoid publicity. Diplomatic pressure was brought to bear — Harold Wilson was attempting to get his Labour government re-elected within weeks — and Moore was "bailed" to play in the World Cup.

The case belatedly died when the mysterious witness disappeared. In 1972 the perpetrators were charged with conspiracy.

GOLF

Jacklin easily tames controversial course

THE restyled Hazeltine course at Chaska in Minnesota was the second longest course in US Open history — and the most unpopular. There were blind shots to 11 greens and many of the bunkers could not be seen from the tees. Dave Hill, an American professional, suggested "a monkey could play this course as well as a man. All the course lacks is 80 acres of corn and four cows". His remarks brought a $150 fine from the US Golf Association.

A 40mph wind turned Hazeltine into a nightmare for the best in the world on the opening day. Arnold Palmer scored 79, Gary Player 80 and Jack Nicklaus 81. But while criticism of the course raged, Tony Jacklin went three under par in the first six holes and took a two shot lead with a first-round 71. Jacklin, bubbling with confidence after his victory in the Open the previous year, increased his lead to three shots in the second round and four in the third. He posted a final round of 70 to win by seven shots, only the third Briton after Ted Ray and Harry Vardon to win both the British and US Open titles.

Jacklin: won by seven

THE JACKLIN DOUBLE

The Open 1969					The US Open 1970				
280 Tony Jacklin	68	70	70	72	281 Tony Jacklin	71	70	70	70
282 Bob Charles	66	69	75	72	288 Dave Hill	75	69	71	73
283 Peter Thomson	71	70	70	72	289 Bob Lunn	77	72	70	70
Roberto de Vicenzo	72	73	66	72	Bob Charles	76	71	75	67

Nicklaus triumphs as Sanders slips away

THERE was no doubting Tony Jacklin's determination to retain the claret jug when the 99th Open championship started under leaden skies at St Andrews. He was out in 29 in the first round but a storm halted play and Jacklin had lost his touch when he completed his round the next day.

Doug Sanders, an American who had come through the qualifying rounds, needed a four on the last hole to beat Jack Nicklaus but hit his second shot long, putted to within four feet and then missed. They went to a play-off.

Sanders birdied the last hole in the play-off, but it was too late. Nicklaus was down in three and had won his second Open after three years without a major title.

MOTOR RACING

McLaren: engine exploded in high-speed crash at Goodwood

FOR THE RECORD

CRICKET
■ Batsmen could be dismissed leg before if they offered no stroke to a ball pitching outside the off stump, provided the ball would have hit the wicket.

MOTOR RACING
■ Bruce McLaren, the New Zealand driver who had developed the McLaren company, was killed testing a sports car at Goodwood.

Pele and Brazil on top of the world

FOR many people, the "real final" of the World Cup in Mexico was between England, the holders, and Brazil, twice world champions and the favourites, drawn together in the group matches in Guadalajara on June 7.

England still had six of the team that had triumphed in the final four years earlier and had added several exciting players: Terry Cooper, Alan Mullery, Colin Bell and Francis Lee. Brazil were formidable opponents, and in this World Cup probably fielded their best ever side. As well as the incomparable skills of Pele, they could call on such prodigies as Tostao, Rivelino, Gerson and Jairzinho.

The "real final" lived up to all expectations, despite the 98-degree heat. England had two good chances squandered by Geoff Hurst and Lee but held Brazil to a goalless first half, principally because of an outstanding save by Gordon Banks in the tenth minute. From a perfect centre Pele had headed the ball down with great power towards Banks's right-hand post and was already celebrating when Banks leapt across his goal and, with one hand, pushed the ball over the bar.

In the second half Tostao created the goal that settled the match after 14 minutes when he dribbled past three English defenders and passed to Pele in the area, who instantly pushed the ball into the path of Jairzinho.

Brazil now were struggling to hold on to their lead as England made, but threw away, several chances, notably an horrendous miss by Jeff Astle.

England travelled to Leon for the quarter-finals, and a replay of the 1966 final against West Germany. The game on Sunday June 14 was probably lost the day before when Banks drank a bottle of beer, developed food poisoning and was unable to play.

With 40 minutes left in the match England were 2-0 up with goals from Mullery and Martin Peters and coasting to an easy victory. Then Franz Beckenbauer sent a low shot towards goal and Peter Bonetti, the substitute goalkeeper, dived over it. German tails were up and their substitute Grabowski's pace and domination of Cooper on the wing gave them great heart. They took the match to extra time where, with an England goal inexplicably being ruled offside, they triumphed 3-2.

West Germany lost their semi-final to Italy, who met Brazil in the final in Mexico City. It was a classic encounter: Old World v New; two countries who had won the World Cup twice; and the the most defensive side in the world against the most attack-minded.

Latin flair destroyed Latin fear in a final that would have graced any World Cup. The inflexible Italian man-for-man marking simply caved in when the Brazilians ran at them. Pele played one of his most magnificent games, scoring one goal and creating two others in a 4-1 exhibition of sheer beauty.

One goal above all stood out, the fourth. With three minutes left, Jairzinho found Pele with a delightful through ball. He instantly played a perfectly controlled ball into space and Carlos Alberto arrived to meet it, as if they had made an appointment, to thunderously drive the ball into the net.

Rosewall misses out in yet another final

ROGER TAYLOR was Britain's perennial great hope. And when he ended Rod Laver's 31-match unbeaten run at Wimbledon in the fourth round the nation was agog. But their hopes were shattered when Taylor was tripped up by Ken Rosewall in the semi-finals.

Rosewall's solid groundstrokes had won him five major singles titles but Wimbledon proved elusive. He lost to Jaroslav Drobny in the 1954 final and Lew Hoad in 1956, and met fellow Australian John Newcombe this time.

Rosewall won the opening set 7-5, dropped the next two and then fought back to take the match to a fifth set. But he double-faulted at break point in the third game and Newcombe skipped away to a 5-7 6-3 6-2 3-6 6-1 victory in 2hr 39min. Another Wimbledon had slipped through his grasp.

Rosewall: lost his third Wimbledon final

KEN ROSEWALL'S MAJOR TITLES

1953 Australian championship, French championship;
1955 Australian championship; **1956** US championship;
1968 French Open; **1970** US Open; **1971** Australian championship; **1972** Australian championship

and the finals that got away
1953 US championship; **1954** Wimbledon; **1956** Australian championship, Wimbledon; **1969** French Open; **1970** Wimbledon; **1974** Wimbledon, US championship; **1977** Australian championship

SEPTEMBER

1970

DECEMBER

RACING

Nijinsky acclaimed the best

MANY runners have laid claim to the title of "horse of the century" but only one has, undoubtedly, deserved the accolade — Nijinsky. The Northern Dancer colt cost $84,000 dollars as a yearling in Canada, largely on the strength of his pedigree and good looks. When he arrived at Vincent O'Brien's stables it did not take long for the Irish trainer to realise he had the talent to match.

The 2,000 Guineas was Nijinsky's seventh win in as many starts, but even that was nothing compared with the Derby. If Sir Ivor's victory the previous year had been dazzling then Nijinsky's triumph in a record time that spreadeagled the field was blinding. And he still wasn't finished. Nijinsky showed scant respect for his elders in the King George VI and Queen Elizabeth Stakes, winning by a comfortable two lengths.

O'Brien and Nijinsky's owner then faced a difficult choice: go for the St Leger and the first Triple Crown since 1935, or the Arc de Triomphe which carried the greater prestige.

The answer was simple. Go for both. The decision, though, was to prove Nijinsky's undoing. He had suffered an attack of worms and did not have the strength for two tough races. The Triple Crown was won, but Nijinsky was finally beaten, though only by a head, in the Arc.

BOXING

Ali's emphatic return makes a smash hit

MUHAMMAD ALI had been away from the ring for 3½ years when he squared up to Jerry Quarry in Atlanta on October 26. Times were a changing, and the America that had been outraged with the champion that "didn't have no fight with them Viet Cong" had begun to realise that the Vietnam war had been ill-advised, and that possibly Ali had a point.

Ali's comeback fight, in Atlanta

> **❝ I could announce that tomorrow Muhammad Ali will walk across the Hudson river and charge $20 admission, and there would be 20,000 down there to see him do it. Half of them would be rooting for him to sink, the other half to do it ❞**
>
> **Terry Brenner**
> The matchmaker at Madison Square Garden

of all places, was a glitzy affair with black celebrities and black spectators outnumbering whites in Georgia, a city and a state notorious for its bigotry. Times were a changing all right.

But not for The Greatest. The years slipped away as he danced, floated and stung. By the third round Quarry was a beaten man, and a cut over his left eye stopped the fight. Six weeks later Ali conquered the unstoppable Argentinian Oscar Bonavena in a hard 15-round battle. Ali was back, and looking for the return of his title.

Joe Frazier was his obstacle. Frazier had become the undisputed heavyweight champion in February when he had embarrassed Jimmy Ellis over four rounds. In Ali's absence Frazier had stepped in and proved himself to be a convincing world champion, not somebody just keeping the seat warm.

And Frazier was uncontroversial while Ali, although partially forgiven for his refusal to be drafted, still split the nation in two. You loved him, or you hated him. Everybody was eagerly anticipating the showdown.

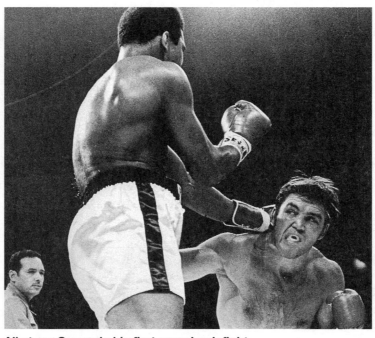

Ali stops Quarry in his first comeback fight

Monzon: middleweight king

FOR THE RECORD

BOXING

■ **Ken Buchanan won the WBA lightweight title in Puerto Rico on September 26 when he gained a stylish split decision over the Panamanian world champion Ismael Laguna. As the British Boxing Board of Control were not affiliated to the WBA they did not recognise Buchanan as the world champion.**

■ **Carlos Monzon of Argentina captured the world middleweight title from Italy's Nino Benvenuti in Rome on November 7. Monzon went on to dominate the division like no boxer since Sugar Ray Robinson.**

■ **Sonny Liston was found dead of a drug overdose in his house in Las Vegas on December 30.**

CRICKET

■ **Kent celebrated their centenary by winning the county championship for the first time in 57 years.**

ICE HOCKEY

■ **The Southern League was formed, although two clubs, the Sussex Senators and the Wembley Vets, were homeless.**

KARATE

■ **Japan won the team competition in the first world championships, held in Tokyo. Kouji Wade won the men's individual Kumite.**

KENDO

■ **Mitsuru Kobayashi became the first world champion. Japan also won the team title.**

RUGBY LEAGUE

■ **Australia retained the World Cup with a 12-7 victory against Britain in a final attended by only 18,776 people at Headingley.**

242

Umpires give England hard time in Australia

ANY illusions England might have entertained about easily regaining the Ashes in Australia were shattered on the first morning of the six-match series.

Keith Stackpole, the Australian opener, appeared to be run out for 18 but was given not out. Seven hours later he was dismissed for 207 and it took defiant batting by England to repair the damage.

Peter Lever was called up for the second Test but was overshadowed by another debutant, Greg Chappell, who scored 108. England went on to win the Ashes in the spring, but they were bitter about the umpiring. No Australian batsman was given out lbw in the entire series.

Grand Slam crowns Court's comeback

MARGARET SMITH'S thirst for titles had been quenched when she married Barry Court in 1967. She had won more championships than any other player and decided to retire. But Mrs Court began to miss the circuit and, encouraged by her husband, she was back to add to the largest silverware collection in the sport.

Court was unbeatable in 1970, sweeping aside Kerry Melville in the Australian Open final and beating Helga Niessen in the French Open final. Wimbledon proved a tougher test. Court injured her ankle and needed pain-killing injections before the final against the top-seeded Billie Jean King. It proved one of the finest on the Centre Court.

They traded blows in a record 26-game opening set which Court took 14-12. Then King fought back to save four match points at 9-10 but missed a fifth and Court won 14-12 11-9 after 2hr 26min.

Rosie Casals provided only token resistance in the US Open final and Court cruised to a 6-2 2-6 6-1 victory. She was the second woman after Maureen Connolly in 1953 to win the Grand Slam. It was the crowning achievement in a career that reaped 67 Grand Slam titles and 92 tournaments throughout the world.

Court: beat King

MARGARET COURT'S 24 MAJOR TITLES

1960 Australian championship; 1961 Australian championship; 1962 Australian championship, French championship, US championship; 1963 Australian championship, Wimbledon; 1964 Australian championship, French championship; 1965 Australian championship, Wimbledon, US championship; 1966 Australian championship; 1969 Australian Open, French Open, US Open; 1970 Australian Open, French Open, Wimbledon, US Open; 1971 Australian Open; 1973 Australian Open, French Open, US Open

Sobers stands out in team of all talents

Sobers leads the teams from the field at The Oval

A GLITTERING array of talent representing the Rest of the World stepped in to fill the gap left by South Africa's cancelled tour of England and beat their hosts 4-1 in an unofficial Test series.

The combination, under Garry Sobers, were made to struggle despite boasting players of the calibre of Intikhab Alam, Lance Gibbs, Rohan Kanhai, Clive Lloyd, Graeme Pollock, Mike Procter and Barry Richards. Sobers was the most consistent. He helped dismiss England for 127 in the first match with six for 21 and then scored 183. Only a defiant Ray Illingworth delayed England's defeat by an innings and 80 runs.

The England captain led his side to victory in the second match at Trent Bridge. But Sobers and Pollock had the final say at The Oval. The left-handers plundered 135 runs in a memorable two hours, for a four-wicket victory.

Board loses battle with cancer

LILLIAN BOARD'S six-month fight against cancer ended on Boxing Day. The 22-year-old athlete had risen to fame in the 1968 Olympics, when she finished 0.07sec behind the 400m winner Colette Besson of France. She hid her disappointment by joking that she would have the silver medal sprayed gold.

She won the 800m in the European championships the next year, was awarded the MBE and named Sportswoman of the Year. Six months before her death she was running in club meetings with her sights on the 800m in the 1972 Olympics.

Instead, she flew to a Munich clinic in October after doctors in England had given up hope. The bulletins on her condition made the newspaper headlines and when she died Britain mourned the loss of one of its youngest and most talented athletes.

CRICKET

Knott misses record pair

ALAN KNOTT'S opportunities to cement his place were crumbling when the selectors gave Bob Taylor his chance in the first Test against New Zealand. But Knott was recalled for the second Test and made a fine 101 in the first innings. In the second he was denied a place in the records as the first wicketkeeper to score a century in each innings of a Test when Bob Cunis bowled him for 96.

FOR THE RECORD

CRICKET

■. Brian Close was dismissed by Yorkshire in the winter after he fell out with the committee.

■ Sunil Gavaskar made his debut in the second Test in Trinidad, hitting the winning runs in India's first victory against West Indies.

FOOTBALL

■ Fourth Division Colchester provided one of the greatest shocks of the FA Cup when they knocked out Leeds 3-2 in the fifth round.

■ Tranmere, of the Third Division, drew 22 of their 46 League matches, a record.

GOLF

■ Alan Shepherd, an Apollo astronaut, hit a golf ball with a six-iron during his walk on the moon.

ICE HOCKEY

■ Murrayfield Racers were the first team to win the British Grand Slam of the Icy Smith Cup, the Northern League, and the Spring and Autumn Cups.

MOTOR RACING

■ Bernie Ecclestone, a former Formula 3 driver, bought Brabham cars outright after Jack Brabham had sold up and returned to Australia the previous year.

Smokin' Joe extinguishes Ali

Frazier floors Ali with a left hook in the final round

IT WAS called the Fight of the Champions, and it certainly was. For 15 brutal rounds on March 8 the two unbeaten champions battled like fury. Muhammad Ali used his 6½-inch reach advantage to sidestep, counter, and jab and jab, while Joe Frazier bored in on Ali's body to get in his left hooks.

Both fighters took a pounding as 20,000 in Madison Square Garden and 300 million on TV in 46 countries watched in awe. In Chicago, fight fans were so angry that their closed-circuit show was cancelled because of projector failure that they wrecked the venue.

For war-torn America the clash was perceived as a battle of ideologies. In the red corner, Ali, the hero of the liberals, the refuseniks and the blacks. In the blue corner, Frazier, the flag-bearer of the establishment, the red-necks and the moral majority. Amazingly, Frazier had been burdened with the role of the Great White Hope.

It did not seem to bother Smokin' Joe Frazier. A proud champion, he disdained Ali's antics, and gave better than he got, slamming into Ali's body time after time. In the 15th round he floored Ali for only the third time in his career. Ali jumped up after the mandatory eight count but Frazier had won an unanimous points decision, and sportingly Ali accepted his defeat graciously.

CRICKET

Fiery Snow freezes out Australia

AUSTRALIA was no place for fainthearted English cricketers, as Ray Illingworth and his troops found on their gruelling winter tour. The Ashes were at stake and the Australians were not about to surrender them without a fight in the six-match contest — the longest series in Test history.

They gave the gloves to Rod Marsh, blooded Greg Chappell and Dennis Lillee and when things began to go wrong dropped their captain for the first time in 70 years. But in John Snow, England had the firepower to counter the Australians. The Sussex fast bowler thrived on the hard pitches with a flowing bowling action and a vicious bouncer. A mean and moody player, he relished the intensity of the competition.

Snow stirred up a section of the Sydney crowd in the seventh Test when he hit Terry Jenner in the face with a short-pitched delivery, earning a warning from the umpire Lou Rowan. A shower of beer cans greeted the Englishman when he returned to the fine-leg boundary and a heckler grabbed his shirt. An incensed Illingworth led his team off the field to return only when the crowd had calmed down.

Bill Lawry, the Australian captain, was dropped for the last Test and Ian Chappell took over. But he was unable to stop England winning the series 2-0. Snow spearheaded the bowling with 31 wickets and Boycott anchored the batting, with 657 runs at 93.85.

Arsenal come from behind to win the title

FEW people outside the Highbury dressing room considered Arsenal as title contenders, though there were signs that under Bertie Mee and Don Howe Arsenal were learning to rid themselves of the ghosts of triumphs past and become a winning team.

Their spirited campaign, and ultimate victory in the previous season's Fairs Cup was one. However, overshadowed by England's attempt to retain the World Cup and Leeds's extraordinary collapse when they were within sight of three trophies, Arsenal's achievement had largely gone

unnoticed. Except at Elland Road. When Don Revie was asked which team, other than Leeds of course, he fancied for the title he plumped for the 14-1 shots Arsenal.

By the beginning of the year it was a two-horse race but by the end of February Leeds were seven points clear of Arsenal, although the North Londoners had two games in hand. Then Arsenal truly came into their own and the match-winning machine took shape.

Between March 2 and May 3 Arsenal played 13 League matches and won 11, drawing one. Their only loss was to Leeds at Elland

Road. In that awesome run Arsenal scored 20 goals and conceded a mere four, all away. They also recorded six 1-0 victories.

The last, and most gratifying, was at White Hart Lane. Leeds had already completed their programme and Arsenal either had to beat Tottenham or draw 0-0 to win the title (because of the vagaries of goal average any score draw would have given the title to Leeds). Arsenal had won the championship with 65 points, and the runners-up had amassed the highest number of points, 64, that had never secured the title.

Mee: best manager

66 die, 140 injured at Old Firm disaster

The fateful steps where the crowd was crushed

THE year began in the worst possible way in Scotland on January 2. At the annual New Year Old Firm match between Rangers and Celtic 66 spectators died and 140 were injured when thousands streaming down the steps to leave the game early rushed back up and met hundreds more on the way down. Bodies fell and hundreds were crushed in the ensuing chaos.

Celtic had been leading 1-0 with time running out, then Colin Stein equalised for Rangers and the Ibrox crowd were cheering madly. Those leaving rushed back to find out the cause of the excitement and inadvertently created Britain's worst football disaster. A government inquiry was set up which eventually produced legislation that covered ground safety.

Rain starts one-day international

THE traditional New Year fixture between Australia and England in Melbourne had been washed out during the first three days so it was agreed to stage a 40 eight-ball overs knockabout game to compensate the crowd. The unique match attracted 46,00 people and pointed the way to the future with

gate receipts of $Aus33,000.

John Edrich became the first player to score a half-century in one-day internationals with an innings of 82 that earned him the Man-of-the-Match award. But it was not enough to stop the Australians winning by five wickets with 42 balls to spare.

John galvanises runaway Welsh

WALES, inspired by the brilliance of their fly-half Barry John, won their first Grand Slam in 19 years. The King scored 31 points as Wales piled up 73 points in their four matches, more than twice the total they conceded.

The powerful Welsh pack provided their talented backline with clean ball to dominate the com-

petition. They thumped England 22-6, shaded Scotland 19-18 and beat Ireland 23-6.

Then John provided the coup de grace in Paris when he gathered the ball from a heel against the head and darted through for a 9-5 win. The victory helped put 13 Welshmen in the 30-man British Lions party to New Zealand.

Wales scored 73 points in four matches

The dragon roared their names

Stephen Jones

It is difficult to know which was the more remarkable — the magnificence of Welsh rugby in the 1970s, when the most vivid and self-confident rugby ever played poured from the dragon, or the barrel-scraping dive which the same nation made in the late 1980s and early 1990s. Yet it is probable that history will forgive the dive quicker than it will forget the glories, for glories were in abundance. In the 11 seasons from 1969 to 1979 Wales finished top or joint top of the Five Nations championship in every season bar three, a remarkable feat which almost certainly will never be equalled. There were three Grand Slams and six Triple Crowns in that era and Wales never lost a championship match at Cardiff Arms Park.

As ever, the bare statistics tell nothing. There was a wonderful élan and theatre about the Welsh style. Until the late 1960s international matches plodded along and a 14-6 result was regarded almost as an extravaganza. Suddenly, Wales started scoring 20 and 30 points regularly, scoring try after try and revolutionising the sport as a spectacle.

Welsh rugby always had household names but never so many in one era. The five archangels of the game, J P R Williams, Gerald Davies, Barry John, Gareth Edwards and Mervyn Davies were so well loved that they lost their surnames. Everybody knew that if you were talking about Gerald then you did not mean Gerald your brother, or Gerald from next door or Gerald from down the shop. You meant GERALD, from the right wing. Likewise with Barry and Gareth and Mervyn. All five are still recognised widely, and probably unanimously, as the greatest players ever to play in their positions.

Significantly, Wales had been the first to embrace the new coaching philosophies. Until the end of the 1960s British teams met up, ran round the pitch and went out and played.

Coaching in its early forms — a concept frowned upon by the large numbers of ultra-Corinthians in the sport — meant simply organising yourselves, having a few plans and a little understanding. Wales, through the visionary Ray Williams, the first technical officer appointed by any Union, and through the fierce motivational powers of Clive Rowlands, coach at the start of the 1970s, were five years ahead before the other European countries awoke.

John Dawes, a radical thinker and master tactician, also played a central part. He was not a centre of blistering talents but his leadership transformed Welsh rugby and he led the 1971 British Lions to victory in New Zealand. More to the point, his vision transformed his club, London Welsh, from middle rank to sublimity. From 1968 to 1973 the club touched off the golden days of Welsh rugby by playing a breathtaking attacking game. The club nurtured the likes of Dawes, Gerald and Mervyn Davies, J P R Williams, John Taylor, Mike Roberts and Geoff Evans.

The national team at the start of the 1970s was so good that they actually created their own blueprints for the first coaching manuals, or at least rewrote previous theories.

J P R Williams made the fullback position one of attack for the first time with his spectacular charges from deep. The extraordinary length of Edwards's pass wrote off back row aspirations to get at the fly-half because John, operating on the end of that pass, had already gone. Mervyn Davies was so superb as a ball-winner at the tail of the lineout that everyone began to throw there. And there was so much more in the approach and in the set moves that was revolutionary.

The incomparable Welshmen: Gerald Davies, Gareth Edwards, and J P R Williams, whose exploits made them household names in the 1970s . . .

There are so many memories of swaggering, attacking rugby. The first signpost to the era came in 1967 when Wales were battling to avoid the wooden spoon in their last match. They played England at Cardiff, and at fullback was a young man who had just left school and had never even been to Cardiff Arms Park, let alone played there. He was Keith Jarrett and he was the most brilliant rugby talent I have ever seen. On that day in Cardiff he gave a phenomenal performance, scoring 19 points in an astonishing 34-21 win.

The pace picked up. There was a superb Grand Slam in 1971, with Gerald Davies on the wing in dazzling form. There was the tumultuous match in Edinburgh that year which was won by a dramatic conversion in the dying moments by John Taylor. His boot still lies in a glass case in London Welsh's trophy room.

The original team broke up in the mid 1970s, but such was the momentum that a new model immediately installed itself with a remarkable 25-10 win in Paris. Throughout the decade, however, the best performances were usually reserved for England, who were downed by a barrage of tries almost annually. It took England until 1991 to recover from the Welsh onslaught.

Another band of folk heroes played together for the first time in that match in Paris in 1975. The Pontypool front row of Charlie Faulkner, Bobby Windsor and Graham Price underlined another of the great truths about the Welsh team of the time; that although the focus was usually on John and Edwards, Williams and Davies, Wales were producing the most fearsome and productive packs.

For Welsh people who grew up in the era it was an orgasmic experience. The self-confidence of the rugby team pervaded the nation. It was a time when rugby glossed over anything, any dip in the economy or in national esteem. Rugby was so dominant in Welsh hearts and minds that academics and literary men made plaintive noises about there being more to Wales than 15 men in scarlet jerseys.

There was, but for the massed millions it existed unsuspected for long years. There was great ritual associated with the colossal pilgrimages to the shrine of the Welsh team. Every club or other gang had its own meeting place — perhaps the Angel Hotel or the Old Arcade or the Rummer Tavern. They all became tourist attractions even when there was no rugby on.

To obtain a ticket was a ritual in itself, and, as the kick-off approached and panic and market prices increased, there was the feeling that all 70,000 of your blood brothers were attending a feast and that you, only you, would be left outside.

Even parts of the stadium became sub-cathedrals. Some people would prefer the West Enclosure, others the East. Most would covet the grail of a ticket for the heart of the ground, the North Enclosure, where before the Safety at Sports Grounds Act the pilgrims massed in a steaming and happy crush, desperate for the bellowing songs and the reflected glory. We became the most outrageously lucky, over-fed sports followers there have ever been. Wales established the Five Nations championship, once and for all, as the most glamorous fixture in the post-Christmas sporting calendar. And a hundred cottage and souvenir industries sprung up. The team spawned plays, films and poetry, and also pulled in a massed band of bandwagon jumpers and all the flotsam and jetsam that stunning success frequently trails in its wake.

Yet, to be fair, it was also a time of high good humour and the players, to a man, remained unaffected. Perhaps it was that sort of temperament that made them such good players. The accusations of arrogance levelled at the game in Wales could not be aimed at players, rather at some of the hangers-on.

Not even Liverpool or Jahangir Khan have disproved the theory that all sporting success is cyclical. Results dipped in the 1980s and the team broke up and, eventually, shattered. Perhaps there is a regret that, at the time, when we watched Wales play we never realised that this was the best we would ever feel about sport. Or perhaps, deep down, we did realise we understood that nothing could be so good again.

. . . and with Barry John, Phil Bennett, J J Williams and Mervyn Davies forged a side so strong that no rugby team in the world could live with them.

TENNIS

Shy Goolagong comes of age

Goolagong: charms fans

EVONNE GOOLAGONG, an enchanting 19-year-old whose surname meant "tall trees by still water", provided a pleasant contrast in an era when the big and the brash had dominated the women's singles at Wimbledon. She was so popular on her Wimbledon debut the previous year that she played on Centre Court, only to be crushed by Jane Bartkowicz.

Now she was back as the French champion. Goolagong sliced her forehands, had a soft and short second serve and occasionally went "walkabout", losing concentration and matches against weak opponents. But she more than matched the brash Billie Jean King in the semi-finals and then beat Margaret Court 6-4 6-1 in the final. Court and King had won six of the previous eight championships but a new belle had come to the ball.

FOR THE RECORD

FOOTBALL

■ Leeds won the Fairs Cup for the second time and were the first club to achieve victory on away goals when they tied 3-3 on aggregate with Juventus.

■ Chelsea won the European Cup Winner's Cup by beating Real Madrid 2-1 in Athens in extra time after a replay.

■ Kevin Keegan joined Liverpool from Scunthorpe for £33,000 and wages of £50 a week.

HOCKEY

■ Pakistan became the first men's World Cup champions.

POWERLIFTING

■ The first official world championships were held two years after an unofficial championship.

CRICKET

Run feast for Zaheer

PAKISTAN'S penchant for choosing prodigies provided Imran Khan with his first taste of Test cricket at the age of 18. But it was Zaheer Abbas, five years his senior, who stole the show in the opening Test against England at Edgbaston.

He scored 274 in 9hr 10min, becoming the first Pakistani to hit a double century against England. He also featured in a second-wicket stand of nearly 300 with Mushtaq Mohammad. Only rain prevented England losing in Colin Cowdrey's 114th and last Test.

Imran was run out for five, failed to take a wicket and was dropped. But Zaheer had established himself as a batsman of class and after England won the series 1-0 he signed for Gloucestershire.

ZAHEER'S RECORD

	FIRST-CLASS	TESTS (78)
Innings	768	124
Not out	92	11
Runs	34,843	5,062
Highest	274	274
Average	51.54	44.79
Hundreds	108	12
Wickets	28 at 37.82	3 at 44.00
Catches	262	34

GOLF

Joker Trevino laughs his way to a hat-trick

LEE TREVINO, the joker in the pack, came up trumps in 24 days of stunning golf. The 31-year-old had emerged from the wrong side of the tracks to become the leading money-winner on the US Tour in 1970 within four years of joining the circuit. In the summer of 1971 he put the seal on his status as a great.

Trevino, with the typical banter that had made him a fairway favourite, won the US Open at Merion in Pennsylvania after a play-off with Jack Nicklaus, coming home in 33 to win by three shots.

A fortnight later he won the Canadian Open at Richelieu Valley in Montreal, coming back from four shots down after two rounds to beat the 47-year-old Art Wall with a birdie at the first hole of a sudden-death play-off.

The next stop was Royal Birkdale for the Open centenary and Trevino was charging. He shot a 69 on the opening day, sank a 40-foot eagle putt at the last on the second day and grabbed a one-shot lead in the third round ahead of Tony Jacklin and Liang-Huan Lu of Taiwan.

Mr Lu, as he became known, endeared himself to the crowd by doffing his trilby each time he was applauded. But in the final round he had to take his hat off to Trevino. The Texan turned five shots ahead, ran into trouble at the 17th with a seven and then birdied the last for a one-shot victory and an unique championship hat-trick.

THE WORLD ACCORDING TO LEE TREVINO

ON LIFE: I can't wait to wake up in the morning to hear what I have to say.

ON GROWING UP: My family was so poor they couldn't afford any kids. The lady next door had me.

ON GOLFERS: There are two things that won't last long in this world — dogs that chase cars and pros that putt for pars.

ON COURSES: If I were designing a golf course for myself, there would be a dog-leg right on every hole and the first hole wouldn't count. That would be a warm-up hole.

ON PRESSURE: You don't know what pressure is until you play for five bucks with only two in your pocket.

ON BEING STRUCK BY LIGHTNING: There was a thunderous crack like cannon fire and suddenly I was lifted a foot and a half off the ground. Damn, I thought to myself, this is a helluva penalty for slow play. I guess I learnt that day when God wants to play through, you stand aside.

ON WINNING: I am going to win so much money this year my caddie will make the top 20 money-winners' list.

ON CADDIES: Caddies are a breed of their own. If you shoot a 66 they say 'Man, we shot a 66!' But go out and shoot 77 and they say 'Hell, he shot 77!'

and his major titles
1968 US Open; 1971 US Open, The Open; 1972 The Open; 1974 US PGA; 1984 US PGA.

TENNIS

Wimbledon break with tradition

WIMBLEDON broke with tradition and introduced the tie break. But they compromised by using the innovation at 8-8, unlike the rest of the world who brought it in at 6-6. But no new-fangled ideas could stop John Newcombe successfully defending his title.

Leeds blow up as Arsenal steal Double

LEEDS, acknowledged by everybody (including Bill Shankly!) as the greatest club side of the day, once again had their hopes dashed. And this time they could unequivocally point to the referee Ray Tinkler as the man who virtually extinguished those hopes.

As the championship race was coming to the boil on April 17 Tinkler overruled his linesman and allowed a West Brom goal that was the most controversial of the season. The ball cannoned off the West Brom forward Tony Brown, who started to chase it, but then stopped, as did all the other players, because the linesman was pointing at another West Brom forward, Colin Suggett, who was in an offside position and running in support of Brown.

Incredibly, Tinkler waved play on, and Brown, almost reluctantly, was able to pass to Jeff Astle, who also looked offside, to sidefoot the ball past the stranded Gary Sprake. Chaos ensued. Fans invaded the pitch and 23 were arrested. Leeds were fined £750 and ordered to play their first four home games of the next season away from Elland Road.

Arsenal had experienced their own hiccups three weeks earlier. In the FA Cup semi-final against Stoke they had been 2-0 down with half an hour gone and should have been three down minutes later when Jimmy Greenhoff, with only the keeper to beat, blasted high and wide.

Arsenal got one back but with time added on they were still in pursuit of an equaliser when they were awarded a hotly-debated penalty. Peter Storey beat Gordon Banks and gained them a replay.

This was probably the turning point of the season. Arsenal still had 10 League matches to play and they had demonstrated a mettle that perhaps Leeds did not possess. Having won the League on Monday May 3, and celebrated until the Wednesday, Arsenal now had to beat Shankly's Liverpool in the Cup final on the Saturday if they were to emulate their neighbours Tottenham and achieve the Double.

Liverpool fully tested the new

Shankly and the Arsenal team congratulate Charlie George

champions. The two best defences in the land had kept the first 90 minutes scoreless, then two minutes into extra time Steve Heighway beat Bob Wilson with a near-post shot. Eddie Kelly equalised for Arsenal, and with nine minutes remaining Charlie George, the darling of the North Bank, blasted a right-footed shot past Ray Clemence for the FA Cup, and the historic Double.

Mill Reef sprints to record-breaking career

IT WAS almost too much to hope that, after Nijinsky's heroics the previous year, English racing could enjoy another spectacular season. But while Nijinsky was sweeping all before him three two-year-olds were also starting to make a name for themselves.

The long awaited showdown came in the 2,000 Guineas, with Mill Reef just the favourite even though he had been beaten by My Swallow the year before. The third contestant, Brigadier Gerard, was nowhere near as heavily fancied because he had not run so far this season and was rated behind My Swallow and Mill Reef in the Free Handicap.

My Swallow, as anticipated, set the pace but coming up the hill it was Mill Reef and Brigadier Gerard who fought out a stirring finish, with Brigadier Gerard pulling away by three lengths.

My Swallow's career went into decline but Mill Reef and Brigadier Gerard went from strength to strength, particularly Mill Reef, who never lost again. He had little trouble in winning the Derby and then over the course of the rest of the summer he proved he was undoubtedly the best middle-distance horse of the year as he ran away with the Eclipse in record time, the King George VI and then, just to round off the year, the Arc de Triomphe in a record time as well.

Mill Reef races away with the King George VI Stakes

Lions devour New Zealand

AUGUST

1971

DECEMBER

Title backing for Buchanan

Buchanan: lightweight king

WHENEVER the British Lions went south of the equator they turned into pussycats. The mighty forwards of New Zealand and South Africa battered and bruised them through the 1950s and 1960s. Now it seemed the 1970s would be no different.

The Lions lost to Queensland and struggled against New South Wales before they even set foot in New Zealand. But the captain, John Dawes, Carwyn James, the coach, and the manager Dr Doug Smith had done their homework.

Their combination, built around the Welsh Grand Slam team, was dedicated, enthusiastic and talented. With men such as Gordon Brown, Mervyn Davies, Willie John McBride and Ian McLauchlan, they could dominate the forward play. And when they ran in seven tries against Waikato, New Zealand realised these were not the pushovers of the past.

McLauchlan, nicknamed Mighty Mouse, turned the first Test in Dunedin, charging down a kick to score after 15 minutes of relentless pressure from the All Blacks, and the Lions won 9-3. But a 50-yard try by Ian Kirkpatrick lifted New Zealand to a 22-12 victory in the second Test.

Enter The King. Barry John, the Welsh fly-half, kicked two conversions and a penalty goal, scored a try and kept the All Blacks at bay in a 13-3 triumph in the third Test. Then the tourists came back from 8-0 down to draw the final Test 14-14. They were the first Lions to win a series in New Zealand. When they clambered aboard Qantas flight 530 for Heathrow, they looked like the cats who had eaten the cream.

THE PRIDE OF THE LIONS

May 12	Queensland 11-15
May 15	New South Wales 14-12
May 22	Counties and Thames Valley 25-3
May 26	King Country and Wanganui 22-9
May 29	Waikato 35-14
June 2	Maoris 23-12
June 5	Wellington 47-9
June 9	South and Mid-Canterbury, North Otago 25-6
June 12	Otago 21-9
June 17	West Coast and Buller 39-6
June 19	Canterbury 14-3
June 22	Marlborough and Nelson Bays 31-12
June 26	NEW ZEALAND (Dunedin) 9-3
June 30	Southland 25-3
July 3	Taranaki 14-9
July 6	New Zealand Universities 27-6
July 10	NEW ZEALAND (Christchurch) 12-22
July 14	Wairarapa-Bush 27-6
July 17	Hawkes Bay 25-6
July 21	Poverty Bay and East Coast 18-12
July 24	Auckland 19-12
July 31	NEW ZEALAND (Wellington) 13-3
Aug 4	Manawatu 39-6
Aug 7	North Auckland 11-5
Aug 10	Bay of Plenty 20-14
Aug 14	NEW ZEALAND (Auckland) 14-14

Tour Record

	P	W	D	L	F	A
In Australia	2	1	0	1	25	27
In New Zealand	24	22	1	1	555	204
Total	26	23	1	2	580	231

THE British Boxing Board of Control finally recognised Ken Buchanan as the world lightweight champion when he outpointed Ruben Navarro in Los Angeles on February 12. But then the WBC stripped Buchanan of their part of the title when he agreed to a rematch with Ismael Laguna, from whom Buchanan had taken the title the previous year. The WBC had wanted Buchanan to fight their No 1 rated contender, Pedro Carrasco of Spain. This time the BBB of C stood by their man and continued to recognise Buchanan as the champion.

He retained the title in Madison Square Garden in September with a tremendous performance to gain an unanimous points decision after he had had to soldier on with a badly cut eye.

The Lions pack gives Edwards time to get the ball away during the third Test

Stewart still dominant

JACKIE STEWART won his second world championship in a Tyrrell designed by Ken Tyrrell and unveiled late the previous year, the 001. Once Tyrrell had ironed out the teething problems the car — now the 003 — was almost unbeatable. Stewart won six of the 10 Grands Prix, was on pole six times, and his teammate Francois Cevert won the US GP.

Although the season was virtually a procession for Tyrrell and Stewart, one GP the dominant Scot did not win was the most exciting five-way battle ever seen on a motor racing circuit. From the outset of the Italian GP at Monza the lead kept changing hands and every time a driver made the tiniest of errors he dropped back half-dozen places. With three laps remaining Peter Gethin, Francois Cevert, Ronnie Peterson, Mike Hailwood and Howden Ganley were all in contention.

In the last lap Cevert led but going into the parabolic curve he braked late, Peterson passed but went too wide and was overtaken on the inside by Gethin and then Cevert. As all five dashed for the chequered flag there was next to nothing in it. Gethin got home first, just, and Peterson stole second from Cevert. A mere 0.09sec separated first and third, and 0.61sec spanned the first five finishers.

THE SPLIT-SECOND GRAND PRIX

1	Peter Gethin (GB)	1hr 18min 12.60sec
2	Ronnie Peterson (Swe)	1hr 18min 12.61sec
3	Francois Cevert (Fra)	1hr 18min 12.69sec
4	Mike Hailwood (GB)	1hr 18min 12.78sec
5	Howden Ganley (NZ)	1hr 18min 13.21sec

Stewart: on the way to his second championship

India finally break their duck

THERE was a mighty cheer from the Indian dressing-room at The Oval at 2.42pm on August 24. Abid Ali cut Brian Luckhurst to the boundary to give his country their first-ever Test victory in England after 39 years. The four-wicket win ended England's record run of 26 Tests without defeat and gave the home side their first loss in 20 matches under Ray Illingworth's captaincy.

Lancashire put Kent lights out

LANCASHIRE beat Kent to win the Gillette Cup for the second year running but had to work hard for success. Their three-wicket victory against Gloucestershire in the semi-final came at 8.50pm in what became known as The Lamplight Match. In an exciting finish, David Hughes hit 24 runs off an over from John Mortimore, including two sixes and two fours, with the lights bright in the pavilion.

Princess Anne and Doublet: two European gold medals

FOR THE RECORD

CRICKET
■ Surrey finished level on points with Warwickshire, but took the championship because they had won 11 matches to Warwickshire's nine.

EQUESTRIANISM
■ Princess Anne and Doublet won individual and team gold medals at the European Three-Day Event championships at Burghley.

FOOTBALL
■ Ted MacDougall scored a record nine goals for Bournemouth in their 12-0 victory over Margate in the FA Cup in November.

■ Alvechurch finally won their FA Cup qualifying match 1-0 against Oxford City in the fifth replay in November. At 11 hours, it was the longest ever FA Cup match.

■ The Professional Footballers Association threatened to take referees to court under the Industrial Relations Act to challenge unfair decisions as part of its campaign for higher standards of refereeing.

■ Graeme Souness made his only appearance for Spurs in an Uefa Cup tie in Iceland on September 14 and was substituted for Alan Mullery.

GOLF
■ The United States reasserted their domination of the Ryder Cup, winning 16-11 with five matches halved at the Old Warson Country Club in St Louis on September 18.

■ Jack Nicklaus became the first player to win the four major tournaments twice when he won the US PGA championship at Palm Beach Gardens, Florida.

■ Britain had only their second victory in the Walker Cup, winning 13-11 at St Andrews on the event's 50th anniversary.

MOTORCYCLING
■ Phil Read of Britain, riding a Yamaha, won the 250cc world championships.

RUGBY UNION
■ The value of a try was increased from three points to four in an attempt to encourage attacking play.

SAILING
■ Edward Heath captained the British team that regained the Admiral's Cup from the United States. Seventeen countries took part and the Cup was held under IOR rules for the first time.

SQUASH
■ The first court with a glass back wall opened near Sheffield.

FOOTBALL

Rangers banned after Cup riot

Willie Johnston scores his first goal in the win over Moscow Dynamo

Hurricane takes world title in a whirlwind

FROM his first qualifying match to his week-long final with John Spencer in February, it took Alex Higgins 13 months to win the world professional title at his first attempt and change the face of snooker forever. He was the first champion who did not even aspire to come from the right side of the tracks; he commanded prodigious support from those similarly disaffected.

His quick, instinctive style and one-against-the-world approach carried him to victory over Spencer in a final which stimulated press interest for the first time for 20 years, took the championship into more salubrious venues and convinced sporting entrepreneurs that snooker had possibilities. This is why, the following year, the championship ceased to run through a whole season and was instead encapsulated into a fortnight.

Higgins: people's champion

RANGERS finally won a European trophy to assuage the pain of Celtic's victory in the European Cup in Lisbon in 1967. Unfortunately, only the Rangers players did themselves proud, while their fans did them a great disservice.

After the 3-2 victory over Moscow Dynamo in the Cup-winners Cup final Barcelona the jubilant Glaswegians, many the worse for drink, had a pitched battle with Franco's Guardia Civil. The orgy of violence left one person dead and hundreds injured.

Rangers were banned from European competition for a year. Their supporters had wreaked terrible damage on a club that had swept magnificently to the final. Probably their finest performance in European competition was when they beat Bayern Munich 2-0 at Ibrox. Bayern went on to win three European Cups in succession.

In the final, Rangers had won the match in the first 50 minutes when they raced to a 3-0 lead with a goal from Colin Stein and two from from Willie Johnston. Dynamo grabbed two late goals, but Rangers were never put out of their stride.

After their triumph, and disaster, the manager Willie Waddell moved upstairs and Jock Wallace took over the running of team affairs.

FOR THE RECORD

CRICKET

■ Lawrence Rowe became the first batsman to score centuries in both innings on his debut when he hit 214 and 100 not out for West Indies against New Zealand in Kingston, Jamaica.

■ Garry Sobers played what he described as his finest innings, scoring 254 for a Rest of the World XI against Australia in Melbourne. He hit 29 off Dennis Lillee in his first three overs.

FOOTBALL

■ West Germany virtually knocked England out of the European championships with a 3-1 victory at Wembley on April 29. A fortnight later the formalities were complete when England could do no better than a goalless draw in Berlin.

■ Southern League Hereford knocked First Division Newcastle out of the third round of the FA Cup 2-1. Hereford held West Ham, another First Division side, to a goalless draw in the next round before losing the replay 3-1 at Upton Park. Their Cup exploits did not go unrewarded and they were elected to the Fourth Division at the end of the season.

■ Stoke, the League's second oldest club, won their first trophy when they beat Chelsea 2-1 and George Eastham, at the age of 35, scored the winning goal — his first for three years.

■ Partick Thistle beat Celtic 4-1 in the League Cup final. When the half-time score of 4-0 was relayed to crowds around the country it was greeted first with disbelief, then derision. Then they had to believe it.

■ Gordon Banks, who kept goal for England on 73 occasions, had to retire from the game when a car crash cost him the sight of an eye.

■ Aldershot, of the Fourth Division, drew 22 of their 46 League matches to equal Tranmere's record of the previous season.

RUGBY LEAGUE

■ Halifax won the first Knockout Trophy, beating Wakefield Trinity 22-11 in the final at Odsal.

■ Britain won the World Cup in France after drawing 10-10 with Australia.

RUGBY UNION

■ Ireland were denied an opportunity to win their first Five Nations championship in 21 years when Scotland and Wales refused to play in Dublin because of violence in the Irish capital. Ireland beat England 16-12 and France 14-9 in a disrupted season.

■ Gloucester beat Moseley 17-6 in the first final of the knock-out competition. Neath beat Llanelli 15-9 in the inaugural Welsh Cup final in Cardiff.

TENNIS

■ Virginia Wade won her first major tournament when she beat Evonne Goolagong 6-4 6-4 in the final of the Australian Open.

Leeds's Double hopes dashed at end of cruellest season

IF THE destiny of the League championship was a close run thing the previous season then the twists and turns of the 1972 championship and its eventual denouement were surely beyond even the feverish brain of any thriller writer.

Once again Leeds were chasing more than one trophy: the Double of League and Cup. But this was an even deadlier Leeds. They overwhelmed Southampton 7-0 and then, to emphasise their utter authority, strung together some 30 passes without an opposition player getting a sniff of the ball.

They had reached the Cup final where they would meet Arsenal, last year's winners of the Double. Now Leeds were going to emulate that achievement at the expense of the team that had "stolen" their title.

If it had not been for the punishment hanging over from the previous season they probably would have been League champions by Cup final day. Because of the riot that was provoked by referee Ray Tinkler's controversial offside decision Leeds had to play their first four home games away from Elland Road. They dropped two points in those four "home" games, exactly the same number they dropped in their genuine 17 home games. Mr Tinkler's actions may have cost Leeds two championships, not one. With a week to go to the Cup final the top of the First Division looked like this:

	P	Pts
Manchester City	42	57
Liverpool	40	56
Derby	41	56
Leeds	40	55

Only Liverpool, Derby and Leeds could win the title, because Derby had still to play Liverpool so it was mathematically impossible for Manchester City, who had finished their programme, to become champions.

Leeds had three matches left to clinch the Double. In midweek they beat Chelsea, and Derby did them a favour by beating Liverpool. On the Saturday Leeds beat Arsenal with a goal from Allan Clarke in a sterile Cup final and left for the Midlands without even attending their official banquet. They had a League fixture to fulfil 48 hours after the final. Don Revie had personally petitioned Alan Hardaker, the League secretary, to move the match to a more amenable day.

But no, the League secretary was intransigent. So on the Monday Leeds had to face middle-of-the-table Wolves. A draw would have given Leeds the Double. Inexplicably they lost 2-1. Even stranger, Liverpool drew 0-0 with Arsenal on the same night and Brian Clough's Derby were the surprising champions. When the news broke, Clough was on holiday in the Scilly Isles and his team was relaxing in Majorca.

Leeds's FA Cup success, the first in their history, was forgotten in the gloom. "It was as if we had won nothing," Clarke said. "We wanted that League championship so badly." For the second successive season it had eluded them by a single point.

Brian Clough's Derby County team that won the Championship while on holiday in Majorca

Austrian banned over cash rewards

Schranz: hero's welcome

A CROWD of 200,000 people gave Karl Schranz a hero's welcome in Vienna after he had been kicked out of the Winter Olympics in Sapporo, Japan. The leading Austrian skier was expelled because he had allowed his name and photographs to be used for paid advertising.

Schranz was used as a scapegoat by the IOC, who alleged that nearly 40 competitors had broken the strict amateur code. Austria withdrew in protest but re-entered when Schranz pleaded that his countrymen be given a chance to compete. The Austrians took one gold medal, two silver and two bronze in a Games dominated by the Soviet skier Galina Kulakova, who won three Nordic events. The Dutch speed skater Ard Schenk also won three gold medals.

George Best
The misunderstood genius

Eamon Dunphy

George Best arrived at Old Trafford in the summer of 1961. He was 15, a slim dark boy, careful of his appearance, shy and watchful of manner. There was something different about Best from the beginning. He wasn't as coarse as the rest of us players. He didn't swear or talk dirty about girls. He used shampoo instead of soap on his silky black hair. Best was a popular lad but never a Lad in the true dressing-room sense of that word.

People first began to notice him in the improvised 15-a-side games that were the highlight of a morning's training at Matt Busby's Manchester United. Apprentices, pros and internationals all joined in these car park epics, every man or boy for himself. Here Best was no longer self-effacing. The quiet kid from east Belfast was poised and self-possessed amid the fierce competitiveness. Where others of his age learnt the hard lessons about the difference between the schoolyard and the pro game George astonishingly prevailed, gliding past the lunging challenges of powerful men irritated by the impudence of this elusive urchin who didn't seem to understand that the flicks, shimmies and nutmegs of schoolboy imagination wouldn't get you far when you began to play with men. Best never learned this lesson. His genius was to retain the joyous innocence of the streets and impose it on the professional game in a way that only the greatest footballers have done. Busby's genius was to allow Best to be himself at a time when coaching was becoming fashionable.

In 1963, after a dreadful League campaign which saw them narrowly avoid relegation, United won the FA Cup, their first triumph since Munich. Best was still an A-team player unable to command a place in the reserve side. He was an enigmatic figure to Old Trafford insiders. On the car park Best continued to astonish, but the brilliance was not reflected on Saturday afternoons. When, in the spring of 1963, he replaced the injured first-choice winger for a Youth Cup tie at Sheffield Wednesday the team lost 1-0. The consensus was that his presence hadn't helped the cause.

Best's problem was a lack of physical strength. But some among the senior pros offered other reasons for his apparent failure. They blamed Busby. Best was cited as an example of the folly of allowing players to express themselves, the principle Busby had always adhered to even in the darkest days when relegation threatened. Somebody, it was argued, ought "to get hold of George". In other words, coach his bad habits away.

Busby's legendary patience paid off when he introduced the uncoached Best to the First Division in the autumn of 1963. After a promising debut against West Brom, in which he delighted the crowd by tormenting the experienced Welsh international Graham Williams, who tried desperately to kick him, Best was rested for a few months before returning to the team for good at the turn of that year. His emergence enabled Bobby Charlton to return from exile at outside-left, where he had languished for years, and the foundation of Busby's last great side was laid.

Best in the First Division was the boy from schoolyard and car park grown strong and even more confident. He was the complete footballer, a master of every facet of the game, a scorer of goals and maker of chances, the slim dark handsome tormentor of bullies, of which there were many in the First Division of that era. Best was also profoundly courageous, relishing his duels with Ron Harris, Norman Hunter and Tommy Smith, hard men who made less noise but inflicted more damage than Vinny Jones.

United won the championship in 1965. In March the following year they travelled to Lisbon to play Benfica in the European Cup. The Portuguese were Europe's most formidable side but United won 5-1, a

sensational result achieved in magnificent style. George Best scored twice in a display which confirmed his greatness. Best returned to England to find himself a national hero, the "Fifth Beatle", his fame transcending the simple world of sport. He became an icon of the Swinging Sixties, the most dashing and virile symbol of those non-conformist times. Life, he would later reflect, was never the same again.

They say that fame destroyed George, who now became known as "Georgie". They say he couldn't "handle it", but this is not the case. The real Best bore no resemblance to the mythic hero. The "Fifth Beatle" lived in digs. His pleasures were the bowling alley, the movies, the snooker hall and penny games of crib with his land-lady. Also girls because, lacking the machismo coarseness of other men, Best found solace in the warmth and sensitivity of women's company.

Fame made life's simple pleasures less accessible and attracted a different kind of girl: models, actresses and beauty queens on the make who knew that a date with George was a photo opportunity. He wanted a woman's company; they wanted a tryst with an illusion. Fame also deterred real friends while attracting those who liked to bathe in reflected glory.

Best had always been different, a loner. Fame accentuated this. But fame did not destroy Best. He became an even greater player between 1966 and 1968. The thing he loved most was football. He once confessed to being sexually aroused by the idea of playing. If he turned to women for company it was in football he sought love. United won the championship again in 1967. George played in every match. The next season he missed one game and was joint leading goalscorer in the First Division with 28 goals. On May 29, 1968 Manchester United beat Benfica 4-1 at Wembley to take the European Cup that Busby's young players had died for a decade earlier.

After a scrappy 90 minutes the scoreboard read 1-1. A few minutes into extra time Best seized on an error in Benfica's defence, mesmerised a couple of desperate pursuers, rounded the goalkeeper and guided the ball into the net. Socks down around his ankles, hair long and shining in the cool night air, the street urchin imposing his will on the greatest football night; that will always be my memory of Best.

Something came to an end that night at Wembley; the crusade into Europe — tragic and glorious — for which Matt Busby and Manchester United will always be remembered. The club would go on but the great romance was over. Busby retired and Manchester United became just another side in the years after Wembley. This is what was to cause finally the downfall of George Best as a great player.

He fell out of love with football. According to myth his decline was rapid. In fact, he fought courageously while the club fell to pieces around him. In the three seasons after that great night at Wembley Best missed a mere handful of games, but the battle was a losing one.

Best fought harder than anyone. He lost more than anyone for he loved the game more than most. Drink and girls became a refuge. The myth of George Best suggests that he precipitated United's downfall. The truth is that he was a victim.

A more worldly man might have settled for the money and the glory. Best always wanted to be great, and wanted every football day to be an adventure as it had been in the playground and remained through the romantic years of Busby's European crusade. Best couldn't live with ordinariness, the stuff of coaches' imagination, the evil of the game post-Busby when people "got hold" of youngsters with genius and turned them into players.

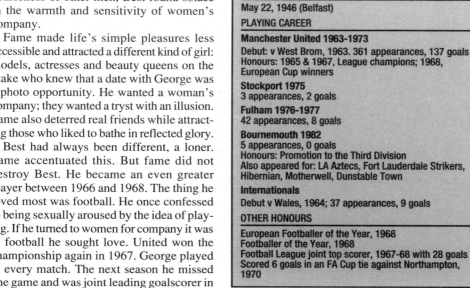

BORN

May 22, 1946 (Belfast)

PLAYING CAREER

Manchester United 1963-1973
Debut: v West Brom, 1963. 361 appearances, 137 goals
Honours: 1965 & 1967, League champions; 1968, European Cup winners

Stockport 1975
3 appearances, 2 goals

Fulham 1976-1977
42 appearances, 8 goals

Bournemouth 1982
5 appearances, 0 goals
Honours: Promotion to the Third Division
Also appeared for: LA Aztecs, Fort Lauderdale Strikers, Hibernian, Motherwell, Dunstable Town

Internationals
Debut v Wales, 1964; 37 appearances, 9 goals

OTHER HONOURS

European Footballer of the Year, 1968
Footballer of the Year, 1968
Football League joint top scorer, 1967-68 with 28 goals
Scored 6 goals in an FA Cup tie against Northampton, 1970

From the back streets to oblivion: the boy wonder from east Belfast became the wizard of Old Trafford. But his playboy image as the fifth Beatle seemed to eclipse his talents and he drifted out of the game he loved.

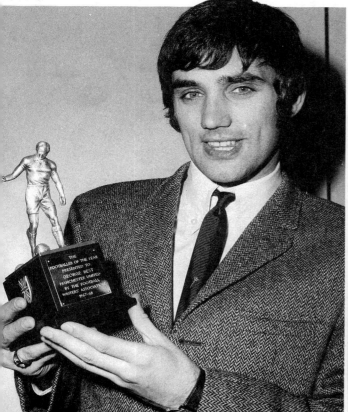

BOXING

Buchanan robbed by Dirty Duran

KEN BUCHANAN'S reign as the world lightweight champion came to an end on June 26 in New York to a boxer who had been on the undercard of Buchanan's successful defence nine months previously, Roberto Duran. The 21-year-old Panamanian had been a professional boxer since he was 15, and was unbeaten in 25 fights. His explosion on to the lightweight scene had caused a sensation. He was a rough, tough, swaggering bully and a record crowd flocked to Madison Square Garden to watch the championship bout, paying more than $200,000 — the largest receipts ever for an indoor lightweight contest.

Although Duran narrowly outfought the stylish Scot much of his work was quite dirty and he could easily have been disqualified at the very end of the 13th round, when he caught Buchanan with a savage low blow that left the champion holding his groin in serious pain. Instead, the referee stopped the fight when the champion, for obvious reasons, did not come out for the 14th.

Duran, now the champion, swaggered his way through the division for the next seven years and was arguably the greatest ever lightweight. Significantly, he never entertained a re-match with Buchanan, and 10 years after the fight Duran acknowledged that Buchanan had been his toughest and most difficult opponent.

Massie's magic wears off

ENGLAND had been given ample warning about the new tearaway in the Australian ranks and Dennis Lillee was bristling for another crack at Ray Illingworth's men. The pace he generated off a 22-stride run up sent shock waves through the England team in the first Test at Old Trafford. Lillee took six for 66 and only two determined innings of 57 and 62 from Tony Greig saw England home by 89 runs.

Australia struck back at Lord's, but not with Lillee. Instead, England were bamboozled by Bob Massie, a 25-year-old fast-medium swing bowler making his debut.

The bank clerk from Perth chose to bowl round the wicket and took a phenomenal 16 for 137 to earn Australia an eight-wicket victory. Massie's magic was never repeated. Only 190 days later he was dropped after taking 31 wickets in a six-match Test career.

England had mastered Massie by the fourth Test at Headingley, where a fungal attack left the pitch without grass and ideal for Derek Underwood to take 10 for 82 and dismiss Australia twice within three days. Lillee dominated the final Test to finish the series with 31 wickets, but it was too late to stop England retaining the Ashes.

Massie: massive swing

Money row disrupts Wimbledon

JOHN NEWCOMBE was barred from winning a third successive Wimbledon title when he became one of the pawns in the battle between the International Lawn Tennis Federation and World Championship Tennis. The Australian had signed a contract with the WCT, an organisation controlled by the oil millionaire Lamar Hunt. But the ILTF were in dispute about the fees paid to the WCT players and banned them from January 1.

So Newcombe, Arthur Ashe, Rod Laver and Ken Rosewall were not allowed to play at Wimbledon. Instead, Jimmy Connors took the spotlight with his cracking two-handed backhand. The 19-year-old unseeded American reached the quarter-finals, where he lost to Ilie Nastase of Romania. But Nastase went down 4-6 6-3 6-3 4-6 7-5 to Stan Smith in the 2hr 40min final.

Evonne Goolagong accounted for the new American sensation Chris Evert in the women's semi-finals but lost 6-3 6-3 to Billie Jean King in the final. Britain's Buster Mottram reached the junior final, only to lose 6-3 4-6 7-5 to a 16-year-old Swede who came back from 5-2 down in the final set. His name was Bjorn Borg.

Smith beats Nastase in the Sunday final

Injury denies Mill Reef revenge

IT WAS the rematch that everybody wanted. Mill Reef, the 1971 Derby, Eclipse, King George and Arc winner, versus Brigadier Gerard, his conqueror in the 2,000 Guineas and the country's best miler. But, sadly, it was not to be.

The two great horses were expected to meet in the Eclipse but a virus kept Mill Reef out of the race. Then, in late August, disaster struck. Mill Reef shattered a leg in training, an accident so terrible that it made front page news. Any other horse would probably have been put down, but the little horse with a big heart was saved by a minor miracle of veterinary science. With his leg patched up he retired to stud the record stakes winner of all time.

Brigadier Gerard, meanwhile, just kept on winning. And to prove that he wasn't just a miler he won the King George VI Stakes only a third of a second slower than Mill Reef's time the year before. That was his fifteenth successive triumph but, like Mill Reef, all good things had to come to an end. He was finally beaten by Roberto in the Benson and Hedges Cup at York and, at the end of the season, with another two wins to his credit, he, too, retired.

Brigadier Gerard: won 15 races in succession

Tricky Trevino's greatest escape

THE ungainly swing that made Lee Trevino one of golf's greats had its critics. Even Trevino admitted that "no one who ever had lessons would have a swing like mine". But because it was flat at the bottom of the arc and his follow through was perfect it was one of the most consistent swings in the game. Even on bad days Trevino could challenge the best.

Supermex and Tony Jacklin led a cluster of players in the Open and were paired for the last two rounds at Muirfield. Jacklin spent two days watching one of the greatest escapes in golf.

Trevino finished the third round with five successive birdies for a 66, including a bunker shot at the 16th which hit the flag and dropped into the hole. Trevino continued to ride his luck on the last day, but at the par-five 17th he drove into a bunker, pulled his third into the rough, hit his fourth across the green into more rough and appeared to have given up hope of retaining the title.

There was one last trick. He chipped in for a par, a stunned Jacklin three-putted and Trevino won by one shot from Jack Nicklaus with Jacklin two behind. Trevino quipped: "God is a Mexican."

Trevino: stunned Jacklin

England silence Springboks

ENGLAND pulled off one of their finest victories by beating the Springboks 18-9 on a seven-match tour of South Africa. John Pullin's side were facing a hiding to nothing. They had failed to win a game in the disrupted Five Nations programme and struggled to stay unbeaten before the only Test in Johannesburg. Then they silenced the Springboks as Sam Doble scored 14 points with four penalties and a conversion and Alan Morley scored a try.

First time lucky for Leicester

LEICESTERSHIRE proudly placed a piece of silverware in their trophy cabinet for the first time in their 78-year history. And it was the newest trophy on offer, the Benson and Hedges Cup.

The county, thriving under the captaincy of Ray Illingworth, beat Yorkshire by five wickets in the inaugural final. The B&H Cup was slotted in at the start of an already busy summer and soon acquired the status of the Football League Cup, something to win but not quite the big one.

FOR THE RECORD

CYCLING
■ Eddie Merckx won his fourth successive Tour de France.

FOOTBALL
■ Spurs became the first British club to win two European trophies when they beat Wolves 3-2 on aggregate to clinch the Uefa Cup. It was also the first all-British final.

TENNIS
■ The Association of Tennis Professionals was formed at Forest Hills. Cliff Drysdale was elected president and Jack Kramer executive director.

AUGUST

MOTOR RACING

Speedy title for Fittipaldi

EMERSON FITTIPALDI, at 25 years and eight months, became the youngest ever world champion. The Brazilian seemed destined from birth to be the first driver from his country to capture the world crown.

The son of a motor racing journalist, he was the Brazilian karting champion at 18 and Formula Vee champion at 20. At 23 he won his first Grand Prix after the tragic death of Jochen Rindt elevated Fittipaldi into the position of Lotus team leader.

The season was supposed to have been dominated by Fittipaldi's continuous tussle with the previous season's champion, Jackie Stewart. But although the Brazilian's Lotus-Ford gave him five GP victories compared with the Scot's Tyrrell-Ford's four, Fittipaldi had the championship wrapped up by the Italian GP in September.

Fittipaldi: youngest champion

GOLF

Nicklaus quick to strike again

JACK NICKLAUS was one of the slowest players in professional golf, but the fastest collector of major titles. He took his fourth Masters crown with a one under-par 286 at Augusta and then added the US Open with a three-shot win at Pebble Beach, California.

The victories put Nicklaus on course for the Grand Slam, but he was denied by Lee Trevino in the Open. A second place at the Open and a tie for 13th in the US PGA was the closest Nicklaus came to achieving the Grand Slam.

FOOTBALL

Allison: in charge

FOR THE RECORD

FOOTBALL

■ Joe Mercer quit as the manager of Manchester City in August and handed over to his assistant, Malcolm Allison.

■ Mansfield, of the Third Division, did not score a League goal at home until December 18 against Plymouth, 833 goalless minutes of football.

MOTORCYCLING

■ Giacomo Agostini won a record seventh successive 500cc world championship on his MV. He also rode to his fifth victory in a row in the Isle of Man Senior TT race.

RUGBY LEAGUE

■ The Rugby Football League changed the four-tackle rule to six tackles.

TENNIS

■ The United States retained the Davis Cup for the fifth successive year. It was the first time the challenge round was abolished.

OLYMPIC GAMES

All-American nightmare

THE Olympic Games were remarkable for a series of unusual incidents involving Americans. Jim Ryun, the world 1500m record holder, was put in the wrong heat when his best time submitted by the American team was interpreted as a slow 1500m run instead of a fast one-mile time. Ryun fell and failed to make the final.

Then three American sprinters confused their race times and were in their room when they heard their 100m event announced on the television. Robert Taylor was the only one to reach the stadium in time, and he won the silver medal.

The Americans' basketball reign had a bizarre ending after 63 successive victories since 1936. The United States were leading 50-49 in the final against the Soviet Union when the horn sounded for full-time. An official overruled the referee and ordered another second to be played. Then the English secretary-general of FIBA, Dr William Jones, said the clock had been incorrectly set and another three seconds had to be played. The Soviet Union threw a pass the length of the court and Aleksandr Belov knocked over two American defenders to score, giving his team a 51-50 victory. The furious Americans went home without their silver medals.

Another man who did not take a medal home was Norbert Sudhaus, who joined the marathon just outside the stadium and was cheered home by the crowd who believed he had won. The 22-year-old student was led off by officials.

GOLF

Jacklin denied revenge

THE World Matchplay at Wentworth was won by Tom Weiskopf, but the lasting memories were of a great battle between Tony Jacklin and Lee Trevino in the semi-finals. Trevino had beaten Jacklin at the last green in the Ryder Cup and snatched the Open title from him. This time Jacklin was four down at the halfway stage of their 36-hole semi-final, shot 63 in the afternoon and still lost by one hole.

MOTORCYCLING

Agostini: 500cc champion for the seventh time

Massacre eclipses Spitz's feat

THE Olympic complex in Munich echoed to cheers for Mark Spitz during a glorious first week of the XX Games until 11 Israelis were gunned down in a Palestinian terrorist attack.

The 11th day of the Games was about to dawn when a group of Palestinian guerrillas scaled the fence surrounding the Olympic Village, made their way to 31 Connollystrasse and gunned down two Israeli athletes. They took another nine hostages.

After lengthy negotiations, the terrorists were allowed to take their hostages to the nearby Fürstenfeld-bruk airport by helicopter. As soon as the helicopters landed, a gun battle started and the nine hostages, one German policeman and five guerrillas were killed.

The Games were suspended for 24 hours and the next morning a memorial service for the Israelis was held in the Olympic stadium. The Israeli team went home and several other athletes withdrew.

The incident cast a shadow over the performance of the 24-year-old Spitz, who won a remarkable seven gold medals in the 100m and 200m freestyle, the 100m and 200m butterfly, the 4x100m and 4x200m freestyle relays and the 4x100m medley relay. All seven times were world records.

The water bubbled with records all week. A total of 34 world and 84 Olympic records were broken or equalled, with the United States taking 17 of the 29 gold medals. But it was not all plain sailing for the Americans. Rick DeMont was disqualified after winning the 400m backstroke. American officials forgot to tell the IOC that he was using ephedrine to alleviate his asthma, and when the banned substance showed up in a drugs test he was disqualified.

As well as Spitz, there were many other memorable performances during the Games. The Finn Lasse Viren won the 5,000m and 10,000m, John Akii-Bua of Uganda broke David Hemery's 400m hurdles world record and the Cuban heavyweight Teofilo Stevenson won his boxing gold medal in less than six rounds. Shane Gould of Australia won three gold medals, a silver and a bronze in the swimming pool.

Britain took home four gold medals, five silver and nine bronze. The 33-year-old Mary Peters broke the pentathlon world record with 4,801 points and Britain retained the three day eventing title. Richard Meade, on Laurieston, won the individual gold medal.

Spitz: seven golds

> ❛ *The medals weighed a lot. They have heavy, crazy chains. Really, it was hard to stand up straight wearing them all at one thing* ❜
>
> **Mark Spitz**

THE MAGNIFICENT SEVEN

100m freestyle
1 Mark Spitz (US) 51.22sec
2 Jerry Heidenreich (US) 51.65
3 Vladimir Bure (USSR) 51.77

200m freestyle
1 Mark Spitz (US) 1min 52.78sec
2 Steven Genter (US) 1:53.73
3 Werner Lampe (France) 1:53.99

100m butterfly
1 Mark Spitz (US) 54.27sec
2 Bruce Robertson (Canada) 55.56
3 Jerry Heidenreich (US) 55.74

200m butterfly
1 Mark Spitz (US) 2min 00.70sec
2 Gary Hall (US) 2:02.86
3 Robin Backhaus (US) 2:03.23

4x100m freestyle relay
1 United States 3min 26.42sec
2 Soviet Union 3:29.72
3 East Germany 3:32.42

4x200m freestyle relay
1 United States 7min 35.78sec
2 France 7:41.69
3 Soviet Union 7:45.76

4x100m medley relay
1 United States 3min 48.16sec
2 East Germany 3:52.12
3 Canada 3:52.26

Peters: world record 4,801 points in the pentathlon

Frazier and Ali blow up

Foreman and Frazier: one-sided battle in Kingston, Jamaica

RUGBY LEAGUE

Grand kick-off by Watkins

SALFORD were desperate to find a kicker in 1970 and crossed their fingers when they handed the job to David Watkins. But the former Welsh rugby union captain proved a sensation and two seasons later kicked a record 221 goals.

Watkins used the then unusual round-the-corner style while others were still toe-punting. He helped Salford win the Lancashire Cup and reach the John Player Trophy final, and came within four points of beating the record 496 points in a season by Lewis Jones in 1957. But he was overlooked for the three Tests when Britain could well have done with his kicking as Australia regained the Ashes.

SQUASH

No stopping Barrington

JONAH BARRINGTON won his sixth British Open title with the dedication and determination that made him one of the greatest players in history. It was his fourth successive victory.

The left-hander, who was born in Cornwall but played for Ireland, broke the Australian, Egyptian and Pakistani domination with intense training. His regimen made him arguably the fittest man in the world. He had been a greenkeeper, a milkman and an artist's model before turning professional in February 1969. He then lost 13 of his 15 exhibition matches against Australian rival Geoff Hunt.

JOE FRAZIER and Muhammad Ali proved that nothing in the world of boxing is certain. As the world was whetting its appetite for the re-match both of them blew up in the ring.

In Kingston, Jamaica, on January 22 Frazier defended his title against George Foreman. Still dining out on his fabulous victory over the legendary Ali, he took the challenge too lightly. Foreman had followed Frazier as the Olympic champion and then won 37 fights in succession as a professional, with 34 inside the distance.

FOOTBALL

Charlton: Bobby's last game

Frazier, meanwhile, had enjoyed two easy defences of his title and seemed more preoccupied with working out with his rock group, The Knockouts.

Then the hit parade took on a new meaning. Frazier attacked continuously but Foreman would not take a step backwards. Instead, he attacked the champion's jaw. Two rounds and six knockdowns later, an out-of-tune and reeling Frazier was an ex-champ when the referee stopped the fight.

Ali, meanwhile, had been taking his boxing more seriously.

Having finally won his appeal against his draft conviction, he quickly rattled off 10 victories across the globe until March, when he ran into the ex-marine Ken Norton, in San Diego. Norton broke Ali's jaw and stole a points decision.

Ali recaptured some of his pride by beating Norton in his next fight, but even then he had to pull out all the stops in the last round. Now Ali and Frazier would have to meet again, not for the world title, but for the right to fight the new king, George Foreman.

FOR THE RECORD

CRICKET
■ Dennis Amiss failed by a single run to score three centuries in successive Tests during England's tour of Pakistan.

DOGSLED RACING
■ Dick Wilmarth was the first winner of the Iditarod Trial from Anchorage to Nome in Alaska.

FOOTBALL
■ Jack Charlton retired from the game on April 28. On the same day, his brother Bobby played his last game for Manchester United.

■ Malcolm Allison resigned as manager of Manchester City in April after only eight months in the job.

GOLF
■ Peter Oosterhuis led by three shots going into the final round of the Masters but finished third with a 74.

RUGBY LEAGUE
■ After flirting with a Second Division on two previous occasions, the sport tried a third time and succeeded. Bradford Northern were the first champions, gaining promotion with York, Keighley and Halifax.

RUGBY UNION
■ Wales won the Five Nations championship for the fourth consecutive occasion when all five countries finished level on points for the first time in the 63-year history of the competition.

Welsh wizards conjure epic try

WHEN Phil Bennett fielded a deep kick a few feet from his tryline he was expected to kick for touch. But in true Barbarians style he launched a bold attack in the second minute of the traditional end-of-tour fixture against New Zealand at a packed Cardiff Arms Park.

Bennett side-stepped one advancing All Black, then another, then another. He swung the ball to JPR Williams, who held off a tackle from Bryan Williams and passed to John Pullin. Then, in a breathtaking break down the left flank involving passes between backs and forwards, the ball moved from John Dawes to Tommy David to Derek Quinnell and finally to Gareth Edwards. The little Welsh scrum-half had the crowd on its feet as he dived into the corner to score The Try.

It was acclaimed as the greatest try of all time, was preserved on film and in later years became available in almost every video store in the country. The Try sparked a scoring spree by a Barbarians combination built around the successful Welsh contingent in the 1971 British Lions party.

They led 17-0 at half-time and held off the All Blacks to win 23-11 in one of the finest matches on British soil. Local supporters were quick to realise that Pullin was the only person involved in The Try who was not a Welshman, but they gave credit where it was due. They were so impressed with David Duckham, the English wing, they dubbed him Dai Duckham.

The All Blacks had lost four of their previous 32 matches on the gruelling tour, including a 9-3 defeat against Llanelli in the club's centenary year. A 10-10 draw with Ireland robbed them of the Grand Slam.

Red Rum overhauls Crisp in agonising finish to the Grand National

Crisp cut down in final strides

CRISP was going to win the Grand National. There was no doubt about it. He was at least 20 lengths clear at Becher's on the second circuit and jumping like a stag. It was no matter that he wasn't really a stayer and he was carrying top weight. He was cruising and the fences just flew by.

It did matter. Two fences from home he started to slow. Richard Pitman, Crisp's jockey, was anxiously looking over his shoulder and Fred Winter, his trainer, feared the worst.

Even then, though, it looked as if his lead, although shrinking by the second, would just be enough. There was only one fence to go and Crisp, the best jumper in the land,

hit it hard. He lurched on and, still, he was not beaten.

But, inexorably, Brian Fletcher was catching up. As Crisp looked like he was sinking in quicksand the gap narrowed — four lengths, two lengths, one length. And in the final strides Red Rum squeezed past to win by ¾ of a length in record time.

Indian spin quartet strike a chord

ENGLAND were teased and tormented for eight weeks by four of the world's leading spinners who proved a nightmare for batsmen and typists alike. Bishan Singh Bedi, Bhagwat Subramanya Chandrasekhar, Erapally Anantharao Srinivasa Prasanna and Srinivasaraghavan Venkataraghavan bowled India to a 2-1 triumph in their five-match series.

England had learned to live with the lethal fast bowling of the Australians and West Indians down the years. Now they faced an examination at a different tempo and failed. The Four Musketeers, as they became known, took 197 of the 244 wickets on their tour of England in 1971. They were even more dominant on familiar ground, thriving on the dry, hard pitches.

They captured 70 of the 73

Bedi bamboozles Keith Fletcher in the third Test

English wickets to fall to an Indian side who only employed opening bowlers to take the shine off the ball. Chandra was the most suc-

cessful, taking 35 wickets at 18.91. His haul was an Indian record. Bedi took 24 wickets, Prasanna 10 and Venkat one.

GOLF

Miller hits his way to first major

AMERICA was looking for a successor to Jack Nicklaus even when the Golden Bear was in his prime. And in Johnny Miller, tall and blond and hungry, they believed they had found their man.

Miller appeared to confirm his new-found status with one of the greatest comebacks in the US Open. He was six strokes behind when he set out for his final round one hour ahead of the leaders at Oakmont, Pennsylvania. But he stirred the field with birdies on the first four holes, dropped a shot at the eighth and picked it up at the next to turn in 32. Three more birdies brought him charging home in 31 for a record 63. It was a long wait but when John Schlee finished one behind Miller celebrated his first major victory.

Nicklaus was also collecting major titles. His US PGA victory in Cleveland took his tally to 14 majors, one ahead of Bobby Jones.

Miller: great comeback

TENNIS

Leading players veto Wimbledon

Kodes: winner of the men's singles at Wimbledon

THE All England Lawn Tennis and Croquet Club believed its Wimbledon championships were bigger than the players. Some would agree. With overpriced strawberries and cream, cold champagne and exclusive seating for the well-heeled, the event was regarded by many as a social rather than a sporting occasion. In the summer, the Wimbledon hierarchy showed their true colours. The well-being of the players and the quality of the field counted for nought.

The Yugoslav Nikki Pilic had failed to turn out for a Davis Cup match and was suspended. He then went ahead and played in the French Open, reaching the final. The International Lawn Tennis Federation ruled that his suspension would start after the Paris event. But Pilic went to Rome and was admitted into the Italian Open.

His next stop was Wimbledon. The fledgling Association of Tennis Professionals regarded the suspension as invalid, but Wimbledon officials would not budge. So the case went to a High Court judge who ruled for the establishment. Pilic was out.

The ATP asked their players to withdraw and 79 of their 82 members pulled out. Only Ilie Nastase, Roger Taylor and the Australian Ray Keldie refused and were fined. Wimbledon officials hastily scrapped the qualifying rounds, seeded the remaining players and put novices into the tournament.

The biggest drawcard was Bjorn Borg, a 17-year-old Swede with blue eyes and blond hair who was mobbed by female teenagers wherever he went. He showed a cool temperament in his first match on the Centre Court by beating Premjit Lall 6-3 6-4 9-8. The tie-break lasted a record 38 points before Borg won 20-18. But the title went to the Czech Jan Kodes who beat Alex Metreveli of the Soviet Union 6-1 9-8 (7-5) 6-3 in the final.

RUGBY UNION

England rise to the occasion

ENGLAND startled the world for the second time in two years by beating New Zealand 16-10 in Auckland. John Pullin's side struggled to a 13-12 win against Fiji and lost all three of the matches against provincial opposition. However, the English scrum-half Jan Webster set up two tries to complete a rare rugby double. England had beaten the Springboks and the All Blacks on their home grounds.

GOLF

Weiskopf shoots to the front

TOM WEISKOPF used his skill at golf to finance his great passion for hunting. He added £5,500 to his bank balance by shooting enough birdies at Troon to stay in front from start to finish in the Open. Gene Sarazen, 50 years after his first appearance in the Open, reached the eighth hole, the Postage Stamp, in the first round, took a five-iron from his bag and hit a hole in one. Sarazen said: "I want a copy of the shot on film to take to heaven and show Walter Hagen what a 71-year-old can still get up to."

Weiskopf: uncatchable

Sunderland's dream comes true

THIS was the fairytale Cup final. Second Division Sunderland came to Wembley on May 5 with a huge army of fans from Wearside who roared themselves hoarse and believed they would stuff Leeds, the team that kept saying they were the greatest club side in Europe.

This was no ordinary team they were intent on embarrassing — they were the Cup holders, a team who had in the past five years won the League championship, the Fairs Cup twice, the League Cup and been runners-up in Leagues and Cups so many times that everybody had stopped counting.

Leeds were the hottest favourites for years until Ian Porterfield swivelled and lashed a right-foot shot from a corner into the Leeds net. For the next 60 minutes Leeds hurled white shirt after shirt at the Sunderland goal. But Jim Montgomery was having the time of his life, including one double save that broke the hearts of the Leeds players.

The 1-0 victory will always be remembered for the moment after the final whistle when Sunderland's manager, Bob Stokoe, raced ecstatically right across Wembley to embrace Montgomery, two men whose belief in fairytales had come magically true.

Bedford: world record

England crash to record defeat

West Indian fans celebrate their victory calypso-style at Lord's

RAY ILLINGWORTH'S tenure of the England hot seat came to an abrupt end after an embarrassing defeat by West Indies in the third Test at Lord's. The Yorkshireman, who led the team for 31 of his 61 Tests, was given the boot after the West Indians won by an innings and 226 runs.

Illingworth could offer no excuses. "We were outbatted, outbowled and outfielded," he said.

The tourists dominated the series, ending a 20-match run without victory in the first Test with a 158-run triumph. The second Test was drawn. The West Indians were in ascendancy, the English in decline. The West Indies captaincy had been handed from Garry Sobers to Rohan Kanhai and most of the party were familiar with English conditions, having honed their skills on the county circuit.

Sobers and Kanhai signed off in their last Test in England by scoring 150s at Lord's. A crowd of 28,000 packed the ground on the Saturday afternoon only to find themselves evacuated after a bomb hoax during the height of an IRA bomb campaign.

Sobers played a minor role in the one-day series which was drawn 1-1. He was dismissed for a duck in his only innings and failed to take a wicket. So the world's greatest all-rounder, whose attacking batting would have been ideally suited to the demands of the abridged game, had a career average of 0.00 in one-day internationals.

FOR THE RECORD

ATHLETICS
■ Dave Bedford slashed nearly eight seconds off Lasse Viren's 10,000m world record with a time of 27min 30.8sec in London on July 13.

CRICKET
■ Colin Cowdrey became the 16th batsman to score 100 first-class centuries.

■ Durham became the first Minor County to beat a first-class team, winning by five wickets against Yorkshire at Harrogate in the Gillette Cup.

■ New Zealand came within 38 runs of winning their first-ever Test in England after a mammoth fourth innings total of 440 at Trent Bridge. It was a remarkable turnaround after they had been dismissed for only 97 in the first innings.

■ England won the first women's World Cup.

FOOTBALL
■ The Greek referee Christos Michas was suspended for cheating after Leeds lost the European Cup Winners Cup final 1-0 to Milan in Salonika.

■ Liverpool won the Uefa Cup 3-2 on aggregate from Borussia Moenchengladbach and became the first English side to win the League and a European trophy in the same season.

■ Bobby Moore became England's most capped player when he played in his 107th, and penultimate, international for England against Italy at Turin in June.

HOCKEY
■ Holland triumphed in the men's World Cup.

SWIMMING

Winner just keeps on going

THE touch-timing board at the first world championships in Belgrade was moved in one centimetre after the pool was measured. But despite their attention to detail, bungling officials forgot to blow the warning whistle for the last lap in the 1500m freestyle.

So after Steve Holland won the 16-length event he kept swimming. It was only 2½ lengths later that the penny dropped and the 15-year-old Australian stopped. Along the way he had broken the 800m world record by 6.2sec and the 1500m mark by 14.8sec.

TENNIS

King scores in battle of sexes

BILLIE JEAN KING fought long and hard to close the vast gap between men's and women's prize-money. Bobby Riggs provided her with the finest opportunity to put her cause on the world stage. The 55-year-old, who had been triple champion at Wimbledon in 1939, challenged her to a "Battle of the Sexes". King turned the event into a spectacle in front of 30,500 people in the Houston Astrodome, the largest crowd to watch a match, and millions of television viewers. She was paraded into the arena in a glittering dress and won 6-4 6-3 6-3.

FOOTBALL

Clown makes a fool of England

THE clown had the last laugh at Wembley on October 17. England needed to beat Poland to qualify for the World Cup finals in West Germany the following summer. According to Brian Clough, TV pundit and Derby County manager, the game was in the bag because the Polish goalkeeper, Jan Tomaszewski, was "a clown".

England hit all parts of the woodwork and were awarded 26 corners to Poland's two. But, apart from a penalty, they could not get past the clown. He stopped England's scoring attempts with every part of his body: foot, leg, torso, hand, fingertip, fist. He was brilliant, he was lucky and sometimes just plain crazy.

The Poles scored first in the 57th minute when Lato and Domarski pounced on an error by Hunter as England were committed to attack. Six minutes later, with Allan Clarke's penalty, they were level. But try as England might, including last minute substitutions, there was some part of the clown's body, or a defender clearing off the line, to thwart them. The score stayed at 1-1 and England were out of the World Cup finals for the first time.

Tomaszewski: denied England a place in the finals

MOTOR RACING

Tragedy drives Stewart to quit

Stewart: won 27 Grands Prix out of 99 starts

JACKIE STEWART won the world championship, pulled out of the last race of the season when his teammate was killed and quit the racetrack for good. Stewart had won five of the year's Grands Prix when his colleague Francois Cevert was killed in practice for the United States GP at Watkins Glen on October 6. Stewart and the Tyrrell team immediately withdrew.

Stewart had little else to prove. He was a three-times world champion and out of 99 starts he had won 27. When he won the Dutch GP he had surpassed the late Jim Clark's world record of 25 wins.

Stewart had survived a bad accident at Spa in 1966 and retiring at the top, and alive, was a characteristically brave decision by one of the greatest champions to have graced the circuit. Too many colleagues, friends and fellow-stars of his time had paid the ultimate price of the sport and lost their lives.

Clough and Taylor desert Derby

BRIAN CLOUGH, Britain's most outspoken manager, and his Svengali assistant Peter Taylor walked out on Derby County, the club they rescued from the doldrums and took to dizzying heights. So dizzying it seemed that the club was not big enough for both the manager and the chairman, Sam Longson.

Somebody had to go, and it was Clough. But not without a public, and acrimonious, row that spilled over into the dressing room and the streets. The players were so unhappy that they threatened a strike. The town was up in arms and there were pickets and and placards outside the ground.

In 1967, when they joined Derby County, then languishing in the Second Division, Clough and Taylor were unknown quantities from lowly Hartlepools. By 1969 they had completely rebuilt the team and their young side had run away with the Second Division championship. Last year they won the League championship for the first time in Derby's history, and followed that with a European Cup

Happier days: Clough and Taylor with Derby's first-ever championship trophy

semi-final place. It was little wonder players and public were distraught at losing a pair of apparent miracle workers.

The clash between Clough and Longson had been boiling over for some time. Clough frequently went behind the board's back to buy, or attempt to buy, players for large

sums of money. His frequent appearances on TV and his articles in the press infuriated the old guard. His published outspokenness angered football's establishment and embarrassed Longson and his board. Clough was given an ultimatum: Desist or go. Clough decided to call Longson's bluff.

The chairman moved quickly to find a replacement for the disruptive duo and Dave Mackay, a former captain, was installed. He quelled the players' mutiny, but could do little about the fans. Clough and Taylor, surprisingly, went to Third Division Brighton. Attendances trebled overnight.

FOR THE RECORD

BOXING
■ Britain and New York withdrew recognition of Roberto Duran in September for failing to honour a contract with Madison Square Garden to defend his lightweight title against Ken Buchanan.

FOOTBALL
■ The first change in promotion and relegation for nearly 80 years was introduced for the 1973-74 season. There would be three clubs relegated from the First and Second Divisions with three promoted from the Second and Third.

■ Willie Ormond took over from Tommy Docherty as the Scotland manager.

■ Denis Follows retired as the FA secretary and was replaced by Ted Croker.

GOLF
■ The United States retained the Ryder Cup when they beat Britain 16-10 with six matches halved at Muirfield. It was the first time the event was held in Scotland.

■ Gary Player beat Graham Marsh at the 40th hole in the longest final of the World Matchplay championship at Wentworth.

■ Kathy Whitworth was the leading money-winner on the US LPGA Tour for a record eighth year with $82,864.25.

MOTORCYCLING
■ Phil Read won his first 500cc world championship. The British rider had previously won titles in the 125cc and 250cc classes.

RACING
■ Lord Leverhulme, the Senior Steward, announced in October that women were to be allowed to ride as amateurs in 1974 and as full professionals in 1975.

TAEKWONDO
■ South Korea dominated the first world championships in Seoul.

TENNIS
■ Australia broke the United States' five-year domination of the Davis Cup, winning 5-0 in Cleveland in the first indoor final.

Read: 500cc crown to go with his other titles

GOLF

Gritty Player confounds his many critics

A TYPICALLY tenacious round of 66 at Augusta proved the turning point in one of Gary Player's finest years. Many believed that the South African was past his best before the third round of the Masters. Player had other ideas. He came back from five shots behind to join the leaders for the final day, then nosed ahead of the field to win by two shots from Dave Stockton and Tom Weiskopf. Player added the Open at Royal Lytham to his honours, beating Peter Oosterhuis by four shots in strong winds. It was the first Open where the big ball was compulsory.

He also recorded the 100th win of his career when he took the Australian Open and finished the year with a spectacular 59 to win the Brazilian Open.

Player: spectacular year

CRICKET

England spoil grand finale

ENGLAND ruined the farewell party for Rohan Kanhai and Garry Sobers in Port of Spain, Trinidad on April 5.

Everything was set up for a grand send-off for one of the world's finest batsmen and the sport's greatest all-rounder. The West Indies were 2-1 up in the series and heading for another victory when they began the final day at 30 without loss chasing 266 to win.

Alas, Tony Greig, who had taken eight for 86 in the first innings, captured five for 70 to

KANHAI'S RECORD

	FIRST-CLASS	TESTS (79)
Innings	669	137
Not out	82	6
Runs	28,774	6,227
Highest	256	256
Average	49.01	47.53
Hundreds	83	15
Wickets	18 at 56.00	0 for 85
Catches	318	50
Stumpings	7	–

> ❝ I never doubted my batting ability from the day I could hold a piece of wood between two small grimy hands ❞
>
> **Rohan Kanhai**

help England to a 28-run victory with an hour to spare. Kanhai was out for seven and Sobers for 20.

But the pair had played their part in an eventful series. Kanhai, the captain, blended the young and old in his side to lay the foundations for the most successful era in West Indian cricket. Although he had a disappointing series with the bat, the Guyanese right-hander displayed his characteristic sweep, which usually ended with him lying on his back and the ball in the stands. Sobers's contribution with both bat and ball was the swansong of an unparalleled career.

Greig took 24 wickets in the series and was involved in an explosive incident in the first Test, running out Alvin Kallicharran on the last ball of the day when the West Indian strayed from his crease. He was given out but England withdrew the appeal overnight and the little left-hander added 16 runs the next day.

Kanhai: laid foundations

FOOTBALL

Ramsey pays the price of failure

SIR ALF RAMSEY was never going to survive as manager after England were embarrassingly eliminated from the World Cup finals by Poland at Wembley.

Ramsey had never been a popular manager with the public or press. He was diffident, stand-offish and uncommunicative. By 1974 his myriad critics had forgotten the euphoria of the 1966 World Cup triumph and the knives were out.

Sir Harold Thompson, the vice-chairman of the FA, was adamant that Ramsey should be sacked and he was on April 21, although the decision was not made public until May 1. Joe Mercer, the former manager of Manchester City, was appointed as caretaker manager

and enjoyed a wonderful spell, losing only one of seven matches.

On July 4, Don Revie, of Leeds, and the outstanding English manager of the day, was appointed England manager. When Alan Hardaker, the secretary of the League, found out he told the FA secretary: "You must be off your heads." And later Hardaker wrote: "Revie as England manager was a classic case of poacher turning gamekeeper."

Revie's first full match in charge was against Czechoslovakia at Wembley in a European championship qualifier on October 30. Two goals from Colin Bell and one from Mike Channon gave Revie a 3-0 victory. It was heralded as a new dawn.

Ramsey: sacked

RAMSEY'S RECORD AS ENGLAND MANAGER

1962-74	
Played 113	Lost 17
Won 69	Goals For 224
Drawn 27	Goals Against 99

Bayi storms away to smash 1500m record in breathtaking race

Beaten again: Foster can only finish second in the 5,000m

NEW ZEALAND were expecting great things from their talented middle-distance runners Rod Dixon and John Walker in the Commonwealth Games in Christchurch. Instead they witnessed a great 1500m run on February 2.

Filbert Bayi, a 20-year-old Tanzanian who loved to run from the front, set a cracking pace, with 54.4sec for the first 400m and 1min 51.8sec for the 800m. He was 10 metres ahead of a strong field and after tiring in the final stretch came home in 3:32.2 to break Jim Ryan's world record by nearly a second. The next six runners all set personal bests or national records, including Brendan Foster whose 3:37.64 broke the British record even though he was only seventh.

Persistent Amiss hits hot streak

DENNIS AMISS would have provided an excellent advertisement for suntan lotion. The England opener spent more hours at the crease than in any of his previous 15 years in first-class cricket.

He was the most prolific scorer of the year, amassing 1,379 runs in 13 Tests at an average of 68.95. His first great deed was to save England from certain defeat in the second Test against the West Indies in Kingston when he made an unbeaten 262 in 9½ hours.

Warwickshire's right-hander, whose repertoire was chiefly limited to scoring off the front foot, hit 663 runs in the series at an average of 82.87. He returned home to help England to a clean sweep in the three-match series against India and maintained his form in the drawn series against Pakistan later in the summer.

Amiss then took his bat to Australia where he completed his tally with a solid 90 off Dennis Lillee and Jeff Thomson.

Ali dances to sweet revenge over Frazier

ALI-FRAZIER II followed much the same script as the original, except this time, on January 28, Ali won. Ali danced, counter-attacked and kept hitting Frazier's head. Smokin' Joe kept relentlessly pursuing Ali's body. Frazier was fortunate in the second round when the referee mistakenly thought he had heard the bell and stopped Ali from finishing off Frazier.

Once again, the fight went the distance in Madison Square Garden and although Ali was in serious trouble in the seventh and eighth rounds he rallied to gain an unanimous points decision and a title fight with George Foreman.

Hartono: seventh title

FOR THE RECORD

BADMINTON
■ Rudy Hartono of Indonesia won a seventh successive All England title.

CRICKET
■ Greg Chappell, with 247 not out and 133 against New Zealand in Wellington, scored the then highest aggregate in a Test.

■ Australia beat New Zealand by an innings and 25 runs in the first official Test between the two countries in Australia.

FOOTBALL
■ Leeds were unbeaten in their first 29 games and ran away with the League title, finishing five points clear of Liverpool.

■ Denis Law, in his last League match, scored a late goal for Manchester City on April 27 and sent his former club, Manchester United, down to the Second Division. In 1963, Law, then playing for Manchester United against Manchester City, won a penalty that relegated City and kept United up.

■ Middlesbrough won the Second Division championship by the record margin of 15 points.

MOTOR RACING
■ The Philip Morris cigarette company signed a deal with McLaren to have their cars painted in the red and white colours of Marlboro.

RUGBY LEAGUE
■ Britain failed to regain the Ashes in Australia when they were beaten 22-18 in the final Test.

RUGBY UNION
■ Hawick became the first Scottish club champions. They held the title for five years.

RUGBY UNION

McBride's Lions stay undefeated

THE Springboks had never lost a major series on home soil, but 31 players were moulded into the greatest-ever British Lions side under the Irishman Willie-John McBride and they went rampaging through the veldt. The Lions knocked over all their opposition until a local referee robbed them of a perfect record in the last game of their 22-match tour.

The score was 13-13 in the fourth Test in Johannesburg when Fergus Slattery crossed the Springbok line in the closing minutes. The referee was one of only a few people in the stadium who believed that the Irishman had not scored.

The Lions started the tour with trepidation. Three of their key backline players — Gerald Davies, David Duckham and Mike Gibson — were unavailable and several stars of the successful 1971 visit to New Zealand were missing.

But McBride, on a record fifth Lions tour, instilled pride in his players that produced the application and discipline to break down the invincibility of the South Africans. The Lions, who won the first Test 9-3 in the mud in Cape Town, gave their best display in the second Test in Pretoria, running in five tries to win 28-9 — a record defeat for the Springboks. The panic-struck South African selectors made 11 changes for the next match, but again the tourists

McBride: record tour

were devastating, winning 26-9.

However, it was not all hard work for the Lions. Two planes were hired to take them to the Kruger National Park for a few days' relaxation. One plane was stocked with beer and was sent back to Johannesburg a day later for a refill.

THE LIONS ON SAFARI

May 15	Western Transvaal 59-13
May 18	South West Africa 23-16
May 22	Boland 33-6
May 25	Eastern Province 28-14
May 29	South Western Districts 97-0
June 1	Western Province 17-8
June 4	Proteas 37-6
June 8	SOUTH AFRICA (Cape Town) 12-3
June 11	Southern Universities 26-4
June 15	Transvaal 23-15
June 18	Rhodesia 42-6
June 22	SOUTH AFRICA (Pretoria) 28-9
June 27	Quaggas 20-16
June 29	Orange Free State 11-9
July 3	Griqualand West 69-16
July 6	Northern Transvaal 16-12
July 9	Leopards 56-10
July 13	SOUTH AFRICA (Port Elizabeth) 26-9
July 17	Border 26-6
July 20	Natal 34-6
July 23	Eastern Transvaal 33-10
July 27	SOUTH AFRICA (Johannesburg) 13-13

Tour record

P	W	D	L	F	A
22	21	1	0	729	207

CYCLING

Merckx reaches peak

EDDY MERCKX and the yellow jersey worn by the Tour de France leader had become synonymous by the time the Belgian powered into Paris. The 29-year-old had equalled the five victories by Jacques Anquetil.

Merckx reached other great milestones on the road to Paris which put him a notch above his rivals. The world's greatest cyclist donned the yellow jersey a record 96 times in seven races during his illustrious career. In 1969 he was the first to win the Tour, the points classification and the King of the Mountains in the same event. A year later he won a record eight stages and when he retired in the spring of 1978 to concentrate on manufacturing bikes he had collected a record 35 stage wins.

His career was blemished only once. He was disqualified in the 1969 Giro d'Italia for failing a drugs test but was later cleared. On another occasion when positive the drug was cough mixture.

> **‚ I don't need dope, I win on the strength of my legs ‛**
>
> **Eddy Merckx**

But Merckx was remembered better for his bravery, such as his ride in the 1975 Tour. He fractured a cheekbone after falling six stages from the finish and soldiered on against medical advice to finish second behind Bernard Thevenet. He said: "If I had not finished this race Thevenet's victory would not have looked as great as it is."

THE MERCKX MACHINE

Tour de France 1969, 1970, 1971, 1972, 1974

World championship 1967, 1971, 1974

Giro d'Italia 1968, 1970, 1972, 1973, 1974

Vuelta de España 1973

Milan-San Remo 1966, 1967, 1969, 1971, 1972, 1975, 1976

Tour of Flanders 1969, 1975

Paris-Roubaix 1968, 1970, 1973

Fleche Wallonne 1967, 1970, 1972, 1975

Liege-Bastogne-Liege 1969, 1971, 1972, 1973, 1975

Tour of Lombardy 1971, 1972

Paris-Nice 1969, 1970, 1971

Tour of Switzerland 1974

TENNIS

Love match has its points

CHRIS EVERT and Jimmy Connors were the talk of the circuit, the media and every women's magazine. The American pair were on top of the world — and engaged.

While Connors was winning three major titles, Evert broke through to take the French and Wimbledon titles. She thumped Olga Morozova 6-1 6-2 in the French final and then beat her 6-0 6-4 at Wimbledon. Her engagement to Connors was not made in heaven though, and they parted company later in the year.

The happy couple

Total Football wins the day

SCOTLAND were Britain's lone representatives in the World Cup in West Germany, and despite being the only country to be unbeaten in the tournament failed to reach the second round.

They had been drawn in a tough, but not impossible group with Brazil and Yugoslavia. Brazil were now without Pele, who had refused to play in another World Cup, and believing it was necessary because the Cup was being held in Europe, had virtually abandoned their "samba" style for a physical approach.

The minnows of the group were Zaire, whom Scotland met first. The naivety of the Scots was to prove their undoing as they only won 2-0. Yugoslavia promptly thumped nine past Zaire, and despite creditable draws against Brazil and Yugoslavia, Scotland were on the plane home courtesy of goal difference.

Poland had qualified at the expense of England and were the revelation of the tournament and unfortunate not to reach the final. Instead they finished third.

But most of all this was the World Cup of Total Football, when two players utterly bestrode the tournament, Johann Cruyff of Holland and Franz Beckenbauer of West Germany. Total Football was a positive response to the negative, defensive tactics perfected by the Italians. For the Germans it meant that the sweeper was free to spring

Opening shot: Cruyff wins a penalty in the first seconds

from behind his defence and launch attacks. In this role Beckenbauer was the pioneer and arch exponent.

For Holland it meant that attackers would suddenly become defenders, and vice versa. The conductor of this orchestra was Cruyff. The two countries and players clashed in a memorable final.

Before a German had touched a ball Cruyff had won a penalty. Holland kicked off and Cruyff began a stupendous run into the penalty area, swerved round one defender only to be brought down by another. Johann Neeskens promptly scored the fastest goal in a World Cup final. Ironically it

did Holland no good. Although they teased the Germans for the next 25 minutes they did not add to their score. The Dutch were too confident and too composed.

They paid for their casual attitude when Paul Breitner won a penalty and converted it and the Germans sensed the trophy was theirs. Two minutes from half-time the Germans scored again when Gerd Muller dragged a cross back and swept it into the net. The Dutch had their chances in the second half but inspired goalkeeping kept the score the same. So 20 years after West Germany had first won the World Cup they captured it again.

Brash Connors overwhelms popular Rosewall

THERE was no doubt who the Centre Court crowd were supporting when Jimmy Connors and Ken Rosewall stepped on to the green grass of Wimbledon for the men's singles final.

Connors was a 21-year-old American with a grunt, a blistering double-handed backhand and a mother prone to dressing in a purple trouser-suit and yelling: "C'mon Jimbo, c'mon Jimbo."

Rosewall, a 39-year-old Australian, was the sentimental favourite who had lost finals to Jaroslav Drobny in 1954, Lew Hoad in 1956 and John Newcombe in 1970. He had come back from match point down in the semis to beat Stan Smith 6-8 4-6 9-8 6-1 6-3 for one last crack at the crown 20 years after his first final.

But Jimbo wasn't bowing to sentiment. "People don't seem to

understand that it's a damn war out there," he said. "I don't go out there to love my enemy, I go out there to squash him."

Connors did just that. After losing the opening game, he took the next 10 on the trot. Rosewall staged a brief revival in the third set but went down 6-1 6-1 6-4. Connors then squashed Rosewall 6-1 6-0 6-1 in the US Open final to take his third major title of the year.

> *Jimmy Connors is loud, aggressive and with the face and hairstyle of a medieval varlet, he personifies a generation which tips its hat to no man*
>
> **Ian Wooldridge**

269

Muhammad Ali
The sting was in the tale

Harry Mullan

Few athletes have made the transition from the back of the paper to the news pages with more impact than Muhammad Ali, whose social significance matched his central role in rescuing his sport from terminal boredom in the 1960s. In both incarnations, first as Cassius Marcellus Clay and then, most memorably, under his adopted Moslem name he reflected and occasionally instigated the upheavals which America went through during his 20 years as the most recognisable face on earth.

His parents followed the creed of the upwardly-mobile blacks of those segregated times: work hard, fear God and keep out of trouble. The moderately comfortable lifestyle the young Cassius Clay enjoyed in Louisville, Kentucky, was far removed from the more stereotypical background of his arch-rival Joe Frazier, who deserted the poverty of a South Carolina cotton plantation for the ghettoes of Philadelphia. But it was Clay, not Frazier, who changed American blacks' perception of themselves.

Initially, he was a charmer. His outrageous self-praise, doggerel verse and correct predictions of the rounds in which his opponents would fall made him the world's most talked about sportsman. Clay's highly original approach to his trade, immortalised in the slogan "Float like a butterfly, sting like a bee" raised boxing from the depths of boring mediocrity in which it had floundered since Rocky Marciano and Sugar Ray Robinson left the stage.

Within three years of winning the Olympic light-heavyweight title in 1960 he had established himself as the leading contender for the heavyweight championship, and only Henry Cooper, with one glorious left hook which earned the Englishman sporting immortality, came close to beating him. When he forced a bewildered and demoralised Sonny Liston to surrender the heavyweight title on his stool at the end of the sixth round on February 25, 1964, it was the biggest upset the game had seen for nearly 30 years.

The dour, intimidating Liston had been considered unbeatable, with an unsavoury history and known Mob connections which cast a shadow over the sport. He was, in the literal as well as the theatrical sense of the word, a villain and Clay's victory should have ensured national hero status for the new champion. Instead, the morning after the fight he made an announcement which dramatically reversed the roles. His declaration of membership of the so-called Black Moslems, which he had secretly joined a few months previously, electrified and divided America. The Moslems were seen then as a subversive, revolutionary movement, preaching racial hatred and separation. When Clay went public the impact could not have been greater had he announced that he was also a communist gay.

His propaganda value to the movement was incalculable: his immediate renunciation of the "slave name" Clay was a powerfully symbolic act which made white Americans consider, probably for the first time, the fact that so many of their fellow countrymen had been robbed of their family's history. He gave the Moslems status and a platform from which to reach out to the rootless and disadvantaged. They used him, of course, but he was a willing tool and even his enemies eventually had to acknowledge his sincerity.

When he refused conscription for the Vietnam war in 1966 on the grounds that he was a minister of religion, boxing's various ruling bodies stripped him of his world title and banished him from the ring, although his action had no relevance to any country but his own. Ali's comment that "I ain't got no quarrel with those Viet Cong" outraged public opinion, yet his anti-war views, which he advanced at every opportunity, gradually came to be shared by the majority of young Americans. Eventually, in October 1970, he was relicensed by Atlanta of all places — once the heartland of white supremacy — and the second phase of his remarkable career was launched.

His long years of exile cost him his prime, and robbed him of the speed and extraordinarily fluent movement which was central to his style. Ali Mark 2 was a wholly different performer from the boxer who had danced unscathed through 10 title fights. Now, he relied on the ability to improvise, to devise ploys and strategies to defeat specific opponents. He turned puncher to knock out the Argentinian Iron Man Oscar Bonavena, and introduced the "rope-a-dope" in an unsuccessful bid to frustrate Joe Frazier in the first of their three epic clashes.

That fight, in March 1971, was more a world event than a boxing match — 300 million people watched on TV and closed circuit in 46 countries as, for the first time, two undefeated heavyweight champions clashed for the title and for an unprecedented purse of $2.5m apiece. Ali lost narrowly in a magnificent fight, but the grace and dignity with which he accepted defeat served to cement his rehabilitation in public affection.

> **❝ I ain't got no quarrel with those Viet Cong ❞**

Before they could be rematched, Frazier lost the title to the hulking George Foreman, a ferocious puncher whose crushing defeat of Ken Norton (who had out-pointed Ali in 1973) seemed to remove any hopes of a Second Coming. Foreman v Ali was made by Don King, who persuaded Zaire to put up $10m in government money for the privilege of becoming the first African country to host a heavyweight title fight. Ali, ever the unpredictable, shocked the world again by letting Foreman (arguably the hardest hitter in history) pound himself into exhaustion before Ali at last came off the ropes in the eighth to knock him out. It was a strategy requiring courage and endurance of superhuman dimension, and the punishment he soaked up that night must surely have contributed to his later, tragic decline.

He became a busy champion, defending 10 times in three years against opponents of assorted quality. Some were little more than exhibition matches, but there were also desperate struggles with Frazier (the "Thriller in Manila"), Norton and Earnie Shavers. Leon Spinks, a seven-fight novice whom he faced in Las Vegas in February 1978 was expected to be one of the easier jobs, but instead he hustled the ill-conditioned champion to a shock points defeat. Seven months later Ali became the only three-times heavyweight champion when he outboxed Spinks in the rematch in the New Orleans Superdome.

He should, of course, have quit on the spot. But his ego would not permit it, nor would the financial demands imposed on his resources by a large and parasitic entourage. A brief retirement ended in a pathetic attempt to reclaim the title from Larry Holmes, who was once his sparring partner, before his career finally petered out with an embarrassing points loss to the obscure Trevor Berbick in an episode which shamed the game. The illness which had such a harrowing effect in the subsequent decade had already taken hold. There were those in his camp who knew it, but nothing could be allowed to stand in the way of one last pay day. The greatest entertainer of them all surely deserved a better exit.

Rebel with a cause: The Louisville Lip conquered the world, and his stand on Vietnam made him a role-model for young blacks. A spectacular comeback enhanced his reputation but, sadly, his career faded with a pathetic display against Larry Holmes.

SEPTEMBER

1974

DECEMBER

CRICKET

Lillee and Thomson's deadly act

ENGLAND had found Dennis Lillee more than enough to handle during Australia's tour of England in 1972. Now he had a partner.

Jeff Thomson of New South Wales, who was even quicker than his teammate, devastated Mike Denness's team, who were two Tests down in the Ashes series by Christmas. Lillee and Thomson took 13 wickets in the first Test and 11 in the second. And the England injury toll was mounting. Dennis Amiss had a broken thumb, John Edrich a broken hand, David Lloyd a sore groin and Colin Cowdrey a long trip from England to help out. It was going to be a hard winter tour.

Devastating pace pair

BOXING

Ali shatters George's world

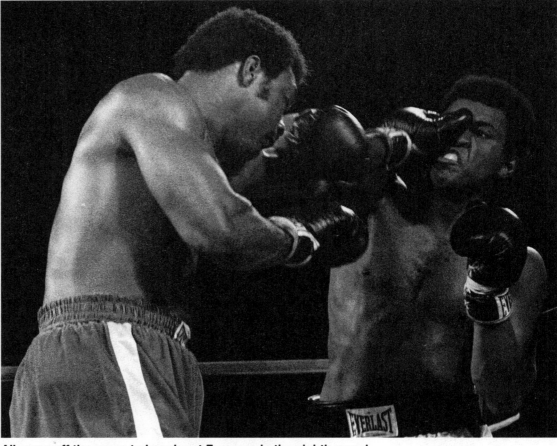

Ali came off the ropes to knock out Foreman in the eighth round

MUHAMMAD ALI out-foxed the bookmakers, George Foreman, and the entire world to recapture his heavyweight crown in his greatest, perhaps *the* greatest, title fight in Kinshasa, Zaire on October 30. Foreman was the 3-1 favourite. Boxing writers around the world had not given Ali a prayer, and even his supporters were doubtful.

How was a dancing counter-attacker at 32 going to handle, let alone defeat, a champion seven years younger who attacked with a relentless two-fisted barrage that had destroyed every opponent he had ever met?

Ali knew how. For eight rounds Foreman had Ali banged up against the ropes, hitting him with everything he had, but although the champion was belting away at Ali's body, connecting with his rib-cage and arms, he was singularly unsuccessful with blows to Ali's head.

The challenger was cleverly,

> **❛I told you all I would do it, but did you listen? He was scared, he was humiliated. I told you I was the greatest heavyweight of all time. I kept telling him during the fight to show me something, to come on and punch. Come on, you're the champion! Show me something❜**
>
> **Muhammad Ali**

almost wickedly, using the ropes to his advantage, sliding and slipping punches and crucially avoiding any serious damage. And he was not dancing around the ring with his butterfly sting, instead he was flat-footed and virtually static,

cleverly conserving his energy.

By the fifth round, Foreman started to look a little weary. His remorseless battering of Ali still had not put him down, and Ali's tactic of counterpunch, cover-up, and hide on the ropes, was still soaking up Foreman's all-out barrage. But even at this point observers at ringside, and television commentators — let alone Foreman — did not realise that Ali's gameplan was working. They still thought they were witnessing a one-sided hammering.

With less than 20 seconds remaining in the eighth round Ali exploded off the ropes, hit Foreman with a left hook, a right to the jaw and another left hook. The champion hit the canvas as if the roof had caved in. With only two seconds left Foreman was counted out. Muhammad Ali was the world champion again, and only the second man to have regained the world heavyweight title.

272

Leeds United's dangerous liaison

Fittipaldi wins close contest

Clough arrives at Elland Road but only stayed 44 days

THE most unlikely marriage in football was consummated on July 22 when Brian Clough, the most vitriolic critic of Leeds United, took over the manager's chair at Elland Road. The honeymoon lasted 44 days before Clough was sacked.

In that brief month and a half Clough managed to spend £500,000 on three players, attempt to sell Terry Cooper, a popular figure with the fans, alienate the entire playing squad by treating them like children and, worst of all, win only one League match of the eight he was in charge.

When the divorce was finalised on September 12 with a £44,000 golden handshake, Leeds were fourth from bottom of the First Division. Managerless, Leeds won their next match 5-0. Subsequently Jimmy Armfield took over.

THREE drivers arrived at Watkins Glen, the last Grand Prix in the calendar, with the world championship in their sights. Emerson Fittipaldi and Clay Regazzoni both had 52 points, and Jody Scheckter 45. Fittipaldi was the narrow favourite because he had won more GPs than Regazzoni and would therefore claim the title if their points were equal. All three were down the grid and fought their own private race as winning was not as important as how they finished in relation to each other.

With 14 laps left in the season Fittipaldi won his second world championship when Scheckter had to retire with a broken fuel pipe and Regazzoni, having struggled with his Ferrari, was out of the points. Fittipaldi finished fourth but had won the race that counted.

Fourth in the championship was the new driver for Ferrari, the Austrian Niki Lauda, who in his first F1 season won the Spanish and Dutch GPs.

FOR THE RECORD

BOXING

■ Don King, who was once convicted for manslaughter, suddenly became a major figure in world boxing when he persuaded the Zaire government to put up the money for the fight between Muhammad Ali and George Foreman, the first world title fight ever staged in Africa.

CRICKET

■ Gordon Greenidge became the first West Indian to score a century on his debut in a Test outside the Caribbean against India in Bangalore.

FOOTBALL

■ Bill Nicholson, the manager of Spurs for 15 years, resigned on August 28 after Tottenham's worst start to the season for 62 years. Nicholson recommended either Danny Blanchflower or Johnny Giles as his successor. The board chose Terry Neill, a former Arsenal player.

■ Sir Stanley Rous was succeeded as the Fifa president by the Brazilian João Havelange who was elected on a tide of Third World votes when he promised to give them a greater representation in world football.

■ Ron Greenwood became general manager at West Ham. John Lyall took control of playing matters.

■ The FA formally abandoned amateurism in football.

MOTORCYCLING

■ Giacomo Agostini switched from MV to Yamaha and won a record seventh successive 350cc world championship. Phil Read of Britain retained the 500cc title.

RACING

■ Pat Eddery, at 22, was the youngest champion jockey since Sir Gordon Richards in 1925.

RUGBY LEAGUE

■ Britain devalued the drop goal from two points to one three years after Australia had done so.

RUGBY UNION

■ Hugo Porta, the Argentinian fly-half, scored 23 points but could not prevent his team losing 31-27 to France.

TENNIS

■ South Africa won the Davis Cup when India refused to play them in the final.

Conteh dazzles rough diamond

Conteh: bruising battle with Ahumada

JOHN CONTEH captured the vacant WBC light heavyweight title when he won a thrilling unanimous points victory over Argentina's diamond-hard Jorge Ahumada at Wembley Arena on October 1. Conteh had boxed brilliantly, using his wondrous speed to devastate the Argentinian with his lightning combinations. Any doubts that Conteh was just a fancy dan fighter hiding behind a fabulous jab were dispelled when he slugged it out with Ahumada over the closing rounds and saw off the hard man's onslaught.

Kiss of life saves Chatfield

EWEN CHATFIELD, the New Zealand tailender, was struck on the temple by a delivery from Peter Lever, swallowed his tongue and was saved by mouth-to-mouth resuscitation administered by the England physiotherapist Bernard Thomas in the first Test at Auckland. Chatfield, whose heart had stopped, regained consciousness in hospital an hour later.

RUGBY UNION

Face-saving tour backfires on England

ENGLAND, who won only one game in the Five Nations championship, embarked on a short tour of Australia with the intention of repairing the damage. But the Australians were not such generous hosts, winning the first Test 16-9 in Sydney and the second 30-21 in Brisbane. There was further embarrassment for the tourists in Brisbane when Mike Burton became the first-ever Englishman to be sent off in an international.

A driving wind played its part in the All Blacks beating Scotland 24-0 at Eden Park in what became known as the Waterpolo Test. Four inches of rain in 12 hours turned the ground into a lake and the Scots, playing into the gale, were 6-0 down at half-time. But during the interval the wind swung 180 degrees and the All Blacks splashed to a comfortable victory.

MOTORCYCLING

Sheene bounces back from horrific crash

Lucky escape: Sheene slid at 180mph at Daytona

AN HORRIFIC crash at Daytona nearly cost Barry Sheene his life and appeared to have ended his career. But Sheene was not about to give up. The son of a motorbike fanatic and the nephew of a speedway driver had racing in his blood and he was soon back on a bike.

He won the 500cc world championship for the next two years and he had learnt one thing from sliding down the tarmac at 180mph on his backside: "Just don't move your foot — it might snap off."

TENNIS

Navratilova defects

THE attraction of life in the West proved a strong magnet for Martina Navratilova. The 19-year-old Czech defected to America after the US Open to begin a new life as one of the sport's finest and richest players. Earlier she was runner-up to Chris Evert in the French Open and to Evonne Goolagong in the Australian Open.

It was also an eventful year for Goolagong. She married the British businessman Roger Cawley, split with her long-time coach Vic Edwards and lost 6-0 6-1 to Billie Jean King in the Wimbledon final.

GOLF

Nicklaus star of Masters drama

THE 39th Masters became known as the best of them all. As usual, Jack Nicklaus was at the centre of the drama. He was six ahead after two rounds but surrendered his lead when Tom Weiskopf shot a 66 in the third round and Johnny Miller came home with six consecutive birdies.

Nicklaus went out first in the final round and swapped the lead with Weiskopf three times. With the tension mounting, Nicklaus rattled his 45-foot putt at the 16th towards the hole. It broke one way, then the other before dropping in for a birdie. Miller and Weiskopf had putts to tie at the last, but missed to give Nicklaus his fifth Masters.

CRICKET

■ Garry Sobers was knighted on New Year's Day.

FOOTBALL

■ For the third year in succession Ron Saunders led out his club for the League Cup final. In 1973 it was Norwich, in 1974 Manchester City and this year Aston Villa. He won for the first time, beating Norwich 1-0.

■ Derby proved there was life after Brian Clough when, under the managership of Dave Mackay, they won their second League championship — with 53 points the lowest since Chelsea in 1955.

■ Brian Clough took over at Second Division Nottingham Forest on January 5. His first match in charge was a 1-0 FA Cup Third Round replay victory at First Division Tottenham Hotspur.

■ Orient finished 12th in the Second Division with 42 points, having scored only 28 goals.

■ Manchester United bounced back into the First Division as the Second Division champions.

MOTOR RACING

■ James Hunt seemed to have successfully graduated from his tempestuous days in Formula Ford when he won the Dutch Grand Prix in a Hesketh, and the car's, first victory. But by the end of the year Hesketh had folded and Hunt signed for McLaren.

■ Lella Lombardi of Italy became the first woman to pick up F1 points when she finished sixth in the Spanish Grand Prix in a March on April 27.

RUGBY LEAGUE

■ Leeds beat Halifax 26-11 in the first Premiership Trophy final.

SKIING

■ Gustavo Thoeni of Italy won a record fourth men's overall title in the World Cup, and Annemarie Moser-Proll won her fifth successive women's overall championship.

SKIING

Moser-Proll: fifth title

Demon pace duo adds injury to insults

"ASHES to ashes, dust to dust, if Thommo don't get ya, Lillee must." That was the greeting English batsmen received from the crowd when walking out to face the most lethal fast bowling combination in the world. It was an adaptation of the catchphrase used for Jim Laker and Tony Lock in 1956. The major difference was that the English spinners did not break bones.

England knew Dennis Lillee. He had tormented them in England in 1972. They did not know Jeff Thomson, who delivered the ball at nearly 100mph.

Thommo struck like a bolt of lightning, taking nine wickets in the first Test as Mike Denness's team buckled to a 166-run defeat. He captured seven wickets in the second Test to help Australia to a nine-wicket win, and took another eight in the drawn third Test.

Denness dropped himself for the fourth Test but his replace-ment, John Edrich, ended up in hospital when he was hit in the ribs by a delivery from Lillee. He returned later but could not prevent Australia winning by 171 runs with 35 balls to spare.

Lillee, who had recovered from stress fractures of the lower spine that threatened his career, collected two wickets in each innings of the first four matches in his come-back. Then he moved up a gear.

He took eight wickets in the fifth Test to bowl Australia to a 163-run victory without his part-ner in crime for the second innings.

Thomson injured his shoulder playing tennis on the rest day and took no further part in the series.

Lillee bruised his foot after six overs of the sixth Test and England thrived against a team without its deadly duo. The visitors triumphed by an innings and four runs. But it was too late — Australia had won back the Ashes a month before. Thomson took 33 wickets and Lillee 21.

> ❝ I don't want to do the batsman permanent injury, just to cause him concern, to hurt him a bit ❞
>
> **Dennis Lillee**

> ❝ I enjoy hitting a batsman more than getting him out. It doesn't worry me in the least to see a batsman hurt, rolling around screaming and blood on the pitch ❞
>
> **Jeff Thomson**

LILLEE'S RECORD

	FIRST-CLASS	TESTS (70)
Innings	223	90
Not out	65	24
Runs	2,220	905
Highest	73 not out	73 not out
Average	14.05	13.71
Wickets	845	355
	at 22.86	at 23.92
Catches	62	23

Lillee: eight wickets in the fifth Test

Tiny Wimbledon scare First Division giants

SOUTHERN LEAGUE Wimble-don embarked on a stupendous FA Cup run when they knocked out First Division Burnley 1-0 at Turf Moor in the third round when their goalkeeper, Dickie Guy, played a blinder. Wimbledon were the first non-League club to beat First Division opposition away since the formation of the Third Division in the Twenties.

Wimbledon travelled to mighty Leeds in the next round and held them to a goalless draw. The inter-est in the replay was so great that it was held at neighbouring Sel-hurst Park to accommodate the spectators. Wimbledon went out to a fortuitous goal that was deflected off Dave Bassett's backside.

The Dons flowing not so quietly to FA Cup glory

Steady Watson comes of age

JACK NICKLAUS had seen young pretenders to his throne come and go. The latest was Tom Watson, a 25-year-old who had won his first title in the Western Open the previous year but was still wearing the scars of missed opportunities in two US Opens and a Masters when he headed for Carnoustie.

Watson's first experience of links golf went largely unnoticed until the final hole of the Open. He played steady golf while the leaders were wayward, and a 15-foot putt at the last earned him a play-off against the Australian Jack Newton. Watson won the play-off at the 18th when he made par and Newton dropped a shot.

Watson: won play-off

CRICKET

West Indies simply the best

Lloyd runs out Ian Chappell for 62 in the World Cup final

THE advent of one-day cricket provided a quick answer to the sport's eternal question: Who are the world champions?

For years people had wondered who were the best team: England in 1932, Australia in 1948, West Indies in 1950 or South Africa in 1970. But nobody could call themselves the real world champions, until Clive Lloyd's West Indians at 8.42pm on June 21.

Four-and-a-half years after the first-ever one-day international, eight teams gathered in England for the inaugural 60-over World Cup. The limited-over game would never provide a true gauge of the strengths and weaknesses of teams; there was too much left to chance. But during a sunny fortnight in June it was the nearest the sport could come to finding its finest team of the era.

The event did not look destined to be a success when several early matches attracted disappointing crowds and produced poor cricket, particularly from East Africa and Sri Lanka. But when Andy Roberts and Deryck Murray hit 64 runs for the last West Indian wicket to beat Pakistan with two balls to spare the World Cup came alive.

The West Indians reached the final with a five-wicket win over New Zealand while Australia bowled out England for 93 on their way to a four-wicket victory in the other semi-final.

The finest teams in the 15-match competition produced a stirring final on the longest day of the year. Lloyd, the newly-appointed West Indian captain, rescued his team from 50 for three with a century off 82 balls to set Australia the task of scoring 292 at 4.85 runs an over. The West Indians showed their skills in the field, running out five batsmen as the frantic Australians fell 17 runs short. They were crowned kings of cricket by the Duke of Edinburgh.

FOOTBALL

Harsh decisions spark Leeds riot

LEEDS lost the European Cup final to the holders Bayern Munich 2-0 in Paris on May 28. Leeds were unlucky to be beaten as two good claims for penalties against Franz Beckenbauer were waved away by the French referee and a good goal was disallowed for offside.

Disgracefully, the Leeds fans massed behind the West German goal were so incensed by the referee's cavalier decisions that they went berserk, broke up seats and hurled them towards the pitch. Their aim was indiscriminate and a photographer was blinded in one eye, and a policeman and a ball boy were knocked spark out.

The German goalkeeper Sepp Maier had kept Bayern alive for more than 70 minutes of a brutal game that forced the European champions to make two substitutions. But two splendid goals, the last from Gerd Muller, dashed Leeds's hopes.

Jockeys rescued by punters

PUNTERS are quick to blame jockeys for their losses, but, for once, they were quick to come to the jockeys' rescue. Stable lads were on strike in pursuit of a pay rise and they took their campaign to the 1,000 Guineas in May.

Willie Carson was making his way down to the start when he was pulled from his horse by the demonstrators. The crowd was outraged and they rushed on to the course to protect the riders. Order was eventually restored, although the protesters made a further attempt to disrupt racing when they used a bulldozer to dig up part of the course overnight.

Grundy fights his way to an awesome victory

THE King George VI and Queen Elizabeth Stakes was the richest race in England when it was inaugurated during the Festival of Britain and it had provided Ascot with a feast of top-flight races.

None though could match this race for its jewels and, true to form, it produced a right royal finish. Eleven of the best horses in Europe went to the start on a scorching hot day, and two of them produced possibly the most blazing finish ever seen.

Lady Beaverbrook's four-year-old Bustino had not one but two pacemakers, and they set off at a phenomenal rate. One then the other faded away with their job done, leaving Bustino with just under half a mile to run and a four-length lead.

The rest of the field were left in breathless pursuit, all apart from Grundy, the Derby winner, who refused to be left behind. With little more than a furlong left Grundy had caught up, but it looked as if the effort of closing the gap had drained all of his reserves of strength.

Bustino, still showing no signs of slowing the relentless pace, rallied. Grundy fought back again. Still Bustino refused to concede. The two horses stormed on, separated by little more than a nostril. Grundy edged ahead. Bustino made another effort until, just yards from the finishing post, he had to give second best by half a length.

The crowd that had been hushed with expectation at the start was awestruck, and even hardened racing journalists were moved. One summed it all up with the title of his book about the duel: "The Race of the Century".

The breathtaking finish: Grundy edges Bustino by half a length

Ashe makes his point in outsmarting Connors

Ashe: overcame racial prejudice to reach the top

ARTHUR ASHE was on a winning streak. He played blackjack in the Playboy club until well after midnight and won. A little more than 12 hours later he played Jimmy Connors in the Wimbledon men's singles final and won.

Spectators at both venues were surprised. They need not have been. Ashe had been winning against the odds all his life. His toughest battle was against the prejudice he faced in a sport that was the exclusive preserve of white, middle-class Americans. The triumph against Connors was the icing on top.

It was also a victory of precision over power. Connors was all brawn. He had a strong serve, an even stronger return and a two-handed backhand that fired shots down the line like bullets.

Ashe found the perfect riposte. He slowed the pace with angled returns wide of Connors and mixed his play with soft, short shots, slices and top-spin. Connors had no answer until a supporter shouted: "C'mon Connors." His reply: "I'm trying, for Chrissake!"

But Ashe was having what he described as a serene high. He won the first two sets 6-1 6-1, then he stuttered. Connors took the next set 7-5 and went ahead 3-0 in the fourth set. But the comeback ran aground. Ashe rose like a phoenix to win six of the next seven games and the applause for his 6-1 6-1 5-7 6-4 victory was deafening.

FOR THE RECORD

HOCKEY
■ India won the men's World Cup.

KARATE
■ Britain won the men's team event in the world championships.

TENNIS
■ The United States won the first Nations Cup, an eight-team men's event, in Kingston, Jamaica.

TUG-OF-WAR
■ England dominated the inaugural world championships, winning both the 720kg and 640kg divisions.

AUGUST

1975

DECEMBER

Lauda puts Ferrari on course

NIKI LAUDA fulfilled the promise of his previous season when he steered his Ferrari to five Grand Prix victories, the world championship and the constructors' championship. It was a crucial success for Ferrari. In 1969 Enzo Ferrari had found the cost of competing at the highest levels of motor sport prohibitive and had sold out to Fiat.

Five barren years had disillusioned the giant Italian company. So Ferrari's first success in the drivers' and constructors' championships since 1964, and with a newly redesigned car, was timely and sweet.

Lauda: sweet success

CRICKET

Steele is the mettle in England

NOTHING had changed in five months since Dennis Lillee and Jeff Thomson left England shell-shocked in a disastrous tour of Australia. Mike Denness's team folded up again like deck chairs against Australia in the first Test at Edgbaston.

Geoff Boycott had gone into self-imposed exile and Graham Gooch, the great new hope in the side, failed dismally. He was dismissed for a pair on his debut and Australia won by an innings and 85 runs.

Tony Greig took over the captaincy and the selectors decided to opt for experience rather than youth. They surprised many by picking the 32-year-old David Steele, a bespectacled Northamptonshire batsman who was overweight and unfit in his benefit season. He had displayed little more than solid defence in 13 summers on the county circuit. It was an odd choice.

But Steele was a great find. In his first six innings he scored 50, 45, 73, 92, 39 and 66. He averaged 60.83, and earned a boost for his benefit and admiration from Ian Chappell. "His application and concentration were faultless," the Australian captain said. "Sometimes I felt he concentrated so hard that he didn't know there was anyone on the field apart from himself and the bowler."

Steele's determination gave the England batting enough backbone to draw the remaining three Tests. The third Test at Headingley was abandoned on the last day when vandals campaigning for the release of a criminal sabotaged the pitch with knives and oil. Australia needed 225 runs to win with seven wickets left.

In a lighter moment, Michael Angelow became the first streaker at a Test match in England when he hurdled over each set of stumps at Lord's.

Steele (left) an unlikely hit for England

FOR THE RECORD

BOXING

■ John H Stracey, the British and European champion, got off the floor in the first round to wrest the world welterweight title from the legendary José Napoles with a sixth-round stoppage in Mexico City on December 6.

CRICKET

■ Greg Chappell took over the Australian captaincy from his brother Ian and in his first match scored hundreds in both innings against the West Indies.

FOOTBALL

■ The Football League decided to use goal difference rather than goal average to separate teams level on points.

■ Scotland decided to scrap their existing League format and replace it with a 10-club Premier Division and 14-strong First and Second Divisions.

GOLF

■ The United States retained the Ryder Cup with an 18-8 victory at Laurel Valley, Pennsylvania. Six matches were halved.

MOTORCYCLING

■ Giacomo Agostini powered his Yamaha to a record eighth 500cc world championship. Agostini won a record 122 Grands Prix in his career, 54 in the 350cc class and 68 on his 500cc bike.

TENNIS

■ Bjorn Borg helped Sweden to a 3-2 victory against Czechoslovakia in the Davis Cup final.

Balderstone's twin peaks

LEICESTERSHIRE won the championship for the first time in their 102-year history with a victory against Derbyshire at Chesterfield after an eventful three days for Chris Balderstone. After batting for Leicestershire, he sped off in the evening to play football for Doncaster Rovers, returned the next morning to reach his century and then helped dismiss Derbyshire to win the title.

RUGBY LEAGUE

Global launch for World Cup

THE World Cup went global for the first time when the organisers decided to play a nine-month tournament on a home and away basis. Britain's challenge was split into England and Wales, but the new format did not help the English. They were pipped by one point in the final table by Australia despite beating and drawing with them. England were undone by a 12-7 loss in Brisbane to Wales, who were declared the home side.

Revie pays high price for dithering

DON REVIE'S stewardship of England which had begun so brightly against Czechoslovakia the previous October dimmed dramatically when his team failed to qualify for the European championships. A 0-0 draw against Portugal at Wembley had followed the initial euphoria, but was dismissed as a hiccup. England then went on to beat West Germany, the world champions, 2-0 using 11 players from 10 different clubs, and hammer Cyprus 5-0 with all the goals coming from Malcolm Macdonald. A 5-1 rout of Scotland to clinch the home international championship rounded off Revie's first season in charge. His record was near to perfect: played eight, won five, drawn three, lost none.

But the writing was already on the wall. In those eight matches Revie used 27 different players and only Dave Watson was an ever-present. Such wholesale changes were the product of his anxiety and inability to make the leap from club manager to international manager.

His continual dropping of players, frequently for no apparent reason, unsettled the squad and the individuals. Alan Hudson lost his club form because of it and Kevin Keegan stormed out of the England camp and had to be coaxed back.

When the real task of qualifying for the European championships came around England promptly lost 2-1 to the Czechoslovakians in Bratislava, having been ahead with a Mick Channon goal. Their quarter-final place was slipping away as the full horror of the point dropped at home to Portugal dawned. England needed to win in Lisbon, but only scraped a 1-1 draw and Czechoslovakia were through.

And Revie got a taste of what his predecessor, Sir Alf Ramsey, had experienced in the last years of his reign — a baying pack of newshounds scenting blood.

Hot shot: Macdonald scored all five goals against Cyprus

Frazier stuns Ali with the fight of his life

THE third meeting of Muhammad Ali and Joe Frazier was even more bruising than their previous encounters. Ali, now the defending champion, was convinced that Frazier was shot as a fighter and decided to slug it out with the former champion when they met in Manila on October 1.

For four rounds Ali's battle plan was working as he seemed able to hit Frazier at will. But Frazier would not give up and his bull-like determination got him back into the fight as he won the fifth round and had the champion in desperate straits in the sixth. Ali hung on somehow, and by the tenth round the fight was even and both boxers were going to dig deep into their reserves if they were to win.

Ali found the strength in the 11th and caught Frazier with a couple of long shots and effectively turned the fight in his favour. For the next three rounds Frazier was the shot fighter that Ali thought he was before the contest began, but Ali too was drained and could not put him away.

Frazier stumbled around, unable to offer any real resistance. By the end of the 14th Frazier could hardly see and had blood dripping from his mouth. His manager refused to allow Frazier out for the 15th, and final, round. Ali sank to the canvas, shattered and grateful that it was all over.

Ali did not gloat over his victory. He said that he had thought of quitting after the 10th and that at one point he had felt like fainting. "A fight like that was next to death," he said. "It was the closest thing I know of to dying."

The thriller in Manila: 15 brutal rounds

Keegan thunders to the title

WINTER OLYMPICS

Artful Curry figures out winning way

JOHN CURRY, who always had aspirations to act in a West End play, instead went on centre stage at the winter Olympics Games in Innsbruck. He took advantage of a change to the scoring, winning the men's figure skating gold medal.

Previously, marks were divided equally between set figures and free skating, but a greater emphasis on artistic imagination suited Curry, whose perfectly co-ordinated balletic display was too hot for his rivals. Rosi Mittermaier of France was the star of the Games, but failed by 0.13sec to win the giant slalom, having won the downhill and slalom.

Curry: balletic style

Liverpool defeat Bruges to do the League and Uefa Cup double a second time

BOB PAISLEY, in his second season as the successor to Bill Shankly, won his first trophy as manager on May 4 at Molineux. Liverpool pipped Queen's Park Rangers for the League championship by beating Wolves 3-1. But when the season had started nobody could have forseen the outcome. Liverpool had begun by losing at QPR 2-0, which appeared to be two points thrown away. They continued in similar sluggish form by only winning a half-dozen of their first 12 matches.

Liverpool were kept afloat throughout the season by the striking force of Kevin Keegan and John Toshack, with a little help from David Fairclough. The flame-haired teenager had made such a habit of coming on as a substitute and scoring critical goals that he was universally acclaimed as "Supersub". Indeed, as the season reached its peak, he came on three times, scored four goals and secured three crucial victories.

But the night Liverpool won Paisley his first title belonged to Keegan and Toshack. QPR had already completed their 42 matches and could only hope that Wolves, who needed to win to avoid relegation, would rise to the occasion. That they certainly did. Roared on by a capacity crowd, they scored after 13 minutes and valiantly held on until 13 minutes from the end. Then Keegan popped up out of nowhere to equalise. Wolves threw everything into attack and exposed their frail defence. Within minutes Toshack and Ray Kennedy had made it 3-1.

Fifteen days later Paisley had a second trophy, the Uefa Cup when Liverpool, defending a slender 3-2 lead from the first leg, drew 1-1 against Bruges in Belgium. Bruges took an early lead from a penalty which, if the scores had stayed the same, would have given them the trophy. But before they could marshal themselves Keegan had already bent a shot past the keeper, and it was Liverpool's chance to hang on and, for the second time, win the League and Uefa Cup in the same season.

Barker enjoys French affair

SUE BARKER became more famous for dating Cliff Richard than for her tennis. But in the summer it was her much-improved backhand that kept her on song in the French Open. She was the first English player since Ann Jones in 1966 to win the women's singles title in Paris, beating Renata Tomanova 6-2 0-6 6-2.

Barker: on song

Near-fatal last match for Merv the Swerve

ONE of the great careers in rugby came to an abrupt end in a televised Welsh Cup semi-final between Swansea and Pontypool on March 28. Mervyn Davies, the Swansea and Wales captain, collapsed on the field and nearly died of a brain haemorrhage.

Merv the Swerve played 38 internationals and had recently led Wales from the back of the pack to the Grand Slam in a momentous winter. The Welsh, who kicked off the season with a 28-3 win against the touring Australians, scored a record 102 points in the Five Nations championship, for their sixth title in eight years.

Docherty's Babes prove no match against McMenemy's wise men

SUNDERLAND had prepared everybody for this result three years earlier. If a Second Division side could topple Leeds and win the FA Cup, why not Second Division Southampton? All giants were there for slaying. And Lawrie McMenemy's astute blend of youth and experience duly obliged.

Southampton overwhelmed Tommy Docherty's young Manchester United and captured the FA Cup for the first time. United never got back into the game when, after early pressure, Sammy McIlroy's header hit the wood-work. Southampton worked tire-lessly and never let the occasion unnerve them, as it did United. With eight minutes remaining Bobby Stokes scored the only goal from a pass by Jim McCalliog, whom Docherty had sold to Southampton 15 months before.

BADMINTON
■ Rudy Hartono of Indonesia won the All-England championship a record eighth time.

BOXING
■ Wilfred Benitez became the youngest ever world champion when, aged 17½, he outpointed Antonio Cervantes for the WBA light-welterweight crown in San Juan, Puerto Rico on March 6.

CRICKET
■ Lance Gibbs became the leading wicket-taker in Tests when he had the Australian Ian Redpath caught on the long-on boundary by Michael Holding. He then dismissed Gary Gilmour to finish his career with 309 wickets, two more than Fred Trueman.

■ India, set to score 403 runs in 595 minutes against West Indies in Port of Spain, won with seven overs to spare. Their total of 406 for four was the highest fourth innings to win a Test.

FOOTBALL
■ Jock Wallace, a manager with firm ideas on physical fitness, guided Rangers to the Treble of League championship, Cup and League Cup.

■ West Ham lost the Cup Winners Cup final to Anderlecht 4-2.

GOLF
■ Ray Floyd led from start to finish to win the Masters. He took an eight-stroke lead into the final round and won by the same margin.

RUGBY UNION
■ Ireland, hoping to play Fiji, stopped off on the island on their way to New Zealand only to find the Fijians were touring Australia. The Irish lost 11-3 to the All Blacks.

TENNIS
■ Mark Edmondson was the last Australian to win his national title when he beat John Newcombe 6-7 6-3 7-6 6-1 in the final.

Heavenly moment: Second Division Southampton celebrate their 1-0 upset of Manchester United

BOXING

Tired Stracey loses his title

Stracey: unwanted defence

JOHN H STRACEY defended his world welterweight title twice. The first time he won with a 10th round stoppage against the fading Hedgemon Lewis, who promptly retired. The second time, against the classy Carlos Palomino at Wembley on June 22, was a defence Stracey did not want to make at that time.

Stracey thought he needed a rest, but his manager Terry Lawless and matchmaker Micky Duff eventually talked him into the fight. After all, his advisers had skilfully engineered Stracey's rise through the rankings by astutely picking highly rated opponents who were no longer formidable, and invariably never boxed again. However, this time their counsel was ill-advised and Stracey was bludgeoned to defeat in 12 rounds with a searing accumulation of body punches.

GOLF

Seve's dramatic debut

Ballesteros: six under par after three rounds

EVERYTHING pointed to Johnny Miller taking over Jack Nicklaus's mantle as the world's best player. He was blond, American, had a sure, upright swing and was seven years younger than the Golden Bear.

He had won the US Open in 1973, finished the leading money-winner on the US tour the next year and was second to Nicklaus in 1975. He had also signed a clothes endorsement contract worth $1 million and was on top of his game when he arrived at Royal Birkdale for the Open.

But Miller, and even Jack Nicklaus, were outplayed on the first three days by a little known Spanish teenager. Severiano Ballesteros, a 19-year-old from Pedreña, scored a brace of 69s to head the leaderboard. Ballesteros slipped a little in the third round with a 73 but still led Miller by two shots and Nicklaus by five. His name was on everybody's lips even if they had difficulty pronouncing it.

Then the wheels came off.

> *‘ Happiness is knowing that even your worst shot is still going to be pretty good ’*
>
> **Johnny Miller**

Ballesteros struggled to the turn while Miller began a charge, finishing with 66 and a six-shot victory. It was his second major victory. Ballesteros hit a string of birdies and an eagle over the closing holes to tie with Nicklaus for second place.

But in years to come it was Ballesteros and not Miller, who took over Nicklaus's crown. Miller failed to live up to the high standards set by the Golden Bear and his game faded. "I climbed to the top of my personal mountain and decided to sit back and relax," he said. He devoted his time to his wife Linda, their six children and his Mormon religion.

Pate's shot hits the bullseye

JERRY PATE provided the US Open with one of its most dramatic finishes at the Atlanta Athletic Club in Georgia. The 22-year-old rookie with a flowing swing and bubbling confidence played the shot of the year at the last hole to win by two strokes from Al Geiberger and Tom Weiskopf.

Pate needed par at the 460-yard final hole to win. But he drove into thick grass 190 yards from the hole and needed to clear a pond guarding the hole and land close to the flag, tight against the fringe of the green. Fortunately, his ball was sitting up. He struck a sweet five-iron, the ball landed four feet from the hole and rolled to within two feet. After this the birdie putt was a formality.

TENNIS

Iceman melts Nastase's fire

WIMBLEDON was prepared for a battle of fire and ice. The tempestuous Ilie Nastase against Bjorn Borg for the men's singles crown. But after four games the fire was extinguished by the stoic Swede, who surprised even himself by taking the title without dropping a set.

Ice Borg, as he became known, had worked four hours a day on strengthening his weak serve and it paid off. He won 6-4 6-2 9-7 despite needing pain-killing injections for a stomach muscle he injured while playing doubles. He never competed in a major doubles tournament again, and instead concentrated on winning five successive Wimbledon singles titles.

Borg: stoic Swede

FOR THE RECORD

CRICKET
■ The Women's Cricket Association celebrated their Golden Jubilee with a one-day match between Australia and England at Lord's on August 4. It was the first time women played at the sport's headquarters.

HOCKEY
■ West Germany won the women's World Cup.

MOTOR RACING
■ Tyrrell launched a six-wheeled F1 car and the two Tyrrell-Ford Project 34 cars amazed the world of motor racing when they finished first and second in the Swedish Grand Prix on June 13.

RUGBY UNION
■ Cantabrians won the first Hong Kong Sevens tournament.

Walker benefits from African boycott

A GROUP of New Zealand rugby union players intent on becoming the first All Blacks to win a series in South Africa sparked a boycott of the Olympic Games.

The New Zealanders ignored world opinion and went ahead with their tour and mounting criticism threatened their attendance at the XXI Olympics in Montreal. When New Zealand refused to withdraw 20 African countries boycotted the Games in protest only two days before the opening ceremony.

Their absence caused chaos in the seedings for several events and devalued the athletics and boxing. One of the biggest beneficiaries was a New Zealander. John Walker took advantage of the absence of the powerful Africans to win the 1500m, one of New Zealand's two gold medals. But Walker missed his rivalry with the Tanzanian world record holder Filbert Bayi

and his time of 3min 39.17sec was slower than the four previous 1500m gold medal winners. Lasse Viren, the tall Finnish policeman who had fallen in Mexico before winning the 10,000m, became the first man to retain the 10,000m and 5,000m titles.

Edwin Moses won the 400m hurdles a year after he began hurdling, but America's domination on the track was dented by the Caribbean in the shorter distances. Hasely Crawford of Trinidad and Tobago won the 100m, Don Quarrie of Jamaica won the 200m and the Cuban Alberto Juantorena won an unique double in the 400m and 800m. His time of 1min 43.5sec for the 800m was a world record.

The West German Annegret Richter, who took the 100m, was the only woman from outside Eastern Europe to win on the track.

The muscular East German swimmer Kornelia Ender won four gold medals and her countrymen won the football crown, beating Poland 3-1. Sixteen of the finalists played in the 1974 World Cup.

Leon Spinks displayed his sparkling teeth and boxing skills to win the light-heavyweight gold medal two years before the took the world heavyweight title from Muhammad Ali. But not everybody was smiling. Canada were the only host nation in a modern summer Olympics not to win a gold medal; several weightlifters tested positive for drugs and Boris Onischenko was thrown out of the modern pentathlon in disgrace. The indicator light on his épée flashed before he touched his opponent and closer scrutiny revealed it had been tampered with. The Soviet team was disqualified.

Their disgrace was replaced by

British delight. Adrian Parker lifted his three-man modern pentathlon team from fourth place to the gold medal with a brilliant victory in the cross-country, the last of the five disciplines.

David Wilkie won Britain's first swimming gold medal since 1908, taking the 200m breaststroke title, and the sailing pair of Reg White and his brother-in-law John Osborne completed the golden haul in the Tornado class. Britain won five silver medals and five bronze.

Comaneci first to be perfect

NADIA COMANECI earned better marks in gymnastics than in school. The little 14-year-old Romanian earned the first-ever perfect score to catapult her sport on to the world stage. Her faultless performance on the asymmetrical bars captivated a worldwide television audience, who watched the sensation of the Olympic Games score another six ultimate marks of 10.0.

Olga Korbut, the hero of the 1972 Olympics, took a back seat while her unsmiling rival attracted a record crowd of 18,000 people to the women's finals. Comaneci won three gold medals, one silver and one bronze. Korbut shared in the Soviet team victory and took the silver medal on the beam.

Long-distance double: Viren was the first man to retain the 5,000m and 10,000m titles

Comaneci: faultless

MOTOR RACING

MOTOR RACING
Twists of fate favour Hunt

Hunt: snatched the championship from Lauda by one point in the final race

FOOTBALL

Revie's days are numbered

IF THE price of failure to qualify for the World Cup is the sack then Don Revie must have been a worried man. Hard on the heels of England's exit from the previous season's European championships, a similar fate loomed in the qualifying rounds of the World Cup. However, this time the performance of Revie's teams before the qualifying games had given an indication of what might be to come.

Although England beat Ireland and Wales they failed to retain the Home international championship when goals by Don Masson and Kenny Dalglish in Glasgow crowned Scotland instead.

England had beaten Finland, the minnows of the World Cup group, 4-1 in Helsinki but could only muster a scrappy 2-1 victory at Wembley. A huge goal difference had been vital to put pressure on the innately cautious Italians, the favourites for the single qualifying spot.

Revie needed a good result in Rome in November. He made six changes from the side that had failed to put away the Finns the month before. Italy fielded a world-class side, including seven players from Juventus, and won 2-0 at a canter. England now had an impossible task: they had to beat Italy at Wembley and hope the Finns took a point off the Italians.

JAMES HUNT'S reputation as a driver had preceded him when he lined up on the grid on January 25 for the first race of the season, the Brazilian Grand Prix.

His days in the lower formulas, where the temperamental ex-public schoolboy had earned the nickname "Hunt the Shunt", were well known. So it was no surprise that the 29-year-old hothead had stolen pole from the world champion Niki Lauda, nor that he then crashed his McLaren on the 33rd lap. But that turned out to be only the beginning of a dramatic season to end all seasons.

Lauda won the Brazilian GP, and the next race, but only by a second from Hunt. The inevitable happened in the third race: Hunt crashed. Then Hunt won the Spanish Grand Prix, only to be disqualified because his car was 1.8cm too wide, with Lauda promoted to first place.

By June, Lauda's lead in the world championship was a massive 45 points. Then at the French Grand Prix the season turned upside down. Lauda retired with mechanical failure, Hunt won and the day afterwards his victory in the Spanish Grand Prix was restored. Lauda's lead was back to a more realistic 26 points.

Hunt then won the British Grand Prix, only to have that victory stripped two months later because his car had been illegitimately repaired after Hunt collided with Clay Regazzoni in the first lap.

But fate had not finished with the two protagonists. At Nurburgring, in the German Grand Prix, Lauda was involved in an horrific accident on the second lap when his Ferrari hit a kerb and burst into flames. Lauda, scarred for life from the burns, was lucky to escape with his life. Hunt won the race.

Six weeks later, incredibly, Lauda was back behind the wheel and in the points. Hunt then won successive races in North America, and the whole season came down to the last event, the first Japanese Grand Prix, with Lauda only two points ahead.

The race was held in appalling conditions, with pouring rain, a track covered in puddles and visibility down to 100 metres. When Hunt took an early lead Lauda found himself driving into a huge cloud of spray and, sensibly and nobly, retired after two laps.

Hunt had to finish fourth or better to snatch the title. As Hunt had led for most of the race this seemed to be a formality. Then it stopped raining and Hunt was in trouble. His wet weather tyres were not suitable for a drying track, and one of them was badly worn.

He decided to ease up and risk it. With six laps remaining Hunt was third when the worn tyre gave way and he limped into the pits. Thirty seconds later Hunt, with four new tyres, was fifth and apparently out of the world championship. Then luck turned his way as two drivers ahead of him suffered the same tyre problems and he was able to overtake them. Hunt finished third, and Lauda's crown passed to him by a single point.

CRICKET

Lever starts on the right foot with 10 wickets

NINE years after making his debut for Essex, John Lever finally received an invitation to play for England. And he took it with open arms, grabbing 10 wickets in Delhi to sweep England to their first victory by an innings in India. The left-arm swing bowler took seven for 46 in the first innings and then completed his work with three for 24 in the second innings.

Lever: beat India

Greig's taunt rebounds on him in spades

TONY GREIG was not the most tactful of England captains. The Sussex all-rounder had a tendency to talk, and then think.

When he discussed the impending visit by the West Indians, he predicted: "We will make them grovel." It was an unfortunate remark that had the connotations of a racist slur from a South African-born player, and it fired up Clive Lloyd's tourists. Not that they needed much firing up. They had five pace bowlers in their party and were about to introduce England to life in the fast lane.

Wayne Daniel, Michael Holding, Vanburn Holder, Bernard Julien and Andy Roberts were the aces in a winning hand. The West Indian skipper had been taught a lesson by the Australians who used Dennis Lillee and Jeff Thomson to thrash them 5-0 earlier in the year. Now he employed the same methods to soften up England.

The relentless pace attack wore down Greig's team in the first two

Eating his words: Greig is bowled for a duck by Roberts

Tests and then moved in for the kill at Old Trafford. The tourists won by 425 runs, and they kept up the pressure to triumph by 55 runs and 231 runs in the remaining Tests. The fast bowlers took 84 of the 92 English wickets with Holding and Roberts capturing 28 scalps each. Holding had an average of 12.71.

Viv Richards confirmed his emergence as one of the world's finest batsman by scoring 829 runs at an average of 118.42 in four matches. He had innings of 232 at Trent Bridge and 291 at The Oval. The West Indies won the Test series and one-day series 3-0 and it was time for Greig to grovel.

LLOYD'S RECORD

FIRST-CLASS	TESTS (110)	
Innings	730	175
Not out	96	14
Runs	31,232	7,515
Highest	242 not out	242 not out
Average	49.26	46.67
Hundreds	79	19
Wickets	114 at 36.00	10 at 62.20
Catches	377	87

FOR THE RECORD

BOXING
■ Muhammad Ali successfully defended his world heavyweight title four times.

CRICKET
■ Javed Miandad scored 163 for Pakistan on his debut against New Zealand in Lahore on October 9.

FOOTBALL
■ Blackburn's David Wagstaffe was the first player in the Football League to be shown the red card when he was dismissed in his club's Second Division match at Orient on October 2.

GOLF
■ Jack Nicklaus was the leading money-winner on the US PGA tour for the eighth year. He won $226,438.57, almost twice as much as his first victory in 1964.

■ Severiano Ballesteros was the leading money-winner on the European Tour for the first of three years running when he won £39,504.

■ Dave Stockton holed from 10 feet on the last hole to win the US PGA championship by one shot from Don January and Ray Floyd.

■ David Graham beat Hale Irwin at the 38th hole in the final of the World Matchplay championship.

MOTORCYCLING
■ Barry Sheene won his first of two successive 500cc world championships.

RACING
■ The French horse Trepan was disqualified in August, having failed drug tests at Royal Ascot and in the Eclipse Stakes.

SQUASH
■ Geoff Hunt of Australia won the first men's World Open championship. It was his first of four successive titles. Heather McKay won the women's final.

Title race turned into gentle spin

A LONG hot summer turned the county championship into a canter for Middlesex. With the experienced Mike Brearley as captain they were better off than most even

before the campaign began. The astute leader was blessed with three high quality spinners who thrived on the dry turning pitches. Phil Edmonds, Norman Featherstone

and John Emburey added variety to an attack which also starred Mike Selvey. The runners-up were Northamptonshire who won their first trophy, the Gillette Cup.

Brearley leads the celebrations for Middlesex, who prospered on the dry pitches

CRICKET

100 years on, nothing changes

Gary Cozier takes a brilliant catch to dismiss Randall for 174

THE greatest gathering of Test players took place at the Melbourne Cricket Ground. In mid-March 218 of the 244 living cricketers who had played in Tests between Australia and England attended the Centenary Test.

Melbourne was swamped with souvenirs, including a specially minted gold coin used for the toss.

Tony Greig called correctly and appeared justified in fielding first when Australia crashed to 138 all out. But England struggled against the pace of Dennis Lillee and Max Walker and before the sun had set on the first day were out for 95.

Australia were again in trouble until their 21-year-old new cap David Hookes responded to jibes from Greig by hitting the England captain for five successive fours. When the dust had settled England needed 463 runs to win, and with a brilliant 174 from Derek Randall came close.

But Lillee had the final say and Australia's victory by 45 runs was identical to their win in the first Test at the same ground in 1877.

RUGBY UNION

France make the perfect choice

France beat England 4-3 en route to their second Grand Slam

THE French selectors picked their team for the Five Nations championships, and then might as well have gone on holiday. The 15 chosen men played all four matches, did not concede a try and gave France its second Grand Slam.

The unchanged side included one of the finest back-row trios to grace a rugby field, Jean-Pierre Bastiat, Jean-Pierre Rives and Jean-Claude Skrela, who played in 18 Tests together. Rives, with his flowing blond hair, had the speed,

Bastiat the height and Skrela the tackling ability to turn France into a combination capable of challenging Welsh supremacy. Jacques Fouroux's side beat Wales 16-9, England 4-3, Scotland 23-3 and Ireland 15-6.

Red Rum is National hero

Beach boy: Red Rum exercising on Southport sands before his third Aintree triumph

GINGER McCAIN had just two words to describe Red Rum's record third triumph in the Grand National: "Bloody marvellous." And what a marvel it was. Red Rum had run in the race five times in succession and the only two times he did not win, in 1975 and 1976, he was second.

It was a fairytale finale for a horse that had been passed around from pillar to post. Indeed, Tommy Stack, the tearful jockey, had even trained Red Rum for a while.

Eventually Red Rum had been bought by a retired millionaire for a few thousand guineas and sent to McCain to train in the humble surroundings of Southport sands.

As Red Rum galloped home by 25 lengths, ears pricked to the cheers of the crowds, he might have sensed that his moment had come. His first victory at Aintree in 1973 had been dismissed as the race that Crisp should have won.

But Red Rum's courage soon captured the public's imagination and he was elevated to almost superstar status. Like the Aintree fences, though, Red Rum just took the endless round of celebrity appearances to open supermarkets and the other stunts in his stride.

Longest course concedes the lowest score

AL GEIBERGER became Mr 59 with one of the most remarkable rounds in golf. He had six pars, 11 birdies and an eagle in the second round of the Memphis Classic. His 59 at the 7,249-yard Colonial Country Club — the longest course on the US PGA Tour — broke the tour record of 60 by Al Brosch in 1951.

Conteh stripped of world title with glittering career in tatters

THE troubles that had dogged John Conteh since he won the world light-heavyweight title in 1974 finally caught up with him when he was stripped of his crown for refusing to go through with a contracted defence against the Argentinian Miguel Cuello in Monte Carlo.

Conteh, once tipped to be Britain's golden boy of boxing, never fulfilled his early promise. He had made only three defences of his title while his career was beset with recurring hand injuries and promotional and managerial problems. At one time it seemed that Conteh was reserving his fisticuffs for the court rather than the ring.

Conteh: hand injuries

Missing Welshmen deflate the Lions

THE British Lions came down to earth after the heady visits to New Zealand in 1971 and South Africa in 1974, and they were three down before they even took off. The Welsh trio of JPR Williams, Gerald Davies and Gareth Edwards were unavailable and the lack of midfield talent and a wet winter did not augur well.

They lost the opening Test to New Zealand 16-12 and won the second 13-9. However, tries by Ian Kirkpatrick and Andy Haden lifted New Zealand spirits in the third Test, which the hosts won 19-7. British hopes rested on the Scottish scrum-half Dougie Morgan in the final Test. He scored all their points but missed a penalty late in the second half to give the All Blacks a 10-9 victory.

Crucible becomes top venue

SINCE 1976, the World Professional championship has retained the same sponsor, Embassy, and since 1977 it has always been held at the Crucible Theatre, Sheffield. The wife of Mike Watterson, snooker's leading promoter of the day, saw a play there and told him that its in-the-round setting and intimate atmosphere would be ideal for snooker.

John Spencer's third world title made him the Crucible's first champion. His 1969 title had marked the championship's return to a knockout basis after 12 years in the wilderness of challenge matches; his 1970 title in Sydney was the first championship to be held abroad.

MAY

AUGUST

1977

TENNIS

Superbrat hits town in style

McEnroe: a native New Yorker

A BRASH New Yorker named John Patrick McEnroe burst on to the Wimbledon scene with the greatest touch and worst temper to prowl a tennis court. The unseeded 18-year-old became the first qualifier to reach the semi-finals, where he was beaten by Jimmy Connors, not somebody to be put off his game by a tempestuous brat. Connors won 6-3 6-3 4-6 6-4 but then ran into an iceberg and sank.

Bjorn Borg, the defending champion, used his superb stamina to win 3-6 6-2 6-1 5-7 6-4 in two-and-a-half hours. Borg was expected to be a spent force after taking 3hr 3min to beat his practice partner Vitas Gerulaitis 6-4 3-6 6-3 3-6 8-6 in a stirring semi-final. He played 97 games in three days.

Liverpool defy their doubters

WHEN the year began Liverpool were universally written off. They had ended 1976 by being thrashed 5-1 by Aston Villa, their biggest defeat for 13 years, eliminated from the League Cup and had only stuttered into the European Cup quarter-finals.

Then they dismissed their critics with a swagger. From January 22 to May 14 they never lost another League game and won the championship. In the European Cup they gave one of their most riveting performances to oust St Etienne, the previous year's finalists, with an unforgettable solo goal from "Supersub" David Fairclough, and then strolled into the final. Reaching the FA Cup final had been a canter. Everton in the semi-final had provided their only real opposition.

From next to nowhere Liverpool were 12 days and three matches from the Treble. A point at Anfield against West Ham secured the first leg. Eight days later, at Wembley, they faced Tommy Docherty's youthful Manchester United who had been distraught when Second Division Southampton had stolen their thunder and the Cup the previous year.

But United were a year older, and a year wiser. And this time the luck was running their way. Five minutes after a scoreless first half Stuart Pearson put United ahead only for Jimmy Case to equalise two minutes later. Within two minutes United were ahead again when Lou Macari's solidly struck shot deflected off Jimmy Greenhoff's chest into the goal. Liverpool would now have to settle merely for a League and European Cup Double — if they were up to it.

Four days later in Rome, Liverpool, only the second English club to reach the European Cup final, faced Borussia Moenchengladbach, the West German champions, in Kevin Keegan's last match for the Merseysiders. They put Wembley behind them and played like European champions.

Steve Heighway cleverly set up Terry McDermott in the 27th minute and although the Germans equalised after half-time and pressed for a second goal, Liverpool weathered the storm. In the 65th minute Tommy Smith, of all people, headed home a corner. Keegan and Liverpool now let rip, so much so that Keegan's marker, Berti Vogts up-ended him to concede a penalty that Phil Neal coolly slammed home. Paisley had finally fulfilled Bill Shankly's dream: the European Cup.

Liverpool parade the cup that fulfilled Shankly's dream

Docherty sacked for love affair

SIX weeks after Manchester United had won the FA Cup Tommy Docherty publicly announced that he was leaving his wife and four children to live with Mary Brown, the wife of the club's physiotherapist. Docherty was one of the most controversial figures in the game and had held a string of managers' jobs.

Before United he had been in charge of Chelsea, Rotherham, Aston Villa, Porto and the Scottish national side. He had a wicked sense of humour and was famous for his quips. This made him fair game for the media and although his statement was supposed to stifle press speculation about his three-year affair, it had the opposite affect.

Instead they had a field day hounding Docherty and Catholic Manchester United. The pressure on the club from without and within became great and within 10 days Docherty was sacked for breaking the club's "moral code".

The Daily Express claimed on their front page of July 5: "Club Wives Oust Doc". The utterly safe Dave Sexton replaced him. The Doc soon was back in management with Derby and living up to his celebrated quote: "I've had more clubs than Jack Nicklaus."

Watson and Nicklaus on a different planet

Watson set a record aggregate as he shredded Turnberry

TOM WATSON and Jack Nicklaus were in a world of their own at Turnberry. The links course was hosting its first Open, and the rough had perished under the blazing sun, there was no wind, and the greens were fast. It was a week for low scores, as the American Mark Hayes showed with a record 63 in the second round.

However, the third round belonged to Nicklaus and Watson, who thrilled the crowd by matching each other stroke for stroke with 65s. The rest were trailing.

On the final day the leaders tore Turnberry to shreds. Nicklaus birdied the second and fourth for a three-shot lead and turned one ahead in 33. Few punters would have put money on Watson when

he struck his four-iron at the short 15th on to a down slope 60 feet from the hole. But he drew level when his putt ran in and another birdie at the 17th for a one-shot lead shattered Nicklaus.

But there was one last trick in the Nicklaus's bag. He drove into gorse at the par-four last, hit a brilliant eight-iron recovery to 30 feet and holed the putt. Suddenly Watson needed a three-footer to win. One of the surest putters in the game stroked his ball into the middle of the cup for a 65 and a record low aggregate of 268.

Hubert Green, 10 shots behind Nicklaus in third place, remarked: "Two gods of golf played their own game. I won the tournament for the mortals."

WATSON'S MAJOR VICTORIES

1975 The Open. **1977** The Masters, The Open.
1980 The Open. **1981** The Masters. **1982** The US Open,
The Open. **1983** The Open.

TENNIS

Wade's triumph crowns Queen's silver jubilee

IT WAS a glorious summer. The Queen was celebrating her Jubilee and Wimbledon was staging its centenary. To crown it all Virginia Wade won the singles title.

Wade beat Betty Stove 4-6 6-3 6-1. Her victory at the 13th attempt brought rapturous applause from a patriotic crowd. They sang the national anthem before the final and broke into a rendition of "For she's a jolly good fellow" when the Queen stepped on to the Centre Court to present one of her subjects with the winner's plate.

Wade used her solid serve to beat Chris Evert 6-2 4-6 6-1 in the semi-final but struggled at the start

of a final littered with errors. Wade, nearly 32 years old and 16 days younger than Stove, appeared to have lost until she won seven games on the trot to turn the tide.

She was one of the five winners of major tournaments in a year when the Australian Open was held twice. The January tournament was moved to December to avoid a clash with the Grand Prix Masters in New York. Kerry Reid won in January and Evonne Cawley in December. Roscoe Tanner took the first men's singles title and Vitas Gerulaitis beat John Lloyd of Britain 6-3 7-6 5-7 3-6 6-2 in December.

Wade won seven games to turn the tide

CRICKET

Bowler is the best batsman

RAYMOND PAUL BAKER, a medium pace bowler with Surrey, chalked one up for the tailenders. He could muster only 204 runs in 10 innings in the county championship. But eight not outs lifted his average to 102.00. He finished top of the batting averages, above Viv Richards and Gordon Greenidge who scored more than 1,500 runs.

FOR THE RECORD

ATHLETICS
■ East Germany won the men's team event and Europe the women's in the first World Cup. Britain's only success was Steve Ovett in the 1500m.

BOXING
■ Muhammad Ali successfully defended his world heavyweight title twice.

FOOTBALL
■ Kevin Keegan was the first British player to be transferred for £500,000 when he moved from Liverpool to Hamburg. Liverpool replaced him by luring Kenny Dalglish away from Celtic for £400,000.
■ Wimbledon were elected to the Fourth Division.

GOLF
■ The United States retained the Ryder Cup by beating Britain 12-7 with one match halved at Royal Lytham. It was the last event before European players bolstered the Great Britain and Ireland team.

MOTORCYCLING
■ Phil Read of Britain became the first TT Formula One world champion.

WATERSKIING
■ Mike Hazelwood became the first Briton to win the men's overall title in the world championships.

CRICKET

Boycott comes back with a bang

GEOFF BOYCOTT returned to Test cricket after a self-imposed exile of 30 matches to help England regain the Ashes. The Yorkshire opener looked as though he had never been away, scoring 442 runs in five innings at an average of 147.33.

Boycott marked his comeback in the third Test at Trent Bridge with a century and an unbeaten 80 in a seven-wicket victory. He then celebrated his 100th century in first-class cricket by on-driving Greg Chappell for four in a marathon innings of 191, appropriately at Headingley.

His home ground was packed to watch one of Yorkshire's favourite sons become the first player to reach the auspicious mark in a Test. It was possibly the greatest moment for an opener described as the finest slow scorer in cricket.

The Australians were divided between pro and anti-Packer members and only rain prevented them losing the Jubilee Test at Lord's. They were beaten 3-0 in the Test series and 2-1 in the one-day internationals.

Geoff Boycott reaches his hundredth hundred at Headingley

BOYCOTT'S RECORD

	FIRST-CLASS	TESTS (108)
Innings	1,014	193
Not out	162	23
Runs	48,426	8,114
Highest	261 not out	246 not out
Average	56.83	47.72
Hundreds	151	22
Wickets	45 at 32.42	7 at 54.57
Catches	264	33

GEOFF BOYCOTT . . .

ON HIS SLOW BATTING "Nobody's perfect. You know what happened to the last man who was — they crucified him."

ON SCORING "Given the choice between Raquel Welch and a hundred at Lord's I'd take the hundred every time."

ON W G GRACE "Unless I'm crackers or something, I've scored a bloody sight more runs than that bearded old bugger."

MOTOR RACING

Lauda proves second is best

NIKI LAUDA put the horror and disappointment of the previous season behind him and captured his second world championship for Ferrari. Although he won only three Grands Prix, the same as Jody Scheckter and James Hunt, and one fewer than Mario Andretti, his racing strategy gave him six second places and the title.

Lauda: back in action after his crash last year

CRICKET

Pakistani emulates Boycott

MUDASSAR NAZAR was determined to impress the Pakistani selectors on his home ground when he was recalled after a disappointing debut the previous season. Nine hours and 17 minutes later the opener may well have put the selectors to sleep with the slowest century in Test cricket. His innings of 114 in nearly 10 hours ensured a boring draw against England in the first Test, which was only enlivened by crowd disturbances.

Packer rocks cricket to its foundations

WHEN Kerry Packer knocked on the Australian Cricket Board's door and asked if they would like bags of money in exchange for the rights to televise Test matches they bluntly refused. Packer was miffed. Believing the ACB had not given him a fair hearing, he went away and staged the biggest revolution in the 100-year history of Test cricket.

The multi-millionaire owner of the Channel Nine television station decided to hold his own series and signed 35 of the world's leading players. The establishment was in a flap. For years they had refused the players a fairer monetary deal. Now the underpaid were queuing at Packer's door for a slice of the cake. All but four of the Australian team signed up for World Series Cricket and the best players in the rest of world followed.

The Test and County Cricket Board's reaction was to strip Tony Greig of the England captaincy when they heard he had recruited players. The International Cricket Conference held an emergency meeting on June 14 and agreed to meet Packer. But when he reiterated his request to televise Australian Tests, the talks broke down. The ICC took a hard line and gave the players until October 1 to turn down Packer or face a ban.

Packer's players went to the High Court and 31 days later won their case against restraint of trade and inducement to breach their contracts. The judgment by Mr Justice Slade on 221 foolscap-size pages took 5½ hours to deliver and took nearly £200,000 out of the ICC and TCCB coffers in costs.

World Series Cricket started in the Australian summer but attracted only small crowds to a variety of unusual venues because the games were barred from playing on the establishment's grounds. So on showgrounds, trotting tracks and football fields, the Australian, West Indian and Rest of World teams began what was to become all the rage the following season.

Packer: money talks

THE PACKER PLAYERS

The 66 who played World Series Cricket

AUSTRALIA Ian Chappell (captain), Ray Bright, Greg Chappell, Trevor Chappell, Ian Davis, Ross Edwards, Gary Gilmour, David Hookes, Martin Kent, Bruce Laird, Rob Langer, Dennis Lillee, Ashley Mallett, Mick Malone, Rod Marsh, Rick McCosker, Graham McKenzie, Kerry O'Keeffe, Len Pascoe, Wayne Prior, Ian Redpath, Richie Robinson, Jeff Thomson, Max Walker, Doug Walters, Graeme Watson, Dennis Yagmich, Kepler Wessels.

WEST INDIES Clive Lloyd (captain), Jim Allen, Richard Austin, Colin Croft, Wayne Daniel, Roy Fredericks, Joel Garner, Gordon Greenidge, Desmond Haynes, David Holford, Michael Holding, Bernard Julien, Collis King, Deryck Murray, Albert Padmore, Viv Richards, Andy Roberts, Lawrence Rowe.

REST OF THE WORLD *England* Tony Greig (captain), Dennis Amiss, Alan Knott, John Snow, Derek Underwood, Bob Woolmer. *Pakistan* Asif Iqbal, Imran Khan, Majid Khan, Javed Miandad, Mushtaq Muhammad, Sarfraz Nawaz, Haroon Rashid, Zaheer Abbas. *South Africa* Eddie Barlow, Garth le Roux, Mike Procter, Clive Rice, Barry Richards. *New Zealand* Richard Hadlee.

> *Cricket is the easiest sport in the world to take over. Nobody paid the players what they are worth*
>
> **Kerry Packer**

Revie takes the Arab money and runs away

DON REVIE quit as England manager in the most shocking way. Having failed to qualify for the European championships and on the point of being eliminated from the World Cup finals, Revie felt his time was up and he looked around for a safety net.

While his squad was on a successful summer tour to South America, Revie was supposed to be watching Italy, their opponents in the World Cup qualifiers, play Finland in Helsinki. Instead, he went to Dubai and negotiated a four-year contract as the football supremo of the United Arab Emirates worth £340,000 tax free.

Then he quietly approached the FA and offered "to save trouble and go" if they paid up the remainder of his England contract, £50,000, and gave him a £5,000 golden handshake. The FA officials asked him if he had another job to go to, because Manchester United had suddenly sacked Tommy Docherty, and he said: "No".

Revie revealed his decision to quit in the Daily Mail on July 12. The following day he revealed the details of his new job in the same newspaper. The FA deplored his actions and charged him with acting deceitfully and damaging the image of football and the FA. Revie refused to appear before an FA hearing and they suspended him from any involvement with football under the FA until he did.

Ron Greenwood took over as caretaker manager while the FA interviewed prospective candidates. Brian Clough was the people's choice but the FA establishment were terrified that he would be uncontrollable. To mollify public opinion they interviewed him and, to their surprise, he almost won them over. However Greenwood was confirmed as England team manager in December.

Revie: sold out

RUGBY LEAGUE

Briton helps Australia to beat Britain

BOBBY FULTON was born in Warrington but his parents decided to move to Australia and Britain lost one of its finest stand-offs.

Fulton led the Kangaroos to a 2-1 victory in the Ashes series. They won 13 of their 16 tour matches. The Australians clinched the first Test 15-9, lost the second 18-14, but were too powerful in the decider, winning 23-6.

CRICKET

Gatting a victim of lbw record

MIKE GATTING was given his first experience of Test cricket, and Pakistani umpires. The chunky Middlesex batsman was one of a record six lbw victims in England's first innings in Karachi. Gatting, making his debut in the third Test, was given out by the Pakistani umpire Shakoor Rana to a delivery from Abdul Qadir which pitched well outside the leg stump.

There was no respite in the second innings. He was dismissed lbw to Iqbal Qasim as the match petered out to an 11th successive draw between the two countries.

Gatting played one more Test against New Zealand before he was dropped for two years. He would have words with Shakoor Rana another day.

RUGBY UNION

Welsh epic ignited by fired-up Bennett

FOLKLORE suggests that dragons were slain because they breathed fire. On March 4 the Welsh dragon was nearly slain because it did not breathe fire.

Phil Bennett's team looked as though they had played one match too many in the Five Nations championship when France took a 7-0 lead in Cardiff. Both teams were unbeaten, the Grand Slam was up for grabs and Wales were fading. But shortly before half-time the captain provided the spark to ignite the Welsh fire. He side-stepped his way through for a try, Gareth Edwards kicked a drop goal and when Bennett scored again Wales were 13-7 ahead at the interval. They were on their way to a 16-7 victory.

It was a hard winter for the champions of the 1970s. They opened their campaign in driving rain at Twickenham, where rolling touch kicks from Edwards and Bennett's three penalties provided a 9-6 win. A 14-point scoring burst in 10 minutes against Scotland took them to a 22-14 triumph, and then Steve Fenwick applied the finishing touches against Ireland. The centre scored a try and four penalties in a 20-16 win that gave Wales a record third successive Triple Crown.

That was the end of an era. The illustrious Edwards, with 53 consecutive caps, retired and one more championship title closed the book on the fairy-tale about the Welsh dragon.

THE DECADE OF THE DRAGON

Wales in the Five Nations championship

Year	Position	Honours
1969	First	Triple Crown
1970	First	Triple Crown
1971	First	Grand Slam/Triple Crown
1972	—	—
1973	First (tie)	—
1974	Second (tie)	—
1975	First	—
1976	First	Grand Slam/Triple Crown
1977	Second	Triple Crown
1978	First	Grand Slam/Triple Crown
1979	First	Triple Crown

Wales and Scotland did not play their matches against Ireland in 1972 because of violence in Dublin. No table is provided because of the disruption to fixtures.

CRICKET

Hadlee humiliates England as New Zealand break their duck

THERE was no love lost between Richard Hadlee and England's batsmen on St Valentine's Day. The New Zealand fast bowler left England floundering at 53 for eight, chasing 137 for victory in Wellington. He returned the next day to clean up the tail in New Zealand's first-ever victory against England after 48 matches. The tourists were dismissed for 64 and Hadlee took six for 26.

England squared the series in the second Test when Ian Botham hit his maiden Test century and took eight wickets.

SNOOKER

Cameras catch all the angles

RAY REARDON'S sixth and last world title was achieved in the dawning of a new era for the championship and for snooker: blanket BBC television coverage for all 17 days of the tournament. This gave a portrait of an event rather than a sketch of the final.

Such coverage enabled the length and complexity of the matches to be appreciated more fully than ever before and set the model for television's coverage of other sporting events. Through heavily increasing screen time a huge advance in snooker's sponsorship levels was achieved.

Reardon: sixth title

GOLF

Shifting sands trap Nakajima

TOMMY NAKAJIMA earned an invitation to the Masters as one of the most consistent players in Japan. Three months later he was known throughout the golfing world as the Sands of Nakajima.

His notoriety was achieved at Augusta's 13th hole when he landed in a bunker and took 13 shots to complete the hole. He then went to St Andrews for the Open and was in contention until he landed in a greenside bunker at the Road Hole. He failed to clear the lip, took three more shots in the bunker and scored nine for the hole. "I'm now a very good friend of sand," he suggested afterwards.

New boys Forest teach Liverpool a lesson

NEWLY promoted Nottingham Forest surprised everybody, except of course Brian Clough and Peter Taylor, when they cruised to the First Division championship seven points clear of Liverpool.

They had begun the season well but an early 3-0 defeat at the hands of Arsenal prompted knowing heads to shake. However, after they were beaten by Leeds in November they never lost another League match. They had taken a five-point lead into the New Year, which by February had been stretched to eight. Liverpool helped Forest's cause by losing four matches in six weeks between January and March. And although Liverpool moved into overdrive in their last 12 games, winning nine and drawing three, so did Forest.

Clough had now joined Herbert Chapman as the only English managers ever to have taken two different clubs to the League title.

Parade of champions: Forest show off the silver to their fans

Even more extraordinary was that for each of those clubs it was their first League title. Chapman with Huddersfield and Arsenal, Clough with Derby and Forest.

Liverpool's vain attempts to hang on to Forest's coat-tails had not been confined to the race for the title. The two had also clashed in the League Cup final. The first meeting at Wembley on March 18 was a dour, scoreless draw. Four days later at Old Trafford it became a livelier affair which Forest won with a controversial penalty when Phil Thompson brought down John O'Hare outside the penalty area.

Three weeks later Clough clinched the title and celebrated his return to the spotlight with two trophies.

Player steals Masters with a rousing charge

GARY PLAYER, at 42 in the twilight of his career, confirmed the golfing cliché that the Masters is won on Sunday afternoon. The tournament that Bobby Jones founded was regularly decided on the final nine holes, and this time was no different.

Player, who won his first green jacket in 1961, was seven shots behind the leader Hubert Green and well down the field at the start of the final round. But Player made seven birdies over the last 10 holes to win by one shot from Rod Funseth. He came back in 30 for a 64 and his third Masters title 17 years after his first.

Tom Watson presents Player with his third green jacket

Stenmark: third successive overall title in the World Cup

FOR THE RECORD

CRICKET
■ Bhagwat Chandrasekhar became the first Test batsman to be dismissed for a pair on four occasions.

DARTS
■ Leighton Rees of Wales became the first world professional champion.

FOOTBALL
■ The FA imposed a 10-year ban on Don Revie.

SKIING
■ Ingemar Stenmark of Sweden won his third successive men's overall title in the World Cup.

TRIATHLON
■ Gordon Haller became the first Hawaii Ironman in Oahu on February 18. The American beat 14 other competitors in 11hr 46min 58sec. He swam 3.8km, cycled 180km and then ran a marathon of 42.195km.

1978

CRICKET

Botham runs rings all round poor Pakistan

Botham: 8-34 at Lord's

IAN BOTHAM became the toast of England with three superb performances against Pakistan. The Somerset all-rounder helped to end a run of 12 draws against the tourists.

The Pakistanis had no answer to his bat, which hit 212 runs in three innings, including two centuries. His 100 in the second Test required only 104 balls. He then bowled career-best figures of 20.5-8-34-8.

David Gower also had a glorious summer. He entered the Test arena with a flourish, hitting the first ball he faced from Liaquat Ali to the boundary. The left-hander secured a place in the middle order with two half centuries against a Pakistani side who were saved from a clean sweep by rain in Leeds.

TENNIS

Navratilova wins as a Yankee-doodle dandy

Evert: lost 12 of the last 13 points in the final

THE land of French fries, hamburgers and Coca-Cola turned Martina Navratilova into a podgy player after her defection to the United States. But she had a burning desire to become the best player in the world. So, after a series of poor results, she teamed up with the golf professional Sandra Heynie.

Their hard work paid rich dividends at Wimbledon. Navratilova, who had lost 20 of her previous 25 matches against Chris Evert, took 12 of the last 13 points in their final to win 2-6 6-4 7-5. It was the start of her love affair with the Centre Court.

Navratilova: successfully fought the flab

Borg stumbles but makes it three in a row

A GENTLE giant nearly hacked down Bjorn Borg's growing reputation as Wimbledon's greatest champion in the first match on the Centre Court. Victor Amaya, a 6ft 7in American, caught Borg on an off day. He was on the verge of a stunning victory when leading two sets to one with a break point for 4-1. But Amaya slapped his return into the net and Borg recovered to win 8-9 6-1 1-6 6-3 6-3.

The close shave snapped the Swede out of his trance and he was never again troubled. He took 105 minutes to beat Jimmy Connors 6-2 6-2 6-3 in the final and then dropped to his knees, raised his hands and celebrated a third successive title. Connors had his revenge though. He beat Borg 6-4 6-2 6-2 in the US Open final later in the year.

FOR THE RECORD

CYCLING
■ Bernard Hinault won the first of a record five Tours de France.

FOOTBALL
■ Ipswich, who narrowly avoided relegation from the First Division, won the FA Cup for the first time in their history. Almost as memorable was Margaret Thatcher's choice as man of the match: Trevor Whymark. He wasn't playing.

■ Liverpool retained the European Cup when Kenny Dalglish scored the only goal with a chip against Bruges at Wembley on May 10.

GOLF
■ Nancy Lopez strung together a record five successive victories on the US LPGA Tour.

HOCKEY
■ Pakistan won the men's World Cup, and the inaugural Champions Trophy, played for by the leading six teams in the world.

RACING
■ The American jockey Willie Shoemaker, riding in the Derby for the first time, was beaten by inches by Greville Starkey and Shirley Heights in a photofinish.

Kempes sends home fans into raptures

THE World Cup almost never took place in Argentina because of the military junta that had seized power two years earlier. Thousands of people had been murdered or had mysteriously disappeared, there was rampant terrorism, a stricken economy and doubts that the stadiums would be ready in time.

Rumours abounded that the tournament would be moved to Belgium and Holland. Johann Cruyff, Holland's glittering jewel, refused to go, others signed Amnesty International petitions, but the tournament went on as planned. England, having been eliminated by Italy, were absent once again and Scotland were the sole British representative. They had an excellent side, but their manager, Ally MacLeod, indulged in a kind of nationalistic buffoonery that seemed to go down well with the myopic Scottish fans and press alike.

He arrogantly paid no attention to Peru, and their gifted goalscoring midfielder Teofilo Cubillas, and paid the price with a shattering 3-1 defeat. When Willie Johnston tested positive for drugs and was sent home in disgrace Scottish morale was at its nadir. They promptly rolled over and drew with Iran.

Then, quixotically, when they had to play Holland, one of the favourites, and win by three goals to qualify, they miraculously produced fabulous football. With Graeme Souness finally in the team they took a 3-1 lead with an Archie Gemmill goal that dumbfounded the Dutch as he weaved his way through three defenders. But there was to be no happy ending, and a 25-yard blast from Johnny Rep shut the door in their faces. Once again, Scotland had failed to survive the first round.

Holland marched on to the final where they faced the hosts, Argentina, whose path had been somewhat smoothed for them. A number of controversial refereeing decisions had been in their favour. But the most damning example of Argentina's easy ride was in the match against Peru, where they needed to win by four goals to make the final. Quiroga, the Peruvian goalkeeper born in Argentina, conceded six. After the tournament it was alleged that members of the military junta had bribed some of the Peruvian players.

The final was a thrilling match with both sides, strangely vulnerable in defence, allowing several good chances that only fine goalkeeping kept out. Mario Kempes scored the only goal of the first half with the Dutch substitute Dirk

Kempes scores the first two goals to beat Holland 3-1

Nanninga equalising with a header. The Dutch were now in the ascendant and should have won the match in the very last minute of normal time. Rob Rensenbrink was clear through, but his fierce shot hit the foot of the left-hand post with the keeper beaten.

That effectively was the end of Holland. In extra time Argentina roused themselves as the Dutch wilted. Kempes scored again and, as the Dutch vainly pursued the equaliser, Daniel Bertoni sent the whole of Buenos Aires into night-long raptures with a third goal.

Oosterhuis fails to stem the American tide

A BOLD putt at the penultimate hole ruined Peter Oosterhuis's opportunity to end America's domination of the Open. The Briton, with a record crowd providing vociferous support, was in strong contention for his first major title over the final nine holes at St Andrews.

But in his moment of truth he let his heart rule his head and he finished fifth, three strokes behind the winner Jack Nicklaus. It was the American's third Open triumph and his second at St Andrews. His first was in 1970 when the then 22-year-old Oosterhuis finished with rounds of 69, 69 and 76 for fifth place. Nicklaus's victory began America's nine-year supremacy in the Open which was broken only by Gary Player's victory in 1974.

A crowd of 125,271 attended the 1978 Open, the first to attract more than 100,000 people. But the most ecstatic person at golf's headquarters was, naturally, Nicklaus. He was so garrulous in the post-tournament press conference that his wife Barbara pleaded: "Can you get him to stop talking, we've a plane to catch."

> ❝ There are three Opens – the one played in England, the one played in Scotland and the one played at St Andrews ❞
>
> **Jack Nicklaus**

Oosterhuis: fatal error

CRICKET

England's G-men open fire

ENGLAND, beaten by New Zealand on their winter tour for the first time in history, were determined to put the record straight. And with runs from Graham Gooch and David Gower and wickets from Ian Botham they completed three comfortable victories.

The elegant Gower hit his maiden Test century in the opening match and was the leading run-scorer in the series. Gooch returned to open the innings after a two-year absence, scored a duck and then a confident, unbeaten 91 that took England to their first win. Botham was the leading wicket-taker with 24 victims at an average of 14.04.

Gower: maiden century

FOOTBALL

Spurs scoop world with Argentine aces

Gotcha: Burkinshaw swooped for Villa and Ardiles

KEITH BURKINSHAW, Tottenham's mild-mannered manager, staged the transfer coup of the decade, if not the century, when he flew to Argentina two weeks after their World Cup victory and came away with Osvaldo Ardiles, their midfield genius, and Ricardo Villa for the pauperly sum of £750,000.

The story made the front pages of every newspaper. The audacity of Spurs and Burkinshaw to filch two World Cup stars from under the noses of the free-spending Spaniards and Italians was breath-taking, particularly as Spurs had just scraped back into the First Division on goal difference and were not seen as any threat to the likes of Forest and Liverpool. The deal was completed in just 72 hours and announced to a gawping press on July 10. They lapped it up. It was described as "shattering new ground in the British game."

On August 19 the two Argentinian aces could not have had a better stage for their English debut. It was a wonderful sunny day for South American football and Spurs were away to Forest, the League champions. With 26 minutes gone and Spurs 1-0 down Villa demonstrated his deft touch to outwit Peter Shilton and Archie Gemmill and flick the ball into the corner of the goal. The final score was 1-1 and the Argentinians had landed. "Viva Villa" was the inevitable headline as the press reached for their Spanish dictionaries.

> **❛ It was as if the janitor had gone to buy a tin of paint and come back with a Velasquez ❜**
>
> **David Lacey**
> In the Guardian

RUGBY UNION

Munster dent mighty All-Blacks

GRAHAM MOURIE was regarded in New Zealand as one of the greatest players to lead the All Blacks. The flanker from Taranaki enhanced his reputation by captaining his country to their first-ever Grand Slam in Britain.

But there was one hiccough on the tour. Munster became the first-ever Irish team to beat New Zealand. They won 12-0 in Limerick on October 31 and the match programme — sold out before the kick-off — was reprinted as a souvenir after the game.

Packer and Willis rout Australia

The England party which proved too strong for under-strength Australia

KERRY PACKER'S World Series Cricket was beginning to flourish when the official England team arrived in Australia to defend the Ashes. And it took only 14 overs from Bob Willis to expose the extent of Packer's revolution.

The England paceman captured four for 44 as the under-strength Australians crumbled to 116 all out. It set the tone for a one-sided series which England won 4-1.

The tourists triumphed in the opening two Tests for the first time in Australia since 1936, with Willis capturing five for 44. Geoff Boycott scored 77 in 7½ hours, which prompted Lindsay Hassett to comment that "it was an exceptional innings by someone who could not find the middle of the bat".

Australia's answer to their predicament was to call up a young left-hander who would provide the backbone to a shattered batting line-up. Allan Border struggled in his maiden Test but did enough to help Australia to their only victory in the series.

Ali regains crown for a third time

Spinks: upset victory

MUHAMMAD ALI went from the ridiculous to the sublime in seven months, made heavyweight history, and inadvertently plunged his prized title into anarchy.

On February 15 in Las Vegas he managed to contrive a listless defence of his title against Leon Spinks, the 1976 Olympic light-heavyweight champion with only seven professional fights under his belt, and lost on a split decision. The frenetic youngster was even more of a shock winner than Ali was 14 years previously against Sonny Liston. Spinks quickly agreed to a re-match.

A month later the WBC stripped Spinks of his title because he was fighting Ali and not their No 1 contender, Ken Norton, who was immediately proclaimed the world champion. In June, Norton lost the WBC version of the title to Larry Holmes on points in Philadelphia. However the boxing world still saw Spinks, the WBA holder, as the legitimate champion.

Then on September 15, Ali bamboozled everybody when he regained the title (at least one half of it) from Spinks with a performance that belied his 36 years. Ali had now virtually confirmed his immortality. He had taken part in 24 world title bouts and became the first man to win the world heavyweight championship three times. But would he retire and leave the way clear for Holmes?

Patrese blamed for fatal crash

LOTUS and their two drivers were having a wonderful year until the Italian Grand Prix on September 10. Mario Andretti, their team leader, had won six of the 13 GPs, and Ronnie Peterson two, and both drivers were storming away with the drivers championship.

Then at Monza disaster struck. Riccardo Patrese, in only his second season in F1, attempted to overtake on a narrow part of the circuit and hit James Hunt's McLaren, which caught Peterson's car. Peterson did not survive the crash. Patrese, an Italian who had something of a reputation for reckless overtaking, was charged with manslaughter but was eventually acquitted in 1981.

For Andretti, the American who was weaned on motor racing in Italy as a kid, it cast a shadow over his world championship success. He had been born in Pisa and emigrated to the United States with his family in 1955.

Andretti had been a successful driver in all forms of racing in the United States and had won the Indianapolis 500 nine years earlier. Despite his teammate's sad death Lotus took the constructors' championship and first and second places in the drivers' championship.

Peterson: died at Monza

297

Clough's £1m gamble on Francis pays premium European dividend

BOXING

Hope: world champion

FOR THE RECORD

BOXING

■ Roberto Duran relinquished his world lightweight title in February and moved up to the welterweight division.

■ Jim Watt was able to capture the vacant WBC version of the lightweight title by stopping the Colombian Alfredo Pitula in the 12th round in the Kelvin Hall, Glasgow on April 17.

■ Maurice Hope, born in Antigua but based in London, won the WBC version of the world light middleweight title at San Remo when the Italian defender, Rocky Mattioli, retired after eight rounds.

FOOTBALL

■ Brighton, under Alan Mullery, won promotion to the First Division and had successfully graduated from the Third to the First in three seasons.

■ West Bromwich Albion bought David Mills from Middlesbrough in the first domestic £500,000 transfer in January.

RACING

■ Monksfield, one of the few entire horses to race in the top flight of National Hunt, won the Champion Hurdle at Cheltenham for the second year running. His victory on March 14 was also the second time he had beaten Sea Pigeon into second place.

SKIING

■ Annemarie Moser-Proll of Austria won a record sixth overall title in the women's section of the World Cup.

Francis's European Cup debut was marked with the winning goal

NEVER underestimate Brian Clough's ability to shock. On February 9, a month after the British transfer record of £500,000 was broken, Clough smashed it into little pieces when he paid £1m to Birmingham City for Trevor Francis. Everybody believed Clough was mad, particularly as Nottingham Forest's chief target was the European Cup and Francis would only be eligible for one game, the final — if Forest got that far.

Francis, 24, had been a teenage prodigy, making his debut for Birmingham at the of 16 and going on to score 118 goals in 278 appearances. He was one of the brightest talents on the English football horizon and one of the few English players who could have commanded such a fee.

Francis repaid a significant slice of it when he made his European debut on May 30 in Munich in the European Cup final. He headed the only goal and Forest, two seasons out of the Second Division, were the champions of Europe.

Mean Liverpool a league apart

LIVERPOOL had begun the season in their characteristically sluggish style. Within a month they had been knocked out of the European Cup and the League Cup. Bizarrely, this did not seem to apply to their League form.

While Nottingham Forest were pursuing European glory, Liverpool were squirrelling away points. From Christmas 1978 to the end of the season they only lost one League game, and although Forest won the European Cup they finished eight points adrift.

It was a remarkable performance by Liverpool. They garnered 68 points, a record, and lost only four games. Statistically, their defence was the key. In 42 matches they conceded only 16 goals, and their goalkeeper, Ray Clemence, kept a clean sheet on 27 occasions. But League titles are also won with goals. Kenny Dalglish, bought from Celtic in 1977 to replace the irreplaceable Kevin Keegan, scored 21 times.

Clemence: 27 clean sheets

Brearley dominates weakened Australia

MIKE BREARLEY led England to an unprecedented 5-1 victory against Australia, becoming only the second captain after Len Hutton to regain and then retain the Ashes. But the gloss was taken off the triumph by the fact that England had beaten an Australian team devastated by defections to Kerry Packer's World Series Cricket.

England would have been happy to beat Australia 5-1 every summer, but the call from Australia was for peace with Packer and the recall of the best players to redress the balance.

England's victory was achieved mainly by their bowling quartet of Ian Botham, Mike Hendrick, Geoff Miller and Bob Willis. Miller, with 23 wickets at 15.04, was top of the averages while Botham took 23 wickets, Willis 20 and Hendrick 19.

The England batting was solid throughout and in Graham Gooch, David Gower and Botham the team found a middle order they could depend on. Rodney Hogg, with 41 wickets, gave Australia a glimmer of hope. The paceman also provided one of the rare moments of light relief when he brought out an artificial snake to greet Derek Randall's appearance at the crease in the sixth Test. Australia had shown about as much backbone as the snake.

Brearley: second captain to regain and retain the Ashes

Old guard cave in to Packer's revolutionaries

KERRY PACKER'S World Series Cricket, initially shunned by Australian cricket followers, produced a slick marketing campaign to turn around public opinion. There had been unforeseen problems in the first season, such as the West Indians complaining they were being called the Pink Panthers because of the colour of their strip. They preferred maroon.

More than 50,000 people watched the first day/night match at the Sydney Cricket Ground while attendances in the one-sided official Ashes series slumped dramatically. The Australian Cricket Board, realising they had been beaten, made peace with Packer on April 24 by granting his Channel Nine exclusive rights to televise Test matches. The WSC players were reinstated and cricket's spectacular two-year revolution ended.

Zoeller proves nice guys can come first

Zoeller: won first sudden-death play-off at the Masters

FRANK ZOELLER was never going to become a champion, according to his coach at Houston University. He was too much of a gentleman who would clap and congratulate an opponent for making a good shot. So the coach dropped him.

But Zoeller proved that good guys do come first. He was the first player since Gene Sarazen in 1935 to win the Masters on his first appearance. And it was a dramatic victory.

Fuzzy, as he was known, was six shots behind Ed Sneed at the start of the final round. He was in the clubhouse in 70. But Sneed dropped shots at the last three holes for a 76 and lost confidence for the first sudden-death play-off at Augusta. Tom Watson was also in the play-off, and Zoeller won at the second extra hole.

There was also a sudden-death play-off in the US PGA championship, where the Australian David Graham took six on the last hole for a 65 and then beat Ben Crenshaw at the third extra hole.

Cronin kicks Lions off the park

THE round-the-corner kick favoured by most players in the late 1970s was shunned by Mick Cronin. The centre said: "I set the ball on the lace as I found I could get more distance that way."

Doug Laughton's touring British Lions would be the last to disagree. They watched Cronin kick Australia to their first-ever clean sweep in the Ashes. Cronin scored nearly two thirds of Australia's points. He kicked 48 points and took his tally to 54 with two tries as Australia won 35-0, 24-16 and 28-2.

Wayward Seve tames Open

SEVERIANO BALLESTEROS stayed off most of the fairways in the final two rounds of the Open at Royal Lytham. The 22-year-old struck the ball everywhere else on his way to becoming the youngest champion this century.

He landed on only two fairways in 36 holes. It was not quite championship form, but then Ballesteros had a reputation for being wild and wayward off the tee. His idea was to hit the ball as hard as he could and then use his brilliant short game to recover. It was a skill he had learned as a schoolboy with a battered three-iron on the Santander Bay course in Spain. It stood him in good stead.

He estimated that he had been down in two from bunkers 15 times. There was no better example than his eventful finish. He started the last round one behind Hale Irwin, the US champion. When he reached the turn he had the bit between his teeth. He landed in the sand at the 13th and was down in two for a birdie. He finished in the car park at the 16th. A miraculous recovery from among the television vehicles gave him a 15-foot putt for birdie. He sank it.

A bunker at the 17th failed to ruin his par and, with a three-shot advantage, the gallery thought he would play safe on the 18th. Not Ballesteros. He hooked his tee shot and was short with his second. But

Ballesteros: hit almost everything apart from the fairways

another exquisite recovery and a three-foot putt gave him the title, three shots ahead of Jack Nicklaus and Ben Crenshaw. He was the first professional from the continent to win since Arnaud Massy in 1907.

Americans called him the first "car park champion". One sug-

gested he spent so much time off the fairways he was mistaken for a gallery marshall. But Ballesteros had the last say. He suggested the Royal Lytham course should be changed. "I'd like to see the fairways more narrow," he said. "Then everybody would have to play from the rough, not just me."

Borg withstands Tanner's blitz

Tanner: 140mph serve

ROSCOE TANNER, a left-hander from Chattanooga, possessed one of the fastest serves in the game. He was once timed at 140mph and a succession of opponents found the thunderbolts too fast at Wimbledon. Even Bjorn Borg, seeking his fourth successive title, struggled against the American in the final.

Wimbledon had joined the rest of the world by introducing the tie-break at 6-6 instead of their original 8-8, and with both players holding serve, Tanner won the tie-break in the opening set. But the Tanner serve lost its sting, Borg levelled in a 19-minute second set and although there were minor hiccups he won 6-7 6-1 3-6 6-3 6-4. An exhausted Borg sank to his knees and held his hands in prayer. He had survived 2hr 49min with the Chattanooga Express.

Elegant King Viv rules the world

ENGLAND'S hopes of winning the World Cup went up in smoke when Viv Richards strode to the crease at a packed Lord's on June 23 and showed the world why he was regarded as one of the sport's finest batsmen.

England had improved their chances in the final by capturing the first four West Indian wickets for only 99 runs. They nearly had Richards trapped leg before with the second ball he faced, but when

he got into his stride he batted with the arrogance of a master.

Richards was joined by Collis King and they put on 139 in 21 overs to turn the match in favour of the defending champions. Richards scored an unbeaten 138 off 157 deliveries and treated the crowd to 11 fours and three sixes in an innings which earned the Man-of-the-Match award. England's selectors loaded Mike Brearley's team with batsmen and

paid the price for being one recognised bowler short. A combination of 12 overs from Geoff Boycott, Graham Gooch and Wayne Larkins cost 86 runs.

England made a solid but slow start to their innings and were well behind the required run rate of 4.78 per over when the middle order were forced to throw caution to the wind. That was the cue for Joel Garner to take five wickets for four runs in 11 balls.

Billie Jean proves the perfect team player

King: doubles victory gave her a record 20th Wimbledon title

BILLIE JEAN KING crowned her career by winning a 20th title at Wimbledon. Her moment of glory came in the women's doubles final when she teamed up with Martina Navratilova to beat Betty Stove and Wendy Turnbull 5-7 6-3 6-2. Six of her titles were singles, 10 were women's doubles and four mixed doubles.

The bespectacled American, who was the leading campaigner for women's equality in the game, eclipsed the record held by Elizabeth Ryan, who died at Wimbledon the day before.

King's strong serve-volley repertoire and fighting qualities made her one of the sport's greats.

She played in 265 matches at Wimbledon and was a quarter-finalist 20 times in 22 years. She did not play in 1976, when she retired temporarily, and in 1981, when she became a television commentator and was unsuccessfully sued by her former lover Marilyn Barnett for palimony.

> *We wouldn't be where we are without Billie Jean King*
>
> **Martina Navratilova**

BILLIE JEAN KING'S MAJOR SINGLES TITLES

1966 Wimbledon. 1967 Wimbledon, US championship.
1968 Australian championship, Wimbledon. 1971 US Open.
1972 French Open, Wimbledon, US Open. 1973 Wimbledon.
1974 US Open. 1975 Wimbledon.

FOR THE RECORD

FOOTBALL

■ Liverpool became the first British club to sign a shirt sponsorship deal, on July 24, with Hitachi. Television quickly orchestrated a ban on the shirts being shown on the screen.

■ Celtic beat Rangers 4-2 with only 10 men on May 21 to capture the League in a match that was virtually a play-off for the title.

GOLF

■ Sam Trahan needed only 18 putts in the final round of the Philadelphia Classic, a US PGA Tour record.

MOTOR RACING

■ Seventy-three years after their first victory in the French Grand Prix Renault won it again, the first success for a turbocharged car.

RACING

■ The crowd at Epsom celebrated the 200th running of the Derby and Troy gave them something to cheer with a runaway seven-length victory, the biggest winning margin for more than 50 years.

■ Kris was almost unbeatable over a mile. He won 10 of 11 races and his only defeat was by Tap On Wood in the 2000 Guineas.

WATERPOLO

■ Hungary won the first World Cup to add to their triumph in the inaugural world championship in 1973. It was the only time they won either competition. The United States won the women's final.

Arsenal's marathon run ends in sprint finish

THE FA Cup began in arctic conditions — it took nearly a month to complete the third round — and finished on a stifling hot day in May. Arsenal required five matches involving 16 goals and 540 minutes to dispose of Jack Charlton's Third Division Sheffield Wednesday in the third round. But when they got to Wembley in a marathon FA Cup campaign they eventually triumphed by outsprinting Manchester United over just five minutes.

United were the favourites but with five minutes remaining Arsenal were comfortably 2-0 ahead in a dull final. Terry Neill, the Arsenal manager, foolishly disrupted his defence by bringing on Steve Walford as a substitute in order to give him a winner's medal. Four minutes later Gordon McQueen and Sammy McIlroy had levelled the scores.

United were on a roll, anticipating extra time and extra glory, so when Liam Brady picked up the ball from the kick-off, his only thought was to keep hold of it and prevent a third United goal before full-time. Graham Rix had other ideas. He raced down the wing, received Brady's pass and put the ball neatly into Alan Sunderland's path for the winner. United could hardly draw breath before the referee blew the whistle.

Brian Talbot scores Arsenal's first goal in the Cup final

SEPTEMBER
1979
DECEMBER

CRICKET

Essex break 103-year duck

IT TOOK Essex 103 years to win the county championship. But when they triumphed they did it in style. John Lever took 53 wickets in June to put them top of the table and the title was sealed with four matches to play. Earlier in the season they won the B&H Cup, beating Surrey by 35 runs.

But the talking point in the competition was Somerset's group match against Worcestershire on May 24. Somerset led the group with a superior strike rate and, to ensure they were not overtaken, their captain Brian Rose batted first and declared after only one over. Worcestershire won the match but Somerset qualified for the quarter-finals until the TCCB disqualified them for bringing the game into disrepute. The match lasted 20 minutes and admission money was refunded.

SOMERSET'S SHAME

Benson and Hedges Cup group match
Worcestershire v Somerset, Worcester, May 24

Somerset
B C Rose not out	0
P W Denning not out	0
Extras (1nb)	1
Total (for no wkt dec)	1

Bowling V A Holder 1-1-0-0.

Worcestershire
G M Turner not out	2
J A Ormrod not out	0
Total (for no wkt)	2

Bowling C H Dredge 1-0-1-0;
K F Jennings 0.4-0-1-0

Worcestershire won by 10 wkts

CRICKET

India stretch England to limit

ENGLAND, hoping to make up for their disappointment in the World Cup final, were frustrated by the weather in their Test series against India. But there were moments of brilliance to satisfy their rain-drenched supporters.

David Gower put them on the road to victory in the first Test at Edgbaston with his maiden first-class double century. He hit 24 boundaries in six hours. England won by an innings and 83 runs.

Ian Botham and the ubiquitous rain dominated the second and third Tests and India had their say in the fourth match. Botham took five for 35 at Lord's and hit a century off 121 balls at Headingley in drawn matches. The tourists came close to squaring the series at The Oval where, set 438 to win in 498 minutes, they needed 15 off the last over with two wickets left. They scored six runs and the match was drawn.

FOR THE RECORD

BOWLS
■ David Bryant of England, who had become the inaugural outdoor world champion in 1966, repeated his feat indoors.

BOXING
■ Larry Holmes made three successful defences of the WBC version of the world heavyweight title, and Muhammad Ali relinquished the WBA version and announced his retirement.

■ Sugar Ray Leonard, the 1976 Olympic light-welterweight champion, captured the world welterweight title from Wilfred Benitez in Las Vegas on November 30.

CRICKET
■ Pakistan's first Test on Indian soil in 19 years was halted for several minutes on the first day when a swarm of bees forced the players and umpires to lie flat on the ground with hands over ears.

FOOTBALL
■ Alan Hardaker, the secretary of the Football League, retired. Hardaker was a tough administrator and his sobriquets reflected his image: from "Cagney of the

League" to "the League's most celebrated enforcer".

■ The 10-year ban imposed by the FA on Don Revie was overturned in the High Court because of the probable bias of the FA chairman Sir Harold Thompson during Revie's disciplinary hearing.

MOTOR RACING
■ Niki Lauda announced his retirement after the practice session for the Canadian Grand Prix in Montreal on September 29.

■ Alain Prost won the European F3 crown and signed with McLaren-Ford for the 1980 season.

■ James Hunt retired to become a television commentator.

RUGBY UNION
■ Wales struggled to a 13-12 win against Romania in the first Test between the two countries in Cardiff on October 6.

SPEEDWAY
■ Ivan Mauger of New Zealand took a record sixth world championship 11 years after he had won his first title.

Mauger: record at Wembley in British speedway's golden jubilee

Thomson fastest of them all

Thomson: 99.688 mph

A CAMERA and computer in Perth put the final stamp on Jeff Thomson's claim as the fastest and most accurate Test bowler in the world. The Australian was recorded bowling more than four miles an hour faster than his West Indian rival Michael Holding on November 22. Each bowler had eight balls. Bob Willis of England, Sylvester Clarke of Barbados and the Australian Rodney Hogg were the only leading players missing from the line-up.

THE FAST LANE

1 Jeff Thomson (Australia) 99.688mph
2 Michael Holding (West Indies) 87.76mph
3 Imran Khan (Pakistan) 86.77mph
4 Garth le Roux (South Africa) 86.58mph
5 Colin Croft (West Indies) 86.45mph
6 Andy Roberts (West Indies) 86.08mph
7 Dennis Lillee (Australia) 84.72mph
8 Wayne Daniel (West Indies) 82.90mph
9 Len Pascoe (Australia) 81.73mph
10 Richard Hadlee (New Zealand) 80.62mph
11 Mike Proctor (South Africa) 79.87mph
12 Safraz Nawaz (Pakistan) 78.88mph

Storm kills 15 in Fastnet race

Helicopters flew hundreds of missions to rescue survivors of the Admiral's Cup disaster

THE fleet had little idea of what they were about to face as they set off in moderate winds on the Fastnet race, the last event in the Admiral's Cup. And after a day the wind was getting lighter, with no indication that a storm was about to break.

But as the leaders were approaching the Fastnet rock the wind suddenly roared up to force 10 and more and the seas became tempestuous. The yachts took a fearful pounding and many of the crews had cause to regret experimenting with lightweight carbon-fibre rudders, which could not stand the strain.

Lifeboats had to tow several craft to safety, and the crew of the Irish Cup yacht Golden Apple of the Sun were winched to safety by a helicopter.

Many of the smaller yachts in the fleet were not able to withstand the battering and, in all, 15 people died. At the height of the storm the coastguards dealt with more than 10,000 messages in 60 hours.

When the survivors limped back to Plymouth Australia had won the Cup, but the usual end of race celebrations were cancelled and replaced with a memorial service for those who had been lost.

Dashing Scheckter coasts home

TWO Ferrari drivers finished first and second in the world championship, with Jody Scheckter taking the title and Gilles Villeneuve the runner-up's spot, four points adrift. The championship was effectively settled at the Italian Grand Prix in Monza on September 9 when Scheckter won and his teammate was second. With only two races remaining Villeneuve had an insurmountable task, and despite winning one and finishing second in the other, a simple fourth place in Canada clinched it for the South African.

Scheckter's triumph at Monza virtually wrapped up the title

Australia back in contention

AUSTRALIA, celebrating the recall of their leading players from World Series Cricket, invited England and the West Indies for hastily arranged tours. But the Australians were miffed when the Test and County Cricket Board decided not to put the Ashes up for stake.

Their hopes of regaining the urn would have to wait until 1981, but three comfortable victories gave them confidence. A triangular series of one-day matches was staged for the World Series Cup, which West Indies won by beating England in the first two games of the three-match final.

Europe in Ryder Cup

EVER since the decline of British golf after the Second World War there was a wave of support for changing the composition of the Ryder Cup team. The United States had turned the event into a one-sided contest, their only blemish being a narrow loss in 1957.

After the emergence of the Australian Peter Thomson and Bobby Locke of South Africa there were suggestions that the British team should include Commonwealth players. Nothing came of it. America kept on winning.

It took the growth of the European Tour in the 1970s to realise the merits of expanding the Great Britain and Ireland team to include Europe. So, with the agreement of the USPGA, the Ryder Cup team under John Jacobs flew to the United States with two Spaniards aboard.

Severiano Ballesteros and Antonio Garrido were unable to end the American domination at The Greenbrier in West Virginia, but they played well enough to provide Europe with a glimmer of hope. The United States won 16-10 with two matches halved.

1980s

The killing fields that broke our hearts

Strangely, for a decade that will be forever remembered as one of disaster, British sport came off the starting blocks to beat the politicians. President Carter, in an election year, demanded that the West boycott the 1980 Olympic Games in Moscow in retaliation for the Soviet Union's invasion of Afghanistan the previous year. Margaret Thatcher agreed, but British Olympians (with the exception of hockey and equestrianism) stood firm and, to their credit, defied the Iron Maiden.

Much was wonderful in the 1980s. Seb Coe's two successive 1500m Olympic gold medals; Ian Botham's exploits at Headingley and Edgbaston in 1981; Martina Navratilova's six consecutive Wimbledon singles titles; Liverpool's European and domestic dominance; the emergence of Essex as a cricketing power; the pre-eminence of Steve Davis on the green baize; the resurgence of British and European golfers . . . the list is endless. But, unfortunately, history will probably place greater store on our failings.

Football let us all down. English fans simply went from bad to worse. Not content with bringing shame on the clubs that they "supported", they also latched on to the national side. Uefa fined the Football Association £8,000 in 1980 after English fans had brawled with Italians in Turin during the European championships. By 1984 the problem had become so acute that Uefa warned the FA that English clubs would be banned from Europe unless the government took action to stop hooligans travelling abroad. But the FA and the government could not even control fans in this country.

Football in England could never face up to the fact it was running a slum sport in slum stadiums. Then in three fateful months in 1985, the roof caved in.

On March 13, the nation watched appalled when TV showed Millwall fans running amok at Kenilworth Road as their team lost to Luton in the FA Cup quarter-finals. Luton knew what to do. They promptly banned away fans from their ground, even though the club incurred the displeasure of the rest of the League. Football, though, did not have a clue. Summoned to 10 Downing Street on All Fools' Day by a Prime Minister who wanted to know what was going to be done, Ted Croker, the FA secretary, came out with the immortal words: "These people are society's problem and we don't want your hooligans at our sport."

Europe didn't want English hooligans destroying its sport either. So when Liverpool fans charged Juventus supporters before the European Cup final at Heysel, leaving 39 people dead and more than 400 injured, the response was swift. All English clubs were banned from playing any matches in Europe.

English hooligans were not the only culprits. Heysel was a disgrace. It was an old, crumbling stadium and this contributed to the death toll. The tragedy at Heysel was the time bomb that football had manufactured for itself: violent fans in an unsafe environment. The hooligan problem was self-evident, but the danger posed by antiquated grounds should also have been fully understood. Particularly as less than three weeks before Heysel, tragedy had struck at Bradford. What

should have been a day of celebration — Bradford had won promotion to the Second Division — became a day of mourning. Fifty-six people died when they were unable to escape from an ancient wooden stand that turned into a blazing inferno within minutes.

English football had hit rock bottom. But it still had further to sink. Mr Justice Popplewell, charged with finding ways of making sure such terrible events could never happen again, produced a report. Yet, once again, little was done. Football was up to its usual party trick: sitting on its hands while sticking its head in the sand. Sadly such inertia costs lives.

Four years after Heysel 95 Liverpool supporters lost their lives through no fault of their own when they went to Hillsborough to watch the FA Cup semi-final against Nottingham Forest. Caged in like animals — the belated response to hooliganism — the supporters, many of them boys and girls, had nowhere to run when they were crushed to death on an overcrowded terrace. It was the most damning indictment of the way the national game was run. As Kenny Dalglish said: "Football is irrelevant now."

This time the nation was mortified, and the report by Lord Justice Taylor called for the most sweeping changes in the game, including the introduction of mandatory all-seat stadiums. The report was universally praised for breathing new life into football. Unfortunately by 1992, the backsliding had begun all over again. The lower Division clubs bleated that they could not afford the ground improvements. Local authorities stalled on planning permission for new stadiums, and fans at West Ham and Arsenal protested against schemes to raise the required money. Football, it seems, is like the Bourbons: "It remembers everything, but learns nothing."

Our faith in sport was also rocked by scandals that shook the very foundations. Lester Piggott, the greatest jockey this century, was jailed for a multi-million pound tax fraud and Ben Johnson, the fastest man on earth, was caught using drugs to win an Olympic gold medal. Our idols really did have feet of clay.

One had a suspect hand that he blamed on god. When Diego Maradona, one of the most complete footballers ever to grace this earth, used his arm to "score" against England in the 1986 World Cup in front of a television audience in the billions, he tarnished his talent and the game. Worse, he demonstrated, at the highest possible level and in the most public of ways, that cheating is deeply rooted in professional football. Argentina won that game by a one-goal margin, and went on to take the World Cup. Did he devalue the trophy, the tournament? Yes. Do we care? Yes, but not because it was England that suffered, but because it was football — dammit, it was all sport — that paid the price.

As sport goes into the 1990s and beyond it has to understand one thing. Winning might be most of the story — but it isn't all of it. The be all and end all of it is: the love affair. Take the love out, the passion, the emotion, the sorrow, the anger, the despair, and you may as well do crossword puzzles. And try selling that to television.

AMERICAN FOOTBALL

■ *Super Bowl*
1980 Pittsburgh Steelers
1981 Oakland Raiders
1982 San Francisco 49ers
1983 Washington Redskins
1984 Los Angeles Raiders
1985 San Francisco 49ers
1986 Chicago Bears
1987 New York Giants
1988 Washington Redskins
1989 San Francisco 49ers

ATHLETICS

■ *British Olympic gold medals*
1980 *100m* Allan Wells; *800m* Steve Ovett; *1500m* Sebastian Coe; *decathlon* Daley Thompson
1984 *1500m* Sebastian Coe; *javelin* Tessa Sanderson; *decathlon* Daley Thompson

BASEBALL

■ *World Series*
1980 Philadephia Phillies
1981 Los Angeles Dodgers
1982 St Louis Cardinals
1983 Baltimore Orioles
1984 Detroit Tigers
1985 Kansas City Royals
1986 New York Mets
1987 Minnesota Twins
1988 Los Angeles Dodgers
1989 Oakland Athletics

BOXING

■ *British world champions*
1980 *Middleweight.* Alan Minter
1983 *Flyweight.* Charlie Magri (WBC)
1986 *Welterweight.* Lloyd Honeyghan
1986 *Light-heavyweight.* Dennis Andries (WBC)
1987 *Junior welterweight.* Terry Marsh (IBF)
1987 *Welterweight.* Lloyd Honeyghan (WBC/IBF)
1988 *Flyweight.* Duke McKenzie (IBF)
1988 *Welterweight.* Lloyd Honeyghan (WBC)
1989 *Flyweight.* Dave McAuley (IBF)
1989 *Light-heavyweight.* Dennis Andries (WBC)

CRICKET

■ *World Cup*
1983 India *bt* West Indies by 43 runs
1987 Australia *bt* England by 7 runs
■ *County championship*
1980 Middlesex
1981 Nottinghamshire
1982 Middlesex
1983 Essex
1984 Essex
1985 Middlesex
1986 Essex
1987 Nottinghamshire
1988 Worcestershire
1989 Worcestershire
■ *Gillette Cup*
1980 Middlesex *bt* Surrey by 7 wickets
■ *Nat West Trophy*
1981 Derbyshire *bt* Northants, fewer wickets lost
1982 Surrey *bt* Warwickshire by 9 wickets
1983 Somerset *bt* Kent by 24 runs
1984 Middlesex *bt* Kent by 4 wickets
1985 Essex *bt* Nottinghamshire by 1 run
1986 Sussex *bt* Lancashire by 7 wickets
1987 Nottinghamshire *bt* Northants by 3 wickets
1988 Middlesex *bt* Worcestershire by 3 wickets
1989 Warwickshire bt Middlesex by 4 wickets
■ *B&H Trophy*
1980 Northamptonshire *bt* Essex by 6 runs
1981 Somerset *bt* Surrey by 7 wickets
1982 Somerset *bt* Nottinghamshire by 9 wickets
1983 Middlesex *bt* Essex by 4 runs
1984 Lancashire *bt* Warwickshire by 6 wickets
1985 Leicestershire *bt* Essex by 5 wickets
1986 Middlesex *bt* Kent by 2 runs
1987 Yorkshire *bt* Northamptonshire, fewer wickets lost
1988 Hampshire *bt* Derbyshire by 7 wickets
1989 Nottinghamshire *bt* Essex by 3 wickets
■ *Sunday League*
1980 Warwickshire
1981 Essex
1982 Sussex
1983 Yorkshire
1984 Essex
1985 Essex
1986 Hampshire
1987 Worcestershire
1988 Worcestershire
1989 Lancashire

CYCLING

■ *Tour de France*
1980 Joop Zoetemelk
1981 Bernard Hinault
1982 Bernard Hinault
1983 Laurent Fignon
1984 Laurent Fignon
1985 Bernard Hinault
1986 Greg LeMond
1987 Stephen Roche
1988 Pedro Delgado
1989 Greg LeMond

FOOTBALL

■ *World Cup*
1982 Italy 3 West Germany 1
1986 Argentina 3 West Germany 2
■ *European championship*
1980 West Germany 2 Belgium 1
1984 France 2 Spain 0
1988 Holland 2 USSR 0
■ *European Cup*
1980 Nottingham Forest 1 Hamburg 0
1981 Liverpool 1 Real Madrid 0
1982 Aston Villa 1 Bayern Munich 0
1983 Hamburg 1 Juventus 0
1984 Liverpool 1 AS Roma 1 (Liverpool won 4-2 on penalties)
1985 Juventus 1 Liverpool 0
1986 Steaua Bucharest 0 Barcelona 0 (Bucharest won 2-0 on penalties)
1987 Porto 2 Bayern Munich 1
1988 PSV Eindhoven 0 Benfica 0 (Eindhoven won 6-5 on penalties)
1989 AC Milan 4 Steaua Bucharest 0
■ *European Cup Winners' Cup*
1980 Valencia 0 Arsenal 0 (Valencia won 5-4 on penalties)
1981 Dynamo Tbilisi 2 Carl Zeiss Jena 1
1982 Barcelona 2 Standard Liege 1
1983 Aberdeen 2 Real Madrid 1
1984 Juventus 2 Porto 1
1985 Everton 3 Rapid Vienna 1
1986 Dynamo Kiev 3 Atletico Madrid 0
1987 Ajax 1 Lokomotiv Leipzig 0
1988 Mechelen 1 Ajax 0
1989 Barcelona 2 Sampdoria 0
■ *Uefa Cup*
1980 Eintracht Frankfurt *bt* Borussia Moenchengladbach 2-3 1-0 (Frankfurt won on away goals)
1981 Ipswich *bt* AZ Alkmaar 3-0 2-4
1982 IFK Gothenburg *bt* SV Hamburg 1-0 3-0
1983 Anderlecht *bt* Benfica 1-0 1-1
1984 Tottenham *bt* Anderlecht 1-1 1-1 (Tottenham won 4-3 on penalties)
1985 Real Madrid *bt* Videoton 3-0 0-1
1986 Real Madrid *bt* Cologne 5-1 0-2
1987 IFK Gothenburg *bt* Dundee Utd 1-0 1-1
1988 Bayer Leverkusen *bt* Espanol 0-3 3-0 (Leverkusen won 3-2 on penalties)
1989 Napoli *bt* VFB Stuttgart 2-1 3-3
■ *Football League*
1980 Liverpool
1981 Aston Villa
1982 Liverpool
1983 Liverpool
1984 Liverpool
1985 Everton
1986 Liverpool
1987 Everton
1988 Liverpool
1989 Arsenal
■ *FA Cup*
1980 West Ham 1 Arsenal 0
1981 Tottenham 3 Manchester City 2
1982 Tottenham 1 QPR 0 (after 1-1)
1983 Manchester Utd 4 Brighton 0 (after 2-2)
1984 Everton 2 Watford 0
1985 Manchester Utd 1 Everton 0 (aet)
1986 Liverpool 3 Everton 1
1987 Coventry 3 Tottenham 2 (aet)
1988 Wimbledon 1 Liverpool 0
1989 Liverpool 3 Everton 2 (aet)
■ *League Cup*
1980 Wolverhampton 1 Nottingham Forest 0
1981 Liverpool 2 West Ham 1 (after 1-1)
1982 Liverpool 3 Tottenham 1 (aet)
1983 Liverpool 2 Manchester Utd 1 (aet)
1984 Liverpool 1 Everton 0 (after 0-0)
1985 Norwich 1 Sunderland 0
1986 Oxford 3 QPR 0
1987 Arsenal 2 Liverpool 1
1988 Luton 3 Arsenal 2
1989 Nottingham Forest 3 Luton 1
■ *Scottish League*
1980 Aberdeen
1981 Celtic
1982 Celtic
1983 Dundee Utd
1984 Aberdeen
1985 Aberdeen
1986 Celtic
1987 Rangers
1988 Celtic
1989 Rangers
■ *Scottish Cup*
1980 Celtic 1 Rangers 0
1981 Rangers 4 Dundee Utd 1 (after 0-0)
1982 Aberdeen 4 Rangers 1
1983 Aberdeen 1 Rangers 0
1984 Aberdeen 2 Celtic 1
1985 Celtic 2 Dundee Utd 1
1986 Aberdeen 3 Hearts 0
1987 St Mirren 1 Dundee Utd 0
1988 Celtic 2 Dundee Utd 1
1989 Celtic 1 Rangers 0
■ *Scottish League Cup*
1980 Dundee Utd 3 Aberdeen 0 (after 0-0)
1981 Dundee Utd 3 Dundee 0
1982 Rangers 2 Dundee 1
1983 Celtic 2 Rangers 1
1984 Rangers 3 Celtic 2
1985 Rangers 1 Dundee Utd 0
1986 Aberdeen 3 Hibernian 0
1987 Rangers 2 Celtic 1
1988 Rangers 3 Aberdeen 3 (Rangers won 5-3 on penalties)
1989 Rangers 3 Aberdeen 2

GOLF

■ *The Open*
1980 Tom Watson
1981 Bill Rogers
1982 Tom Watson
1983 Tom Watson
1984 Severiano Ballesteros
1985 Sandy Lyle
1986 Greg Norman
1987 Nick Faldo
1988 Severiano Ballesteros
1989 Mark Calcavecchia
■ *US Open*
1980 Jack Nicklaus
1981 David Graham
1982 Tom Watson
1983 Larry Nelson
1984 Fuzzy Zoeller
1985 Andy North
1986 Raymond Floyd
1987 Scott Simpson
1988 Curtis Strange
1989 Curtis Strange
■ *US PGA*
1980 Jack Nicklaus
1981 Larry Nelson
1982 Raymond Floyd
1983 Hal Sutton
1984 Lee Trevino
1985 Hubert Green
1986 Bob Tway
1987 Larry Nelson
1988 Jeff Sluman
1989 Payne Stewart
■ *US Master*
1980 Severiano Ballesteros
1981 Tom Watson
1982 Craig Stalder
1983 Severiano Ballesteros
1984 Ben Crenshaw
1985 Bernhard Langer
1986 Jack Nicklaus
1987 Larry Mize
1988 Sandy Lyle
1989 Nick Faldo
■ *Ryder Cup*
1981 United States 18½-9½
1983 United States 14½-13½
1985 Europe 16½-11½
1987 Europe 15-13
1989 Drawn 14-14

MOTOR RACING

■ *World championship*
1980 Alan Jones (Williams-Ford)
1981 Nelson Piquet (Brabham-Ford)
1982 Keke Rosberg (Williams-Ford)
1983 Nelson Piquet (Brabham-BMW)
1984 Niki Lauda (McLaren-TAG)
1985 Alain Prost (McLaren-TAG)
1986 Alain Prost (McLaren-TAG)
1987 Nelson Piquet (Williams-Honda)
1988 Ayrton Senna (McLaren-Honda)
1989 Alain Prost (McLaren-Honda)

RACING

■ *The Derby*
1980 *Henbit*
1981 *Shergar*
1982 *Golden Fleece*
1983 *Teenoso*
1984 *Secreto*
1985 *Slip Anchor*
1986 *Shahrastani*
1987 *Reference Point*
1988 *Kahyasi*
1989 *Nashwan*
■ *Grand National*
1980 *Ben Nevis*
1981 *Aldaniti*
1982 *Grittar*
1983 *Corbiere*
1984 *Hallo Dandy*
1985 *Last Suspect*
1986 *West Tip*
1987 *Maori Venture*
1988 *Rhyme 'N' Reason*
1989 *Little Polveir*

ROWING

■ *Boat Race*
1980 Oxford
1981 Oxford
1982 Oxford
1983 Oxford
1984 Oxford
1985 Oxford
1986 Cambridge
1987 Oxford
1988 Oxford
1989 Oxford

RUGBY LEAGUE

■ *Challenge Cup*
1980 Hull KR 10 Hull 5
1981 Widnes 18 Hull KR 9
1982 Hull 18 Widnes 9 (after 14-14)
1983 Featherstone 14 Hull 12
1984 Widnes 19 Wigan 6
1985 Wigan 28 Hull 24
1986 Castleford 15 Hull KR 14
1987 Halifax 19 St Helens 18
1988 Wigan 32 Halifax 12
1989 Wigan 27 St Helens 0

RUGBY UNION

■ *Five Nations championship*
1980 England
1981 France
1982 Ireland
1983 France and Ireland
1984 Scotland
1985 Ireland
1986 France and Scotland
1987 France
1988 Wales and France
1989 France

SAILING

■ *America's Cup*
1980 *Freedom* (US, Dennis Conner)
1983 *Australia II* (Aus, John Bertrand)
1987 *Stars & Stripes* (US, Dennis Conner)
1988 *Stars & Stripes* (US, Dennis Conner)
■ *Admiral's Cup*
1981 Team: Great Britain. Individual: *Victory* (GB)
1983 Team: West Germany. Individual: *Diva* (Fra)
1985 Team: West Germany. Individual: *Phoenix* (GB)
1987 Team: New Zealand. Individual: *Propaganda* (NZ)
1989 Team: Great Britain. Individual: *Jamarella* (GB)

SNOOKER

■ *World championship*
1980 Cliff Thorburn 18 Alex Higgins 16
1981 Steve Davis 18 Doug Mountjoy 12
1982 Alex Higgins 18 Ray Reardon 15
1983 Steve Davis 18 Cliff Thornburn 6
1984 Steve Davis 18 Jimmy White 16
1985 Dennis Taylor 18 Steve Davis 17
1986 Joe Johnson 18 Steve Davis 12
1987 Steve Davis 18 Joe Johnson 14
1988 Steve Davis 18 Terry Griffiths 11
1989 Steve Davis 18 John Parrott 3

TENNIS

■ *Wimbledon*
1980 Bjorn Borg *bt* John McEnroe; Evonne Cawley *bt* Chris Evert Lloyd
1981 John McEnroe *bt* Bjorn Borg; Chris Evert Lloyd *bt* Hana Mandlikova
1982 Jimmy Connors *bt* John McEnroe; Martina Navratilova *bt* Chris Evert Lloyd
1983 John McEnroe *bt* Chris Lewis; Martina Navratilova *bt* Andrea Jaegar
1984 John McEnroe *bt* Jimmy Connors; Martina Navratilova *bt* Chris Evert Lloyd
1985 Boris Becker *bt* Kevin Curren; Martina Navratilova *bt* Chris Evert Lloyd
1986 Boris Becker *bt* Ivan Lendl; Martina Navratilova *bt* Hana Mandlikova
1987 Pat Cash *bt* Ivan Lendl; Martina Navratilova *bt* Steffi Graf
1988 Stefan Edberg *bt* Boris Becker; Steffi Graf *bt* Martina Navratilova
1989 Boris Becker *bt* Stefan Edberg; Steffi Graf *bt* Martina Navratilova
■ *Australian Open*
1980 Brian Teacher; Hana Mandlikova
1981 Johan Kriek; Martina Navratilova
1982 Johan Kriek; Chris Evert Lloyd
1983 Mats Wilander; Martina Navratilova
1984 Mats Wilander; Chris Evert Lloyd
1985 Stefan Edberg; Martina Navratilova
1987 Stefan Edberg; Hana Mandlikova
1988 Mats Wilander; Steffi Graf
1989 Ivan Lendl; Steffi Graf
■ *French Open*
1980 Bjorn Borg; Chris Evert Lloyd
1981 Bjorn Borg; Hana Mandlikova
1982 Mats Wilander; Martina Navratilova
1983 Yannock Noah; Chris Evert Lloyd
1984 Ivan Lendl; Martina Navratilova
1985 Mats Wilander; Chris Evert Lloyd
1986 Ivan Lendl; Chris Evert Lloyd
1987 Ivan Lendl; Steffi Graf
1988 Mats Wilander; Steffi Graf
1989 Michael Chang; Arantxa Sanchez Vicario
■ *US Open*
1980 John McEnroe; Chris Evert Lloyd
1981 John McEnroe; Tracy Austin
1982 Jimmy Connors; Chris Evert Lloyd
1983 Jimmy Connors; Martina Navratilova
1984 John McEnroe; Martina Navratilova
1985 Ivan Lendl; Hana Mandlikova
1986 Ivan Lendl; Martina Navratilova
1987 Ivan Lendl; Martina Navratilova
1988 Mats Wilander; Steffi Graf
1989 Boris Becker; Steffi Graf

Piquet: two world championships in three years

Minter's reign a brief affair

ALAN MINTER became the world middleweight champion the hard way, as the first British fighter since Ted "Kid" Lewis to win a title in America. The Crawley southpaw did it on March 16 by outpointing the rugged Vito Antuofermo on a split decision at Caesars Palace, but the apparently lopsided scoring of the British judge Roland Dakin provoked howls of outrage from the American camp. Dakin gave Minter 12 of the 15 rounds, but the official whose competence deserved to be questioned was the Venezuelan Adaslad Sanchez, who had the Englishman winning only five rounds.

Minter settled the argument by stopping Antuofermo three months later at Wembley, where his short reign ended on September 27, when Marvin Hagler cut him to defeat in the third round. Racial tensions which the fight generated exploded into a bottle-throwing riot, and Hagler needed a police escort to his dressing room.

Minter: temporary champion

306

Cousins follows on in Curry's footsteps

Cousins: won Britain's only medal in Lake Placid

JOHN CURRY had paved the way for British skating with his balletic style and when he retired Robin Cousins, with his more athletic approach, took over the mantle. Cousins, like Curry, was coached by Carlo Fassi, a former Olympic skater who spent a lot of time working on the compulsory exercises, which were often Cousins's weak point.

The effort paid off when the 22-year-old Cousins, the youngest son of a professional footballer, won the European championships in Gothenburg before he went to the Winter Olympics in Lake Placid, America, in February. Cousins, like Curry before him, won Britain's only medal of the games,

and once again it was the gold. The improvement in his technique was apparent when he was fourth after the compulsories. Going into the final day, after the short programme, Cousins was only in second place, behind Jan Hoffman of East Germany. But an excellent free skating programme, which earned nine 5.9s and eight 5.8s just won him the gold.

Cousins tried to repeat Curry's feat of a hat-trick of gold medals at the world championships in West Germany the following month, but he could only finish second to Hoffman. He turned professional later in the year, building a successful career as an ice rink manager and coach.

Watford end Harlow's dream run

HARLOW TOWN of the Isthmian Premier Division continued the glorious tradition of giant-killing by knocking Southend and Leicester out of the FA Cup after replays. Their run ended in the fourth round when they were

beaten dramatically at Watford.

Harlow led 1-0, only for Watford to rattle in four goals early in the second half. The Essex side fought back with two goals but the equaliser was beyond them and they succumbed 4-3.

Seve is youngest master

SEVE BALLESTEROS began playing golf when he was seven. Sixteen years later he became the youngest winner of the Masters.

Ballesteros started his quest for the green jacket on his 23rd birthday with a 66 and a share of the lead. He concentrated on accuracy off the tee rather than distance and missed only one fairway in the first round. Although he was wayward on the second day, a 69 gave him a three-shot lead, which he extended to seven shots over Ed Fiori in the third round.

On the last day, Ballesteros was threatening Jack Nicklaus's record victory of nine shots in 1965 when he moved 10 ahead with three birdies in the first six holes. Then he three-putted the 10th for a bogey and ran into trouble at Amen Corner, splashing into Rae's Creek for a double bogey at the 12th and a dropping a shot at the 13th. Ballesteros was now only two shots ahead but a birdie at the 15th put him back on course for a two-shot victory over Gibby Gilbert and Jack Newton.

Ballesteros: two-shot victory

Fate plays tricks on tired Arsenal

Cruel blow: Brooking, with a rare header, steals the FA Cup from Arsenal

FOR Arsenal it was the cruellest end to an arduous season ever devised. They reached their third consecutive FA Cup final, the first club to do so in the century, having taken three replays to dispose of Liverpool in the semi-final.

In the final on May 10 they faced Second Division West Ham, and in a forgettable game lost 1-0 to a bizarre goal from Trevor Brooking, who stooped and deflected a mis-hit shot with his head. It was only the third time Brooking had scored with a header.

Four days later Arsenal travelled to Heysel to confront Valencia, managed by Alfredo di Stefano and boasting Argentina's World Cup striker Mario Kempes, in the European Cup Winners' Cup final. David O'Leary nullified Kempes in another forgettable final that did not see a goal in 120 minutes of defensive sparring. In the penalty shoot-out Kempes and then Liam Brady missed. At 5-4 Graham Rix stepped up to shoot, the goalkeeper moved and having guessed right dashed another Cup from Arsenal's grasp. It was their 16th game in 46 days.

The fates had not finished with Arsenal yet. There was still a Uefa Cup place if they could win their last two League matches. They won the first, but five days after Heysel they lost 5-0 to Middlesbrough. Arsenal had played 70 matches, a British record, reached two finals and come away with nothing.

BOXING

■ Jim Watt retained his world lightweight title in March by stopping Charlie Nash of Derry in Glasgow.

■ Bob Taylor equalled Wasim Bari's record of seven catches against India in February.

FOOTBALL

■ Wales beat England at home for the first time in 25 years on May 17 when they won 4-1 at Wrexham.

■ England made 10 changes for the match against Northern Ireland at Wembley on May 20, but could only draw 1-1.

■ Tommy Docherty and QPR parted company on May 6. It had been Docherty's second term as their manager, the first lasting 28 days. This time he had survived for nearly a year. Nine days later he was reinstated, only to be replaced in October by Terry Venables.

■ Always full of surprises, Ian Botham signed for Scunthorpe on March 5.

■ Eight players were booked in the Doncaster v Hereford match on April 11, seven of them at once when the Hereford defensive wall were dilatory about retreating 10 yards.

ROWING

■ Oxford won the Boat Race by a canvas on April 5, the shortest winning margin ever. They finished with only seven men rowing when their bow, Francis, collapsed with exhaustion during the race.

TABLE TENNIS

■ John Hilton, ranked only No 3 in England, became the first Briton to win the European singles title in Berne in April.

TENNIS

■ Chris Evert-Lloyd announced in January that she would retire later in the year. In fact, she kept on playing until 1989.

Swing low, sweet champions

THE coach carrying the England team to Murrayfield was a few minutes from its destination when Bill Beaumont gave his team talk. He kept it short. "We know why we're here," he said. "If everybody does their job we can win." The team listened to their captain, did their job and beat Scotland 30-18. It was England's first Grand Slam in 23 years.

John Carleton and Dusty Hare provided most of the points. Carleton, a powerful wing, became the first Englishman to score three tries in one Test for 56 years. Hare, in his first season, took his points tally in four matches to 32 with two conversions and two penalties.

England's campaign was an eventful one. Hare scored half the points in a 24-9 win against Ireland, and the 17-13 victory against France was their first triumph in Paris in 16 years. England then entertained Wales.

It was a fiery encounter in which the Welshman Paul Ringer was sent off for striking John Horton in the face. Hare saw England home 9-8 with three penalty kicks and Ringer was banned for eight weeks. He complained later: "People have been inventing things about me ever since. I was said to have shot a cow in Brecon."

Beaumont: driving force

' *They should send Borg away to another planet. We play tennis. He plays something else* '

Ilie Nastase

OLYMPIC GAMES

Britain defies Carter's boycott

THE invasion of Afghanistan by Soviet troops at the end of 1979, and the swift reaction from President Carter, meant that a seven-month political debate raged before the opening of the Moscow Olympic Games. Carter wanted the United States, and as many other countries as he could influence, to boycott the Games unless the Soviet Union withdrew. He also, not understanding the Olympic charter, wanted the Games moved to another country: an impossibility.

The Soviet troops stayed in Afghanistan, and eventually an estimated 45-50 countries boycotted the Moscow Games in protest, most notably the United States, West Germany and Japan. But Britain, despite strong pressure from the government to boycott, fully supported the Games.

TENNIS

Borg and McEnroe's epic duel leaves Centre Court spellbound

BJORN BORG staked his claim as one of the sport's greatest players when he won a fifth successive Wimbledon title, beating John McEnroe 1-6 7-5 6-3 6-7 (16-18) 8-6 in arguably the finest final in Wimbledon history. For nearly four hours Borg and his arch rival thrilled the Centre Court in a dramatic 55-game match.

Borg worked hard on improving his play at the net, and his only chink was an inability to stretch wide on his left because he employed a two-handed backhand. It was a flaw exposed by left-handers with swinging serves like McEnroe.

The American abandoned the boorish behaviour he had displayed in a bitter semi-final against Jimmy Connors and with some exquisite play took the first set in 20 minutes. Borg came bounding back to win the next two sets and was on the brink of victory at 5-4 and 40-15 in the fourth set. McEnroe saved both match points, won the game and then forced the champion into a memorable tie-break. It lasted nearly 23 minutes. McEnroe saved five championship points and Borg seven set points before McEnroe levelled the match.

Most other players would have fallen in a heap after missing seven championship points. Not Borg. He maintained his peak form and when McEnroe could not answer a two-handed cross-court shot on the eighth championship point Borg won the title in 3hr 54min.

Borg wins his fifth successive Wimbledon title after a 55-game marathon

BORG'S FIVE WIMBLEDON TITLES

1976 Ilie Nastase 6-4 6-2 9-7
1977 Jimmy Connors 3-6 6-2 6-1 5-7 6-4
1978 Jimmy Connors 6-2 6-2 6-3
1979 Roscoe Tanner 6-7 (4-7) 6-1 3-6 6-3 6-4
1980 John McEnroe 1-6 7-5 6-3 6-7 (16-18) 8-6

. . . and his major titles
1975 French Open. 1976 Wimbledon.
1977 Wimbledon. 1978 French Open,
Wimbledon. 1979 French Open,
Wimbledon. 1980 French Open,
Wimbledon. 1981 French Open,
Wimbledon.

Triumph and disaster in battle of Britons

THE two races between Sebastian Coe and Steve Ovett, both in classic showdowns at the Moscow Olympic Games, would have captured the attention of the sporting world wherever they happened. That they were on the Olympic stage merely heightened the drama.

In 1979 the paths of the two Britons had never crossed competitively. The speculation over who would win, should they meet, was intense. By the summer of 1980 it was clear that both were still in top form, but had no intention of racing each other before the Olympics, where each would run the 800m and 1500m.

In the weeks preceding the Games both produced performances guaranteed to add fuel to the anticipatory flames: on July 1, in Oslo, Ovett broke Coe's world mile record with 3:48.8, while on the same track the same night Coe set a 1,000m world record of 2:13.40. A fortnight later, Ovett equalled Coe's 1500m world record of 3:32.1.

Yet the first of their Olympic clashes, at 800m on July 26, was almost an anticlimax. Ovett won after Coe, most people's favourite for the shorter distance, had run a poor tactical race in which he was last at the bell. Coe simply left himself too much to do in the home straight after the inevitable upsurge in speed. With the last 200m run in under 25sec Coe did well to move from fourth to second, but he could not come within half a second of Ovett. "I threw it away on the second lap," Coe admitted.

With Ovett having won his less favoured event, and taking a string of 43 successive victories into the 1500m final on August 1, he was heavily favoured to complete the double. But Coe had been smouldering all week. Roundly criticised even by his own father and coach for his poor run in the 800m, he poured every ounce of competitiveness into the 1500m.

After a slow first 800m, the East German Jurgen Straub took the lead and injected a sizzling third lap of 54.2sec, trying to burn out the Britons' finishes. The field stretched out behind him, and with 200m left Straub was leading by four metres from Coe, and six from Ovett.

Then, entering the home straight, all of Coe's frustration was suddenly transformed into useable energy. He kicked past Straub with 80 metres left and raced on to victory. Ovett was unable even to catch Straub, and had to settle for third. "Seb was a worthy winner," he said. "I just couldn't lift myself after the 800m."

Both races had their share of drama and competitiveness, and one Olympic title each was probably the fairest result for the pair. Even if each was effectively an own goal.

Ovett pips Coe

Forest lock up Cup

Forest kept the European Cup in England for the fourth year

A BELOW strength Nottingham Forest put on a below-par performance in the European Cup final in Madrid on May 28 but still managed to retain the trophy.

Trevor Francis was out injured with a ripped Achilles tendon, Peter Shilton had pulled a calf muscle and needed an injection to play, and the unpredictable Stan Bowles had walked out of the club because he had been left out of the team for a testimonial match.

These setbacks prompted Brian Clough and Peter Taylor to play a cagey game against a Hamburg team who had Kevin Keegan and Manny Kultz, an attacking fullback, in their side. Forest strung five men across the midfield and waited for something to happen.

And it did. In the 20th minute John Robertson ran at Kultz and shot fiercely. The ball ricocheted in off the far post. Forest shut up shop and went on to become the second British side to successfully defend the trophy.

European fiasco for England

ENGLAND'S trip to the finals of the European championships proved disappointing on the field and disastrous off it. In the opening match against Belgium in Turin on June 12, England seemed to have got off to a good start when Ray Wilkins sprang Belgium's offside trap to score. But then the Belgians scored and everything went horribly wrong.

Italian fans taunted the English fans, many of whom had been drinking. Seats were torn up and fierce fighting started behind the England goal. The Italian police instantly moved in with batons and fired tear-gas into the crowd. The game was stopped for five minutes to allow the smoke on the pitch to clear. And that effectively was the end of England's tournament. No more goals were scored,

more than 70 fans had to go to hospital, and the next day Uefa fined the FA £8,000.

In the final, the only decent match in the championships, West Germany beat Belgium 2-1.

Belgium deny England

Duran finally takes no more

Duran beat Leonard but quit in the re-match

No sting in Ali's sham comeback

IT WAS the fight which should never have happened. But for Muhammad Ali the temptation to make one last bid to become world heavyweight champion for an unprecedented fourth time was too great.

He could have learned from Jack Dempsey and Joe Louis the truth of the old cliche "they never come back", but the man who was now champion, Larry Holmes, had once been Ali's sparring partner and the leeches who lived off Ali convinced him that nothing had changed.

They pumped him full of weight reducing drugs (without the knowledge of his long time trainer Angelo Dundee) so that by the time he entered the ring at Caesars Palace, Las Vegas, his 38-year-old body at least looked trim and athletic. But it was all a cruel illusion; Ali had nothing left, except his shining and unbreakable spirit, and for round after painful round Holmes dominated the man who had once been his idol.

Repeatedly, Holmes pleaded with the old champion to quit, and each time he rocked Ali he would look to the referee as if willing him to intervene. Ali's pride kept him in there until, at the end of the tenth round, Dundee over-ruled the vociferous protest of camp follower Bundini Brown and refused to let his man answer the bell for the eleventh.

ROBERTO DURAN, the Panamanian they called Hands of Stone, stepped out of the lightweight division he had dominated for eight years and won the welterweight title by outslugging Sugar Ray Leonard in The Brawl in Montreal on June 20.

It was a magnificent fight, 15 rounds where the wills and skills of two of boxing's immortal warriors blended to provide an hour of greatness. Duran won a close, unanimous decision. But if that night brought Duran to a phenomenal peak the return in the New Orleans Superdome on November 25 all but ruined him.

Leonard had discovered the madness of standing toe to toe with Duran, so in the rematch he produced a wonderful exhibition of speed and pure fighting cunning at long range, and Duran simply could not handle it. In the eighth round, suddenly, unbelievably, Duran waved his arm at Leonard in disdain, turned away and told the astonished referee "No mas" (no more).

Leonard went on to seal his place in history, but for Duran the disgrace was acute. His people forgave him only when he battered the light-middleweight title away from Davey Moore, and defied the mighty Marvin Hagler for 15 rounds in a bid for the middleweight title.

Owen killed in pursuit of title

UNTIL he fought the Mexican Lupe Pintor for the world bantamweight title, Johnny Owen's skeletal frame seemed only to suggest a terrible fragility. His record of one controversial defeat in 27 fights indicated that appearances were deceptive: the 24-year-old Welshman, who cheerfully mocked his physique by calling himself the Merthyr Matchstick, was the European, British and Commonwealth champion.

On his own admission, he was so consumed by boxing that he had never even dated a girl. He was obsessively dedicated, unusually strong. But the dreadful truth was exposed in Los Angeles on September 19.

Knocked out in the 12th round, Owen never regained consciousness and died in California Hospital on November 4. The post-mortem examination revealed that he had an abnormally thin skull.

Muhammad Ali: lost to Holmes in his last title bid

Rain gatecrashes the Test party

Hollow ring to Lillee's bat

David Constant ignored the run-out appeal although Border was seemingly well out

THE celebration of 100 years of Test cricket in England became little more than a celebration of 100 years of rain disrupting Test cricket in England. The match between England and Australia at Lord's ended in an inevitable draw when 10 hours of play were lost to rain.

England were outplayed by the Australians, who amassed 385 for five declared. Geoff Boycott, who batted nearly six hours in scoring 201 runs in the match, and David Gower were the only Englishmen to show any form with the bat while the newly-appointed captain Ian Botham failed dismally.

Several members of the MCC assaulted the umpire David Constant after his return from a fifth pitch inspection. He had a police escort through the Long Room.

DENNIS LILLEE forced another line to be added to the rule book when he had the temerity to use an aluminium bat. His break with tradition prompted the inclusion of the words "the bat shall be made of wood" in the laws of the game.

Lillee had faced four balls from Ian Botham with his innovative bat in the first Test in Perth in December 1979 when the umpires asked him to change it. He threw a tantrum and the bat. He then took out his frustration on the unfortunate England batsmen, and when the three-match series ended in mid-February he had taken 23 wickets at 16.86. Australia won the series 3-0, but England had refused to put the Ashes at stake.

Cheap but illegal: aluminium was half the price of willow

FOR THE RECORD

BILLIARDS
■ Fred Davis won the world professional title at the age of 66.

BOXING
■ Frank Warren promoted his first contest licensed by the British Board of Control in December.

CRICKET
■ John Arlott was given a standing ovation by the crowd and the players when he completed his last radio commentary during the Centenary Test at Lord's.

FOOTBALL
■ West Ham had to play the second leg of their European Cup Winners' Cup tie against Castilla behind closed doors on October 1 because of the drunken antics of their fans at the first leg in Madrid. West Ham won 5-1.

■ Octogenarian Sam Phillips was banned from watching Ledbury Town's home matches for allegedly assaulting a referee. However, he still watched through a hedge surrounding the pitch.

ICE HOCKEY
■ Gordie Howe retired at the age of 52, having played a record 26 seasons in the National Hockey League, plus another six with the World Hockey Association.

RUGBY LEAGUE
■ The sport was relaunched professionally in London when Fulham were admitted to the Second Division.

RUGBY UNION
■ Stuart Lane played for the British Lions for only 45 seconds on their tour of South Africa. The Cardiff and Welsh flanker was chosen for the opening match but tore his knee ligaments in the first minute and never represented them again.

SPEEDWAY
■ Michael Lee of England won the world championship.

SQUASH
■ Heather McKay was beaten for the first time since 1962. The Australian won 16 British Open titles.

John Arlott: standing ovation for his last radio commentary

JANUARY

1981

APRIL

Death and deportation haunt tour

ENGLAND had an unhappy tour of the Caribbean marred by controversy and tragedy. Robin Jackman, who flew in as a replacement for the injured Bob Willis, was served with a deportation order by the Guyanese government because he had broken the Gleneagles Agreement by coaching in South Africa. The second Test in Georgetown was cancelled and only after a prolonged debate was it agreed to continue with the tour.

Roland Butcher became the first black West Indian to represent England in the third Test in Bridgetown. But the match was overshadowed by the death of Ken Barrington, the England coach and former Test batsman, who suffered a heart attack. The West Indians won the four-match series 2-0.

Butcher: England debut

ATHLETICS

London sets out on a long and winding road

More than 7,000 runners set off from Greenwich

THE inaugural London Marathon, conceived by the 1956 Olympic steeplechase gold medallist Chris Brasher after he had taken part in the established New York City Marathon, was staged from Greenwich Park, with 7,055 runners actually lining up from an entry of 7,700, and 6,418 finishing.

The race was jointly won by Inge Simonsen of Norway and Dick Beardsley of America, who crossed the finish line at Constitution Hill in a mutually agreed tie in 2:11.48. Joyce Smith, aged 43, won the women's event in 2:29.57, setting the fifth British marathon record of her career. Brasher, aged 52, clocked under three hours. It was the start of something big.

SNOOKER

Davis sets the agenda

STEVE DAVIS'S first world championship presaged his dominance of the 1980s with an immaculately tailored technique, relentless application and supreme consistency. Even his six world and six UK titles do not do full justice to the epitome of class and professionalism he became.

Davis had already won the English professional title and three other tournaments when he met Doug Mountjoy in the final at The Crucible, Sheffield, in April. Mountjoy was in good form, having made a 142 clearance in his semi-final against Ray Reardon, but he had no answer to Davis, who won £20,000 for his 18-12 victory.

Davis's manager, Barry Hearn, carried his off-table earnings into new realms for a snooker player and used him as the foundation of his own Matchroom snooker empire.

Underarm call is underhand

NEW ZEALAND needed six runs off the last ball to tie their one-day international against Australia in Melbourne when Greg Chappell discovered what little brothers were for: to do the dirty work. The Australian captain instructed Trevor Chappell to bowl underarm to Brian McKechnie who pushed the ball forward and threw down his bat in disgust.

Richie Benaud called the underarm delivery "the most gutless thing I have seen on a cricket field". Robert Muldoon, the New Zealand Prime Minister, said it was no surprise the Australians were playing in yellow, and his countrymen began printing T-shirts with the words "Australians have an underarm problem".

FOOTBALL

Palace do the hot-seat shuffle

CRYSTAL PALACE had four managers in a single season. They had begun with Terry Venables, who left in October 1980 to take over at QPR. Ernie Walley replaced him, only to be joined by Malcolm Allison two months later.

Allison became sole manager but the farce continued when Ron Noades gained control. He promptly installed Dario Gradi, Wimbledon's manager. But come the new season it started all over again and so, on November 10, Gradi was sacked after poor results and Steve Kember became the latest occupant of Palace's hot seat.

Venables: went to QPR

Against all odds, a Champion is reborn

NATIONAL HUNT racing is not known for its sentiment, but the world was visibly moved when both runner and rider overcame the most terrible of odds to win the Grand National on April 4.

Bob Champion was in his prime as a jockey in 1979 when doctors broke the terrible news that he had cancer and less than a year to live. But Champion refused to be beaten and embarked on a long and debilitating course of chemotherapy.

For 18 months Champion endured treatment that left him so weak that he could not even stand. Only one thing kept him going — a burning will to win the Grand National. Finally, early in 1980, the doctors announced that the cancer had gone into remission. Champion fought through the year to regain his strength and in August he was back in the saddle, celebrating his return with a winner in his first race.

Throughout the long months in hospital, Josh Gifford had stood loyally by Champion. The trainer kept his stable jockey's spirits up with discussions about the progress of Aldaniti, who they both agreed was a Grand National prospect.

However, Aldaniti had problems of his own. His legs were so fragile that several times it was said that he would never race again. But while Champion was recuperating Aldaniti was also healing well, and the stage was set for the impossible dream to come true.

But, on a sunny afternoon, it looked as if the dream would turn into a nightmare when Aldaniti hit the first fence so hard he barely recovered. Somehow, Champion kept his mount on his feet. By the eleventh fence they had taken the lead and they stayed in front throughout. For a brief moment on the run-in it looked as if Aldaniti might be overhauled by Spartan Missile, but with one flourish of the whip from Champion the fairytale came true.

> ❛ I rode this race for all the patients in hospital. My winning shows them that there is always hope, and all battles can be won ❜
>
> **Bob Champion**

Champion and Aldaniti overcame illness, injury and Aintree

Hunt: titanic battle

FOR THE RECORD

AMERICAN FOOTBALL
■ The Oakland Raiders became the first wild-card team to win a Super Bowl when they beat the Philadelphia Eagles 27-10 in New Orleans on January 25.

BOXING
■ Joe Louis died on April 12, aged 66. Muhammad Ali was moved to admit: "I idolised Joe. I just gave lip service to being the greatest — Joe was the greatest."

FOOTBALL
■ England and Wales refused to play Northern Ireland in Belfast because of political unrest and so the Home championship was abandoned.

■ Aston Villa won the League championship for the first time in 71 years and their manager Ron Saunders only needed to use 14 players.

■ Red and yellow cards to indicate sendings-off and cautions were abolished by the FA Council from January 19.

MOTORCYCLING
■ Mike Hailwood was killed in a car crash in March.

ROWING
■ Sue Brown became the first woman cox in the Boat Race and Boris Rankov was the first don to take part.

SQUASH
■ Geoff Hunt broke Hashim Khan's record when he won his eighth British Open title. Hunt beat the 17-year-old Jahangir Khan in a titanic battle that lasted 2hr 13min.

TABLE TENNIS
■ China won all seven titles at the world championships in Yugoslavia, the only time this has happened in the history of the sport. China also had five of the losing finalists.

Brown: first woman cox

313

Botham's blitz upsets odds

GOLF

Rogers: mistaken identity

Graham: overseas winner

IAN BOTHAM booked out of his Leeds hotel on the morning of the fourth day of the Test against Australia. And soon after he walked to the crease with England 105 for five, his captain, Mike Brearley, changed and prepared to face defeat and the press. England still required 122 runs to make Australia bat again.

The England team and Botham were shattered. They had lost a bitter three-match series in the West Indies, were 1-0 down after two Tests against Australia and now faced humiliation in the third Test at Headingley.

Botham, who had given up the captaincy after a poor spell with the bat, was shoring up the innings when Graham Dilley joined him at 135 for seven, still 92 runs from saving an innings defeat. Odds of 500-1 were offered against an England victory. Australia were 4-1 on and the draw 5-2.

Kim Hughes, the Australian captain who enforced the follow on, had used his bowlers in long spells and Terry Alderman, Geoff Lawson and Dennis Lillee were showing signs of exhaustion.

So Dilley played aggressively, the bearded Botham joined in the fireworks and their stand was worth 117 in 80 minutes. Botham raced to his century off 87 deliveries and added 67 valuable runs with Chris Old before booking

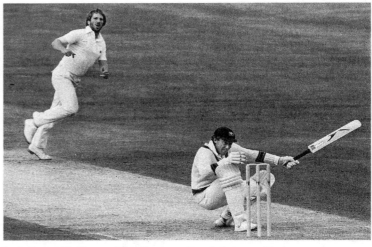

In full cry: Botham virtually won the Ashes on his own

back into the hotel at the close of play. When Bob Willis was the last man out early on the fifth day he had helped Botham add 37 for the last wicket. Botham remained undefeated on 149 and England's total was 356. Australia needed 130 runs for victory.

Botham was again in the spotlight by dismissing Graeme Wood early in the innings, but the Australians looked comfortable at 56 for one shortly before lunch. Then Willis struck. He returned career-best figures of eight for 43 and in a sensational turnaround England became only the second side to win a Test after following on. The feat was last achieved by England in 1894.

Botham's summer was not over.

The fourth Test at Edgbaston provided another opportunity for him to pull England out of the fire. There was a sense of déjà vu about Australia chasing 151 for victory. Botham was reluctant to bowl with Australia's score at 105 for five, but Brearley overruled him. In 29 deliveries Botham took five wickets for one run to achieve an astonishing 29-run victory.

He plundered 118 runs off 102 balls in the fifth Test at Old Trafford, hitting six sixes in a century off only 86 deliveries. The innings turned a match which England won by 103 runs to retain the Ashes. He then captured 10 wickets in a drawn sixth Text at The Oval to take his tally in the series to 34 wickets.

Shergar leaves the rest standing

SHERGAR quite simply strolled away with the Derby. And then, just to prove how good he was, he walked off with the Irish Derby and the King George VI and Queen Elizabeth Stakes as well.

The Aga Khan's horse had been lightly raced as a two-year-old, with one win and one second to his credit, but there was nothing to touch him as a three-year-old. His first race of the summer was won by 10 lengths, and then the tight track of the Chester Vase yielded an even bigger victory.

It was no wonder that Shergar started the strongest favourite for the Derby for more than a decade. He won, once again, by 10 lengths — the biggest margin ever. And it might have been more than that except for Walter Swinburn easing up in the last furlong.

The Irish Derby was won by a "mere" four lengths but Peter O'Sullevan summed up the majesty of the horse when he described the manner of Shergar's victory: "He's only in an exercise canter."

Shergar: majestic champion

Paisley's third triumph a European Cup first

BOB PAISLEY became the first British manager to have won the European Cup three times when Liverpool scored the only goal of a scrappy final against Real Madrid in Paris on May 27.

Real Madrid were a shadow of the fabulous side that had dominated the competition in the 1950s, and fear of losing seemed to grip both sides. With eight minutes left to extra time, Ray Kennedy's throw-in was chested down by Alan Kennedy, who began a run towards goal. A crass error by Cortes, Real's right-back, gave him the space he needed, and from a sharp angle he beat the keeper.

PAISLEY MANAGER OF THE DECADE

His nine year record as Liverpool's manager

1975 First Division runners-up
1976 League champions; Uefa Cup winners
1977 League champions; European Cup winners; FA Cup finalists
1978 European Cup winners; First Division runners-up; League Cup finalists
1979 League champions
1980 League champions
1981 European Cup winners; League Cup winners
1982 League champions; League Cup winners
1983 League champions; League Cup winners

Liverpool celebrate Alan Kennedy's winning goal

Villa's singular goal meets Spurs's destiny

IF THE centenary FA Cup final was not the greatest one ever, it was certainly won by the greatest goal to grace the occasion. With 15 minutes left in the replay, and the scores level at 2-2, Ricardo Villa, Tottenham's Argentinian, innocuously picked up the ball midway in Manchester City's half and set off on a weaving run that devastated the opposition and delighted the millions watching worldwide.

At first there was no apparent danger as Villa ran at the heart of the defence, but he twisted and turned, changed pace, held his balance, kept the ball, beat Tommy Caton three times, Ray Ranson twice, Nicky Reid once and slipped the ball under the body of the onrushing Joe Corrigan. It was a courageous and audacious goal and it gave Tottenham their sixth FA Cup and compensated Villa for his humiliation at the first final.

On May 9, Tottenham had been fortunate to get a draw. And Tommy Hutchison was unfortunate to become the second man to score for both sides in an FA Cup final when he attempted to block a swerving Glenn Hoddle free kick only to deflect it off his shoulder and past a stranded Corrigan.

Minutes before, an ineffective Villa had been substituted, much to his annoyance, and he trudged off clearly upset and in tears. Just as he reached the mouth of the tunnel he stopped to watch the free kick.

Fate gave him a second chance and confirmed the superstitions of Spurs fans. Ever since Tottenham won the Cup as a non-League side in 1901, they have expected success in years that end with a one. And in 1901, 1921, 1951, 1961 and 1971 Tottenham had delivered with a trophy.

Hinault trounces the field again

Hinault: won at a record speed

"MADE to measure for him," the critics said of the route. And for once they were right as Bernard Hinault was to prove when he won his third Tour de France at a record average of 37.844kh (23.6mph).

With four individual time trial stages during the three-week race, the format certainly suited the stocky Hinault. He had won in 1978 and 1979 and was forced to retire in 1980 with tendinitis after winning the Giro d'Italia.

Hinault immediately took the race leader's yellow jersey when he won the opening test against the clock at Nice. He lost it on stage two but was again wearing yellow at the end of stage seven, another time trial.

Strong in the mountains, Hinault demolished the opposition to reach Paris 14min 34sec clear of the Belgian Lucien van Impe.

Ian Botham
Boy's Own hero who never grew up

Peter Roebuck

Not since the days of William Gilbert Grace can any English cricketer have entertained as many people, provoked as much apoplexy, swung as many games or seized as many headlines, as did Ian Terence Botham in the decades after his first appearance as a raw, vulgar Somerset all-rounder in 1973.

As a cricketer, and as a man, he led the life of Riley, fishing, drinking, gambling, hitting hard, bowling lustily, catching flies, shattering stumps with an athleticism astonishing in one who grew bulky. His appeal reached far beyond cricket's customary conservatism, reached into pubs so that cricket was followed by working men who saw in Botham a product of a secondary modern school and a town, Yeovil, industrialised by Somerset standards.

Botham also touched the hearts of children who sensed his spontaneity, his generosity, even his naughtiness, who saw him as he saw himself, as a champion, a comic strip hero, a man capable of rescuing a lost cause or a damsel in distress, a man who walked thousands of miles for children's charity and once smashed two posh cars in one afternoon. A man who did not want to grow old.

Botham yearned for such a following, yearned for this affection because he was lonely and vulnerable, characteristics to which was added a mulish will which made him utterly loyal to friends and an intense hater of enemies; they threatened him so, and reminded him of mortality and solitude. Above all, Botham worried about being an outsider, yet he wanted to be a maverick.

> **' Never mind the footwork – see where the ball has gone '**

Those close to him, yet not within his immediate circle, were apt to have mixed emotions, including affection and frustration, and it is perhaps significant that he felt called upon to move from Somerset to Worcester via Queensland and on to Durham, searching for fresh challenges and for companions who had not tired of him.

Besides his valour, documented daily in tabloid newspapers which had replaced Homer as our chief source of myths, he was a man who could go too far, a man convicted of possessing cannabis, a man sometimes lured into notoriety by a hot pursuance of fantasy. This trait was typified by a visit to Hollywood in his halcyon days, where, expecting to find acclamation, he discovered only puzzlement. Significantly, if surprisingly to his public, England's selectors were for long periods reluctant to include in their team this mercurial cricketer, particularly towards the end of the 1980s, this despite numerous defeats and despite Botham's magnificent Test record.

Perhaps this was because Botham had risen by seizing every opportunity and shaking it for all it was worth, thrusting himself into the spotlight, brave and ambitious, even calculating, in a manner beyond less brave and combative men. Plainly the empire built around him needed constant injections of exhilaration and publicity, which did not always allow such plans as his captains or managers may have developed in these pragmatic times. Curiously, towards the end of an illustrious, brilliant, and controversial career, Botham did learn to cut his cloth according to prevailing opinion and, in 1991, he returned to the England colours after an absence of two years, even winning selection for the World Cup, this despite a commitment to act in a pantomime and a record in limited-overs cricket less impressive than might have been anticipated in so dynamic a cricketer.

Few players can have launched their careers with more flair than this youngster from Somerset. Having risen through the local ranks and having served two seasons on the ground staff at Lord's, having defied all attempts to change his rude ways ("never mind the footwork, see where the ball has gone") he burst into Test cricket in 1977, and survived a wayward first spell during which, and for the only time in his career, he appeared lost and inhibited. He took five Australian wickets in his first innings, using swing pitched to a full length and mixed with occasional faster bumpers to persuade batsmen to play apparently reckless shots.

This haul was considered lucky by connoisseurs used to the more subtle ways of Sobers and Snow. But Botham continued to take wickets, trusting to his spirit and to a brain more sharply analytical than was commonly supposed. Moreover, he was a far better bowler than he appeared on his worst days, could swing the ball either way once Tom Cartwright had taught him to disguise his in-swinger, could vary his pace and use surprise as a weapon in a manner beyond those of more orthodox persuasion.

Botham's wickets could be taken with deadly spells of swing bowling, as in 1982, when Pakistani batsmen found him irresistible, or with a trusted instinct capable of plotting downfalls. He raced to 100 Test wickets in record time and if, later, as his body grew heavier and his back gave him pain, he was apt to be expensive, apt to buy his wickets since he had lost his swing, he nevertheless continued to trap men and his Test tally rose past 350. Those who doubt his bowling should study his eight wickets in an innings against Pakistan in 1982, rather than his later incarnations.

As a batsman he grew in stature, changed from a thumper to a player capable of constructing Test match hundreds. In the epic Ashes series of 1981 spectators saw him in both veins, as first he led an extraordinary England fightback at Leeds by smiting a rapid and unbeaten 149 which was followed a fortnight later by a more majestic and authoritative hundred in Manchester. This was after he had resigned as captain of England, a post bestowed upon him at an early age, 24, and a crown he never wore easily. Nevertheless, he was a good enough batsman to score 13 Test hundreds, and the third fastest Test 200 by an Englishman.

After savouring such heady glories at such an early age, life was perhaps never quite as smooth again, especially in county cricket of which Botham soon tired. Yet he remained, throughout his career, a mostly popular and always sporting cricketer. Beyond doubt, he cheered many a dark hour and if he was not the greatest all-rounder ever — and his failure to score Test hundreds against the West Indies rather than his overall record denies him this title — it is certain that cricket the world over would have been poorer without him.

The many faces of Botham: the master batsman and master bowler with a wonderful pair of hands in the slips. And, if that wasn't enough, he also made his mark as a footballer for Scunthorpe and as an indefatigable fund-raiser.

FOOTBALL

Swansea rush to the top

Toshack: inspiration

AFTER 10 League matches Swansea City had 22 points and were leading the First Division. It had been an astonishing climb for the club brilliantly managed by the former Liverpool striker John Toshack.

In four breathtaking seasons they had ascended from the Fourth Division to the heights of the First. They finished the season in sixth place but their meteoric rise was matched by a spectacular fall. By 1986 they were back in the Fourth Division.

ATHLETICS

Mile record becomes private race

THE Coe-Ovett saga reached another peak in a nine-day purple patch during which, between them, they broke the world mile record three times. The record had stood to Ovett, whose 3:48.8 in 1980 had dispossessed Coe of the mark.

On August 19 Coe regained the record, running 3:48.53 in perfect conditions in Zurich. He was paced by the American Tom Byers and even declared himself somewhat disappointed with his record, as he had been hoping for a time closer to 3:46 or 3:47. Earlier in the summer he had already improved his own world records at 800m and 1,000m.

In response, just one week after Zurich, Ovett, recovering from a leg injury, asked for a scheduled 1500m race at Koblenz on August 26 to be changed to a full mile. Paced by his training partner Bob Benn, Ovett clocked 3:48.40 to regain the record. But Coe's one-week tenure as the mile world record holder proved lengthy compared to Ovett's.

Just two days later, on August 28 in Brussels, Coe bettered the mark yet again with 3:47.33. "I still don't think the mile record has been tapped yet," he said. But this record, the third in nine days, was to last nearly four years, and proved the final word in the Coe-Ovett dominance of this distance.

Coe: retrieved record

WINTER SPORTS

Perfect start for ice pair

JAYNE TORVILL and Christopher Dean only teamed up in 1975 because neither of them had a partner at the Nottingham rink where they trained. A one-month trial soon become a spectacular ice dance pairing.

Under the tutelage of Betty Calloway they made steady progress, and 1981 was the year they started to take the world by storm. In a sign of things to come, they were awarded seven maximum marks in the British championships at their home rink, and then they went on to win the European and World titles in the same year.

Torvill and Dean

DARTS

Bullseye: Jocky Wilson is first British professional champion

FOR THE RECORD

DARTS
■ Jocky Wilson of Scotland won the first British professional championship.

FOOTBALL
■ The season opened with the most fundamental change in the rules since the offside law was altered in 1925. A win was to be rewarded with three points instead of two, and it was believed that this would encourage more attacking football.

■ Bill Shankly died in a Liverpool hospital on September 29, aged 67. Shankly, who retired in July 1974, had been Liverpool's manager for 15 years and is credited with transforming a club fallen on hard times and languishing in the Second Division into one of the world's greatest.

■ Luton were the guinea pigs in September when they were the first visitors to play a League match on artificial turf. QPR had installed the £350,000 surface at Loftus Road amid much acrimony, and they lost 2-1.

GOLF
■ Kathy Whitworth became the first woman to win $1m when she finished third in the US women's Open at La Grange, Illinois, on July 26.

ICE HOCKEY
■ The sport began its resurgence with the re-formation of the English and Scottish National Leagues and the opening of the Peterborough rink.

RUGBY UNION
■ The International Rugby Board outlawed the "pile-up".

TENNIS
■ More than a year after she said she was going to retire, Chris Evert-Lloyd beat Hana Mandlikova in the Wimbledon final.

Raging bull McEnroe takes Borg's title

THE brat was back. John McEnroe, who had behaved impeccably at Wimbledon on his way to losing a memorable final against Bjorn Borg the previous year, returned to his old tricks.

He spent a fortnight ranting and raging his way to another final against Borg on July 4. He would throw a tantrum whenever he was not getting his way. His opponent, usually playing a big point, would have his concentration disrupted and invariably McEnroe's gamesmanship would bring about his opponent's downfall.

The American was aided and abetted by weak officials who did little to curb his volley of obscenities, boorish behaviour and gamesmanship. They broke tradition after McEnroe incurred two penalty points in his first-round match against Tom Gullikson by fining him $1,500 and issuing him with the first-ever warning at Wimbledon.

But on he went, serving and swearing his way to a meeting with Borg who had beaten Jimmy Connors in a stirring five-set semi-final that lasted more than three hours. Borg came back from two sets down to cling to his quest for a record sixth successive title.

In the final, Borg had the only break of serve in the first set and although he was outplayed by McEnroe in the tie-break in the second set, he appeared in control by going 4-1 ahead in the third set. But McEnroe rebounded. He won the next three games, saved four set points and grabbed the lead in a second tie-break. McEnroe kept his nerve and his temper to win 4-6 7-6 (7-1) 7-6 (7-4) 6-4. Borg's run of 41 matches without defeat at Wimbledon had ended.

McEnroe: fined $1,500

FROM THE MOUTH OF McENROE . . .

TO UMPIRES I am not having points taken off me by an incompetent old fool. You are the pits of the world.
When I said: 'You're a disgrace to mankind,' I was talking to myself, not you.

TO A POLICEMAN You must arrest him, he's the worst umpire I've ever seen.

TO THE CROWD I am so disgusting you shouldn't watch. Everybody leave.

. . . AND WHAT OTHERS SAID Mister McEnroe, I must warn you that you are abusing your racket. Please behave — Edward James, Wimbledon umpire.
Mister McEnroe called me a four-letter word. It was not a very serious one — Fred Hoyles, Wimbledon referee.

McENROE'S TITLES

1979 US Open
1980 US Open
1981 Wimbledon, US Open
1983 Wimbledon
1984 Wimbledon, US Open

Norway's finest hour is England's nightmare

ENGLAND suffered a humiliating defeat in Oslo when they lost 2-1 to Norway in a World Cup qualifying match on September 9. It was their most embarrassing defeat since 1950, when they were beaten by the United States, and put their qualification for the World Cup finals in jeopardy.

England were on top of their group with seven points from seven games but only had one match left, at home to Hungary. But then fortune smiled on them. A series of improbable results meant that Hungary had qualified and England only needed a point.

A single goal from Paul Mariner against an uninterested Hungarian side was sufficient to see England to the finals for the first time since 1970. Scotland, for the third successive time, and Northern Ireland, for the second, were the other British teams set for Spain.

❝ We are the best in the world. We have beaten England. Lord Nelson, Lord Beaverbrook, Sir Winston Churchill, Sir Anthony Eden, Clement Attlee, Henry Cooper, Lady Diana. We have beaten them all. Maggie Thatcher, can you hear me? Maggie Thatcher, your boys took a hell of a beating. Norway have beaten England at football ❞

Norwegian radio commentator

Humiliation in Oslo: England lose to Norway

Torvill and Dean find perfection

THERE seemed to be no stopping Jayne Torvill and Christopher Dean. They really started to cash in on a £50,000 training grant from Nottingham council and the Sports Aid foundation with repeat victories in the European and World championships.

Judges were starting to find it ever harder to find fault with their performances. They were awarded 11 maximum scores of 6.0, three for technical merit and eight for presentation, at the European championships, and another five perfect scores for artistic impression in their Mack and Mabel routine at the World championships.

Faultless pair

FOOTBALL

Spurs shrug off missing stars

Glenn Hoddle's penalty in the sixth minute of the replay won Tottenham the Cup

THE SHADOW of the Falklands war hung over the FA Cup final between Spurs and Second Division QPR.

Twenty-four hours before the semi-finals Argentina had invaded the Falklands and this placed Tottenham's two Argentinians, Osvaldo Ardiles and Ricardo Villa in an impossible position. Ardiles rose to the occasion, making the first goal in a brilliant set-piece from a corner, but promptly went to Buenos Aires to join his country's World Cup squad and did not return.

Then 24 hours before the Cup final the British Task Force landed in the Falklands and Villa and the Spurs manager, Keith Burkinshaw, decided on the morning of the match that it would be impolitic for him to play.

So Spurs had to take the field without their two inspirational South Americans. And what players remained were shattered from a long and arduous season where they had been chasing four trophies. By May 22 Spurs had lost the League Cup final to Liverpool in extra time, the European Cup Winners' Cup semi-final to Barcelona by one goal and finished fourth in the League.

Inevitably the final suffered. In extra time Spurs went ahead with a Glenn Hoddle goal that was deflected by an opponent (shades of the final the year before) only

to be caught with a set-piece goal from Terry Fenwick. The replay five days later was, if anything, less inspiring, particularly as QPR were without the injured Clive Allen and the suspended Glenn Roeder, and a Hoddle penalty in the sixth minute settled matters.

For Spurs it was their seventh FA Cup (only Aston Villa have won it as often) and they did not finish the season empty-handed as they once feared. However, doubts about the future of Ardiles and Villa in English football muted the celebrations, and on July 5 Ardiles agreed to play for Paris St Germain for a year.

LONDON PRIDE

London clubs' dominated the FA Cup from 1961 to 1982. In the previous 60 years London clubs had won the FA Cup only six times.

1961	Tottenham
1962	Tottenham
1964	West Ham
1967	Tottenham
1970	Chelsea
1971	Arsenal
1975	West Ham
1979	Arsenal
1980	West Ham
1981	Tottenham
1982	Tottenham

In the same period, Arsenal (three times), Chelsea, Fulham and QPR were losing finalists

CRICKET

Boycott reaches record and packs his bag

GEOFF BOYCOTT became the most prolific run-scorer in Test cricket and then went home midway through the series in India, claiming he was too ill. The England opener took his tally to 8,114 runs in his final Test, beating the record of 8,032 runs by Garry Sobers. India won the six-match series 1-0 thanks to solid batting by Sunil Gavaskar, who later eclipsed Boycott's record.

England finished their tour on an historic note when they visited Colombo for Sri Lanka's maiden Test. Keith Fletcher's side won by seven wickets.

Boycott: 8,114 runs

CRICKET

Dirty dozen succumb to the rand

England's rebels were banned from Tests for three years and many never returned

GEOFF BOYCOTT, who had spent most of his life counting runs, showed he was also a dab hand at counting money. The England opener grabbed a lucrative contract to mastermind a rebel tour of South Africa. But the one-month dalliance with apartheid earned the team a three-year ban from Test cricket.

Boycott, never far from controversy, was the brains and backbone behind the side led by Graham Gooch. The party slipped quietly into South Africa on Sunday, February 28 and were soon dubbed the "Dirty Dozen". They were later joined by three others.

South Africans, starved of Test cricket for 11 years, were starstruck by their arrival but were soon brought down to earth. There was no Ian Botham and a team of has-beens, hired hands and holiday-makers were hardly a match for a side champing at the bit to prove they were still world-beaters. The South African XI dominated a series of four-day matches despite showing the rust of more than a decade in isolation. Only a productive partnership between Barry Richards and Graeme Pollock in a one-day victory brought back memories of 1970.

The tour ended the Test careers of Boycott, Mike Hendrick, Alan Knott, Chris Old and Derek Underwood and took a great bite out of the England appearances of the remainder of the party.

The South African cricket officials, backed by their government's money, then bid to buy up any Test player who would swallow his conscience for money and launched a succession of rebel tours by highly-paid teams from Australia, Sri Lanka and the West Indies. Their plans came unstuck when an English side led by Mike Gatting were forced to abandon a 1990 tour because of protests.

THE DIRTY DOZEN

Graham Gooch (captain), Dennis Amiss, Geoff Boycott, John Emburey, Mike Hendrick, Alan Knott, Wayne Larkins, John Lever, Chris Old, Les Taylor, Derek Underwood, Peter Willey.

SNOOKER

Davis: screen heroics

MOTOR RACING

Canadians' tribute to Villeneuve

GILLES VILLENEUVE, the French Canadian driver, was killed in practice at the Belgian Grand Prix at Zolder in April. To honour their brave driver the Canadians renamed their Grand Prix circuit after him. Villeneuve had won the first world championship held on the circuit in 1978.

Villeneuve: fatal crash

FOOTBALL

Argentina's Diego Maradona: record transfer fee

FOR THE RECORD

CRICKET
■ Gladstone Small delivered an 18-ball over for Warwickshire against Middlesex. He bowled 12 no-balls, had two runs scored off him and took two wickets.

FOOTBALL
■ Bobby Robson was appointed England manager on July 7. Robson had enjoyed 13 successful years as manager of Ipswich, a modest club. They had won the FA Cup in 1978, the Uefa Cup in 1981, had been First Division runners-up that year, and were runners-up again this season.

■ Irving Scholar and his associates succeeded in a shares coup at Tottenham's AGM and took control of the club. The old board's troubles stemmed from the escalating costs of building a new stand at White Hart Lane.

■ Alan Mullery became Crystal Palace's sixth manager in 20 months on June 24.

■ On July 23, the Football League instructed referees to send off players committing professional fouls.

MODERN PENTATHLON
■ Wendy Norman of Britain won the women's World championships with 5,311 points. Britain also won the team event.

TENNIS
■ The United States won the Federation Cup for the seventh successive year.

FOOTBALL

Robson: England manager

TENNIS

Connors steals McEnroe's thunder

Connors at full stretch in the battle of the big hitters

WHEN the rain finally cleared to bring a little sunshine to one of the wettest Wimbledon championships on record, the two biggest guns in the game lifted the tournament from the mire in a memorable final. Jimmy Connors and John McEnroe went at each other hammer and tongs for 4hr 16min before Connors triumphed 3-6 6-3 6-7 (2-7) 7-6 (7-5) 6-4.

For a fortnight the main talking point was the merit of putting a roof over the Centre Court. But that was forgotten for another year when Connors broke in the first game of the third final between left-handers. He went 3-1 ahead before the champion reeled off five games on the trot to take the opening set. Connors, nearly 30 and enjoying his 11th visit to Wimbledon, levelled the match and appeared in control when he served for the third set at 5-4. Inexplicably he double-faulted twice and then lost the tie-break.

But he was more than a match for McEnroe and strutted his stuff from then on with some blistering returns that won him the fourth set on a tie-break, the deciding set and the title eight years after his first Wimbledon victory.

Chris Evert, the defending women's singles champion, also lost in the final, 6-1 3-6 6-2 to Martina Navratilova, the first of her six successive titles.

FOOTBALL

Low gates push clubs to the brink

WOLVES, crippled by debts of £2.5m because of falling gates, reckless spending in the transfer market and their £10m stadium, avoided bankruptcy on July 30 by three minutes when the receiver and the Football League accepted Derek Dougan's package to rescue the club.

And Bristol City, who had been in the First Division from 1976 to 1980 but now languished in the Third, were also brought to the brink of bankruptcy by their massive wage bill of £350,000. The wages of eight players alone totalled £250,000 and after considerable pressure the "Ashton Gate Eight" finally agreed on February 3 to their contracts being cancelled.

Matters were almost as bad at Hereford, where the cash crisis prompted the directors' wives to volunteer on March 23 to do the office cleaning at Edgar Road.

Part of the problem of football's tottering finances was caused by a slump in attendances at League matches. The crowds hit rock bottom on September 19, when there were only 390,451 spectators for a full programme, 71,000 down on the corresponding day the previous season and the lowest for any September since the war.

Italy scintillate after negative start

ENGLAND began the finals of the World Cup in the best possible fashion with a goal after 27 seconds from Bryan Robson against France in Bilbao on June 16. They easily qualified for the second phase winning all their games, scoring six goals and only conceding one. But this was only the phoney part of the competition.

When they met West Germany in Madrid, a sterile 0-0 draw left them needing to beat the hosts Spain 2-0 to reach the semi-finals. Ron Greenwood, the manager, had been blighted by injuries to Kevin Keegan and Trevor Brooking and neither had yet played in the competition. Bizarrely, he decided in advance to bring them on as a double substitution just after the hour. The gamble never paid off as both missed good chances and the match was scoreless. England went out, unbeaten.

Scotland, yet again, failed to qualify for the second phase. This time they had a good excuse: they were in the same group as Brazil and the Soviet Union. They actually led, briefly, against Brazil and drew with the Soviet Union, but were eliminated from the next stage on goal difference.

Northern Ireland were the shock side of the tournament, beating Spain with a goal from Gerry Armstrong to top their group and reach the second phase. Unfortunately France were too strong for them.

Italy stuttered into the second phase, drawing all three games and only qualifying by virtue of having scored two goals to Cameroon's one. Then they, and Paolo Rossi, exploded. In successive matches they beat Argentina, the holders; Brazil, the favourites; Poland, who finished in third place; and in the final, West Germany, the European champions. They were the only four games Italy won in the whole of 1982, and it made them World champions for the third time.

Unfortunately, the 1982 World Cup will not only be remembered for Rossi's six goals and Italy's stunning renaissance, but also for disgraceful Germanic cynicism. In their final match in the first phase against Austria, who had already qualified, both sides knew a 1-0 win for West Germany would edge out Algeria on goal difference. The Austrians duly succumbed 1-0 to their cousins in a match that was played at walking pace. Then in West Germany's semi-final with the flamboyant French, Harald Schumacher, the West German goalkeeper, committed the most atrocious foul on Patrick Battiston, and went unpunished. The French, unsettled, were eliminated on penalties.

Rossi powers Italy's first goal in the final

Robson heads England's second against France in Bilbao

Watson comes up with the shot of a lifetime

TOM WATSON became the fifth player to win the Open and the US Open in the same year. But even Watson agreed he was fortunate to join Bobby Jones (1926 and 1930), Gene Sarazen (1932), Ben Hogan (1953) and Lee Trevino (1971).

Jack Niklaus had taken the chill out of a crisp Sunday afternoon in California with one of his classic charges. Nicklaus was running hot in the US Open and five successive birdies on the final day at Pebble Beach left only Watson with an opportunity to deny his rival a fifth title. Watson, though, needed par on the last two holes to tie.

There were groans in the gallery when he pulled his two-iron at the par-three 17th into lush Kikuyu grass about 12 feet from the edge of the green and 20 feet from the pin. Watson was ankle deep in the rough when he took back his sand iron and delicately lobbed the ball towards the hole. It bounced twice and dropped into the hole. Racing out of the rough with his arms aloft, he did a victory jig around the green. He finished with a 15-foot birdie putt at the last for a two-shot victory.

And so to sunny Scotland for the Open at Troon. Watson had done well north of Hadrian's Wall and all three of his Open titles had been won there. Soon the talk of Troon was Bobby Clampett, who took a five-shot lead with rounds of 67 and 66. However, the 22-year-old Californian struggled to 78 in the third round and on the final day gave way to Nick Price. The unassuming Zimbabwean led Watson by three shots with six to play and Watson admitted he had prepared his second-place speech. He did not need it.

Price dropped a shot at the 13th, two at the 15th and missed a seven-foot putt for par at the 17th. Then he left a birdie putt short at the final hole to finish one behind and tie for second with Peter Ooster-huis. Watson changed his speech and gratefully gripped the old claret jug for the fourth time.

Watson: bravura year

CRICKET

Botham grabs last-gasp win

IAN BOTHAM provided England with another miracle on the penultimate day of the year. Botham, who had almost single-handedly retained the Ashes in 1981, ended a last-wicket stand of 70 to give England a three-run victory on the final morning of the fourth Test in Melbourne.

Botham's 100th Australian wicket broke the partnership between Allan Border and Jeff Thomson, who had resumed from the overnight score of 255 for nine, chasing 292 for victory. A crowd of 15,000 people turned up for what might have been only one ball. The Australian pair declined 29 comfortable singles in their 128-minute stand.

England's victory lifted their morale after Australia had taken a 2-0 lead in the series despite missing Terry Alderman. The pace bowler injured his shoulder tackling one of about 20 spectators who invaded the field in the first Test in Perth.

Alderman: injured in tackle

CRICKET

England's astute leader retires

MIKE BREARLEY led Middlesex to their fourth championship title in seven summers and called it a day after an illustrious career as captain of county and country.

The 40-year-old right-hander was never more than a mediocre batsman in the Test arena. He averaged a mere 22.88 in 39 matches and regularly required innings of substance to retain his place in the team. Instead, it was as a leader that he earned his glowing reputation, winning 18 of his 31 Tests as captain and losing only four — all to Australia. He won seven out of nine series, drew one and lost one.

Brearley had an excellent rapport with his players, and with his psychoanalyst's training was able to get the best out of a sometimes tempestuous Ian Botham, particularly in the memorable Ashes series against Australia in 1981.

He was revered at Middlesex, where he led the county to four championship titles and two Gillette Cups after taking over the reins in 1971 from Peter Parfitt.

Middlesex had also come close to winning other trophies. In 1975 they lost by five wickets in the B&H Cup final and by seven wickets in the Gillette Cup final. They also finished runners-up to Sussex in the Sunday League in Brearley's last season.

England soon realised they were missing Brearley's leadership, but neither India nor Pakistan were able to capitalise on Bob Willis's inadequate captaincy. Allan Lamb hit a century in his third Test as England made sure of a 1-0 victory against India and then Botham's bowling inspired the team to a 2-1 triumph against Pakistan. Imran Khan took seven for 52 in the first innings but lacked the support to trouble the home side in the decisive third Test.

But it was not all rosy in the English garden. No sooner had Willis's team arrived in Australia then they were struggling to stay the pace against an Australian team rebounding from a 3-0 loss in Pakistan.

Brearley: leadership missed

ATHLETICS

Thompson possesses all of the title deeds

DALEY THOMPSON responded superbly to the European championships challenge of the West German Jurgen Hingsen, who just three weeks earlier had relieved him of the world decathlon record with a score of 8,723 points.

In Athens on September 7 and 8 Thompson outran, outjumped, outthrew and outtalked the German not only to win the gold medal, but also regain the world record with 8,743 points. In doing so, he became the first man in any event to hold simultaneously the Olympic, European and Commonwealth titles, as well as the world record.

Thompson wins Athens European showdown

Ruthless Australians rampage through Europe

THE cream of Britain did not appreciate the skills of 28 Australian Kangaroos. They were on the receiving end. But 67,000 people enjoyed watching possibly the greatest touring team in history.

They flocked to three Tests to witness the sublime skills, tactics and fitness of Max Krilich's side. The Australians took the sport into a new dimension and it showed in their scores against the best Britain could offer. They won the Tests 40-4, 27-6 and 32-8, completing a clean sweep of Britain and France. And the leading club sides were not spared either. The League champions Leigh were beaten 44-4 and in-form Leeds lost 31-4.

The Kangaroos scored an impressive 97 tries in Britain and conceded only seven. They got 69 in France and gave away only two.

Their success was achieved by discipline and a quest for perfection. Players were fined for seemingly trivial misdemeanours, such as not wearing the official blazer to post-match functions, and some men were still not satisfied with their fitness despite rigorous training sessions under the coach Frank Stanton. Ray Price, a former rugby union international, showed why he was called Mr Perpetual Motion by running eight miles each morning, and his partner Wayne Pearce used the stairs at his Leeds hotel to improve his stamina.

Australia's Ray Price evades Jeff Grayshon during the 1st Test

AUSTRALIA'S TOUR RECORD

IN BRITAIN: Hull Kingston Rovers 30-10; Wigan 13-9; Barrow 29-2; St Helens 32-0; Leeds 31-4; Wales 37-7; **Great Britain (First Test) 40-4**; Leigh 44-4; Bradford Northern 13-6; Cumbria 41-2; Fulham 22-5; Hull 13-7; **Great Britain (Second Test) 27-6**; Widnes 19-6; **Great Britain (Third Test) 32-8**.

IN FRANCE: Roanne 65-0; **France (First Test) 15-4**; Selection Aquitaine 67-2; French Under-24 42-3; Catalans de France 53-2; Selection Pyrenees-Rouergue 26-0; **France (Second Test) 23-9**.

	P	W	D	L	F	A
In Britain	15	15	0	0	423	80
In France	7	7	0	0	291	20
Total	22	22	0	0	714	100

Many of the players in the Invincibles became Australian legends: the Parramatta half-backs Brett Kenny and Peter Stirling, the vice-captain Wally Lewis, the centre Mal Meninga and, of course, Pearce and Price. Britain had no answer.

Chapman, creator of Lotus, dies

COLIN CHAPMAN, one of the sport's greatest innovators, died of a heart attack at the age of 54 in his Norfolk home in December. Chapman's energy and enthusiasm had created the Lotus marque and a host of world champions from Jim Clark in 1963 and 1965, Graham Hill in 1968, Jochen Rindt in 1970, Emerson Fittipaldi in 1972 and Mario Andretti in 1978.

Chapman's contribution to his sport included ground-effect cars, gas turbine engines and sponsor-ship. It was Chapman's idea to have his cars painted in the colours of the sponsors and in 1968 he unveiled the John Player Lotus in the colours of their Gold Leaf brand. Although he was criticised at the time, the whole of motor racing quickly followed suit.

His relationship with Jim Clark was something special, and together they clocked up a record 25 Grand Prix victories. Chapman was never the same after his friend, and the world's best driver, was killed at Hockenheim in 1968.

Chapman, who had studied engineering at London University, cut his teeth on modifying Austin Sevens, which proved immensely successful. In 1952 he decided to branch out and formed Lotus with £25 borrowed from his girlfriend (later to become his wife). Always ambitious, he set his sights on Formula One, and by 1958 a Lotus had appeared in F1. Then Jim Clark appeared, and a great partnership and F1 marque was born.

Chapman in the JPS Lotus

FOOTBALL

Maxwell starts a right royal row

ROBERT MAXWELL put the cat among the pigeons when he announced on April 16 that although the chairman of Oxford United he had bought a controlling interest in Reading and intended to merge the two clubs and form the Thames Valley Royals.

Within five days the Oxford board unanimously backed Maxwell's controversial plan, and the Football League said five clubs would be promoted from the Fourth Division if the merger went ahead. However, Maxwell underestimated the opposition.

Two weeks after he unveiled his plans Reading supporters paraded a coffin around the town before a home match. The merger finally collapsed on May 13 when the Reading chairman and two directors resigned, opening the way for a new chairman. Maxwell insisted that he would leave Oxford United unless the council provided a site for a new stadium.

CRICKET

Boycott's supporters overthrew the Yorkshire committee

Boycott in local feud

THE Yorkshire committee decided that watching Geoff Boycott bat for 20 years was quite enough. They refused to renew his contract but agreed to award the 43-year-old opener a benefit season the following summer. The committee did not last long.

They were overthrown in the elections in March by a pro-Boycott coup and the former England player was presented with a new contract. He celebrated by scoring 1,941 runs at an average of 55.45, but it was not enough to stop Yorkshire propping up the championship table for the first time in their 120-year history. The only county who refused to sign players born outside their boundaries began to feel the effects of their insular policy.

THE FALL OF YORKSHIRE

(Overseas players were accepted into the championship in 1968)

Year	P	W	L	D	Pos
1963	28	13	3	11	1
1964	28	11	3	14	5
1965	28	9	4	14	4
1966	28	15	5	8	1
1967	28	12	5	9	1
1968	28	11	4	13	1
1969	24	3	6	15	13
1970	24	8	5	11	4
1971	24	4	8	12	13
1972	20	4	5	11	10
1973	20	3	5	12	14
1974	19	4	7	8	11
1975	20	10	1	9	2
1976	20	6	6	8	8
1977	21	6	5	10	12
1978	22	10	3	9	4
1979	21	5	3	13	7
1980	22	4	3	15	6
1981	22	5	9	8	10
1982	21	5	1	15	10
1983	23	1	5	17	17

RACING

Dickinson knocks Cheltenham for six with a bunch of fives

MICHAEL DICKINSON had an even busier day than usual at the Cheltenham Festival on March 17. With five runners out of the 11 in the Gold Cup there was a lot of work to do, particularly because his assistant trainer Dermot Browne was one of the jockeys.

When the field turned into the finishing straight all of Dickinson's runners were well placed. "Come on my lot," he shouted. And they did. Led home by Bregawn, Dickinson's horses filled

DICKINSON'S NAP HAND

1 BREGAWN (G Bradley)
2 Captain John (D Goulding)
3 Wayward Lad (J J O'Neill)
4 Silver Buck (R Earnshaw)
5 Ashley House (D Browne)

the first five places in the race and, to mark the feat, the Stewards allowed all of them to return to the unsaddling enclosure.

Bregawn: the first of Dickinson's five

Mystery of vanishing Shergar

SHERGAR was last seen alive on the evening of February 8. What happened after that reads like a half-finished Dick Francis novel.

The Aga Khan's stallion had been retired at the end of the 1981 season. With victories in the English and Irish Derbys and the King George VI to his credit, he was worth at least £10 million and he stood at the Aga Khan's Ballymany Stud in Ireland.

There, he was snatched by an armed gang. Nobody has ever claimed responsibility for the kidnapping, but it is generally accepted to have been the work of the IRA. A ransom demand was made, but it soon became apparent that the Aga Khan had no intention of paying the £2 million asked for the safe return of his horse.

On one hand, it seemed impossible that a horse as well known and as instantly recognisable as Shergar could vanish into thin air. And, as the story dominated the headlines, there were dozens of reported sightings. But in the wilder regions of Ireland there were any number of barns or outbuildings that could be used to hide a horse. Despite an enormous operation, the police soon had to admit that they did not have any real clues to what had happened.

The search for Shergar soon took on an air of farce with ever wilder theories being advanced about his whereabouts. As the days dragged by it became more apparent that Shergar would never be seen again. The most likely explanation is that the kidnappers, once they knew a deal could never be done, killed the horse and buried him, or otherwise destroyed the evidence of their crime.

FOR THE RECORD

CRICKET

■ Eddie Hemmings came within five runs of scoring a century as a nightwatchman for England against Australia in the fifth Test in Sydney. But it was not enough to take his side to victory and Australia regained the Ashes for the first time in 5½ years.

FOOTBALL

■ The latest Chester report was published on March 28. Chester recommended a reduction of clubs in the First Division; the Third and Fourth being reorganised into regional groups; and home clubs retaining all the gate money. Four weeks later club chairmen indicated very little support for his ideas.

■ Bishop's Stortford of the Isthmian League stunned Malcolm Allison's Middlesbrough at Ayresome Park with two second-half equalising goals from their reserve midfield player Richard Bradford in the third round of the FA Cup on January 8. Six thousand packed into Stortford's ground for the replay to see Lyndon Lynch give them a half-time lead but Middlesbrough rallied to win 2-1.

■ The heated debate about how much football there should be on television took a novel turn on February 22 when Brian Clough suggested the game should be taken off the screens for three years.

ICE SKATING

■ It was six of the best yet again for Jayne Torvill and Christopher Dean. When they won the World championships in Helsinki all nine judges gave them perfect 6.0 scores for artistic impression.

SQUASH

■ Jahangir Khan and Gamal Awad played the world's longest match — 2hr 46min — at Chichester. Khan won in four games.

Stenmark and Klammer are still the greatest skiers in the world

Stenmark powering his way to that 8th win

INGEMAR STENMARK, possibly the richest amateur in sport, won a record eighth World Cup slalom title to confirm his status as one of the greatest ever skiers.

The arrogant Swede, who bathed in the inflated glory of a lucrative contract with the Yugoslav ski manufacturers Elan, had dominated the men's slalom in the 1970s, winning seven successive titles before the American Phil Mahre broke his sequence.

Now Stenmark was back from his home in Tarnaby, a fishing resort 20 miles south of the Arctic Circle, hoping to show the world he was still the best. Although he was still a sporting god in Sweden — tourists stole stones from his garden as mementoes — he was no longer the fastest on the slopes. That honour went to Mahre, who retained the giant slalom crown and won his third successive overall title.

Franz Klammer, the dominant downhill racer in the 1970s, also had his moment. The Austrian won a record fifth downhill title. It was the last hurrah for the 1976 Olympic gold medallist.

Seve puts one over Americans

SEVERIANO BALLESTEROS had one complaint about playing in America. "In the United States I'm lucky, in Europe I'm good," he said of his status across the Atlantic. A four-shot victory in the Masters changed that.

At last Americans began to appreciate the genius of Ballesteros, who won his second green jacket at Augusta with a spectacular charge in the final round. Ballesteros began the day one shot behind, but with a birdie, eagle, par and birdie in the first four holes he was suddenly three shots ahead.

He turned in 31, four in front, and found the tricky homeward trip through Amen Corner plain sailing. The two Texans Ben Crenshaw and Tom Kite were left behind. Kite suggested that "trying to catch Seve is like a Chevy pickup trying to catch a Ferrari".

Kite knew what it was like chasing champions. He seemed destined to go down in history as one of the finest players never to win a major tournament. Instead, he had to be content as runner-up to Jack Nicklaus in the 1978 Open and 1986 Masters and second to Ballesteros at Augusta.

Ballesteros masters Augusta

1983

FOOTBALL

Elton and Taylor in harmony

Elton John: on song

THE season ended on a perfect note for Watford. They beat Liverpool, the champions, 2-1 at Vicarage Road on May 14 to finish as runners-up, a point ahead of Manchester United. For their chairman, Elton John, and manager, Graham Taylor, it was the culmination of seven years of near-miracle working.

Watford were a modest, mid-table Fourth Division outfit when Elton John took control in 1976. He pumped in his own money and recruited Taylor as manager and Bertie Mee as his assistant. Within two years they had escaped from the Fourth Division and over the next five seasons steadily worked their way up to the First with a blend of experienced and young players. En route Taylor discovered, and introduced, precocious talents such as John Barnes and Luther Blissett.

CRICKET

Outsiders India stun the world champions

THE first signs that the third World Cup in England would be an eventful fortnight came on the opening day when Zimbabwe beat Australia by 13 runs. A day later India ended the unbeaten run of West Indies with a prophetic victory against the champions.

Although the format favoured Australia they were unable to recover from their shock defeat and failed to qualify for the semi-finals. Not so the West Indians. They looked in good form for a third successive title after an eight-wicket victory against Pakistan with 68 balls to spare in the semi-final.

Their opponents in the final were the 66-1 outsiders India, who had scored a comfortable six-wicket victory against England in their semi-final at Old Trafford. Few people expected the Indians to challenge West Indian superiority, and when Kapil Dev's team mustered only 183 in 54.5 overs there were even fewer who gave them much chance.

The victory drums began to sound at Lord's despite the early loss of Gordon Greenidge, and they gathered momentum when Viv Richards began hitting the ball with a devil-may-care attitude. But he played one risky shot too many. He attempted to lift a delivery from Madan Lal over the mid-wicket boundary, mistimed the shot and Kapil made much ground to take

Richards: began collapse

an excellent high catch in the deep.

That was the beginning of the end for the great West Indian team. Desmond Haynes soon followed Richards to the Long Room and the team were struck by stage fright. The calypso had become a collapso. Their total of 50 for one had progressed to 76 for six when Malcolm Marshall joined Jeff Dujon.

They posted 43 runs for the seventh wicket but the recovery was scuppered when Amarnath slipped a delivery between Dujon's bat and pad and the favourites were back on the rack. Amarnath and Madan Lal kept a tight rein on the scoring and when Michael Holding was trapped lbw the Indians celebrated a memorable 43-run victory. A national holiday was declared in India the next day.

GOLF

Eighth major for Tom

TOM WATSON, dressed in a plain white shirt and grey trousers, resembled a marshal controlling the crowd which had come to Royal Birkdale to watch him win a fifth Open. The furrowed brow and two-iron at the 18th gave him away.

Watson produced one of the great shots in golf at the 473-yard last to win by one stroke from Andy Bean and Hale Irwin. Needing a par to retain the title, he hit a straight drive that landed 210 yards from the pin. Then out came the two-iron and his magnificent effort under pressure covered the flag, bounced twice and finished 15 feet and two putts from the hole. It was his eighth major title in nine years.

TENNIS

McEnroe too streetwise for novice Lewis

CHRIS LEWIS, a little New Zealander with a headband and an ability to fight for every point, preferred to play tennis on clay courts. It showed. John McEnroe carved him up in only 85 minutes on the grass at Wimbledon to win a second title.

McEnroe's 6-2 6-2 6-2 victory was swift and clinical. Lewis was exhausted before he even started. He had taken nearly four hours to beat Kevin Curren 6-7 (3-7) 6-4 7-6 (7-4) 6-7 (3-7) 8-6 in a gripping semi-final. Curren, a gangly South African with a big serve, had eliminated the defending champion Jimmy Connors with 33 aces. But Lewis, the 1975 Wimbledon junior champion, played what he described as the match of his life to become the first New Zealander to reach the finals since Tony Wilding in 1914. However, McEnroe was far too street-wise for an opponent obviously overawed by the occasion.

One who had not been overawed by expectations a month earlier was Yannick Noah, who became the first Frenchman since Marcel Bernard in 1946 to win in Paris. Noah, who had grown up in Cameroon, broke the 37-year drought with a 6-2 7-5 7-6 victory against the defending champion Mats Wilander.

McEnroe: 85-minute win

Brighton's wonderful campaign yields nothing

ALTHOUGH Brighton's four-year stint in the First Division came to an end, this was still the greatest season in their history. In the fifth round of the FA Cup they travelled to Anfield with the pundits' predictions of a Liverpool Double ringing in their ears, and knowing they had never gone beyond this round.

Nevertheless, they triumphed 2-1. It was the Cup upset of the year. Brighton's former Anfield hero Jimmy Case did the damage with a late goal, and when Phil Neal missed a penalty Brighton believed it was to be their year.

The victories that proved so elusive in the League just kept flowing in the Cup and on May 21 Jimmy Melia's team faced Manchester United in the final. Unfortunately, Brighton were without Steve Foster, their captain and the heart of their defence, suspended because of a booking in a League match. Perhaps his absence inspired them.

In the 14th minute a Gordon Smith header put the outsiders in the lead, but in the second half Frank Stapleton equalised for

Smith's lunging tackle just prevents Whiteside shooting for Manchester United

United and Ray Wilkins seemed to have wrapped it up when he curled in a second goal with 17 minutes left.

Yet there was still life in relegated Brighton and Gary Stevens, the man of the match, levelled the scores with 180 seconds remaining. In extra time, Smith had a wonderful opportunity to snatch the Cup but hesitated and the moment was lost. The replay five days later followed the form book: Brighton were put in their place with a 4-0 trouncing.

Paisley: bowed out

FOR THE RECORD

FOOTBALL

■ Bob Paisley, the most successful manager in British football, carried out his promise and retired as Liverpool manager on May 14. Nine days later, Joe Fagan, a stalwart of the Boot Room, was named as his replacement.

■ Aberdeen achieved a remarkable Cup double. First, they overcame Real Madrid 2-1 in extra time in the final of the European Cup Winners' Cup then, 10 days later, they snatched the Scottish Cup by wearing down Rangers in extra time.

■ On July 18 the FA referees' committee rejected last season's instruction to send off players for professional fouls or intentional handball.

TENNIS

■ Bill Scanlon did not drop a point in the second set of a 6-2 6-0 victory against Marcos Hocevar in Del Ray, Florida. It was the only known occasion in a professional event that a player won all 24 points in a set.

Black scores Aberdeen's first goal against Real Madrid

World tournament rivals Olympics

WITH the Olympic Games having previously been considered the unofficial world championships of athletics, the governing body of the sport, the International Amateur Athletic Federation, established its own rival quadrennial World championships in August.

Some people felt that the sport wanted an alternative to the Olympics if there was any major disagreement between the International Olympic Committee and the IAAF, which now had an ambitious president in the Italian Dr Primo Nebiolo.

The venue chosen for the inaugural championships was Helsinki's historic Olympic Stadium, where the athletics-mad spectators gave the event their full support, even though many of the individual stars of the show were Americans: Carl Lewis, who took gold medals in the 100m, long jump and relay; Ed Moses, the hottest favourite of the week, who won the 400m hurdles by more than a second; and Mary Decker, who took the 1500 and 3,000m double in the face of stiff Soviet competition.

Britain's only champions were Steve Cram in the 1500m and Daley Thompson, who added yet another title to his collection, and could now call himself Olympic, World, European and Commonwealth decathlon champion.

Cram: 1500m gold

Whitbread: javelin silver

The most dramatic moment, though, came in the women's javelin. All of the host nation's hopes of success rested with their world record holder, Tiina Lillak. But the competition was blown open in the first round when Fatima Whitbread threw a near personal best of 69.14m.

It seemed a winner, with Lillak's best, in second place, only 67.46m. Then, on Lillak's sixth and last throw, with the spear almost being held aloft by the collective will of thousands of Finns, she threw 70.82m to snatch the title amid near-pandemonium.

Of such drama are not only gold medals won, but entire championships nurtured. And with none of the boycotts which had plagued the Olympic movement in recent years, the sport's fans gave silent thanks that the championships had well and truly established themselves.

FOOTBALL

Spurs float their shares

FOR THE RECORD

FOOTBALL

■ Tottenham's 3.8m shares on offer at £1 each were oversubscribed 4½ times. When the Stock Exchange opened on October 13, 1.5m shares changed hands in 20 minutes.

■ In perfect summer conditions the season got under way on August 27 and attracted the lowest number of spectators ever recorded on the opening day.

■ Second Division Swansea, faced with debts of more than £1.5m, put their entire side up for sale on November 20.

GOLF

■ Tom Watson beat Bernard Gallacher 2 and 1 in the final singles match to help the United States retain the Ryder Cup 12-11 with five matches halved.

ICE HOCKEY

■ The rebirth of the sport got a boost when the British Ice Hockey Association signed a five-year sponsorship deal with Heineken, worth £100,000 in the first season.

RUGBY LEAGUE

■ Points for a try were increased from three to four, the sin bin was introduced, teams had to relinquish possession of the ball after six tackles and the international transfer ban was lifted.

MOTOR RACING

Piquet clings on to thwart Prost

NELSON PIQUET snatched his second world title much the same way as he did his first in 1981, in the last race of the season. Going into the South African Grand Prix at Kyalami on October 13 he was two points behind Alain Prost, with Rene Arnoux breathing down their necks if either of them made a mistake.

Piquet took an early lead, and a third of the way through the race had a lightning-fast pit-stop of 9.2sec that still left him in first place. Prost had a terrible pit-stop and soon withdrew, but as the title beckoned Piquet's turbocharged Brabham began to fail.

His team-mate Riccardo Patrese easily overtook him and with two laps to go Andrea de Cesaris pushed him into third place. However, Piquet managed to hang on to third place and the four points needed to pip Prost for the title by two points.

Piquet: second title

America's Cup leaves home

THE New York Yacht Club had done away with the need for boats challenging for the America's Cup to be entirely designed and built in their home country. It was a decision that in the end was to cost them the Cup.

Ben Lexcen scoured the world for the very best in technology, and for the flamboyant Australian Alan Bond money was no object. Lexcen produced a design so radical that when Australia II was out of the water in Newport, Rhode Island, its hull was shrouded from prying eyes. The secret was in the keel, which was fitted with wings to increase speed and stability.

There was no doubt that the winged design was very fast, as was shown when Australia II easily beat the conventionally designed British entry, Peter de Savary's Victory 83, in the challengers' final. Even Dennis Conner, defending the Cup in Liberty, knew that Australia II was the fastest boat on the water.

However, during September, it looked as if the novel design would be let down in the finals. Equipment failures cost Australia II, skippered by John Bertrand, the first two races. Bond's syndicate pulled a race back, but then Conner won again to give the Americans a 3-1 lead in the best of seven final.

Then the competition hotted up. It was Liberty's turn to be hit by an equipment failure, and then Australia II raced away with the sixth round by 3min 25sec to tie the series at 3-3.

Everything was at stake in the final race, and it looked as if the Cup would be staying put as Conner led almost from the start. On the penultimate leg, though, Bertrand edged ahead and the race was on with a vengeance.

Conner started a close-quarters duel, tacking 47 times on the final leg, but Bertrand was able to match his every manoeuvre and hold on for victory by 41sec, forcing the New York Yacht Club to unbolt the trophy from their floor and hand it over for the first time in 132 years.

John Bertrand, in Australia II, ends the longest winning streak in history

English hooligans run riot in Europe

TOTTENHAM beat Feyenoord 2-0 in Rotterdam on November 2 and went through to the last 16 of the Uefa Cup 6-2 on aggregate. However, their achievement was marred by rioting fans. More than 30 people were injured and Uefa fined Tottenham £8,000 and Feyenoord £3,000.

English fans abroad continued to shame their country when England beat Luxembourg 4-0 away a fortnight later. Despite the win, England failed to qualify for the finals of the European championships and their fans wreaked thousands of pounds of damage as they rampaged through the town.

Three weeks after the riot, the Luxembourg courts handed down prison sentences of one to four months to nine of the 13 who were arrested and fines of up to £300.

Fluctuating fortunes dog Essex charge

ESSEX looked like a team on a roller-coaster ride. Keith Fletcher led them to his second county championship after a mixed bag of results, and they threw away the B&H Cup in a sensational final at Lord's. Essex appeared certain to overhaul Middlesex's 196 for eight when they needed 12 runs in four overs with five wickets in hand. But Mike Gatting, the Middlesex captain, kept his head and pulled off a stunning four-run victory at 8.50pm.

Essex's championship run also had its share of drama. They dismissed Surrey for 14 — their lowest-ever score — at Chelmsford but watched Middlesex score 634 for seven at the same ground.

Lester Piggott
The consummate winner

John Karter

Lester. He inspired a billion bets, spawned a thousand stories and transcended the sport of racing like no other. Revered by pin-stickers and serious horse players alike, Piggott was by general consensus the greatest jockey of all time. When he finally retired in 1995 at the age of 59, Piggott had netted 30 British Classics, including an unprecedented nine Derby victories. He gained the last of those Classic wins aboard Rodrigo de Triano in the 1992 2,000 Guineas at the age of 56. Eleven times British champion jockey, Piggott amassed over 4,500 victories in Britain and some 800 overseas.

However, mere statistics cannot remotely portray the full picture of Piggott's almost unearthly brilliance in the saddle. His uncanny empathy with horses acted like the most powerful stimulant and enabled him to perform the impossible on a daily basis. Being so tall, Piggott was in one sense not a natural jockey, so he adopted a unique and instantly-recognisable style. Clad in flamboyant silks as he perched over his mount with his bottom thrust absurdly high in the air, he looked like one of those exotic African birds that cheekily hitch a ride on a hippo's back. In full flight he was more like a hawk swooping on his prey.

He could be incredibly subtle on a horse, cajoling an unwilling partner to produce that little bit extra with a seductive touch. When necessary, however, he was also the most ruthless finisher in the game. Under the updated rules on the use of the whip he would not have got away with some of the floggings he inflicted on his mounts in his heyday.

Piggott's complete lack of nerves manifested itself in an extraordinary nonchalance on the big occasion. He faced every race with the same icy detachment whether it was the Derby in front of 250,000 people at Epsom or the most humble selling race on a quiet Monday at Catterick. His nursing of Sir Ivor, a colt with doubtful stamina, to win the 1968 Derby was acclaimed as possibly the greatest piece of race riding ever. Piggott's sang froid was almost beyond belief as he restrained Sir Ivor until the shadow of the post before cutting down Connaught with contemptuous ease. Sandy Barclay, Connaught's rider, was in tears afterwards and it was a fatherly Piggott who comforted him.

Piggott's triumph on Roberto in the 1972 Derby was utterly contrasting in every respect. You could almost hear the merciless crack of his whip above the baying crowd as he brought it down repeatedly on Roberto's quarters to snatch victory by the width of a nostril from another young rider, Ernie Johnson, on Rheingold. No other rider could have won on Roberto, they said. Yet Piggott was for once greeted in stoney silence as the racing world showed exactly what they thought of his eleventh-hour substitution for the Australian rider Bill Williamson. Procuring the mount on Roberto appeared to be another example of Piggott's practice of "jocking off" other riders by using his reputation and relationship with leading owners and trainers to secure himself a big-race ride at the expense of a colleague. In Roberto's case though, Piggott was not totally to blame, as it was largely at the owner's insistence that the substitution was made.

This disregard for his fellows had manifested itself at the start of his career when, in the first of his constant brushes with authority, he was suspended for his riding of Never Say Die at Ascot a fortnight after win-

ning his first Derby on the same horse at the age of 18. The Stewards of the Jockey Club, racing's ruling body, said: "In spite of continuous warnings Piggott continued to show complete disregard for the rules and the safety of other riders."

Piggott's bizarre personality, distorted to monstrous proportions by endless stories (some factual but most apocryphal) often overshadowed his extraordinary feats on the race track. He frequently appeared aloof and totally uncaring about his adoring public, although that was probably due largely to the fact that his partial deafness and consequent speech impediment made him shy and introverted. His impassive features looked as if they had been hewn from rock, hence his nickname Old Stoneface. A trainer who once rashly suggested that Piggott might give the ecstatic fans a smile met with a predictable rebuke. "Why should I?" Piggott retorted in that famous nasal monotone. "They'd be throwing things at me if I lost."

Riding at Deauville at the height of his career, he dropped his whip at a crucial moment in a rare loss of concentration. Unfazed, he grabbed the whip of the jockey alongside him and renewed his challenge to finish second. Asked about the incident, he said the other rider had no chance of winning anyway.

Many Piggott stories concern his meanness and hoarding of money, which, according to medical theory, can be a syndrome common to those who starve themselves constantly. Piggott's emaciated face told the story of his constant struggle to keep his body a stone below its natural weight. During the season his diet was said to consist of thin air and a fat cigar. Obsessive hoarding eventually brought about the downfall of a man who was believed to be Britain's highest-paid sportsman, with a personal fortune estimated at £20m. In October 1987, two years after he retired from the saddle to take up training, he was given a three-year jail sentence for cheating the Inland Revenue of £2.8m in what was described as a "massive, deliberate and persistent fraud".

Piggott's conviction led to the loss of his OBE and almost certainly deprived him of a knighthood. He received universal support and sympathy from within the racing world when he went to prison. Many felt,

> **❝ Why should I [smile]? They'd be throwing things at me if I lost ❞**

probably with justification, that he had been made a scapegoat for under-the-counter financial practices that were widespread in racing.

He was given his freedom after serving 12 months of his sentence and for two years he assisted his wife, Susan, with their training operation at Newmarket. However, his yearning for the irreplaceable thrill of the race track was eating away at him and a month short of his 55th birthday Piggott stunned the racing world by taking out his licence again five years after hanging up his riding boots. Faithful fans were ecstatic at this totally unexpected second coming, but fellow professionals were more dubious. They felt the legend could only be tarnished and that Piggott's magic could never be rekindled.

How wrong they were. By common consent Piggott was soon demonstrating so much of the old skill and sorcery that it seemed as if he had never been away. Within a few weeks he had lifted the most valuable prize of his career when he spirited home the Irish colt Royal Academy to win the $1m Breeders' Cup Mile in New York. For the fans who backed Piggott to win fortunes and the housewives who annually entrusted him with their 50p bets in the Derby, exhorting him to nerve-tingling feats in the saddle with frenetic cries of "Come on, Lester", there can never be another like him.

As a professional tribute, the words of Jimmy Lindley, one of Piggott's most successful riding colleagues, could hardly be bettered. "The Americans used to say that a cavalry officer would ride a horse until it dropped dead and then an Apache would come along and get it to go another 20 miles. That is how it was with Lester."

The man who dominated racing for half a century: from boy wonder to the king of Epsom, where he won the Derby nine times. Piggott shocked the world when he was jailed for tax evasion, and then stunned everybody by making a triumphant comeback.

FOOTBALL

Maxwell plays fast and loose

LOUD, bullying, and promising everything, Robert Maxwell strutted across club boardrooms from the beginning of the year. Undismayed by his failure to merge Oxford and Reading into the Thames Valley Royals earlier, he used his position as the proprietor of Mirror Group Newspapers to exclusively reveal to his readers his £10m bid for Manchester United on February 3.

Amazingly, the Edwards family were seduced by the offer and haggled with Maxwell over the price. Fans were shocked, United was like an Edwards heirloom. Fortunately for them, Maxwell would not increase his offer and the deal fell through 10 days later.

Then Maxwell turned his sights on a club that would give in to his bullying ways, Derby County. They had fallen on hard times and were in danger of being wound up with debts of £1.5m. Within a fortnight of being rebuffed by Manchester United Maxwell was offering to assist Derby.

Despite the fact that he was the chairman of Oxford, and therefore disbarred by League regulations in having dealings in any other League club, and despite a ruling by a High Court judge in March that Maxwell's takeover bid of Derby would not be approved, he would not desist. By August 13, his son, Ian Maxwell, was Derby's chairman.

ATHLETICS

South African Budd becomes British with unseemly haste

THE isolation of South Africa from world sport meant that much of its natural talent was never fully developed.

Zola Budd, a gifted young distance runner from Bloemfontein, first came to notice when she set an unofficial world best of 15:01.83 for 5,000 metres in Stellenbosch on January 5, nearly seven seconds faster than the official record held by Mary Decker.

With South Africa's membership of the IAAF suspended, a way for her to compete in the forthcoming Los Angeles Olympics was found through claiming British citizenship. Zola's grandfather, it transpired, had been born in London in 1886 and emigrated to South Africa at the turn of the century. Her own father was thus able to claim British citizenship through his emigrant father and, once granted, this in turn allowed Zola to make the same claim.

Assisted by the Daily Mail, which had signed her to an exclusive contract, she arrived in London on March 24, and was issued with citizenship papers on April 6. The application, which was rushed through with unusual speed to the annoyance of immigrant groups, had to be lodged before her 18th birthday on May 26 or else she would have had to serve a five-year residency in the United Kingdom.

Budd returns to roots

WINTER OLYMPICS

Top marks for Torvill and Dean

THERE was only one fear for Jayne Torvill and Christopher Dean: had they peaked too soon? In a sport where careers were brief, they had already spent three years at the very top. But the British public need not have worried. The pair carried on getting better.

They spent six months designing their costumes for the Bolero routine and a year dazzling the world and even the most hard-bitten of judges. They coasted to victory in the European championships in Budapest with 11 perfect scores and then, on February 14, they set the ice alight at the Winter Olympics in Sarajevo. They were awarded 6.0 a total of 19 times, which included all nine

> ❝ They have opened up a new era, if only the rest of the world can grasp what they do ❞
>
> **Courtney Jones**

judges giving them top marks for Bolero's artistic impression.

Still there was more to come. They went on to the World championships in Ottawa, where they earned an unprecedented set of 29 maximum points. After such a spectacular career, which would have been almost impossible to improve, they turned professional.

T & D coasting to victory

Dods steps in to kick Scots to Grand Slam

THERE was a tinge of sadness about Scotland's charge to their first Grand Slam in 59 years. One of their great players was missing.

Andy Irvine, a brilliant fullback who had served his country in 51 internationals in 10 years, had retired two seasons before Scotland's greatest hour. Irvine's willingness to broaden the horizons of the role of the fullback into attack epitomised the style of Scotland's success.

The Scots' determination to play running rugby earned high praise, although most of their 86 points came from the accurate boot of Irvine's replacement, Peter Dods. He kicked 46 points and scored a try. The Scots beat Wales 15-9, England 18-6, France 21-12 and Ireland 32-9.

Their policy of playing open rugby was copied the following winter by the brilliant Australians, who thrilled crowds with their flair. The star in Andrew Slack's team was their fly-half Mark Ella, who

Scotland overcoming France en route to the Grand Slam

had caught the imagination of the British public when touring with the unbeaten Australian schoolboys in 1977-78. Ella, who with his brothers Gary and Glen had a big influence on Australian rugby, became the first player to score tries in all four internationals on the tour of Britain. The Wallabies won their first Grand Slam, beating England 19-3, Ireland 16-9, Wales 28-9 and Scotland 37-12.

Cup minnows wreak havoc with big boys

IT WAS the year of the underdog in the FA Cup. In the third round, on January 7, six First Division clubs were knocked out. The most spectacular was Bournemouth's 2-0 humiliation of Cup-holders Manchester United. Three weeks earlier United had been humbled by another Third Division side, Oxford, in the League Cup.

On January 29, Brighton proved they had the Indian sign over Liverpool when they knocked them out of the Cup for the second successive season. But it was Plymouth who enjoyed the most extraordinary Cup run, becoming only the sixth Third Division club to reach the semi-finals. An Andy Rogers goal direct from a corner kick in the sixth round replay against Derby put them through to meet Watford. But despite 20,000 Argyle fans travelling to Villa Park on April 14 they went down 1-0.

Plymouth (in dark strip) against Watford in the FA Cup semi-final

335

1984

FOOTBALL

Europeans knocked for six by British

THE night of March 21 was extraordinary for British clubs in Europe. All six went through to the semi-finals: in the European Cup, Liverpool and Dundee United qualified; in the European Cup Winners' Cup, Manchester United and Aberdeen went through; and in the Uefa Cup, Tottenham and Nottingham Forest.

In the subsequent draws, all the British clubs were kept apart. However, the prospect of three all-British European finals was shattered when only Liverpool and Tottenham made it to their finals.

Both finals were nerve-tingling. Liverpool were playing Roma on their home ground and were fortunate to end all square after 120 minutes. In the penalty shoot-out Liverpool should have been outsiders, given the number of penalties they had missed all season, and true to form Steve Nicol missed their first. But with two misses by Roma it fell to Alan Kennedy and Liverpool secured their fourth European Cup.

It was a similar story in the two-legged Uefa Cup final, scores level, extra time, another penalty shoot-out. But on this occasion Tottenham were playing at home and Anderlecht away. The Tottenham keeper, Tony Parkes, produced two breathtaking saves to win the Cup.

FOOTBALL

Aberdeen top dogs

ABERDEEN, under the canny managership of Alex Ferguson, achieved the near-impossible in Scotland, not only denying Celtic and Rangers a major trophy, but winning both the League championship and Cup. Ferguson had laid the foundations for his team to believe they could win the Double the season before, when they had won the Cup and the European Cup Winners' Cup and missed the League title by a point.

Although winning the championship was almost a doddle — Celtic were seven points behind in second place — the Cup Final on May 19 was another matter. It was only settled in extra time, after six players had been booked and

Ferguson: Double winner

Celtic's Roy Aitken had suffered the ignominy of being the first player sent off in a Cup final since 1929.

Platini composes and plays perfect score

MICHEL PLATINI and France finally fulfilled all the promise they had demonstrated in the 1982 World Cup finals when they swaggered through the European championships. Platini was incomparable. He was the orchestrator and chief soloist, scoring nine of France's 15 goals. With Giresse and Tigana playing in harmony, Platini and France looked the best side in the world.

However, on the day of the final in Paris, they froze. The memories of their catastrophic defeat in the World Cup semi-final against West Germany still haunted them, and the French nation. Their own sports press did not help either as they harked back to France's dismal failure in the 1958 World Cup semi-final as well. It was as if they were expected to lose to Spain.

Fortunately for France the Spaniards were even more daunted and France were 2-0 victors in an insipid final that bore no comparison with their earlier performances.

Michel Platini overcame his nerves to score in the final

GOLF

Seve exploits Watson's slip

THE notorious Road Hole had been the graveyard for many potential Open champions and Tom Watson became another victim of the 461-yard 17th hole at St Andrews.

Watson was chasing Severiano Ballesteros and his sixth crown. Both proved elusive. Ballesteros was determined not to fall into the trap of taking short cuts and landing in the pot bunkers as he had done when finishing 17th six years before. So he kept to the left for the four days and stayed on course for a second Open title.

Ballesteros turned in 34 on the final day to lead by one shot from Watson, playing in the group behind. They swapped the lead until the penultimate hole, where Ballesteros struck his tee shot into the rough on the left. His recovery with a six iron was immaculate, clearing the bunker and landing on the green. Two putts gave him par.

Watson drove well but pulled his approach shot, which skipped across the road and ricocheted off the wall. His recovery came too late. Ballesteros sank a 15-foot birdie putt at the last and Watson's hopes of a third successive title were dead and buried. Ballesteros won by two shots from Watson and Bernhard Langer.

> ❛ Seve hits the ball further than I go on my holidays ❜
>
> **Lee Trevino**

BALLESTEROS'S MAJOR TITLES

1979	The Open
1980	The Masters
1983	The Masters
1984	The Open
1988	The Open

Decker blames Budd for tearful down fall

AS BEFITTED any event staged in Los Angeles, the United States turned on all the Hollywood-style glitz it could muster for an extravagant opening ceremony to the 23rd Olympic Games on July 28. But some of the gloss was taken off the event at the last moment when the Soviet Union, citing fears over their team's security but probably in revenge for the boycott of the Moscow Olympics, pulled out in May. All of the Eastern bloc countries, with the exception of Romania, followed their lead.

There was drama on the track to match. The controversy was still raging about Zola Budd's hasty qualification for Britain, and the partisan American crowd were keen to see their golden girl Mary Decker put the upstart Budd in her place, particularly because Budd had broken Decker's 5,000m world record earlier in the year. Decker and Budd faced each other in the 3,000m and the controversy got even greater when, in a bunched field, they clashed. Decker was sent sprawling and, in tears, was carried from the track by her husband Richard Slaney. Decker blamed Budd for her fall, but replays showed it was almost

certainly an accidental collision.

There was still more drama, and a sign of things to come in later years, when 12 competitors were disqualified for taking drugs, including the 10,000m silver medalist Martti Vainio of Finland.

There were many high spots as well, even though the absence of the eastern Europeans took some of the competitive edge off the Games. Carl Lewis equalled Jesse Owens's feat of winning four gold medals when he won the 100m, 200m, 4x100m relay, and long jump. And another American, Valerie Brisco-Hooks, won three athletics golds.

Britain had a relatively successful Games, winning five gold medals, 11 silvers and 21 bronzes. Their challenge was spearheaded by Daley Thompson, who broke the world record to win the decathlon, and Seb Coe, who won the 1500m gold and added an 800m silver.

The Games also marked the emergence of China as a world power. They won their first ever gold medal at Los Angeles and by the time the Games closed on August 12 had added 14 more to finish fourth in the medals table.

The fateful moment of collision between Budd and Decker

FOR THE RECORD

FOOTBALL

■ Crystal Palace's saga of ever-changing managers continued with Alan Mullery's dismissal on May 14. He was replaced by Dave Bassett three days later. Bassett then had second thoughts and returned to Wimbledon after four days in the job saying: "I made a mistake." On June 3, Steve Coppell, who had no experience of managing a club, was appointed. He was Palace's eighth manager in 44 months.

■ Liverpool became the third club to win the League championship in three successive seasons on May 12. It was their 15th League title.

■ Wolves appointed Tommy Docherty as their manager on June 8. It was the 17th time Docherty had been given a managerial job in football.

Gold-medallist Thompson

Carl Lewis equalled Jesse Owens four gold medals

ATHLETICS

Bubka: four world records

FOR THE RECORD

ATHLETICS

■ Sergei Bubka of the Soviet Union broke the world pole vault record four times in the year, lifting the mark from 5.85m to 5.94m. He was unable to compete at the Olympic Games because of the Soviet boycott.

■ Spanish footballers, unhappy with unpaid wages and broken contracts for players in the lower divisions, went on strike on September 9. The first week of the League programme was played by teams made up of amateurs and junior players. The second week was suspended and after 13 hours of talks a compromise was reached.

■ The European Commission demanded complete freedom of movement between clubs for all players of member countries.

ICE HOCKEY

■ Four new rinks — Gillingham, Lee Valley, Oxford and Telford — opened, the largest number ever in one year.

KARATE

■ Britain won the men's team title at the World championships.

TENNIS

■ Sweden won the Davis Cup for the first time in their history, beating the United States 4-1. The Swedes, who were beaten 3-2 by Australia the previous year, played in seven successive finals until 1989.

338

CRICKET

Blackwash engulfs England

FOUR West Indian fast bowlers — Joel Garner, Malcolm Marshall, Michael Holding and Eldine Baptiste — battered, bruised and beat England 5-0 in a series that became known as the Blackwash. The clean sweep was sandwiched between six consecutive victories against Australia, which gave Clive Lloyd's team the longest winning sequence in Test cricket. They were also the first visiting side to win a series 5-0 and were unbeaten in a record 27 Tests before defeat by Australia the following January.

Records were of little concern to Lloyd's team. They played with a professionalism and ferocity never before seen in cricket. They had the batsmen, bowlers and fielders to dominate any team in the world under almost any conditions. And during a sunny English summer conditions were perfect.

The pack of four fast bowlers hunted down English batsmen while the opening combination of Desmond Haynes and Gordon Greenidge softened up the bowling for the likes of Viv Richards, Larry Gomes, Jeff Dujon, and Lloyd to plunder.

Richards, arguably the best batsman since Don Bradman, set the tone early in the tour with the highest score in a one-day innings. He hit an unbeaten 189 off 170 balls, laced with 24 fours and five sixes, one of which flew out of Old Trafford.

Then came the Blackwash. England were torn to shreds in four

Holding strikes again to dismiss Broad at The Oval

days by Garner in the first Test at Edgbaston, where Andy Lloyd's Test career lasted only 33 minutes. He was hit on the helmet by a bouncer from Marshall and spent several days in hospital with blurred vision.

Greenidge hit an unbeaten double century at Lord's to take West Indies to an unexpected victory

and Marshall scored 59 while batting one-handed in a comfortable victory at Headingley. Paul Terry became the next victim at Old Trafford when he was forced to bat with a broken arm.

England were at such a low ebb that even Sri Lanka dominated their only meeting, a draw at Lord's later in the summer.

RICHARDS'S TEST RECORD

Matches	121
Innings	182
Not out	12
Runs	8,540
Highest	291
Average	50.23
Hundreds	24
Wickets	32 at 61.37
Catches	122

THE WEST INDIES' TESTS IN 1984

Date	Opponents	Venue	Result
Mar 2-7	Australia	Georgetown	Match drawn
Mar 16-21	Australia	Port of Spain	Match drawn
Mar 30-Apr 4	Australia	Bridgetown	Won by 10 wickets
Apr 7-11	Australia	St John's	Won by innings and 36 runs
Apr 28-May 2	Australia	Kingston	Won by 10 wickets
Jun 14-18	England	Edgbaston	Won by innings and 180 runs
Jun 28-Jul 3	England	Lord's	Won by nine wickets
Jul 12-16	England	Headingley	Won by eight wickets
Jul 26-31	England	Old Trafford	Won by innings and 64 runs
Aug 9-14	England	The Oval	Won by 172 runs
Nov 9-12	Australia	Perth	Won by innings and 112 runs
Nov 23-27	Australia	Brisbane	Won by eight wickets
Dec 7-11	Australia	Adelaide	Won by 191 runs
Dec 22-27	Australia	Melbourne	Match drawn

Essex snatch the championship with some help from Somerset

Essex celebrate after winning the title in the final match

ESSEX won the county championship when Nottinghamshire narrowly failed to beat Somerset in the final match of the season. Notts, inspired by Richard Hadlee and Clive Rice, needed 14 off the last over for the title. After scoring 10 off four balls they looked likely to triumph. But Mike Bore lofted the fifth ball to long off where the substitute fielder Richard Ollis held the catch to deny them victory.

Lauda's second best is just good enough

NIKI LAUDA won his third world championship, edging out Alain Prost, his McLaren teammate, by the narrowest of margins: half a point. It had come down to such fine tuning because when Prost had won the Monaco Grand Prix only half points had been awarded because rain had halted the race.

When the pair lined up at Estoril on October 21 Prost was second on the grid and Lauda was 3½ points ahead. Lauda was 11th on the grid, and knew that if he finished second he would regain his title, however Prost performed.

Prost swept into the lead in the ninth lap but then was helpless as he watched Lauda carve his way through the field. On the 33rd lap of 70 Lauda had reached third place, and then 18 laps later Nigel Mansell's pit stop gave Lauda second. The rest of the race was a procession. Prost won the race, but Lauda took the championship.

Lauda at rainy Monaco, where only half points were awarded

Gandhi's assassination haunts England's tour

ENGLAND'S winter tour of India was twice thrown into jeopardy. Indira Gandhi, the Indian Prime Minister, was assassinated soon after the team arrived, and the British deputy High Commissioner was murdered hours after entertaining the tourists.

England were more fortunate on the field, although they had no answer to Laxman Sivaramakrishnan in the opening Test in Bombay. The 18-year-old leg spinner took 12 for 181 to bowl his side to an eight-wicket victory. But David Gower's side recovered to become the first team to win a series in India after trailing 1-0.

The highlight of the tour was the strokeplay of Mohammad Azharuddin, who was the first batsman to score centuries in his first three Tests. He averaged 109.75 in five innings.

Sivaramakrishnan: 12-181 in Bombay for eight-wicket victory

Exposed: the deal that held sway over boxing

ON DECEMBER 9 an astonishing four-way partnership between the major British boxing figures Jarvis Astaire, Mickey Duff, Mike Barrett and Terry Lawless was revealed by the Sunday Times. In 1979 the four had agreed to divide equally the income from their various boxing activities. Lawless was the manager of the world champions Jim Watt, Maurice Hope and Charlie Magri as well as a thriving stable of lesser lights, all of whom worked virtually exclusively on shows which were staged by Duff and Barrett and screened by BBC television.

Amid a general furore over possible conflicting interests (a principle belatedly established in the High Court in 1991 by the ill-fated Michael Watson) the British Boxing Board of Control investigated the agreement and announced, in February 1985, that they had found nothing improper. But the quartet would never again enjoy the degree of unchallenged monopoly with which they had dominated big-time British boxing for so long.

FOOTBALL

Millwall fans run amok at Luton

Millwall fans invade the pitch and have a full-scale battle with 200 police

GOLF

Strange lets in Langer

BERNHARD LANGER knew what Curtis Strange was going through during the final nine holes of the Masters at Augusta — he had been there before. Strange, four strokes ahead with nine to play, saw his lead evaporate when Langer charged past to win by two shots.

Langer was familiar with adversity. Twice in his career he had battled to overcome the dreaded yips. Now, with an unorthodox left-handed putting stroke, he posted two rounds of 68 to win his country's first major golf trophy. Four birdies in the last seven holes enabled him to beat Strange, Severiano Ballesteros and Raymond Floyd.

Langer: two 68s

SPECTATOR violence was increasing at an alarming rate. But on March 13 a riot occurred at Luton that shocked the nation watching it on television.

Luton were playing Millwall in an FA Cup quarter-final when hundreds of Millwall fans ripped up plastic seats, hurled some of them on to the pitch and used the rest as shields, batons and weapons as they launched into a full-scale battle with 200 policemen. The referee had no option but to take the

players off the field for 25 minutes.

After the match the Millwall hordes rampaged through the town causing thousands of pounds of damage to shops, cars and houses. For good measure they wrecked their train home. Forty-seven people, including 31 policeman, were injured, and Luton subsequently announced that they would ban away fans.

The scenes were so disgraceful that the Prime Minister summoned football chiefs to Downing Street

on April 1 to discuss what they were going to do about hooliganism. Whereupon Ted Croker, the FA secretary, perpetrated the blunder of the decade when he told Margaret Thatcher: "These people are society's problem and we don't want your hooligans at our sport."

Relations between the government and football had never been good, now they were to be nonexistent, as it was plain that football was incapable of putting its own house in order.

SNOOKER

Francisco row brings drugs into the open

SILVINO FRANCISCO beat Kirk Stevens to win the British Open, and in accusing him of playing under the influence of drugs brought the issue of drugs and snooker into the open. A few weeks later Stevens confirmed that he was "helplessly addicted to cocaine".

The World Professional Billiards and Snooker Association, forced by this scandal to introduce drug testing, had to include all drugs on the Sports Council's banned list. Embarrassingly, these included beta blockers, which several players, including the then WPBSA chairman, Rex Williams, were taking.

Taylor shatters Davis

Taylor came back from a seemingly impossible position

DENNIS TAYLOR'S epic recovery to win the world title shattered Steve Davis's aura of invincibility in a way which was never quite repaired. Davis led 8-0 in the final but, at 17-17, missed the deciding

black of a 68-minute final frame. The highest BBC2 audience ever recorded, 18.5 million, also the highest British audience for a sporting event, watched Taylor, well after midnight, pot that black.

Bradford inferno kills 56

ON MAY 11, the last day of the season, Bradford City were celebrating their Third Division championship and promotion to the Second Division at home to Lincoln. Then just before half-time a fire started in the wooden main stand.

Within five minutes the entire 76-year-old stand was a raging inferno from end to end and the hurrahs turned to howls of terror. Those that survived clambered on to the pitch, which provided the only safe means of exit. Fifty-six people died and hundreds were burnt, many seriously.

The cause of the fire was identified as years of accumulated rubbish under the main stand, which was probably set alight by a cigarette or dropped match.

On the same day, 100 miles to the south, Leeds fans rioted at their match in Birmingham and a wall collapsed, a boy was killed and 96 police were injured. These two incidents pinpointed the malaise that gripped football: unsafe, antique stadiums and hooliganism. Bradford was the worst sporting disaster in England. Until the next one.

The day that celebration turned into tragedy when Bradford's wooden stand caught fire

Everton's treble chance vanishes

EVERTON were poised to have one of the most successful seasons ever enjoyed by an English club. They were League champions and on May 15 had swamped Rapid Vienna 3-1 in Rotterdam to win their first European trophy, the Cup Winners' Cup.

Three days later they attempted to complete the last leg of a unique treble in the FA Cup final against Manchester United. But the shadow of the Bradford disaster hung over their magnificent achievements and the final was a very muted affair.

And so was the football. Everton's treble probably disappeared when Kevin Moran of Manchester United was given his marching orders, the first man to be sent off in a Cup final. A 10-man United

Cup Final: muted affair

fought back with spirit and Norman Whiteside snatched the Cup with the only goal of a subdued game in extra time.

Francome hangs up his boots

JOHN FRANCOME retired on April 9 and bowed out with a crashing fall in his last race, at Chepstow, in the World jockeys' championship. Francome was the champion jockey for the seventh time when he hung up his saddle.

He decided to try his hand as an apprentice with the great Fred Winter after a promising career as a showjumper, when he turned down a chance to ride Harvey Smith's second string of horses. Francome rode his first winner in 1969 and, in all, had a record 1,138 victories, passing Stan Mellor's previous mark of 1,035 in May 1984.

FOR THE RECORD

ATHLETICS

■ Ingrid Kristiansen ran a women's world best time of 2hr 21min 6sec in the London Marathon on April 21.

BADMINTON

■ There was controversy in the women's final at the world championships in Calgary when Wu Jianqiu of China was faulted for time-wasting. She was unsettled by the decision and her compatriot Han Aiping came back from 6-11 11-11 to win 6-11 12-11 11-2.

BASKETBALL

■ Manute Bol of Sudan became the tallest player in NBA history when he turned out for the Washington Bullets. He was 7ft 6¾ tall.

CRICKET

■ Ravi Shastri became the second player after Garry Sobers to score 36 runs off an over in first-class cricket. He hit 200 runs off 123 balls in 113 minutes for Bombay against Baroda.

■ Australia scored 323 for two and bowled Sri Lanka out for 91 for the biggest victory in a one-day international in Adelaide on January 28.

FOOTBALL

■ Chelsea announced on April 19 that they intended to erect electrified fencing to deter hooligans. However, the GLC threatened to seek an injunction against the electrified fencing unless Chelsea promised not to turn it on and they reluctantly complied.

■ Arsenal suffered one of their periodic hiccups in the FA Cup when they were beaten 1-0 by Third Division York on January 26. It was the seventh time since the war that the Gunners had been knocked out of the competition by a club from a lower division.

■ Garth Crooks's goal in the 70th minute ended one of football's longest losing streaks when Tottenham Hotspur managed to beat Liverpool at Anfield for the first time since 1912.

ICE HOCKEY

■ Tony Hand, the 18-year-old Murrayfield Racers forward, became the first Briton to be drafted by an NHL club, the Edmonton Oilers.

MOTOR SPORT

■ Co-driver Terry Harryman of Britain helped the Finn Ari Vatanen win the Monte Carlo rally in a Peugeot 205. The pair had won the RAC rally the year before and the Safari rally in 1983.

RUGBY LEAGUE

■ Wigan beat Hull 28-24 in the highest scoring Challenge Cup final on May 4. Wigan also won the inaugural Charity Shield on the Isle of Man.

ATHLETICS

Cram keeps on getting better

THE frustration of Steve Cram, the World, European and Commonwealth 1500m champion, at being unable to add the Olympic title to his set in 1984, when he finished second to Sebastian Coe in Los Angeles, found an outlet in a spree of world record breaking.

It began on July 16 in Nice, where he defeated Said Aouita of Morocco over 1500m in 3:29.67, as the pair became the first two men to break 3½ minutes. Then in Oslo's Dream Mile on July 27 he gained some revenge on Coe by beating him and taking his world mile record with 3:46.32.

On August 4 in Budapest he just scraped under John Walker's 2,000m world record with 4:51.39, his third global mark in 19 days. But to many his UK all-comers 1,000m record of 2:12.88, set on August 9, the second best ever time for the distance and set on a cold, windy night at Gateshead, probably constituted his best run of the year. Several weeks later Cram's season was curtailed by injury.

Cram: three world records

FOOTBALL

Showpiece plumbs the depths

The Heysel terracing where 39 fans were crushed to death before the European Cup final

ENGLISH football hit its nadir at the Heysel stadium in Brussels on May 29. All the ills of the game came together at the summit of European football: the final of the Champions Cup, Liverpool v Juventus. And when the dust had settled 39 people were dead and more than 400 injured.

The catalogue of mistakes that led to this tragedy indicted everybody involved in the game. The stadium was a crumbling dinosaur; the fans were drunk, many of them ticketless, and there was no proper segregation; the policing was so inadequate that sticks, bottles and iron bars were easily smuggled into the stadium; there was no closed circuit television to monitor the situation; the emergency services were pitiful.

The facts of the incident were commonplace, it could have oc-curred at almost any average English ground. The outcome was appalling. Two sets of rival fans taunted each other, hurling insults and missiles, and Liverpool fans charged Juventus fans three times.

The third time the Juventus fans attempted to run to safety, but there was no way out. An old wall collapsed under the pressure and in the ensuing panic people tumbled over each other and crushed each other to death. Meanwhile, the police were using batons to clear the area while people lay dying.

The political response was swift. The FA withdrew English clubs from European competition and Margaret Thatcher demanded quick solutions. Now all the backsliding by football for 100 years was coming home to roost, but still they tried to muddle their way out of the solution. Thatcher banned the sale of alcohol at grounds and demanded an ID card scheme for entry to grounds. Football prevaricated.

Despite Heysel, despite Bradford, despite Thatcher, football saw no need for root and branch reform. Until the next disaster.

FOR THE RECORD

CYCLING
■ Bernard Hinault won the Tour de France a fifth time, equalling the record held by Jacques Anquetil and Eddy Merckx.

FOOTBALL
■ Kenny Dalglish was named player-manager of Liverpool on May 30.

RUGBY UNION
■ A High Court injunction by two New Zealand lawyers caused the All Black tour of South Africa to be cancelled only days before the team departed.

Wee Barry lands greatest prize

McGuigan outpointed Pedroza to take the WBA featherweight title at Loftus Road

ONLY Barry McGuigan could outdraw Ian Paisley in Belfast and the Pope in Dublin, as the Clones Cyclone did on his triumphant return to Ireland with the world featherweight title.

The appeal of the articulate and handsome fighter transcended sport, politics or religion. Despite the simplistic claims of the tabloids, McGuigan did not unite the warring factions in the North, but at least on those unforgettable nights when he went to work in the Kings Hall the violence was confined to the ring.

He was at his considerable peak and not even the magnificent Eusebio Pedroza, a survivor of 19 defences of the WBA title, could cope with the Irishman's exhilarating, surging aggression. The veteran Panamanian risked his championship in front of a 25,000 crowd at QPR's Loftus Road ground on June 6, and although he boxed with style and defiance, there was never much doubt that the title would change hands.

Three months later McGuigan retained it in Belfast against the brilliant American Bernard Taylor. But already there were signs of decline. He struggled to beat Danilo Cabrera in Dublin, before an ill-advised match in the desert heat of Las Vegas brought defeat by a competent but unexceptional Texan, Steve Cruz.

Becker scatters all of the seeds

Becker: youngest winner

THE thunder showers that swept London in the summer were not the only thing that took Wimbledon by storm. A more lasting impression was created by Boris Becker, a German with a game for grass.

The ginger-haired Becker, who was four years old when Jimmy Connors made his Wimbledon debut in 1972, became the youngest player, at 17 years and 227 days, to win the men's singles crown. He was also the only unseeded player to win.

Becker's game consisted of blasting his opponent off the court. If he couldn't do it with his booming service, he would hit shots that could have been fired from a cannon. It was all stirring stuff for a Centre Court crowd who had grown complacent on a diet of five years of Bjorn Borg on the baseline interspersed with John McEnroe and his touch game.

But the precocious Becker nearly failed to make it. He twisted his left ankle during a fourth-round match against Tim Mayotte and started to walk to the net with his arm outstretched as though he had retired. His coach, Günter Bosch, shouted at him to keep fighting and Becker went on to win.

His opponent in the final was Kevin Curren, who had beaten Connors 6-2 6-2 6-4 and McEnroe 6-2 6-2 6-1. But the tall South African froze on the big occasion, his serve went off the boil and Becker won 6-3 6-7 (4-7) 7-6 (7-3) 6-4.

Lyle's victory surprises him

MODERN British golf came of age at Sandwich on a windy day in July when Sandy Lyle won the Open. The Scot and his English rival Nick Faldo had been trying for several years to break the 16-year drought. Then Faldo went away to remodel his swing, lost form and left Lyle as the standard bearer.

Lyle did Britain proud at Royal St George's, becoming the first British winner since Tony Jacklin in 1969. But it was a tense wait. Lyle believed he had lost his chance with a bogey at the last, fluffing a chip and taking three to get down from the fringe of the green. He fled the scene to agonise over his failure. But those behind him fell by the wayside and the English-born Scot was summoned by a radio announcer to collect his first major trophy.

Lyle had started the day three shots behind Bernhard Langer and David Graham and only moved into contention with birdies at the 14th and 15th. He sank a 45-foot putt at the 14th after ploughing through the rough and took the lead at the next hole. His final round of 70 gave him a one-shot victory over Payne Stewart. It was a long-awaited breakthrough. British players won six more majors in the next six years.

Lyle: fled the scene

343

FOOTBALL

Chairmen dither as TV money dwindles

FOOTBALL is never quite sure what to make of television. Is it a good thing, a showcase for the game? Or a bad thing, keeping potential customers indoors? But mostly it is seen as a cash cow, there to be milked.

This was the attitude that predominated throughout the year. The Football League chairmen kicked off on January 17, when they threw out a four-year deal worth £16m. With attendances falling and many clubs in dire financial straits TV money was seen as a convenient solution. But television refused to play ball.

Despite warnings from the League that not accepting the offer could prove financially disastrous, the chairman stuck to their guns. In May, the BBC and ITV gave the chairmen a one-month deadline. Then came the twin disasters of Bradford and Heysel and televised football was suddenly a soiled commodity. But still football did not appreciate its predicament and the even greater need for income.

Protracted negotiations continued through to Christmas, including one meeting on December 5 that lasted just five minutes. By December 20 football caved in and signed a deal worth £1.3m and football returned to the small screen on January 5, 1986, having lost half a season.

CRICKET

Gower good as gold

Gower pulls another boundary during his halcyon summer

DAVID GOWER celebrated a golden summer by regaining the Ashes in his finest season. The polished left-hander whose flowing strokes made him one of the world's most attractive batsmen, led the charge against the Australians with 732 runs at an average of more than 80.

The series was tied 1-1 when the England captain inspired his team to a decisive victory in the fifth Test at Edgbaston with an innings of 215 — his highest score in Test cricket. He declared at a mammoth 595 for five, Richard Ellison took four wickets in 15 balls and Australia collapsed to defeat by an innings and 118 runs.

The visitors did little better in the final Test at The Oval. Gower and Graham Gooch posted 351 runs for the second wicket and Ellison and Ian Botham, his hair dyed blond, shared the bowling spoils, taking England to victory by an innings and 94 runs.

They won the series 3-1 after outplaying the Australians throughout a wet summer. The tourists relied too heavily on the batting of

❛It's difficult to be more laid back without being actually comatose❜

Frances Edmonds
on David Gower

GOWER'S TEST RECORD

Matches	114
Innings	199
Not out	16
Runs	8,081
Highest	215
Average	44.15
Hundreds	18
Wickets	1 at 20.00

their captain Allan Border and the fast bowling of the strapping Craig McDermott, who took 30 wickets in the series.

FOOTBALL

Stein goes out on winning note

JOCK STEIN, Scotland's manager, collapsed from a heart attack and died in the tunnel at Ninian Park seconds before the end of Scotland's vital World Cup qualifying match against Wales. Stein, who had created the legendary Celtic side that won the European Cup in 1967, was the most successful manager in Scottish history. His final act showed his acumen.

Scotland needed a point to go into a play-off for the World Cup finals. At half-time Wales were 1-0 up and the Scottish dressing room was despondent. But as the second half wore on Stein sensed that the Welsh were concentrating on preserving their slender lead.

He brought on Davie Cooper for Gordon Strachan and the match was transformed. Ten minutes from time Scotland were awarded a dubious penalty, which Cooper casually struck home. The maestro had pulled his final masterstroke.

MOTOR RACING

Prost comes in winning at last

Prost: Formula 1 champ

ALAIN PROST proved he was not just an also-ran when he finally captured the world championship, having narrowly missed it the two previous years. This time he was not going to allow anybody to pip him in the last race and snatch the title. Prost won five Grands Prix in his McLaren and cruised home comfortably, 20 points ahead of Michele Alboreto.

Jacklin's men shift balance of power in favour of Europe

AMERICA'S 28-year reign in the Ryder Cup was at stake when Sam Torrance and Andy North stepped on to the 18th tee at the Belfry on September 15. When North put his drive into the lake, a tearful Torrance followed his ball straight up the fairway to claim the crown for Europe.

It was an emotional day for Tony Jacklin's team, who won for the first time since 1957. In those days the team was called Great Britain and Ireland. Now it was Europe and bolstered by four Spaniards — Seve Ballesteros, José-Maria Canizares, Manuel Pinero and José Rivero — and the West German Bernhard Langer. The British contingent was Ken Brown, Howard Clark, Nick Faldo, Sandy Lyle, Sam Torrance, Paul Way and Ian Woosnam.

There were indications that America's domination was under threat at the previous clash at Palm Beach Gardens in Florida in 1983 when the United States were lucky to scrape through 12-11 with five matches halved.

At the Belfry it took victories by Ballesteros and Pinero in the four-somes and fourballs to keep Europe in touch on the first day as the Americans took a 4-3 lead. The tide turned on the second day when the home side finished 8-6 ahead with 12 singles matches to play.

However, the trophy was again heading towards the United States until Ballesteros provided the inspiration with a 50-foot birdie putt at the 14th and two more birdies in the closing holes to tie with Tom Kite. In a spectacular comeback, Europe won 15-10 with three matches halved.

Spaniards Pinero and Ballesteros helped Europe to victory

FOR THE RECORD

FOOTBALL
■ According to a business survey, 56 of the 92 Football League clubs were in the red at the end of the last financial year. And on December 20 Swansea was wound up because it owed £106,000 in taxes.

■ A life sentence was imposed on a football hooligan for the first time on November 8. Two Chelsea fans were convicted after an orgy of violence when Manchester United beat Chelsea 3-1 at Stamford Bridge the previous December. The second man received a jail sentence of eight years.

■ Charlton announced on September 6 that they had decided to share Crystal Palace's ground at Selhurst Park. At their last match at The Valley on September 21, in front of their largest crowd of the season, 8,858, supporters cut out pieces of the turf as souvenirs.

■ Thirteen fans were arrested and four policemen injured at Millwall's game with Leeds on November 9. The FA instructed Millwall to make their home games all-ticket with no provision for away supporters.

■ Twelve leading clubs agreed plans for a Super League and submitted them to the Football League on November 11. They wanted a First Division of 20 clubs and a Second of 24 with the Third and Fourth Divisions going part-time.

GOLF
■ Seve Ballesteros won the World matchplay title for the fourth time in five years at Wentworth.

■ Australia won the inaugural Dunhill Cup at St Andrews, beating the United States 3-0.

SQUASH
■ England's women won the first of their four successive world team titles.

TENNIS
■ Ivan Lendl won his first of three successive US Open titles. Lendl, who had lost the previous three finals, beat John McEnroe 7-6 6-3 6-4.

■ West Germany reached the Davis Cup final for the first time. Although Boris Becker won both his singles matches, Sweden retained the title.

Lendl on the way to three successive US Open wins

FOOTBALL

Top order sink to the bottom

THE third round of the FA Cup on January 4 was full of thrills and spills. Bristol Rovers of the Third Division provided the former with three goals in 24 minutes to dispose of First Division Leicester. And Peterborough of the Fourth Division provided the latter when they lost their goalkeeper with a broken leg and, despite playing with 10 men for the final 20 minutes, dispatched Second Division Leeds 1-0.

Altrincham, of the Gola League, kept up the giant-killing spree 10 days later when they eliminated Birmingham 2-1 at St Andrews. The winning goal came from Robert Hopkins who passed back to his goalkeeper, only to find the net. The defeat, coupled with 17 League matches without a win, was so distressing for Ron Saunders, Birmingham's manager, that he resigned two days afterwards.

FOR THE RECORD

FOOTBALL
■ **Oxford passed their entrance exam in the First Division with flying colours when they won the League Cup by trouncing QPR 3-0 at Wembley on April 20. It was Oxford's first major trophy and to complete their first season in the top flight they managed to avoid relegation by finishing 18th.**

ROWING
■ **Cambridge ended Oxford's 10-year winning streak in the Boat Race.**

GOLF

Parting shot by Golden Bear

THE Golden Bear's 46-year-old back was creaking, his sight was failing and his $5 million swing looked ready for the Seniors Tour. He had slumped to 44th in the money winners' list and had not won a tournament in two years or a major in six years.

But there was something about the Masters that brought out the best in Jack Nicklaus. The 50th gathering at Augusta was billed as a parade of the foreign big hitters: Seve Ballesteros, Bernhard Langer, Sandy Lyle and Greg Norman. Instead, it became the last hurrah for one of America's favourites.

Nicklaus was four shots behind Norman on a crowded leaderboard starting the final round. He did nothing to suggest a memorable late charge until the ninth, where he picked up a birdie to turn in 35. He birdied the 10th and the 11th too as the adrenalin in his old veins began to flow. And as his charge gathered steam the applause from the galleries grew thunderous. The Bear was having a picnic.

There was more. He collected a birdie at the 13th, an eagle at the 15th and another birdie at the 16th to storm home in 65. The last 10 holes were played in seven under. The field faded. Ballesteros went

into the water at the 15th, Tom Kite took too many putts and Norman went into the gallery at the last. Nicklaus had become the oldest Masters champion at 46 years, two months and 21 days. Norman's frustration continued. He led after the third round in all four major tournaments but won only one, the Open at Royal Birkdale, with a second round of 63.

Nicklaus: late charge

> ❝When Nicklaus plays well he wins; when he plays badly he comes second; when he plays terribly he's third❞
>
> **Johnny Miller**

> ❝I wouldn't care if I got beat by 20 shots. I'd still like to see how God does it❞
>
> **Ed Fiori**
> on being paired with Nicklaus

NICKLAUS'S MAJOR TITLES

1962 US Open **1963** The Masters, US PGA **1965** The Masters **1966** The Masters, The Open **1967** US Open **1970** The Open **1971** US PGA **1972** The Masters, US Open **1973** US PGA **1975** The Masters, US PGA **1978** The Open **1980** US Open, US PGA **1986** The Masters

---

FOOTBALL

Steep drop in attendance forces reluctant chairmen to face reality

FOOTBALL'S sponsors were so concerned about the game's future that 49 of them warned the Football League on January 28 that they must be seen to get their act together, and ensure that there was never another six-month television black-out.

Their warning was timely because, after Bradford and Heysel, fans voted with their feet. Less than 17m went through the turn-

stiles in 1985-86, compared with 40m in 1950. So clubs, in need of income, paid heed to the advice about television. Unlike the protracted negotiations the previous year, the Football League came to a speedy agreement on a two-year £6.2m deal on June 3.

There was also, eventually, a measure of agreement that saw threats of a Super League apparently recede on January 9. The

Second Division clubs accepted that the voting system shift in favour of the elite, but it required an ultimatum by First Division chairmen to force the issue.

The need for change in favour of the top clubs was not confined to England. Nine of the 10 Scottish Premier Division clubs announced on February 22 that they would form a breakaway League unless demands were met.

Fiery Souness starts revolution at Rangers

Souness broke the mould by importing Englishmen to Scotland

RANGERS pulled off the managerial coup of the decade when they persuaded Graeme Souness to quit Sampdoria and become their player-manager. It was an expensive decision for Rangers. Not only had Souness a year to go on his contract, he wanted to plunder the transfer market. On top of that, at a press conference on April 7 to announce his appointment, Souness vowed that he would end the 113-year-old religious sectarianism at Ibrox and sign a Catholic.

"How could I have possibly taken on this task if I could not have signed Catholics? I am married to one," he said. "The best players will be signed, no matter what they are. It is not a thorny question as far as I am concerned."

Souness duly went on a spending spree. When he paid £450,000 for Graham Roberts, the Tottenham player was the fifth Englishman in six months he had lured north of the border.

The Rangers manager also made news on the field. In his first game, he was sent off after a punch-up and nine other players were booked as Hibernian won 2-1.

Fridge provides food for thought

AMERICAN FOOTBALL had started to catch on in Britain, and William "The Refrigerator" Perry became its first household name. Perry, a defensive lineman with the Chicago Bears, was given his nickname by a teammate because of the prodigious amount of food he ate to maintain his weight at well over 300lbs. Soon, television audiences were cheering Perry on as he sacked opposing quarterbacks and flattened running backs. And on the night of January 26 they had more to cheer when Perry lumbered in for a touch-down as the Bears routed the New England Patriots 46-10 in Super Bowl XX.

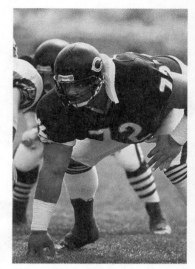

Perry: forever eating

Johnson emerges from nowhere to rock Davis

JOE JOHNSON won the world title as a 150-1 outsider, making two centuries in the last four frames to beat Terry Griffiths from three down with four to play in the quarter-finals, and maintaining much of this inspiration to beat Steve Davis 18-12 in the final.

"I knew I could win when I beat Terry. That's when I knew I was a good player," the unassuming Yorkshireman, then lead singer in a semi-pro rock group, said.

A hometown boy at heart, he was soon weighed down by the pressures of celebrity and a disastrous management entanglement. Although he reached the 1987 world final he sank down the rankings and his career continued in 1991 only through surviving a life-threatening heart attack.

Johnson, a 150-1 outsider, won the final 18-12

Maxwell rescues Games fiasco

THE 13th Commonwealth Games were certainly unlucky for Edinburgh. Influenced by the $250m profit made by the Los Angeles Olympics, the government ordered that the Games had to be self-financing.

But efforts to raise money made little progress, and matters were not helped by countries boycotting the event over Britain's attitude to sanctions against South Africa. On June 19, with the Games just over a month away, and millions of pounds still needed, Robert Maxwell came to the rescue and took over as chairman of the fund-raising operation.

Maxwell, in his usual larger than life fashion, poured his energies into making sure the Games went ahead. But after the competition ended the recriminations started. It was revealed that the organisers owed more than £4m and the financial disputes were not settled until the next year.

Dalglish manages to grasp elusive Double

Ian Rush scores Liverpool's third goal in the Cup Final

KENNY DALGLISH, in his first season as Liverpool's manager, achieved what had eluded his illustrious predecessors and numerous other managers throughout the century: the League and FA Cup Double. And he did it in the most difficult of circumstances, the season after Heysel.

The championship was a strange pass-the-parcel affair and Liverpool did not go to the top of the table until Easter Monday, when they beat Manchester City 2-0, and even then it was only on goal difference that they led.

In the run-in Liverpool needed to win their final seven games, five of which were away. Always at their best in adversity, they completed the task with aplomb. Dalglish himself delivered the coup de grace, catching a flighted ball on his chest at Stamford Bridge to score the goal that won the title.

A week later, on May 10, Liverpool faced their arch-rivals Everton in the FA Cup final. Everything was at stake in the first Merseyside FA Cup final. Everton had been denied the Double the previous year by Manchester United. Liverpool hadn't won the Cup since 1974. The whole of Liverpool invaded London for The Match.

Everton, with Gary Lineker, were formidable foes, and it was no surprise that the champions went in at half-time 1-0 down to a Lineker goal. Liverpool were still rattled after the re-start, but an Ian Rush equaliser settled them and the football began to flow.

Rush and Jan Molby combined to give Craig Johnston a close-range goal. Rush ended matters with six minutes remaining, and Liverpool became the third club this century to achieve the Double.

LeMond upstages Hinault's last assault on Tour victories record

BERNARD HINAULT lost his fight to become the first rider to win the Tour de France six times when he arrived in Paris 3min 10sec slower on overall time than his teammate, the American Greg LeMond.

Hinault, a brilliant rider against the clock in the Tour's time trial stages and a great climber, had looked set to depose the five times winner, the great Eddy Merckx.

All went well until the ninth stage, a 61.5km time trial, which Hinault won. But LeMond was second, 44sec behind his captain after being delayed by a puncture which lost him time and also his pedalling rhythm when he changed bikes.

Three days later in the Pyrenees, Hinault finished one second down on Pedro Delgado to take the yellow jersey. But LeMond, third on the mountainous stage, also improved to third overall, five minutes adrift.

The next day, seemingly unaffected by his earlier efforts, LeMond rode as though he had wings on another mountain stage from Pau to Luchon, leaving all his rivals 16km from the summit of Superbagneres, including Hinault, who rolled across the line four minutes behind, still the overall leader but by only 40sec.

LeMond's strength held; four days later he became the first American to wear the yellow jersey and he kept it to the finish, where Hinault had ridden his last Tour de France.

LeMond: strength held

FOR THE RECORD

■ Hearts surrendered the League title to Celtic in the cruellest way. Unbeaten in 27 League games, they lost the last game of the season 2-0 away to Dundee while Celtic hammered St Mirren 5-0 to steal the championship on goal difference. If Celtic had only won 1-0, then Hearts would have been champions.

■ The FA decided on May 14 to allow two substitutes in Cup ties for the coming season.

■ Raymond Floyd became the oldest winner of the US Open at 43 years and 284 days.

■ Warrington scored the biggest victory in a Premiership Trophy final when they beat Halifax 38-10 on May 18.

■ Boris Becker retained his Wimbledon title, beating Ivan Lendl 6-4 6-3 7-5 in the final.

Hand of God lifts Cup for Argentina

DIEGO MARADONA and Argentina deservedly won the World Cup in Mexico on June 29. They were the best team with the world's best player. But the abiding memory of the tournament will surely be Maradona cheating against England in the quarter-finals.

Peter Shilton, England's goalkeeper, and Maradona together went up for a lofted ball. Maradona palmed it over Shilton's head and the goal was allowed by a Tunisian referee who should have known better. "The hand of God," Maradona called it after the match.

Within minutes of his devilish behaviour, Maradona had bewitched almost the entire England team to score a solo goal of scintillating brilliance. Thus the modern demigod.

England were somewhat fortunate even to have got to the second phase. Bobby Robson had picked his ideal team for the first two games. And what happened? A 1-0 defeat at the hands of a squabbling Portuguese team and a dispiriting goalless draw against a craven Moroccan side.

But every cloud has a silver lining: Bryan Robson was unavailable because he was injured (again) and Ray Wilkins was suspended because, in a fit of pique, he had thrown the ball at a Paraguyan referee and had been sent off. The team had to be re-shaped and virtually picked itself. England duly murdered Poland 3-0 with a Gary Lineker hat-trick.

Luck did not favour Scotland and Northern Ireland. Scotland were in a particularly tough group but failed to go through when faced with the cynicism of Uruguay. Despite Uruguay being reduced to 10 men for more than 89 minutes Scotland could not score the vital goal they needed. So they left Mexico with one goal from Gordon Strachan and one point. Northern Ireland, despite having the incomparable Pat Jennings, were no match for Brazil and Spain.

The final, between West Germany and Argentina, was a pulsating affair. Argentina took a two-goal lead, surrendered it, then with six minutes remaining Jorge Burruchaga won Argentina's second World Cup.

Maradona celebrates his second goal against England

Bad Botham bounces back after drugs ban

Botham returned with a quickfire 59 against New Zealand

ENGLISH cricket fell apart at the seams and the man at the centre of the decline was Ian Botham, whose antics on and off the field moved him from the sporting pages at the back to the front pages of the country's newspapers.

Botham had appeared before the Test and County Cricket Board to explain his behaviour in the series against Australia and was under pressure to stay on the straight and narrow during England's visit to the Caribbean.

While the relationship between the players and the press on the tour deteriorated, so too did Botham's form. He averaged only 16.80 with the bat and took 11 expensive wickets as the West Indians under Viv Richards repeated their 5-0 Blackwash of 1984. There was also little joy for the tourists in the one-day internationals and in the second match Mike Gatting's nose was fractured by a bouncer.

There was more to come. On his return, Botham admitted in an article in the Mail on Sunday, written under his name, that he had previously smoked marijuana. The TCCB was aghast. They kicked him out of the squad to play India and suspended him from first-class cricket for two months.

Botham's return could not have been better scripted. He took a wicket with his first ball against New Zealand to equal Dennis Lillee's world record of 355 Test wickets, and 10 balls later dismissed Jeff Crowe to break the record. He then hit 24 runs off one over in an unbeaten 59.

AUGUST

1986

DECEMBER

Cruel fortune robs Mansell

NIGEL MANSELL was desperately unlucky not to have ended the year as the world champion. In the Spanish Grand Prix on April 13 he had a furious battle with Alain Prost for second place over the last three laps. Mansell won that battle but the duelling meant that he could not quite catch the race leader, Ayrton Senna, although he was quicker than him, too. Mansell finished second to Senna by 0.014sec.

Come the last race in Adelaide on October 26, Mansell was the championship leader with 70 points, Prost and Nelson Piquet were both on 63. If Mansell finished third he was the champion. If neither Prost nor Piquet won, then it did not matter whether Mansell finished or not, he would still be the champion.

Mansell started on pole, but with nine laps remaining a rear tyre on his Williams-Honda disintegrated and he did extremely well to steer himself out of a serious collision. But he was out of the race and could only spectate as Piquet and Prost battled it out over the last few laps.

To the winner would go everything: the Grand Prix and the world championship. Prost triumphed and took his second world title. But by only two points. If Prost had not sparred for second place back in Spain and Mansell had caught Senna, then Britain would have had its first world champion since James Hunt in 1976.

Mansell: narrow loser

Curry destroyed by Honeyghan

NO BRITISH challenger for a world title ever faced a more intimidating task than that tackled by Bermondsey's Lloyd Honeyghan when he travelled to Atlantic City to meet the undefeated and seemingly unbeatable Texan Don Curry for the undisputed welterweight championship on September 7.

Honeyghan owed his No 1 rating to clever managerial manoeuvring by Mickey Duff, but the American had cleaned up the division and was, by common consensus, the world's best pound for pound performer.

Yet Honeyghan's self belief was so absolute that he backed himself to win $25,000 at odds of 5-1, and he treated Curry like a third class sparring partner, pummelling the American around the ring until, demoralised and battered, the champion quit on his stool at the end of the sixth round.

Honeyghan: title upset

England twice fail simple test

DAVID GOWER'S golden summer of 1985 was a distant memory. Instead, Kapil Dev came to haunt him at Lord's. The Indian all-rounder, who had spearheaded the bowling attack for eight years, taught his team never to give up the ghost.

The Indians, following their captain's advice against an England team who had reached their nadir, recorded their second victory in 33 Tests in England. It ended Gower's two-year reign as captain.

Mike Gatting took charge, but failed to reverse the trend. India won the second Test early on the fourth day by 279 runs to seal the three-match series, their second series win on English soil.

There was further embarrassment for England. Their next opponents were New Zealand, regarded as the fall-guys of world cricket — until they played England. Richard Hadlee took 10 for 140 in the second Test at Trent Bridge and poor England were stunned, losing by eight wickets. It was New Zealand's first victorious series in England.

Botham walks out as Somerset sack stars

Richards, Garner and Botham in discussion at Hove

SOMERSET was divided by a row about whether to retain two of the best cricketers in the world: Viv Richards and Joel Garner. The West Indians were signed in the mid-1970s in the vain hope of winning the championship for the first time. But when the crown went to Essex for the third time in four summers, Richards and Garner were summarily dismissed in an episode that stirred controversy.

Ian Botham, who had been dismissed as captain in favour of Peter Roebuck at the start of the season, was bitter about the dismissal of his two friends and signed for Worcestershire during the winter.

Norman demonstrates Jahangir is beatable

Norman: lucky numbers came up despite row with referee

SINCE Jahangir Khan lost to Geoff Hunt in the final of the British Open in 1981, he had never been beaten. But, on November 11, his reign was finally brought to an end by Ross Norman of New Zealand in the final of the World Open. And, in just under two hours, Norman toppled the man regarded as being without equal in the history of squash despite what he regarded as a series of bad calls by the referee in the first game.

Norman was 5-3 down when he demanded that the referee be replaced. His protest was rejected and, still seething, he fought back to take the first two games 9-5 9-7. Khan stopped a clean sweep by taking the third game 9-7, but he was merely delaying the inevitable as Norman ran away with the fourth game 9-1. Norman could hardly believe the result. He said: "It's like rolling the dice — lucky numbers."

OLYMPIC GAMES

Favourites Barcelona humble Birmingham

THE DECISION on the venue for the 1992 Olympic Games was made at the 91st session of the IOC in Lausanne on October 17, and Britain's bid, Birmingham, with a contingent led by Denis Howell, was quiet, satisfied and contemplative, and "leading on to the floodtide of victory".

Alas, that confidence soon faded. In the first round of voting for the six candidate cities, with an overall majority of 47 required to win, only one city, Amsterdam, got fewer than Birmingham's eight votes and was eliminated. In the second round, Birmingham, again with eight, was itself eliminated, and in the third round, to nobody's great surprise, Barcelona, the home city of the IOC President Juan Antonio Samaranch, carried the day over the remaining candidates, Brisbane, Paris and Belgrade.

Tyson knocks out Berbick to become the youngest champion

FOR THE RECORD

BOXING
■ Mike Tyson, aged 20, became the youngest heavyweight champion of the world when he beat Trevor Berbick of Canada for the WBC title.

CRICKET
■ Yorkshire announced on September 23 that they would not retain the services of Geoff Boycott.

■ Sri Lanka were dismissed for 55 — the lowest total in a one-day international — by West Indies in Sharjah on December 3.

FOOTBALL
■ Middlesbrough, still trying to wriggle free of their debts, were unable to play their first home game of the season at Ayresome Park on August 23 because the Official Receiver had locked up the ground. They were forced to play their Third Division match against Port Vale at Hartlepool.

■ Luton dropped out of the League Cup rather than compromise their ban on visiting fans.

■ Aston Villa scraped through their third round League Cup tie with Derby on October 29 in suspicious circumstances.

Somebody in the crowd blew a whistle and the Derby players came to a standstill as Tony Daley scored the equaliser.

■ Dave Bassett's Wimbledon, who were in the Southern League nine seasons previously, found themselves on top of the First Division on September 2.

■ Queen of the South announced on October 9 that they had leased their car park for 125 years to a property company that intended to build a supermarket on the site. The annual rent was greater than the club's annual gate receipts.

KARATE
■ Britain won the men's team title at the World championships.

RUGBY LEAGUE
■ Joe Lydon became the first player to be transferred for £100,000 when Wigan signed him from Widnes.

TENNIS
■ The Australian Open was not staged because the Grand Slam event was moved from December to January to avoid a clash with the Grand Prix Masters.

CRICKET

Boycott leaves Headingley after being sacked by Yorkshire

1987

SAILING

America's Cup back to Conner

THE Royal Perth Yacht club staged the defence of the America's Cup that Alan Bond and John Bertrand had won four years before, but they were unable to keep the trophy in the waters off Fremantle.

Bond's syndicate did not even make it to the final, where Kevin Parry's Kookaburra III represented the Australian hopes. But this time it was the Americans who had done the best preparation and design work, and Dennis Conner, who had lost the Cup, had no difficulty winning it back with a 4-0 triumph in Stars and Stripes.

Conner's vengeance

FOOTBALL

Coventry stun Spurs

Coventry inflicted a first FA Cup final defeat on Tottenham

COVENTRY astounded Tottenham and football historians when they won the FA Cup 3-2 for the first time on May 16. Tottenham, who had won the Cup seven times, had never lost a Cup final and had begun to regard Wembley as their home from home.

That myth collapsed in the cruellest way in the sixth minute of extra time when the Tottenham captain Gary Mabbutt deflected a cross from Lloyd McGrath into his own net. Coincidentally, Tottenham had taken a 2-1 lead with another own goal from Coventry's

Brian Kilcline. Their first goal had come from Clive Allen, his 49th of a remarkable season.

Tottenham had been forewarned about Coventry. They had reached the final by beating Leeds 3-2, also in extra time, with a scrambled goal from Dave Bennett.

Terry Venables, who had walked out on Barcelona a month earlier, was then appointed the Tottenham manager on October 27. David Pleat, the previous manager, resigned after allegations about his private life were published in The Sun.

Rangers' triumph is Hay's loss

RANGERS won their first League title for nine years on May 2 when they drew 1-1 at Aberdeen while their rivals, Celtic, amazingly lost 2-1 at home to Falkirk.

It was Celtic's first home defeat of the season, and it did not go down well with their supporters. The police had to call for reinforcements to disperse demon-

strators who were demanding that David Hay, the Celtic manager, should be sacked.

Within four weeks the board bowed to the supporters' wishes and Billy McNeill replaced the hapless Hay. McNeill, who had just been sacked by relegated Aston Villa, had quit Celtic four years earlier.

CRICKET

Inferior England still too good

THEY were the team who could not bat, could not bowl and could not field. But after a long winter tour of Australia, the English team returned home with the Ashes, the Perth Challenge Trophy, the World Series Cup and the Sharjah Cup.

Mike Gatting's side won nine of their 14 one-day internationals in a crowded programme and retained the Ashes with a 2-1 triumph

against a weak Australian team. Their biggest triumph was in the fourth Test in Adelaide. They won by an innings and 14 runs and the opener Chris Broad became the third Englishman to score centuries in three successive Tests in Australia.

Of his place in history, he said: "Hobbs, Hammond and Broad. It doesn't quite ring true, does it?"

CRICKET

Gavaskar hits Test milestone

SUNIL GAVASKAR became the first batsman to score 10,000 runs in Test cricket when he late-cut a ball from the off-spinner Ijaz Faqih through the slips for two. The remarkable milestone was reached shortly after tea on March 7, exactly 16 years after the Indian opener scored his first Test run against West Indies.

The crowd invaded the field for 20 minutes to celebrate the occasion with their 37-year-old hero. The great moment came on the third day of the drawn fourth Test against Pakistan in Ahmedabad.

Gavaskar: first to 10,000 runs

GAVASKAR'S TEST RECORD

Matches	125
Innings	214
Not out	16
Runs	10,122
Highest	236 not out
Average	51.12
Hundreds	34
Wickets	1 at 206.00
Catches	108

RUGBY UNION

All-Blacks prove all-conquering

NEW ZEALAND confirmed their status as the most powerful rugby nation by winning the first World Cup. The All Blacks beat France 29-9 in an unimaginative final of a competition that had taken years to get off the ground.

The International Rugby Board, convinced a World Cup would be the first step towards professionalism, had passed a resolution in 1958 that forbade member nations from organising a World Cup. But when the inaugural competition finally kicked off, it produced some entertaining, and one-sided, matches. New Zealand opened the event with a 70-6 victory against Italy and then beat Fiji 74-13 and Argentina 46-15. England thrashed Japan 60-7 and France and Scotland had big wins in their group games. The French crushed Romania 55-12 and Zimbabwe 70-12, and Scotland hammered Romania 55-28 and Zimbabwe 60-21.

The latter stages provided closer contests, none more so than France's 30-24 win against Australia in the semi-final in Sydney.

France's victory was sealed by their exciting fullback Serge Blanco, who darted over in the left corner for a try in the final minute.

But the French were no match for New Zealand in the final on June 20 at Eden Park in Auckland. Once the All Black fly-half Grant Fox put on his kicking boots, David Kirk's team cruised to victory. Fox scored 17 of their 29 points.

New Zealand: world's best

THE FIRST WORLD CUP

Quarter-finals
June 6 Christchurch: New Zealand 30 Scotland 3
June 7 Sydney: Australia 33 Ireland 15
June 7 Sydney: France 31 Fiji 16
June 8 Brisbane: Wales 16 England 3

Semi-finals
June 13 Sydney: France 30 Australia 24
June 14 Brisbane: New Zealand 49 Wales 6

Final
June 20 Auckland: New Zealand 29 France 9

FOR THE RECORD

ATHLETICS
■ Ed Moses was beaten for the first time in 122 races by Danny Harris in Madrid on June 4.

FOOTBALL
■ Play-offs were used for the first time in May to decide some of the Football League promotion and relegation places.
■ The proposed merger of Fulham and Chelsea was called off after an emergency meeting of the Football League blocked the move on March 1.
■ The Walsall defender Andy Dornam finally broke the deadlock in their marathon FA Cup tie with Watford by scoring an own goal on March 2. In the first replay of their fifth round match, Walsall equalised in extra time to produce the first ever 4-4 draw in the competition proper.
■ Dundee United became the first Scottish club to reach the Uefa Cup final, but a 1-1 draw at home on May 20 handed the trophy to Gothenburg.
■ Wigan reached the FA Cup quarter-finals for the first time in their history with a 3-0 victory over Hull.

RUGBY LEAGUE
■ Wigan beat Manly 8-2 in the first World Club Challenge.

RUGBY UNION
■ Bath won the Cup for a record fourth successive season, beating Wasps 19-12 in the final.

ROWING

Oxford successfully resist American mutiny

Donald MacDonald (standing) put down the challenge to his authority and won with the team that he had chosen

THE quiet waters of the Isis and the Thames were stirred by a mutiny as Oxford tried to prepare for the Boat Race. The dispute started in late January when the president of the Boat Club, Donald MacDonald, dropped the American Chris Clark from the squad in a dispute over the seating order in the boat and the team selection.

Seven other rowers, including four Americans, then refused to train until Clark was reinstated. MacDonald, with the backing of Oxford's chief coach Daniel Topolski, survived a series of challenges to his authority. Finally, many rebels backed down.

With all the bickering, Cambridge were made favourites for the race but in the end, on March 28, Oxford won by four lengths even though five of the rebels were not in the boat.

FOR THE RECORD

FOOTBALL
■ **Merthyr Tydfil** enjoyed one of their greatest results when they beat the Italian side Atalanta 2-1 in the European Cup Winners' Cup on September 16. They lost the away leg 2-0 and went out 3-2 on aggregate.

■ **Ken Bates**, the controversial Chelsea chairman, made an unusual contribution to the interminable wrangling over television on September 24. He suggested that football should start its own TV channel to break the ITV-BBC duopoly.

■ The irrepressible **Tommy Docherty** took up his 15th managerial post on September 28 at Altrincham in the GM-Vauxhall Conference.

GOLF
■ **England** beat Scotland 2-1 in the final of the Dunhill Cup.

■ **Laura Davies** became the first British winner in the US women's Open with a total of 285.

TENNIS
■ **Ivan Lendl** won his third consecutive US Open title and a record fifth Grand Prix Masters title.

GOLF

Davies: conquered America

MOTOR RACING

Crowd fuels Mansell's charge

Mansell overhauled his teammate Piquet to win a third British Grand Prix

NIGEL MANSELL won the British Grand Prix at Silverstone on July 12 in thrilling fashion. He overtook his teammate Nelson Piquet with just two laps remaining and finished a mere 1.9sec ahead of him. Then Mansell's Williams-Honda ran out of fuel on his victory lap, indicating how close he had been to defeat.

Piquet had led from the start, but an unscheduled pit stop by Mansell halfway through the race laid the foundation for his victory. When Mansell returned to the track with fresh tyres he was 27sec behind his teammate, and he furiously attacked the deficit.

Mansell broke lap record after lap record as he hauled the Brazilian back by a second a lap. Then, on Stowe corner, Piquet offered Mansell the narrowest of gaps and the Englishman was through and on the way to his third British GP victory.

"I was driving on crowd power," Mansell said. "They put five seconds on me. I could see them waving me on at every corner for the last 20 laps." The result left Mansell and Piquet joint second in the championship, one point behind Ayrton Senna.

However, Piquet won three of the next four Grands Prix, and after Mansell crashed in practice at the Japanese GP in October Piquet cruised to the world title.

BOXING

Tyson shows he has no equal

IRON Mike Tyson, the one time New York street delinquent moulded into the perfect fighting machine by the eccentric and enigmatic Cus D'Amato, unified the heavyweight championship for the first time since 1978. He became the youngest heavyweight king in history when he won the WBC title by trouncing Trevor Berbick in two rounds in Las Vegas in November 1986, and added the WBA belt with a laborious points win over James "Bonecrusher" Smith on March 7. In Las Vegas on August 1, he completed the set by out-pointing the tough and durable IBF champion Tony Tucker. After years of fat men and non-entities, the world at last had a heavyweight champion who looked the part.

Tyson: youngest champion

CYCLING

Miraculous recovery by Roche

THE Irish prime minister, Charles Haughey, was on the Champs Elysees to congratulate Stephen Roche on becoming the first Irishman to win the Tour de France and only the fifth rider also to win the Giro d'Italia in the same year.

Only four days before, in the Alps, Roche had collapsed at the finish of the climb to the summit of the 1970m La Plagne and was wrapped in a foil blanket and given oxygen for 15 minutes. He made an amazing recovery to take the overall lead from Pedro Delgado on the penultimate stage and coast to victory by 40 seconds.

Frustrated Lendl lost in the grass yet again

IVAN LENDL started to believe that grass was for cows and golf. He appeared allergic to the surface when he lost a second successive Wimbledon final, 7-6 6-2 7-5 to Pat Cash. It was a frustrating loss for the world's leading player, who had won the Wimbledon junior title in 1978 and said he would swop a Wimbledon victory for all his other Grand Slam titles.

Cash was so excited after his win that he scrambled over spectators and climbed into the players' box to embrace his entourage. Lendl went back to playing golf and dreaming about the next Wimbledon championship.

Lendl: quick defeat

IVAN LENDL'S MAJOR TITLES

1984 French Open **1985** US Open **1986** French Open, US Open **1987** French Open, US Open
1989 Australian Open **1990** Australian Open

. . . and the missing jewel in the crown

Lendl at Wimbledon

Year	Round	Opponent	Year	Round	Opponent
1983	Semi-final	John McEnroe	1988	Semi-final	Boris Becker
1984	Semi-final	Jimmy Connors	1989	Semi-final	Boris Becker
1985	Fourth round	Henri Leconte	1990	Semi-final	Stefan Edberg
1986	Runner-up	Boris Becker	1991	Third round	David Wheaton
1987	Runner-up	Pat Cash			

Six in a row for Martina

THE signs pointed to Martina Navratilova being a spent force. She was on her third coach in a year, had not won a tournament in seven months and had lost the Australian Open final to Hana Mandlikova and the French title to Steffi Graf.

But Wimbledon brought out the best in her and she reversed the trend with a record sixth successive title, beating Graf 7-5 6-3 in the final. Graf was seeking her 46th consecutive victory but lacked the experience of her opponent, whose serve and volley game went a long way to making her the highest earning player of all time.

Navratilova was only the second left-hander after Ann Jones to take the Wimbledon women's singles title. She made up for the lost years, winning the crown nine times. Her domination was phenomenal. She had a 74-match unbeaten streak in 1984 and won 109 consecutive doubles matches with Pam Shriver.

Seve marches to Ryder Cup

SEVE BALLESTEROS and Tony Jacklin, the two golfers who did most to put the European Tour on the map, lifted the continent to its zenith at Muirfield Village in Columbus, Ohio. The pair helped Europe win the Ryder Cup on American soil for the first time in its 61-year history.

Ballesteros was the anchor in the visiting team's 13-11 victory with four matches halved. He won four of his five matches and Jacklin, the non-playing captain, moulded a strong team around his leading player.

The Europeans took a 10-5 lead into the last day and withstood a determined comeback by their hosts. Apart from Ballesteros, the European line-up included Gordon Brand Jnr, Ken Brown, Howard Clark, Eamonn Darcy, Nick Faldo, Bernhard Langer, Sandy Lyle, José-Maria Olazábal, José Rivero, Sam Torrance and Ian Woosnam.

Fame swings Faldo's way

NICK FALDO decided in 1983 that his swing was not consistent enough to challenge the best players in the world despite finishing top of the Order of Merit on the European Tour with £140,761.

So he went away and worked on a new swing for three years, changing it from an upright motion to a flatter one. After some fine-tuning by the Florida-based coach Dave Leadbetter, Faldo began his climb to the top of the world rankings.

In the summer of 1987 he enjoyed the first major return on his decision to risk his game when he won the Open at Muirfield.

The triumph at Muirfield was a victory for consistency. Faldo made par at all 18 holes in his final round to take his first of four major titles in three years. He won the Masters in 1989, retained the title the next year, won the Open at St Andrews and was regarded as the best player in the world at the end of the decade.

Johnson 'fastest' in world

THE defeat of the 100m world and Olympic champion Carl Lewis by the muscular Canadian Ben Johnson was the competitive highlight of the second World championships in Rome.

Such was the standard of the race that Lewis equalled the existing world record of 9.93, yet still finished a full metre behind the Jamaican-born Johnson, who took the world record with 9.83sec.

Johnson's powerful physique and superb pick-up helped him to the victory and record. He had opened that crucial metre lead on Lewis during the first 10m, and although subsequent technical analysis of the race showed that both men reached a peak speed of 42.35kh (26.32mph) during the race, the gap remained constant.

It had been a remarkable year for Johnson, who won 21 of his 100m races between January and September, and set three indoor world records at 60m, including victory in the World Indoor championships in March. He had become transformed in a relatively short time to the greatest sprinter in history. Before much longer, we were to find out how.

Johnson: smashed Lewis

FOOTBALL

Maxwell fails in Watford bid

ROBERT MAXWELL resigned as chairman of Oxford United on May 31 and immediately installed himself as the chairman of Derby County, displacing his son Ian. Another son, Kevin, was appointed Oxford's chairman.

Then, on November 20, Elton John announced his intention of selling his controlling interest in Watford to Robert Maxwell for £2m. However, within a week, the Football League refused to sanction the deal because of Maxwell's interests in three other League clubs: Derby, Oxford and Reading.

The tale took another strange turn on December 5 when, at a secret meeting, the League president, Philip Carter, and Maxwell came to an agreement that enabled Maxwell to take over Watford providing he sold his shares in Oxford. However, by the 20th Maxwell was persuaded to pull out of the Watford deal, and he sold his shares in Reading.

Maxwell: too many clubs

CRICKET

Gatting in cheating showdown

IT TOOK intervention from the Foreign Office and Lord's to save England's tour of Pakistan midway through the second Test in Faisalabad.

The visit came under threat when the Pakistani umpire Shakoor Rana refused to officiate on the third day unless the England captain Mike Gatting provided a written apology after their finger-wagging confrontation. Gatting had moved the field after Eddie Hemmings had started his run-up. Rana accused the England captain of cheating and the incident quickly developed into a shouting match which culminated with Bill Athey leading Gatting away.

Then Rana made his stand after the close on the second day and it took 65 hours and 35 minutes of accusations and negotiations before play resumed. A day was lost, the match was drawn and Pakistan scored a hollow 1-0 victory in a bitter series.

Gatting, under pressure from the Test and County Cricket Board, issued an apology, but the TCCB decreed later that the England players should each receive a £1,000 bonus because of the problems they had encountered.

The root of the row went back to a match in Karachi in 1978. Gatting was playing in his first Test. A delivery hit him on the pad well outside the leg stump and he was given out lbw. The umpire was Shakoor Rana.

Gatting and Shakoor Rana exchange angry words

> *Pakistan have been cheating us for 37 years and it is just getting worse and worse*
>
> **Tom Graveney**

BOXING

Honeyghan beaten by rule book

LLOYD HONEYGHAN rampaged through the welterweight division after his incredible sixth round victory over Don Curry. The brash south Londoner caused a sensation by relinquishing his WBA belt in an anti-apartheid protest, but then rebuffed a triple American challenge.

Steamroller wins over the former light welterweight champions Johnny Bumphus and Gene Hatcher sandwiched a gruelling points triumph over Maurice Blocker, who later became a two-time world champion.

Then, on October 29 at Wembley, Honeyghan lost his WBC title on a technical decision. Jorge Vaca of Mexico was too badly cut to continue after an accidental clash of heads, but was judged to be ahead on points at the eighth round finish.

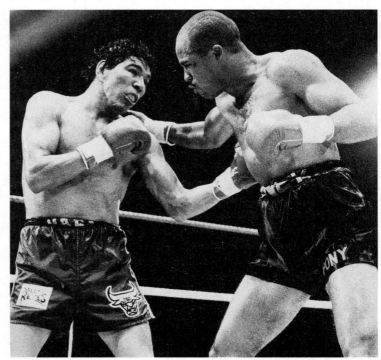

Vaca won because he was ahead when the fight stopped

Piggott jailed for tax fraud

Piggott was sentenced to three years after failing to declare earnings of £3m

LESTER PIGGOTT had always had a reputation for being mean with money. Unfortunately, one of the people he was not too keen on paying was the taxman. And on October 23, at Ipswich Crown Court, Piggott was sentenced to three years in jail after he admitted 10 charges of tax evasion.

The case arose from an Inland Revenue investigation of secret deals between Piggott, the trainer Henry Cecil and several leading owners. It was claimed that Piggott made £1.36m over 12 years from bets placed on his behalf by owners, even though jockeys are not allowed to bet on races. Further deals to top up his retainers, provide more money for riding winners and give him shares in horses that went to stud took the total amount of undeclared earnings to in excess of £3m, the court was told. It was estimated that, in all, Piggott had failed to pay £1.7m in tax.

Mr Anthony Hidden, QC, prosecuting, said: "It was a massive evasion of corporation tax and

income tax over a period of more than 10 years." Piggott had been investigated twice by the Inland Revenue, in 1970 and 1981. Even as late as 1983, when he had paid £168,000 in tax, Piggott had claimed that he only had three bank accounts. In fact, as he eventually admitted to another investigation, he had 17, some in false names, including ones in Jersey and the Isle of Man.

> **ʕ If I was to pass over this behaviour it would be an incentive to others to cheat the tax authorities ʔ**
>
> **Mr Justice Farquharson**

Piggott served most of his time in Highpoint open prison, and although his sentence was extended by seven days when he was caught using a smuggled phone card to call home, he was

released on parole after a year. To add to his disgrace, he was also stripped of his OBE while he was in prison.

FOR THE RECORD

CRICKET
■ The West Indies scored 360 for four — the highest total in a one-day international — against Sri Lanka in Karachi on October 13.

FOOTBALL
■ The Berwick physiotherapist Bobby Gordon was on the pitch for longer than he had anticipated. Their goalkeeper's car broke down and he was late arriving for the match, so Gordon had to keep goal for the first six minutes.

■ Huddersfield suffered their worst defeat on November 7 when they were destroyed 10-1 by Manchester City at Maine Road.

GOLF
■ Ian Woosnam became the first player to win more than one million pounds in a year — £1,042,662.

RUGBY UNION
■ New Zealand beat Japan 106-4 in Tokyo on November 1, the highest score in an international.

Border turns his boys into full-grown champions

ALLAN BORDER took a bunch of boys to the sub-continent and within a month they had completed a man-sized job: winning the World Cup. His team of rookies was expected to be a push-over in a contest many hoped would climax in a dream final between the host nations India and Pakistan. Instead, the Australians held on to beat their old rivals England by seven runs.

It was nearly 111 years since the two oldest cricket nations had played in the first Test match. Now they had come to ruin the party organised by the sport's emerging powers. England, who finished second to Pakistan in their group matches, surprised India with an easy 35-run victory in their semifinal in Bombay. Graham Gooch led the way with an impressive 115 in 136 deliveries.

Australia were upset that Zaheer Abbas, a former Pakistan player, had called them a bunch of club cricketers. "Our boys take a fancy to that sort of talk," Border said after an 18-run win in the semifinal against their hosts in Lahore.

The final started at nine o'clock in the morning. England only started playing at eleven, and by then David Boon had put the underdogs in command at 95 for one after 25 overs. The stocky opener hit 75 off 125 balls and when 79 runs came off the last 10 overs England needed more than five runs an over.

England badly needed their captain, Mike Gatting, to produce a match-winning innings. But after scoring 41 at nearly a run a ball he foolishly attempted to reverse sweep the first delivery from Border. All he did was top-edge the ball to the wicketkeeper and England were on their way to defeat.

Martina Navratilova
The Queen of Wimbledon

Sue Mott

Billie Jean King was the brazen militant and Suzanne Lenglen the bandeau-ed madame superstar. Evonne Goolagong displayed balletic poise and Steffi Graf blitzkrieg power. Ginny had us all in tears and Chrissie had Burt Reynolds. Martina Navratilova was simply the greatest.

To win one Wimbledon as a portly and recently-defected 21-year-old Czechoslovak was an achievement, to win six in succession was phenomenal, and to surpass the record of Helen Wills Moody, established in 1938, by winning nine Wimbledon singles titles was a feat bordering on the impossible. Even then, Navratilova wanted 10. It was the prerogative of the great champion not to know where to stop.

She began life, like Evert, as a brunette in tennis whites, but there the similarities ceased. Evert had Floridian sunshine, an indulgent father's coaching and a fiancé called Jimmy Connors. The young Martina Subertova lived in somewhat more spartan surroundings and disturbing times in a town near Prague. She was nine when her father, Kamil, committed suicide and 11 when the Russian tanks rolled across the border. Tennis was already both her passion and distraction. By 16 she was possessed of a devilishly cunning serve, a fine forehand, an awful (formerly two-fisted) backhand, abundant aggression and a new name, Navratilova, after her stepfather.

That was the guise under which she launched her international tennis career, losing 6-4 6-4 to Goolagong in her first match in the United States in 1973. That same year she made her debut at Wimbledon, beating Christine Truman in her first match and reaching the third round. Seventeen years later, on the Centre Court she called home, Navratilova made history. Defeating Zina Garrison 6-4 6-1 in the final granted her a wish she had made many years before. "Even as a young girl, I knew I was going to be the greatest tennis player in the world one day." She might have added: "The greatest of all time."

The 1991 final may have had an anti-climactic air about it – Garrison, overawed and overpowered, offered no significant resistance – but as an elated Navratilova said: "They don't put an asterisk beside your name in the history book saying, 'She broke the record but didn't play well.'"

Not playing well was an unusual departure for Navratilova. A fitness fanatic and shot-maker fantastic, playing well was her forte. So well that she amassed 18 Grand Slam singles titles in a career which spanned three decades, plus a formidable quota of doubles titles. So well that at Wimbledon alone she won seven women's doubles, once with Evert, once in partnership with Billie Jean and five times alongside her longtime sidekick Pam Shriver. So well that an ugly resentment surfaced, both within tennis and among the spectating hordes, that one woman should be so dominant. It was deemed unfair that a player of such fitness should muscle her way to victory over frailer, and by implication, more feminine rivals. In 1984, between January 15 and December 6, she won 74 matches in succession. In the doubles with Shriver she remained undefeated for more than two years.

Navratilova sadly accepted a level of public hostility. While Evert continued to radiate Disney cartoon perfection, Navratilova was perceived as a grasping, butch ex-Communist defector. And then she dared criticise Wimbledon for awarding women less prize money than men. "It was as if I'd insulted God," she said. She would hear voices in the crowd shouting: "Come on Chris. I want a real woman to win." This was a reflection on Navratilova's open bisexuality and the muscle-pounding

> **' Even as a young girl, I knew I was going to be the greatest tennis player in the world one day '**

workouts she put herself through, having discovered that double chocolate chip cookies and athleticism don't mix. This knowledge was not only to transform her game and physique, but also hastened the advent of the modern female tennis player to whom power, muscle and utter professionalism are essential.

Before this, Navratilova had cut a swathe of acquisition across America during her early years in the country to which she defected in 1975. Encouraged by Evert, who knew a tough rival when she saw one, Navratilova tucked into pancakes, hamburgers and ice cream with a will. She swelled to more than 12 stone and became known as The Great Wide Hope. Teddy Tinling, the tennis couturier, suddenly noticed he was using an awful lot of material for her dresses. "I Big Mac-ked across America," she said.

At one point her garage contained a Toyota Supra, a Pontiac J, a BMW 733, a silver Mercedes, a Porsche 928, a 1975 Rolls Royce Silver Cloud and a white Rolls Royce Corniche convertible. One of them had a registration plate "X-CZECH."

Not surprisingly, Navratilova suffered a slump. Emotional, impulsive, and outspoken she found the aftermath of her defection difficult to handle. Friends feared poison-tipped umbrellas in KGB hands; Navratilova feared losing tennis matches, which she did most famously at the US Open in 1976. Cameras zoomed in to picture her distraught and sobbing, having lost in the first round to Janet Newberry, a name not destined to be writ large in the annals of women's tennis.

"She had that dramatic Slav temperament that requires the stimulus of a crisis," Tinling once explained. She goes direct from arrogance to panic with nothing in between. The panic button has been pressed on a number of conspicuous occasions. Against Tracy Austin in the 1981 US Open final, Navratilova won the first set 6-1 but lost the championship with a double fault on match point. The dreaded double struck again against Steffi Graf in the 1987 French Open final and again when Jennifer Capriati, 19 years her junior, defeated her at Wimbledon in 1991.

But the slumps have been magnificently counterpointed by sustained brilliance. Evert, who once led the celebrated rivalry 18 victories to two, was caught and overhauled by the sheer quality and versatility of Navratilova's attacking game. This did not always sit well with Miss Chris America. In 1983 Navratilova was rash enough to announce: "I want to be the greatest player of all time," within Evert's hearing. The tart response was: "Martina's had one great year and I've had seven."

So the multi-millionairess who did, indeed, become the greatest always had to struggle for the recognition she craved. The affection of a crowd, the cover of magazines, the approval of corporate sponsors came slowly and reluctantly, even after she proudly attained American citizenship in 1981. She donated fortunes to charity, cracked witty jokes in self-taught English and cared passionately about the ozone layer, whales and equal prize money for women, and then discovered the world's prurient interest was focused on her lawsuit with her one-time lover Judy Nelson. But sporting history will be kinder to Navratilova. As she herself said, there are no asterisks in the record books.

Simply the best: From her first Wimbledon singles title in 1978, Navratilova reigned supreme to her record ninth championship in 1990.

FOOTBALL

Courts punish dirty players

TWO Rangers players, Chris Woods and Terry Butcher, were convicted of disorderly conduct and a breach of the peace at Glasgow Sheriff Court on April 15. The charges stemmed from a goal-mouth incident during the Rangers-Celtic match the previous October.

They were fined £500 and £250. The case against Graham Roberts of Rangers was not proven, and Celtic's Frank McAvennie was found not guilty.

Three days later, Swindon's Chris Kamara became the first footballer in England to be punished by a civil court for an incident on the field. Kamara was fined £1,200 and ordered to pay £250 compensation after pleading guilty in a magistrates' court to causing grievous bodily harm to Shrewsbury's Jim Melrose.

BOXING

Strange times for Honeyghan

LLOYD HONEYGHAN regained the WBC welterweight title by knocking out Jorge Vaca in the third round at Wembley Arena on March 29. Four months later, Honeyghan made a bizarre defence in Atlantic City, stopping Young-Kil Chang of Korea in five rounds. When a body punch strayed accidentally low, Chang writhed on the canvas like a bad B-movie actor for several minutes and, ignoring the warnings of the referee, refused to continue.

GOLF

Masterly Lyle sets the trend for Britain

Lyle won by one stroke from Mark Calcavecchia

SANDY LYLE became the first Briton to win the Masters after an eventful final fling at Augusta. He appeared to have sealed the title at the turn in the last round, when he led by three shots. But disaster struck at the notorious Amen Corner. He dropped a shot at the 11th and two at the short 12th when he went into the water. By the time he reached the last Lyle needed a birdie three to win.

He overhit his one-iron from the tee, landing in a fairway bunker 150 yards from the hole. But he had a good lie and the chance to reach the green. Out came his seven iron and a clean hit took the ball towards the green. It was a brilliant shot. The ball landed on the green and rolled to within 10 feet of the pin. Lyle holed his birdie putt for a one-shot victory over Mark Calcavecchia. The traumas of the afternoon had been forgotten. One of the most talked-about shots in golf secured the first of Britain's three successive Masters titles.

FOR THE RECORD

CRICKET

■ The West Indies conceded a record 71 extras in a Test against Pakistan in Georgetown.

FOOTBALL

■ On May 3, Uefa announced the most dramatic change to their regulations. From the 1988-89 season clubs entering their competitions would only be allowed to field four "foreign" players. As England, Wales, Scotland and the two

Irelands competed as separate countries, their players were also regarded as "foreign". The ruling did not apply for three seasons to players already registered at their clubs.

■ Chelsea beat Middlesbrough 1-0 in the second leg of the play-offs, but lost 2-1 on aggregate and were relegated to the Second Division on May 28. Their fans reacted angrily and had to be dispersed by mounted police. There were more than 100 arrests.

WINTER OLYMPICS

The Eagle dares to come last

IT WAS the year of Eddie the Eagle. Michael Edwards was a plasterer from Cheltenham with thick glasses and an ability to ski-jump. Not very well, but he could jump all the same. So he turned up for the 15th Winter Games in Calgary, Canada, and stole the show.

He was Britain's first entry in the ski-jumping, and to the amusement of millions finished last in both jumps. Although he broke the British record of 71m, he finished 20 metres behind the rest of the field. "Everybody back home thinks I'm crazy," he said. "They're probably right."

There was also traditional success for Britain. Martin Bell surprised himself by finishing eighth in the men's downhill, won by Pirmin Zurbriggen of Switzerland. Bell had clocked mediocre times in training, but produced a world-class performance on the big day.

The East German Katarina Witt became the first individual skater since 1952 to retain a figure-skating title, although she was accused of attempting to influence some of the judges by wearing skimpy costumes.

Edwards: "I'm crazy"

Budd forced out by South African rumpus

ZOLA BUDD, never far from controversy, reluctantly withdrew from the British team selected for the World Cross-country championships in Auckland on March 26 after the IAAF had put pressure on the British Amateur Athletic Board to remove her.

Demonstrations to disrupt the championships were threatened by New Zealand anti-apartheid campaigners if Budd competed in a race she had already won for England in 1985 and 1986.

Budd had spent much of 1987 training in South Africa and recovering from injury. The IAAF, fearing demonstrations, used reports of a trivial incident in which Budd had run round a cross-country course in South Africa during a race the previous summer as a means of raising questions over whether she had illegally competed while there.

Budd insisted that she had just been training and spectating, but it proved a sufficient lever for the IAAF to keep her from Auckland. The BAAB declared itself prepared to stand behind Budd, but she said: "I must put my country and teammates first and for the sake of saving this event for them I must now withdraw myself from the British team."

Budd: withdrew from the world cross-country championships

Beasant save denies Liverpool

Unfashionable Wimbledon deny Liverpool the Double

WIMBLEDON perpetrated one of the most staggering upsets in Cup final history when they beat Liverpool 1-0 on May 14. Not only did they deny Liverpool their second League and Cup Double, they inflicted defeat on a team who had only lost twice in the League.

Liverpool began the Cup final at 4-1 on, the hottest favourites since the war. But when the referee disallowed Peter Beardsley's "goal" in the 35th minute, awarding a Liverpool free-kick instead, it looked as if the gods were not going to smile on the League champions. A minute later, with Liverpool still complaining, Lawrie Sanchez snatched the lead with a header from a free-kick. Wimbledon's defence, coached by Don Howe, resolutely held out.

However, Liverpool did have one clear-cut chance to stop the underdogs when they were awarded a penalty in the second half. John Aldridge, who had not missed one all season, stepped up to take it and Dave Beasant dived at full stretch to his left to make the save. The team who 11 years previously had been in the Southern League had conquered England's most successful club side.

Hick left short of top score

GRAEME HICK was 19 runs away from the highest score in English first-class cricket when his captain declared at Taunton. Phil Neale, the Worcestershire skipper, was unaware that the Zimbabwean-born batsman was about to eclipse Archie MacLaren's record of 424 for Lancashire, also against Somerset at Taunton, in 1895.

Hick went in to bat when his team had lost their first wicket for 78. He stayed 555 minutes, faced 469 deliveries and sent the Somerset fielders to the boundary to collect 35 fours and 11 sixes. When Neale called his players in Hick was unbeaten on 405 in a score of 628 for seven declared. He admitted afterwards: "I didn't know the record existed. I just kept going."

Later in the month, Hick became the eighth player to score 1,000 runs in May. He hit 172 against the West Indies three days before the end of the month to pass the mark with an average of 101.90. Hick, still serving his English residential

Hick: 405 not out

qualification, was the first player to reach the milestone since 1973, when the New Zealander Glenn Turner achieved the feat, also playing for Worcestershire.

CRICKET

Gatting sacked for bedroom romp

IT RANKED as one of the most bizarre dismissals in Test cricket. Mike Gatting, England's captain, was given the sack for inviting a blonde barmaid to his hotel room to celebrate his 31st birthday.

Gatting claimed he did not have sex with the barmaid, the TCCB said they believed him but then took away the captaincy. It was a case of "too many black marks and you're out old boy".

The captain's dismissal after the drawn first Test at Trent Bridge did nothing to repair the team spirit in an England side attempting to improve an atrocious record against West Indies. John Emburey took the helm and lost the next two Tests. So Chris Cowdrey was appointed captain. A gateman refused him entry to the Headingley ground and he then lost his sole match as skipper by 10 wickets. Graham Gooch, the only England player to appear in all five Tests, got the nod but dislocated his finger during the final game and his deputy, Derek Pringle, became the fifth England captain in as many matches. Not surprisingly, West Indies won 4-0.

Gatting: denied having sex

GOLF

Play-off ends Faldo's dream

NICK FALDO'S hopes of emulating Tony Jacklin's feat of holding both the Open and US Open titles were destroyed by Curtis Strange in a play-off at Brookline.

Although Faldo finished level with Strange on 278 after four rounds he was beaten by four shots in the play-off. Strange became the first player in 38 years to retain the US Open title when he won at Oak Hill the next year.

FOOTBALL

Game split by television bidding wars

TELEVISION nearly split the League. ITV negotiated in secret with the elite First Division clubs and offered them £33m over four years for League and League Cup matches, it was revealed on July 10. BBC and British Satellite Broadcasting also weighed in with a counter-offer. As the weeks went on the money spiralled.

The acrimony over the secret negotiations cost Philip Carter of Everton the League presidency and David Dein of Arsenal his position on the League management committee.

In the end, ITV got the League and League Cup, and the BBC and BSB the FA Cup and England internationals. The threat of a breakaway Super League receded as the top clubs were to receive the lion's share of the TV money.

BOXING

Tyson on the slide

Tyson pounds the ageing Holmes in the fourth round

AS MIKE TYSON reached his professional peak, his personal life crumbled. Tyson's year began with a four-round destruction of the 38-year-old Larry Holmes, whose participation in the tasteless episode after a 21-month retirement was a shameful reflection on the sport's governing bodies.

That was followed by the death from leukaemia of Tyson's co-manager Jim Jacobs, and his ill-fated marriage to the actress Robin Givens. Meanwhile, Tyson travelled to Tokyo to brush aside the blubbery Tony Tubbs, a former WBA champion, in two rounds.

With Cus D'Amato and Jacobs dead, Tyson's life altered direction.

Some said his wife influenced his move towards the predatorial Don King and away from his surviving co-manager Bill Cayton. As the year wore on, the marriage began to crack further.

Cayton, later to make a public and unsuccessful plea for Tyson to "come home", said the champion's greatest performance was his 93-second destruction of the undefeated Michael Spinks in the showdown billed as "Once and For All," at Atlantic City on June 27. Tyson was talked about as one of the great heavyweight champions in history, but there were also those who feared he would never be the same again.

CYCLING

Delgado wins Tour on drugs

PEDRO DELGADO of Spain won the 75th Tour de France on a technicality that allowed him to go unpunished after testing positive for drugs. Probenecid, detected in his sample and known to be a masking agent for anabolic steroids, was not due to be included on cycling's proscribed list of drugs for another fortnight, although it was already "outlawed" by the Olympic movement.

Delgado claimed that he had used the drug to flush an excess of uric acid from his system.

Delgado: tested positive

England blow up on and off the field

FOR Bobby Robson, England and all those who wished to see the end of hooliganism, the finals of the European championships in West Germany in June were an unmitigated disaster.

For the first time, England lost all their games in the finals of a major tournament. And off the field English supporters clashed with Dutch and German fans in scenes televised worldwide. There were more than 100 arrests before and after England's game with the Republic of Ireland.

Jack Charlton's Irish team, who had shocked England with a 1-0 defeat in the opening game, were desperately unlucky. They held the Soviet Union and were very unfortunate to lose to Holland.

Both of these teams contested the final. Holland were worthy winners and in Marco van Basten they had the man of the tournament. He scored a hat-trick against England and a fabulous goal in the final.

The violence in Germany increased the government's desire for identity cards to be used at all football stadiums. On June 16 the government announced a package of proposals including a mandatory national membership scheme and the powers to confiscate passports. And by October the government was also suggesting a levy on transfer fees to finance the ID card scheme.

Van Basten celebrates the first goal of his hat-trick

Jenkins jailed for seven years

DAVID JENKINS, who became the youngest ever individual male European athletics champion when he won the 400m title for Britain in 1971, was given a seven-year jail sentence and a $75,000 fine after pleading guilty to smuggling steroids in California.

Jenkins had admitted using steroids himself from 1975. After his competitive retirement in 1982, he had lived in the United States and built up a business smuggling steroids from across the border from Mexico.

He was released from prison after serving just 10 months in return for supplying information and handing over all the money he had made to the US government.

Senna and Prost set an impossible target

AYRTON SENNA'S McLaren-Honda defied the treacherously wet conditions to win the British Grand Prix at Silverstone on July 10, and Senna took himself to within six points of his teammate Alain Prost in his quest for the world championship.

But the bravest drive was from Nigel Mansell, who hauled himself from 11th on the grid to finish in second place, 23.3sec behind Senna. Mansell had predicted before the race that wet conditions would suit his Williams car. But it was an extraordinary performance from the Briton given that the Williams mechanics had worked through the night between practice and the race to convert his suspension from reactive to conventional.

It was the last season of the turbocharged car and McLaren were utterly dominant, scoring 199 constructors' points — two points less than all the other marques put together. And McLarens finished first and second no fewer than 10 times in the season.

Senna, with eight wins, snatched the world title from his teammate Prost, who had seven victories.

Senna: snatched title

Prost had scored more points overall, but under the rules only the best 11 results of the 16 races could be counted.

FOR THE RECORD

■ **Joey Dunlop won the Isle of Man senior TT title for the third time. The Irishman won 13 TT races in 10 years, one fewer than Mike Hailwood's record.**

Dunlop: master of the Isle of Man circuit

363

1988

BOXING

Sugar Ray five times the champ

Leonard: back in the ring

WITH a cavalier disregard for the massed ranks of contenders, Sugar Ray Leonard emerged from a 19-month retirement to take the WBC light-heavyweight championship from Donny Lalonde of Canada on November 7. The new fangled super-middleweight (12 stone) title was thrown in to enable Leonard to become the first man to win versions of world championships at five different weights.

Lalonde, a glamorous but predictable fighter, almost ruined the script when he floored Leonard in the fourth round, but the great man rallied brilliantly to knock out the Canadian in the ninth.

Johnson stripped of gold and sent home for using steroids

TO FUTURE historians, the dominance of Ben Johnson in setting a world record of 9.79sec in winning the 1988 Olympic 100m title on September 24 in Seoul would not have appeared inconsistent with his 1987 World title victory over Carl Lewis in the former world mark of 9.83. But to those who had seen Johnson decisively beaten by Lewis in a 100m race at Zurich on August 17, just a few weeks before the Games, it seemed that Lewis was on his way to retaining the Olympic crown. Even in the preliminaries at Seoul, Johnson was not convincing and only survived the quarter finals as the fastest loser after misjudging what he had to do to qualify.

In the final, however, Johnson appeared a different man. He pulled ahead of Lewis early in the race, and won by more than a metre, 9.79 to 9.92. In the time-honoured cliche, Johnson expressed his preference afterwards for the title over the world record: "They can break my record, but they can't take my gold medal away." He was wrong.

Three days later, Canadian Olympic officials were informed in the early hours of September 27 that Johnson had been disqualified because traces of an anabolic steriod, stanozolol, had been found after the mandatory drug test for Olympic medallists.

Johnson was rushed out of Seoul amid a media stampede. His disqualification ranked as probably

Johnson wins the 100m race of shame

the biggest, and certainly the most publicised, Olympic scandal of all time. His gold medal and world record performance in Seoul were rescinded, and he received an automatic two-year competitive ban from the IAAF. More humiliating, perhaps, was the publicity of being seen as a cheat, and a host of lucrative sponsorship agreements — existing, planned and potential — fell around his ears.

His early protestations that he had not taken drugs, and that his urine sample must have been tampered with, were eventually aban-

doned, and he admitted and repented the following year during the hearings of the Dubin inquiry, an investigation into drug-taking in sport ordered by the Canadian government in the wake of the Johnson case.

Carl Lewis was awarded the title of Olympic 100m champion, with Britain's Linford Christie elevated from bronze to silver medallist. But although their names are in the history books, Johnson's cheating had taken away the moment from them, and that can never be recaptured.

FOOTBALL

Maxwells keep it in the family

THE League tightened its rules on individuals having a financial interest in more than one club on January 19. However, the rules were not retrospective so Robert Maxwell's dealings with Derby and Oxford were unaffected.

This did not stop Maxwell from

seemingly abusing his position. On October 23 Robert Maxwell, as the chairman of Derby, signed Oxford's Welsh striker Dean Saunders for £1m from his son Kevin, the chairman of Oxford.

Kevin failed to tell his manager, Mark Lawrenson, what he was up

to and Lawrenson complained publicly about the transfer and threatened to quit. Lawrenson was sacked after eight months in the job. Within a fortnight Oxford received a petition with more than 4,000 signatures calling for Kevin Maxwell's resignation.

Graf smashes all the opposition off court

WOMEN'S tennis had never seen anything like it. Suzanne Lenglen threw off her corsets in the 1920s, Billie Jean King won a battle for recognition in the 1970s and Martina Navratilova won a battle for equal pay in the 1980s. Now came Steffi Graf to catapult the sport into a new era.

The West German possessed the most powerful serve and ferocious forehand on the circuit, honed and strengthened by practising against men. And she took the game by the scruff of the neck,

winning everything in sight. The 19-year-old became the third woman after Maureen Connolly and Margaret Court to win the Grand Slam in a calendar year. She also took the gold medal in Seoul, where tennis returned to the Olympic Games after 64 years.

Graf won 71 of her 74 matches in the year, losing twice to Gabriela Sabatini and once to Pam Shriver. Her most significant victory was at Wimbledon, when she came back from a set down to defeat Martina Navratilova.

Graf came from behind against Navratilova at Wimbledon

STEFFI GRAF'S GOLD SLAM

Tournament	Opponent	Result
Australian Open	Chris Evert	6-1 7-6
French Open	Natalia Zvereva	6-0 6-0
Wimbledon	Martina Navratilova	5-7 6-2 6-1
US Open	Gabriela Sabatini	6-3 3-6 6-1
Olympic Games	Gabriela Sabatini	6-3 6-3

Bryant and Tony Allcock with their medal haul from Auckland

FOR THE RECORD

BOWLS

■ David Bryant of England won a record third men's singles title in the World championships.

FOOTBALL

■ Ian Rush returned to Liverpool on August 18 for £2.8m, 15 months after he was transferred to Juventus for £3.2m.

■ The FA and the Scottish FA announced on September 24 that all future England-Scotland matches would be played midweek because of the history of violence associated with the fixture. In May there had been more than 200 arrests even though the match had been played on a Sunday.

■ On October 22 Southampton fielded a side with three brothers: Danny, Ray and Rodney Wallace. It was the first time in 68 years that three brothers appeared in the same First Division team.

GOLF

■ Ireland beat Australia 2-1 in the final of the Dunhill Cup.

■ Curtis Strange became the first player to win more than one million dollars on the US PGA Tour in a year.

KARATE

■ Britain won the men's team title at the World championships.

RUGBY LEAGUE

■ Australia beat New Zealand 25-12 in the final of the World Cup in Auckland on October 9.

■ Jonathan Davies, the former Welsh rugby union international, joined Widnes in one of the most publicised switches between the two codes.

SAILING

■ The America's Cup was reduced to a shambles by a series of court cases disputing the type of boats that should be used. While the arguments continued, Stars and Stripes II, an American catamaran, beat New Zealand off San Diego in September.

TENNIS

■ Mats Wilander of Sweden won three of the four Grand Slam titles — the Australian Open, the French Open and the US Open.

■ West Germany, inspired by Boris Becker, won the Davis Cup for the first time, beating Sweden 4-1.

Selection wrangle denies Coe

SEBASTIAN COE'S dreams of becoming the first man to win three successive Olympic 1500m titles got no further than the AAA championships, the UK Olympic trials, in Birmingham on August 6.

Coe, having come down from altitude training, caused a sensation as he ran listlessly in the 1500m preliminaries, finishing only fourth in his heat and not qualifying for the final. With lit-

tle of Coe's form earlier in the season to consider, and a rigid policy of the first two in the trials being automatically selected for the Olympic team, plus one other, Coe was sunk.

Despite a public outcry, the selectors had little choice but to give the third 1500m place to Steve Cram, who had chosen to run the 800m at the trials but would contest both events in Seoul.

1989

BOXING

Iron Mike wobbled by Bruno

Bruno: lasted 5 rounds

FOR five or six seconds, Frank Bruno had the heavyweight championship of the world in his grasp as the supposedly indestructible Mike Tyson reeled across the open-air ring at the Las Vegas Hilton from the impact of an almighty hook. But then reality intruded on the longest lived dream in sport as, halfway through the fifth round, yet another British challenge faltered and failed.

Bruno had done well to survive the first round as Tyson had battered him to his knees before the sound of the opening bell faded. At least Bruno had the satisfaction of finishing on his feet, and that electrifying moment when the impossible almost happened was his passport to folk hero status.

Desert Orchid rises to occasion

DESERT ORCHID was already the leading money winner in jump racing before he went to Cheltenham on March 16. The only people who did not want him to win again were the bookmakers, who stood to lose more than £2m if Dessie won the Gold Cup.

> **❛ The emotion that horse generates is unbelievable. We all love him dearly ❜**
>
> **Richard Burridge**
> **Desert Orchid's owner**

On the morning of the race it looked as if their money might be safe. The weather was dreadful, with rain lashing down, and the fire brigade had to pump water off the course. Richard Burridge almost pulled out his horse, but his trainer David Elsworth persuaded him to let Desert Orchid run.

It looked like the wrong deci-

Desert Orchid's Gold Cup victory cost the bookmakers £2m

sion, particularly because the horse was said to dislike left-handed courses and heavy going. Desert Orchid only went to the front when Ten Plus, who was leading by three lengths, fell three fences out and had to be put down.

Coming over the last fence

Desert Orchid was headed again, by the 25-1 outsider Yahoo. But the crowd only wanted one result. "Dessie, Dessie," they roared. The grey pricked up his ears and bravely fought his way up the hill for an emotional victory that left Elsworth in tears.

MOTOR RACING

Mansell's great start for Ferrari

NIGEL MANSELL amazed himself and his rivals when he commandingly won the opening Grand Prix of the season in Brazil on March 26. It was Mansell's first race for Ferrari, and given the utter dominance of the McLaren-Honda stable the previous year, it suggested that the post-turbo era may

be more competitive. Gerhard Berger, Mansell's teammate, accidentally helped him by colliding with Ayrton Senna early in the race. However, the power of Mansell's Ferrari was awesome, particularly when he shot past Alain Prost's McLaren to take the lead and the race.

Mansell's triumph in Brazil broke McLaren's stranglehold

SQUASH

British women in command

MARTINE LE MOIGNAN became the first British woman to win the world title on March 12, with a courageous fightback against Susan Devoy of New Zealand, the defending champion.

Le Moignan, from Guernsey, lost the first game and was behind at some stage in every other game but she battled on to win 4-9 9-4 10-8 10-8. It was the first time Devoy had been beaten in the World championships or British Open since 1983.

There was further celebration for Le Moignan a week later when, with Suzanne Horner and Lisa Opie, England won the women's team title for a record third time.

95 die in Hillsborough tragedy

Hendry on cue to break the Davis mastery

STEPHEN HENDRY, at 20, burst into the top flight when he won the B&H Masters. Although the young Scotsman was little known to the public at large, inside the game his prodigious talent had been apparent when he won the Scottish professional championship in 1986 at 17 and retained it for two years.

He seemed destined to be the player of the next decade, when, at the age of 21 years and 106 days, Hendry become the youngest ever world champion in 1990, superseding Alex Higgins who had been a 22 year old champion in 1972. Fast, fluent and instinctive, Hendry overtook Steve Davis in 1991 and made the world No 1 sport commandingly his own.

Fans at the Leppings Lane end attempt to drag people to safety

Hendry: fast and fluent

THE ultimate disaster in British sport eventually occurred at Hillsborough on a beautiful spring Saturday. It was April 15, FA Cup semi-final day, Liverpool v Nottingham Forest. Although the disasters at Ibrox in 1971 and at Bradford and Heysel in 1985 should have shocked football into taking responsibility and new initiatives for crowd safety and security, they hadn't.

So, between 2.30 and 3.06pm more than 1,000 policemen, the administrators of the FA and of Sheffield Wednesday watched as 95 supporters, including women and children, needlessly died. Some 53,000 people had come to watch a football match, but instead of arriving at a place of entertainment and drama they streamed into a death-trap.

Hillsborough, like most major stadiums, was now a place that imprisoned the paying spectators by fencing them in. Stewards and police saw all spectators as potential hooligans. Thus it was that a series of serious police blunders at the Leppings Lane end meant that 95 people perished when they were crushed to death.

Kenny Dalglish summed up the numbed feelings of a nation when he said: "Football is irrelevant now, nobody is even asking after the other scores."

That such a tragedy could happen so soon after Heysel and Bradford was a shocking indictment of English football. On the day of Hillsborough, The Sunday Times said: "Despite disaster after disaster, nothing seems to shake the complacency and incompetence of those who run the country's most popular spectator sport".

"Football stadiums, and their administration, remain a disgrace. They are filthy, dangerous places that spectators only put up with because of their enthusiasm for what happens on the pitch."

Lord Justice Taylor was given the task of conducting a wide-ranging inquiry into the events.

FOR THE RECORD

■ Millions of television viewers watched in amazement as Brian Clough cuffed two of the jubilant Forest fans who invaded the pitch after their 5-2 defeat of QPR had put them in the semi-finals of the League Cup on January 18. The FA charged him with bringing the game into disrepute, fined him £5,000 and banned him from the touchline for the remaining League games of the season.

■ Uefa announced on April 11 that the ban on English clubs would be lifted in 1990-91 provided the British government agreed.

Sutton recite their lines perfectly

SUTTON UNITED pulled off one the great FA Cup upsets when they outplayed Coventry, winners of the trophy in 1987, and knocked them out of the competition 2-1 on January 7.

Sutton, of the GM-Vauxhall Conference, were inspired by their literary manager Barrie Williams, who exhorted his players with quotes from Kipling. Both Sutton goals were well-rehearsed and came from set-pieces from flicked-on corners, though in training on the morning of the match both set-pieces had been missed.

John Sillett, Coventry's manager was gallant in defeat: "It will be worse when we open the papers and realise we made history the wrong way round."

APRIL

1989

JULY

FOR THE RECORD

FOOTBALL
■ Steve Bull scored both goals for Wolves in their 2-0 defeat of Bristol City on May 1. This brought his tally to 48 for the season.

■ Relegated West Ham broke with tradition on June 5 and sacked John Lyall. Lyall, who had been their manager for 15 years, was only the fifth person to have held the post.

GOLF
■ Nancy Lopez, who won her first US LPGA title at the age of 21 in 1978, came back to win her third title 11 years later.

POLO
■ The United States beat Britain 7-6 in the final of the inaugural world championship in West Berlin.

SURFING
■ Martin Potter of Britain won the world professional championship.

GOLF

Lopez: winning return

FOOTBALL

Liverpool denied by last kick of season

LIVERPOOL had to put the anguish of Hillsborough behind them as they entered the last week of the season poised to become the only club to have done the Double twice. But first they had to win the FA Cup. Their opponents on May 20 were Everton.

On a brilliantly sunny day the two Merseyside communities mingled before and during the match, maintained a minute's silence for the Hillsborough dead, and sang "You'll never walk alone" with Gerry Marsden. Then the football had to take over.

Liverpool burst out of the starting gates and John Aldridge scored in the first five minutes. For more than an hour Liverpool dominated without adding to their score. Gradually, Everton got into the match, but with seconds remaining it seemed Liverpool's Cup.

Then Bruce Grobbelaar fumbled a shot and Stuart McCall equalised. In extra time, Ian Rush, now on for Aldridge, restored Liverpool's lead only for McCall to snatch the equaliser yet again. But Rush wasn't finished. A cross from John Barnes, a flashing header, and Everton were finished. Now Liverpool had to beat West Ham

and Arsenal for the Double.

West Ham were thrashed 5-1 at Anfield two days later, leaving Arsenal the most difficult of tasks: they had to win by two goals on May 26 to win the League championship. At Anfield.

It was one of the most ferocious matches ever witnessed, and at half-time it was still scoreless. The second half was just as frantic, but with seven minutes gone Arsenal scored a disputed goal from an indirect free-kick when a linesman briefly raised his flag. Did Alan Smith touch it or not? Had there been a foul? The referee allowed the goal and set up the most extraordinary finale to a season this century.

Arsenal pressed and pressed for the vital goal, but each wave of attack foundered on Liverpool's rock-hard defence. Seconds to go. A clearance from Arsenal's goal fell to Lee Dixon whose long ball to Alan Smith was lobbed straight in the path of the onrushing Michael Thomas.

Thomas evaded Steve Nicol's tackle, waited for Grobbelaar to commit himself and flicked the ball over him for the most dramatic goal in League history.

RACING

Scudamore's supremacy

PETER SCUDAMORE spent the 1988-89 National Hunt season rewriting the record books. He rode the fastest 50 winners in a season (on October 24), reached 100 before Christmas, became only the third jockey to have 1,000 career victories on February 14, and passed Jonjo O'Neill's record of 149 three days later.

Then on the evening of April 27, despite suffering from flu, he rode a four-timer at Towcester to become the first ever jump jockey to have 200 winners in a season. A measure of his achievement was

that the last time any jockey had exceeded the double century was in 1952, when Gordon Richards had 231 winners on the Flat.

Scudamore owed much of his success to Martin Pipe. The Somerset trainer had started in a small way, earning a reputation for landing gambles on the smaller West Country tracks, but he had built up his yard with the most modern technology available.

The appliance of science paid rich dividends for Scudamore, who got nearly two-thirds of his winners from Pipe's stable.

GOLF

Faldo gets it right in last round

Faldo: changed putter

NICK FALDO was not averse to changing things in his eternal quest for perfection. He had changed his golf swing in 1983 and won the Open within four years. Now he changed his putter for the final round of the Masters after scoring a horrendous 77.

It worked wonders. Faldo knocked the ball in from 50 feet at the first hole, 10 feet at the second, 15 feet at the fourth, 20 feet at the seventh, turned in 32 and was back in contention. Then four birdies in the last six holes, including a 30-foot putt at the 17th, and a round of 65 put him in a play-off with Scott Hoch.

The Amercian missed a three-footer at the first sudden-death hole for the title and Faldo won at the next green. He whacked the ball with his mallet-headed putter, watched it climb the rise and drop into the hole 25 feet away. He raised his arms in triumph, looked into the sky and was probably thinking: "Thank heavens I changed my putter."

Precocious youth has a great fling in Paris

Chang: youngest winner of a men's Grand Slam singles

THERE was a belief that the slow clay courts at Roland Garros were made for experienced players. Michael Chang took a fortnight to destroy that myth.

The American made up for his lack of experience with tenacity, to become the youngest winner of a men's singles title in a Grand Slam event. He was only 17 years and 109 days old when he won the French Open with a five-set victory against Stefan Edberg.

He triumphed 6-1 3-6 4-6 6-4 6-2 and was the first American to win in Paris since Tony Trabert in 1955. Trabert was full of praise. "I have never seen a player show such courage on a tennis court," he said.

Chang, who was seeded 15th when John McEnroe and Thomas Muster withdrew, staged his most remarkable fight in the fourth round against Ivan Lendl. The match between two players with excellent footwork and a determination to fight for every point lasted 4½ hours. Chang came back from two sets down, but was so exhausted in the deciding set that he served underarm. He eventually overcame cramp to beat the top seed 4-6 4-6 6-3 6-3 6-3.

The women's event produced an equally surprising champion in Arantxa Sanchez, a 17-year-old Spaniard who upset Steffi Graf by taking 16 of the last 19 points in their final. Sanchez won 7-6 3-6 7-5. It was the only flaw in Graf's attempt to retain the Grand Slam, and the first chink in her hitherto impenetrable armour.

Johnston stuns all of Glasgow

CELTIC announced on May 12 that they had agreed to pay Nantes £1.2m for Mo Johnston. It was the first step in a convoluted transfer saga that would end in bitterness and divide Glasgow.

On the 29th the deal had apparently fallen through. However, four weeks later, the Fifa general secretary, Sepp Blatter, said he had scrutinised the case and that Johnston should be a Celtic player from July 1. Johnston said that he had not signed a contract.

Then, on July 10, the sky fell in. To a stunned Glasgow, Graeme Souness paraded his latest signing, Johnston. Not only had Souness snatched him from under Celtic's noses, he had finally signed a Catholic. The Rangers bigots branded Souness a traitor, and the wags said that the only shock was that Johnston wasn't English.

Johnston: first Catholic

Campese gaffe gifts series to the Lions

DAVID CAMPESE, the Australian wing who had turned try-scoring into an art form, handed Findlay Calder's British Lions the series on a platter in the deciding Test in Sydney on July 15.

Campese, the leading try scorer in Test history, uncharacteristically lost possession on his own tryline and gave the tourists a 19-18 win in the dying minutes.

The Lions lost the first Test 30-12 but came back to win a bitter second Test in Brisbane 19-12 that soured the remainder of the tour. However, the Lions were not complaining. They went home having won 11 of their 12 matches.

Campese: Australia's leading try scorer made a fatal error

AUGUST
1989
DECEMBER

BOXING

Marsh hits headlines

Warren (left) and Marsh: broke up acrimoniously

TERRY MARSH lost his first nine amateur fights, but persevered to become the only British professional to win a world title and retire undefeated. The Cheeky Cockney Chappie double act featuring Marsh and his brash young manager Frank Warren made great newspaper copy, but then their relationship ended amid a flurry of writs and recriminations. Marsh quit the ring via The Sun's front page on the morning after he had signed to make the second defence of his IBF light welterweight championship on a bill to be promoted by Warren.

When Warren was shot and seriously wounded in November as he arrived at a boxing show in Barking, Marsh found himself the chief suspect. He was brought to trial at the Old Bailey, but the singularly inadequate prosecution case collapsed.

So too did Warren's financial empire. "Banks don't like doing business with people who get shot," he reflected. But by 1992 the irrepressible Warren was on the way back, while Marsh was completing the first year of a degree course in politics and social science at London's City University.

FOOTBALL

Knighton's United bid falls through

The MANCHESTER UNITED faithful were amused on the opening day of the season when Michael Knighton made a surprise entrance on to the Old Trafford pitch. The property owner, decked in Manchester United training kit, blew kisses, saluted the crowd, juggled the ball and fired shots into an empty net.

It transpired that Martin Edwards, United's majority shareholder, had agreed to sell his shares to Knighton in exchange for £10m cash and £10m to spend modernising the stadium. Knighton, then, was now the owner of Manchester United.

The intended deal attracted the attention of a generally hostile press who poured scorn on the new "owner". Knighton claimed that the newspapers were hounding him and were unjustly misrepresenting his future intentions for Manchester United. Some of the most vitriolic criticism was found in the Daily Mirror whose proprietor, Robert Maxwell, some suspected, harboured designs of his own concerning the future ownership of United.

The whole affair became intolerable for United and for Knighton. In October Knighton decided to withdraw his offer. Knighton received a non-executive seat on the board and the episode was over.

MOTOR RACING

Prost wins feud with Senna

ALAIN PROST won the world championship in the Japanese Grand Prix on October 22, when his McLaren-Honda teammate Ayrton Senna collided with him and was assisted in re-starting his car. Prost immediately retired after the shunt but Senna, who crossed the finishing line in first position, had illegally re-entered the track and was therefore disqualified.

The incident came five laps from the end of the race when Senna made a desperate attempt to overtake Prost. Senna needed to win in Japan and Australia to retain his world title. The bad blood between the two drivers had been such they had not spoken directly to each other for six months.

Prost wins the British Grand Prix

FOR THE RECORD

CYCLING
■ Sean Kelly of Ireland won the inaugural World Cup, judged on places in the six classic races during the year.

FOOTBALL
■ A brave performance from Terry Butcher, who required 10 stitches in his head at half-time, saw England through in a goalless draw in Sweden on September 6 and virtually guaranteed them a place in the 1990 World Cup finals. Another goalless draw in Poland on October 11 confirmed England's place in Italy.

■ Arsenal's injury-time penalty at Highbury on November 4 against Norwich provoked a 30-second burst of madness that eventually cost both sides dear. Lee Dixon's late winner resulted in a melee involving almost all the players and was broken up by police having to come on to the pitch. Three weeks later Arsenal were fined £20,000 and Norwich £50,000 by the FA.

■ Manchester United's signings of Paul Ince and Danny Wallace took their spending on players to £12m in less than three years.

GOLF
■ Britain beat the United States in the Walker Cup for the first time since 1971.

ICE HOCKEY
■ Wayne Gretzky became the most prolific scorer in the National Hockey League, beating Gordie Howe's record of 1,850 points on October 15.

■ Britain took part in the World championships for the first time in eight years.

MOTOCROSS
■ Britain's David Thorpe won his third world 500cc title on a Honda.

MOTORCYCLING
■ Eddie Lawson retained the world 500cc title on a Honda. It was his fourth win in six years.

TABLE TENNIS
■ Chen Xinhua, who won two world titles for China, made his debut for England after a long dispute about his eligibility.

TENNIS
■ Boris Becker beat Ivan Lendl in the US Open final. It was Lendl's eighth consecutive appearance in the final, having won three.

■ West Germany retained the Davis Cup, beating Sweden 3-2.

TRIATHLON
■ Mark Allen of America won the men's title in the first world championships. The women's event was won by Erin Baker of New Zealand.

Border humiliates bedraggled England

ALLAN BORDER became the first Australian captain to regain the Ashes on English soil since Bill Woodfull in 1934. And only rain prevented his touring team from completing a 6-0 whitewash against David Gower's embattled side.

England were in a sorry state by the end of a hot summer which produced the sun-baked pitches that were meat and drink for the Australian batsmen. England were hoping for a repeat of their Ashes triumph at home in 1985 when they recalled Gower to lead the team. In the end, the only similarity was that Terry Alderman took a lot of wickets. Alderman, the West Australian medium pacer, captured 41 scalps, one fewer than his haul four years before. And much to the chagrin of the English batsman, 19 of his dismissals were lbw decisions.

Australia set the tone in the opening match when Mark Taylor and Steve Waugh scored at will and Alderman took 10 wickets. England left out their spinner, put

> *There is a possibility that your ability as a player may well be analysed by future generations on your one-day statistics. That's the day I dread most*
>
> **Allan Border**

Australia in to bat against the groundsman's advice and lost by 210 runs. Taylor scored the first tranche of his 839 runs in the series and Waugh hit an unbeaten century. He was not dismissed until the third Test after scoring a total of 393 runs, and he got 506 runs in the series at an average of 126.50.

There was nothing for England to cheer about. They used 19 players in the first three Tests and recalled Ian Botham after a break of 15 Tests in the vain hope that

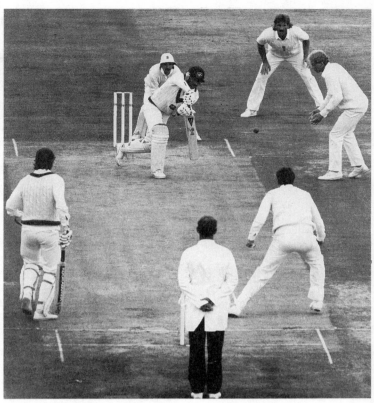

Border guides Australia to the Ashes at Old Trafford

he would repeat his splendid achievements of 1981. But the latter-day Australians were not fooled. They claimed back the Ashes in the fourth Test at Old Trafford on the day the South African Cricket Union announced it had signed 16 Englishmen to

play in a rebel series the next year.

It was another knife in the gaping wound and 10 days later Taylor and his opening partner Geoff Marsh batted all day, scoring 301 runs on their way to a first-wicket stand of 329. Australia won 4-0 and England were at their nadir.

'Old man' Moorhouse proves he can still be a world beater

Moorhouse: record-breaker at the European championships

AGE did not show any signs of diminishing Adrian Mooorhouse's talents at the European championships in Bonn in August. Aged 25, he equalled Michael Gross's record when he won a gold medal at the event for the fourth consecutive time.

To top it all, his victory in the 100m breaststroke came in a world record time, making Moorhouse, at 25, the oldest man to break a record for nearly 20 years. Another Briton was among the records. Nick Gillingham equalled the world's best for 200m breaststroke.

MOORHOUSE'S MEDALS

1982 Commonwealth gold 100m breaststroke

1983 European gold 200m breaststroke, European silver 100m breaststroke

1985 European gold 100m breaststroke

1986 Commonwealth gold 200m breaststroke, Commonwealth silver 100m breaststroke

1987 European gold 100m breaststroke, European bronze 200m breaststroke

1988 Olympic gold 100m breaststroke

1989 European gold 100m breaststroke, world record 100m breaststroke

FOOTBALL

Stadiums condemned

LORD Justice Taylor's report on the safety of football grounds was published on January 29 and it provided a radical vision of the future. Taylor did not just confine his work to preventing accidents and fatalities, he tackled the modernising of football head-on.

Taylor recommended that football grounds should be all-seat stadiums by 1999, with First and Second Division clubs all-seat by August 1994. A new body, the Football Licensing Authority, would oversee the change. Taylor also dismissed the government's identity card scheme as potentially dangerous and impractical.

The government and the football authorities accepted the report in full. However, within days there were moans about the cost from football chairmen.

FOR THE RECORD

BOXING

■ George Foreman, aged 42 and weighing 18st, whipped the upstart Gerry Cooney, nine years his junior, by stopping him in the second round on January 16.

DARTS

■ Phil Taylor, a 100-1 outsider, won the World professional championship.

FOOTBALL

■ The government gave football a financial windfall in the budget on March 20, reducing betting duty from 42½ per cent to 40 per cent. The extra income produced was to help pay for all-seat stadiums.

BOXING

Tyson dealt a busted flush

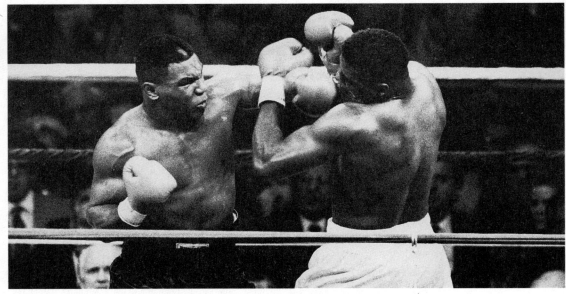

The great upset: Buster Douglas shattered the myth of Tyson's invincibility

IRON Mike Tyson finally met his comeuppance in Tokyo when he was knocked out by Buster Douglas in the 10th round. It was the biggest upset since Leon Spinks overturned Muhammad Ali. February 11 will go down as the day that the myth of the invincible Tyson was destroyed.

When Tyson, the undisputed world heavyweight champion, had to battle with a journeyman pro who was prepared to take the fight to him, Tyson showed he did not have the mettle.

Tyson's chaotic, almost self-destructive, lifestyle contributed to his downfall. His failed marriage to Robin Givens, his discharging of all of the people who had guided him in his formative years, and his relationship with Don King all helped.

It was King who made the 23-year-old champion's demise even more of a nadir when he claimed that the "long" count in the eighth round, when the referee started the count late after Tyson had knocked Douglas down, nullified the result.

King used his promotional muscle, and a fear of millions of dollars disappearing from his pocket, to persuade the presidents of the WBA and WBC to object. For once in boxing, logic eventually prevailed. The count is the count, no matter how long the referee takes. Tyson had officially lost the crown. But King lost more.

Douglas's reign was short-lived. On October 26 he lost the title in his first defence to Evander Holyfield in the third round. But Douglas did pick up $24m.

TENNIS

McEnroe kicked out for tantrum

JOHN McENROE stood in stunned silence. The umpire had struck back. "Code violation, verbal abuse, default McEnroe. Game, set and match Pernfors," Gerry Armstrong called.

The maverick McEnroe had become the first player to be defaulted from a Grand Slam tournament. He was kicked out of the Australian Open on January 21 for swearing during his fourth round match against Mikael Pernfors. McEnroe led 6-1 4-6 7-5 2-4 when he erupted once too often in a career remembered for his temper rather than his talent.

McEnroe's punishment is officially confirmed by Ken Farrar

Gatting's rebels sent packing

SOUTH AFRICA'S insistence on snubbing world opinion by organising rebel tours backfired when mass protests forced the visit by Mike Gatting's team to be abandoned in late February.

The former England captain and his outcasts were greeted on their arrival in Johannesburg on January 18 by opponents of the tour clashing with heavy-handed police. Then staff at the team's hotel refused to serve the players, blacks were bribed to watch the matches and by the time the anti-apartheid leader Nelson Mandela was released from prison the tour was a lost cause. The visit was cut short and a second tour planned for the following summer called off.

Milk farmer whips cream

SIRRELL GRIFFITHS did not even mean to enter the Cheltenham Gold Cup. The Welsh farmer had intended to enter Norton's Coin for another race at the festival. But the horse that spent most of his time rounding up sheep was not qualified. So Griffiths entered him for the Gold Cup instead.

On the morning of March 15, Griffiths milked his 70 cows before driving Norton's Coin, one of only three horses he trained, to Cheltenham. He did not rate his prospects highly: "Like everyone else, I thought Desert Orchid would win. I worked out that with a bit of luck we might be third." The bookmakers were not even that optimistic. They rated Norton's Coin at 100-1.

Two fences from home it looked as if Griffiths's third-place prediction was going to be proved right, as Norton's Coin disputed the lead with Toby Tobias and the incomparable Desert Orchid. But, for once, Dessie did not have the finish. Norton's Coin outlasted Toby Tobias in the run-in and all of west Wales celebrated for days.

Gooch's heroes stun West Indies

GRAHAM GOOCH described England's victory against West Indies in the first Test in the Caribbean as the sweetest moment in his sporting life. It was their first win against West Indies in 16 years and 30 Tests. The England captain had waited a decade to beat the world's leading team. Even the victors were surprised.

Inspired bowling by Angus Fraser in Kingston reduced the home side to 164 all out. Fraser took five for 28, England took a 200-run lead and won by 10 wickets on March 1. But the established order was soon restored when the West Indians won the series 2-1.

Famous victory: the England team that beat West Indies for the first time in 16 years

Glittering prizes cap Hadlee's farewell

THE Christchurch crowd erupted. Richard Hadlee had become the first bowler to take 400 Test wickets when he forced the Indian batsman Sanjay Manjrekar to drag an inside edge on to his stumps on February 4.

Two girls brought a bouquet of 400 flowers on to the field, the Indian team manager Bishen Bedi ran on to congratulate Hadlee and the Indian captain Mohammad Azharuddin joined in the back-slapping and hand-shaking.

There was more. The former Nottinghamshire all-rounder collected another 31 wickets before announcing his retirement after a series in England. Awarded a knighthood in the Queen's Birthday Honours, Sir Richard suggested he was the first bowler to be knighted since Francis Drake.

HADLEE'S RECORD		
	FIRST-CLASS	TESTS (86)
Innings	473	134
Not out	93	19
Runs	12,052	3,124
Highest	210 not out	151 not out
Average	31.71	27.16
Hundreds	14	2
Wickets	1,490 at 18.11	431 at 22.29
Catches	198	39

Arise Sir Richard

Scotland upstage England

THE smart money was on England winning the Grand Slam when they ventured into Murrayfield for the title decider on March 17. They had thumped France 26-7, Ireland 23-0 and Wales 34-6, while Scotland had beaten France 21-0 but struggled to win 13-10 against Ireland and 13-9 against Wales.

However, inspired by an enthusiastic crowd, Scotland saved their best until last. They took an early lead and stayed ahead until the final whistle, winning 13-7.

Craig Chalmers kicked three penalty goals and Tony Stanger breached the English defence for a try to earn Scotland their third Grand Slam. The Scottish tackling was decisive, particularly a superb effort by Scott Hastings, who tackled Rory Underwood when the England wing looked like scoring after a dramatic dash through the middle.

FOOTBALL

Hearts fail to take over Hibs

HEARTS made an ambitious £6.12m bid for Hibernian on June 3. Hearts argued that the only way for an Edinburgh club to break the Glasgow duopoly was to have one strong club in the capital.

However, the Hibs fans and board were completely opposed to the merger. Hibs fans even campaigned for people holding accounts with the Bank of Scotland, who were backing Hearts, to close them. Under such pressure, Hearts abandoned the bid on July 13.

FOR THE RECORD

ATHLETICS
■ Simon Mugglestone ran the second sub-four-minute mile at Iffley Road, Oxford, after Roger Bannister 36 years before.

FOOTBALL
■ Fifa announced the first change in the offside law since 1925 on June 28, with players who are level no longer offside. The professional foul also became subject to automatic dismissal.
■ Uefa decided to allow English clubs back into Europe on July 10.
■ The Football League chairmen voted on August 2 to increase the size of the First Division from 20 to 22 for the 1991-92 season and increase the League to 94 clubs.

GOLF
■ Tom Kite became the first player to win $6 million on the US PGA Tour on August 5.

SNOOKER
■ Alex Higgins was banned for 10 months in July for threatening to have Dennis Taylor shot.

CRICKET

Almighty Gooch has field day

MOHAMMAD AZHARUDDIN won the toss for India in the first Test at Lord's on July 26, put England in and watched Graham Gooch rewrite the record books.

Gooch plundered 333 runs, the highest score at cricket's headquarters, in his 627 minutes at the crease. He faced 485 deliveries, hit 43 fours and three sixes and passed a cluster of records, including Jack Hobbs's record score at Lord's of 316 not out for Surrey in 1926. Gooch then made 123 in the second innings for a record aggregate of 456 runs in a Test.

India also had their moments. Azharuddin blazed a century off 87 balls and Kapil Dev, needing 24 to save the follow-on, smote four deliveries from Eddie Hemmings into the building site that was to become the Compton and Edrich Stands. India saved the follow-on by one run but lost by 247 runs.

England, who had beaten New Zealand 1-0 earlier in the summer, beat India by the same margin, restoring their pride after the humiliation against Australia the previous summer.

Gooch: triple century

FOOTBALL

Leeds go up on day of shame

THE League season ended on a sour note when Leeds fans ran amok at Bournemouth on May 5 and 120 people were arrested. The fans rioted, looted and committed assaults before and after the 1-0 victory that took them back to the First Division. The police were particularly unhappy because they had warned the Football League not to hold that particular fixture on a Bank holiday weekend.

TENNIS

Navratilova outsmarts the bright young things

Child's play: Capriati, the 14-year-old debutante

EIGHT different players won the eight Grand Slam titles for the first time since 1966. But there was one familiar name among the cast of champions: Martina Navratilova. She won a record ninth Wimbledon crown, eclipsing Helen Wills Moody's tally, with a 6-4 6-1 victory against Zina Garrison in 75 minutes.

It was a memorable triumph for the 33-year-old Navratilova, who had been under pressure from a troupe of teenagers through the years. The latest member of the young brigade was the prodigious Jennifer Capriati. She made her professional debut 23 days short of her 14th birthday and became the youngest to win at Wimbledon, aged 14 years and 89 days.

Capriati had set the stage for her Wimbledon debut by reaching the semi-finals in the French Open, where she lost to Monica Seles. The Yugoslav, aged 16 years and 6 months, beat Steffi Graf 7-6 6-4 in the final to become the youngest winner of a Grand Slam event since Lottie Dod in 1887.

Penalties hijack world's top flight

Crying shame: a tearful Gascoigne after he was booked

NOTHING boded well for England as they began their World Cup campaign in Italy. Bobby Robson, the manager, had been the victim of a sustained press witch-hunt for more than 18 months. Uefa and the government had made it plain that misbehaviour by English fans would prevent English clubs returning to Europe. And once again there was a question mark over Bryan Robson's fitness.

Only Bryan Robson let England down, limping home because of an Achilles tendon problem. The rest worked out wonderfully. Without him, England reached the semi-finals and were eliminated by West Germany in a penalty shoot-out. Even Paul Gascoigne's tears in that match when he was booked, and therefore not eligible for the final if England had won, could not compete with the abiding image of Italia 90: the penalty. It seemed to have decided everything.

Jackie Charlton's Republic of Ireland got to the last eight with three draws and a penalty shoot-out. In the quarter-finals only two matches were decided by goals from the run of play. In the others Argentina eliminated Yugoslavia in a penalty shoot-out, and two penalties from Gary Lineker put paid to a game Cameroon side that had thrilled the tournament and scared the daylights out of England.

As the competition reached its climax, it got worse. Both semi-finals were settled on penalty shoot-outs, a craven Argentina eliminated Italy, and England bowed out having participated in the best match of the World Cup.

The final was a travesty, made worse as it was Diego Maradona's last international performance. The superstar was now a parody of a sportsman: he was a cheat, a whinger and a bad loser. West Germany deservedly won the World Cup with a dubious penalty six minutes from time.

Betting scandal mars Swindon's finest hour

SWINDON enjoyed their most successful season in their 109-year history and suffered their greatest humiliation.

Under the visionary management of Osvaldo Ardiles, the Second Division side won through to the play-offs in May and secured a place in the First Division for the first time. However, within three weeks, the Football League cancelled their promotion and relegated Swindon to the Third Division for irregular payments to players.

The scandal had started in January, when it was revealed that their chairman, Brian Hillier, and Lou Macari, their manager at the time, had placed a bet that they would lose an FA Cup tie at Newcastle in 1988. Swindon lost 5-0.

Hillier admitted the charge and was suspended from any involvement in football for six months. The club was fined £7,500 and Macari, now the West Ham manager, was fined £1,000 and censured. Macari resigned a week later.

Gradually, the full horror had come out. In April, Hillier, Macari, the club captain and the former

Macari: resigned

chief accountant were arrested for an alleged tax fraud conspiracy. They were released on bail.

However, it was not all bad news for the club. The FA reinstated Swindon to the Second Division after an appeal in July. But they were instructed by the League to pay an additional £67,000 for previous transfers.

Backley grabs record back at the double

STEVE BACKLEY became the first Briton to set a world record on home soil in 17 years when he threw a borrowed javelin 90.98m at Crystal Palace on July 20. Backley's throw with the controversial Nemeth javelin, which has a rough section behind the grip to help its flight, was his second world mark in 18 days. Backley first broke the record in Stockholm with an effort of 89.66m, but his Czechoslovakian rival Jan Zelezny eclipsed the mark 12 days later.

Backley: borrowed javelin

375

MOTOR RACING

Senna destroys the opposition

LIKE the previous year, the world championship boiled down to a duel between Alain Prost and Ayrton Senna. And once again it was acrimoniously decided at the Japanese Grand Prix in October. This time Prost had the most to lose if the arch-rivals collided.

Prost had to win, or at least finish ahead of Senna, to keep his hopes alive for the last Grand Prix in Australia. Before the race there was wild talk of revenge, aggravated by Prost having left McLaren to drive for Ferrari.

Senna's McLaren was on pole but on the slower side of the track, with Prost in second position but on the faster side. Prost burst into the lead and moved to the left to take the first corner. Senna, knowing that this was the best overtaking possibility on the circuit, decided that there was a gap, and went for it. Prost would not give way and the two crashed and were out of the race.

But Senna was world champion — in a race of just 10 seconds.

Senna: 10-second champion

Faldo proves his open and shut case

Faldo on his way to victory at St Andrews

NICK FALDO was the best golfer in the world. Everybody knew that except the computer that produced the rankings each week. Now he had an opportunity to change even the computer's mind.

Faldo and Greg Norman were level halfway through the Open at St Andrews. Many hoped it would match the memorable showdown between Jack Nicklaus and Tom Watson at Turnberry in 1982. Alas, it was not to be.

Faldo had six birdies and one dropped shot in a third round of 67. Norman shot 76 and the contest was over. Faldo charged to a five-shot victory on July 22 to add to his Masters and become only the sixth player to win the Masters and Open in the same year. The computer took another seven weeks before it recognised Faldo as the world's leading player.

Faldo had become only the second player after Jack Nicklaus to retain the Masters on April 8. But his hopes of the elusive Grand Slam were left on the lip of the cup at the final hole in the US Open, when he missed a putt and the play-off by one shot. Hale Irwin, aged 45 years and 15 days, became the tournament's oldest winner.

THE BRITISH RENAISSANCE

1985 The Open:	Sandy Lyle (Scotland)
1987 The Open:	Nick Faldo (England)
1988 The Masters:	Sandy Lyle (Scotland)
1989 The Masters:	Nick Faldo (England)
1990 The Masters:	Nick Faldo (England)
The Open:	Nick Faldo (England)
1991 The Masters:	Ian Woosnam (Wales)

RUGBY LEAGUE

Battling British underdogs draw first blood

GREAT BRITAIN grabbed a rare opportunity to put the code on the centre stage when they shocked Australia 19-12 in front of a record Test crowd of 54,569 at Wembley on October 27.

It took a moment of inspiration from the stand-off Garry Schofield to win the first Test. With Great Britain holding on to a 13-12 lead nine minutes from the end, Schofield chipped the ball over the defence, gathered it and passed to Daryl Powell, who sent Paul Eastwood in for the winning try.

The Australians won the second Test 14-10 when Ricky Stuart ran 80 metres to set up Mal Meninga for the decisive try with 20 seconds remaining. And despite Britain's 14-0 defeat in the third Test the sport enjoyed unprecedented publicity.

CRICKET

Runs galore as hot summer takes its toll

COUNTY cricket's battle between bat and ball swung decisively in favour of the bat during a hot, dry summer. Ten men scored more than 2,000 runs.

Cherished records fell each week, including Percy Fender's famous hundred in 35 minutes in 1920. Tom Moody was fed some choice long hops and full tosses in his 26-minute century off 36 balls for Warwickshire against Glamorgan, who were seeking a declaration on July 27. It was hardly cricket.

There were records galore at The Oval in early May when Surrey scored 707 for nine declared on a batting paradise. Lancashire replied with 863, the highest championship total of the century and second only to Yorkshire's 887 in 1896. Neil Fairbrother led the run glut with 366.

Piggott silences critics with dream comeback

IT WAS one of the most sensational combacks of all time. Lester Piggott, retired for five years, jailed for a year for tax evasion, and weeks away from his 55th birthday, was granted a licence to resume riding by the Jockey Club on October 11.

The wags joked that he needed the money, his fellow professionals were divided, and the experts thought that he would never be able to recapture his old skills.

Piggott, who became the oldest ever British flat race jockey, once again proved all his critics wrong. Within weeks he had gone to America to partner Royal Academy in the Breeders' Cup Mile and, in his own inimitable fashion, pulled off yet another outstanding victory.

Piggott: back to his old winning ways

Seaman steers clear of tempest

OLD TRAFFORD witnessed the most extraordinary scenes when 21 of the Manchester United and Arsenal players on the field engaged in a brawl on October 20. Only David Seaman was not involved. The FA charged both clubs with bringing the game into disrepute.

Three days after the fracas, Arsenal fined George Graham, their manager, and five players two weeks' wages. This did not deter the FA from taking a strong line and, on November 12, they deducted two points from Arsenal, and one from Manchester United. Both clubs were fined £50,000.

Costly clash: £100,000 in fines and three points deducted

Sampras: charitable

Warwick: fortunate

FOR THE RECORD

ATHLETICS

■ Athens, believing it had a right to stage the 1996 Games on the 100th anniversary of the birth of the modern Olympics in the Greek capital, lost out to a slick bid from Atlanta on September 18.

■ Sebastian Coe retired to a career in politics. He was awarded the OBE.

BOXING

■ Terry Marsh was charged with the attempted murder of Frank Warren, his former manager, on January 17. He was acquitted on November 7.

FOOTBALL

■ Tony Adams of Arsenal was sentenced to nine months for a drink-driving offence on December 19. He became the third player jailed for a similar offence in the past few years.

■ The Faroe Islands had the best possible start to international competition, beating Austria 1-0 on September 12 in a European championship qualifier.

MOTOR RACING

■ Lotus had a terrible September. First, Derek Warwick crashed at the Italian Grand Prix on the 9th, but fortunately was able to walk away. Then Martin Donnelly crashed at 160mph in practice for the Spanish GP on the 30th and was much more seriously injured.

■ Alessandro Nannini's arm was severed in a helicopter crash in Italy on October 12, but doctors sewed it back.

RACING

■ The Aga Khan withdrew all his horses from England in a dispute with the Jockey Club about drug-testing procedures after his 1989 Oaks winner Aliysa was disqualified in November for testing positive.

TENNIS

■ Pete Sampras became the youngest winner of the US Open at the age of 19 years and 28 days. He then collected $2m for winning the inaugural Grand Slam Cup, and donated $250,000 to charity.

Maxwell deal forces Scholar to quit Spurs

TOTTENHAM, crippled by debts of £12m, had secret negotiations with Robert Maxwell about him taking control of the club, it was revealed on September 9.

Irving Scholar, the Tottenham chairman, had agreed with Maxwell that he would inject £13.2m into the club, and had borrowed £850,000 from the publishing tycoon to meet the final payment to Barcelona on the transfer of Gary Lineker. The rest of the board did not know of this deal.

Because Tottenham were a publicly quoted company, Scholar's and Tottenham's extraordinary fiscal arrangements were scrutinised by the Stock Exchange. Six weeks later Tottenham's shares were suspended and Scholar was forced to resign as company chairman.

However, a new actor came on the stage just before Christmas, when it was revealed that Terry Venables, Tottenham's manager, had put together a consortium that would enable him to buy the club.

Northern Dancer
Grandest daddy of them all

John Karter

The grand daddy of them all — that was the legendary stallion Northern Dancer, who was put down in the summer of 1990 at the age of 29. Northern Dancer was a breeding phenomenon; no thoroughbred stallion has created such an international dynasty of champions. Arab owners such as the Maktoum family bought their pre-eminence with black gold, but the crimson gold flowing through Northern Dancer's veins was the currency that guaranteed him a far greater, and more lasting place in the annals of horse racing.

Not only did his own countless progeny such as Nijinsky and The Minstrel hammer home their supremacy on the race tracks; many of his sons have become super sires in their own right, producing strings of champions almost to order. Furthermore, Northern Dancer's grandsons such as Caerleon and Ile de Bourbon have shown that his sphere of influence is increasing daily. When the brilliant colt Generous, a son of Caerleon, romped home in the 1991 Derby he became the seventh product of the Northern Dancer male line to win the Epsom classic. Seven years earlier, two of Northern Dancer's sons, Secreto and El Gran Señor, fought out one of the most enthralling Derby finishes in memory, separated by the width of a nostril at the finish.

Northern Dancer's bloodlines are not only dominant in Europe and the United States, but also in Australia, South Africa, India and Japan. Bernard McCormack, general manager of Windfields Farm in Canada where Northern Dancer was born and buried, made the following impressive claim after the horse's death: "Very soon, if it has not happened already, more than 50 per cent of the world's thoroughbred population will have Northern Dancer's blood in their pedigrees."

The blind faith that the world's normally finicky racehorse breeders placed in Northern Dancer was unprecedented. Breeding is arguably even less of an exact science than the study of racing form, but the arrival of Northern Dancer made the business of breeding racehorses of the highest class almost a production-line affair. In his book Thoroughbred Stallions, Tony Morris, the leading bloodstock writer, contends that 95 per cent of stallions are failures in terms of the racecourse performances of their progeny. Northern Dancer stood that notion on its head. "Breeders breed on the basis that like begets like and most of the time it doesn't," Morris said. "What Northern Dancer did was prove that in certain cases it does happen. He was the most reliable source of class in the world; he gave breeders something they could have faith in."

Ironically, nobody had the slightest belief in Northern Dancer at the beginning. He was unfashionably bred and was so small as a yearling that he failed to reach his reserve of $25,000 at the sales. His breeder, Eddie Taylor, the owner of Windfields Farm, was forced to keep him and decided rather half-heartedly to put him into training. Northern Dancer won seven of his nine races in his first season and as a three-year-old galloped off with two legs of the American Triple Crown, the Kentucky Derby and the Preakness Stakes. In all, Northern Dancer won 14 out of 18 races before injury ended his career.

Northern Dancer may not have been the greatest horse to race in the United States, but his courage and competitive fire captured the imagination of breeders and they flocked to his barn door when Taylor retired him to stud. His covering fee was then $10,000. Twenty years later breeders were allegedly paying an astonishing $1m for his services without the guarantee of a foal.

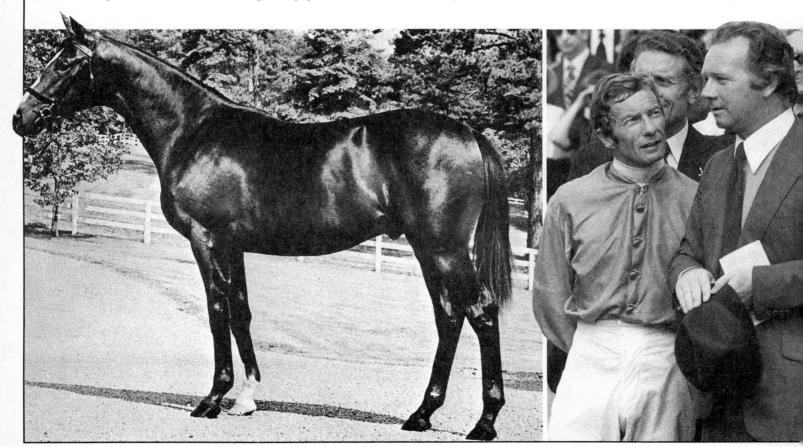

Northern Dancer could be described as a freak of nature, yet in one respect this extraordinary founding father of modern racing was man-made. Robert Sangster, the multi-millionaire racehorse owner who dominated the British scene in the late 1970s and early 1980s, was responsible for sending Northern Dancer's stallion career into a heady orbit that changed the face of the bloodstock world. Sangster, working in partnership with the master trainer Vincent O'Brien, realised he had tapped into a vein of gold in Northern Dancer and virtually cornered the market in his progeny, raiding the famous Keeneland yearling sales in Kentucky time and again to buy his offspring.

The Northern Dancer factor was largely responsible for sending bloodstock prices spiralling to previously unimagined levels. When Northern Dancer began his career in 1965 the world record price for a yearling was $170,000. During the 1980s, when the market reached its peak, one of his sons, Snaafi Dancer, was to fetch $10.2m and a grandson, Seattle Dancer, was sold for $13.1m, figures that are unlikely to be surpassed for years.

Charles Taylor, Eddie's son and the owner of Windfields, said that Northern Dancer had an extraordinary will to win which he passed on to his progeny. But he revealed that there was so much more that made the chunky little bay unique.

"We were all a bit tearful when the end came," Taylor said. "It might sound ridiculous to attribute human qualities to a horse, but Northern Dancer definitely had them. He was a feisty, gutsy, complex character, who always knew he was No 1. He hated it when mares were brought to be mated with other stallions on the farm. He thought they should all be for him and he would go berserk. "When it was his turn you could hear him trumpeting 100 yards away. He would dance out on two legs in a state of high excitement, then get straight on and mount the mare. Afterwards he would snort as if to say: 'Where's the next one?'"

Northern Dancer retired from breeding at the grand old age of 26 (about 104 in human terms). "Sadly, he was not the same at the end of his stud days," Taylor said. "He would carry out his duties just as proficiently, but he seemed embarrassed to do so. He knew his powers were waning." While the blood of his universal family continues to flow, Northern Dancer's light will never be dimmed.

The almighty trinity who changed the face of racing: Robert Sangster and Vincent O'Brien tapped into Northern Dancer's vein of gold.

NORTHERN DANCER AT STUD

- Northern Dancer sired 635 foals and produced 410 winners from 511 runners up to 1991.
- 295 of his first generation progeny were sold at public auction for a total of $183,758,632 (an average of more than $620,000).
- He sired a record 144 winners of stakes races (internationally-recognised prestige events), a record. His son Nijinsky is next with 137 up to 1991.
- Eight of his youngsters were among the 12 highest-priced yearlings sold at auction in North America. Nijinsky sired three of the other four.
- Northern Dancer's sons and daughters have earned in excess of $30m in prize money worldwide.

HIS BEST WINNERS (first generation)

NIJINSKY, winner of the 2,000 Guineas, Derby, King George VI and Queen Elizabeth Diamond Stakes and the St Leger in 1970.

THE MINSTREL, Derby, Irish Derby, King George VI and QEDS, 1977.

NUREYEV, 2,000 Guineas, 1979. Controversially disqualified from first place.

SHAREEF DANCER, Irish Derby, 1983.

LOMOND, 2,000 Guineas, 1983.

EL GRAN SEÑOR, 2,000 Guineas, Irish Derby and a close second in the Epsom Derby, 1984.

SADLER'S WELLS, Irish 2,000 Guineas, Eclipse Stakes, Champion Stakes, 1984.

SECRETO, Derby, 1984.

HIS BEST SIX SONS AT STUD

NIJINSKY: Sire of many champions including Shahrastani and Golden Fleece (winners of the Derby); Shadeed (2,000 Guineas); Caerleon (French Derby); Royal Academy (July Cup and Breeders' Cup Mile).

LYPHARD: Sire of Dancing Brave (2,000 Guineas, Eclipse Stakes, King George VI and Queen Elizabeth Diamond Stakes and Prix de l'Arc de Triomphe and an unlucky second in the Epsom Derby); Three Troikas (French 1,000 Guineas, Arc de Triomphe); Ensconse (Irish 1,000 Guineas).

SADLER'S WELLS: Sire of Salsabil (1,000 Guineas, the Oaks, Irish Derby); Old Vic (French and Irish Derbys).

NUREYEV: Sire of Miesque (English and French 1,000 Guineas and dual winner of the Breeders' Cup Mile); Sonic Lady (Irish 1,000 Guineas); Soviet Star (French 2,000 Guineas); Zilzal (champion miler).

THE MINSTREL: Sire of Musical Bliss (1,000 Guineas); L'Emigrant (French 2,000 Guineas); Melodist (Irish Oaks); Silver Fling (champion sprinter).

DANZIG: Sire of Shaadi (Irish 2,000 Guineas); Dayjur and Green Desert (champion sprinters).

FOOTBALL

Dalglish abandons Liverpool

KENNY DALGLISH astounded everybody when he suddenly quit as the manager of Liverpool on February 22. In Dalglish's six-year reign Liverpool had won three League titles and two FA Cups, and in his first season had become the third club this century to win the Double.

The resignation seemed inexplicable: Liverpool were top of the table and still in the FA Cup, having drawn 4-4 with Everton two days previously. Dalglish cited the enormous pressure he put himself under to be successful as the reason. But as Howard Wilkinson said: "If he has resigned because of the pressures, the rest of us have no chance."

For once the smooth Liverpool tradition of continuity was broken. Ronnie Moran was made caretaker manager, and the search for a successor was on. One by one candidates ruled themselves out, including the Rangers manager Graeme Souness who said: "I would never contemplate leaving Ibrox." However, on April 16, Souness did move to Anfield.

But in the championship the damage had been done. Liverpool lost the title to an Arsenal side that had only lost one League match all season. And, curiously, Dalglish shrugged off the self-imposed pressure and accepted the manager's job at Blackburn before the end of the year.

RUGBY UNION

Carling's men finally reap their just reward

Revenge: England beat Scotland on the way to the Grand Slam

ENGLAND, wrestling with the ethics of shamateurism and an inability to win the Five Nations championship, finally got their act together. Will Carling's men, who had twice come close to capturing the Holy Grail, beat France 21-19 in a pulsating Grand Slam decider at Twickenham on March 16.

England took the lead when Rory Underwood flew past the French defence, but his try was a pale shadow of the effort engineered by Serge Blanco and scored by Pierre Saint-André. The French fullback ran 80 yards.

RUGBY LEAGUE

Hard road to record for Wigan

WIGAN, inspired by their captain Ellery Hanley and Andy Gregory, won a record fourth successive Challenge Cup with a 13-8 victory against St Helens at Wembley on April 27. It was their 20th consecutive Cup match victory.

They also retained the League title by winning 11 of 12 matches in 34 days at the end of the season, which prompted their coach John Monie to suggest: "The side has been held together by needles and sticking plaster."

Hanley: driving force

WONDERFUL WIGAN

1987 League championship, Premiership, Regal Trophy, Lancashire Cup
1988 Challenge Cup, Lancashire Cup
1989 Challenge Cup, Regal Trophy, Lancashire Cup
1990 League championship, Challenge Cup, Regal Trophy
1991 League championship, Challenge Cup

CRICKET

England hit rock bottom

ENGLAND crash-landed on their winter tour of Australia. Graham Gooch's team were thrashed 3-0 in the Ashes series, failed to qualify for the finals of the three-team World Series Cup and were embarrassingly beaten in a one-day series in New Zealand.

They won only one first-class match and it was the sour manner in which they took defeat that made them one of the most unpopular teams to leave England. Phil Tufnell turned his back on his captain when Gooch attempted to congratulate him after the spinner had taken his first Test wicket, and Eddie Hemmings and Alec Stewart were fined for a petulant exhibition after an appeal had been turned down.

David Gower and John Morris were also on the receiving end of the wrath of the tour management when they took a joyride in a Tiger Moth which buzzed the ground during a match against Queensland. Their high jinks cost the pair a £1,000 fine.

Bobby Simpson, the Australian manager, had a suggestion to repair the game in England. He said: "If I could recommend one change in the way English cricket is run it would be to have a four-day championship." English cricket thought otherwise.

FOOTBALL

Maradona flees from sex and drugs scandals

DIEGO MARADONA's fabulous career ended in disgrace. He was accused of being involved in a sex and drugs vice ring, was tested positively for cocaine after a League match for Napoli, and hours before the Italian FA were due to suspend him on April 2 he fled to his native Argentina.

Sugar Ray leaves sour taste

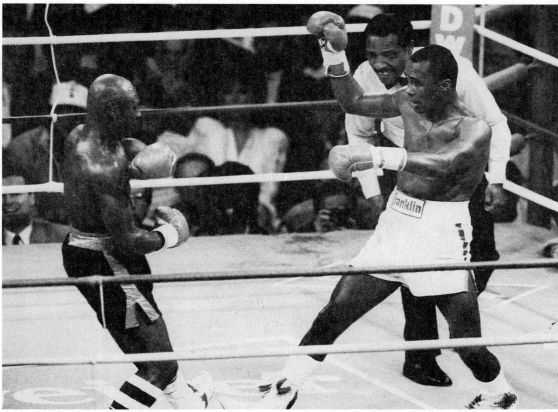

Master of the comeback: in 1987 Leonard mocked Marvin Hagler to take his middleweight crown

SUGAR RAY Leonard looked all of his 34 years when he struggled to cope with Terry Norris, 10 years his junior, in Madison Square Garden on February 10.

Leonard, who was challenging the WBC super-middleweight champion, took a beating, lost on points and retired again. This time it looked as if it was for good. "My son said I was an old man, and he was right," Leonard said. "I want to do what I planned to do a long time ago: take golf lessons."

Leonard's record was extraordinary: five world titles spanning nine years and 21lb across the different weight divisions. In that glittering decade Leonard met the best and stopped them all. His victims included Marvelous Marvin Hagler, Roberto Duran, Thomas Hearns and Wilfredo Benitez. But despite his remarkable fighting ability there was always a question mark over Leonard the man.

Many disliked his taunting of Hagler and the way he forced Hearns to wait eight years for a rematch, and saw him as a strutting poseur who bent the rules to suit his every whim. Thus when Leonard wanted to fight for the light heavyweight title, and make history, he forced the holder Donny Lalonde to box at 12st instead of 12st 11lb and won.

Blessed with a remarkable talent, Sugar Ray Leonard was the best of his time. But his namesake, Sugar Ray Robinson, will be remembered more fondly.

Elite bogged down in the mud

CALL it the Super League or the Premier Division or what you will, the arguments went on all year, eventually to the point that most fans were mystified as to what was going on and what difference it would make.

The bald facts were that the First Division clubs announced in May that they intended to break away from the Football League and establish an autonomous League under the auspices of the FA, and that this Premier Division would commence in August 1992.

The thorny question of whether it would have 18, 20 or 22 clubs and whether there would be promotion and relegation, and of what type, provoked acrimonious discussions. The FA launched its Blueprint for the Future on June 19, but within months the document seemed to be superseded as the row escalated.

The Football League took the FA to court to stop the breakaway and lost on July 30 but the rows went on. By the end of the year everything was as clear as mud.

ATHLETICS
■ Ben Johnson made a comeback after his two-year ban for testing positive for steroids at the Olympics. Johnson clocked 10.46sec in his lucrative return race against Carl Lewis, which was won by Dennis Mitchell.

BOXING
■ At 42, George Foreman failed to regain the world heavyweight crown from Evander Holyfield on April 19, losing on points. Foreman said: "I proved that 40 is no death sentence."

CRICKET
■ New Zealand's Martin Crowe and Andrew Jones overtook the highest Test partnership record set by Don Bradman and Bill Ponsford with a partnership of 467 in the first Test against Sri Lanka in Wellington on February 4.

FOOTBALL
■ Chelsea were fined a record £105,000 on January 11 by the Football League for making illegal payments to players.

■ After Worthing lost 13-0 to Carshalton on February 2 their manager, Joe Boon, said: "The defeat wasn't as bad as it sounds. But we gave away five bad goals."

■ Manchester United beat Barcelona 2-1 on May 15 to win the European Cup Winners Cup. Mark Hughes, a failure at Barcelona, scored both goals.

■ Liverpool were readmitted to European competitions on April 19.

RUGBY LEAGUE
■ Runcorn Highfield ended a run of 61 defeats in the Second Division when they drew with Carlisle on February 3. They beat Dewsbury 9-2 a month later, their first win since October 30, 1988.

SQUASH
■ Lisa Opie became the first British winner of the women's Open title since Fran Marshall in 1961.

BOXING

Foreman: still going strong

GOLF

Awesome Daly puts longitude firmly on the map

THIRTY years ago there was a podgy blond-haired golfer who took America by storm, hitting the ball further than anyone before him. His name was Jack Nicklaus. In the summer of 1991 there was a podgy blond-haired golfer who took America by storm, hitting the ball further than anyone before him. His name was John Daly.

The 25-year-old rookie, a late replacement after the withdrawal of Nick Price, stormed to a three-shot victory in the US PGA championship at the 7,289-yard Crooked Stick course, the longest in the tournament's history. Daly's triumph on August 11 was in only his third professional tournament.

When Nicklaus first saw Daly

hit the ball all he could say was: "Goodness gracious. What a coil, what an unleashing of power." Ray Floyd said: "I watched him hit a few balls on Saturday and went home with a bad back."

Bob Verdi, of the Chicago Tribune, wrote: "He's longer than Greg Norman, he's even longer than War and Peace."

FOOTBALL

Tottenham make a drama out of crisis

Gascoigne writhes in agony after his moment of madness that nearly cost Tottenham the Cup

TOTTENHAM, beset with £18m of debt and with the Midland Bank breathing down their neck, somehow managed to lead a charmed life. Paul Gascoigne and Gary Lineker swept them serenely to the FA Cup while Terry Venables worked furiously and put together a deal that rescued the ailing club from bankruptcy.

Gascoigne, whose £8.5m transfer to Lazio was in the pipeline, had scored five crucial goals to take Tottenham into the semi-final against Arsenal. On Sunday April 14 the two clubs met in the first

Wembley semi-final, and Tottenham were playing for the very existence of the club. Winning the Cup, and playing in Europe, would ease the worries of their creditors.

In the fifth minute Gascoigne took a free kick from 35 yards. He hit the ball with all the ferocity of a club on the edge of extinction. The shot bent and dipped all the way and was unstoppable. Six minutes later Gascoigne combined electrifyingly with Paul Allen for Lineker to make it 2-0. The game was over, Tottenham eventually winning 3-1.

The final against Nottingham Forest on May 18 was equally dramatic. Gascoigne, completely manic, fouled Gary Parker in the opening minutes and was fortunate not to be booked. Fifteen minutes later he lunged at Gary Charles and committed an horrendous foul. Gascoigne was taken off on a stretcher and his knee injury threw his transfer to Italy, and his team's hopes of the Cup, into doubt.

Worse was to follow. Stuart Pearce converted the free-kick into a goal when the referee failed to spot Lee Glover, in the wall, shov-

ing Gary Mabbutt out of the way. Lineker had a goal disallowed for offside, and missed a penalty.

Stewart rescued Tottenham's crusade with the equaliser in the second half, and in extra time Des Walker, attempting to head a flicked-on corner away, put through his own net. It was to be Tottenham's year after all.

By the end of June, despite last-minute interference by Robert Maxwell, Venables had found the backer he needed in the shape of the Amstrad giant Alan Sugar, and together they owned the club.

CRICKET

Tufnell turns series upside down

GRAHAM GOOCH, his face etched with determination, became the fifth Englishman to carry his bat, scoring 154 in the second innings total of 252 against West Indies at Headingley. But, more importantly, he inspired a spectacular turnaround.

England had been petulant and pathetic in losing to Australia. But a few astute personnel changes altered the character of the team and, with Gooch leading from the front, England gained their first home victory against West Indies since 1969. It was the start of an intriguing series.

The West Indians came back to win easily at Trent Bridge and Edgbaston and appeared likely to present their captain, Viv Richards, with a series victory in his final Test at The Oval. But the Middlesex spinner Phil Tufnell ruined the

Spinning his web: Tufnell has Richards caught behind

script with six for 25 and Richards's swansong ended with a five-wicket defeat.

It was not all rosy for England. Their great hope, Graeme Hick, proved a dismal failure after a seven-year fanfare leading up to

the most publicised Test debut. Hick made 6 in his first innings, then scored 6, 0, 43, 0, 19 and 1 and was dropped. Ian Botham was recalled and hit the winning runs in the final Test. It was the stuff of which pantomimes were made.

TENNIS

Sunday opening a winning service

Stich: surprised Becker

IT WAS quite a Wimbledon. Andre Agassi wore angelic white, Monica Seles went missing, the 66-1 outsider Michael Stich won the men's title and Martina Navratilova met her Waterloo against a 15-year-old who once described Napoleon as "that short little dead dude". But, above all, they played on the middle Sunday.

Stich, a strapping 6ft 4in with a 125mph serve which delivered 97 aces, beat Boris Becker 6-4 7-6 6-4 in the men's final. Steffi Graf recaptured the women's crown after defending champion

Navratilova was beaten in the quarter-finals by Jennifer Capriati.

But the moment to savour was People's Day. A week of rain forced the All-England club to open their gates on the middle Sunday for the first time. Tickets were issued on a first-come first-served basis and a young and boisterous crowd thrilled the players with cheers, wolf whistles and the Mexican Wave. Jimmy Connors was moved to remark: "This is my kind of crowd. I wish they were like this the last 20 years. Where have they been?"

FOOTBALL

Atkinson the mover and shaker

RON ATKINSON, the manager of Sheffield Wednesday, newly promoted to the First Division and the winners of the League Cup, denied he was moving to Aston Villa on May 31. "I would be barmy to think of leaving Sheffield. I would be leaving the best job in football."

Seven days later Atkinson joined Aston Villa. "I suppose I let Sheffield Wednesday down in a way," he said. The Football League computer seemed to have a wicked sense of humour and arranged for Villa's first match of the next season to be against Sheffield Wednesday on August 17.

TENNIS

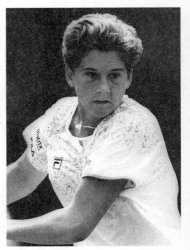

Seles: three titles

GOLF

Langer blows it at last hole

BERNHARD LANGER was called on to make the most important putt of his life: a six-footer with a break of a few inches at the final hole of the Ryder Cup. He missed.

As the agony rippled across his face and he broke into tears, the Americans celebrated a rare victory, winning 12-11 with five matches halved including the last between Langer and Hale Irwin. Langer had recovered a two-hole deficit over the last four holes at Kiawah Island as the Europeans launched a late charge to retain the Cup they had virtually given away with poor performances from star players.

The most telling contribution came from the Spaniards Seve Ballesteros and José-Maria Olazábal, who had cause to bemoan the decision that the 1993 Ryder Cup would be staged at The Belfry rather than in Spain.

Langer: agonising miss

CRICKET

Fletcher's band hits the top note

ESSEX had finished runners-up in the county championship two years in a row. Now they needed to beat Middlesex in the last match of the season to pip Warwickshire for the title. Surprisingly, there were few signs of nerves. They bowled out the defending champions for 51 on the first morning. Graham Gooch hit 259 and Chelmsford celebrated their fifth title in 13 years.

Essex had taken 103 years to find a winning formula. And when Keith Fletcher moulded his band of players into a strong team they became the most powerful and popular combination in cricket, winning 10 trophies in 13 years.

Their bonhomie was in contrast to the conflicts tearing apart struggling Somerset and Yorkshire at the foot of the table. But there was hope for Yorkshire. They finally agreed to get outside help and eventually signed the Indian teenage batting sensation, Sachin Tendulkar, as their first overseas player.

Essex await the final wicket against Middlesex

ESSEX: 13 YEARS OF SUCCESS
1979 County champions, B&H Cup champions
1980 B&H Cup runners-up
1981 Sunday League champions
1983 County champions, B&H Cup runners-up
1984 County champions, Sunday League champions
1985 NatWest Trophy champions, Sunday League champions, B&H Cup runners-up
1986 County champions
1989 County runners-up, B&H Cup runners-up
1990 County runners-up
1991 County champions

MOTOR RACING

Loose screw unhinges Mansell

NIGEL MANSELL's hopes of the world championship slid away in the Portuguese Grand Prix at Estoril on September 22. Mansell had been dominating the race when he came in for a routine change of tyres on the 30th lap. Unfortunately, the Williams mechanics did not fully secure the right rear wheel

and it flew off as Mansell went to re-enter the race.

Mansell stopped in the pit acceleration lane. A replacement wheel was hastily installed and he roared back into the race, but 20 laps later he was disqualified for working on a car in the acceleration lane.

It was a sad end to Mansell's season. He and the Williams cars had mounted a stiff challenge to Senna and McLaren. Mansell had won the French, British and German Grands Prix in July, and the Italian and Spanish in September, but Senna and comfortably won his third world title.

FOR THE RECORD

ATHLETICS
■ Sergey Bubka broke his 27th world pole vault record on August 5 in Malmo when he cleared 6.10m.

BOXING
■ Mike Tyson's chances of regaining his title from Evander Holyfield dimmed on October 23 when he was charged with rape.

MOTOR RACING
■ Jean-Marie Balestre was ousted as the Fisa president on October 9 and replaced by Max Moseley.

RACING

Desert Orchid brought down to earth with a resounding bump

THE YEARS finally caught up with Desert Orchid at Kempton Park on Boxing Day. A record crowd of 25,000 flocked to see him in the King George VI Chase, a race he had made his own with four previous victories, and were stunned when he took a crashing fall at the third-last fence.

Desert Orchid only suffered

minor bruising, and still received a rousing cheer when he crossed the finishing line without his jockey, but for his owner, Richard Burridge, the time had come.

At the age of 12, Britain's favourite grey, who had won 34 races and more than £650,000, was retired to the stud where he was bred by Burridge's father.

Campese's deceit is decisive

Western Samoa slay the Welsh dragon at the Arms Park

IT TOOK an act of cheating to win the second World Cup. David Campese, the Australian wing, broke the laws of rugby union to deny England a try in the final at Twickenham in November.

The Australians won 12-6 with a rock-solid defence that had earned them a ticket to Twickenham after conceding only three tries in the tournament. England, who had been criticised earlier for playing conservatively, played with verve and enterprise. But a pass to Rory Underwood, which would have left the England wing a clear run to the line, was deliberately knocked-on by Campese. The referee, Derek Bevan, awarded a penalty and not a penalty try as many believed would have been appropriate.

England had reached the final with close victories against France in Paris and Scotland at Murrayfield, while Australia had accounted for the defending champions New Zealand. The revelations of the tournament was Western Samoa, who beat Wales 16-13 and gave Australia a scare. They had not been invited to the previous World Cup.

THE SECOND WORLD CUP

Quarter-finals: Scotland 28 Western Samoa 6; England 19 France 10; Australia 19 Ireland 18; New Zealand 29 Canada 13.

Semi-finals: England 9 Scotland 6; Australia 16 New Zealand 6.

Final: Australia 12 England 6

Title fight puts Watson in coma

MICHAEL WATSON lost more than the vacant WBO world super-middleweight title on September 21 at White Hart Lane. In a keenly contested, savage fight, Watson was caught by an uppercut from Chris Eubank in the 12th round, and his head hit the bottom rope as he fell. The whiplash effect put Watson into a coma and on a life-support machine and he underwent two brain operations.

Eubank turned the fight around in the 11th when he climbed off the floor to smash Watson against the ropes as the 15,000 crowd howled for his defeat.

Controversy had dogged Eubank throughout his career. In February he had butted Dan Sherry with the back of his head and won the WBO middleweight title when Sherry could not continue. Eubank was fined £10,000 for the incident and said: "I've never been called nigger in the ring before and I completely lost my composure."

It was a long time in coming

MIKE POWELL took a leap into the 21st century in Tokyo on August 30. The American jumped 8.95m to beat Bob Beamon's famous record set at the Mexico Olympics 23 years and 316 days previously.

Beamon's 8.90m was so astonishing that many people thought it would last into the next century. But for 10 years and 65 long jump competitions, the unbeaten Carl Lewis had been edging closer.

To Lewis's chagrin, the oldest record in athletics was broken at the third World championships by the unheralded Powell. Lewis had eclipsed the record before in the competition, but his jump was ruled out because of wind assistance. However, Lewis did secure a place in history five days earlier, winning the fastest-ever 100m in 9.86sec in a race that produced six sub-10sec times.

Britain took two gold medals, with Liz McColgan winning the 10,000m from the front in 31min 14.31sec and Kriss Akabusi passing the American Antonio Pettigrew down the final straight to take the 4x400m relay. Akabusi said: "He may be world champion, but he is only a kid when it comes to relay."

Liz McColgan: 10,000m gold

ATHLETICS

Krabbe caught in a fix after cheating row

KATRIN KRABBE, the German sprinter, and her teammates Silke Moeller and Grit Breuer were suspended for four years by the German Athletics Federation on February 15 when their drug test samples were found to have been tampered with while they were training in South Africa. Krabbe, who won the 100m and 200m at the world championships in Tokyo in 1991, and her colleagues submitted identical urine samples. They appealed and their ban was cut to four months, enabling Krabbe to launch a bid for the sprint double at the Olympic Games in Barcelona.

Krabbe: identical sample

CRICKET

Pakistan fight back to thwart England

Mushtaq celebrates one of his three wickets in the final

IMRAN KHAN took his talented and temperamental Pakistan team on a roller-coaster ride to the top of the world. In two weeks, Imran's hand-picked heroes went from being 25-1 outsiders to World Cup champions with a 22-run victory against England at the Melbourne Cricket Ground on March 25. It was England's third defeat in a World Cup final. Pakistan lifted the trophy a fortnight after they appeared destined for a quick flight home. The Pakistanis lost three of their first five games and were bowled out for 74 by England, but saved by rain. They won their remaining three matches in the qualifying stage and watched Australia, the favoured co-hosts, and West Indies crack under pressure.

But it still looked like being England's tournament after the round-robin series. They had swept aside New Zealand on their winter tour and retained their winning streak. Then Graham Gooch's team ran aground. They were beaten by New Zealand and Zimbabwe and were plagued by injuries. England reached the final by beating South Africa, whose return to international cricket was

marked by a controversy over the rules. Kepler Wessels showed that the South Africans were certainly not naive when he slowed down the over rate while England were in full flow. The South Africans were presented with a simpler target, but their attempts backfired when the ridiculous rain rule made sure of England's victory.

In the final, England were in command as Pakistan struggled to 34 for two off 16 overs. Then Imran and Javed Miandad, the only men to have played in all five World Cups, used their experience to build a patient partnership of 139. Inzamam-ul-Haq and Wasim Akram's blazing bats lifted Pakistan's total to 249 for six. England faltered when Ian Botham was dismissed for a duck in his World Cup swansong. The leg spinner Mushtaq Ahmed bamboozled the middle order with his googly and when Akram added the fire England were all out for 227. The financial benefits of a tournament ruled by Australian television helped Imran realise his dream of building Pakistan's first cancer hospital in memory of his mother, who died of the disease.

FOOTBALL

Keegan returns as the saviour

KEVIN KEEGAN, once a favourite son at Newcastle United, was given a hero's welcome back to St James's Park when he took over as manager from Ossie Ardiles, who was sacked after Newcastle had floundered precariously close to the foot of the Second Division.

Keegan was hailed as the new Messiah on Tyneside when despite public rows with the chairman, Sir John Hall, he saved the team from relegation. Ardiles moved on to manage West Bromwich Albion.

BOXING

Iron Mike convicted of rape

MIKE TYSON, the former world heavyweight champion, was sentenced to six years in jail for raping Desiree Williams, an 18-year-old beauty contestant, in his hotel room in Indianapolis the previous July.

Tyson, the youngest and richest heavyweight champion, denied raping Williams after meeting her at a Miss Black America pageant, and delivered a 12-minute monologue from the witness box before being sentenced on March 26.

Tyson, who was described by his reform school supervisor as "a tulip among the weeds", was expected to serve three years with good behaviour.

Tyson: six-year sentence

Tomba swoops to golden double

King of the mountains: Tomba drove his Italian supporters wild with delight

ALBERTVILLE, the French ski resort, became known as Albertoville for a fortnight in February. The man who prompted the change was Alberto Tomba, a charismatic Italian who took the winter Olympics by storm. Tomba won his second successive gold medal in style when he retained the giant slalom, but he had to be content with the silver medal in the slalom despite a stirring second run.

The British two-man bobsleigh team of Mark Tout and Lenny Paul were on the brink of winning a medal when they led the field after the first run. But a slow second run relegated them to sixth place.

Britain's medal hopes slipped even further when Wilf O'Reilly crashed into a barrier during the 1,000m semi-final in the short-track speed skating. The world champion from Sutton Coldfield, who had carried the Union Jack at the opening ceremony, was the favourite to return with a medal in the new Olympic discipline.

Eddie Edwards, who had earned a degree of notoriety at the 1988 Games, was not even selected because he failed to achieve the qualifying distance.

England sweep the field again

ENGLAND came charging back from their defeat in the World Cup final to retain the Grand Slam in the Five Nations championship. It was the first time successive Grand Slams had been won since England did so in 1923 and 1924. Although their finest hour was not as sweet as they might have wished, England's 24-0 victory against Wales at Twickenham on March 7 lifted their points tally to a record 118, surpassing the 102 scored by Wales in 1976. Will Carling's team beat Scotland 25-7 under cloudy skies at Murrayfield on January 18. But there were no dark clouds for England. The Scots proved the toughest hurdle, and England grew in strength through the winter, thrashing Ireland 38-9, outplaying France 31-13 in a brawl in Paris and sealing their clean sweep against the improving Welsh.

England were so dominant that they were immediately installed as 2-1 favourites to win an unprecedented third Grand Slam, despite the threat of mass retirements before their next campaign.

Carling: commanding role

Waqar: jury still out

CRICKET

Pakistan accused of cheating

PAKISTAN'S tour of England will be remembered less for the bowling of Wasim Akram and Waqar Younis than allegations that their feats were achieved by tampering with the ball.

Rumours started to circulate that the Pakistanis were able to impart reverse swing on the ball by scratching its surface and picking the seam, and matters came to a head during the one-day international at Lord's in August.

The ball was changed during the lunch interval, and Don Oslear, the third umpire that day, was convinced that it had been deliberately damaged. Fearful of creating a diplomatic incident by accusing Pakistan of cheating, cricket's authorities tried to play the incident down.

They said that the ball had merely gone out of shape and the matter was closed. The Pakistan tour manager strenuously denied any wrong-doing, saying that the "insinuations are a distortion of the facts and are totally unfounded".

But more fuel was poured on the fire when Allan Lamb claimed that his Northamptonshire teammate Sarfraz Nawaz had shown him how to doctor the ball. Sarfraz sued for libel, and Oslear, who had made a series of reports to the TCCB alleging ball-tampering, told the High Court that he was convinced that the ball used at Lord's had been deliberately interfered with.

A host of big names, including Ian Botham, Graham Gooch,

David Gower and Robin Smith had been subpoenaed as witnesses, but the case was settled when Lamb made a statement to the court that Sarfraz had never cheated in a match in which they had played together.

In between times, Waqar's club, Surrey, had been reported several times for alleged ball-tampering, and were eventually fined £1,000 by the TCCB, a fifth of the penalty imposed on Lamb by Lord's for speaking out.

Ultimately, credence was given to Lamb's claims when Imran Khan, a former Pakistan captain, admitted on television that he had used a bottle-top to gouge the surface of the ball during a county championship match.

FOOTBALL

Leeds profit as United blow up on the last lap

JUST AS it seemed that Manchester United would finally win their first championship for 25 years they utterly collapsed and were overhauled by Leeds United. It was a surprising end to a season that had begun so brightly for United as they were unbeaten in their first 12 League matches. Leeds, however, were a dogged and determined side who refused to give up.

Each week the two sides swapped places at the top of the table and the fierce rivalry between the pair left all the other clubs trailing miles behind. In January fate played a cruel card and matched United and Leeds in both Cup competitions, with a League fixture

At long last: signing Eric Cantona inspired Leeds to their first League title in 18 years

thrown in for good measure. The three fixtures, played over 11 days and tagged "The Battle of the Titans", probably decided the outcome of the title. For when United knocked Leeds out of both Cups, Howard Wilkinson's men no longer had any distractions.

Even so, United were dis-

tinctly careless when in sight of the winning post. In April they were in pole position: two points ahead with a game in hand. Then in 11 days they blew the title by drawing with Luton, and losing to Nottingham Forest, relegated West Ham and Liverpool. Thus the title went to Elland Road for the first time

since Don Revie's days in 1974.

One of the principal reasons Leeds were able to overtake United in the final straight was the inspirational play of the French international Eric Cantona. So it came as a complete shock when Wilkinson suddenly sold his mercurial genius to United in November for £1.2m.

TENNIS

Agassi's triumph leaves his critics crestfallen

Proving his point: Agassi did not choke in the Wimbledon final

THE CRITICS were starting to write off Andre Agassi. The flamboyant Las Vegan was all show and no substance, they claimed. His form was terrible, his world ranking was in decline. And, to top it all, this was only the second time he had deigned to play at Wimbledon.

The brash American delivered the perfect riposte to those who said he lacked the temperament after losing two French Open finals and a US Open final.

Agassi breezed past Boris Becker and John McEnroe to meet the big-hitting Goran Ivanisevic in the final. It was one of the most pulsating contests that Agassi's screaming army of female fans had ever seen.

Despite losing the first set on a tie-break, Agassi withstood all the rocket serves Ivanisevic launched at him to lead two sets to one. Ivanisevic, warned by the umpire for swearing in Croatian, vented his spleen on Agassi instead, running away with the fourth set 6-1 in 17 minutes.

When Ivanisevic held a break point at 3-3 in the final set it looked as if Agassi was just about to cave in again. But this time he dug deep, hit a sublime volley and then unleashed an ace of his own to claw his way back.

Now it was Ivanisevic's turn to crack. Down 5-4, he served two double faults to trail 0-30. Ivanisevic subsided tamely and Agassi won his first Grand Slam title, 6-7 6-4 6-4 1-6 6-4.

FOR THE RECORD

CRICKET

■ In only their third match, Durham beat Glamorgan by an innings and 104 runs to record their first county championship victory.

■ Keith Fletcher, the former Essex captain, was appointed England team manager.

FOOTBALL

■ The long-running feud in the English game ended when the FA Council sanctioned the formation of a Premier League in February. In May, the new League announced it had signed a five-year deal worth £304m with BSkyB and the BBC.

■ Eleven people died and hundreds were injured when a temporary stand collapsed in Corsica during the French Cup semi-final between Bastia and Marseille. The French FA cancelled the final.

■ Rangers completed the Scottish League and Cup Double for the first time since 1978 when they beat Airdrie 2-1 in the Cup final.

■ Cash-strapped Maidstone followed Aldershot out of the League in August, unable to guarantee their fixtures.

SAILING

■ Bill Koch's America³ beat the Italian boat Il Moro di Venezia 4-1 to keep the America's Cup in America.

TENNIS

■ Dan Maskell, the voice of tennis, died aged 84.

■ India consigned Britain to the basement of the Davis Cup, the Euro-African group, when they won the first three matches in New Delhi.

RACING

■ Lester Piggott, 56 and a grandfather, won his 30th British classic when he rode Rodrigo de Triano to victory in the 2,000 Guineas. In November, Piggott was crushed by his mount, Mr Brooks, at the Breeders Cup in Florida and suffered a broken collarbone, broken ribs, concussion and internal injuries.

RUGBY LEAGUE

■ Martin Offiah, the costliest player in world rugby, scored two tries as Wigan trounced Castleford 28-12 to win their fifth successive Challenge Cup.

■ Australia retained the World Cup by beating Great Britain 10-6 at Wembley after Britain had led 6-4 at half-time.

RUGBY UNION

■ Stuart Barnes scored a drop goal with the last kick of the Cup final to complete a League and Cup Double for Bath as they beat Harlequins 15–12 in extra time. If he had missed, the trophy would have been shared for only the second time.

RUGBY LEAGUE

No way through: Ellery Hanley cannot stem the Australian tide

389

Jensen: Great Dane

FOOTBALL

Lineker left in lurch by England's European fiasco

THE European championships were supposed to be Gary Lineker's grand finale and the high spot of Graham Taylor's tenure as the England manager. Instead they were a complete fiasco for both men.

Lineker began the tournament with 48 international goals and England's captain seemed set fair to overhaul Bobby Charlton's record of 49. Taylor had enjoyed the luck of the draw and England were in the weaker of the two groups.

But three matches are a long time in football. When the dust had settled England had failed to win a match, drawing twice and losing once, and Lineker's goal tally was still stuck on 48. Taylor compounded England's shame by substituting Lineker 29 minutes from the end of the final match against Sweden.

It was a match that England had to win to reach the semi-finals. Instead they lost 2-1 and finished bottom of their group. It was a sour ending to Lineker's career — he had announced his international retirement before the championships — and made Taylor even more unpopular back home.

Denmark's exploits in the tournament highlighted what a golden opportunity England had missed. They were brought in as late substitutes for Yugoslavia, who had been excluded because of UN sanctions. The Danes drew their first match, against England, and went on to meet Holland in the semi-finals.

The Dutch, overwhelming favourites, found the Danes formidable opponents and twice fell behind before scrambling a 2-2 draw. Extra time was goalless and in the penalty shoot-out Manchester United's Peter Schmeichel saved Marco van Basten's kick to put his country into the final against Germany, the world champions.

The Germans had been fortunate to even reach the semi-finals. They had scraped a remarkable win over Scotland when they could easily have lost and only qualified ahead of the CIS because Scotland beat them 3-0. But the Germans' luck ran out against Denmark.

The underdogs played a canny, containing game and once John Jensen had put them ahead in the 18th minute they refused to be overawed by their illustrious opponents. With 12 minutes remaining and the Germans scrambling for the equaliser, Kim Vilfort added the coup de grace and the tiny Scandinavian nation had won their first major trophy.

OLYMPICS

Spain's golden armada

THE SPANISH were determined that the Barcelona Olympics would be a success, but even they could not have guessed how well their own competitors would perform. Spain had only won four gold medals in the history of the Games but this time they collected 13, much to the shock of a local insurance company which was left with an enormous bill for a chain of shops' offer to refund the cost of everything they sold during the Olympics if Spain won more than 10 medals.

In the end, there was no doubt that the Games were a success but not before the usual drug scandals reared their ugly head. Jason Livingston, Andrew Davies and Paul Saxton were all banished from the British team for testing positive; Gwen Torrence claimed that two runners who finished ahead of her in the 100m had taken drugs; and all three medals in the men's shot were taken by athletes who had served bans for drug abuse.

The Games marked the return of South Africa to the Olympic movement and the swansong of Carl Lewis. The American had failed to qualify for the 100m but showed his enduring strength by winning the long jump again. He was called into the 4×100m relay team as a late substitute when Mark Witherspoon was injured, and he turned on all his old power in the final. Lewis anchored the team to a world record time and collected the eighth gold medal of his career.

Christie: fastest in the world

Some people argued that the 100m was devalued by Lewis's absence, but Linford Christie was having none of it. He had been beaten by Leroy Burrell in the semi-finals, but was the most relaxed as the runners took their places for the final, less than two hours later. A false start, caused by Burrell, did not faze Christie. He stormed away in the second half of the race to take the gold by half a metre from Frankie Fredericks of Namibia, with Burrell trailing in fifth.

Christie's achievement as the captain of the men's team was matched by the women's captain Sally Gunnell, whose determined run took the gold medal in the 400m hurdles.

There was another equally assured performance from Steven Redgrave. He won his third successive Olympic gold, this time with Matthew Pinsent, leading the finals of the coxless pairs from start to finish.

But perhaps the most extraordinary gold medal was won by the cyclist Chris Boardman in the 4,000m pursuit. He took the track by storm with his outlandish looking Lotus super-bike. The ultra-light ultra-streamlined design enabled him to smash the Olympic record and beat Jens Lehmann, the world champion, by more than a lap in the final.

BOXING

Lewis given trash title

BRITAIN gained only its second world heavyweight champion since Bob Fitzsimmons when Riddick Bowe unceremoniously dumped his WBC belt in a dustbin days after beating Evander Holyfield for the undisputed title. It meant Lennox Lewis, who was the No 1 contender for Bowe's title, automatically became the champion.

Lewis, although only a paper champion to many commentators, had earned his No 1 status the hard way: in the ring. And it was a measure of his credibility that Bowe refused to honour his commitment to fight Lewis, preferring to discard one of his three belts instead. Boxing politics and boxing economics, meant that hanging on to the WBA and IBF titles made more sense than risking the lot.

But for Lewis it was a cruel way to reach the top. He had proved his capabilities in stunning style when he knocked out Donovan "Razor" Ruddock in the second round of their final eliminator at Earl's Court. Perhaps that was what frightened Bowe. It was awesome: a chopping, downward right at the end of the first round so rocked Ruddock that the second round knock-out was inevitable.

GOLF

Jittery Faldo did it his way

BOOKMAKERS had no doubts about who was going to win the Open — Nick Faldo. He went to Muirfield on the very top of his game, with nine successive top-10 finishes.

For the first two days Faldo tore up the course, setting a two-round tournament record of 130. When Faldo (by now 6-1 on) still led by four strokes after three rounds the title did, indeed, seem his for the taking. Midway through his final round, Faldo still led by three strokes.

But then he dropped shots at the 11th, 13th and 14th holes. John Cook, playing just ahead of him, made a 6ft birdie on the 15th and a 20ft birdie on the 16th. Suddenly, Faldo was two strokes behind the American with four holes to play.

Faldo pulled himself together sufficiently to hit a perfect tee shot for a birdie two at the 15th. Now it was Cook's turn to feel the pressure. The American, on the 17th, just missed with a 30ft eagle attempt. He was left with a two-footer for a birdie. Inexplicably, he missed again. His chance to snatch victory had come and gone.

But Faldo was faring little better. He only just managed to save par on the 16th after over-

Faldo: sweet success

shooting the green and was still a stroke adrift. The demons, though, were with Cook. On the 18th an indecisive approach shot missed the green and cost him another stroke.

On the 17th, Faldo attacked the hole, just failed to make an eagle but he sunk the birdie putt to go back into the lead. A par at the last hole and the title would be his.

His first two shots were typical Faldo, and he was left with a one-foot putt for the championship. Shaking like a leaf, Faldo tapped the ball in and burst into tears.

The stress had been so great that the first Briton to win the Open three times since Henry Cotton was incoherent afterwards.

MOTOR RACING

Mansell: finally a champion

Mansell's flying start leaves his rivals standing and brings home a long-awaited world championship

AT THE Hungarian Grand Prix in August, five races before the end of the season, Nigel Mansell crossed the finishing line in second place to Ayrton Senna. It was enough. Mansell had won the world championship for the first time and became the seventh Briton to have captured motor racing's blue riband.

Mansell's achievement was astonishing by any standards.

He won the first five Grands Prix and in the season's 16 races he was on pole a record 14 times, winning nine in total. He took the title with 108 points. The distant runner-up was his Williams teammate Riccardo Patrese with 56.

Mansell, never seen as a charismatic personality by his colleagues, had worked hard for his success, once having to sell his house to finance his career.

He made his F1 debut in 1980, driving in 180 GPs. Three times a runner-up (in 1986, 1987 and 1991) it had seemed the ultimate prize would always elude him. Sadly, his season of success was marred when a contractual dispute with Frank Williams forced him to walk out on the team. Mansell angrily packed his bags and promptly went to America to join the Newman-Haas IndyCar team instead.

DIEU ET MON DROIT

FOOTBALL

'Sweeteners' sour Sugar's dream ticket

TWO YEARS earlier, the Alan Sugar–Terry Venables alliance that had rescued Tottenham Hotspur had been called the dream ticket; now it was most definitely a nightmare. Sugar had never really been convinced that Venables was a businessman and it was Sugar's concern about this aspect of Venables' performance, and the people he associated with, that finally caused the rift.

On the eve of the FA Cup final Sugar had Venables voted off the board and dismissed as Tottenham's chief executive. Venables responded by taking his case to the High Court seeking reinstatement. The acrimonious dispute split the club's support with the majority plumping for Venables.

Sugar, however, soon fought back in the popularity war. In court he alleged that Brian Clough, the Nottingham Forest manager, had wanted "a bung" during the Teddy Sheringham transfer. Then Sugar appointed Osvaldo Ardiles as Tottenham's manager. It was a masterstroke and stopped all the threats of boycotts in their tracks.

Venables' legal action also came to a halt when the judge ruled that Sugar's action in dismissing his chief executive was entirely permissible and therefore Venables would not be reinstated.

BOXING

Question time as Lewis and Eubank hang on to titles

LENNOX LEWIS's first defence of the WBC title he had won outside the ring confirmed his status as a world champion but also raised serious questions about his stamina. Tony Tucker was a creditable opponent and Las Vegas a perilous venue, as Barry McGuigan, Frank Bruno and Lloyd Honeyghan had all discovered to their cost.

Lewis easily built up a solid lead against the American but faltered in the later rounds. By the 10th Lewis was looking slow and easy to hit and was reduced to a strategy of survival. Tucker was unable to take advantage and Lewis won on points.

Five months later Lewis fought Bruno in Cardiff and seemed to have learnt nothing from his bout against Tucker in May. Once again, the champion retained his title but only because Bruno showed his usual failings. His wooden muscularity cannot cope at world level and he freezes when he takes a solid punch.

By the sixth round Bruno had managed to achieve a slender

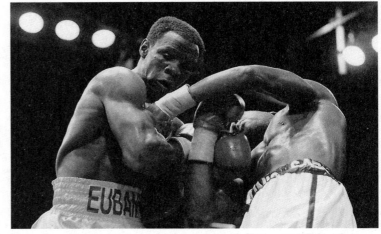

Hung jury: the judges could not separate Benn and Eubank

points lead but Lewis then caught him with left hooks to the head, leaving him dazed. The seventh was a formality as Lewis moved in for the kill and the referee stopped the fight. The worst of Lewis had beaten the best of Bruno. It was a sad indictment of British boxing in the first world heavyweight contest between Britons this century.

By contrast, the world super middleweight fight at Old Trafford was a cracker. Chris Eubank, the WBO champion,

and Nigel Benn, his WBC counterpart, fought 12 brutal and uncompromising rounds and ended honours even.

The fight that was billed as Judgment Day ended with the judges unable to split them, although Benn could claim a moral victory. The referee, having cautioned Benn twice for low blows, had no option in the sixth round but to deduct a point when another left strayed below the belt. Without that penalty Benn would have won.

FOOTBALL

Cantona casts his magic spell again

THE arrival of Eric Cantona from Leeds galvanised Manchester United in just the way Alex Ferguson had hoped. With the French maestro knocking in the goals United soon overhauled Norwich, who had unexpectedly opened up an eight-point lead at the top of the table at the beginning of the year.

As Norwich slipped away, Aston Villa emerged as United's main rivals. But in March the nightmares of the previous season, when Leeds had pipped them for the title, returned as

United went four matches without a win.

The lesson from the previous season had been learnt. United finished the season with an awesome display of form, winning their last seven matches. This time it was Villa who cracked, and on May 2 they lost to relegation-threatened Oldham and United had won their first championship since 1967.

Ferguson also entered the record books. He was the first manager to have won the League title in both England and Scotland.

About time: United's title

The race that never was

THE Grand National, one of Britain's sporting institutions, was reduced to an utter shambles by two false starts, and the race had to be declared void.

Nerves were already on edge when an animal rights protest at the first fence delayed the race for seven minutes. Then when the starter, Captain Keith Brown, tried to send the field on their way the starting tapes did not rise properly and became entangled with the field.

The runners were recalled and after another delay the starter tried again. Amazingly, the tapes failed again, wrapping around the runners and riders.

Down the course, most of the horses thundered straight past Ken Evans, the flag man who was supposed to stop the race if there was a false start. The chaos was unbelievable to the watching millions.

Some jockeys were still trying to disentangle themselves from the tapes and others were milling around waiting for the next restart. But most were off and running. Owners and trainers leapt out on to the course in a frantic attempt to stop the race, but to no avail.

Thirty of the 39 runners reached the first fence and from that point the "race" was out of control. Esha Ness eventually crossed the finishing line "first", but under Jockey Club rules the result would not count. His rider, John White, was devastated and his trainer, Jenny Pitman, was reduced to tears.

Brown and Evans needed a police escort away from the track and the recriminations went on for days. Did Brown unfurl his red flag to indicate the second false start? Did Evans see the signal?

The jockeys insisted they had not seen a flag to stop the race

Beyond recall: Captain Brown's flag waving failed to halt the race

and everybody else raged at the officials. The trainer John Upson fumed: "I think it is an absolute disgrace that the world's No1 National Hunt race should be run like this. It would not happen in a point to point in a little country like Ireland."

With no realistic prospect of the race being re-run, bookmakers had to return £75m to disgruntled punters.

FOR THE RECORD

ATHLETICS

■ The validity of the 100m and long jump world records set in the world championships in Tokyo in 1991 were in doubt when it was revealed that the Japanese had flouted IAAF regulations and built a super-fast track.

■ Chinese women were shredding world records at an alarming rate. Qu Yunxia took more than two seconds off the 1500m record only days after Wang Junxia slashed the 10,000m record by an awesome 42.94sec. Questions about whether the records were the result of performance-enhancing drugs were angrily rebutted.

BOXING

■ Steve Robinson beat Jim Davison from Newcastle on a split points decision to take the vacant WBO featherweight title. The Welshman was a last-minute substitute for Ruben Palacio, the defending champion, who had tested positive for HIV.

CRICKET

■ Pakistan, the one-day world champions, were dismissed for 71 in Brisbane by West Indies, the lowest score in one-day internationals. West Indies easily knocked off the 72 runs required and the match finished before lunch.

■ Four Pakistan cricketers — Wasim, Waqar, Mustaq and Aqib Javed — were arrested for "constructive possession" of marijuana on a beach in Grenada.

FOOTBALL

■ Bobby Moore, who had captained England to the World Cup in 1966, died of cancer at the age of 51. During his time as the captain of West Ham he also won the FA Cup in 1964, and the European Cup Winners Cup in 1965.

■ After 18 years at the helm of Nottingham Forest, Brian Clough decided to call it a day. Sadly for the man who had taken the club from the depths of the Second Division to the heights of two European Cups, Forest were relegated in his final season.

■ Arsenal became the first side to win the FA Cup and League Cup in the same season when they beat Sheffield Wednesday in both finals.

GOLF

■ Bernhard Langer became the eighth European in 14 years to win the Augusta Masters when he repeated his triumph of 1985.

HOCKEY

■ England had to return home when the Indira Gandhi five-nation tournament in Bombay was cancelled because of bomb attacks.

ICE SKATING

■ Oksana Bayul, a Ukrainian 15-year-old, won the women's world title on her debut.

MOTOR CYCLING

■ Wayne Rainey, three times the world 500cc world champion, crashed in Italy and was paralysed from the waist down.

OLYMPIC GAMES

■ Sydney, with 45 votes, were narrowly elected by the IOC to host the 2000 Games ahead of Peking (43). Manchester only received 11 votes and were eliminated in the penultimate round.

ROWING

■ Cambridge won the Boat Race for the first time since 1986 and in the fastest time since 1984.

RUGBY UNION

■ France won the Five Nations championship when they beat Wales 26-10 in Paris. Their only defeat was at Twickenham, where they lost 16-15.

■ Bath came back from 13-11 down with eight minutes remaining against Saracens to win their third consecutive League title.

TENNIS

■ Arthur Ashe died, aged 49. He had previously contracted Aids from a blood transfusion during a heart operation. He became the first black player to win a major men's single title, the US Open.

FOOTBALL

Clough: bowing out

393

CRICKET

Gooch admits defeat and hands Atherton the poisoned chalice

TWO disastrous series brought Graham Gooch's reign as England captain to an ignominious close.

The winter tour started badly for Gooch with uproar over the failure to select David Gower and the tabloids going to town on the news that he had split up with his wife, Brenda. And there was no respite in India — either on or off the field.

Political unrest, poor organisation and complaints about the food and heat dogged the tour, but they were hardly excuses for England's inept performances. They lost all three Tests and were beaten by Sri Lanka to boot.

That was nothing compared with what happened when the Australians arrived in England with their chief tormenter Shane Warne. The leg-spinner's first delivery in the first Test was one of the most amazing ever seen.

It looked like it was drifting away down the leg side and Mike Gatting was content to pad up and watch the ball pass safely by. But when the delivery pitched it turned back almost at

Spin doctor: Warne mesmerised the England team

a right-angle, removed the off bail and left Gatting, and the rest of England, gobsmacked.

England lost by 179 runs and Gooch, horrified by another collapse, gave his team an ultimatum: "Show some fighting spirit or I'll quit." So much for fighting spirit. Australia raced to 632-4 dec in the second Test and had no difficulty in winning by an innings.

England escaped with a draw in the third Test, but when Australia bludgeoned their way to 653-4 dec at Headingley and England lost by an innings, yet again Gooch had had enough and resigned the captaincy.

Gooch admitted: "The sad truth is that England are just not good enough. We haven't been playing as a team. There is too

> ❝ **We're not just losing Test matches, we're getting stuffed** ❞
>
> **Graham Gooch after he resigned as England's captain**

much you have no control over, however hard you try."

Mike Atherton was handed the poisoned chalice but there was little he could do to stop the rot as England lost the fifth Test as well. The only consolation for Gooch was in the final Test. He surpassed Gower as the country's leading run-scorer as England, for once, actually managed to win a Test.

Next in the firing line: Atherton tried to stop the rot

Mansell's brave New World

MOST British motor racing experts rated Nigel Mansell's foray into Indy Car racing as complete folly. They argued he would not be able to handle oval circuits and his English diffidence would go down like a lead balloon in America. Mansell proved them all wrong.

He began by winning the first race, a street circuit in Surfers' Paradise, Australia. His critics felt they were vindicated when he had a serious crash in practice at Phoenix in April. But it turned out to be the making of him as an Indy Car driver. Mansell described it as his "wake-up call".

A month later Mansell made his oval debut at Indianapolis and finished a close third in the legendary Indianapolis 500. Now he was firing on all cylinders. He reeled off victories in four of the season's six races on ovals (Milwaukee, Michigan, New Hampshire and Nazareth) and became the first driver to win Formula One and Indy Car championships in successive seasons.

He also won respect with the American public and the American media, despite his often fractious relationship with the other Indy Car drivers as he complained about rolling starts and driver tactics. But then that's motor racing.

Winning formula: Mansell successfully transfer to Indy Cars

Seles stabbed on court by Graf fan

AN unemployed East German lathe operator turned women's tennis upside down when he stabbed Monica Seles at a tournament in Hamburg. Seles, the No 1-rated player in the world, was sitting at the edge of the court when Günther Parche jumped over a barrier and plunged a knife into her back.

Parche, who idolised his compatriot Steffi Graf, claimed that he attacked Seles so that Graf could regain her No 1 status. Seles was traumatised by the attack and was unable to face another tennis tournament.

Her fears were compounded when the German courts only gave Parche a two-year suspended jail sentence. The decision was widely condemned with Graf saying: "The rest of the world can only shake its head when it looks at us." With Parche at large, Seles found it impossible to return to the tennis court. She received psychiatric counselling for her post-traumatic stress disorder but still became a virtual recluse.

In 1995 Parche's suspended sentence was confirmed on

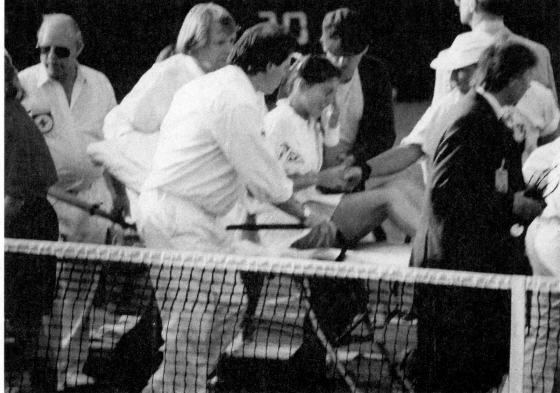

Near-fatal attraction: Seles is wheeled away on a stretcher after being knifed in the back

appeal. The judge said: "Our law does not operate on the principle of an eye for an eye." The feeling in tennis was that unless Parche was put in jail Seles would feel unable to play

again. Her father said: "She is afraid of sitting on the bench with her back to the public."

Arantxa Sanchez Vicario spoke for the sport when she said: "We need Monica back,

and this is terrible for her and tennis not putting the guy in jail." Seles finally plucked up the courage to return, although it was not until 1995 that she felt able to play again.

GOLF

Cook brings USA to the boil and Floyd garnishes the dish

THE United States dug themselves out of a hole to retain the Ryder Cup 15-13 at the Belfry. And they had Chip Beck and John Cook to thank for starting the fight back.

Below par: Ballesteros' withdrawal left Europe in a sorry state

Midway through Saturday, things looked good for the European team. Their $4^1/_2$-$3^1/_2$ advantage from the first day had been extended to a $7^1/_2$-$4^1/_2$ lead after the morning foursomes.

Before the four-balls started, Tom Watson, the American captain, told Beck and Cook: "I need your point." The only problem was that Beck and Cook, who had not played so far, were up against one of Europe's strongest pairings, Nick Faldo and Colin Montgomerie.

Cook had been suffering indifferent form before he came to England, but he showed no sign of letting his dramatic defeat by Faldo in the Open the previous year affect him. He plugged away with Beck to win by two holes.

"What turned us around was when Beck and Cook beat Faldo and Montgomerie," Lanny Wadkins said. "After that, our spirit went through the roof."

Europe were dealt another blow when Seve Ballesteros and Bernhard Langer asked to be rested in the afternoon. Ballesteros was tired and had back-ache, and Langer was suffering from a neck injury. So Europe were forced to break up another

of their great pairings, Ballesteros and José-Maria Olazabal, and throw the inexperienced Costantino Rocca into the fray.

Rocca and Mark James lost 5 and 4, and Olazabal and Joakim Haeggman lost 2 and 1 as the United States revival gained momentum. Europe's three-point lead had been cut to one — $8^1/_2$-$7^1/_2$.

The singles on the final day were cut to 11 matches when Sam Torrance was forced to withdraw. He was still suffering from a chest injury he received when he crashed into a pot plant while sleep walking, and he had a septic toe which meant he could hardly walk.

Watson's dilemma about who to leave out was solved for him when Wadkins volunteered to stand down.

Wadkins' gesture meant that Ray Floyd, another wild-card member of the team and the player thought to be one of the most likely to be omitted, retained his place. And it was Floyd, at 51 the oldest man to play in the Ryder Cup, who made sure that America took the trophy home when he beat Olazabal by two holes to secure the crucial 14th point.

ATHLETICS

Gunnell smashes world record

GREAT BRITAIN returned in triumph from the World Championships in Stuttgart with a record 10 medals and a pair of world records. Sally Gunnell ran the race of her life to take two-tenths of a second off the seven year old record in the women's 400m hurdles. She produced a near-perfect finish to overhaul Sandra Farmer-Patrick and became the first woman to break a track world record in five years.

The next day, Colin Jackson

broke the 100m hurdles record, with Tony Jarrett following him across the line to take the silver. Linford Christie also won a gold medal, although his time in the 100m was just outside the world record. Christie, Jackson, and Jarrett also won silver medals in the 4×100m relay, and Gunnell anchored the 4×400m team to a bronze.

There was also delight for Sonia O'Sullivan, who won Ireland's first medal, a silver in the 1500m.

FOR THE RECORD

BOXING

■ Evander Holyfield regained his WBA world heavyweight title when he got a majority points decision against Riddick Bowe, who had taken his title a year previously. Bizarrely, the fight was interrupted by a parachutist who landed in the ring, but this was not enough to disrupt Holyfield's determination.

■ Michael Bentt, born in south London but based in New York, floored Tommy Morrison three times in the first round to become the WBO heavyweight champion.

■ Eamonn Loughran won the vacant WBO welterweight title with a

unanimous points decision over the American Lorenzo Smith in Belfast.

FOOTBALL

■ Danny Blanchflower, who captained Spurs to the Double in 1961, died at the age of 67.

■ Celtic's managerial duo of Liam Brady and Joe Jordan walked out on the club on the eve of its AGM. Lou Macari, a former Celtic player, replaced Brady.

ICE HOCKEY

■ Wayne Gretzky became North America's highest paid sportsman when he signed a three-year $25.5m contract to play for the LA Kings.

Humiliated Taylor finally bites the bullet and falls on his sword

GRAHAM TAYLOR'S job as the England manager was always going to depend on qualifying for the 1994 World Cup. Only two England managers had failed to qualify, Sir Alf Ramsey in 1974 and Don Revie in 1978. The first was sacked, the second walked the plank. Much the same fate befell Taylor.

It was no more than he deserved. The results and the performances were disastrous. England dropped precious points at home by drawing, first to Norway and then in April to Holland having been ahead 2-0.

Then in the summer Taylor's team could only scrape a draw in Poland and were lucky to lose only 2-0 to Norway. As if to rub salt in their wounds, England then lost 2-0 to the United States in a friendly.

Everything now hinged on England's match in Rotterdam. A bad decision by the referee, when Ronald Koeman should have been sent off for bringing down David Platt, probably cost them the match. England lost 2-0 and had only a mathematical chance of qualifying. They had to beat San Marino by seven

Taylor: down and out

goals and pray that Holland lost to Poland. After eight seconds Taylor's international career hit rock bottom as the tiny republic scored only their second goal in the group. England eventually won 7-1, but Poland succumbed to the Dutch.

Taylor did the decent thing and resigned almost immediately. The search for a successor was bedevilled by the number of candidates who instantly ruled themselves out but eventually the FA settled on Terry Venables, who despite his travails at Spurs, was the popular choice.

Lions wound All Blacks and England finish them off

THE All Blacks were, for once, shown to be mortal. And were it not for a mistake by an Australian referee, the British Lions could have returned from New Zealand with an historic series victory.

The Lions lost the first Test in Christchurch 20-18, but only because the referee awarded the All Blacks a try in the opening minutes which television evidence clearly showed should not have been allowed. To add to the heartbreak, the referee awarded the All Blacks a debatable penalty near the end that allowed them to snatch victory.

But the Lions were not disheartened, even after a mistake by their captain Gavin Hastings gifted the All Blacks a 7-0 lead in Wellington. They came storming back to level the series, and one of the most stirring performances seen for a long time had the stadium resounding to choruses of Rule Britannia. Hastings kicked four penalties, Rory Underwood outsprinted the defence for a try and Rob Andrew kicked a drop goal as the All Blacks wilted under the onslaught and lost 20-7.

The decider was a let down for Hastings, who saw his team surrender a 10-0 lead and lose 30-13 in an acrimonious game. Both sides traded insults after the match and the bad feeling was still lingering when the All Blacks came to Britain on tour in the autumn.

Phil de Glanville was nearly blinded when, horrifyingly, his face was split open playing for the South-West against the tourists, and Hastings and several other players were left nursing injuries as Scotland were swamped 51-15 at Murrayfield.

The pundits gave a below-strength England little chance, but the team played with outstanding commitment. Four penalties from Jonathan Callard and a drop goal from Andrew gave England a 15-9 victory that their captain, Will Carling, described as "our greatest win ever".

Forward charge: Nick Popplewell leads the way as the Lions demolish New Zealand 20-7

Harding loses out in ice war

EVERYBODY at the Winter Olympics took a back seat to two ice skaters — and they weren't Jayne Torvill and Christopher Dean.

The saga of Nancy Kerrigan and Tonya Harding had gripped the world ever since the day in January when Kerrigan was attacked at the United States championships.

When it emerged that the attempt to break Kerrigan's legs had been carried out by associates of Harding, Kerrigan's main rival on the American team, the world was amazed. Sporting rivalry was one thing, but this was something else.

And when Harding's former husband, Jeff Gillooly, and her former bodyguard, Shawn Eckardt, not only admitted being involved in the attack but claimed that Harding was part

of the plot as well, the world was agog. This was something that not even Hollywood could have invented.

With Harding facing the threat of not being allowed to go to Lillehammer, that other great American institution — their legal system — went into overdrive as well. Threatened with a $25m case, the United States Olympic Committee decided that it would let Harding compete in the Games.

And still there was high drama to come. In the final programme Harding took to the ice, fluffed her first jump and stopped. She skated over to the judges, brandished a boot lace that she claimed had broken, and was allowed to start again.

Not that the histrionics did her any good. Harding finished in eighth place, with Kerrigan

collecting the silver medal behind Oksana Baiul of the Ukraine.

In a classic American piece of plea-bargaining Harding subsequently admitted the minor felony of "hindering prosecution" and was fined $100,000 and sentenced to three years' probation and 500 hours' community service. Eventually, Harding was also banned for life by the United States Figure Skating Association.

Back in the real world, the other news from the ice was good and bad for Britain. Nicky Gooch won the bronze medal in the 500m short track speed skating. He had previously gone one better in the 1,000m, finishing in second place but missing out on the silver medal when he was disqualified for charging Derrick Campbell of Canada.

Face-off: Kerrigan and Harding

FOOTBALL

Hughes turns United's hotheads into winners

ALEX FERGUSON'S brilliant squad of immensely talented and immensely expensive players at Old Trafford had one serious flaw. They all seemed to be on a short fuse. And their hotheadedness very nearly cost United dear in March.

Before that month United were set fair for a unique triumph: the treble. They had begun their League campaign in near-perfect fashion and at the beginning of the year they were 16 points clear of Blackburn. Even when they were beaten at home by Chelsea, their first defeat at Old Trafford for 17 months, nobody thought twice about it.

Yet it seemed to precipitate a month of sheer madness as four players were sent off in the space of five matches. Eric Cantona managed to get sent off in successive matches. Peter Schmeichel was dismissed in the FA

Cup quarter-final and Andrei Kanchelskis got his marching orders in the League Cup final.

That final dismissal ended their hopes of the treble. The others enabled Blackburn to whittle away at United's colossal lead and, at one point, the teams were level on points. United's season could so easily have gone to tatters.

The turning point was probably Mark Hughes's superbly executed last-second equaliser in the FA Cup semi-final against Oldham. It was as if the Welshman had knocked some sense into his teammates. United breezed to the final and it was Blackburn's turn to deal with the pressure. They failed and United retained their title with a match to spare.

Even the prospect of Chelsea in the final did not unnerve Ferguson's men. Chelsea, who had beaten United twice in the

First leg: United clinch the title and go on to collect the FA Cup

League, could have been their nemesis. And for the first 45 minutes an upset seemed on the cards. But two Cantona penalties, the second highly questionable, blew away Chelsea's challenge and they were beaten 4-0. And so United became only the fourth side this century to complete the Double.

T&D give their fans six of the best despite the judges' whims

WHEN Jayne Torvill and Christopher Dean returned to competition they had to start at the bottom and work their way back up.

Not that it took them long. A perfect set of nine 6.0s for artistic impression at the British ice dance championships suggested that they were going to carry on where they had left off.

But the first sign that everything was not going to continue as normal came at the European championships in Copenhagen, where Torvill and Dean had curbed their exuberance in favour of the more technically precise skating demanded by the sport's governing body.

In the free dance, Torvill and Dean, perhaps lacking some of their old sparkle, were marked below the Russians Maya Usova and Alexsandr Zhulin. Then, skating last, came another Russian pair, Oksana Gritschuk and Evgeny Platov.

Gritschuk and Platov's routine seemed to ignore the new guidelines yet they were awarded the best marks and won the free dance. Even more confusingly, Gritschuk and Platov's triumph in the free dance handed the gold medal to Torvill and Dean. The final verdict hinged upon the fact that six judges had placed Torvill and Dean in second place while only five had put Usova and Zhulin second.

The great British public (nothing if not blinkered Torvill and Dean fans) were happy but utterly baffled. The scoring system seemed to need a degree in obscure maths and the interpretation of the rules of what was, or wasn't, good ice dancing was extremely confusing.

Torvill and Dean decided, in the wake of Gritschuk and Platov's performance, to revamp their routine for the winter Olympics even though they only had a few weeks to make the changes.

The great British public (nearly 24 million watched on television) thought the new version was even better. The judges thought otherwise, awarding the gold medal to Gritschuk and Platov, the silver to Usova and Zhulin and the bronze to Torvill and Dean.

The great British public were outraged. "Gold robbery", one newspaper shouted. They included an illegal lift, the governing body said.

Dean was diplomatic. "We like to think the audience were our judges," he said. The crowd at the skating gala at the end of the Games gave their own verdict — holding up a line of cards all marked 6.0.

"We think that the audience were our judges" — Christopher Dean

FOR THE RECORD

ATHLETICS
■ Andy Norman, the promotions officer of the British Athletics Federation, was sacked for "inappropriate conduct". Norman's sacking followed the suicide of Cliff Temple, the athletics correspondent of *The Sunday Times* in January. Norman had falsely accused Temple of sexually harassing a female athlete after Temple had written articles critical of Norman's role in the sport.

BOXING
■ Jersey Joe Walcott, who was the oldest man to win the world heavyweight title when he knocked out Ezzard Charles in 1951 at the age of 37, died in New Jersey at the age of 80.

■ Bradley Stone, 23, collapsed at his girlfriend's flat and subsequently died from brain injuries after he lost his super-bantamweight British title to Richie Wenton in the 10th round in the York Hall, London.

■ Evander Holyfield lost his WBA and IBF world heavyweight titles to Michael Moorer by a majority verdict.

■ Michael Bentt lost the WBO heavyweight title to Herbie Hide and was taken to the Royal London Hospital after he could not remember his name in the dressing room.

CRICKET
■ Needing 117 to win the second Test match against South Africa in Sydney, Australia lost by five runs following inspirational bowling by Allan Donald and Fanie de Villiers.

FOOTBALL
■ Sir Matt Busby, who single-handedly created the modern Manchester United, died at the age of 84.

■ After 33 months in charge, Graeme Souness resigned as the Liverpool manager following a shock defeat in the FA Cup by Bristol City. Roy Evans took over.

■ John Toshack quit as the manager of Wales after only 47 days in the job. Toshack retained his job as the manager of Real Sociedad.

GOLF
■ José-Maria Olazabal won the Masters, his first major.

ICE SKATING
■ John Curry, the European, World and Olympic champion in 1976, died of an Aids-related illness.

RACING
■ Willie Carson, a 51-year-old grandfather, won his fourth Derby when he took Erhaab from the back of the field over the last furlong.

RUGBY LEAGUE
■ Great Britain lost the home Test series 2-1 to Australia. Britain had started as the underdogs but a stirring 8-4 victory in the first Test, despite Shaun Edwards being sent off midway through the first half, seemed to have shifted the odds in their favour. However, Australia went into overdrive to win the other two Tests.

RUGBY UNION
■ Wales won the Five Nations championship for the first time since they shared it with France in 1988.

■ South Africa roared back to defeat England 27-9 in the second Test at Newlands and draw the series after England had won the first Test at Loftus Versfeld 32-15.

■ Bath maintained their record of never losing a Cup final (their eighth in 11 years) when they beat Leicester 21-19 for their third League and Cup double.

SKIING
■ The 26-year-old Austrian Ulrike Maier, twice the world super-G champion, died in a World Cup downhill race at Garmisch, Germany.

GOLF

Olazabal: his first major

Tour de force by Boardman

CHRIS BOARDMAN became the first British rider since Tommy Simpson to wear the Tour de France's yellow jersey with a blistering performance in the opening time trial. The 15-second victory over Miguel Indurain, himself something of a time trial specialist, was enough to enable him to keep the overall lead until the end of the fourth stage.

Boardman's exploits created a surge of interest when the Tour visited Britain for the first time since 1974. The excitement was increased when Sean Yates also claimed the yellow jersey for a day.

But when Indurain took over the lead the outcome of the race was hardly in doubt. Indurain swept to victory to become only the third man to win the Tour four years in a row.

There was consolation for Boardman, who won two titles at the world championships, but nothing but grief for Graeme Obree. The world hour record holder was disqualified in Sicily after a row about his riding style. Then, later in the year, he lost his record to Indurain as well.

Boardman: time-trial triumph

Brazil keep the flame burning

BRAZIL satisfied even their own exalted expectations by winning their first World Cup since 1970. It was an important victory for Fifa as much as it was for Brazil. For 24 years successive Brazilian national teams had been burdened with the memories of that legendary side, arguably the greatest team ever assembled.

Now the land of the samba has another litany of heroes to replace Pele, Gerson, Tostao and Rivelino. They can dance instead to the tune of Romario, Bebeto, Jorginho, Aldair and da Silva. For this was a modern Brazil. There was no throwing caution to the wind for Carlos Alberto's team. Brazil 1994-style could defend as well as attack.

They blazed their way to the final with only Holland giving them the merest of scares. Italy, their opponents, had slunk into the final. They were the worst of the third-place sides to qualify for the second round; they were seconds away from elimination by Nigeria and only poor refereeing let them off the hook against Spain.

The final, inevitably, was an anti-climax. Italy retreated into their shell for 120 minutes and, in the penalty shoot-out, Roberto Baggio blasted his kick over the bar. In the end justice was done.

For Fifa this had been a crunch World Cup. Not only had they taken the gamble of staging it in the United States, where there was no real football tradition, they had also decided to fundamentally overhaul the rules.

After the sterility of the 1990 World Cup in Italy something had to be done if football wanted to retain its global dominance as a spectator sport. The decline in the average number of goals in the tournament had gone hand-in-hand with an

Brazil showed that they could defend as well as attack

increase in drawn matches. In 1970 each game averaged exactly three goals. By 1990 it was down to 2.2.

Fifa's intention had been to make the game more open by tilting the balance away from defenders and in favour of attacking play. They introduced three points for a win in the first round, insisted on a liberal interpretation of the offside rule and banned the tackle from behind. By and large their revolution succeeded, with the average goals per game shooting up to 2.7. Apart from the final, only two other matches were 0-0 draws.

The principal beneficiaries were flair sides such as Brazil, who revelled in the freedom this gave their forwards. Sides like Jack Charlton's Republic of Ireland soon found their dogged, negative play was much more ineffective and never responded to the new rules.

They went out 2-0 to Holland in the second round, having qualified by winning one and drawing another of their first three matches. En route to their departure Charlton had managed to pick up a £10,000 fine and a touchline ban from Fifa for arguing with officials about a delayed substitution.

Still, at least they got there. All four Home nations failed to make the trip, the first time this had happened since they had first entered the World Cup in 1950. The surprise packages of the tournament were the former Communist countries, Romania and Bulgaria, who reached the quarter-finals and semi-finals respectively, and capitalist America, who were perfect hosts, bowing out 1-0 to Brazil in the second round.

FOR THE RECORD

SWIMMING
■ China's Zhong Weiyue, who broke two world records in two days, the 50m butterfly and the 100m butterfly, at the World Cup, was banned for two years, and her records expunged, after she failed a drugs test.

TENNIS
■ Conchita Martinez made it a fabulous year for her country when she beat Martina Navratilova 6-4 3-6 6-3 to become the first Spanish woman to win the Wimbledon singles title. A month earlier her compatriots, Arantxa Sanchez Vicario and Sergi Bruguera had won both singles' titles at the French Open. Then in September Sanchez Vicario put the icing on the cake with the US Open title, beating Steffi Graf despite having lost the first set 6-1.

■ Vitas Gerulaitis, the flamboyant American, died of carbon monoxide poisoning, aged 40.

World Cup tragedy

TWO terrible events cast a deep shadow over the glittering success of the World Cup. Andres Escobar, a member of the Colombian side, was gunned down when he returned to his country after they were knocked out. And Diego Maradona failed a drugs test and was expelled from the competition.

Colombia had been one of the pre-tournament favourites but when Escobar unluckily put through his own goal in the match against the United States they were left with no realistic chance of qualifying for the next round. Nine days later he was dead.

He was leaving a restaurant in Medellin with his fiancée when he was attacked by three men. One of them said: "Thanks for the own goal" and repeatedly shot Escobar in the chest and face. As each bullet struck home the assailants shouted: "Goal". At his funeral, 100,000 Colombians wept and demanded justice. A year later Humberto Munoz Castro was convicted and sentenced to 43 years in jail.

The Escobar tragedy came hard on the heels of Maradona's disgrace. The Argentinian claimed that he had only been taking a cold cure, but Fifa

Maradona: shamed again

rejected this defence stating that Maradona had tested positive for a cocktail of five banned drugs.

The Argentine FA immediately threw Maradona out of the tournament and Fifa banned him worldwide. Initially, Maradona claimed that he never took drugs and that he was a victim of a conspiracy. However, on reflection, he said he had "forgotten" to tell the team doctor he was taking medicine. "I was taking them like aspirin," he said. "Thousands of players do it, but the cost is always higher when it is Maradona."

The cost to his team was high. With Maradona gone they were beaten 3-2 by Romania and knocked out of the World Cup.

Lara: the man who wielded a golden bat

BRIAN LARA spent the year rewriting the record books. The West Indian batsman started by overhauling the record score in a Test, Sir Garry Sobers' 365 not out, by plundering England's hapless bowlers for 375 in Antigua in April.

Then, for good measure, Lara smashed Durham's bowlers to every corner of the ground, setting the highest first-class score ever, 501 not out, for Warwickshire at Edgbaston in June.

The match was heading for a draw when Lara went out to bat on the final morning on 111. Including Antigua, it was already his seventh century in eight innings, but there was no hint of the carnage to come. By the time the players went in for lunch Lara had already plundered another 174 runs.

Trevor Penney, almost a spectator while batting at the other end, said: "Durham were not bowling badly. Lara was frightening."

Lara had reminded his captain, Dermot Reeve, that the record was Hanif Mohammad's 499 and was promised that Warwickshire would not declare until he was out. Throughout the afternoon, Lara just marched on

— he reached 418 by tea.

For one instant Lara's chance of breaking the record was in jeopardy. He did not seem aware that play could finish at 5.30pm. His partner, Keith Piper, warned him that only two balls remained. Lara just leaned back, smashed the ball to the ropes and history was his. The 501 not out had been scored in 474 minutes from 427 balls, 62 of which went for fours and another 10 for sixes.

With batting like that, Warwickshire were almost unbeatable. They took the county championship by 42 points, beat Worcestershire in the B&H Cup final, were denied a grand slam by Worcestershire in the the NatWest Trophy final, and then collected their third trophy of the season in the Sunday League.

Lara: smash hit

Malcolm is the only shaft of light in England's gloom

WHILE Brian Lara was enjoying a wonderful year Mike Atherton was having a torrid time. He could have been excused for thinking things could not have got any worse when England, only needing 194 to beat West Indies in Trinidad, were shot out for 46, their second-lowest total ever.

Despite a victory in Barbados, things did, indeed, get much worse. South Africa were confirming their return from the wilderness by playing at Lord's, when television cameras twice caught Atherton reaching into his pocket and apparently doing something to the ball.

Peter Burge, the match referee held an investigation and announced that nothing untoward had occurred. But Atherton was not going to get off that lightly.

With ball-tampering hysteria raging once again, Atherton was forced to admit that he had been rather economical with the truth and had had dirt in his pocket, which he was using to dry the ball. Ray Illingworth hit him with a £2,000 fine but ignored the clamour to sack Atherton.

Almost unnoticed, England were hustled out for 99 in their second innings to lose by 356 runs. That they managed to level the series was entirely thanks to Devon Malcolm. Malcolm had felled Jonty Rhodes in the first innings, so it was hardly surprising he received the same treatment in return from Fanie de Villiers.

"You guys are going to pay for this," he said as he picked himself up. "You guys are history." So it was. South Africa were blown away by one of the most breathtaking displays ever seen from an England fast bowler. Malcolm took nine for 57 in 99 balls, the sixth-best Test performance of all time.

Graham: banned by the FA

Wave after wave of scandals

THREE stories threatened to rock the game to its very foundations. First, Bruce Grobbelaar, the Southampton goalkeeper, was accused of match-fixing. Second, Paul Merson, the Arsenal striker, confessed that he had been hooked on cocaine, was an alcoholic and was also addicted to gambling. And to cap it all, it was alleged that George Graham, the Arsenal manager, had personally received large sums of money from transfers involving Scandinavian players.

Grobbelaar had been secretly video-taped discussing with Chris Vincent, a former business partner and fellow soldier, how he had thrown matches for money. A newspaper alleged that a syndicate of Asian businessmen had paid the former Liverpool goalkeeper £40,000 to throw the match at Newcastle in 1993. It was also claimed that he had accepted £2,000 with more to come if he would throw a match later in the season. Grobbelaar vehemently denied the allegations and issued a writ for libel. The FA said they would charge him with bringing the game into disrepute but would wait until police had finished their inquiries.

Merson admitted that he had often spent up to £150 a night on cocaine, had run up gambling debts of £108,000 and had been drinking 14 pints of lager an evening. The FA and Arsenal heeded his pleas for mercy and the 26-year-old enrolled in a drink and drug rehabilitation clinic for six weeks.

Graham repaid Arsenal £425,000 plus interest, money that he had received from Rune Hauge, a Norwegian agent, in the course of the transfers of John Jensen and Pal Lydersen to Arsenal in 1991 and 1992. Graham claimed that he thought the money was an "unsolicited gift" and when he discovered that, it was not, he returned the money to his club. As a consequence Arsenal sacked him in February 1995. An FA commission subsequently banned Graham for 12 months.

Senna's fatal accident robs F1 of a genius

A DARK cloud hung over Formula One after the San Marino Grand Prix at Imola. Not only had the sport suddenly lost Roland Ratzenberger, who was killed in practice, it had also lost one of its greatest champions, Ayrton Senna, killed in the seventh lap of the race when he drove into a concrete barrier at 140mph.

The two deaths were a profound shock. Formula One believed that such tragedies were a thing of the past, indeed there had been no fatalities for 12 years. Two at one Grand Prix was unthinkable.

Senna's accident was also inexplicable. Had one of the most calculating drivers in history made an error? Was the car, or the Williams team, at fault? Or were the bumps at the Tamburello corner responsible? Was a fault in the steering column to blame? Nobody knew.

Controversy continued to dog Formula One. Michael Schumacher and Benetton, having won six of the first seven races,

Senna and Roland Ratzenberger were the first F1 drivers to be killed in 12 years

contrived to go into reverse. At Silverstone they ignored a black flag, Schumacher was disqualified and banned for two races. Then in Belgium Schumacher, having finished first, was disqualified because the skid-block on his car was too thin.

Damon Hill took full advantage of Schumacher's misfortune and whittled away the German's lead in the world championship. By the final race in Australia, Hill was only one point behind. For 36 laps the two battled it out, with Schumacher never more than a half second ahead.

Then the German struck a wall, virtually wrecking his car, and shunted back on to the track. As Hill moved to the left to overtake, Schumacher, knowing his race was over, blocked him. Hill then moved to the right and the German blocked him again. This time the cars collided and both men were out of the race. Schumacher was the world champion.

ATHLETICS

Glittering prizes tarnished by drug scandals

THE achievements of athletes were, once again, overshadowed by drug abuse. Colin Jackson appeared invincible, and Linford Christie and Sally Gunnell retained their Commonwealth titles, but the more indelible images were of Diane Modahl and Paul Edwards returning from Canada in disgrace.

Modahl tested positive for steroids while training in Portugal and was found to have 42 times the normal level of testosterone in her system. There was also something deeply ironic about Edwards testing positive after he had complained that other shot-putters were only winning medals because they had taken drugs.

Both athletes denied that they had done anything wrong, but when the result of Modahl's test was upheld it caused even more problems. The British women's team only qualified for the World Cup because of Modahl's victory in the European Cup. Because Modahl's case was still pending, they competed anyway, but all their performances were later expunged from the record books. Modahl continued to deny the accusations and in July 1995 her appeal to the British Amateur Athletic Board was upheld on the grounds that her sample had been incorrectly stored. Ultimately, the International Amateur Athletic Federation will decide her fate.

Solomon Wariso also received a ban after testing positive. And Horace Dove-Edwin was a short-lived hero for "winning" Sierra Leone's first medal at the Games. He finished second but was stripped of his medal after failing a test.

China was also dogged by controversy. Nobody could understand how the country's athletes had made such great advances in such a short period

Jun Xia: Chinese whispers

of time, and the finger of suspicion was pointed at the unorthodox training methods employed by "Ma's Army".

The Chinese regarded this a gross slur on their reputation, but when Ma fell foul of his own athletes (for being too strict) and his governing body (for being too unconventional), and Chinese competitors disgraced themselves in drug tests at the Asian Games there was a queue of people waiting to say: "We told you so."

Everybody wanted to live in glass houses and throw stones at the same time. An indication of how far the sport had sunk was soon to come: in 1995 the International Amateur Athletic Federation announced that a 14-year-old South African girl had failed a test, the youngest ever athlete to test positive.

Liza de Villiers was given a four year ban after she was caught using an anabolic steroid and a stimulant during her country's junior championships.

BOXING

Over 40 and over the hill?

GEORGE FOREMAN definitely had the last laugh. He had come out of retirement after 10 years' inactivity and, at the age of 45, was once again fighting for the world heavyweight title. His opponent, Michael Moorer, was 18 years younger and had taken the WBA and IBF titles from Evander Holyfield. Almost without exception, boxing pundits thought the contest was a farce.

With only six minutes and 57 seconds of the fight remaining they seemed to be right. Moorer had built up an unassailable lead and was able to hit Foreman at will. Then Moorer got careless. He stepped back from an attack and left Foreman an opening. The veteran caught the champion with a left and promptly followed up with a short right. It was enough. Moorer was counted out and Foreman had become the oldest man to be the world heavyweight champion.

Two months earlier, in September, the WBC version of the title also surprisingly changed hands. Lennox Lewis, who had successfully defended his title three times, also got careless against the 4-1 outsider Oliver McCall. Lewis, perhaps through over-confidence, simply dropped his hands 30 seconds into the second round and the challenger took full advantage, beating the British fighter.

Foreman: the daddy of boxing regained the title

FOR THE RECORD

BASEBALL
■ Major League players went on an indefinite strike over salary capping on August 12. Both the team owners and the players stubbornly refused to compromise and, for the first time since it started in 1904, the World Series was cancelled. The case against team owners went to court, with the players seeking an injunction.

BOXING
■ Jack Sharkey, oldest of the world heavyweight champions, died at the age of 91. Born Joseph Paul Zukauskar, Sharkey won his first title in 1930, defeating Max Schmeling.

CRICKET
■ Peter May, the former England captain and the chairman of selectors from 1982 to 1988, died at the age of 64.

FOOTBALL
■ Billy Wright, the former Wolves and England centre-half and captain who won 105 international caps, died aged 70 in north London.

RACING
■ Four days after jump jockey Declan Murphy survived a kick in the helmet at Haydock, Steve Wood was killed by a kick in the chest in a race at Lingfield. It was the first flat-race fatality since 1981.

Ayrton Senna

A celestial talent who was a demon on the track

Chris Nawrat

When Ayrton Senna's body was being laid to rest in the Morumbi cemetery in Sao Paulo the Brazilian airforce flew over the cemetery and drew a huge S and a heart in the sky. A million Brazilians lined the streets of the city. To Brazil, Senna was a demi-god, and now he was gone, killed in the San Marino Grand Prix on May 1, 1994. He was 34. In a country where the official religion is football, Senna had captured their hearts in a way that no other athlete had done since Pele.

Hyperbole is the stock in trade of sports writing as superlatives are bandied around on a daily basis. But if ever the words 'tragedy' and 'genius' were appropriate then the death of Senna merited both. Whether Senna was actually a better driver than Juan Fangio or Jackie Stewart is irrelevant. A debate over the accolade of 'the greatest driver in Formula One' would be otiose. Senna was a genius and, in the late 1980s and early 1990s, utterly dominated his sport. He was the driver to beat, the one by which all other drivers measured themselves.

Ayrton Senna da Silva was born in Sao Paulo on March 31, 1960, to wealthy parents. His destiny was shaped at the age of four when his millionaire father, Milton, encouraged him to take up kart racing. The young Senna was a professional kart racer at 13 and South American kart champion at the age of 17. In 1981 he abandoned his university studies to ply his trade in Europe and was an immediate success in Formula Ford races.

Senna's climb to Formula One was meteoric as he negotiated his way through the lesser Formulas. His first season for Toleman in F1 in 1984 saw Senna finish second in Monaco, third in the Portuguese Grand Prix and ninth in the world championship. But already the two different sides of Senna had begun to emerge. On the one hand, a total confidence in his own ability, almost as if he thought himself invincible and, on the other, a brooding quietness. "He was so shy when he came to Britain," recalled Denis Rushden, who owned the Formula Ford team for which Senna raced in 1981. "He was always the guy you found standing quietly in the kitchen at parties."

Senna's obsessive determination to become world champion manifested itself when he announced in mid-season that he intended to abandon Toleman for Lotus. Senna wanted to drive the better car; team loyalty was not in his make-up. A furious team manager immediately suspended him for the Italian Grand Prix.

And, in his way, Senna was right. It was in a Lotus that he secured his first Grand Prix victory, in Portugal in 1985. His second followed shortly afterwards in Belgium. During his three years at Lotus, Senna won a total of six Grand Prix, two a season, and, in the world championship, the Brazilian finished fourth twice, and third once. He had also developed a reputation as a consummate professional.

Unlike many drivers, Senna was utterly absorbed by the inner workings of his car. He would spend hours locked in deep conversation with the mechanics and his pin-point analysis of how the car performed, and why, was uncanny. With Senna as your driver you didn't need telemetry. This deep knowledge was translated to his driving. Senna was more than fast, he was electrifyingly fast, and right from the green light. But his speed was not manic, his control of the car was frighteningly awesome. Many thought his imperious, self-obsessed driving was manic. Woe betide you if you caught sight of Senna's car in your mirrors and didn't make way for him. Senna soon became the most feared and resented driver in Formula One. His intense privateness added to the

demonology. In a very real sense, Senna lived in a world of his own, not only as a person but as a world-beating driver.

The flowering of Senna's career came with his move to McLaren-Honda in 1988. Together with his team-mate Alain Prost, then regarded as the best driver in the world, they simply blew away the opposition, winning 15 of the 16 Grand Prix. Senna's eight victories gave him the edge over Prost's seven, and his first world championship by the slim margin of three points. The explosive competitiveness of the two superstars also generated one of the most bitter feuds ever seen in the world of sport.

Temperamentally the team wasn't big enough for the two of them, and there could only be one world champion. It is likely that Senna started the bad blood in the 1988 Portuguese grand prix. Both drivers were racing wheel to wheel down the long straight in Estoril when the Brazilian deliberately swerved at the Frenchman. Prost went on to win the race.

The rift deepened at Imola in the 1989 season. Because both drivers were theoretically equal 'No 1s' it was agreed that whichever of them got to the first corner before the other would not be challenged by his team-mate. Senna breached that deal at Imola and won the race. Although Senna was forced to apologise to Prost the two drivers did not speak to each other for the rest of the season. This time Prost won the world championship, with Senna second.

Ron Dennis, the head of McLaren, found himself powerless to quell their feuding. "The fundamental requirement of being the best in the world," he once explained, "is that you believe yourself to be the best. When you have two people believing they're the best, you have a time bomb ticking away."

Their rivalry continued the following season, although now Prost, thoroughly fed up with his so-called team-mate, had jumped ship to Ferrari. "I appreciate honesty," Prost said, "Ayrton is not honest." And, as Dennis predicted, the time bomb did go off. In the penultimate Grand Prix of the season, at Suzaka, the arithmetic was simple. Prost had to win, or at least finish ahead of Senna to keep his championship hopes alive for the final Grand Prix. Despite being second on the grid, behind Senna, the Frenchman just got to the first corner before Senna's McLaren. So the Brazilian simply drove into him and pushed Prost's Ferrari off the track. The race was over for both of them, as was the 1990 title race. Senna had won his second championship.

Despite all the photographic and television evidence, Senna adamantly denied he had done it deliberately. Prost saw things differently. "What he did was more than unsporting," he said, "it was disgusting. With Ayrton, racing isn't a sport, it's war." A year later when Senna clinched his third world championship at the same track, he finally admitted that he had done it purposefully and apologised.

Over the next two seasons the Williams-Renault car displaced the McLaren as the dominant Formula One car and Senna could only manage fourth in the 1992 world championship and second in 1993 to Prost, now driving for Williams. Following his victory the Frenchman retired, opening the door for Senna to switch to the Williams, pursuing what he always wanted: the best car. Senna's final race for McLaren saw him take his Grand Prix victories to 41, second only to Prost.

Senna was relishing the challenge of driving for Williams in 1994 but was fearful of the potentially dangerous effects of the modifications imposed on the sport by FIA, Formula One's governing body. It was thought that the ever-increasing use of high-tech in F1 was becoming too big an advantage to the richer teams, so they banned them. "It's a great error to remove the electronics from the cars," he said. "The cars are very fast and difficult to drive. It is going to be a season of accidents. We'll be really lucky if something really serious doesn't happen."

Sadly, Imola fulfilled his prediction. On the day before the Brazilian's fatal accident, Roland Ratzenberger, an Austrian in his first F1 season, lost control of his car in a qualifying lap, flew off the track and was killed. It was the first death in F1 in 12 years. The incident deeply affected Senna. That evening he walked alone to the scene of the accident and gazed into the sky, barely able to hold back the tears.

When the race began the next day, there was a crash at the start and the first five laps were raced under the caution flag. When the caution flag was lifted Senna and Michael Schumacher, who had won the first two Grand Prix of the season, roared away. Then, on the seventh lap, accelerating into the Tamburello curve at 180mph, Senna lost control of his car and crashed virtually head-on into a concrete wall. He was pronounced dead of massive head injuries four hours later.

An Italian court is still investigating what caused the accident and is hearing manslaughter charges against six Formula One officials. The prosecutors believe that Senna's steering column broke because of defective welds. Others believe that it was a bumpy track that caused Senna to lose control.

Niki Lauda, who almost died in an accident in 1976, has a different explanation. "If we start believing that motor racing is not dangerous, then we are all stupid," he said. "It's almost as though God has held his hand over Formula One. At Imola, he took it away." As a devout Christian, and inveterate Bible-reader, Senna would probably have appreciated that. And he definitely would have liked Lauda's estimation of him: "Ayrton Senna was the best driver who ever lived."

Chequered career: Senna enjoyed a meteoric rise on the track from the age of 13 until his death at 34

Gough: fighting spirit

CRICKET

Gough fails to save Fletcher

KEITH FLETCHER paid the price for another England failure when he lost his job as team manager after Australia retained the Ashes 3-1.

With the exception of Darren Gough's spirited batting and bowling (until he had to return home injured) there was precious little for England to cheer about. There just seemed to be an endless succession of batting collapses, slapdash fielding and injuries, plus the ignominy of losing to the youngsters of the Australian Cricket Academy.

The only bright spot came in the fourth Test when, for once, it was Australia's turn to collapse. They subsided to 156 all out in their second innings to give England victory by 106 runs. Any hopes that England could square the series were soon dashed in Perth when they fell apart yet again.

The tour marked the end of the international careers of Mike Gatting and Graham Gooch, who overtook David Gower as England's most capped player. But attention was soon diverted from the record books by a scandal potentially even greater than ball-tampering.

Several Australian players admitted that they had been offered bribes, in some cases as large as £500,000, to throw Test matches. The middle-man was alleged to be the Pakistan captain Salim Malik. Salim denied the claims, but was sacked by Pakistan, whose players were made to swear on the Koran that they were not involved.

Aamir Sohail, another member of the Pakistan team, was claimed to have said: "If I wasn't bound by a code of conduct I could name so many players who have been bribed." Further confirmation came from a former Pakistan player, Qasim Omar, who said that corruption was rife in his country. Qasim alleged that dozens of players, and even some umpires, were in the pay of illegal syndicates.

FOOTBALL

Cantona's mad moment

THE scandals that had rocked the game at the end of 1994 just seemed to be never ending. The first shock came when Eric Cantona decided to take the law into his own hands at Selhurst Park in January.

As Cantona trudged along the touchline after being sent off, Matthew Simmons, a so-called Palace fan, leapt from his seat and allegedly hurled obscenities at the United player. Cantona's reaction was swift. He launched a kung-fu assault on Simmons. Paul Ince also was involved in the general melee.

Cantona was prosecuted for his offence and initially was given a two-week jail sentence. On appeal this was reduced to 120 hours' community service. Manchester United banned him for the rest of the season and fined him two weeks' wages. The FA increased the fine and extended the ban until October 1.

Kung-fu fighting: Cantona kicks out at an abusive fan

And then floodgates opened. In February Chelsea fans invaded Stamford Bridge after they had lost to Millwall; England's "friendly" against Ireland was abandoned because of rioting English fans and Belgian police deported more than 800 Chelsea fans before, and after, their European Cup Winners Cup match against Bruges.

In March, Crystal Palace's Chris Armstrong was tested positive for cannabis; the Chelsea captain Dennis Wise was sentenced to three month's imprisonment for assaulting a taxi driver and Bruce Grobbelaar,

Justin Fashanu and Hans Segers were arrested by police investigating alleged match-fixing.

And in April the Cantona affair returned when Paul Nixon, a 35-year-old Palace fan, was crushed to death by a coach before their FA Cup semi-final against Manchester United when the two sets of fans fought in a pub car park. To compound matters, in the replay four days later, Manchester United's Roy Keane was sent off for stamping on Gareth Southgate. This was after both managers had pleaded for peace in football before the kick-off.

RUGBY LEAGUE

Murdoch's takeover

RUPERT MURDOCH started a revolution in rugby league as divisive as the upheaval that had led to the split between professional and amateur rugby teams exactly a century ago.

His attempt to wrest control of the Australian game turned English clubs against each other as they scrambled to cash in on the TV mogul's money.

The prospect of a £75m 14-team European Super League to run in parallel with Murdoch's newly-announced Australian operation led members of the Rugby Football League to all but vote themselves out of existence.

But fans wanted no part of the mergers and Keighley, the Second Division champions, started court action because they had been denied promotion to the top flight. The RFL was forced to reshape its plans — a 12-team League without any enforced mergers — but the arguments dragged on until the new Leagues kicked off.

Mandela and Springboks unite to stun the world

PLAYING in the World Cup for the first time, South Africa, the hosts, celebrated by beating New Zealand, the clear favourites, 15–12 in extra time of the final. A drop goal by Joel Stransky eight minutes from time sent the rainbow nation of 43 million, and President Nelson Mandela, into joyous hysterics.

Hardly anybody thought the Springboks, who scraped past France in the semi-final, had much of a chance against the all-conquering All Blacks. New Zealand were undoubtedly the team of the tournament and in Jonah Lomu they possessed the man of the tournament. The 20-year-old winger was 6ft 5in, 18st 7lb, and ran the 100m in 10.8sec. His opponents described him as unstoppable, and until the final they were proved right.

Lomu had destroyed England in the semi-final with four tries, the first in the third minute, as the European champions were humiliated 45–29. It was a disappointing end to England's campaign which had promised so much when a Rob Andrew drop goal in injury time eliminated Australia, the defending champions.

England had done well to progress so far after Will Carling had been sacked as captain before the tournament. Carling had inadvertently been caught on television calling the RFU "57 old farts". However, player power forced the RFU to back down and Carling was reinstated.

The All Blacks' style of play — a wide open, passing game — was hailed as the future and labelled Total Rugby. But just as

The rainbow nation was rewarded with the ultimate prize

Holland discovered in two football World Cups in the 1970s there is always the final hurdle to overcome.

Southern hemisphere nations easily dominated the tournament with Wales failing to qualify from their pool and Ireland

and Scotland going out in the quarter-finals. It was little wonder that Rupert Murdoch paid £340m for the television rights for international and provincial tournaments between Australia, New Zealand and South Africa.

FOR THE RECORD

BASEBALL
■ The eight-month dispute ended when the players were granted an injunction against the owners for unfair labour practices.

BOXING
■ Chris Eubank, in his 15th defence of his WBO super-middleweight crown, was comprehensively beaten by the Irishman Steve Collins on points in County Cork. It was Eubank's first defeat in a 10-year career.

■ Mike Tyson was released on parole after serving exactly three years of his six-year jail sentence for rape.

■ Herbie Hide, in his first defence of his WBO world heavyweight title, was knocked out in the sixth round by Riddick Bowe in Las Vegas. It was the ninth time Hide had hit the canvas.

CRICKET
■ Australia became the first country to win a Test series in the West Indies in 22 years. The last time West Indies had lost a series anywhere in the world was in New Zealand in 1980.

■ Tony Lock, the slow left-arm bowler who, with off-spinner Jim Laker, led Surrey to seven successive county championships in 1952-58, died aged 65 in Perth, Australia.

FOOTBALL
■ Arsenal's attempt to become the first side to retain the European Cup Winners Cup foundered when, with only seconds remaining in extra time, Nayim scored a spectacular 50-yard goal to give Real Zaragoza a 2-1 victory.

■ Manchester United's disappointing season continued when they lost to Everton 1-0 in the Cup final. The 30th minute Graham Stuart's shot rebounded from the crossbar leaving Peter Schmeichel stranded. Paul Rideout nodded the ball past him.

■ Liverpool beat Bolton 2-1 to win the League Cup, their first trophy since 1992.

RACING
■ Harayir won the 1,000 Guineas, the first Classic to be held on a Sunday.

■ The 24-year-old jockey, Jason Titley, riding in his first Grand National, confidently brought home the 40-1 outsider Royal Athlete to give trainer Jenny Pitman her second victory.

RUGBY LEAGUE
■ Wigan strolled to their eighth consecutive Challenge Cup and for good measure also won their sixth — and last — successive championship.

RUGBY UNION
■ England won their third Grand Slam in five seasons when Rob Andrew kicked all of their 24 points to defeat Scotland. Scotland were also previously unbeaten, but 12 from the boots of Gavin Hastings and Craig Chalmers were not enough.

■ Leicester broke Bath's stranglehold on the League championship to win the title for the second time.

SNOOKER
■ Peter Francisco was banned for five years for "not conducting himself in a manner consistent with his status" but cleared of allegations of match-fixing after he lost 10-2 to Jimmy White in the World championship.

■ Stephen Hendry became only the third player to record a maximum 147 in the world championships at the Crucible. The feat earned him £147,000.

TENNIS
■ Fred Perry, Britain's last Wimbledon men's singles champion, died.

■ Andre Agassi won the Australian Open at his first attempt when he beat Pete Sampras in the final at Melbourne 4-6 6-1 7-6 6-4.

■ Britain lost 5-0 to Slovakia in the Davis Cup.

Classic contest end in tragedy

IT WAS a tragic end to a classic, brutal contest. Gerald McClellan, the 27-year old American challenger, had to receive emergency surgery for a blood clot on his brain after he was knocked out by Nigel Benn in the 10th round of their WBC super middleweight world title fight.

McClellan, who was noted for his furious punching and fast finishes, seemed to have won the fight in the first few seconds when he sent the title-holder crashing through the ropes. Somehow Benn miraculously used the minute's rest between rounds to launch his own onslaught in the second.

McClellan thought he was going in for the kill; instead the hunted became the hunter. As the fight progressed both men were stretching their endurance to the absolute limit. In the 10th McClellan caved in.

Europe win Ryder Cup

EUROPE regained the Ryder Cup for the first time since 1989 when the American team blew a final-day lead by not being able to make important shots under pressure.

Europe were given little chance of winning in America because their big names were not in the best of form and the rest of the team were regarded as little more than run of the mill players. And the Americans had set up the Oak Hill course to suit their players' style of play – narrow fairways, thick rough and lightning fast greens.

The first day went all America's way. They built a 5-3 lead in the rain, largely because Nick Faldo and Colin Montgomerie lost twice. Europe produced a rally on the second morning, sparked by Costantino Rocca's hole in one at the sixth, only the third ace in the history of the Ryder Cup. But from 6-6 at lunch the Americans pulled away again. When Corey Pavin chipped into the final hole from off the green in the last match of the day, America had won three of four matches in the afternoon session for a 9-7 lead.

Even though, in recent times, no European team had come from behind on the final day to win, Bernard Gallacher, Europe's captain, remained confident: "We're still going to win," he said that night.

As the tension rose on Sunday, America had more than enough chances to make sure they retained the Ryder Cup. But, one by one, they were wasted. The turning point was the match between Nick Faldo and Curtis Strange, an unexpected and widely criticised choice for one of the wild-card places on the American team. Both men sensed that theirs would be the key match. Strange was not putting well and his driving was erratic. Even so, Faldo said he thought that the contest would be close.

A birdie at the 11th hole gave Strange a one-stroke lead. But on the final three holes he went to pieces. Strange's drive at the 16th disappeared into the long rough. His drive at the 17th was almost as wayward. Then, on the final hole, he missed a putt from seven feet. Faldo steadied himself and sunk his four-footer. Strange's inability to make par on any of the final three holes had handed victory to Faldo, levelled the two teams' scores and gave Europe an enormous lift.

Everything now rested on the match between Jay Haas and Philip Walton. The Irishman, leading by one stroke, missed a four-foot putt for par on the 17th hole that would have decided everything. He put the mistake, virtually his only poor shot of the day, out of his mind.

On the final hole Haas cracked. He drove into the trees and was still six feet from the hole after playing five shots. Walton settled over his 15-foot putt knowing that he had two strokes to win. He rolled the ball to within inches of the hole, Haas conceded and Walton was mobbed by his team-mates.

Europe had won 14–13 and Gallacher, captaining the European team for the final time, said: "I can't tell you what this means to me. It's just... I can't..." and he burst into tears of joy.

Gallacher: never doubted that his team could pull off the impossible

Incredible Edwards

THE unfashionable discipline of triple-jumping was thrust into the limelight by two almost unbelievable leaps in late June.

Willie Banks, who had held the world record of 17.97m for 10 years, was incredulous when told that Jonathan Edwards had jumped 18.39m and 18.43m in the European Cup. "Who the hell is this guy? I've never even heard of him."

"This guy" was a 29-year-old vicar's son who had barely taken up athletics when Banks set his record. Edwards's jumps were wind-assisted, so did not count for the world record, but were still far longer than anybody had thought possible.

"The fact that I did it twice makes me think it wasn't a fluke," Edwards said. "But I'm still nonplussed." It most certainly was not a fluke. Within weeks he had broken Banks's record, by one centimetre.

Then he broke his own record twice on the way to winning the gold medal at the World championships in Gothenburg in August. With his first jump in the finals he became the first man to break 18m, raising the record to 18.16m. Then with his second jump he extended the record even further, to 18.29m – more than 60ft.

Edwards modestly said: "I'm still not quite able to come to terms with what I've achieved. I keep thinking it's someone else out there. But I don't want to think I'm now the best thing since sliced bread. After all, it's only jumping into a sand pit. I just don't know why it has all happened. I've tried to analyse it, but all the little things do not add up to the sum total."

In the women's long jump Fiona May won the long jump gold medal, but for Italy. May had competed for Britain, but she gave up because of lack of money and support. She married an Italian and moved abroad and, with better backing from her new home country, her performances were revitalised.

As Edwards's career was taking off, Linford Christie's was drawing to a close. In June, Christie, in an emotional outburst on television, complained that he did not get the respect he deserved and that he was not going to defend his Olympic title.

He had a bad World championship, pulling a hamstring in the semi-finals and only deciding to run in the final at the last moment. There was no way to overcome the injury and he collapsed after finishing sixth behind the winner, Donovan Bailey.

Edwards: broke his own record

Atherton's stand the only saving grace

ENGLAND set out for their winter tour of South Africa in high spirits after a six-Test series with the West Indies finished all square, with two wins each and two draws. But all the good work of the summer was soon undone.

The high spot of the summer was the way England twice bounced back after falling behind in the series. Dominic Cork emerged as a genuine all-rounder in the fourth Test, with an unbeaten 50 and a hat-trick as England won by six wickets.

The low spot on the field was the pitch at Edgbaston, where England lost by an innings and 64 after being shot out for 147 and 89, their third-lowest total of all time against West Indies.

The low spot off the field was an odious article written for Wisden Cricket Monthly, which questioned non-white cricketers' commitment to playing for England. Mike Atherton resigned from the magazine's editorial board in disgust.

England's morale was high when they arrived in South Africa. Then, in October, they ran into Paul Adams. In only his third first-class match, the teenage spinner, whose unconventional action was memorably described as being like watching a frog in a blender, spun South Africa A to a six-wicket victory, taking nine wickets in the match. From that point on, England went downhill fast.

The second Test was only saved by a piece of heroic batting by Mike Atherton and Jack Russell. Batting last, England needed an impossible 479 and the only question was how

Cork: burst on to Test scene with a hat-trick

quickly South Africa were going to win as England slipped to 75 for two and 145 for four.

Atherton had other ideas, though. He batted for 165 overs and nearly 11 hours to score a painstaking and chanceless 185 not out. Russell gave his captain sterling support for nearly five hours, nudging his way to an unbeaten 29.

By the time England were bowled out for 153 and 157 to lose the last Test and the series they were a team in disarray. And when Devon Malcolm complained about the way he was being treated by the Eng-

land selectors, saying: "I have to ask would this have happened if I had been a white bowler?" the question of racism reared its ugly head again.

England's batting, which had looked so promising against the West Indies, suddenly looked totally inept. England lost six of the seven one-day internationals they played against South Africa, including five defeats in a row. It was hardly the best of preparation for the forthcoming World Cup.

Bruno on top of world

AFTER three dismal attempts to capture boxing's most glittering prize, Frank Bruno finally arrived at the summit when he outpointed Oliver McCall at Wembley to become the WBC heavyweight champion of the world. It was a brave and battling performance from the man who had been easily demolished by Tim Witherspoon, Mike Tyson and Lennox Lewis in his earlier attempts to take the crown.

McCall, who snatched the title from Lewis a year earlier, turned out to be not the boxer his admirers thought he was. Indeed a crashing right from Bruno in the first round could have ended the contest there and then as the champion wobbled towards the ropes. However, Bruno stuck to his game plan: hide behind his jab and grab the points. Forget the glory, take the win.

Having easily won the first three rounds, Bruno was deter-

mined not to be out-witted in the battle for points. McCall surged in the middle rounds but, by the twelfth and final round, it was clear that he was miles behind. McCall came out for the finale ready for a bloodbath. The champion barely touched gloves before tearing into a tiring challenger.

To Bruno's immense credit, he withstood the barrage and collected a unanimous points decision. After the fight Bruno broke down in tears. "Thank God I won. I'm elated — on top of the world. All my dreams have come true."

The next stop for Bruno was a lucrative re-match with former champion Mike Tyson. Iron Mike was out of prison and on the comeback trail. He wanted his titles back and he looked hungry again.

Bruno: title at the fourth attempt

The glittering prize: Dalglish and Sherwood enjoy the moment

FOOTBALL

Walker bankrolls Rovers' return

JACK WALKER was a long-suffering Blackburn Rovers fan who had watched as his team fell on hard times. But Walker was a fan with a difference. He had picked up £365m from the sale of his steel works. So he did what every true blue fan would do, he used his fortune to revive the love of his life, and, in 1995, his wildest dream came true. Rovers won the League championship for the first time since 1914.

Walker laid the foundation for this remarkable achievement by recruiting Kenny Dalglish as Blackburn's manager in 1991. Dalglish promptly achieved promotion from the Second Division. Then the pair set about some serious shopping. Some £30m was spent on players and the British transfer record was shattered twice – Alan Shearer at £3.6m and Chris Sutton for £5.5m. The investment paid off, Shearer scored 37 goals and Sutton 21 in their title-winning season.

Not that Rovers looked like championship material at the start of the season with only eight points from their first four games. Then they moved into overdrive and the League developed into a two-horse race with United chasing their third successive title. The race went to the wire.

On the final day of the season Manchester United had to win at Upton Park and Blackburn had to lose at Anfield for United to snatch the title. Liverpool duly beat Blackburn with a goal in the final seconds, but a stubborn West Ham held out for a 1-1 draw. Blackburn were champions by a single point. Walker's impossible dream had come true.

RACING

Piggott calls a halt

LESTER PIGGOTT finally announced his retirement from race riding in September at the grand old age of 59.

In the end, it was not age that drove him to hang up his whip. The jockey who was famous for being able to survive on fresh air and a large cigar admitted that he was losing the battle to keep his weight down.

Piggott, who had not ridden in a race for months said: "I will miss riding. It is what I have done all my life, but you can't go on for ever."

He rode more than 5,000 winners in a 47-year career, including nine triumphs in the Derby and a record 30 victories in Classic races. He retired once before, in 1985, but made a comeback in 1990 after being sent to jail for tax evasion. Within days, he won the Breeders' Cup Mile and he won his final Classic, the 2,000 Guineas, at the age of 56.

Vincent O'Brien, the legendary trainer whose stable provided many of Piggott's winners, spoke for the entire racing community when he was told of Piggott's decision. "I have no doubt Lester was the greatest," he said.

TENNIS

A Tarango fandango

WIMBLEDON had not seen anything like it since the days of John McEnroe. What started as a minor spat between a player and umpire erupted into a full-scale punch-up.

Jeff Tarango, whose only previous claim to fame was being fined for dropping his shorts during a match in Japan, argued with the umpire when one of his serves was called out. The incident appeared to be no more than a short-lived minor dispute, and the journeyman American prepared to play the next point.

But as Tarango walked back to his side of the court he was jeered by the crowd. The American lost his temper. "Shut up," he snapped at the spectators.

The umpire, Bruno Rebeuh, warned Tarango that he had violated the players' code of conduct. "How come they can say what they want and I can't? Tarango shouted at the umpire. "I want the supervisor."

When a supervisor arrived at Court 13, Tarango was still shouting at Rebeuh. When he was docked a point for verbal abuse his rage boiled over. "You are the most corrupt official," Tarango bellowed before marching off the court in a huff.

That was far from the end of the matter. As Rebeuh left the court, Tarango's wife joined the fray. The volatile Frenchwoman marched up to the umpire and attacked him, slapping him round the face.

Even more amazingly, at a rambling post-match press conference, Tarango claimed Rebeuh was biased in favour of certain players. He said that he had complained to the authorities in the past and had been promised that Rebeuh would never take charge of one of his matches.

Tarango was thrown out of the tournament, fined heavily and banned from playing at Wimbledon the following year. Months later, he apologised to Rebeuh, saying: "I unequivocally apologise to Mr Bruno Rebeuh for any embarrassment or harm that this incident may have caused him and his family. I do not intend to make such a mistake ever again."

Bosman destroys transfer market

A LEGAL dispute between an obscure Belgian footballer and his club was finally resolved by the European Court of Justice and turned the European transfer market upside down. When Jean-Marc Bosman's contract with RFC Liege expired in 1990, the Belgian club offered him a new deal but with a 60% wage cut. Bosman said he would rather move to Dunkerque. Liege demanded a transfer fee of more than £250,000 twice what the French club were prepared to pay.

Effectively this left Bosman unable to play professional football so he took legal action citing restraint of trade. The case was fought all the way to European Court of Justice, who found for Bosman and also announced that the current transfer system was a breach of the free movement of labour between countries. The court also declared that the limit on the number of European Union players a team could field was also unlawful.

The verdict meant that once a player's contract had expired he was able to move to any club in the EU without a transfer fee. Smaller clubs were horrified at the prospect as their very existence depends on selling on players to richer clubs. Others predicted a flood of foreign imports into the British game.

Bosman: permanently changed the labour relations of world football

FOR THE RECORD

ATHLETICS

■ The IAAF were accused of rigging the vote for the 1994 Athlete of the Year to make sure that Jackie Joyner-Kersee beat Sally Gunnell.

BOXING

■ Prince Naseem Hamed stopped Steve Robinson in the eighth round to win the WBO featherweight title in September.

■ James Murray died in hospital the day after his fight with Drew Docherty. While medical staff were trying to help Murray in the ring, drunken spectators brawled in the venue in Glasgow.

■ Steve Collins confirmed his domination of Chris Eubank when he won their rematch in Cork in September on a split decision. A month later Eubank announced his retirement.

BASEBALL

■ Cal Ripken of the Baltimore Orioles broke Lou Gehrig's record of playing 2,130 games.

CRICKET

■ Warwickshire won 14 of their matches as they retained the County championship.

■ Harold Larwood, the former England fast bowler, died in Australia in July, aged 90.

CYCLING

■ Fabio Casartelli, an Italian riding for the Motorola team, was killed in a high-speed crash while descending a mountain during the 15th stage of the Tour de France.

■ No sooner had Chris Boardman started the Tour de France than he crashed out of it. He skidded on a wet bend at the start of the prologue and fell, breaking his wrist and ankle.

FOOTBALL

■ Eric Cantona scored Manchester United's second goal in the 2-2 draw with Liverpool in his first game after serving his eight-month suspension.

■ Jack Charlton resigned as the Republic of Ireland's manager after his team lost a play-off with Holland for the final place at Euro 96.

■ Duncan Ferguson lost his appeal against a conviction for headbutting an opponent and was jailed for three months.

■ Daley Thompson was one of Mansfield's substitutes for their league match against Cardiff.

■ Crowmarsh boys team were all shown the red card in October for singing rude songs about the referee.

GOLF

■ John Daly went some way to putting his wild past behind him when he won the Open at St Andrews.

MOTOR RACING

■ Ferrari announced in August that they had signed Michael Schumacher to a £30m two-year contract. Schumacher retained his driver's title when he won the Pacific GP in October, and secured the constructors' championship for Benetton when he won the Japanese GP a week later.

■ Juan Manuel Fangio, who won the world championship four times in the 1950s, died in July, aged 84.

RACING

■ Sheikh Mohammed withdrew all his horses from Henry Cecil's yard in October after a dispute about the fitness of Mark of Esteem.

■ Six jockeys were suspended in November for taking the wrong route in a race at Taunton.

■ The Aga Khan renewed his involvement with British racing when he said he would send horses to be trained by Luca Cumani.

RUGBY LEAGUE

■ Australia beat England 16-8 to win the centenary World Cup at Wembley.

RUGBY UNION

■ The move to professionalism was hastened by Kerry Packer's abortive attempt to take over the game by signing leading players to his World Rugby Corporation.

TENNIS

■ Monica Seles played for the first time since being stabbed by a fan in 1993 when she beat Martina Navratilova in an exhibition match in Atlantic City in July.

Seles: perfect return. The Czech was immediately installed as joint No 1

JANUARY

1996

AUGUST

Steven Redgrave (above) won an historic fourth gold medal but (below) angrily Linford Christie refused to accept his disqualification after two false starts in the 100m final

The Games that pleased nobody

THERE WAS not a great deal for Great Britain to celebrate at the Olympic Games. A return of just one gold medal (even Kazakhstan managed three) started a chorus of "why are we so bad at everything?"

The answer – Britain is woefully behind the rest of the world when it comes to investing in first-class sporting facilities – has been obvious for years, but that did not make it any more palatable. Just how bad things had become was illustrated by two members of Britain's diving team, who were spotted trying to sell their official kit on a street corner in Atlanta. "We are skint," Robin Morgan said. "We're desperate for money and we are selling our gear to have a night out."

There wasn't a great deal for the Atlanta organising committee to cheer about either. A bomb exploded in a city centre park, transport between the venues was chaotic, and American television coverage was so jingoistic that if an American wasn't taking part in an event then it might as well not have existed. Pointedly, Juan Antonio Samaranch, the president of the International Olympic Committee, failed to give the customary praise of the Games as the best event ever in his speech at the closing ceremony.

Britain's solitary gold medal was won by Steven Redgrave and Matthew Pinsent in the coxless pairs. After an historic fourth successive Olympic triumph Redgrave announced his retirement, saying: "If anyone sees me near a boat again they can shoot me." But Redgrave has always been a driven man, and within a year he was back on the river again, with the next Games in his sights.

There was no stopping the other grand old man of the Olympics – Carl Lewis – either. Age may have dulled his ability as a sprinter but he can still jump, as he proved by winning the long jump gold for the fourth time.

Jonathan Edwards, after his stupendous series of jumps in the preceding year, was widely expected to win a gold medal in the triple jump. But, for once, he was plagued by foul jumps and could only finish second to Kenny Harrison of the United States. One of the few bright spots of the Games was the sporting way that Edwards accepted defeat and congratulated Harrison on breaking the Olympic record, proving that the Olympian ideal is not entirely lost.

In contrast, Linford Christie's exit from the 100m was far less gracious. Christie was held responsible for two false starts and thus disqualified from the final. He argued with the starter and other officials before grudgingly accepting that he was not going to take part in the race. Then, with the crowd's jeers getting ever louder, he completed a "lap of honour" on his way out of the stadium. Christie was unrepentant, claiming: "The crowd booed the judges. They knew they had been robbed of a better race than the one they saw. I'm still the people's champion."

The real champion was Donovan Bailey, who, unfazed by the uproar caused by Christie, won in a world record 9.84sec. There was uproar in the women's 100m as well. In a photo-finish, almost everybody was convinced that the photo showed that Merlene Ottey of Jamaica was the winner. The judges thought otherwise and awarded the gold medal to Gail Devers of the United States.

The men's 200m saw another world record fall, Michael Johnson winning in 19.32sec. The American also won the 400m, a race in which Roger Black took a silver medal for Britain, albeit in a time nearly a second slower than Johnson.

Smith's medals tarnished by back-biting

IT SHOULD have been one of the fairy stories of the Games: "Irish swimmer wins gold medal." But when the headlines became "Irish swimmer wins third gold medal" the fairy story took a decidedly nasty twist.

The problem was that Michelle's Smith's three triumphs in the 200m and 400m individual medley and the 400m freestyle, were not part of the script. Atlanta was supposed to be the final hurrah for Janet Evans, the American swimmer who had won gold medals at the two previous Games.

So when Evans was upstaged she was far from pleased. And American television needed to explain why their local hero hadn't lived up to her billing. Because Smith was married to a Dutch athlete who had been banned for using drugs, the American media, with no little help from Evans, jumped to one conclusion.

Evans claimed to be doing no more than recounting pool-side gossip, but there was little doubt about what the gossips were insinuating. And the American media were even more blunt. One American television interviewer's first question to Smith after she had won a race was about whether she took drugs.

Nightmare ending: Smith was hounded by the American media

The whole episode, with rumour bandied about as if it were fact, was one of the less acceptable faces of an already tarnished Games. The point was not lost on President Clinton, who apologised to Smith, saying: "Sorry for the crap the media are giving you. But I have to put up with it all the time." But even he could do nothing about the fact that the malicious talk had cost Smith a fortune. The deals that an Olympic champion would expect to be offered never materialised, and her pay-day vanished.

Yes, football came home but Southgate missed the party

ENGLAND went into Euro 96 under a dark cloud. At the end of a pre-championship tour to the Far East a number of players were photographed enjoying a late-night drinking binge. The tabloids inevitably whipped up a media frenzy. This was further fuelled when England could only draw their opening match 1-1 with Switzerland. Then England started doing their own talking, and they did it where it mattered – on the pitch.

The Scots, who had held one of the favourites, Holland, to a 0-0 draw were dramatically swept away 2-0. With 12 minutes left, and trailing to an Alan Shearer goal, David Seaman brilliantly saved a Gary McAllister penalty. Then, within seconds, Paul Gascoigne scored a thrilling solo goal. Against Holland, England were simply magnificent. A brace of goals from Shearer and Teddy Sheringham gave the hosts a 4-1 victory.

Sadly for Scotland, the late goal that England conceded eliminated Scotland from the tournament. The media promptly did an about face as England now became the flavour of the month.

England were exceedingly fortunate to get past Spain 4-2 on penalties in the quarter finals. A perfectly good goal from Julio Salinas was disallowed and now England were to face their nemesis, Germany. Fears that the outcome would be much the same as their 1990 World Cup semi-final were confirmed when, once again, the semi-final went to penalties. England had had enough chances to win it in extra time. Darren Anderton hit the post and Gascoigne was a touch away from scoring.

The Stuart Pearce of 1996 turned out to be Gareth Southgate as England were eliminated 6-5 on penalties. The words of the

Euro 96 theme song: "Football's coming home, thirty years of hurt never stopped us dreaming," seemed somewhat ironic as history hurtfully repeated itself. Germany's opponents in the final were the Czech Republic, the surprise package of the tournament.

The Czechs, who had lost 2-0 to Germany in the opening match, played a cautious game and this strategy seemed to have paid off when they went ahead in the 59th minute with a very dubious penalty. The arrival of Oliver Bierhoff, an inspired substitution by coach Berti Vogts, proved to be a match-winning decision. With 17 minutes to go he rose at the far post for the equaliser. Then, in the fifth minute of extra time, Bierhoff, fed by Jürgen Klinsmann, turned and fired in a powerful shot which was deflected into the net.

Germany were the champions, the match was over. But

was Kuntz – clearly offside – interfering with play? The referee thought not. It was the most anti-climactic end to a tournament that one could imagine. Because of the plethora of penalty shoot-outs in major tournaments, Uefa had come up with the wheeze of "the golden goal". The first side to score in extra time won the match there and then. It was such a disappointing end to a final that the football authorities quietly dropped the idea.

FOR THE RECORD

FOOTBALL

■ Bob Paisley, the former Liverpool manager, died aged 77 in February. After Paisley replaced Bill Shankly in 1974, his Liverpool teams won 20 trophies in less than a decade.

■ Paul Gascoigne was voted Scottish Player of the Year as his 19 goals helped Rangers record their eighth successive League title.

■ Matthew Harding, Chelsea's millionaire vice-chairman, was killed in a helicopter crash while returning from a match in October.

■ Terry Venables announced he would stand down as England coach after the European championships. Venables had wanted an extension to his contract six months before the tournament. Glenn Hoddle replaced him in May.

■ Premiership clubs negotiated a four-year £670m TV deal with Sky to run from 1997 to 2001.

■ Tony Adams, the England and Arsenal defender, admitted he was an alcoholic in September, and the FA decided to introduce random breath tests.

■ Mick McCarthy was appointed manager of the Republic of Ireland national team in February.

■ Leyton Orient sacked Roger Stanislaus in February after he tested positive for cocaine. The FA banned him for a year.

SWIMMING

■ Hungary were so desperate to increase the size of their team at the Olympics that they invented a mythical meeting at which several swimmers supposedly made the qualifying times.

Neat Scotch: Paul Gascoigne silenced his critics with a brilliant goal against the Auld Enemy

FEBRUARY

1996

MAY

FOOTBALL

Eric's double twist in United's tale

BY ANY standards, Eric Cantona had the most remarkable of seasons for Manchester United. In October of 1995 he graced his return after a nine-month suspension for attacking a Crystal Palace supporter with a penalty against Liverpool that earned United an important draw. Important goals in important matches became the hallmark of Cantona's extraordinary year.

With Cantona as their inspiration, Manchester United overhauled Newcastle's daunting 12-point lead to win the championship and then beat Liverpool 1-0 in the FA Cup final to capture their second Double. And who scored the

Stranded: Liverpool defenders static as Cantona volleys home

winning goal in the final? Cantona, of course. It was no surprise that Cantona was voted Player of The Year.

Amazingly, the team that made history by making Manchester United the only club ever to win the Double twice, was in transition. Mark Hughes had gone to Chelsea; Paul Ince to Inter and Andrei Kanchelskis was off to Everton. Alex Ferguson gambled on his young players, Fergie's Babes, blending in with his mercurial French genius.

It paid off. Phil and Gary Neville, David Beckham, Nicky Butt and Paul Scholes were all successfully absorbed into the senior squad as the League championship went to Old Trafford for the third time in four

years. With such an impressive array of silverware, it seemed that Ferguson was building a dynasty as dominant as Liverpool had in the 1970s and 1980s.

But did Newcastle throw the title away? Kevin Keegan's side held a 12-point lead in January that was constructed around their impregnable home record. They only lost one match at St James's Park, but that was to Manchester United. And who scored the winner? Cantona.

It was Newcastle's poor away form that did for them, only seven away victories, and the signing of Faustino Asprilla. After the Colombian's arrival in February, Newcastle were nine points ahead with a game in hand. They eventually trailed by four points.

GOLF

The Shark is beached once again

AFTER THREE days' of the US Masters Greg Norman led by six strokes and was on the brink of winning one of the few tournaments to have eluded him. Then everything started to go wrong.

A deathly hush descended over Augusta National as the crowds witnessed one of the

Norman: Amen Corner spelt the death-knell for him

most spectacular collapses ever seen. Norman's game totally fell apart. As he trudged from one disastrous hole to the next he was a broken man.

When, on the final green, Nick Faldo sunk a birdie putt to win by five strokes there was hardly any celebration. Faldo was clearly moved by the suffering that Norman had just been through. The two men embraced, both close to tears and Faldo said to Norman: "I don't know what to say. I just want to give you a hug. I feel horrible about what happened."

It was an unbelievable end to a roller-coaster week for Norman. The day before the tournament started, Norman was wracked by back pains and could hardly swing a club. But after treatment from a therapist he promptly equalled the course record with a first-round 63.

Rounds of 69 and 71 put him so far ahead that even Faldo thought the result was beyond doubt. However, as many commentators pointed out, Norman

had been the leader at the start of the final day of a major seven times before. On six of those occasions he had blown it.

Norman's drive from the first tee disappeared into the trees and he dropped a shot. He had another bogey on the fourth, then Faldo sunk a 20ft putt on the eighth to halve Norman's original lead to three strokes.

Going round Amen Corner was a journey to hell. Norman dropped another shot on the ninth hole, missed from eight feet on the 10th and three feet on the 11th. Faldo was now level. When Norman's ball splashed into the lake at the 12th Faldo led by two strokes.

At the 15th, Norman missed an eagle by a whisker and slumped to the ground in despair. When another ball disappeared into the water at the 16th, all hope sunk with it.

"I screwed up," Norman admitted. "I let this one get away but I'll win here, I will. If I don't, I might as well put my clubs away for good."

FOR THE RECORD

GOLF

■ Tiger Woods turned professional after winning the US amateur title for the third successive time. The 20-year-old prodigy, who signed a £25m-plus deal with Nike, soon set the professional game alight, winning the fifth and eighth tournaments he contested.

■ Steve Jones became the first qualifier to win the US Open since Jerry Pate in 1976.

■ Ivan Lendl took part in the Czech Open in August but failed to make the cut, shooting rounds of 82 and 76.

■ The United States came back from two points down against Europe at the start of the final day to win the Solheim Cup 17-11.

■ Laura Davies, the world No 1, admitted she had lost more than £500,000 gambling.

BOXING

■ Tommy Morrison, the former world heavyweight champion, announced that he was HIV positive in February.

■ Nigel Benn lost his WBC super-middleweight title to Sugar Boy Malinga in March and announced his retirement. He changed his mind, fought Steve Collins and lost again.

■ Chris Eubank, claiming he needed the money to pay tax bills, made a comeback in Egypt against a little-known Argentinian.

■ The British Board of Control decided in November that women would be allowed to fight in amateur contests.

414

Sri Lanka exact full revenge for Australia's snub

FOR SRI LANKA, the World Cup was a joyous occasion as their batsmen scythed through a string of supposedly "superior" teams. Most of the rest of the world slunk away from the month-long event with their reputations in tatters.

Not surprisingly, given their lacklustre tour of South Africa, England made little impression. They lost to New Zealand, South Africa and Pakistan in Group B and only scraped into the quarter-finals by virtue of beating Holland and the United Arab Emirates.

At least England managed to beat the "minnows" they faced. In Group A, West Indies, chasing a mere 167 for victory, were shot out for 93 by Kenya and, like England, only just scraped into the quarter-finals.

And both Australia and West Indies didn't win any friends when they forfeited a match rather than play in Sri Lanka, claiming they feared for their safety because of the political unrest on the island.

Pakistan bowed out in the quarter-finals when they lost to South Africa. The defeat, in Karachi, did not go down to well with the home fans, who burned an effigy of their captain, Wasim Akram, and, for good measure, stoned his house as well.

That was nothing compared to the unrest in the semi-final between India and Sri Lanka (who had hammered England with 10 overs to spare in the quarter-final). The Sri Lankan bowlers tormented their hosts and when the Indians, chasing a target of 252, had limped to 120-8 the 100,000-plus crowd in Calcutta erupted. The Sri Lankan team were pelted with missiles and the match referee, Clive Lloyd, was forced to abandon the game and declare Sri Lanka the victors.

The other semi-final was equally dramatic. Australia slumped to 15-4 before recovering to 207. At 164-2 West Indies looked to have the game in the bag. Then they lost a wicket… and another one… and the team collectively threw in the towel. Apart from their top four batsmen, nobody scored more than three runs. From 44 runs needed with eight wickets in hand they subsided to a five-run defeat.

In the final, Australia were left to rue their snub of Sri Lanka. The Australian score of 241-7 was respectable, but never looked like being enough once the Sri Lankan batsman got into their stride. Gurusinha, De Silva, who scored his second century of the tournament, and the captain Ranatunga, who finished the event with an average of more than 120, were merciless as Sri Lanka raced to a victory that was thoroughly deserved.

FOR THE RECORD

CRICKET

■ Harold "Dickie" Bird, the legendary umpire, retired after officiating in the Test match between England and India at Lord's.

■ Ian Botham and Allan Lamb lost a libel action they brought against Imran Khan and were faced with a bill for £500,000.

■ The Sussex bowler Ed Giddins was banned for 20 months for using cocaine.

■ Devon Malcolm and Phil DeFreitas won an apology and damages when they sued Wisden Cricket Monthly for publishing an article that questioned black players' commitment when playing for England.

■ The MCC's application for lottery money was duly rejected because the MCC do not allow women to become members.

■ Shaun Pollock took four wickets in four balls when he made his debut for Warwickshire in April.

■ Liam Botham, the son of Ian, took five for 67 on his debut for Hampshire in August. He subsequently decided to give up cricket to concentrate on playing rugby union.

■ David Lloyd was appointed England's full-time coach in March.

■ Lancashire won the NatWest Trophy after Essex were dismissed for 57, the lowest ever total in the final.

■ Ray Illingworth was charged with bringing the game into disrepute and fined £2,000 by the TCCB for comments he made in his book, One Man Committee. The punishment was overturned on appeal.

Bruno ends with a whimper

IT WAS the most hyped sports event of the year, and also the biggest let-down. After six minutes and 50 seconds of Frank Bruno's world title defence in Las Vegas in March, Mike Tyson had easily regained his WBC crown. But Bruno's defeat was worse than the loss of his title. He had succumbed to a boxer's worst enemy: fear, and had been humiliated.

Despite all Bruno's bluster of "I refuse to be beaten" in the ludicrous build-up by Sky television for their first pay-per-view event, the world champion just froze. It was evident from the long walk into the ring. Bruno was terrified and his terror was translated into feverish crossing of himself, as if God might save him from the beating that was to come.

Bruno hardly threw a single punch, and what few he attempted were forlorn and half-hearted. It was a measure of the man's terror that he was deducted a penalty point for persistently holding five minutes into the defence of his title. Mercifully the end was quick, early in the third round, when Bruno found himself dazed, confused and marooned on the bottom rope.

Fortunately, Bruno eventually did decide to retire from boxing. His four world title shots had earned him in excess of £10m. And given his obvious shortcomings as a boxer, he can count himself an exceedingly lucky man to have amassed such a nest-egg. Six hundred thousand television viewers had paid nearly £10 a head to watch Bruno's latest farcical debacle.

Nine months later, Tyson's complacency against Evander Holyfield cost him his title. Tyson's preparation for the fight was poor and the champion had hardly trained. Holyfield exploited Tyson's lack of fitness and bludgeoned him into submission and the fight was ended early in the eleventh round.

Bruno: froze like a rabbit caught in the headlights

TENNIS

Henman a smashing hit

BRITISH TENNIS, so long in the doldrums, got a long-overdue fillip with the emergence of Tim Henman from the shadow of Greg Rusedski.

Henman wasn't expected to go far at Wimbledon when he was drawn against the big-serving No 5 seed Yevgeny Kafelnikov in the first round. The unassuming Henman surprised the French Open champion, and the rest of Britain, when he went all the way to the quarter-finals.

Henman beat Kafelnikov in five sets and then dispatched two compatriots, Danny Sapsford and Luke Milligan. Kafelnikov apart, the wags said, it was hardly surprising that Henman had reached the fourth round because beating Britons was not that difficult.

When Henman beat Magnus Gustafsson to become the first Briton to reach the quarter-finals since Roger Taylor in 1973 the joking stopped. With so many seeds having fallen by the wayside in the early rounds, suddenly a place in the final was not such a pipe-dream. It was not to be though, and Henman lost in straight sets to Todd Martin. He went down fighting and his battling display captured the nation's hearts.

Any doubts that Henman's performance was a flash in the pan were soon dispelled. He won a silver medal in the men's doubles at the Olympics and reached the fourth round of the US Open, taking his revenge over Martin in the process. By the end of the year Henman had won more than $400,000 and was on the fringes of a place in the world's top 20.

Henman: surprised everybody with a silver medal at the Atlanta Olympics

RUGBY UNION

Row after row

THE INEVITABLE arrival of professionalism in rugby union was anything but straightforward as assorted groups bickered and fought for control of the millions of pounds flooding into the game. After a year that produced threats, counter-threats and much hot air, most people were left with the distinct impression that nothing much had really changed, and certainly not for the better.

Leading English clubs fell out with the Rugby Football Union and their players boycotted an England training session, raising the spectre of a national side comprised of amateurs drawn from lower division clubs. And England fell out with the other home nations after the RFU broke ranks and signed a television deal with Sky, raising the spectre of England not being able to play anybody, even if they could raise a team.

England were expelled from the Five Nations championship twice in as many months and

Epruc (the group representing the country's top clubs) were on the brink of a breakaway so many times that everybody lost count.

On the field, things were almost as confused. England lost their opening Five Nations match to France, but won the championship on points difference when France lost their final match to Wales by one point. Just about the only thing that was clear cut was that Will Carling announced that he was standing down as England captain.

CYCLING

Mig gunned down

ON THE seventh stage of the Tour de France an era ended. Miguel Indurain, who had won the previous five Tours, seized up on the climb to Les Arcs and his chance of an historic sixth successive victory was gone. The Basque nobly carried on, finishing in 11th position, way behind the winner, Bjarne Riis.

It was the end of a legend, a man who was not only the greatest cyclist of all time, but arguably the greatest athlete of the century. Indurain's nickname was The Extraterrestrial, the man from another planet.

The term was coined in the 1992 Tour when, in the first long time trial, Indurain destroyed the entire field. That stage became known as the Luxembourg Massacre.

Time trials and consistency in the high mountains were his strengths, but what shattered his opponents was that Indurain wasn't built to be a cyclist. He was too big, he didn't like the wind, the cold, or the rain – all the elements that have to be overcome if you wish to win the Tour de France. It was a measure of Indurain's single-minded determination that he became only the fourth man to have won five Tours, and the first to do so with consecutive victories.

Despite pressure from his team, Banesto, and lucrative offers from rivals ONCE, to continue racing, Indurain sensibly decided to retire, his place in history unquestioned.

Handover: Indurain to Riis

RACING

Seventh heaven

FRANKIE DETTORI, whose impish charm had made him a firm favourite with punters, gave his fans plenty to celebrate when he became the first jockey to ride all the winners on a seven-race card.

The Italian, cheered to the rafters by the spectators at the first day of the Ascot festival on September 28 and mobbed in the unsaddling enclosure after his seventh win said: "I always thought that perhaps one day in my life I might do it at a small meeting. But to do it on such a competitive card is beyond me. God was on my side."

The hordes of small punters who routinely back Dettori's mounts definitely thought that God had smiled on them. The cumulative odds on Dettori's feat were in excess of 25,000-1 and the bookmakers were left reeling. They claimed that Dettori's achievement cost them anything up to £30m.

The damage would have been even greater had the big bookmakers not spent a fortune hedging their bets to force down the price of Dettori's mounts as the afternoon progressed. Decorated Hero, his fourth winner, tumbled from 14-1 to 7-1; Fate-

Dettori: flying high after seven wins in seven races

fully, the fifth winner, was cut from 5-1 to 7-4; and Fujiyama Crest, his final triumph, had its odds slashed from 12-1 to 2-1 as the bookmakers desperately tried to reduce their liabilities.

Dettori's third win of the day was in the Queen Elizabeth II Stakes, a race that confirmed Mark of Esteem as Europe's top miler. And there was no doubt that Dettori was one of the country's top jockeys. Although the veteran Pat Eddery won the most races, Dettori took two of the season's Classics – the 2,000 Guineas (also on Mark of Esteem) and the St Leger – was placed in all of the others, and also won more prize money than any other jockey.

MOTOR RACING

Hill beats Villeneuve

WITH defending champion Michael Schumacher having jumped ship from Benetton to Ferrari, this had to be Damon Hill's golden opportunity to emulate his father, Graham, and win the Formula One world championship. Three races into the season, Hill had maximum points, his deadly rival Schumacher four, and the title was assuredly his for the taking.

Not quite. When Hill looked over his shoulder he didn't see a blood-red Ferrari, it was his own teammate, Jacques Villeneuve, that was the principal threat to his first championship. The Canadian won the fourth Grand Prix, at Nürburgring, and then spent the rest of the season harrying Hill. Villeneuve even

had the cheek to spoil Hill's homecoming and take the British Grand Prix at Silverstone.

By the end of July, three more victories, at Montreal, Magny-Cours and Hockenheim, had put Hill in the championship driving seat. Then Hill hit a barren patch as Villeneuve narrowed the gap. Matters were made worse in September when Frank Williams unceremoniously announced that Hill would be surplus to requirements in 1997, preferring Heinz-Harald Frentzen instead.

Perhaps the public vote of no confidence was exactly what Hill needed. He came second at Estoril and, needing only a point in Suzuka, threw caution to the wind and won the race to take the title and leave Villeneuve in second place, 19 points behind the new world champion.

FOR THE RECORD

AMERICAN FOOTBALL

■ William "the Fridge" Perry, former Chicago Bears giant joined the London Monarchs. The Scottish Claymores signed the former Scotland rugby captain Gavin Hastings and won the World Bowl.

ATHLETICS

■ Diane Modahl won a long battle to clear her name when she was cleared of drug-taking by the IAAF in March.

■ Dionico Ceron won the London marathon for the third year in a row. Liz McColgan won the women's race.

BASEBALL

■ The New York Yankees came back from 2-0 down against Atlanta to win the World Series for the first time in 18 years.

■ A couple who were caught having sex during a game between Los Angeles and the New York Mets were found guilty of

lewd conduct. The judge ordered them to buy 50 tickets each for forthcoming games and give them to charity.

BASKETBALL

■ Dennis Rodman of the Chicago Bulls was suspended for six games and fined $20,000 for head-butting a referee.

ICE HOCKEY

■ The championship play-off match between Humberside and Durham in March was an ill-tempered affair. Police were called to the rink when a Humberside player was taken to hospital with concussion after an incident while the two teams were warming up. The game had barely started when police had to break up a mass brawl between the teams.

MOTORCYCLING

■ Joey Dunlop won his 21st Isle of Man TT race at the age of 44.

POOL

■ Minnesota Fats died, aged 82.

RUGBY LEAGUE

■ Wigan were finally beaten in the Challenge Cup after 43 matches and nine years, when they went down 26-16 to Salford in February.

■ Andy Farrell became England's youngest ever captain, aged 20.

RUGBY UNION

■ The Lions had a troubled tour. They had to make 26 substitutions because of the heat during their match against Papua New Guinea. They went on to lose every game played in New Zealand.

FOOTBALL

■ Juventus won the European Cup for only the second time when they beat Ajax, the defending champions, 4-2 on

penalties. Fabrizio Ravenelli had given the Italians an early lead, but an uncharacteristic mistake by Angelo Peruzzi led to a first-half equaliser. In the penalty shoot-out Peruzzi atoned for his gaffe with two saves.

■ Alan Shearer became the first player to score 30 goals in a season in three consecutive years.

■ The fixture list suffered its worst disruption for 36 years because of the weather. On January 27 a total of 55 matches were postponed in England and Scotland.

■ Brighton's announcement that they intended to sell the Goldstone Ground and share with Portsmouth provoked their fans to protest at their final home game of the season. The pitch was invaded, both goals were torn down and the dressing-rooms attacked. The match was abandoned after 16 minutes.

RACING

Grand National beats IRA threat

THE Grand National was called off at the last moment when two telephone warnings, both using recognised IRA code words, said that a bomb had been planted in the Aintree course.

The stands and enclosures were all evacuated and more than 60,000 people flocked into the centre of the course. Although the evacuation was orderly, with no hint of panic, it was obvious that there was no chance of the race going ahead that day as people milled around on the course, some of them even sitting on top of the fences that the runners should have been jumping.

As racegoers streamed away from the course they were united in insisting that the race had to be re-staged. Jenny Pitman, reflected their sentiments when, close to tears, she said: "These people are sick."

Within an hour, the course was deserted. Bookmakers had to leave their satchels in the ring, on the spot television coverage ended when the BBC camera crews were told to leave the area, and Phil Sharp, a stable lad who volunteered to stay behind to look after the racehorses, was also ordered out.

Aintree announced that the race would be run at 5pm on Monday, and the course remained closed for most of the weekend as the police conducted an intensive search. With the entire area sealed off, people were stranded because they were not allowed back to their vehicles. Many of the visitors opted to stay in the Liverpool area rather than go home.

Nobody was quite sure what to expect on Monday evening, but the people flocked back to the course. Another bomb scare was made, but police, confident that it was another hoax, said that the race could go ahead.

Lord Gyllene led virtually from the start and romped home 25 lengths clear of Suny Bay, cheered by a defiant crowd of more than 20,000.

GOLF

Tiger Woods devours Augusta

TIGER WOODS roared around Augusta National, taking the course by the scruff of the neck and breaking records by the dozen on his way to a staggering victory.

The 21-year-old, who only turned professional six months before, was playing in his first Major. His combination of big hitting off the tee and a sublime touch around the greens made him irresistible.

In the first round, Woods's start was hardly the stuff of champions. He had a bogey on the first hole and struggled to save par on the second hole after hitting another wayward drive. But he played a superb back nine to go round in 70. Nick Faldo, the defending champion and his playing partner, shot a 75. In the second round Woods made an eagle at the 13th hole and shot a 66 to lead by three strokes. Faldo, in contrast, took a nine at the 13th, went round in 81 and missed the cut by a long way.

Woods played the third round with Colin Montgomerie, who three strokes behind, thought he was well placed to challenge for the green jacket. Eighteen holes later Woods had had a round of 65 and his lead had stretched to nine strokes.

A staggered Montgomerie conceded that there was only going to be one winner: "It's not humanly possible that Tiger can lose this tournament. I knew how far he hit his driver, but I did not appreciate how he can putt. He is nine clear now and I'm sure it will be more tomorrow.

Indeed it was. Sunday was a triumphant procession for Woods. His total of 270 was a record, his winning margin of 12 was a record, and he was the youngest winner of the tournament for good measure.

The significance of what he had done at a course where non-whites had not been welcome until recently was not lost on Woods, who said: "Winning here will do a lot for the game of golf. It will open a lot of doors and draw a lot of people in who haven't even thought of playing. I think this can do a lot for minorities."

Tiger: tears apart the rest of the field at the 1997 Masters

CRICKET

Compton dies, 78

DENIS COMPTON, England's finest all-rounder of the modern era died, aged 78.

He was a dashing batsman for Middlesex and England, scoring nearly 39,000 runs in his career at an average of over 50. He claimed his left-arm slow bowling was merely experimental, but it was good enough to take 622 wickets.

In autumn, Compton would swap his cricket pads for football boots – winning the League and FA Cup with Arsenal.

In between appearing in adverts the Brylcreem Boy, Compton loved nothing more than having fun. He typified the dashing cavalier.

Denis: the ultimate all-rounder

FOOTBALL

Cantona's final curtain

ANY CHANCE Manchester United had of winning their fourth Premier League title in five years seemed to have evaporated in the autumn. In one amazing fortnight United were thumped 5-0 by Newcastle, similarly thrashed 6-3 by Southampton and then fell to Chelsea 2-1 at Old Trafford. Champions-elect? You must be kidding.

Then, a fortnight after the Chelsea debacle, a David Seaman blunder allowed United to sneak a 1-0 win over Arsenal. It was the defining moment of the season. Fifteen undefeated League matches followed, eleven of them yielding three points. The pattern was set. Win the crucial games and see off the pursuing pack.

In February, Alex Ferguson's team virtually ended Arsenal's title aspirations with a 2-1 triumph at Highbury. Then, in April, they went to Anfield and beat Liverpool 3-1. "You've got to earn the right to be champions," Ferguson said afterwards, "and I think we came to the right place to do that."

United may have been all-conquering on the domestic front. Europe was a different kettle of fish. United did well to reach the semi-finals of the European Champions League, the first English club to do so, but, in all they lost five matches. Juventus and Borussia Dortmund, the eventual finalists, beating them home and away.

A week after United celebrated their championship, their mercurial superstar Eric Cantona dropped a bombshell. On the eve of his 31st birthday the Frenchman announced he was quitting football to pursue a career on the stage and the screen.

Bonne chance, Eric!

Cantona: Au revoir

SNOOKER

Hendry freezes up in the Crucible

THE WRITING was on the wall back in April when Stephen Hendry was thrashed 9-2 by Mark Williams in the British Open. Hendry, ahead 2-1, offered virtually no resistance as the 22-year-old Welshman simply reeled off eight consecutive frames. Suddenly Hendry was no longer invincible.

Losing the British Open was one thing, but could Hendry be toppled at the Crucible where he had been unbeaten for five years? As Hendry cruised to the final of the world championships, it seemed not. Ken Doherty, the world No 7 from the Republic of Ireland, had other ideas.

Despite having won only one ranking event in seven years, Doherty was unfazed by the status of his opponent and comfortably beat the world champion 18-12. Hendry's manager, Ian Doyle, was incensed with his protégé's lacklustre performance. "Perhaps he should take a year off," he said.

BOXING

The Prince shows he is fit to wear the crowns

PRINCE Naseem Hamed proved that he packed a punch to match his showmanship when he demolished Sunderland's Billy Hardy in May to retain his IBF and WBO world featherweight titles.

Hamed's first punch, a massive right, flattened Hardy. The European champion staggered to his feet, was sent sprawling by a another crashing blow and the referee called a halt after 93 seconds of the first round.

Hardy, the No 1 challenger, became the 12th of Hamed's 25 opponents to be stopped inside two rounds. And he has no doubts about how good Hamed is: "He's got a kick like a mule. He's certainly got something special in his hands. I'm certain he will go on to win all four world titles."

1990s STATISTICS

AMERICAN FOOTBALL
■ *Super Bowl*
1990 San Francisco 49ers
1991 New York Giants
1992 Washington Redskins
1993 Dallas Cowboys
1994 Dallas Cowboys
1995 San Francisco 49ers
1996 Dallas Cowboys
1997 Green Bay Packers

ATHLETICS
■ *British Olympic gold medals*
1992 100m Linford Christie; 400m hurdles Sally Gunnell

BASEBALL
■ *World Series*
1990 Cincinnati Reds
1991 Minnesota Twins
1992 Toronto Blue Jays
1993 Toronto Blue Jays
1994 not held
1995 Atlanta Braves
1996 New York Yankees

BOXING
■ *British world champions*
1990 *Middleweight* Nigel Benn (WBO)
1990 *Middleweight* Chris Eubank (WBO)
1990 *Light-heavyweight* Dennis Andries (WBC)
1991 *Featherweight* Paul Hodkinson (WBC)
1991 *Super Middleweight* Christ Eubank (WBO)
1992 *Flyweight* Pat Clinton (WBO)
1992 *Featherweight* Colin McMillan (WBO)
1992 *Super Middleweight* Nigel Benn (WBC)
1993 *Heavyweight* Lennox Lewis (WBC); Michael Bentt (WBO)
1993 *Welterweight* Eamonn Loughran (WBO)
1993 *Featherweight* Steve Robinson (WBO)
1994 *Heavyweight* Herbie Hide (WBO)
1995 *Super Middleweight* Steve Collins (WBO)1995 *Heavyweight* Frank Bruno (WBC); *Super middleweight* Steve Collins (WBO); *Featherweight* Naseem Hamed (IBO)
1996 *Heavyweight* Henry Akinwande (WBO)

CRICKET
■ *World Cup*
1992 Pakistan bt England by 22 runs
1996 Sri Lanka

■ *County Championship*
1990 Middlesex
1991 Essex
1992 Essex
1993 Middlesex
1994 Warwickshire
1995 Warwickshire
1996 Leicestershire
■ *Nat West Trophy*
1990 Lancashire bt Northants by 7 wickets
1991 Hampshire bt Surrey by 4 wickets
1992 Northants bt Leicestershire by 8 wickets
1993 Warwickshire bt Sussex by 5 wickets
1994 Worcestershire bt Warwickshire by 8 wickets
1995 Warwickshire beat Northants by 4 wickets
1996 Lancashire beat Essex by 129 runs
■ *B&H Trophy*
1990 Lancashire bt Worcestershire by 69 runs
1991 Worcestershire bt Lancashire by 65 runs
1992 Hampshire bt Kent by 41 runs
1993 Derbyshire bt Lancashire by 6 runs
1994 Warwickshire bt Worcestershire by 6 wickets
1995 Lancashire by Kent by 35 runs
1996 Lancashire beat Northants by 31 runs
■ *Sunday League*
1990 Derbyshire
1991 Nottinghamshire
1992 Middlesex
1993 Glamorgan
1994 Warwickshire
1995 Kent
1996 Surrey

CYCLING
■ *Tour de France*
1990 Greg LeMond
1991 Miguel Indurain
1992 Miguel Indurain
1993 Miguel Indurain
1994 Miguel Indurain
1995 Miguel Indurain
1996 Bjarne Riis

FOOTBALL
■ *World Cup*
1990 West Germany 1 Argentina 0
1994 Brazil 0 Italy 0 (Brazil won 3-2 on penalties)
■ *European Championships*
1992 Denmark 2 Germany 0
1996 Germany 2 Czech Rep 1 (aet)
■ *European Cup*
1990 AC Milan 1 Benfica 0

1991 Red Star Belgrade 0 Marseille 0 (Belgrade won 5-3 on penalties)
1992 Barcelona 1 Sampdoria 0
1993 Marseille 1 AC Milan 0
1994 AC Milan 4 Barcelona 0
1995 Ajax 1 AC Milan 0
1996 Juventus 1 Ajax 1 (Juventus won 4-3 on penalties)
1997 Borussia Dortmund 3 Juventus 1
■ *European Cup Winners' Cup*
1990 Sampdoria 2 Anderlecht 0
1991 Manchester Utd 2 Barcelona 1
1992 Werder Bremen 2 Monaco 0
1993 Parma 3 Antwerp 1
1994 Arsenal 1 Parma 0
1995 Real Zaragoza 2 Arsenal 1 (aet)
1996 Paris St Germain 1 Rapid Vienna 0
1997 Barcelona 1 Paris St Germain 0
■ *Uefa Cup*
1990 Juventus bt Fiorentina 3-1, 0-0
1991 Inter Milan bt AS Roma 2-0, 0-1
1992 Ajax bt Torino 2-2, 0-0 (Ajax won on away goals)
1993 Juventus bt Borussia Dortmund 3-1, 3-0
1994 Inter Milan bt Casino Salzburg 1-0, 1-0
1995 Parma bt Juventus 1-0, 1-1
1996 Bayern Munich bt Bordeaux 2-0, 3-1
1997 Schalke bt Inter Milan 1-0, 0-1 (Schalke won 4-1 on penalties)
■ *Football League*
1990 Liverpool
1991 Arsenal
1992 Leeds Utd
1993 Manchester Utd
1994 Manchester Utd
1995 Blackburn Rovers
1996 Manchester Utd
1997 Manchester Utd
■ *FA Cup*
1990 Manchester Utd 1 Crystal Palace 0 (after 3-3)
1991 Tottenham 2 Nottingham Forest 1 (aet)
1992 Liverpool 2 Sunderland 0
1993 Arsenal 2 Sheffield Wednesday 1 (after 1-1)
1994 Manchester Utd 4

Chelsea 0
1995 Everton 1 Manchester Utd 0
1996 Manchester Utd 1 Liverpool 0
1997 Chelsea 2 Middlesbrough 0
■ *League Cup*
1990 Nottingham Forest 1 Oldham 0
1991 Sheffield Wednesday 1 Manchester Utd 0
1992 Manchester Utd 1 Nottingham Forest 0
1993 Arsenal 2 Sheffield Wednesday 1
1994 Aston Villa 3 Manchester Utd 1
1995 Liverpool 2 Bolton 1
1996 Aston Villa 3 Leeds 0
1997 Leicester 1 Middlesbrough 0 (after 1-1)
■ *Scottish League*
1990 Rangers
1991 Rangers
1992 Rangers
1993 Rangers
1994 Rangers
1995 Rangers
1996 Rangers
1997 Rangers
■ *Scottish Cup*
1990 Aberdeen 0 Celtic 0 (Aberdeen won 9-8 on penalties)
1991 Motherwell 4 Dundee Utd 3
1992 Rangers 2 Airdrie 1
1993 Rangers 2 Aberdeen 1
1994 Dundee Utd 1 Rangers 0
1995 Celtic 1 Airdrie 0
1996 Rangers 5 Hearts 1
1997 Kilmarnock 1 Falkirk 0
■ *Scottish League Cup*
1990 Aberdeen 2 Rangers 1
1991 Dunfermline 2 Hibernian 0
1992 Rangers 2 Celtic 1
1993 Rangers 2 Aberdeen 1
1994 Rangers 2 Hibernian 1
1995 Raith 2 Celtic 2 (Raith won 6-5 on penalties)
1996 Aberdeen 2 Dundee 0
1997 Rangers 4 Hearts 3

GOLF
■ *The Open*
1990 Nick Faldo
1991 Ian Baker-Finch
1992 Nick Faldo
1993 Greg Norman
1994 Nick Price
1995 John Daly

1996 Tom Lehman
■ *US Open*
1990 Hale Irwin
1991 Payne Stewart
1992 Tom Kite
1993 Lee Janzen
1994 Ernie Els
1995 Corey Pavin
1996 Tom Lehman
1997 Ernie Els
■ *US PGA*
1990 Wayne Grady
1991 John Daly
1992 Nick Price
1993 Paul Azinger
1994 Nick Price
1995 Steve Elkington
1996 Mark Brooks
■ *US Masters*
1990 Nick Faldo
1991 Ian Woosnam
1992 Fred Couples
1993 Bernhard Langer
1994 Jose-Maria Olazabal
1995 Ben Crenshaw
1996 Nick Faldo
1997 Tiger Woods
■ *Ryder Cup*
1991 United States 14½-13½
1993 United States 15-13
1995 Europe 14–13

MOTOR RACING
■ *World Championship*
1990 Ayrton Senna (McLaren-Honda)
1991 Ayrton Senna (McLaren-Honda)
1992 Nigel Mansell (Williams-Renault)
1993 Alain Prost (Williams-Renault)
1994 Michael Schumacher (Benetton-Ford)
1995 Michael Schumacher (Benetton-Renault)
1996 Damon Hill (Williams-Renault)

RACING
■ *The Derby*
1990 Quest for Fame
1991 Generous
1992 Dr Devious
1993 Commander In Chief
1994 Erhaab
1995 Lammtarra
1996 Shaamit
■ *Grand National*
1990 Mr Frisk
1991 Seagram
1992 Party Politics
1993 race void
1994 Minnehoma
1995 Royal Athlete
1996 Rough Quest
1997 Lord Gyllene

ROWING
■ *Boat Race*
1990 Oxford

1991 Oxford
1992 Oxford
1993 Cambridge
1994 Cambridge
1995 Cambridge
1996 Cambridge
1997 Cambridge

RUGBY LEAGUE
■ *Challenge Cup*
1990 Wigan 36 Warrington 14
1991 Wigan 13 St Helens 8
1992 Wigan 28 Castleford 12
1993 Wigan 20 Widnes 14
1994 Wigan 26 Leeds 16
1995 Wigan 30 Leeds 10
1996 St Helens
1997 St Helens

RUGBY UNION
■ *World Cup*
1991 Australia
1995 South Africa
■ *Five Nations championship*
1990 Scotland
1991 England
1992 England
1993 France
1994 Wales
1995 England
1996 England
1997 France

SAILING
■ *Admiral's Cup*
1991 Team: France. Individual: Corum Saphir (Fra)
■ *America's Cup*
1992 America³ (US, Bill Koch)
1995 Team New Zealand (NZ, Peter Blake)

SNOOKER
■ *World Championship*
1990 Stephen Hendry 18 Jimmy White 12
1991 John Parrott 18 Jimmy White 11
1992 Stephen Hendry 18 Jimmy White 14
1993 Stephen Hendry 18 Jimmy White 5
1994 Stephen Hendry 18 Jimmy White 17
1995 Stephen Hendry 18 Nigel Bond 9
1996 Stephen Hendry 18 Peter Ebdon 12
1997 Ken Doherty 18 Stephen Hendry 12

TENNIS
■ *Wimbledon*
1990 Stefan Edberg bt Boris Becker; Martina Navratilova bt Zina Garrison
1991 Michael Stich bt Boris Becker; Steffi Graf bt Gabriela Sabatini

1992 Andre Agassi bt Goran Ivanisovic; Steffi Graf bt Monica Seles
1993 Pete Sampras bt Jim Courier; Steffi Graf bt Jana Novotna
1994 Pete Sampras bt Goran Ivanisevic; Conchita Martinez bt Martina Navratilova
1995 Pete Sampras bt Boris Becker; Steffi Graf bt Arantxa Sanchez Vicari
1996 Richard Krajicek bt Malivai Washington; Steffi Graf bt Arantxa Sanchez Vicario
■ *Australian Open*
1990 Ivan Lendl; Steffi Graf
1991 Boris Becker; Monica Seles
1992 Jim Courier; Monica Seles
1993 Jim Courier; Monica Seles
1994 Pete Sampras; Steffi Graf
1995 Andre Agassi; Mary Pierce
1996 Boris Becker; Monica Seles
1997 Pete Sampras; Martina Hingis
■ *French Open*
1990 Andres Gomez; Monica Seles
1991 Jim Courier; Monica Seles
1992 Jim Courier; Monica Seles
1993 Sergi Bruguera; Steffi Graf
1994 Sergi Bruguera; Arantxa Sanchez Vicario
1995 Thomas Muster; Steffi Graf
1996 Yevgeny Kafelnikov; Steffi Graf

■ *US Open*
1990 Pete Sampras; Gabriela Sabatini
1991 Stefan Edberg; Monica Seles
1992 Stefan Edberg; Monica Seles
1993 Pete Sampras; Steffi Graf
1994 Andre Agassi; Arantxa Sanchez Vicario
1995 Pete Sampras; Steffi Graf
1996 Pete Sampras; Steffi Graf

Bibliography

Those wishing to read more about the events we chronicle should find these books, among the many we consulted, to be particularly useful.

ATHLETICS

A WORLD HISTORY OF TRACK AND FIELD ATHLETICS; R L Quercetani; Oxford University Press; 1964.

ATHLETICS: A HISTORY OF MODERN TRACK AND FIELD ATHLETICS (1860-1990); Roberto L Quercetani; Vallardi and Associati (Milan); 1990.

ATHLETICS: THE GOLDEN DECADE; Tony Ward; Queen Anne Press; 1991.

AUSTRALIAN AND NEW ZEALAND OLYMPIANS; Graeme Atkinson; The Five Mile Press; 1984.

BRITISH OLYMPIANS: A HUNDRED YEARS OF GOLD MEDALLISTS; Ian Buchanan; Guinness; 1991.

DESMOND LYNAM'S 1998 OLYMPICS; Desmond Lynam; Sidgwick and Jackson; 1988.

ENCYCLOPAEDIA OF BRITISH ATHLETICS RECORDS; Ian Buchanan; Stanley Paul; 1961.

HISTORY OF BRITISH ATHLETICS; Melvyn Watman; Robert Hale; 1968.

HITLER'S GAMES; Duff Hart-Davis; Century; 1986.

JESSE OWENS — AN AMERICAN LIFE; William J Baker; Collier Macmillan; 1986.

THE ENCYCLOPAEDIA OF ATHLETICS; Melvyn Watman; Robert Hale; 1964.

THE GUINNESS BOOK OF ATHLETICS FACTS AND FEATS; by Peter Matthews; Guinness; 1982.

THE GUINNESS OLYMPICS FACT BOOK; Stan Greenberg; Guinness Publishing; 1991.

THE NAZI OLYMPICS; Richard D Mandell; Souvenir Press; 1971.

THE OLYMPIC GAMES; edited by Lord Killanin and John Rodda; Queen Anne Press; 1976.

THE OLYMPIC GAMES 1984; edited by Lord Killanin and John Rodda; Collins; 1983.

BOXING

A PICTORIAL HISTORY OF BOXING; Sam Andre and Nat Fleischer; Hamlyn; 1988.

BOXING'S GREATEST PRIZE; Peter Wilson; Arrow; 1982.

HENRY COOPER'S 100 GREATEST BOXERS; Henry Cooper; Macdonald Queen Anne Press; 1990.

THE BOOK OF BOXING QUOTATIONS; Harry Mullan; Stanley Paul; 1991.

CRICKET

100 YEARS OF ENGLAND V AUSTRALIA; Doug Ibbotson; Ralph Dellor and David Frith; Rothmans Publications; 1982.

A CENTURY OF SOUTH AFRICA IN TEST AND INTERNATIONAL CRICKET 1889-1989; various authors; Jonathan Ball; 1989.

A HISTORY OF CRICKET; Benny Green; Guild Publishing; 1988.

A HISTORY OF THE COUNTY CRICKET CHAMPIONSHIP; Robert Brooke; Guinness Publishing; 1991.

A HISTORY OF WEST INDIES CRICKET; Michael Manley; Guild Publishing; 1988.

ARLOTT AND TRUEMAN ON CRICKET; Gilbert Phelps; BBC; 1977.

ASHES '85; Matthew Engel; Pelham; 1985.

AUSTRALIAN CRICKET: THE GAME AND THE PLAYERS; Jack Pollard, Angus and Robertson; 1988.

BARCLAYS WORLD OF CRICKET; edited by EW Swanton; Willow Books; 1986.

BENSON AND HEDGES CRICKET YEARBOOKS; David Lemmon; Guild Publishing.

BORDER'S HEROES: AUSTRALIA'S ASHES TRIUMPH OF 1989; John Huxley; Lester Townsend; 1989.

CRICKET EXTRAS; David Rayvern Allen; Guinness; 1988.

CRICKET ON THE AIR; David Rayvern Allen; BBC; 1985.

CRICKET STATISTICS YEAR BY YEAR; 1946-1987; Fred Trueman and Don Mosey; Guild Publishing; 1988.

DENIS COMPTON: CRICKETING GENIUS; Peter West; Stanley Paul; 1989.

DOUBLE CENTURY — THE STORY OF MCC AND CRICKET; Tony Lewis; Hodder and Stoughton; 1987.

ENGLAND VERSUS AUSTRALIA, A PICTORIAL HISTORY OF THE TEST MATCHES SINCE 1877; David Frith; Australian Broadcasting Corporation; 1984.

FAMOUS WRITERS ON CRICKET; Roger Adams; Partridge; 1988.

FOLLOW ON; E W Swanton; Collins; 1977.

FROM LARWOOD TO LILLEE; Trevor Bailey and Fred Trueman; Queen Anne Press; 1983.

KEITH MILLER: THE GOLDEN NUGGET; R S Whitington; Rigby; 1981.

LAKER: PORTRAIT OF A LEGEND; Don Mosey; Queen Anne Press; 1989.

LIVING FOR CRICKET; Clive Lloyd with Tony Cozier; Stanley Paul; 1980.

LORD'S; Sir Pelham Warner; Harrap; 1946.

LORD'S 1946-1970; Diana Rait Kerr and Ian Peebles; Harrap; 1971.

ON REFLECTION; Richie Benaud; Willow Books; 1985.

PHOENIX FROM THE ASHES; Mike Brearley; Unwin Paperbacks; 1983.

PURPLE PATCHES; Ralph Barker; Collins; 1987.

RICHARD HADLEE: RHYTHM AND SWING; Richard Becht; Collins; 1989.

SIR GARY; Trevor Bailey; Collins; 1976.

SOBERS: TWENTY YEARS AT THE TOP; Sir Garfield Sobers with Brian Scovell; MacMillan; 1989.

SORT OF A CRICKET PERSON; E W Swanton; Collins; 1972.

TALES FROM FAR PAVILIONS; Allen Synge and Leo Cooper; Arrow; 1987.

THE BEST OF CHAPPELL; Ian Chappell; Lansdowne; 1982.

THE BEST OF CRICKET; Roy Peskett; Newnes Books; 1983.

THE BODYLINE CONTROVERSY; Laurence Le Quesne; Unwin; 1985.

THE BOOK OF CRICKET QUOTATIONS; Peter Ball and David Hopps; Stanley Paul; 1990.

THE CENTURIONS; Patrick Murphy; J M Dent; 1986.

THE COMPLETE WHO'S WHO OF TEST CRICKETERS; edited by Christopher Martin-Jenkins; MacDonald Queen Anne Press; 1987.

THE CRICKETER'S WHO'S WHO; Iain Sproat; Collins Willow.

THE HANDBOOK OF CRICKET; Keith Andrew; Pelham Books; 1989.

THE LAUGH'S ON US; various authors; Swan; 1989.

THE LORD'S TAVERNERS 50 GREATEST; Trevor Bailey, Richie Benaud, Colin Cowdrey and Jim Laker; Heinemann-Quixote Press; 1983.

THE OBSERVER ON CRICKET; Scyld Berry; Unwin Hyman; 1987.

THE PENGUIN CRICKETER'S COMPANION; Alan Ross; Penguin; 1979.

THE PUNCH BOOK OF CRICKET; David Rayvern Allen; Grafton; 1986.

THE SLOW MEN; David Frith; Horwitz Grahame Books; 1984.

THE SPINNERS' WEB; Trevor Bailey and Fred Trueman; Willow Books; 1988.

THE STORY OF CRICKET; Robin Marlar; Marshall Cavendish; 1979.

THE WISDEN BOOK OF CRICKET QUOTATIONS; David Lemmon; Queen Anne Press; 1990.

THE WISDEN BOOK OF CRICKET RECORDS; compiled and edited by Bill Frindall; MacDonald Queen Anne Press; 1986.

THE WISDEN BOOK OF ONE-DAY INTERNATIONAL CRICKET 1971-1985; Bill Frindall and Victor H Isaacs; John Wisden; 1985.

THE WISDEN BOOK OF TEST CRICKET 1877-1984; compiled and edited by Bill Frindall; MacDonald Queen Anne Press; 1985.

THE WISDEN BOOK OF TEST CRICKET VOLUME I 1877-1977; Bill Frindall; Queen Anne Press; 1990.

THE WISDEN BOOK OF TEST CRICKET VOLUME II 1977-1989; Bill Frindall; Queen Anne Press; 1990.

VIV RICHARDS: THE AUTHORISED BIOGRAPHY; Trevor McDonald; Pelham; 1985.

WISDEN CRICKETERS' ALMANACKS; John Wisden.

WISDEN ANTHOLOGY 1864-1900; Benny Green; Queen Anne Press; 1988.

WISDEN ANTHOLOGY 1900-1940; Benny Green; Queen Anne Press; 1988.

WISDEN ANTHOLOGY 1940-1963; Benny Green; Queen Anne Press; 1982.

WISDEN ANTHOLOGY 1963-1982; Benny Green; Queen Anne Press; 1983.

FOOTBALL

A HISTORY OF BRITISH FOOTBALL; Percy M Young; Arrow Books; 1973.

A STRANGE KIND OF GLORY, Sir Matt Busby and Manchester United; Eamon Dunphy; Heinemann; 1991.

AND THE SPURS GO MARCHING ON; Phil Soar, Hamlyn, 1982.

ARSENAL OFFICIAL HISTORY; Phil Soar and Martin Tyler, Hamlyn; 1989.

ASSOCIATION FOOTBALL, VOLUME 1: edited by AH Fabian and Geoffrey Green; Caxton; 1960.

ASSOCIATION FOOTBALL AND ENGLISH SOCIETY 1863-1915; Tony Mason; Harvester Press; 1980.

BACK PAGE FOOTBALL; Stephen F Kelly; Macdonald Queen Anne Press; 1988.

BOBBY MOORE; Jeff Powell; Everest; 1976.

BOOK OF WORLD FOOTBALL; Brian Glanville; Dragon; 1972.

BOYS OF '66; Martin Tyler; Hamlyn; 1981.

CLOUGH; Tony Francis; Stanley Paul; 1989.

FOOTBALL!; Nicholas Mason; Temple Smith; 1974.

FOOTBALL PLAYERS' RECORDS 1946-84; Barry J Hugman; Newnes 1984.

ILLUSTRATED ENCYCLOPAEDIA OF BRITISH FOOTBALL; Phil Soar; WH Smith; 1990.

MANCHESTER UNITED: THE BETRAYAL OF A LEGEND; Michael Crick and David Smith; Pelham Books; 1989.

NEWS OF THE WORLD FOOTBALL ANNUAL 1991-92; edited Bill Bateson and Albert Sewell; Invincible Press; 1991.

PELE: MY LIFE AND THE BEAUTIFUL GAME; Pele with Robert L Fish; New English Library; 1977.

PUFFIN BOOK OF FOOTBALL; Brian Glanville; Puffin Books; 1970.

ROTHMANS FOOTBALL YEAR BOOKS; Queen Anne Press.

SCOTTISH FOOTBALL; Kevin McCarra; Polygon; 1984.

SOCCER, A PANORAMA; Brian Glanville; Eyre and Spottiswoode; 1969.

SOCCER FIRSTS; John Robinson; Guinness Publishing; 1986.

SOCCER SHORTS; Jack Rollin; Guinness Publishing; 1988.

SPURS, A COMPLETE RECORD; Bob Goodwin; Breedon Books; 1988.

STANLEY MATTHEWS; David Miller; Pavilion; 1989.

THE DOUBLE AND BEFORE; Danny Blanchflower; Four Square; 1961.

THE FOOTBALL ENCYCLOPAEDIA; edited by Frank Johnston; Associated Sporting Press; 1934.

THE FOOTBALL FACT BOOK; Jack Rollin; Guinness Publishing; 1990.

THE FOOTBALL LEAGUE 1888-1988, the official illustrated history; Byron Butler; Macdonald Queen Anne Press; 1987.

THE FOOTBALL MANAGERS; Johnny Rogan; Macdonald Queen Anne Press; 1989.

THE HISTORY OF THE WORLD CUP; Brian Glanville; Faber; 1980.

THE LEEDS UNITED STORY; Jason Tomas; Arthur Barker; 1971.
THE NEW SCOTTISH FOOTBALL FACT BOOK; completed and edited by Forrest HC Robertson; Sport Data Services; 1985.
THE OFFICIAL HISTORY OF THE FOOTBALL ASSOCIATION; Byron Butler; Macdonald Queen Anne Press; 1991.
THE ONLY GAME; Roddy Forsyth; Mainstream; 1990.
THE SOCCER TRIBE; Desmond Morris; Jonathan Cape; 1981.
THIS ONE'S ON ME; Jimmy Greaves; Coronet; 1979.
YOU'LL NEVER WALK ALONE; Stephen F Kelly; Macdonald Queen Anne Press; 1991.

GOLF

A HISTORY OF GOLF; Louis T Stanley; Weidenfeld and Nicolson; 1991.
BRITISH OPEN CHAMPIONS; Michael Hobbs; Chapmans; 1991.
GOLF: THE LAST 25 YEARS; Mike Britten; WH Smith; 1991.
GREAT SHOTS; Robert Sommers and Cal Brown; Anaya; 1989.
GREATEST MOMENTS IN GOLF; Paul Gregory; Bison Books; 1987.
GUINNESS GOLF; RECORDS, FACTS AND CHAMPIONS; Donald Steel; Guinness Superlatives; 1987.
THE BOOK OF GOLF QUOTATIONS; Bob Chieger and Pat Sullivan; Stanley Paul; 1989.
THE COMPLETE BOOK OF AUSTRALIAN GOLF; Terry Smith; Australian Broadcasting Corporation; 1988.
THE HANDBOOK OF GOLF; Alex Hay; Pelham; 1985.
THE RYDER CUP: THE ILLUSTRATED HISTORY; Michael Hobbs; Queen Anne Press; 1989.
THE WHO'S WHO OF GOLF; Peter Alliss; Orbis Publishing; 1983.
WHO'S WHO IN GOLF; Ian Morrison; Hamlyn; 1988.

MOTOR RACING

MOTOR RACING; Ian Morrison; Guinness Books; 1989.
POWER AND GLORY, VOLUME 1; William Court; Patrick Stephens; 1988.
POWER AND GLORY, VOLUME 2; William Court; Patrick Stephens; 1990.
THE GUINNESS BOOK OF FORMULA ONE; Ian Morrison; Guinness; 1989.
THE POWER AND THE GLORY; Ivan Rendall; BBC Publications; 1991.

RACING

BACK PAGE RACING, A CENTURY OF NEWSPAPER COVERAGE; George Plumptre; Macdonald Queen Anne Press; 1989.
DERBY DAY 200; Royal Academy of Arts; 1979.
GREAT RACES; Sean Magee; Anaya Publishers; 1990.
HORSE RACING, RECORDS, FACTS AND FIGURES; Tony Morris and John Randall; Guinness Books; 1990.
TALES OF RACING AND CHASING; Terry Biddlecombe; Stanley Paul; 1985.

THE FLAT: FLAT RACING IN BRITAIN SINCE 1939; Roger Mortimer; George Allen and Unwin; 1979.
THE WORLD OF FLAT RACING; Brough Scott and Gerry Cranham; World's Work; 1983.
TURF ACCOUNTS; Graham Sharpe; Guinness Publishing; 1990.

RUGBY LEAGUE

RAY FRENCH'S 100 GREAT RUGBY LEAGUE PLAYERS; Ray French; Queen Anne Press; 1989.
ROTHMANS RUGBY LEAGUE YEARBOOKS; Queen Anne Press.
RUGBY LEAGUE: AN ILLUSTRATED HISTORY; Robert Gate; Arthur Barker; 1989.
RUGBY LEAGUE FACT BOOK; Robert Gate; Guinness; 1991.

RUGBY UNION

A HISTORY OF RUGBY UNION FOOTBALL; Chris Rea; Hamlyn; 1977.
BRITISH LIONS; John Griffiths; The Crowood Press; 1990.
DB RUGBY ANNUALS; Bob Howitt; Moa Publications.
ELLA ELLA ELLA; Bret Harris; Springwood Books; 1984.
ENGLISH RUGBY: A CELEBRATION; Ted Barrett; Mainstream; 1991.
FEET, SCOTLAND FEET!; Derek Douglas; Mainstream; 1991.
FIELDS OF PRAISE: THE OFFICIAL HISTORY OF THE WELSH RUGBY UNION 1881-1981; David Smith and Gareth Williams; University of Wales Press; 1980.
GARETH EDWARDS' 100 GREAT RUGBY PLAYERS; Gareth Edwards; Queen Anne Press; 1987.
GUINNESS RUGBY: THE RECORDS; Chris Rhys; Guinness; 1987.
ROTHMANS RUGBY UNION YEARBOOKS; Queen Anne Press.
RUGBY SHORTS; Chris Rhys; Guinness; 1990.
THE BOOK OF WORLD RUGBY QUOTATIONS; Derek Douglas; Mainstream; 1991.
THE COMPLETE RUGBY FOOTBALLER; Dave Gallaher and Billy Stead; Methuen; 1906.
THE ENCYCLOPEDIA OF WORLD RUGBY; Keith Quinn; Lochar; 1991.
THE FOOTBALL ANNUALS 1990-1910; Charles W Alcock; Merritt and Hatcher; 1900-1910.
THE HISTORY OF THE LAWS OF RUGBY FOOTBALL; Admiral Sir Percy Royds; Walker; 1949.
THE INTERNATIONAL RUGBY CHAMPIONSHIP 1883-1983; Terry Godwin; Willow Books; 1984.
THE WORLD OF RUGBY; John Reason and Carwyn James; BBC Books; 1979.

TENNIS

75 YEARS OF THE INTERNATIONAL TENNIS FEDERATION 1913-1988; Dennis Cunnington; The International Tennis Federation; 1988.
BJORN BORG: MY LIFE AND GAME; Gene Scott; Sphere Books; 1981.

TENNIS, A PICTORIAL HISTORY; Lance Tingay; William Collins Sons and Co; 1977.
THE CONCISE DICTIONARY OF TENNIS; Martin Hedges; Mayflower; 1978.
THE GUINNESS ENCYCLOPEDIA OF INTERNATIONAL SPORTS RECORDS AND RESULTS; Peter Matthews and Ian Morrison; Guinness; 1990.
THE ILLUSTRATED ENCYCLOPEDIA OF WORLD TENNIS; John Haylett and Richard Evans; The Automobile Association; 1989.
THE STORY OF THE DAVIS CUP; Alan Trengove; Stanley Paul; 1991.
WIMBLEDON, CENTRE COURT OF THE GAME; Max Robertson; BBC Books; 1987.
WORLD OF TENNIS 1990; John Barrett; Willow Books; 1990.

OTHER SPORTS

AN ILLUSTRATED HISTORY OF BALL GAMES; Nigel Viney and Neil Grant; William Heinemann; 1978.
BACKPAGE; AUSTRALIA'S GREATEST SPORTING MOMENTS; Ian Heads; Lester-Townsend; 1989.
BLOOD SWEAT AND TEARS: AUSTRALIANS AND SPORT; various authors; Lothian Publishing; 1989.
EVERYMAN'S DICTIONARY OF DATES; revised by Audrey Butler; J M Dent; 1987.
FAMOUS SPORTING FIASCOS; Stephen Winkworth; Sphere Books; 1984.
GAMES AND SETS, THE CHANGING FACE OF SPORT ON TELEVISION; Steven Barnett; BFI Publishing; 1990.
HENLEY ROYAL REGATTA: A CELEBRATION OF 150 YEARS; Richard Burnell; Heinemann Kingswood; 1989.
ILLUSTRATED HISTORY OF BASEBALL; Alex Chadwick; Brompton; 1988.
MICHENER ON SPORT; James A Michener; Corgi; 1977.
PEARS CYCLOPAEDIA; Christopher Cook; Pelham; 1990.
PERSONNA YEAR BOOK OF SPORTS; Robert Martin; Pelham; 1969.
PLAYFAIR WINNERS ANNUAL 1991-92; Edward Abelson; Queen Anne Press; 1991.
POCKET MONEY; Gordon Burn; William Heinemann; 1986.
SHOW JUMPING RECORDS, FACTS AND CHAMPIONS; Judith Draper; Guinness Superlatives; 1987.
SPORT IN BRITAIN, A SOCIAL HISTORY; Tony Mason; Cambridge University Press; 1989.
SPORTS QUOTES OF THE EIGHTIES; Peter Ball and Phil Shaw; Mandarin; 1990.
SUNDAY TIMES: THE SPORTING DECADE—1980s; Chris Dighton; Macdonald Queen Anne Press; 1990.
THE 1991 INFORMATION PLEASE SPORTS ALMANAC; edited by Mike Meserole; Houghton Mifflin; Boston.
THE ADMIRAL'S CUP; Bob Fisher; Pelham; 1985.

THE BEST OF SPORTS ILLUSTRATED; Oxmoor House; 1990.
THE BOOK OF SPORTS QUOTES; Jonathon Green and Don Atyeo; Omnibus; 1979.
THE BREAKS CAME MY WAY; Joe Davis; W H Allen; 1976.
THE COURAGE BOOK OF GREAT SPORTING TEAMS; compiled by Chris Rhys; Stanley Paul; 1985.
THE COURAGE BOOK OF SPORTING HEROES; compiled by Chris Rhys; Stanley Paul; 1984.
THE ENCYCLOPAEDIA OF BADMINTON; Pat Davis; Robert Hale; 1987.
THE ENCYCLOPAEDIA OF SPORT; edited by Charles Harvey; Samson Low, Marston and Co; 1959.
THE GRIDIRON UK GUIDE TO AMERICAN FOOTBALL ALL-TIME GREATS; Ross Biddiscombe; Patrick Stephens; 1986.
THE GUINNESS BOOK OF RECORDS 1992; Donald McFarlan; Guinness; 1991.
THE GUINNESS DICTIONARY OF SPORTS QUOTATIONS; Colin Jarman; Guinness; 1990.
THE HUTCHINSON ENCYCLOPAEDIA; Guild Publishing; 1988.
THE ILLUSTRATED ENCYCLOPAEDIA OF WORLD SAILING; David Pelly; Marshall Cavendish; 1989.
THE NGRC BOOK OF GREYHOUND RACING; the NGRC and Roy Genders; Pelham; 1990.
THE NFL OFFICIAL HISTORY OF PRO FOOTBALL; Beau Riffenburgh and Jack Clary; Hamlyn; 1990.
THE OFFICIAL NATIONAL FOOTBALL LEAGUE RECORD AND FACT BOOKS; Partridge Press.
THE OXFORD COMPANION TO SPORTS AND GAMES; edited by John Arlott; Oxford University Press; 1975.
THE SOUTH AFRICAN GAME: SPORT AND RACISM; Robert Archer and Antoine Bouillon; Zed Press; 1982.
THE SPORTING YEAR; John Rodda and Clifford Makins; Collins; 1977.
THE SPORTING YEAR 2; John Rodda and Clifford Makins; Collins; 1978.
THE SPORTS ILLUSTRATED 1992 SPORTS ALMANAC; Little, Brown and Co.
THE SPORTSPAGES ALMANACS; Matthew Engel and Ian Morrison; Simon and Schuster.
THE SUNDAY TIMES SPORT BOOK; John Lovesey, Nicholas Mason and Edwin Taylor; World's Work; 1979.
THE TOUR DE FRANCE AND ITS HEROES; Graham Watson; Stanley Paul; 1990.
TOUR DE FRANCE: THREE WEEKS TO GLORY; Samuel Abt; Bicycle Books; 1991.
WAR GAMES: THE STORY OF SPORT IN WORLD WAR TWO; Tony McCarthy; Queen Anne Press; 1989.
WORLD OF SPORT SPORTSWATCHER'S GUIDE; Dickie Davies; Collins; 1981.

Index

*Numbers in italics refer
to illustrations*

425

427

Acknowledgments

The publishers would particularly like to thank Michael Roffey, Chris Ball, Dean Burrows, Colin Francis and Mike Stephenson of Times Newspapers Picture Library, and Anna Calvert and Chris Tole of the Hulton Picture Company for their invaluable help in providing pictures for this book.

Photographic acknowledgments

Action Images 393 top, 409 top, 414 top, 417 below, 418 top, /**Allsport** 9 centre, 10 left, l0 right, 18 left, 89 right, 91 bottom left, 161, 161 inset, 213, 369 bottom right, 389 left, 407 below left, 417 top, /**Al Bello** 415, /**Shaun Botterill** 389 right, 392 bottom, 397 top, 419 top, /**Simon Bruty** 390 left, 401 top, 411 right, 412 below, /**Clive Brunskill** 399 top, 416 top, /**David Cannon** 414 below, 418 below left, /**Jose Cardigos** 411 left, /**Russell Chene** 369 top right, /**Jonathan Daniel** 347 top right, Dyi Gptdyrt 413. /**Mike Hewitt** 391 bottom right, /**Joe Mann** 388 top, /**Adrian Murrell** 314 top right, 388 top left, /**Stephen Munday** 391 top right, 396, 399 bottom, /**Mike Powell** 338 left, 403 top left, /**Ben Radford** 394 bottom, 401 bottom, 404 top left, /**Pascal Rondeau** 400 bottom left, 416 below, /**Holly Stein** 392 top, /**Steve Swope** 395 top, **Mark Thompson** 419 below, /**Anton Want** 402 bottom right, 407 below right; **Associated Press** 123 right, 129 top, 140 top, 143 top right, 164, 240 top, 257 bottom, 261 bottom, 282 centre, 297 bottom left, 310 top, 318 top right, 320 bottom right, 329 bottom right, 330 top right, 334 bottom, 348 right, 351 top right, 353 top, 362 bottom right, 376 bottom; **Associated Sports Photography/Stuart D Franklin** 371 bottom, 389 bottom, /**George Herringshaw** 237, 387 bottom; BBC 6 centre; **The George Beldam Collection 12** bottom, 15 top, 19 top, 27; **Mike Brett Photography** 299 right; **British Movietone News** 150 bottom; **Carl Bromwich** 341 top; **Bert Butterworth** 329 bottom left; **Bernard Cahier** 221 bottom; **Calyx Photo** Services 377 top right; **Colorsport** 9 top, 20 right, 44 top, 44 bottom, 103 bottom left, 180 centre, 246 top, 252 top, 266 bottom right, 274 top, 278 bottom, 336 top, 387 top, 388 bottom right, 393 bottom, 394 top, 397 bottom, 398 top left, bottom right, 400, 402 top left, 403 botom right, 404 bottom, 406 below left, 408 below, 409 below, 410, 418 below right, /**Andrew Cowie** 390 right, 412 top, /**Hugh Godwin** 412 centre, /**Neale Haynes** 408 top, /**Sipa** 406 below right, 406 top; **Cornish Photo News** 317 centre bottom left; **CPS Ltd** 33 top; **Derby Evening Telegraph** 265 top; **Patrick Eagar** 227 left, 266 top right, 302 top, 324 top, 339 right, 349; **Tony Edenden (Sportsfocus)** 379 top left; **Robin Eley** 313 bottom left **Empics/Ross Kinnard** 405, **FIFA** 124 top; **David Frith Collection** 28 right, 53 right, 79 bottom right, 83 right; **R E Gate** 25 top, 35 top left, 46 right, 96 bottom, 100 bottom, 102 bottom right, 107 bottom right, 144 bottom, 165 top left, 207 bottom, 208 bottom; **Geoffrey Goddard** 163 bottom left, 175 bottom; **Glasgow Herald** 25 bottom, 29 top, 118 top, 132 top, 132 bottom, 176 bottom, 218 bottom; **Keith Hailey 319** bottom, 356 bottom left, 368 bottom left; **Hulton-Deutsch Collection** 6 bottom centre, 9 bottom, 15 bottom, 17 left, 17 top right, 17 bottom right, 19 bottom, 21 top, 21 bottom, 22 centre, 24 top, 24 bottom right, 26 top, 26 bottom left, 26 bottom right, 29 bottom, 31, 32 right, 35 bottom right, 36 top, 36 bottom, 37 bottom, 39, 40 bottom, 41 right, 42 top, 42 bottom, 43 top, 48 bottom, 49 bottom, 51 left, 51 right, 53 left, 54, 55 top left, 56 top, 57 bottom, 58 top, 59 top, 60 left, 61 bottom, 62, 63 left, 63 top right, 64 top, 64 bottom, 65 top, 65 bottom, 66 bottom, 68 top, 68 right, 69 top, 69 centre, 69 bottom, 71, 72 bottom left, 72 top right, 72 bottom right, 73, 75 left, 75 right, 76 bottom, 77 top left, 77 bottom, 78, 80 bottom, 81 bottom, 83 left, 84 bottom, 86 top, 86 bottom left, 87, 88 right, 95 top left, 95 bottom left, 97 top, 99 top right, 99 bottom right, 100 top, 103 top, 103 bottom right, 104 top, 105, 106 bottom, 107 top left, 108 left, 109 top, 109 bottom, 110 centre, 111 left, 111 bottom, 112 left, 113 top left, 113 bottom left, 114 right, 116 top, 116 bottom, 117 bottom, 118 bottom, 120 left, 120 top right, 121 bottom, 124 bottom, 125 left, 126 top right, 126 bottom, 127 top, 127 bottom, 128, 129 bottom centre, 129 bottom right, 130 right, 131 top, 132 left, 133 left, 133 right, 134 bottom, 135 top, 135 bottom, 137 top right, 137 bottom right, 138 right, 139 right, 140 bottom, 141 right, 142, 143 bottom right, 145 bottom, 147 left, 147 right, 148 left, 148 right, 150 top, 151 top, 151 right, 152 top right, 152 bottom right, 153, 155 bottom, 156, 157 top, 158 top, 158 bottom, 159 top, 162 left, 162 right, 163 top, 165 top right, 166 top right, 166 bottom right, 167 left, 167 bottom right, 169 top, 169 bottom, 170, 171 top, 172 left, 173 bottom, 174 centre, 174 top right, 174 bottom right, 175 top, 176 top, 177 top, 180 bottorn left, 180 bottom right, 181 bottom, 182 top, 183 bottom left, 183 top centre, 183 bottom centre, 183 bottom right, 184 top, 184 bottom, 185 bottom, 185 right, 186 bottom, 187, 188 left, 188 top, 190 top, 190 bottom right, 191 top left, 191 right, 192 top, 194, 195 left, 196 bottom left, 196 top centre, 196 bottom right, 197 left, 197 right, 198,199 left, 199 right, 200 left, 200 right, 201 left, 201 right, 203 top right, 203 bottom right, 207 top, 208 top, 209 left, 209 right, 211 right, 215 bottom, 216 top, 217 top, 217 bottom, 218 top, 220 top, 220 centre, 220 bottom, 221 top, 222 left, 222 right, 223 top right, 223 bottom right, 225 left, 225 right, 230 bottom, 231 top, 238, 239 bottom left, 239 top right, 240 bottom, 241, 242 top, 242 bottom, 243 right, 244, 245 top right, 246 centre left, 246 centre right, 246 bottom, 247 centre right, 247 bottom, 249 top, 249 bottom, 250 bottom, 251 right, 253 bottom, 256 top, 256 bottom, 257 top, 258 bottom right, 262 bottom left, 264 top, 265 bottom, 266 bottom left, 267 right, 268 left, 269, 271 top left, 271 top centre, 271 top right, 272 bottom, 273 top, 273 bottom, 274 bottom, 275 top, 277 bottom, 278 top, 279 top, 281 bottom, 283 left, 284 bottom, 285 top, 286 top, 286 bottom, 287 top, 287 bottom, 288 right, 291 top, 293 bottom right, 294 left, 295 top, 295 bottom, 296 top, 296 bottom, 297 top, 297 bottom right, 298 right, 299 left, 300 left, 301 top, 301 bottom 302 bottom, 303 top, 303 bottom, 307 top, 307 bottom, 309 top, 309 bottom right, 311 top, 311 centre, 314 bottom left, 314 bottom right, 315 top; **HultonDeutsch/Bettmann** 33 bottom, 40 top, 41 left, 48 top, 55 bottom left, 55 right, 81 top, 86 bottom right, 101 bottom right, 136, 271 bottom, 272 top; **The Illustrated London News Picture Library** 13 top, 14 top, 22 bottom right, 37 top, 45 top, 45 bottom, 46 left, 47, 98 inset, 101 left; **Ken Kelly** 231 bottom; **Kent County Cricket Club** 22 bottom left; **E D Lacey** 216 bottom, 247 top, 267 left, 276 bottom; **Le Progres** 320 left; **Steve Lindsell** 326 left; **Graham** Morris 356 top; **David Muscroft** 71 inset, 340 bottom right; **North West Counties Press** 348 left; **Popperfoto** 99 left, 126 top left, 253 right, 258 centre, 259 top, 259 bottom, 260 bottom, 261 top, 279 bottom, 280 top, 280 bottom, 323 left, 323 top right, 323 bottom right, 351 top left, 363 left; **Popperfoto/Reuter** 352 bottom, 364 top, 388 bottom right; **Press Association** 13 bottom, 106 top, 172 right, 176 left, 205 top right, 212 top, 212 bottom, 214 top, 214 bottom left, 224 bottom, 234 top, 292, 293 top, 300 right, 324 bottom left, 325 bottom, 326 right, 328 top, 330 left, 335 bottom, 336 bottom, 343 top, 350 bottom left, 351 bottom right, 365 top, 375 top, 380 right; **Press Association/AFP** 315 bottom, 362 centre, 378 bottom; **Press Association/Reuter** 108 right, 112 top, 119 bottom, 166 left, 189, 254 left; **Presse Sports** 16; **Professional Sport/Tommy Hindley** 313 bottom right, /**Phil Shephard-Lewis** 347 left, 374 bottom; **Reed International Books** 52 bottom, 80 top; **The Ring** 130 left; **W W Rouch** 12 top, 18 right; **Rugby Football Union** 88 left; **The Rugby League** 325 top; **The Scotsman** 179 right; **Phil Sheldon** 306 bottom right, 327 bottom, 346, 360 top, 368 top right, 386 bottom; **Chris Smith** 2-3; **Sport & General** 102 top, 109 centre, 113 right, 120 bottom right, 131 bottom, 141 top, 144 right, 149 right, 171 bottom, 177 bottom, 191 bottom left, 193, 195 right, 219 top, 223 top left, 227 top right, 229 bottom left, 229 bottom right, 232 top, 232 bottom left, 234 bottom, 239 top left, 245 bottom right, 282 left, 290 top, 350 bottom right; **Sporting Pictures (UK)** 252 bottom, 262 bottom right, 276 top, 277 top, 281 top, 291 bottom, 318 left, 318 bottom centre, 321 bottom left, 364 left, **Sportsphoto Agency/Stewart Kendall** 6 centre left, 377 bottom right, **Sygma/Paul Zimmer** 395 bottom, **Syndication International** 254 right, 255 right, 306 bottom left; **Bob Thomas Sports Photography** 205 top left, 227 bottom right, 298 bottom, 312 bottom left, 312 bottom right, 321 top, 322 bottom, 349 bottom, 379 top centre; **Times Newspapers Picture Library** 1, 6 bottom left, 6 bottom right, 59 bottom, 66 top, 67 top, 67 bottom, 76 top, 77 top right, 79 bottom left, 82 top, 82 bottom, 84 top, 85 top, 85 bottom, 89 bottom, 91 top left, 91 centre left, 91 right, 92 left, 92 right, 93 top,93 bottom, 94,95 top right, 97 bottom, 98, 107 top right, 110 bottom, 114 left, 115, 116 centre, 117 top, 121 top, 123 left, 125 right, 129 bottom left, 134 left, 137 left, 138 left, 139 left, 141 bottom, 143 top, 144 left, 145 top, 149 left, 154 bottom, 155 top, 157 bottom, 159 bottom, 163 bottom right, 165 bottom right, 167 top right, 178, 179 top left, 179 bottom left, 182 bottom, 186 top, 192 bottom, 202 left, 202 bottom, 203 bottom left, 205 bottom, 206 top, 206 bottom, 210 left, 210 right, 211 left, 212 top centre, 212 bottom centre, 214 bottom right, 215 top, 219 bottom, 219 right, 224 top, 229 top left, 233, 235, 243 left, 245 left, 248, 251 left, 255 left, 258 bottom left, 262 top, 263 left, 263 right, 264 bottom, 268 right, 275 bottom, 282 right, 284 top, 285 bottom, 288 left, 289 top, 289 bottom, 294 top, 294 bottom, 305, 306 top, 308, 309 bottom left, 310 bottom, 311 bottom, 312 top, 313 top right, 314 top left, 317 top left, 317 centre top left, 317 bottom left, 317 right, 318 bottom right, 319 top, 320 top, 321 top right, 322 top, 328 bottom right, 329 top, 330 top left, 330 bottom right, 332 left, 332 centre, 332 right, 333 left, 333 right, 334 top, 335 top, 337 bottom left, 337 bottom right, 338 right, 339 top left, 340 top, 340 bottom left, 341 bottom, 342 top, 342 bottom, 343 bottom left, 343 bottom right, 344 top, 344 right, 345 top, 345 bottom, 347 bottom right, 350 top right, 352 top, 352 right, 353 bottom, 354 top, 354 bottom left, 354 bottom right, 355 top, 355 bottom, 356 bottom right, 357, 359 left, 359 top right, 359 bottom right, 360 bottom, 361 top right, 361 left, 361 bottom right, 362 top right, 363 top right, 363 bottom, 365 left, 366 left, 366 top, 366 bottom, 367 left, 367 right, 369 left, 370 top, 370 bottom, 371 top, 374 top, 375 bottom, 376 right, 377 left, 378 top, 379 top right, 379 bottom left, 380 left, 381, 382 top, 382 bottom, 383 top, 383 bottom, 384, 385 top, 385 bottom left, 385 bottom right, 386 top, 388 bottom left, 389 top; **Topham Picture Source** 6 top left, 6 top centre, 6 top right, 6 centre right, 52 top, 60 left, 101 top right, 102 left, 104 bottom, 119 top, 146, 152 left, 154 top, 173 top, 174 left, 181 top, 202 top, 228, 230 top, 232 bottom right, 298 left; **Universal Pictorial Press and Agency** 328 left; **UPI/Bettmann** 205 top centre, 250 left, 260 top, 283 right, 290 bottom, 293 bottom left, 324 bottom right, 327 centre, 331, 337 top; **David Williams** 247 centre left; 11 top, 14 bottom, 20 left, 23, 24 bottom left, 28 left, 34, 35 top right, 49 top, 57 top, 61 top, 96 top; **Yorkshire County Cricket Club** 11 bottom, 56 left, 58 bottom, 63 bottom right; **Zooom Photographic/John Dunbar** 339 bottom left.